THE BIRDWATCHER'S YEARBOOK 2018

Edited by Neil Gartshore

Calluna Books

Published in 2017 by
Calluna Books
Moor Edge, 2 Bere Road, Wareham
Dorset BH20 4DD
United Kingdom

phone: 01929 552 560 ~ 07986 434 375
e-mail: yearbook@callunabooks.co.uk
website: www.callunabooks.co.uk

© Calluna Books 2017

ISBN 978-0-9933477-2-6
ISSN 2048-7258

Cover photograph: by Neil Gartshore
Wood Warbler *Phylloscopus sibilatrix*: this summer visitor to the UK (from April-August) spends the winter in sub-Saharan tropical Africa.

Black & white illustrations: by Dan Powell
phone: 01329 668 465
e-mail: danpowell11@btinternet.com
website: www.powellwildlifeart.com

Printed and bound in Great Britain by
Ashford Colour Press Ltd,
Gosport, Hampshire

CONTENTS

CONTENTS

PREFACE

AS I'M SITTING in my office, putting the final touches to the Yearbook before it goes off to the printers, autumn is well under way. I keep getting distracted by mixed flocks of birds coming through the garden, (mainly tits and goldcrests... but who knows what might be with them), whilst hirundines are passing overhead heading south. Further afield in the county we've had a purple patch of American waders with Baird's, Buff-breasted, Least, Spotted and Stilt Sandpipers all being twitchable. Added to these a brief staying Yellow Warbler turned up in late-August and there have been plenty of Wrynecks and Grey Phalaropes around as well. It is easy to see why birders enjoy this time of the year.

For those of us who keep a UK bird list there will be changes from 1st January 2018 as the BOU adopts the International Ornithological Congress (IOC) World Bird List for all its taxonomic needs, including the British List. As the list isn't up and running at the time of going to press, the current BOU list has been used in this edition of the Yearbook. Once the changes come into force there will be a few lumps and splits amongst the species so we'll need to sort through them to update our lists - hopefully any losses will be balanced out by gains!

Another Bird Fair has just passed, my 16th as an exhibitor selling natural history books. Even after all of these years, although there are fluctuations from year to year, it is still a worthwhile event to attend as a 'trader'. One part of the event I really enjoy though is catching up with people I know... ex-colleagues, book buying customers, those who have been on a birding trip with me... as well as meeting new acquaintances. Last year an enquiry for the Yearbook from Bulgaria lead to an article in this edition from Ina Agafonova (see page 8) - it was really nice to actually meet Ina face-to-face at the Bird Fair and to find out more about the project that she's involved with. Maybe a trip to Bulgaria's Black Sea coast is on the cards - it sounds like a fascinating place to visit.

Most of us are members of one bird/natural history club or another. I have always made a point of supporting my local bird club and county trust as well as a few specialist clubs/organisations that, to my mind, do a great job. One club that I've been a member of since it was first launched is the African Bird Club. Having first visited Africa in 1984/85, and having been lucky enough to have worked there, I'm hooked on the continent... once it gets you, it never lets you go! The ABC has now reached a milestone of 25 years since it was formed - Nigel Birch's feature (page 12) highlights the role of the ABC and how it has helped, and is helping, birds and birding in Africa.

Finally I would like to thank, as ever, all of the people who have responded to my queries over information contained in the Yearbook to ensure that it is as up to date and as accurate as possible. I would also like to thank two local teenagers, Amy and Joe, for use of their photos for some of the section headings - hopefully their use will encourage them to carry on taking photos.

If you come across any errors, omissions or changes before the next edition please let me know (contact details on page 6).

I hope you all have some great birding in 2018.

Neil Gartshore
Wareham, September 2017

CONTACT US

The information contained in the *Yearbook* is sourced/checked in a number of ways... websites, magazines, personal contacts, e-mails, phone calls, and so on. Once the *Yearbook* has been published there will inevitably be changes to some of the contact information that will not be amended until the following edition.

In the majority of cases, if you contact someone who has stepped down from a role you should be redirected to the new contact. Where we are notified of any changes to contact information we will list them on an amendments page on the Calluna Books website (go to www.callunabooks.co.uk and follow the *Yearbook* link).

If you have any comments on this edition of the *Yearbook*, corrections to advise us of or suggestions for future editions, we would be pleased to hear from you.

Neil Gartshore, Moor Edge, 2 Bere Road, Wareham, Dorset BH20 4DD

phone: 01929 552 560

e-mail: yearbook@callunabooks.co.uk

Limited back copies of the **Yearbook** are available covering most years from **2001** to **2017**

Please contact us for availability/prices

FEATURES

Neil Gartshore

Little Bittern *Ixobrychus minutus* is a species now breeding in the UK but is found in good numbers through the wetlands of Bulgaria. It is one of 254 species of birds ecologically dependent on wetlands (for part of their year) that are covered under the Agreement on the Conservation of African-Eurasian Migratory Waterbirds (AEWA).

EASTERN BULGARIA

Ina Agafonova introduces us to birdwatching in eastern Bulgaria with an emphasis on the area on the Black Sea known as the Burgas Lake Complex.

BULGARIA, SITUATED IN SE EUROPE and bordering the Black Sea, is a land full of diverse natural treasures. Its mountains and sandy beaches are well known attractions, but there is also a well preserved natural environment which includes three National Parks (Central Balkan, Rila & Pirin), 11 Nature Parks, 55 reserves and several protected areas. The unique geographical location provides for all year round activities such as trekking and hiking, horse riding, caving, paragliding, mountain-biking, rafting and kayaking. Bulgaria also offers many possibilities for birdwatching, photography, botany, ecological, archaeological and rural tourism.

Birdwatching in Bulgaria

The **Eastern Rodope Mountains (1)**, especially near the town of Madzharovo, offers the chance of finding more than 20 species of breeding birds of prey like Black and Egyptian Vultures, Long-legged Buzzard, Imperial, Golden, Lesser Spotted, Booted and Short-toed Eagles. There is also a good variety of passerines in the area including Black-eared and Isabelline Wheatears, Rock Thrush, Masked Shrike, Eastern Orphean and Eastern Olivaceous Warblers and Rock Nuthatch.

The internationally important **Srebarna Nature Reserve (2)** is a remnant of the once numerous lakes that lined the route of the Danube. The area was proclaimed a nature reserve in 1948 and a RAMSAR site in 1975. The reserve was recognized as World Natural Heritage Site under the 1972 Convention for the Protection of the World Cultural and Natural Heritage and included in the UNESCO World Heritage list in 1983. Nearly 100 species of birds breed and a further 80 species migrate/winter here. It has the only colony of Dalmatian Pelican in Bulgaria, as well as the largest breeding populations of four more globally threatened species: Pygmy Cormorant, Ferruginous Duck, White-tailed Eagle and Corncrake. Other birds of interest include Red-necked Grebe, Little Bittern, Red-crested Pochard, Red-breasted Goose, Red-footed Falcon, Kentish Plover, Lesser Grey Shrike, Calandra Lark, Tawny Pipit and Bluethroat.

Durankulak Lake (3) is a coastal lake with a good mix of typical birds: Red-necked Grebe, Glossy Ibis, Little Bittern, Purple Heron, Whiskered and White-winged Terns and Savi's Warbler. A good site to look for Paddyfield Warbler. Autumn passage turns up waders like Curlew and Marsh Sandpipers and in winter Red-breasted, White-fronted and a few Lesser White-fronted Geese may be found.

Purple Heron - Neil Gartshore

EASTERN BULGARIA

Lake Shabla-Ezeretz (4) has breeding
Ruddy Shelduck and Paddyfield, Marsh, Savi's
and Great Reed Warblers and a variety of
other birds in the area including Levant
Sparrowhawk, Bee-eater, Golden Oriole,
Black-headed and Ortolan Buntings and
Rose-coloured Starling.

Black-headed Bunting - Neil Gartshore

The beautiful headland in the Southern Dobrudja
region, **Kaliakra (5)**, offers stunning views of
vertical cliffs reaching 70 meters down to the
sea. It features the remnants of the fortified
walls, water-main, baths and residence of
Despot Dobrotitsa in the short-lived Principality
of Karvuna's medieval capital. The Bolata Cove,
with a small sheltered beach, lies just to the
north at the mouth of a picturesque
canyon and forms part of the nature reserve. The reserve has the biggest and most valuable
steppe habitats still found in Bulgaria and is part of the Via Pontica migratory route. An isolated
colony of Shag (Mediterranean race) breed here, Yelkouan Shearwater, Stone Curlew, Pallid
Harrier, a variety of gulls and terns, Alpine Swift, Short-toed Lark, warblers - including Olive-
tree, Pied Wheatear, Red-breasted Flycatcher can be seen, especially in the autumn, along with
pelicans, storks, harriers, buzzards and eagles passing over.

The area covered by the **Ropotamo Complex (6)** currently supports 236 bird species, 69
of which are listed in the Red Data Book for Bulgaria. This is one of the most important
breeding sites in the country for a number of species closely dependent on the different
types of habitats found here including Yelkouan Shearwater, Spotted and Little Crakes,
Purple and Squacco Herons and Semi-collared Flycatcher. Ten globally threatened species
occur during the breeding season, migration or winter – Pygmy Cormorant, Dalmatian
Pelican, Marbled Duck, Ferruginous Duck, White-tailed Eagle (one of three breeding sites
along the Black Sea Coast), Pallid Harrier, Greater Spotted Eagle, Imperial Eagle, Lesser
Kestrel and Corncrake. At migration time the area is a typical bottleneck where the numbers
of White Stork and Common Buzzard and other species of birds of prey can be considerable.
Other birds of interest in the area include Grey-headed, Middle Spotted and Syrian
Woodpeckers, Wryneck, Red-backed Shrike, Icterine Warbler, Sombre Tit and Hawfinch.

Dalmatian Pelecan - Vaughan Ashby

Pygmy Cormorant - Vaughan Ashby

The Burgas Lake Complex (7)

The Burgas Lake Complex, is one of the three most significant wetland complexes for congregations of waterfowl along the Bulgarian Black Sea coast.

The complex consists of three lakes Atanasovsko, Burgas (or Vaya) and Mandra. The region is well known to birdwatchers from around the world.

a] Atanasovsko Lake. The protected area (1,700ha), lies to the north of Burgas, consisting of the lake, arable land and residential areas. Around the lake there are also many freshwater basins, wet grasslands and a well developed system of channels which 'feed' the lake with fresh water. The main Burgas-Varna road divides the hyper-saline lake into two - to the north a firth in character, to the south a lagoon. Salt has been produced here by traditional, environmentally friendly methods since 1906 which preserves the lakes species - a good example of a harmless economic activity.

The northern half of the lake was designated a reserve in 1980 - with remainder of the lake and some areas along its banks (as a buffer zone) the following year. In 1984, the site was designated a Ramsar site (expanded in 2003). The territory was declared a key ornithological territory (KOT) in 1989 by BirdLife International and the same year the lake was designated a CORINE site for its European importance for the conservation of rare and endangered bird species. Conformity with the Protected Areas Act required re-designation of this protected area as a 'maintained reserve' in 1999. In 2007, the buffer zone became 'The Burgas Salt Pans Protected Area' and as of 2008, Atanasovsko Lake was designated as part of the European Natura 2000 network.

b] Burgas Lake. Burgas Lake (also known as Lake Vaya) is the largest natural lake in Bulgaria, occupying 2,900ha: a shallow brackish coastal lake, an open firth with a weak connection to the sea. It is located to the west of Burgas and its entire eastern part borders the industrial and residential districts of the city. The lake is connected to the sea through a narrow channel with a sluice, the cleaning of which in recent years has been one of the main challenges facing the normal functioning of the lake. The channel provides a usual salinity in the lake of about 10.5%, but there are strong seasonal fluctuations. The channel allows access for marine fish species to enter the lake for spawning, and the return of the young fish to the Black Sea. surrounding the lake are several small marsh pools, fishponds, wet marshy meadows, farmland and pasture.

In 1995, Burgas Lake was included in the National Plan for the Protection of the Most Important Wetlands in Bulgaria, and in the updated plan of 2013. The lake was declared a RAMSAR site in 2000 and is protected under both European Directives - for birds and for habitats.

Via Pontica Foundation

c] Mandra-Poda. The Mandra-Poda Complex includes Mandra Lake with its adjacent wetlands. Until 1940 Mandra Lake hosted the last breeding colony of the White Pelican in Bulgaria. Its disappearance was probably due to the transformation of the semi-saline lake into a freshwater reservoir and the flooding of its western part, which destroyed the huge reedbeds there. The main habitat is the lake itself (covering 1,300ha). Fish ponds, a lagoon preserved between the reservoir wall and the sea and a shallow marine area in Foros Bay are part of the site. Meadows, woodland and farmland surround the site.

EASTERN BULGARIA

The Birds

As mentioned above (sites 1-6), Bulgaria's Black Sea area offers a selection of sites with excellent birding where the UK birdwatcher will find many interesting species. The wetlands around Burgas (site 7), however, forms one of Europe's richest bird areas where a visit in the spring/summer, autumn or winter will be well rewarded. About 340 species have been recorded in the area including some that are globally endangered and 71 species listed in the Red Data Book of Bulgaria (http://e-ecodb.bas.bg/rdb/en/).

The complex lies along Europe's second largest migration route, the Via Pontica. It is a typical 'narrow migration front' site used by migratory birds. Up to 240,000 White Storks, 60,000 raptors and more than 30,000 White Pelicans can be seen here during the spring and autumn and this is the place where migrating White and Dalmatian Pelicans, Marsh Harrier and Red-footed Falcon concentrate in their highest numbers in Europe, and which has - after the Bosphorus - the second highest concentrations of Lesser Spotted Eagles.

Wintering waterbird numbers reach internationally important concentrations. Species include Pygmy Cormorant, Dalmatian Pelican, Cormorant, Great Egret, Whooper and Bewick's Swans, White-fronted Goose, Shelduck, Pochard and Tufted Duck and smaller numbers of Red-breasted Goose, Smew, Ferruginous Duck and White-headed Duck. Gulls include Pallas's and Slender-billed.

The Mandra-Poda complex is of international importance for breeding Spoonbill (the only breeding site along the Black Sea coast) and Avocet while Burgas Lake is one of the most important breeding sites in the country for Little Bittern. Other spring/summer species include White-tailed Eagle, Honey Buzzard, Marsh Harrier, White and Dalmatian Pelican, Pygmy Cormorant, Squacco, Black-crowned Night and Purple Herons, Collared Pratincole, Black-winged Stilt, Curlew and Marsh Sandpipers, Kentish Plover, Slender-billed, Mediterranean and Little Gulls, Gull-billed, Black, Whiskered and White-winged Terns, Marsh, Great Reed and Cetti's Warblers and Penduline Tit.

Visiting

Flights and accommodation are readily available along Bulgaria's 250 mile Black Sea coast for a 'do it yourself' trip, alternatively a number of bird tour companies also visit the area. With both options it would be possible to visit most of the sites mentioned in this feature over a week.

In 2016 the **Via Pontica Foundation's Visitors Centre (8)** on the western shore of Burgas Lake opened to visitors - a good starting point when visiting the area. The Centre is open 24/7 and welcomes groups and individuals. Check out the website: https://viapontica.org/en/

The site provides long walks, bird watching towers, special access to the western shore of Burgas Lake and the possibility for wild camping. Guided tours and lectures are offered on request.

It features 60ha of extensive fish farming of freshwater fishes as an example of a sustainable business that co-exists with bird watching. There is a farmers market on site that offers fresh fruits and vegetables from local farmers and there is a small farm with domestic animals that provides a hands on experience for children and adults.

THE AFRICAN BIRD CLUB - 25 YEARS ON

Nigel Birch, the Representatives Co-ordinator of the ABC, gives an insight into the Club as it celebrates its 25th year.

THE AFRICAN BIRD CLUB (ABC): working for birds and conservation in Africa. So says our motto, but does this mean? Who are we and what do we do?

We are a UK-based charity coming up to our 25th Anniversary - we were set up in 1993. The Club is managed by volunteers and has a worldwide membership which is united by an interest in and love of Africa and its birds, and a desire to improve their conservation. To do this requires increasing our knowledge of them and involving local people in their study and conservation.

Why Africa?

According to BirdLife International's 2013 State of Africa's Birds, of the continent's 2,355 species 245 (c.10%) are globally threatened with extinction. 29 of those are on the Red List of Critically Endangered species.

Many of the threatened species are emblematic such as the Bateleur *Terathopius ecaudatus* and the Martial Eagle *Polemaetus bellicosus*. There are also species that perform important ecosystem services such as the vultures, who, by clearing carrion, reduce the risk of disease. Of the eleven species of vulture in Africa, seven (including five of the six endemic species) are now globally threatened.

Africa is also host to large numbers of Palearctic migrants. Studies in Europe have shown that populations of long-distance migrants are declining faster than those species that are resident or migrate shorter distances. This indicates that conditions in the African wintering grounds are deteriorating and this deterioration will also affect resident African species.

The threats to African birds (and biodiversity generally) are multiple and include agriculture, climate change, invasive species, human disturbance, logging, pollution, the effects of energy developments and mining, commercial and residential development and hunting and trapping.

So what do we do?

We strive to increase the knowledge of Africa and its birds, both on the continent itself and further afield. We do this through our communications: our Bulletin, the website and newsletter, our conservation awards and our network of in-country representatives.

The Bulletin of the African Bird Club is produced twice yearly. The content is very varied but always includes a round-up of the latest birding and conservation news from Africa, Club news, recent sightings as well as major feature articles on birding, identification, conservation, research and guides to top birding sites in Africa. We also keep in touch with members through a regular Newsletter from the Chair, distributed electronically.

THE AFRICAN BIRD CLUB – 25 YEARS ON

Our extensive website https://www.africanbirdclub.org contains a wealth of information, not just about the Club, but also Africa and its birds, with checklists, country descriptions that include information on the major birding areas and links to country recorders and the network of Club representatives in Africa.

The Representatives are an important part of the Club, giving the Council information about issues in their respective countries as well as promoting the work of the Club. They can also provide information to members on, for example, birding opportunities. There are currently 46 representatives: 34 African and 12 non-African.

We also developed and support AFBID, The African Bird Image Database https://africanbirdclub.org/afbid/ This contains more than 25,000 images of 2,230 species.

Our biggest impact, however, is probably through our support for conservation and educational projects. Since 1994 we have awarded more than £300,000 in support of more than 200 projects in more than 40 countries. Funding comes form membership fees and the generosity of donors and sponsors.

We award small grants for conservation awards. These support research on African birds and can include activities such as surveys, educational projects or training courses, production in local languages of guides to the common birds of a country and interpretation material for nature reserves. We also provide grants for expeditions.

This range of activity is reflected in some recent awards which include:

- Kenya: a study into the conservation ecology of the globally endangered Grey Crowned Crane *Balearica regulorum gibbericeps* within the agro-ecosystem landscapes of central Kenya; and testing the feasibility of an acoustic monitoring system for monitoring trends in species richness of forest birds in an important bird area on Mount Kenya Forest Reserve.

- Ghana: an award to derive a population estimate and the distribution of the Critically Endangered Hooded Vulture *Necrosyrtes monachus* in the western region of the country.

- Angola: the distribution of 500 copies of the guide The Special Birds of Angola.

- Tanzania: another species study - the population size, distribution, threats and conservation status of the endemic and endangered Usambara Weaver *Ploceus nicolli* in the Eastern Arc Mountains.

- Benin: an educational project on the conservation of migratory waterbirds in the Ramsar site, Nokoue Lake.

- Cape Verde: a bird biodiversity survey and community engagement on Maio Island.

Perhaps our most significant project, however, is the purchase of land to help protect the critically endangered Taita Apalis *Apalis fuscigularis* in Kenya. Announced in March 2015 to mark our 20th anniversary, this is our largest ever award: £25,000 towards the leasing of part of the Apalis' Taita Hills habitat. The award is in partnership with the RSPB and NatureKenya.

THE AFRICAN BIRD CLUB - 25 YEARS ON

Supporting African Ornithologists

We are also supporting the development of an African Birds Field Guide smart phone app. The intention is that this will be free for African ornithologists, birders, field workers and naturalists, many of whom are not able to afford a traditional field guide. We hope that a trial version with photos, sounds, text and maps for the birds of Mauritius and Rodrigues will be released soon.

Finally, we have always been conscious that, as the African Bird Club, we should be involving Africans more in the membership. With the costs of the Bulletin and particularly postage so high, finding the membership fee is a challenge for many potential African members. Working with publishing software company PageSuite (who produce material for the British Trust for Ornithology, amongst others) we have developed an electronic version of the Bulletin. We are now offering free membership to African members: they receive an electronic copy of the Bulletin rather than the hard copy. We hope this will lead to a larger proportion of our membership being based in Africa, and thus greater involvement in the work of the Club by African members.

If you want to know more, or feel like supporting us, please visit our website where you can find details about the Club and how to join. You can also see us at the British BirdFair or come along to our Annual meeting – the next one is on 21 April 2018 at the Natural History Museum in London – where you can hear presentations on Africa and its birds, as well as the work of the Club.

Details of the projects/awards mentioned in this article, and of our other awards, can also be found on the ABC website.

Photo credits: Martial Eagle & Grey-crowned Crane
© John Caddick

ACCESSIBLE RESERVES... WHY GIVE A MONKEYS?

Bo Beolans, Chairman of Birding For All, has advocated more inclusive access on nature reserves for many years.

FIT ABLE-BODIED TWITCHERS enjoying gripping off their rivals don't, or at least not yet! But most of us don't fit that profile. The overwhelming majority of even the most competitive birders get as much of a kick sharing birds as they get out of seeing them for themselves. Ask 'what's about?' or even for ID help from a more experienced birder and you will find we are a pretty generous lot (although from the paltry funds raised at many twitches might make you think otherwise!) From serious ramblers to weekend strollers we all think countryside public access is a good thing, which should, perhaps be even better... subject, naturally, to the conservation needs of wildlife. But what most of us don't think much about is how we can achieve and grow access, let alone who exactly are the public?

Sixty-five million people cram our land. Around fifteen million are children. Over ten million are of pensionable age and as many as ten million, by some definitions, have a disability. At any time there will be people who are sick or injured and, even given that there is considerable cross-over, one cannot avoid concluding that half the population have needs for access that do not fit the average.

The sad truth is that many facilities only enable some of us to enjoy the countryside... can that really be considered public access?

Not all children are small, not all sick people find distance, gradient or ground conditions difficult and not all older people are infirm. Nevertheless, at any moment in time a great many need more accessible paths, hides, gates and so forth. But take notice, you too will need help or better provision if you break a leg, produce children or get old! So, one way or another we ALL need better access.

As an aside its worth sharing the current 'orthodoxy' about disability. (Oddly here in the UK 'disability' is an acceptable term and 'handicapped' is not, but in the US & Canada it's the exact opposite!) – the current orthodox way of looking at mobility issues is the 'social model'. Simply put disability is not a function of a person and their needs, issues or peculiarities, but rather that it is about society's response to varying needs (or lack of it) which is disabling. Having no use of one's legs isn't disabling so much as society's insistence on limited choices suiting the few, such as only providing steps when ramps would suit everyone; having narrow doors when wide ones fit everyone, or barring the way with a gate when a cattle grid will keep cows in while allowing wheelchairs to pass.

So, in terms of birding and bird reserves what does this actually mean? The dictum many people with an interest in this matter use is 'barrier-free access'.

Before ANY type of provision is made one should ask what it is for. If a gate or stile is to keep cows in a field where a footpath runs, it is not fit for purpose as it stops those with mobility problems from gaining access, whereas a cattle grid would be a barrier to cows but not wheelchairs. Another example would be something designed to stop cars or motorbikes from using a track, such as a narrow kissing gate, when an angled design would prevent motorbikes and cars from entering but allow through walkers, wheelers, and pedal-cyclists.

ACCESSIBLE RESERVES... WHY GIVE A MONKEYS?

You might see a pattern here... ninety-nine times out of a hundred it's about good design and more thought not later adaptation or greater expense.

Something else that requires us to think outside of our historical box is replacing the 'average' with 'variety'. Because people are 'differently abled' and come in all shapes and sizes we shouldn't always try to make one size fit all. You wouldn't go dancing in wellies, any more than you would dig ditches in pretty pink stiletto heels! Provision needs to vary heights and widths in, for example, bird hides. At the moment, at best, provision is made for a 'wheelchair slot'. This is a place with extra knee-room, a lower 'elbow' shelf and a lower viewing slot. All the other viewing positions have fixed benches, a standard distance from the viewing slots which have a standard height elbow shelf and a standard size flap window. Why? Surely larger viewing slots suit more people rather than just those of average height. Lower elbow shelves suit people with unbending backs and moveable benches mean kids don't topple forward only being able to look at what is below the hide window!

There are many, simple things that can be done but the first thing to do is to think! The second is to consult, and the third to test everything from the ramp into a hide to the gate into the reserve by throwing a variety of users at it. For example, distance is a real issue for a great many people with mobility issues. More vehicular access where it can do no

harm helps, so does the provision of regular simple benches or perches to rest on. Birding For All can advise and we have a brochure for reserve wardens with suggestions and some vital dimensions etc. (New reserves should think about the public being inside looking out, rather than outside looking in. Most reserves confine the public to a perimeter circuit, it is far better to create a hidden access drive into a central restricted car park ringed by hides.)

Here is a real example of how a half-thought through decision and provision is incredibly disabling:

A reserve I visit has access for cars along a mile of entrance track. The new car park (with accessible toilets) has a gate to the reserve. Blue-badge holders may drive to the first hide (a mile away). But the gate is kept closed to discourage able-bodied drivers cheating.

So, wheelchair users have to get their wheelchair out, transfer into it, open the gate, get back in their car, re-stow the wheelchair and drive through the gate. They then have to get out of the wheelchair again, get in it to close the gate, then climb back in, re-stow the chair and drive on. An exhausting 20 minutes demonstrating the social model of disability, a problem caused by thoughtlessness or the wrong priority.

And that's why I give a monkeys!

Birding ForAll

Further details about Birding for All can be found on their website: www.birdingforall.com

or by writing to:
Birding for All, 18 St Mildreds Road, Cliftonville, Margate, Kent CT9 2LT

NEWS FROM THE WORLD OF BIRDS

James Lowen offers a selection of interesting stories and titbits about wild birds from across the UK, and occasionally further afield.

Unusual breeders

The 2017 breeding season featured some unusual species, including some for which colonisation appears underway. Following a huge influx in 2016/17, Cattle Egrets bred for the second and third times in the UK, with pairs in Cheshire and Dorset. Black-crowned Night Heron bred for the first time, in Somerset. At least five locations in southeast and eastern England held six breeding pairs of Black-winged Stilts - with more fledglings this year than from all previous nesting attempts between 1983 and 2016. Numbers of breeding Spoonbills in north Norfolk continues to rise, and a pair also bred for the first time in Yorkshire, at Fairburn Ings. Back in 2016, 48 pairs of Crane bred in the UK – the highest number since the species returned in 1978 after an absence of 400 years. They nested successfully in Wales for the first time since departure. Finally, at the time of writing, Bee-eaters look likely to nest in Nottinghamshire.

Winners...

There was plenty of pleasingly good news among regular scarce breeding birds. Bittern continues to increase, with 167 'booming' males in 2016 representing a slight rise on 2015. A pair bred in Wales for first time in 30 years, and two pairs did so in Oxfordshire (for the first time ever). RSPB heathland reserves had a record year in 2016, with a 34% increase in Dartford Warblers, 12% rise in Woodlarks and Nightjar reaching an all-time high of 158 'churring' males.

Thanks to an EU-funded project that helps farmers create suitable nesting habitat, Britain's Stone Curlews raised 144 more chicks in 2016 than they did in 2012/13. In 2016, a national survey revealed that Scottish Golden Eagles have increased by 15% since 2003. The population now stands at 508 pairs. Collaboration between farmers and the RSPB – paying the former for making nature-friendly choices – has enabled Cirl Buntings to shoot past the 1,000-pair milestone, reaching 1,078 pairs in 2016. Following the first successful reintroduction of a passerine in Europe, Cornwall now hosts 65 pairs.

Bearded Tits reached 772 pairs in 2014, the highest since monitoring began in 1995. In 2017, wigwam-style nest boxes installed at RSPB Old Moor enabled the species to breed at this South Yorkshire reserve for the first time. The species also now breeds in Nottinghamshire. Corn Bunting populations have stabilised in northeast Scotland following decades of decline. Intriguingly, Scotland's woodland birds have increased by two-thirds overall since 1994 – probably due to constructive woodland management and some beneficial impacts of climate change. Meanwhile, modelling by the RSPB predicts 221 pairs of White-tailed Eagle breeding in Scotland by 2025, with a conceivable 889-1,005 pairs by 2040.

The State of the UK's birds 2016 report noted that 22 species had moved from Amber to Green on the national list of threatened species, meaning that they are now of low conservation concern. Tellingly, their number included Red Kite, following successful reintroductions in recent decades. In addition, Bittern and Nightjar have moved from Red to Amber on the national list of threatened species.

NEWS FROM THE WORLD OF BIRDS

... and losers

Other species fared less well. A Scotland-wide survey of calling Corncrakes in 2016 revealed 1,059 birds, a decline of 3% on 2015 (and 20% on 2014). The State of the UK's birds 2016 report provided particularly troubling reading. The report highlights a continuing downward trend among upland birds, with five species added to the national Red list including Grey Wagtail. One-quarter of the UK's regularly occurring species are now nationally 'Red listed'. In 2016, Curlew,

Puffin and Nightingale were added to the list of nationally threatened species. Eight regular UK species are now considered globally threatened, including such familiar birds as Pochard and Turtle Dove. Sixty per cent fewer Pochard winter in the UK compared to the 1980s. This reflects declining breeding populations in Europe, which the Wildfowl and Wetlands Trust thinks is due to predation from invasive mammals such as American Mink, increased nutrients in wetlands, and reduced protection from dwindling colonies of Black-headed Gulls.

Non-natives

A report by the Rare Breeding Birds Panel reveals that 25 non-native species bred or may have bred in Britain during 2012-14, eight of which are common. Of the remaining species, only Black Swan, Red-crested Pochard (which has increased by 75% in 15 years) and Monk Parakeet nest in double figures. Many non-native breeders are wildfowl such as Bar-headed Goose, Snow Goose and Ruddy Shelduck. One or two pairs of Eagle Owl persist in Lancashire. Intriguingly, there are now mixed pairs of Harris's Hawk and Common Buzzard; what will their hybrid young look like?

Hen Harriers

The much-loved raptor remained in the news for all the wrong reasons. Britain's population declined by 13% from 2011-17 to around 545 pairs, with a longer-term decline of 39% since 2004. Only Orkney and the Hebrides are bucking the overall downwards trend. Just four pairs bred in England during 2016 – despite there being suitable habitat for 300 pairs. Of 16 fledglings satellite tagged in 2016, 10 had been found dead or were otherwise 'missing' by February 2017. Other species were also involved. A review by the Scottish Government found that one-third of Scottish satellite-tagged Golden Eagles were illegally poisoned or shot.

Conservationists pointed fingers towards those managing grouse-shooting moors. To widespread public condemnation, court proceedings against two gamekeepers were dropped despite apparently compelling evidence. Nevertheless, there were positive signs. In June 2017, the Scottish Government announced an independent enquiry into gamebird-shoot licensing – and conservation organisations including RSPB Scotland called for a progressive partnership with the shooting community that would include regulatory measures. More than 120,000 signed conservationist Mark Avery's e-petition to ban driven grouse shooting, prompting a debate in the Westminster Parliament's Petitions Committee. The organisation Ethical Consumer has also called upon UK companies to treat grouse shooting as a Corporate Social Responsibility issue. The now-annual Hen Harrier Day took place on 5-6 August 2017, seeking to raise awareness of the continuing persecution of the species.

NEWS FROM THE WORLD OF BIRDS

Places... good news and bad

There was encouraging news for several wildlife-rich areas around the UK. RSPB Bempton Cliffs made the Top 10 of the natural outdoor visitor attractions, as ranked by the travel website TripAdvisor. Norfolk Wildlife Trust raised £1 million to purchase 655 hectares adjacent to Hickling Broad in the Norfolk Broads. The RSPB announced two notable reserve successes. It secured a 50-year lease to manage Whitton Sands, in the inner Humber Estuary. The 120-hectare island holds breeding Marsh Harrier, Avocet and Bearded Tit. It also raised nearly £300,000 to expand its Mersehead reserve in the Solway Firth, a key site for wintering Barnacle Geese. Meanwhile, the economic benefits of conservation received a boost when a survey revealed that tourists spent £8.2 million in Dumfries and Galloway from 2004-2015 after travelling to see Red Kites released there.

In less good news, the battle for Lodge Hill (Kent) rumbles on. Medway Council's 2014 decision to grant planning permission for 5,000 houses on a stronghold for Nightingales is set to go to a public inquiry in 2018. Conservationists are fearful that an inquiry verdict that supported building on this Site of Special Scientific Interest would set a precedent for protected sites nationwide.

Also worrying was a court ruling upholding a decision by the Scottish Government to grant planning permission for a £10-billion offshore renewable energy developments in the Firths of Forth and Tay. RSPB Scotland fears that the wind farms threaten thousands of Puffins, Gannets and Kittiwakes. In contrast, a Scottish Natural Heritage report found that seabirds continue to use waters around Orkney's wave and tidal energy infrastructure.

Leaving the EU

A review of Special Protection Areas (SPAs) by the Joint Nature Conservation Committee concluded that the existing suite of these EU-designated sites was sufficient for the effective conservation of 64 bird species, but insufficient for 94 species. It lamented that there were seven species for which SPAs are required but for which no sites have yet been protected. We await with bated breath the fate of SPAs and other EU-derived wildlife protection once the UK leaves the EU.

Talking of which, a House of Lords committee published a report recommending key actions to ensure environmental protections are not eroded as a result of Brexit. Following the snap 2017 General Election, responsibility for ensuring this now falls to new Environment Food and Rural Affairs Secretary of State, Michael Gove, who was – lest we forget – among the figureheads of the Leave campaign. In a welcome move, Mr Gove met with one conservation body (the RSPB) during his first week in office. Birdwatchers nationwide surely hope he will listen to what conservationists say.

NEWS FROM THE WORLD OF BIRDS

The British list

Seven species have recently been formally adopted to the British list - Red-footed Booby, Purple Swamphen, Siberian Accentor, Pale-legged Leaf Warbler, Chestnut Bunting, Eastern Kingbird and Acadian Flycatcher. The list now stands at 610 species. This will increase slightly when the British Ornithologists Union starts following taxonomy of the International Ornithological Congress World Bird List on 1 January 2018. Birds dropped from the list considered as national rarities by the British Birds Rarities Committee included one iconic bird, namely Red-flanked Bluetail. From mythical to scarce migrant in under 25 years.

Research revelations

New research has taught us much about how birds behave and why. Geolocators attached to Common Swifts confirmed long-held predictions: that birds remain in the sky for 99% of the time when they are not nesting, and that they can spend 10 months airborne without landing. Whimbrels were also discovered to be aeronauts, migrating non-stop from Iceland to wintering grounds in West Africa, covering up to 5,500 km in just five days. Up to 90% of all seabirds now eat plastic waste, compared to 5% in the 1960s. Researchers have discovered that this is because plastic covered of algae exudes a smell similar to krill – kidding the seabirds into thinking they are consuming food. Continuing the marine theme, researchers have discovered that cormorants can hear under water. Given that human-made sounds disturb marine mammals, this discovery may have implications for underwater infrastructure developments.

Several studies considered the relationship between human actions and avian survival. A study suggests that feeding birds in spring (as many people do in their gardens) could unintentionally reduce breeding success. This is because feeding stations attract predators such as Grey Squirrels, which then raid nests. A Spanish study also found that high levels of human disturbance adversely affect nestling development in Blue Tits. The issue appears to be frequency of disturbance rather than proximity to humans: what might this mean for nature recreation? Another threat to songbirds comes from traffic noise, which dramatically impairs the effectiveness of their alarm calls. This suggests that passerines living near even moderately busy roads are more vulnerable to predation. One wonders whether this has been considered by those seeking to unravel the decline of urban House Sparrows...

All illustrations: Dan Powell

BEST BIRD BOOKS OF THE YEAR

Another year, another bumper selection of books - Gordon Hamlett casts his eye over the changing book market.

At the risk of sounding stupid, not for the first time, there has been a major sea-change this year, with a huge swing towards books that are designed to be read. Of course, all books are designed to be read, so what am I rabbiting on about? Well, there are far fewer reference books this year: fewer field guides, fewer identification guides, fewer 'where to watch' guides and so on.

The obvious reason for this is that we are reaching saturation point; most countries and regions of the world have their own dedicated field guide. Want to know where to go? Most of that has been done too. Looking for an in depth guide to a particular family of birds? They're all out there: warblers, wildfowl, thrushes, gulls.

If I went to a publisher today and said 'Here's a proposal for a new field guide for British birds', they are going to turn round to me and say 'Is it better than the Collins Guide? Does it present the information in a new and innovative way?' And if the answer is 'no', then they are justifiably going to tell me to sling my hook.

But still we have dozens of books for you to enjoy with plenty of them looking at the relationship between books and something else: history, folklore, literature, music. All these subjects work for me but you will have your own favourites.

A real pleasure over the last few years has been seeing how the science of ornithology has been represented. For years, I grew up on the likes of Poyser monographs. I love these dearly but I'll be the first to admit that they can be heavy going at times. Science is now becoming far more accessible, and we have a series of authors who can explain things in an entertaining and easily assimilated manner.

Books about birds and birdwatching never cease to amaze me. There always seems to be a new way of approaching the hobby. This year was no exception; the idea that there might be a huge craft-related birding market had never even entered my consciousness. Who knows what next year will bring?

Field Guides

Covering over 1,400 species on 248 plates, **Birds of Venezuela** (Ascania et al, Helm, £40) is deservedly guaranteed the number one spot when it comes to field guides for what is the world's sixth largest avifauna. Following the usual Helm format, it is good to see that distribution maps are included on the same page as the text so you that don't have to go cross-referencing a separate section elsewhere in the book.

The **Collins Field Guide to Birds of South-East Asia** (Arlott, William Collins, £40) is a portable guide covering large chunks of China, Burma, Taiwan, Thailand, Laos, Cambodia, Vietnam, Peninsular Malaysia, Singapore and the Coco Islands. Most major subspecies, though no juveniles are illustrated. Text, as you might imagine, is restricted to a few lines for each species. Ideal for anyone heading out east on a gap year.

A Photographic Field Guide to the Birds of India, Pakistan, Nepal, Bhutan, Sri Lanka and Bangladesh (Grewal et al, Princeton, £37.95) certainly gets the award for the most unwieldy title of the year. Covering 1,375 species, the book is just about luggable for any traveller. While the overall standard of the photos is pretty good, most species just get one or two illustrations, with tiny thumbnail pictures for alternative plumages; there are just too many birds for a photo guide to do them justice.

21

BEST BIRD BOOKS OF THE YEAR

Birds of Europe, North Africa and the Middle East - A Photographic Guide (Jiguet & Audevard, Princeton, £24.95) has the feel of a more traditional field guide, with the photos of the birds being cropped out of the rest of the picture, thus freeing up far more space than in the Indian Guide (above). It doesn't have as much depth as last year's runaway hit Britain's Birds (Hume et al, WILDGuides) with e.g. only six photos of Lesser Black-backed Gull as opposed to twelve, but it does have a broader range of 860 species covered.

Fans of Britain's Birds might like to know that there is now a companion guide - **Britain's Mammals** (Couzens et al, WILDGuides, £17.95) which follows the same format.

Where the Birds Are

The only 'where to watch' guide that has come my way this year is **The Best Birdwatching Sites in Yorkshire** (Glenn & Miles, Buckingham Press, £19.95). Very good it is too, though I declare an interest, having written the Scottish Highlands book in the same series. It covers 88 sites, ranging from the famous such as Spurn and Flamborough to smaller sites, previously unknown to all but a few locals. As always with this series, excellent maps are the key to its success.

I have long been a fan of books devoted to a small area of the country, written by, usually, one enthusiast who has put in years of patchwork. **Birds of Caernarfonshire** (Pritchard) is a county avifauna available for the ludicrously low price of £12 + £2 p&p from Rhion Pritchard, Pant Afonig, Hafod Lane, Bangor, Gwynedd LL57 4BU, cheques payable to 'Cambrian Ornithological Society'.

A Lizard Bird Diary (Brian Cave, £25) covers the area around Britain's most southerly point during the period 1970-2015. It is available as a limited edition of 500 from either the author at alizardbird@yahoo.com or from Amazon. Both books contain abundance charts, photos and full species descriptions.

On a slightly different tack, **Birding in the Bristol Region: A celebration** covers the history of the Bristol Ornithological Club over the last 50 years. The central part of the book involves getting 50 club members to write about local birds that have a deep significance to them, ranging from mega rarities to the mundane. It is available from William Earp (£12 incl. p&p) at 4 Pitchcombe Gardens, Bristol BS9 2RH. If you have an interest in birding in any of these three areas, then I urge you to invest in a copy.

Moving to a more international level, **Natural History of Tenerife** (Ashmole, Whittles Publishing, £30) and The New Neotropical Companion (Kricher, Princeton, £27.95) are probably too unwieldy to use in the field, but they do make for excellent reference materials pre- and post-holiday. Both cover a full range of wildlife and habitats and are profusely illustrated. I wouldn't want to visit either of these two areas without having read the appropriate volume first.

Species accounts

Well, this is an unfortunate coincidence; two books on the same subject, identical in size and with near identical covers. **Owls** (Taylor, Ivy Press, £30) covers all 225 species, each bird getting a few paragraphs of text, a large colour photo and distribution map. The illustrations have been cut away from their backgrounds, presumably to save space, but they don't work for me. Full size pull-outs of four species' wings and a poster on the back off the dust jacket are gimmicky.

A Parliament of Owls (Unwin & Tipling, William Collins, £25) concentrates on just over 50 species, but in far more depth. The photographs elevate this title over its rival though. They are of a higher quality and include the backgrounds as well; it is amazing how much a bit of added foliage brings the pictures to life. If you are looking for a coffee table book on owls, this is the one to go for.

BEST BIRD BOOKS OF THE YEAR

Anyone who enjoyed Nick Davies' book Cuckoo: Cheating by Nature (Yearbooks passim) will be interested in **The Cuckoo - The Uninvited Guest** (Mikulica et al, Wild Nature Press, £24.99). The emphasis this time is on the photographs, which reveal an intimate portrait of the species. It is easy to forget that on the continent, other species are parasitised; there are excellent pictures of a Cuckoo being raised by Redstarts for example.

Dave Walker has studied his subject for nearly 40 years, so the odds are reasonable that he knows a fair bit about his subject. **A Fieldworker's Guide to the Golden Eagle** (Whittles Publishing, £19.99) is a study of the eagle's ecology and challenges some long-held views on the species.

Flight Identification of Raptors (Forsman, Bloomsbury, £44.99) should have been included in last year's review but missed out due to a technical hitch. It's far too good to leave out again. Covering Europe, North Africa and the Middle East, over 1,100 photos, plus a totally authoritative text cover every age and plumage you are ever likely to come across. And if you still haven't had your fill of birds of prey, try **Raptors of Mexico and Central America** (Clark & Schmitt, Princeton, £32.95) which does the same sort of thing for a different subset of species.

One of my favourite pieces of trivia is that the Bee Hummingbird is so small that you can send up to 63 for the price of a first class stamp. How small? Well, you can find out in **Hummingbirds** (Fogden et al, Ivy Press, £14.99), which is a photographic field guide to all 338 species, with every species depicted life-size.

Anyone who has explored a massive seabird colony in summer, or watched thousands of birds streaming past a headland on autumn passage will find much to enjoy in **The Seabirds's Cry** (Nicholson, William Collins, £16.99). The ten chapters each cover a separate species and are based largely around observations from the Shiant Isles. A fine mix of science and literature.

If, like me, you missed the original Poyser edition of **The Hen Harrier**, you will be interested to know that it has been relaunched in a different format (Watson, Bloomsbury, £18.99). Always one of the classic Poyser titles, it is interesting to see how much has changed since it was first published in 1977; just look at the distribution maps of Marsh and Montagu's Harriers for example. To that end, it's a pity that an additional chapter couldn't have been added, bringing the story up to date with details of satellite tagging information, increased persecution and so on.

Bird behaviour

Claiming to be 'A Complete Guide to their Biology and Behaviour' might be over-egging the pudding somewhat, but **Birds** (Elphick, Natural History Museum, £16.99) has a lot going for it. Starting with a quick chapter on prehistoric birds, there are highly accessible sections on anatomy, flight, breeding, migration and so on. This is a first rate introduction to the subject.

Bird Brain (Emery, Ivy Press £20) puts to bed forever the idea that birds are stupid and that to call someone a bird brain might actually be complimentary rather than derogatory. Short sections, enhanced by some excellent graphics and illustrations, look at various studies into avian intelligence. The text strikes just the right balance too, neither too erudite nor too condescending. Recommended.

It is not unreasonable to state that our understanding of migration has been considerably advanced over recent years by the use of satellite tagging. **Where the Animals Go** (Cheshire & Uberti, Particular Books, £25) looks at some of the more spectacular discoveries, on land, at sea and in the air. Some of the avian examples include looking at penguin colonies from space, seeing how vultures spiral in thermals and how warblers can sense incoming tornadoes and move accordingly. If you love maps and love wildlife, this is an unbeatable combination.

23

BEST BIRD BOOKS OF THE YEAR

All through the Year

Several authors have used the calendar as a framework for their writings. Following on from last year's **'Spring' and 'Summer'**, it doesn't take a genius to work out the two titles completing the set. **'Autumn' and 'Winter'** (ed Harrison et al/The Wildlife Trusts, £12.99 each) are anthologies of nature writing and ideal for a bit of bedtime writing. They would also make lovely presents if you are not sure of your recipient's exact tastes in books.

The Nature of Autumn (Crumley, Saraband , £12.99) is a personal view of his favourite season by one of Scotland's top nature writers, ranging from childhood memories of thousands of Pinkfeet to riffs on the jazz-like calls of flocks of Whooper Swans.

Wonderland (Westwood & Moss, John Murray, £20) is subtitled 'A Year of Britain's Wildlife' and has entries for every day of the year. I set out with the intention of reading that day's entry just before I went to sleep but got so engrossed that I soon found myself several weeks ahead of schedule.

The January Man – A Year of Walking Britain (Somerville, Doubleday, £14.99) takes its title from a folk song by Dave Goulder. The lines for April read 'Through April rain the man goes down to watch the birds come in to share the Summer'. The walks include Foula, the Lancashire and North Norfolk coasts, Upper Teesdale and the Long Mynd.

Most intriguing title of the year goes to Rosamond Richardson's **Waiting for the Albino Dunnock** (Weidenfield & Nicholson, £16.99). Based on the author's articles in Birdwatching Magazine, each chapter, covering a month of the year, is full of literary and musical references, which I love, even though I accept that they might not appeal to everyone.

Walking Through Spring (Hoyland, William Collins, £9.99) sees the author following the spring as it moves north from the south coast to the Scottish Borders at roughly the same speed as a walking man. As well as all the wildlife, the likes of Lady Chatterley, Tolkien, Theresa May and Vaughan Williams all get name-checked.

Personal memoirs

Fans of Spring/Autumn/Winterwatch should check out **A Wild Life** (Corsair, £8.99), a series of behind-the-scenes and how-on-earth-did-they-film-that anecdotes from presenter Martin Hughes-Games.

No Way But Gentlenesse (Hines, Bloomsbury, £8.99) is by the author of A Kestrel for Knave, later filmed as Kes. It is a sort of working class 'H is for Hawk', showing how nature can soothe even the angriest of breasts.

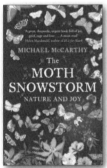

Michael McCarthy looks at the healing power of nature and the forces that oppose it in **The Moth Snowstorm** (John Murray, £20). Not surprisingly, from the author of 'Say Goodbye to the Cuckoo', the Cuckoo satellite tagging scheme features prominently, but there are plenty of other bird references too, ranging from Ivory-billed Woodpeckers to the cards given away in packets of tea.

Not a memoir as such, the exact opposite in fact, but more a labour of love. **Charles Darwin's Life with Birds** (Frith, Oxford UP, £45.99) discusses Darwin the ornithologist, before going on to annotate every single reference Charles Darwin made to birds in his entire published output of works.

BEST BIRD BOOKS OF THE YEAR

Words and music

Songs of Love and War (Couzens, Bloomsbury, £16.99) should properly be placed in the section on bird behaviour, but it dovetails so well with A Sweet Wild Note (Smyth, Elliott & Thompson, £14.99) that it would be perverse not to lump them together.

The former (and here I declare an interest as I know Dominic Couzens), looks at what is going on in the dawn chorus, and the science behind why birds sing. For those of a musical bent, there is a chapter looking at the juxtaposition of Quail, Nightingale and Cuckoo, as they appear in Beethoven's Pastoral symphony. I think that this is one of Dominic's best books.

By way of contrast, Richard Smyth's book looks at the human response to birdsong, including sections on how we record and use sonograms in attempt to transcribe avian warblings into a form humans can make sense of them. There are sections on competitive Goldfinch singing in Victorian England and duets between a Nightingale and Beatrice Harrison's cello, one of radio's earliest hits.

Another war features in Where Poppies Blow (Lewis-Semple, Weidenfeld & Nicholson/Orion, £20). Subtitled The British Soldier, Nature and the Great War, this book looks at birds, horses, vermin, pets etc. as recorded in letters and poems written by those serving on the Western Front. Skylarks feature predominantly with their songs towering above the sound of the shells. There are also the first reports of flocks of migrating birds being seen by pilots of the fledgling Royal Flying Corps. One soldier quoted on the dustjacket states with typical British understatement 'If it weren't for the birds, what a hell it would be.'

Lapwings, Loons and Lousy Jacks (Reedman, Pelagic Publishing, £19.99) looks at the origins of bird names, from dialect names to the scientific names they later acquired. Birds on both side of the Atlantic are discussed and anyone who enjoys words and their origins will find much to entertain them here.

Birds - Myth, Lore and Legend (Warren-Chadd & Taylor, Bloomsbury, £25) was always going to be high on my wish list; everything I love about birds in the one title. I wasn't disappointed. Lavishly produced, what makes this title stand out from other folklore books is that it takes a global rather than purely British approach. I am looking forward to spending many hours with this book in one hand and the other hand rapidly pecking away at the keyboard as I google further information on stories previously unknown to me.

Is it possible to put the beauty of birds into words? Possibly not, but that hasn't stopped writers and poets trying over the years. In As Kingfishers Catch Fire (Corsair, £25) novelist Alex Preston examines how over twenty species, from Peacocks to Peregrines, have been represented over the years. If you enjoy literature, you will love this book and I guarantee that you will find some new authors to explore.

Arts and Crafts

As someone who struggles to draw a stickman, I am in awe of anyone with even a smidgen of artistic talent. I requested a copy of Bird Art from Search Press (Woollett, £17.99) which is an intermediate to advanced guide to drawing birds with graphite and coloured pencils.

What I wasn't expecting was to receive a bundle of other craft books, also themed about birds, including a most impressive looking Stitched Textiles: Birds (Sumner, £15.99), and A Field Guide to Knitted Birds (Arne and Carlos, £14.99). Their back catalogue includes a volume on making birds out of sugar, another book of knitting patterns, and another couple of 'how to draw' books.

BEST BIRD BOOKS OF THE YEAR

I confess that I never knew that this sector of the market existed, and, ever the sceptic, wondered just how niche it was. However, I showed the books to several friends, both birders and non-birders and there is now a queue to borrow them when I have finished this article.

If you love photographs, then one of this year's stand out title is **Raptors in Focus** (Forsman, New Holland, £19.99). The art of a good photograph is to make the viewer think 'Wow! I wish I had seen that in real life' and here, Dick Forsman succeeds in generating considerable amounts of jealousy.

Birds in Pictures (Varesvuo, New Holland, £30) is the sort of book that makes you want to throw your camera away in despair. Apart from the stunning portraits of, mainly of birds of the far North, Varesvuo is not afraid to throw in the odd arty shot too. A double page spread, entirely white apart from a beady black eye and bill of a Ptarmigan and a portrait of a Snowy Owl in which all the white parts of the bird have been made the same shade as the background, leaving only the black feather markings to delineate the bird are memorable. A truly stunning coffee table book.

Perversely, I know of Frank Jarvis not through his art, but from a hide named for him at Sculthorpe Hawk and Owl Trust where I do some work as a voluntary warden. **A Bird Guide to the Fields of Experience** (Jarvis, Chatterpie, £24) is a volume of field sketches and diaries, covering Scotland 1985-6 and Norfolk 1986-93. Utterly charming, this book takes you back to a time when a notebook and pair of binoculars were the only tools of the trade a birder had.

Remarkable Birds (Avery, Thames and Hudson, £24.95) does exactly what it says on the tin, with accounts of 67 or so species ranging from the humble Dunnock to the exotic Resplendent Quetzal. What elevates this book above several other similar titles are the historical prints and paintings of the birds involved, with artists ranging from Audubon to James McCallum. The quality of the paper adds to the appeal of this book.

Stocking fillers and books for children

At just 64 pages, **Skylark** (Crumley, Saraband, £10) is ideal for a last minute present or bit of bedtime reading. The latest in an ongoing series and featuring a lovely cover drawn by Carry Akroyd, the book features a fine mix of first class nature writing with the odd bit of poetry thrown in.

Matt Sewell has written and illustrated a couple of books for children. **A Charm of Goldfinches** (Ebury Press, £12) covers a selection of collective nouns for land, sea and air creatures. I loved his description of Snow Buntings as coming from the 'Badlands of Scotland', accompanied by some delightful cartoonish pictures, drawn in his own inimitable style.

The Big Bird Spot (Pavilion, £9.99) is a sort of avian equivalent of the Where's Wally books. Readers are encouraged to find varying numbers of the key species and a pair of binoculars across a double page diorama of a different habitat type. There are quirky bonus for the more advance birder (or parent) too, such as a cheeky little Wallcreeper in the Alpine scene full of Wheatears.

The Egg (Teckentrup, Prestel, £11.99) is a bewitching mix of science, mythology and art. Ranging from the comparative sizes of Hummingbird and Elephant Bird eggs, via camouflage, different types of nests, fish and reptile eggs through to Fabergé Eggs, and all beautifully illustrated in a series of pastel pictures, this book is a joy throughout.

BIRDWATCHER'S DIARY 2018

Neil Gartshore

The World Seabird Union, an organization comprised of the world's seabird societies (http://www.seabirds.net), held the first annual World Seabird Day on July 3rd, 2017. This date, in 1844, was when the last known sighting of the Great Auk *Pinguinus impennis* occurred. Seabirds, like the Guillemot *Uria aalge*, are indicators of the health of our oceans.

EVENTS DIARY for October 2017~December 2018

The *Yearbook* goes to press in late-Sep so events for Oct/Dec 2017 have been listed here (and will give an indication of similar events to expect in Oct/Dec 2018). **It is advisable to check** the relevant website/contact the organiser to ensure that there are no changes to dates/venues.

OCTOBER 2017

7: RSPB Members' Day & AGM
QEII Centre, Westminster. W: www.rspb.org.uk

13-15: Hawk & Owl Trust Members Weekend
Anglian Water Birdwatching Centre, Rutland Water Nature Reserve, Egleton, Oakham, LE15 8BT
W: www.hawkandowl.org

19-29: Society of Wildlife Artists
The Natural Eye, 54th Annual Exhibition
Mall Galleries, Pall Mall, London.
W: www.swla.co.uk

20-22 Oct: Scottish Ornithologists' Club AGM & Annual Conference
Atholl Palace Hotel, Pitlochry.
W: www.the-soc.org.uk/the-2017-annual-conference/

NOVEMBER

4: Welsh Ornithological Society National Conference
(Raptor Conservation in Wales). Bridges Centre
Drybridge House, Drybridge Park, Monmouth, NP25 5AS.
W: www.birdsinwales.org.uk

18-19: North West Bird Watching Festival
WWT Martin Mere, Fish Lane, Burscough,
Lancashire L40 0TA. T: 01704 895 181
W: www.wwt.org.uk/wetland-centres/martin-mere/whats-on/2017/11/18/north-west-bird-watching-festival/

DECEMBER

8-10: BTO Annual Conference
Hayes Conference Centre, Swanwick, Derbyshire
E: info@bto.org; W: www.bto.org.uk

~~~~~~~~~~

JANUARY 2018

3 Jan-17 Feb: Big Schools Birdwatch (RSPB)
UK-wide event to get children interested in wild birds (first half of Spring Term). For events in your area... W: https://ww2.rspb.org.uk/fun-and-learning/for-teachers/schools-birdwatch/

27-28: Big Garden Birdwatch (RSPB)
UK-wide survey of garden birds.
W: https://ww2.rspb.org.uk/get-involved/activities/birdwatch

FEBRUARY

2: World Wetlands Day
Theme: Wetlands for a Sustainable Urban Future. Various events around the globe celebrating the importance of wetland environments.
W: www.ramsar.org

14-21: National Nest Box Week
A BTO initiative to encourage more people to erect nestboxes. Various events around the UK – see website for details.
W: www.bto.org/about-birds/nnbw

21-24: Pacific Seabird Group
45th annual meeting. La PÁz, Mexico.
W: www.pacificseabirdgroup.org/annual-meeting/

MARCH

17: SOC/BTO Scottish Birdwatchers' Spring Conference
SRUC Barony Campus, Parkgate, Dumfries, DG1 3NE.
W: http://www.the-soc.org.uk/socbto-one-day-spring-conference-the-scottish-birdwatchers-conference/

27-29: BOU Annual Conference
21st century ornithology: challenges, opportunities and decisions. University of Nottingham, UK.
W: www.bou.org.uk/bou-conferences

APRIL

6-8: RSPB Members' Weekend
East Midlands Conference Centre,
University of Nottingham.
W: www.rspb.org.uk/reserves-and-events/events-dates-and-inspiration/events/rspb-weekend/

9-14: American Ornithological Society (136th meeting)
Tucson, Arizona, USA
https://amornithmeeting2018.org/

21: African Bird Club
AGM plus full programme of talks on research & conservation work in Africa.
Flett Theatre, Natural History Museum, Cromwell Road, London SW7 5BD. Door open 10:15am.
E: info@africanbirdclub.org or
W: www.africanbirdclub.org

23-27: 6th International Eurasian Ornithology Congress (IEOC)
University of Heidelberg, Germany.
W: www.eurasianornithology.com/

EVENTS DIARY for October 2017~December 2018

MAY

tba: The Norfolk Bird & Wildlife Fair
(fair was cancelled in 2017 but planned for 2018)
For birdwatchers, photographers, wildlife
enthusiasts & families. Mannington Hall, near
Aylsham, Norfolk. T: 01603 219 119
W: www.norfolkbirdfair.com

JUNE

7-9: AFO/WOS 2018 Meeting
Association of Field Ornithologists (AFO)/Wilson
Ornithological Society (WOS)
Chattanooga, Tennessee, USA.
W: www.wilsonsociety.org/wilsonsoc/meetings/

JULY

AUGUST

2-5: BBC Countryfile Live
Blenheim Palace, Oxfordshire
W: www.countryfilelive.com

17-19: British Birdwatching Fair
Rutland Water Nature Reserve, Egleton, Rutland.
E: callen@birdfair.org.uk; W: www.birdfair.org.uk

19-26: 27th International Ornithological Congress
Vancouver, British Columbia, Canada.
http://www.iocongress2018.com/

SEPTEMBER

14-17: Int. Wader Study Group
Annual Conference
Netherlands. W: www.waderstudygroup.org/

tbc: Spurn Migration Festival
W: www.spurnmigfest.com

OCTOBER - DECEMBER 2018

19-21 Oct: Scottish Ornithologists' Club
AGM & Annual Conference
Atholl Palace Hotel, Pitlochry.
W: www.the-soc.org.uk

13-17 Nov: Annual Meeting of the
Raptor Research Foundation
Skukuza, Kruger National Park, South Africa
W: www.raptorresearchfoundation.org/
conferences/kruger/

See 2017 entries for other likely events during this
period.

Dates unknown:

Oriental Bird Club Autumn Meeting
& AGM (last Sep 2017).
Wilkinson Room, St John the Evangelist, Hills Rd,
Cambridge, CB2 8RN. Starts 11.00am
E: mail@orientalbirdclub.org
W: www.orientalbirdclub.org

OSME (Ornithological Society of the
Middle East, Caucasus & Central Asia)
Summer Meeting & AGM. (last Jul 2017).
BTO, The Nunnery, Thetford, Norfolk.
E: secretary@osme.org; W: www.osme.org

Neotropical Bird Club
General meeting & AGM. (last Sep 2016).
E: secretary@neotropicalbirdclub.org.uk
W: www.neotropicalbirdclub.org

42nd Annual Meeting of The Waterbird Society
(last Aug 2017) W: www.waterbirds.org

VARIOUS DATES THROUGH THE YEAR (BTO)

BTO Garden BirdWatch talks: these are given by
a number of speakers to a wide variety of groups
across the country.

BTO Training Courses: one day courses/residential
courses - subjects include identifying birds; bird
survey techniques; breeding bird survey; & bird
identification/wetland bird survey.

Local Bird Club Conferences: the BTO encourage
& support local bird clubs through their 'Bird Club
Partnership'.

Regional Bird Ringer's Conferences: usually one-day
conferences held in the different regions of the UK.

Check out the BTO's website: www.bto.org.uk or
phone: 01842 750 050 for more information on
BTO-related talks, courses or conferences in 2018.

NOTE:

Due to the printing deadline of the *Yearbook* it
is not always possible to confirm dates or even if
conferences, fairs etc will be running during the
following year.

If you have, or know of, any events for 2019 &
would like them mentioned in this section of the
Yearbook then please contact us by mid-Aug 2018.

[See our contact details on P6.]

DIARY – JANUARY 2018

1	Mon	New Year's Day E&W, NI, S
2	Tue	Bank Holiday S
3	Wed	
4	Thu	
5	Fri	
6	Sat	
7	Sun	
8	Mon	
9	Tue	
10	Wed	
11	Thu	
12	Fri	
13	Sat	
14	Sun	
15	Mon	
16	Tue	
17	Wed	
18	Thu	
19	Fri	
20	Sat	
21	Sun	
22	Mon	
23	Tue	
24	Wed	
25	Thu	
26	Fri	
27	Sat	
28	Sun	
29	Mon	
30	Tue	
31	Wed	

DIARY – FEBRUARY 2018

1	Thu	
2	Fri	
3	Sat	
4	Sun	
5	Mon	
6	Tue	
7	Wed	
8	Thu	
9	Fri	
10	Sat	
11	Sun	
12	Mon	
13	Tue	
14	Wed	
15	Thu	
16	Fri	
17	Sat	
18	Sun	
19	Mon	
20	Tue	
21	Wed	
22	Thu	
23	Fri	
24	Sat	
25	Sun	
26	Mon	
27	Tue	
28	Wed	

DIARY – MARCH 2018

1	Thu	
2	Fri	
3	Sat	
4	Sun	
5	Mon	
6	Tue	
7	Wed	
8	Thu	
9	Fri	
10	Sat	
11	Sun	
12	Mon	
13	Tue	
14	Wed	
15	Thu	
16	Fri	
17	Sat	St Patrick's Day NI
18	Sun	
19	Mon	
20	Tue	
21	Wed	
22	Thu	
23	Fri	
24	Sat	
25	Sun	British Summertime begins (1 hour forwards)
26	Mon	
27	Tue	
28	Wed	
29	Thu	
30	Fri	Good Friday E&W, NI, S
31	Sat	

DIARY 2018

DIARY – APRIL 2018

1	Sun	
2	Mon	Easter Monday E&W, NI
3	Tue	
4	Wed	
5	Thu	
6	Fri	
7	Sat	
8	Sun	
9	Mon	
10	Tue	
11	Wed	
12	Thu	
13	Fri	
14	Sat	
15	Sun	
16	Mon	
17	Tue	
18	Wed	
19	Thu	
20	Fri	
21	Sat	
22	Sun	
23	Mon	
24	Tue	
25	Wed	
26	Thu	
27	Fri	
28	Sat	
29	Sun	
30	Mon	

DIARY 2018

DIARY – MAY 2018

1	Tue	
2	Wed	
3	Thu	
4	Fri	
5	Sat	
6	Sun	
7	Mon	Early May bank holiday E&W, NI, S
8	Tue	
9	Wed	
10	Thu	
11	Fri	
12	Sat	
13	Sun	
14	Mon	
15	Tue	
16	Wed	
17	Thu	
18	Fri	
19	Sat	
20	Sun	
21	Mon	
22	Tue	
23	Wed	
24	Thu	
25	Fri	
26	Sat	
27	Sun	
28	Mon	Spring bank holiday E&W, NI, S
29	Tue	
30	Wed	
31	Thu	

DIARY – JUNE 2018

1	Fri	
2	Sat	
3	Sun	
4	Mon	
5	Tue	
6	Wed	
7	Thu	
8	Fri	
9	Sat	
10	Sun	
11	Mon	
12	Tue	
13	Wed	
14	Thu	
15	Fri	
16	Sat	
17	Sun	
18	Mon	
19	Tue	
20	Wed	
21	Thu	
22	Fri	
23	Sat	
24	Sun	
25	Mon	
26	Tue	
27	Wed	
28	Thu	
29	Fri	
30	Sat	

DIARY – JULY 2018

1	Sun	
2	Mon	
3	Tue	
4	Wed	
5	Thu	
6	Fri	
7	Sat	
8	Sun	
9	Mon	
10	Tue	
11	Wed	
12	Thu	Orangeman's Day NI
13	Fri	
14	Sat	
15	Sun	
16	Mon	
17	Tue	
18	Wed	
19	Thu	
20	Fri	
21	Sat	
22	Sun	
23	Mon	
24	Tue	
25	Wed	
26	Thu	
27	Fri	
28	Sat	
29	Sun	
30	Mon	
31	Tue	

DIARY – AUGUST 2018

1	Wed	
2	Thu	
3	Fri	
4	Sat	
5	Sun	
6	Mon	Summer bank holiday S
7	Tue	
8	Wed	
9	Thu	
10	Fri	
11	Sat	
12	Sun	
13	Mon	
14	Tue	
15	Wed	
16	Thu	
17	Fri	
18	Sat	
19	Sun	
20	Mon	
21	Tue	
22	Wed	
23	Thu	
24	Fri	
25	Sat	
26	Sun	
27	Mon	Summer bank holiday E&W, NI
28	Tue	
29	Wed	
30	Thu	
31	Fri	

44

DIARY – SEPTEMBER 2018

1	Sat	
2	Sun	
3	Mon	
4	Tue	
5	Wed	
6	Thu	
7	Fri	
8	Sat	
9	Sun	
10	Mon	
11	Tue	
12	Wed	
13	Thu	
14	Fri	
15	Sat	
16	Sun	
17	Mon	
18	Tue	
19	Wed	
20	Thu	
21	Fri	
22	Sat	
23	Sun	
24	Mon	
25	Tue	
26	Wed	
27	Thu	
28	Fri	
29	Sat	
30	Sun	

DIARY – OCTOBER 2018

1	Mon	
2	Tue	
3	Wed	
4	Thu	
5	Fri	
6	Sat	
7	Sun	
8	Mon	
9	Tue	
10	Wed	
11	Thu	
12	Fri	
13	Sat	
14	Sun	
15	Mon	
16	Tue	
17	Wed	
18	Thu	
19	Fri	
20	Sat	
21	Sun	
22	Mon	
23	Tue	
24	Wed	
25	Thu	
26	Fri	
27	Sat	
28	Sun	British Summertime ends (1 hour backwards)
29	Mon	
30	Tue	
31	Wed	

DIARY – NOVEMBER 2018

1	Thu	
2	Fri	
3	Sat	
4	Sun	
5	Mon	
6	Tue	
7	Wed	
8	Thu	
9	Fri	
10	Sat	
11	Sun	
12	Mon	
13	Tue	
14	Wed	
15	Thu	
16	Fri	
17	Sat	
18	Sun	
19	Mon	
20	Tue	
21	Wed	
22	Thu	
23	Fri	
24	Sat	
25	Sun	
26	Mon	
27	Tue	
28	Wed	
29	Thu	
30	Fri	St Andrew's Day S

DIARY 2018

DIARY – DECEMBER 2018

1	Sat	
2	Sun	
3	Mon	
4	Tue	
5	Wed	
6	Thu	
7	Fri	
8	Sat	
9	Sun	
10	Mon	
11	Tue	
12	Wed	
13	Thu	
14	Fri	
15	Sat	
16	Sun	
17	Mon	
18	Tue	
19	Wed	
20	Thu	
21	Fri	
22	Sat	
23	Sun	
24	Mon	
25	Tue	Christmas Day E&W, NI, S
26	Wed	Boxing Day E&W, NI, S
27	Thu	
28	Fri	
29	Sat	
30	Sun	
31	Mon	

YEAR PLANNER 2019

JANUARY	
FEBRUARY	
MARCH	
APRIL	
MAY	
JUNE	
JULY	
AUGUST	
SEPTEMBER	
OCTOBER	
NOVEMBER	
DECEMBER	

CHECKLISTS

Joe Mitchell

The Royal Tern *Sterna maxima maximus* found in the USA may soon be split from its West African counterpart (*Sterna maxima albididorsalis*) as recent studies in The Gambia (including DNA analysis) have concluded that the two are distinct species.

CHECKLIST OF BRITISH BIRDS
Based on the British List formulated by the British Ornithologists' Union

THE OFFICIAL BRITISH LIST is maintained by The British Ornithologists' Union (BOU) which sits in judgement on which birds you can count on your lists, and which you can't. The official list can change from year to year in one of two ways:

1): If someone claims to have seen a species never recorded in Britain, a panel of experts (the BOU Rarities Committee) assesses the record, making sure that the identification of the bird was proved beyond all possible doubt. Then the bird's credentials are assessed, to determine whether it was a genuine vagrant, rather than one that had just hopped over the fence from the nearest zoo or aviary.

Only if the bird passes every single strenuous test does it get accepted onto the British List... a process that may take many years. Similarly, historical records may be reassessed in the light of advances in identification skills.

2): The BOU also takes advice from taxonomists on the need to 'split' or 'lump together' sub-species. The current trend towards splitting is usually driven by DNA evidence suggesting that a particular sub-species is sufficiently different to warrant full species status.

With amendments to the 'British List' (8th ed, June 2013), the official list stands at 610 species, made up of 592 species in Category A, eight in Category B and ten in Category C (as of August 2017).

See below for a full description of what the different categories mean.

For further information about the British List visit the BOU's website, www.bou.org.uk

NOTE: there will be changes to the British List from 1st January 2018 - see preface (P5).

SPECIES, CATEGORIES, CODES - YOUR GUIDE TO GETTING THE BEST USE FROM THE CHECKLIST

Species Categories (column 1)

The following categories are those assigned by the British Ornithologists' Union.

A - Species recorded in an apparently natural state at least once since January 1, 1950.

B - Species recorded in an apparently natural state at least once between January 1, 1800 and December 31,1949, but not subsequently.

C - Species that, though introduced, now derive from the resulting self-sustaining populations:

C1 (*Naturalized introduced species*)
Species that have occurred <u>only</u> as a result of introduction, e.g. Egyptian Goose;

C2 (*Naturalized established species*)
Species resulting from introduction by man, but which also occur in an apparently natural state, e.g. Greylag Goose;

C3 (*Naturalized re-established species*)
Species successfully re-established by man in areas of former occurrence, e.g. Red Kite;

C4 (*Naturalized feral species*)
Domesticated species established in the wild, e.g. Rock Pigeon (Dove)/Feral Pigeon;

C5 (*Vagrant naturalized species*)
Species from established naturalized populations abroad. Currently no species in category C5;

C6 (*Former naturalized species*)
Species formerly in C1 whose naturalized populations are either no longer self-sustaining or are considered extinct, e.g. Lady Amherst's Pheasant.

D - This is for species that would otherwise appear in Category A but that there is reasonable doubt that the species have ever occurred in a natural state. Species held here are regularly reviewed with a view to assigning them to either Category A or E. Species placed solely in Category D form no part of the British List, and are not included in the species totals.

E - Species that have been recorded as introductions, human-assisted transportees or escapees from captivity, and whose breeding populations (if any) are thought not to be self-sustaining. Species in Category E that have bred in the wild in Britain are designated as E*. Category E species form no part of the British List (unless already included within Categories A, B or C).

Although the majority of species usually only fall into one category, a few are placed in multiple categories, for example, those species occurring in Category A which now have naturalized populations (e.g. Red Kite).

The British List comprises only those species in Categories A, B and C.

CHECKLISTS

Species List (column 2)

The *Yearbook* Checklist includes all species from categories A, B and C on the British List, based on the latest BOU listing.

Vagrants which are not on the British List, but which may have occurred in other parts of the British Isles, are not included. Readers who wish to record such species may use the extra rows provided. In this connection it should be noted that separate lists exist for Northern Ireland (kept by the Northern Ireland Birdwatchers' Association) and the Isle of Man (kept by the Manx Ornithological Society), and that Irish records are assessed by the Irish Rare Birds Committee.

The species names are those most widely used in the current field guides and each is followed by its scientific name, printed in italics.

Columns 3 to 22

These columns are for personal use and include a Life List, a 2018 list, and monthly lists from Jan to Dec. There are six columns (A-F) which could be used for a variety of reasons including a local patch, birds in the garden, a bird race or holidays.

Generally a tick suffices in each of the columns to record a bird seen. However, added benefit can be obtained by replacing ticks with specific dates.

How you fill in these columns is a matter of preference. For example: you may want to keep your Life List up to date with the first year you saw a species - for example if you see your first King Eider on 10th February 2018 it could be logged as '2/18' in the Life List column (as well as being recorded in the 2018 list as '10/2 and the February column as '10th'). As Life List entries are carried forward annually, in years to come it would be a simple matter to relocate this record into subsequent *Yearbooks*.

As space within the columns is limited it is recommended to use a thin pointed pen or pencil.

ADDITIONAL COLUMNS, make your own list	
A	
B	
C	
D	
E	
F	

BTO species codes (column 23)

The British Trust for Ornithology two-letter species codes are shown in the fourth column from the right. Readers should refer to the BTO if more codes are needed (the other species have been allocated 5-digit codes).

Rare breeding birds (column 24)

The species monitored by the Rare Breeding Birds Panel (see National Directory) comprise of those with a sustained population of fewer than 2000 breeding pairs and rarer non-native species with fewer than 300 breeding pairs. For full details, visit: www.rbbp.org.uk

The following annotations in the charts (third column from the right) reflect the panel's categories:

A) Rare Breeding Birds in UK (Regular);
B) Rare Breeding Birds in UK (Occasional);
C) Rare Breeding Birds in UK (Potential);
D) Rare Non-native Breeding Birds in UK (Regular);
E) Rare Non-native Breeding Birds in UK (Occasional);
F) Rare Non-native Breeding Birds in UK (Potential).

Rarities (column 25)

Rarities are indicated by a capital letter 'R' in the column headed BBRC (British Birds Rarities Committee). For full details, visit: www.bbrc.org.uk

EURING species numbers (column 26)

EURING databanks collect copies of recovery records from ringing schemes throughout Europe and the official species numbers are given in the last column. As they are taken from the full Holarctic bird list there are many apparent gaps. It is important that these are not filled arbitrarily by observers wishing to record species not listed in the charts, as this would compromise the integrity of the scheme.

Similarly, the addition of a further digit to indicate sub-species is to be avoided, since EURING has already assigned numbers for this purpose. The numbering follows the Voous order of species so some species are now out of sequence following the re-ordering of the British List. For full details, visit: www.euring.org

Butterflies & Dragonflies

As most birdwatchers have an interest in other areas of natural history, checklists have been included for two of the most popular groups with a column for a Life List and another for 2018 records.

SWANS, GEESE, DUCKS

			Life list	2018	Jan	Feb	Mar	Apr	May	Jun	Jul	Aug	Sep	Oct	Nov	Dec	A	B	C	D	E	F	BTO	RBBP	BBRC	EU No
AC2	Mute Swan	*Cygnus olor*																					MS			0152
AE	Bewick's Swan	*Cygnus columbianus*																					BS	C		0153
AE*	Whooper Swan	*Cygnus cygnus*																					WS	A		0154
AE	Bean Goose	*Anser fabalis*																					BE	E		0157
AE*	Pink-footed Goose	*Anser brachyrhynchus*																					PG	E		0158
AE*	White-fronted Goose	*Anser albifrons*																					WG	E		0159
AE*	Lesser White-fronted Goose	*Anser erythropus*																					LC	F	R	0160
AC2C4E*	Greylag Goose	*Anser anser*																					GJ			0161
AC2E*	Snow Goose	*Anser caerulescens*																					SJ	D		0163
AC2E*	Canada Goose	*Branta canadensis*																					CG			0166
AE	Cackling Goose	*Branta hutchinsii*																							R	
AC2E*	Barnacle Goose	*Branta leucopsis*																					BY			0167
AE	Brent Goose	*Branta bernicla*																					BG			0168
AE*	Red-breasted Goose	*Branta ruficollis*																					EB	E	R	0169
C1E*	Egyptian Goose	*Alopochen aegyptiaca*																					EG			0170
BDE*	Ruddy Shelduck	*Tadorna ferruginea*																					UD	D		0171
A	Shelduck	*Tadorna tadorna*																					SU			0173
C1E*	Mandarin Duck	*Aix galericulata*																					MN			0178
AE*	Wigeon	*Anas penelope*																					WN	A		0179
AE	American Wigeon	*Anas americana*																					AW			0180
AC2	Gadwall	*Anas strepera*																					GA			0182
AE	Baikal Teal	*Anas formosa*																					IK		R	1830
A	Teal	*Anas crecca*																					T.			0184
A	Green-winged Teal	*Anas carolinensis*																					TA	C		1842
	Sub total																									

DUCKS cont.

AC2C4E*	DUCKS cont.		Life list	2018	Jan	Feb	Mar	Apr	May	Jun	Jul	Aug	Sep	Oct	Nov	Dec	A	B	C	D	E	F	BTO	RBBP	BBRC	EU No
AC2C4E*	Mallard	Anas platyrhynchos																					MA			0186
A	Black Duck	Anas rubripes																					BD	B	R	0187
AE	Pintail	Anas acuta																					PT	A		0189
A	Garganey	Anas querquedula																					GY	A		0191
AE*	Blue-winged Teal	Anas discors																					TB	E	R	0192
A	Shoveler	Anas clypeata																					SV	A		0194
AC2E*	Red-crested Pochard	Netta rufina																					RQ	D		0196
AE	Canvasback	Aythya valisineria																							R	0197
AE*	Pochard	Aythya ferina																					PO	A		0198
AE	Redhead	Aythya americana																					AZ		R	0199
AE	Ring-necked Duck	Aythya collaris																					NG	B		0200
AE	Ferruginous Duck	Aythya nyroca																					FD	B	R	0202
A	Tufted Duck	Aythya fuligula																					TU			0203
A	Scaup	Aythya marila																					SP	B		0204
A	Lesser Scaup	Aythya affinis																					AY	C		0205
A	Eider	Somateria mollissima																					E.			0206
A	King Eider	Somateria spectabilis																					KE	C	R	0207
A	Steller's Eider	Polysticta stelleri																					ES		R	0209
A	Harlequin Duck	Histrionicus histrionicus																					HQ		R	0211
A	Long-tailed Duck	Clangula hyemalis																					LN	C		0212
A	Common Scoter	Melanitta nigra																					CX	A		0213
A	Black Scoter	Melanitta americana																							R	2132
A	Surf Scoter	Melanitta perspicillata																					FS			0214
A	Velvet Scoter	Melanitta fusca																					VS	C		0215
	Sub total																									

DUCKS cont. GAMEBIRDS, DIVERS

Code	Species	Scientific name	Life list	2018	Jan	Feb	Mar	Apr	May	Jun	Jul	Aug	Sep	Oct	Nov	Dec	A	B	C	D	E	F	BTO	RBBP	BBRC	EU No
A	White-winged Scoter	Melanitta deglandi																					VH		R	0216
AE	Bufflehead	Bucephala albeola																							R	0217
AE	Barrow's Goldeneye	Bucephala islandica																							R	0218
AE*	Goldeneye	Bucephala clangula																					GN	A		0218
AE	Hooded Merganser	Lophodytes cucullatus																					HO		R	2190
A	Smew	Mergellus albellus									✓												SY	C		0220
A	Red-breasted Merganser	Mergus serrator																					RM			0221
A	Goosander	Mergus merganser																					GD			0223
C1E*	Ruddy Duck	Oxyura jamaicensis																					RY	D		0225
AE*	Quail	Coturnix coturnix																					Q.	A		0370
C1E*	Red-legged Partridge	Alectoris rufa																					RL			0358
A	Red Grouse	Lagopus lagopus																					RG			0329
A	Ptarmigan	Lagopus muta																					PM			0330
AE	Black Grouse	Tetrao tetrix																					BK			0332
C3	Capercaillie	Tetrao urogallus																					CP	A		0335
AC2E*	Grey Partridge	Perdix perdix																					P.			0367
C1E*	Pheasant	Phasianus colchicus																					PH			0394
C6E*	Lady Amherst's Pheasant	Chrysolophus amherstiae																					LM	D		0397
C1E*	Golden Pheasant	Chrysolophus pictus																					GF	D		0396
A	Red-throated Diver	Gavia stellata																					RH	A		0002
A	Black-throated Diver	Gavia arctica																					BV	A		0003
A	Pacific Diver	Gavia pacifica																							R	0033
A	Great Northern Diver	Gavia immer																					ND	C		0004
A	White-billed Diver	Gavia adamsii																					VW	C		0005
	Sub total																									

ALBATROSSES, PETRELS, SHEARWATERS, CORMORANTS

	Species	Scientific name	Life list	2018	Jan	Feb	Mar	Apr	May	Jun	Jul	Aug	Sep	Oct	Nov	Dec	A	B	C	D	E	F	BTO	RBBP	BBRC	EU No
A	**Black-browed Albatross**	*Thalassarche melanophris*																					AA	C		0014
A	**Yellow-nosed Albatross**	*Thalassarche chlororhynchos*																							R	0150
A	**Fulmar**	*Fulmarus glacialis*																					F.			0020
A	**Fea's Petrel**	*Pterodroma feae*																							R	0026
A	**Capped Petrel**	*Pterodroma hasitata*																							R	0029
A	**Cory's Shearwater**	*Calonectris borealis*																					CQ			0036
A	**Scopoli's Shearwater**	*Calonectris diomedea*																							R	
A	**Great Shearwater**	*Puffinus gravis*																					GQ			0040
A	**Sooty Shearwater**	*Puffinus griseus*																					OT			0043
A	**Manx Shearwater**	*Puffinus puffinus*																					MX			0046
A	**Yelkouan Shearwater**	*Puffinus yelkouan*																							R	
A	**Balearic Shearwater**	*Puffinus mauretanicus*																								0046
A	**Macaronesian Shearwater**	*Puffinus baroli*																						C	R	0048
A	**Wilson's Petrel**	*Oceanites oceanicus*																								0050
B	**Frigate Petrel**	*Pelagodroma marina*																							R	0051
A	**Storm Petrel**	*Hydrobates pelagicus*																					TM			0052
A	**Leach's Petrel**	*Oceanodroma leucorhoa*																					TL			0055
A	**Swinhoe's Petrel**	*Oceanodroma monorhis*																							R	0056
A	**Red-billed Tropicbird**	*Phaethon aethereus*																							R	0064
A	**Gannet**	*Morus bassanus*																					GX			0071
A	**Red-footed Booby**	*Sula sula*									✓	✓													R	
A	**Cormorant**	*Phalacrocorax carbo*																					CA			0072
A	**Double-crested Cormorant**	*Phalacrocorax auritus*																							R	0078
A	**Shag**	*Phalacrocorax aristotelis*																					SA			0080
	Sub total																									

61

	FRIGATEBIRDS, BITTERNS, HERONS, STORKS, SPOONBILL, GREBES		Life list	2018	Jan	Feb	Mar	Apr	May	Jun	Jul	Aug	Sep	Oct	Nov	Dec	A	B	C	D	E	F	BTO	RBBP	BBRC	EU No
A	Ascension Frigatebird	Fregata aquila																							R	0093
A	Magnificent Frigatebird	Fregata magnificens																							R	0095
A	Bittern	Botaurus stellaris																					BI	A		0096
A	American Bittern	Botaurus lentiginosus																					AM		R	0098
A	Little Bittern	Ixobrychus minutus																					LL	B	R	0104
AE*	Night-heron	Nycticorax nycticorax																					NT	E		0107
A	Green Heron	Butorides virescens																					HR		R	0108
A	Squacco Heron	Ardeola ralloides																					QH		R	
A	Chinese Pond Heron	Ardeola bacchus																							R	0111
AE	Cattle Egret	Bubulcus ibis																					EC	B	R	0115
A	Snowy Egret	Egretta thula																								0119
A	Little Egret	Egretta garzetta																					ET	A		0121
A	Great White Egret	Ardea alba																					HW	C		0122
A	Grey Heron	Ardea cinerea																					H.			1230
A	Great Blue Heron	Ardea herodias																							R	0124
A	Purple Heron	Ardea purpurea																					UR	B		0131
AE	Black Stork	Ciconia nigra																					OS		R	0134
AE	White Stork	Ciconia ciconia																					OR	C		0136
AE	Glossy Ibis	Plegadis falcinellus																					IB	C		0144
AE	Spoonbill	Platalea leucorodia																					NB	A		0006
A	Pied-billed Grebe	Podilymbus podiceps																					PJ	B	R	0007
A	Little Grebe	Tachybaptus ruficollis																					LG			0009
A	Great Crested Grebe	Podiceps cristatus																					GG			0010
A	Red-necked Grebe	Podiceps grisegena																					RX	B		
	Sub total																									

	GREBES cont. RAPTORS, RAILS, CRAKES		Life list	2018	Jan	Feb	Mar	Apr	May	Jun	Jul	Aug	Sep	Oct	Nov	Dec	A	B	C	D	E	F	BTO	RBBP	BBRC	EU No
A	Slavonian Grebe	*Podiceps auritus*																					SZ	A		0011
A	Black-necked Grebe	*Podiceps nigricollis*																					BN	A		0012
A	Honey-buzzard	*Pernis apivorus*																					HZ	A		0231
AE	Black Kite	*Milvus migrans*																					KB	B		0238
AC3E*	Red Kite	*Milvus milvus*								✓													KT			0239
AC3E	White-tailed Eagle	*Haliaeetus albicilla*																					WE	A		0243
BDE	Egyptian Vulture	*Neophron percnopterus*																							R	0247
A	Short-toed Eagle	*Circaetus gallicus*																							R	0256
A	Marsh Harrier	*Circus aeruginosus*																					MR	A		0260
A	Hen Harrier	*Circus cyaneus*																					HH	A		0261
A	Northern Harrier	*Circus hudsonius*																							R	
A	Pallid Harrier	*Circus macrourus*																						C	R	0262
A	Montagu's Harrier	*Circus pygargus*																					MO	A		0263
AC3E*	Goshawk	*Accipiter gentilis*																					GI	A		0267
A	Sparrowhawk	*Accipiter nisus*																					SH			0269
AE*	Buzzard	*Buteo buteo*																					BZ			0287
AE	Rough-legged Buzzard	*Buteo lagopus*																					RF	C		0290
B	Spotted Eagle	*Aquila clanga*																							R	0293
AE	Golden Eagle	*Aquila chrysaetos*							✓														EA	A		0296
AE*	Osprey	*Pandion haliaetus*							✓	✓													OP	A		0301
A	Water Rail	*Rallus aquaticus*																					WA	A		0407
A	Spotted Crake	*Porzana porzana*																					AK	A		0408
A	Sora Rail	*Porzana carolina*																							R	0409
A	Purple Swamphen	*Porphyrio porphyrio*																							R	
	Sub total																									

CRAKES cont. GALLINULES, CRANES, BUSTARDS, WADERS

	Name	Scientific	Life list	2018	Jan	Feb	Mar	Apr	May	Jun	Jul	Aug	Sep	Oct	Nov	Dec	A	B	C	D	E	F	BTO	RBBP	BBRC	EU No
A	Little Crake	Porzana parva																					JC		R	0410
A	Baillon's Crake	Porzana pusilla																					VC	B	R	0411
AE*	Corncrake	Crex crex																					CE	A		0421
A	Moorhen	Gallinula chloropus																					MH			0424
A	Allen's Gallinule	Porphyrio alleni																							R	0425
A	Purple Gallinule	Porphyrio martinicus																							R	0426
A	Coot	Fulica atra																					CO			0429
A	American Coot	Fulica americana																							R	0430
A	Crane	Grus grus																					AN	A		0433
A	Sandhill Crane	Grus canadensis																							R	0436
A	Little Bustard	Tetrax tetrax																							R	0442
A	Macqueen's Bustard	Chlamydotis macqueenii																							R	0444
AE*	Great Bustard	Otis tarda																					US	A	R	0446
A	Stone-curlew	Burhinus oedicnemus																					TN	A		0459
A	Black-winged Stilt	Himantopus himantopus																					IT	B		0455
A	Avocet	Recurvirostra avosetta																					AV	A		0456
A	Oystercatcher	Haematopus ostralegus								✓	✓												OC			0450
A	Grey Plover	Pluvialis squatarola																					GV			0486
A	Golden Plover	Pluvialis apricaria						✓															GP			0485
A	American Golden Plover	Pluvialis dominica																					ID			0484
A	Pacific Golden Plover	Pluvialis fulva																					IF		R	0484
A	Dotterel	Charadrius morinellus																					DO	A		0482
A	Killdeer	Charadrius vociferus																					KL	C	R	0474
A	Semipalmated Plover	Charadrius semipalmatus																					TV		R	0471
	Sub total																									

WADERS cont.

	Common name	Scientific name	Life list	2018	Jan	Feb	Mar	Apr	May	Jun	Jul	Aug	Sep	Oct	Nov	Dec	A	B	C	D	E	F	BTO	RBBP	BBRC	EU No
A	Ringed Plover	*Charadrius hiaticula*								√													RP			0470
A	Little Ringed Plover	*Charadrius dubius*																					LP	A		0469
A	Sociable Plover	*Vanellus gregarius*																					IP		R	0491
A	White-tailed Plover	*Vanellus leucurus*																							R	0492
A	Lapwing	*Vanellus vanellus*																					L.			0493
A	Caspian Plover	*Charadrius asiaticus*																							R	0480
A	Greater Sand Plover	*Charadrius leschenaultii*																					DP		R	0479
A	Lesser Sand Plover	*Charadrius mongolus*																							R	0478
A	Kentish Plover	*Charadrius alexandrinus*																					KP	B		0477
A	Upland Sandpiper	*Bartramia longicauda*																					UP		R	0544
A	Little Whimbrel	*Numenius minutus*																							R	0536
B	Eskimo Curlew	*Numenius borealis*																							R	0537
A	Hudsonian Whimbrel	*Numenius hudsonicus*																							R	
A	Whimbrel	*Numenius phaeopus*																					WM	A		0538
A	Curlew	*Numenius arquata*																					CU			0541
A	Black-tailed Godwit	*Limosa limosa*																					BW	A		0532
A	Hudsonian Godwit	*Limosa haemastica*																					HU		R	0533
A	Bar-tailed Godwit	*Limosa lapponica*																					BA	C		0534
A	Turnstone	*Arenaria interpres*																					TT	C		0561
A	Great Knot	*Calidris tenuirostris*																					KO		R	0495
A	Knot	*Calidris canutus*																					KN			0496
A	Ruff	*Calidris pugnax*																					RU	A		0517
A	Sharp-tailed Sandpiper	*Calidris acuminata*																					VV		R	0508
A	Broad-billed Sandpiper	*Calidris falcinellus*																					OA	C	R	0514
	Sub total																									

65

	WADERS cont.		Life list	2018	Jan	Feb	Mar	Apr	May	Jun	Jul	Aug	Sep	Oct	Nov	Dec	A	B	C	D	E	F	BTO	RBBP	BBRC	EU No
A	Curlew Sandpiper	*Calidris ferruginea*																					CV			0509
A	Stilt Sandpiper	*Calidris himantopus*																					MI		R	5150
A	Red-necked Stint	*Calidris ruficollis*																							R	0500
A	Long-toed Stint	*Calidris subminuta*																							R	0503
A	Temminck's Stint	*Calidris temminckii*																					TK	B		0502
A	Sanderling	*Calidris alba*																					SS	C		0497
A	Dunlin	*Calidris alpina*																					DN			0512
A	Purple Sandpiper	*Calidris maritima*																					PS	A		0510
A	Baird's Sandpiper	*Calidris bairdii*																					BP		R	0506
A	Little Stint	*Calidris minuta*																					LX			0501
A	White-rumped Sandpiper	*Calidris fuscicollis*																					WU			0505
A	Least Sandpiper	*Calidris minutilla*																					EP		R	0504
A	Buff-breasted Sandpiper	*Calidris subruficollis*																					BQ	C		0516
A	Pectoral Sandpiper	*Calidris melanotos*																					PP	C		0507
A	Western Sandpiper	*Calidris mauri*																					ER		R	0499
A	Semipalmated Sandpiper	*Calidris pusilla*																					PZ		R	0498
A	Wilson's Phalarope	*Phalaropus tricolor*																					WF		R	0563
A	Red-necked Phalarope	*Phalaropus lobatus*																					NK	A		0564
A	Grey Phalarope	*Phalaropus fulicarius*																					PL			0565
A	Terek Sandpiper	*Xenus cinereus*																					TR		R	0555
A	Common Sandpiper	*Actitis hypoleucos*																					CS			0556
A	Spotted Sandpiper	*Actitis macularius*																					PQ	B	R	0557
A	Green Sandpiper	*Tringa ochropus*																					GE	A		0553
A	Solitary Sandpiper	*Tringa solitaria*																					I.		R	0552
	Sub total																									

WADERS cont. PRATINCOLES, SKUAS, AUKS

	Common name	Scientific name	Life list	2018	Jan	Feb	Mar	Apr	May	Jun	Jul	Aug	Sep	Oct	Nov	Dec	A	B	C	D	E	F	BTO	RBBP	BBRC	EU No
A	Grey-tailed Tattler	Tringa brevipes																					YT		R	0558
A	Spotted Redshank	Tringa erythropus																					DR			0545
A	Greater Yellowlegs	Tringa melanoleuca																					LZ		R	0550
A	Greenshank	Tringa nebularia																					GK	A		0548
A	Lesser Yellowlegs	Tringa flavipes																					LY		R	0551
A	Marsh Sandpiper	Tringa stagnatilis																					MD		R	0547
A	Wood Sandpiper	Tringa glareola																					OD	A		0554
A	Redshank	Tringa totanus																					RK			0546
A	Jack Snipe	Lymnocryptes minimus																					JS	C		0518
A	Short-billed Dowitcher	Limnodromus griseus																							R	0526
A	Long-billed Dowitcher	Limnodromus scolopaceus																					LD		R	0527
A	Woodcock	Scolopax rusticola																					WK			0529
A	Snipe	Gallinago gallinago																					SN			0519
A	Wilson's Snipe	Gallinago delicata																							R	5192
A	Great Snipe	Gallinago media																					DS	C	R	0520
A	Collared Pratincole	Glareola pratincola																							R	0465
A	Oriental Pratincole	Glareola maldivarum																					GM		R	0466
A	Black-winged Pratincole	Glareola nordmanni																					KW		R	0467
A	Cream-coloured Courser	Cursorius cursor																							R	0464
A	Pomarine Skua	Stercorarius pomarinus																					PK			0566
A	Arctic Skua	Stercorarius parasiticus																					AC	A		0567
A	Long-tailed Skua	Stercorarius longicaudus																					OG	B		0568
A	Great Skua	Stercorarius skua																					NX			0569
A	Tufted Puffin	Fratercula cirrhata																							R	3565
	Sub total																									

AUKS cont. TERNS

	Name	Scientific	Life list	2018	Jan	Feb	Mar	Apr	May	Jun	Jul	Aug	Sep	Oct	Nov	Dec	A	B	C	D	E	F	BTO	RBBP	BBRC	EU No
A	Puffin	*Fratercula arctica*																					PU			0654
A	Long-billed Murrelet	*Brachyramphus perdix*																							R	6412
A	Black Guillemot	*Cepphus grylle*																					TY			0638
A	Ancient Murrelet	*Synthliboramphus antiquus*																							R	0645
A	Razorbill	*Alca torda*																					RA			0636
B	Great Auk (extinct)	*Pinguinus impennis*																								
A	Little Auk	*Alle alle*																					LK			0647
A	Guillemot	*Uria aalge*																					GU			0634
A	Brunnich's Guillemot	*Uria lomvia*																					TZ		R	0635
A	Aleutian Tern	*Onychoprion aleuticus*																							R	0617
A	Sooty Tern	*Onychoprion fuscatus*																							R	0623
A	Bridled Tern	*Onychoprion anaethetus*																							R	0622
A	Little Tern	*Sternula albifrons*																					AF	A		0624
A	Gull-billed Tern	*Gelochelidon nilotica*																					TG	B	R	0605
A	Caspian Tern	*Hydroprogne caspia*																					CJ		R	0606
A	Whiskered Tern	*Chlidonias hybrida*																					WD		R	0626
A	Black Tern	*Chlidonias niger*																					BJ	B		0627
A	White-winged Black Tern	*Chlidonias leucopterus*																					WJ			0628
A	Cabot's Tern	*Sterna acuflavida*																							R	
A	Sandwich Tern	*Sterna sandvicensis*																					TE			0611
A	Royal Tern	*Sterna maxima*																					QT		R	0607
A	Lesser Crested Tern	*Sterna bengalensis*																					TF	B	R	0609
A	Forster's Tern	*Sterna forsteri*																					FO		R	0618
A	Common Tern	*Sterna hirundo*																					CN			0615
	Sub total																									

	TRENS cont. GULLS		Life list	2018	Jan	Feb	Mar	Apr	May	Jun	Jul	Aug	Sep	Oct	Nov	Dec	A	B	C	D	E	F	BTO	RBBP	BBRC	EU No
A	Roseate Tern	*Sterna dougallii*																					RS	A		0614
A	Arctic Tern	*Sterna paradisaea*																					AE			0616
A	Ivory Gull	*Pagophila eburnea*																					IV		R	0604
A	Sabine's Gull	*Xema sabini*																					AB			0579
A	Kittiwake	*Rissa tridactyla*																					KI			0602
A	Slender-billed Gull	*Chroicocephalus genei*																					EI	C	R	0585
A	Bonaparte's Gull	*Chroicocephalus philadelphia*																					ON		R	0581
A	Black-headed Gull	*Chroicocephalus ridibundus*																					BH			0582
A	Little Gull	*Hydrocoloeus minutus*																					LU	B		0578
A	Ross's Gull	*Rhodostethia rosea*																					QG		R	0601
A	Laughing Gull	*Larus atricilla*																					LF		R	0576
A	Franklin's Gull	*Larus pipixcan*																					FG		R	0577
A	Mediterranean Gull	*Larus melanocephalus*																					MU	A		0575
A	Audouin's Gull	*Larus audouinii*																							R	0589
B	Great Black-headed Gull	*Larus ichthyaetus*																							R	0573
A	Common Gull	*Larus canus*																					CM			0590
A	Ring-billed Gull	*Larus delawarensis*																					IN	B		0588
A	Lesser Black-backed Gull	*Larus fuscus*																					LB			0591
A	Herring Gull	*Larus argentatus*																					HG			0592
A	Yellow-legged Gull	*Larus michahellis*																					YG	A		5927
A	Caspian Gull	*Larus cachinnans*																								5927
A	American Herring Gull	*Larus smithsonianus*																							R	26632
A	Iceland Gull	*Larus glaucoides*																					IG			0598
A	Slaty-backed Gull	*Larus schistisagus*																							R	
	Sub total																									

GULLS cont. SANDGROUSE, DOVES, CUCKOOS, OWLS

			Life list	2018	Jan	Feb	Mar	Apr	May	Jun	Jul	Aug	Sep	Oct	Nov	Dec	A	B	C	D	E	F	BTO	RBBP	BBRC	EU No
A	Glaucous-winged Gull	Larus glaucescens																							R	5960
A	Glaucous Gull	Larus hyperboreus																					GZ	B		0599
A	Great Black-backed Gull	Larus marinus																					GB			0600
A	Pallas's Sandgrouse	Syrrhaptes paradoxus																							R	0663
AC4E*	Rock Dove / Feral Pigeon	Columba livia																					DV			0665
A	Stock Dove	Columba oenas																					SD			0668
A	Woodpigeon	Columba palumbus																					WP			0670
A	Collared Dove	Streptopelia decaocto																					CD			0684
A	Turtle Dove	Streptopelia turtur																					TD			0687
A	Rufous Turtle Dove	Streptopelia orientalis																							R	0689
A	Mourning Dove	Zenaida macroura																							R	0695
A	Great Spotted Cuckoo	Clamator glandarius																					UK		R	0716
A	Cuckoo	Cuculus canorus																					CK			0724
A	Black-billed Cuckoo	Coccyzus erythropthalmus																							R	0727
A	Yellow-billed Cuckoo	Coccyzus americanus																							R	0728
AE*	Barn Owl	Tyto alba																					BO			0735
A	Scops Owl	Otus scops																						C	R	0739
A	Snowy Owl	Bubo scandiacus																					SO	B	R	0749
A	Hawk Owl	Surnia ulula																							R	0750
C1	Little Owl	Athene noctua																					LO			0757
A	Tawny Owl	Strix aluco																					TO			0761
A	Long-eared Owl	Asio otus																					LE	A		0767
A	Short-eared Owl	Asio flammeus																					SE	A		0768
A	Tengmalm's Owl	Aegolius funereus																							R	0770
	Sub total																									

NIGHTJARS, SWIFTS, BEE-EATERS, KINGFISHERS, WOODPECKERS, FALCONS

	Common name	Scientific name	Life list	2018	Jan	Feb	Mar	Apr	May	Jun	Jul	Aug	Sep	Oct	Nov	Dec	A	B	C	D	E	F	BTO	RBBP	BBRC	EU No
A	Nightjar	Caprimulgus europaeus																					NJ			0778
B	Red-necked Nightjar	Caprimulgus ruficollis																							R	0779
A	Egyptian Nightjar	Caprimulgus aegyptius																							R	0781
A	Common Nighthawk	Chordeiles minor																							R	0786
A	Chimney Swift	Chaetura pelagica																					NI		R	0790
A	Needle-tailed Swift	Hirundapus caudacutus																					SI		R	0792
A	Swift	Apus apus																								0795
A	Pallid Swift	Apus pallidus																						C	R	0796
A	Pacific Swift	Apus pacificus																							R	0797
A	Alpine Swift	Apus melba																					AI			0798
A	Little Swift	Apus affinis																							R	0800
A	Hoopoe	Upupa epops																					HP	B		0846
A	Blue-cheeked Bee-eater	Merops persicus																					MZ		R	0839
A	Bee-eater	Merops apiaster																						B		0840
A	Roller	Coracias garrulus																							R	0841
A	Kingfisher	Alcedo atthis																					KF			0831
A	Belted Kingfisher	Megaceryle alcyon																							R	0834
A	Wryneck	Jynx torquilla																					WY	A		0848
A	Green Woodpecker	Picus viridis																					G.			0856
A	Yellow-bellied Sapsucker	Sphyrapicus varius																							R	0872
A	Great Spotted Woodpecker	Dendrocopos major																					GS			0876
A	Lesser Spotted Woodpecker	Dendrocopos minor																					LS	A		0887
A	Lesser Kestrel	Falco naumanni																							R	0303
A	Kestrel	Falco tinnunculus																					K.			0304
	Sub total																									

FALCONS cont. VIREOS, SHRIKES

	Species	Scientific name	Life list	2018	Jan	Feb	Mar	Apr	May	Jun	Jul	Aug	Sep	Oct	Nov	Dec	A	B	C	D	E	F	BTO	RBBP	BBRC	EU No
AE	American Kestrel	Falco sparverius																							R	0305
A	Red-footed Falcon	Falco vespertinus																					FV			0307
A	Amur Falcon	Falco amurensis																							R	3080
A	Merlin	Falco columbarius																					ML	A		0309
A	Hobby	Falco subbuteo																					HY	A		0310
A	Eleonora's Falcon	Falco eleonorae																							R	0311
AE	Gyr Falcon	Falco rusticolus																					YF	C	R	0318
AE	Peregrine	Falco peregrinus																					PE	A		0320
C1E*	Ring-necked Parakeet	Psittacula krameri																					RI			0712
A	Eastern Phoebe	Sayornis phoebe																							R	0909
A	Acadian Flycatcher	Empidonax virescens																							R	
A	Alder Flycatcher	Empidonax alnorum																							R	9023
A	Eastern Kingbird	Tyrannus tyrannus																							R	
A	Yellow-throated Vireo	Vireo flavifrons																							R	1628
A	Philadelphia Vireo	Vireo philadelphicus																							R	1631
A	Red-eyed Vireo	Vireo olivaceus																					EV		R	1633
A	Golden Oriole	Oriolus oriolus																					OL	A		1508
A	Brown Shrike	Lanius cristatus																							R	1513
A	Isabelline Shrike	Lanius isabellinus																					IL		R	1514
A	Red-backed Shrike	Lanius collurio																					ED	A		1515
A	Long-tailed Shrike	Lanius schach																							R	1517
A	Lesser Grey Shrike	Lanius minor																							R	1519
A	Great Grey Shrike	Lanius excubitor																					SR	C		1520
A	Southern Grey Shrike	Lanius meridionalis																							R	1520
	Sub total																									

	SHRIKES cont. CORVIDS, 'CRESTS', TITS, LARKS		Life list	2018	Jan	Feb	Mar	Apr	May	Jun	Jul	Aug	Sep	Oct	Nov	Dec	A	B	C	D	E	F	BTO	RBBP	BBRC	EU No
A	Woodchat Shrike	Lanius senator																					OO			1523
A	Masked Shrike	Lanius nubicus																							R	1524
AE*	Chough	Pyrrhocorax pyrrhocorax																					CF	A		1559
A	Magpie	Pica pica																					MG			1549
A	Jay	Garrulus glandarius																					J.			1539
A	Nutcracker	Nucifraga caryocatactes																					NC		R	1557
A	Jackdaw	Corvus monedula																					JD			1560
A	Rook	Corvus frugilegus																					RO			1563
A	Carrion Crow	Corvus corone																					C.			1567
A	Hooded Crow	Corvus cornix																					HC			1567
A	Raven	Corvus corax																					RN			1572
A	Goldcrest	Regulus regulus																					GC			1314
A	Firecrest	Regulus ignicapilla																					FC	A		1315
A	Penduline Tit	Remiz pendulinus																					DT	B		1490
A	Blue Tit	Cyanistes caeruleus																					BT			1462
A	Great Tit	Parus major									✓												GT			1464
A	Crested Tit	Lophophanes cristatus																					CI			1454
A	Coal Tit	Periparus ater																					CT			1461
A	Willow Tit	Poecile montana																					WT	A		1442
A	Marsh Tit	Poecile palustris																					MT			1440
A	Bearded Tit	Panurus biarmicus																					BR	A		1364
A	Woodlark	Lullula arborea																					WL			0974
A	White-winged Lark	Alauda leucoptera							✓																R	0965
A	Skylark	Alauda arvensis																					S.			0976
	Sub total																									

73

LARKS cont. MARTINS, SWALLOWS, WARBLERS

	Common Name	Scientific name	Life list	2018	Jan	Feb	Mar	Apr	May	Jun	Jul	Aug	Sep	Oct	Nov	Dec	A	B	C	D	E	F	BTO	RBBP	BBRC	EU No
AE	Crested Lark	Galerida cristata																								0972
A	Shore Lark	Eremophila alpestris																					SX	B		0978
A	Short-toed Lark	Calandrella brachydactyla																					VL	C		0968
A	Bimaculated Lark	Melanocorypha bimaculata																							R	0962
A	Calandra Lark	Melanocorypha calandra																							R	0961
A	Black Lark	Melanocorypha yeltoniensis																							R	0966
A	Lesser Short-toed Lark	Alaudala rufescens																							R	0970
A	Sand Martin	Riparia riparia																					SM			0981
A	Tree Swallow	Tachycineta bicolor																							R	0983
A	Purple Martin	Progne subis																							R	0989
A	Crag Martin	Ptyonoprogne rupestris								✓															R	0991
AE	Swallow	Hirundo rustica							✓	✓	✓												SL			0992
A	House Martin	Delichon urbicum																					HM			1001
A	Red-rumped Swallow	Cecropis daurica																					VR	C		0995
A	Cliff Swallow	Petrochelidon pyrrhonota																							R	0998
A	Cetti's Warbler	Cettia cetti																					CW	A		1220
A	Long-tailed Tit	Aegithalos caudatus																					LT			1437
A	Eastern Crowned Warbler	Phylloscopus coronatus																							R	12860
A	Green Warbler	Phylloscopus nitidus																							R	12910
A	Greenish Warbler	Phylloscopus trochiloides																					NP	C		1293
A	Pale-legged Leaf Warbler	Phylloscopus tenellipes																							R	
A	Arctic Warbler	Phylloscopus borealis																					AP		R	1295
A	Pallas's Warbler	Phylloscopus proregulus																					PA	C		1298
A	Yellow-browed Warbler	Phylloscopus inornatus																					YB			1300
	Sub total																									

WARBLERS cont.

	Common name	Scientific name	Life list	2018	Jan	Feb	Mar	Apr	May	Jun	Jul	Aug	Sep	Oct	Nov	Dec	A	B	C	D	E	F	BTO	RBBP	BBRC	EU No
A	Hume's Warbler	*Phylloscopus humei*																							R	1300
A	Radde's Warbler	*Phylloscopus schwarzi*																								1301
A	Dusky Warbler	*Phylloscopus fuscatus*																					UY			1303
A	Western Bonelli's Warbler	*Phylloscopus bonelli*																					IW	C	R	1307
A	Eastern Bonelli's Warbler	*Phylloscopus orientalis*																							R	1307
A	Wood Warbler	*Phylloscopus sibilatrix*																					WO			1308
A	Chiffchaff	*Phylloscopus collybita*																					CC			1311
A	Iberian Chiffchaff	*Phylloscopus ibericus*																						C	R	1311
A	Willow Warbler	*Phylloscopus trochilus*																					WW			1312
A	Blackcap	*Sylvia atricapilla*																					BC			1277
A	Garden Warbler	*Sylvia borin*																					GW			1276
A	Desert Warbler	*Sylvia nana*																						C	R	1270
A	Barred Warbler	*Sylvia nisoria*																					RR			1273
A	Lesser Whitethroat	*Sylvia curruca*																					LW			1274
A	Western Orphean Warbler	*Sylvia hortensis*																							R	1272
A	Rüppell's Warbler	*Sylvia rueppelli*																							R	1269
A	Sardinian Warbler	*Sylvia melanocephala*																						C	R	1267
A	Moltoni's Subalpine Warbler	*Sylvia subalpina*																							R	
A	Subalpine Warbler	*Sylvia cantillans*																						C		1265
A	Whitethroat	*Sylvia communis*																					WH			1275
A	Spectacled Warbler	*Sylvia conspicillata*																						C	R	1264
A	Marmora's Warbler	*Sylvia sarda*																						C	R	1261
A	Dartford Warbler	*Sylvia undata*																					DW	A		1262
A	Pallas's Grasshopper Warbler	*Locustella certhiola*																							R	1233
	Sub total																									

75

WARBLERS cont. WAXWINGS, NUTHATCHES

		Scientific name	Life list	2018	Jan	Feb	Mar	Apr	May	Jun	Jul	Aug	Sep	Oct	Nov	Dec	A	B	C	D	E	F	BTO	RBBP	BBRC	EU No
A	Lanceolated Warbler	Locustella lanceolata																							R	1235
A	Grasshopper Warbler	Locustella naevia																					GH			1236
A	River Warbler	Locustella fluviatilis																					VW	C	R	1237
A	Savi's Warbler	Locustella luscinioides																					VI	A	R	1238
A	Thick-billed Warbler	Iduna aedon																							R	1254
A	Booted Warbler	Iduna caligata																						C	R	1256
A	Sykes's Warbler	Iduna rama																							R	12562
A	Eastern Olivaceous Warbler	Iduna pallida																							R	1255
A	Olive-tree Warbler	Hippolais olivetorum																							R	12580
A	Icterine Warbler	Hippolais icterina																					IC	B		1259
A	Melodious Warbler	Hippolais polyglotta																					ME	C		1260
A	Aquatic Warbler	Acrocephalus paludicola																					AQ			1242
A	Sedge Warbler	Acrocephalus schoenobaenus																					SW			1243
A	Paddyfield Warbler	Acrocephalus agricola																					PY		R	1247
A	Blyth's Reed Warbler	Acrocephalus dumetorum																						C		1248
A	Marsh Warbler	Acrocephalus palustris																					MW	A		1250
A	Reed Warbler	Acrocephalus scirpaceus																					RW			1251
A	Great Reed Warbler	Acrocephalus arundinaceus																					QW	C	R	1253
A	Fan-tailed Warbler	Cisticola juncidis																							R	1226
A	Cedar Waxwing	Bombycilla cedrorum																							R	1046
AE	Waxwing	Bombycilla garrulus																					WX	C		1048
A	Wallcreeper	Tichodroma muraria																							R	1482
A	Red-breasted Nuthatch	Sitta canadensis																							R	1472
A	Nuthatch	Sitta europaea																					NH		R	1479
	Sub total																									

TREECREEPERS, WREN, STARLINGS, DIPPER, THRUSHES

	Common name	Scientific name	Life list	2018	Jan	Feb	Mar	Apr	May	Jun	Jul	Aug	Sep	Oct	Nov	Dec	A	B	C	D	E	F	BTO	RBBP	BBRC	EU No
A	Treecreeper	Certhia familiaris																					TC			1486
A	Short-toed Treecreeper	Certhia brachydactyla																					TH	A	R	1487
A	Wren	Troglodytes troglodytes																					WR			1066
AE	Northern Mockingbird	Mimus polyglottos																							R	1067
A	Brown Thrasher	Toxostoma rufum																								1069
A	Grey Catbird	Dumetella carolinensis																							R	1080
A	Starling	Sturnus vulgaris			✓	✓																	SG			1582
A	Rose-coloured Starling	Pastor roseus					✓	✓	✓	✓	✓												OE			1594
A	Dipper	Cinclus cinclus																					DI			1050
A	White's Thrush	Zoothera dauma																						R	R	1170
A	Varied Thrush	Ixoreus naevius																					VT	R	R	1172
A	Wood Thrush	Hylocichla mustelina																						R	R	1175
A	Hermit Thrush	Catharus guttatus																						R	R	1176
A	Swainson's Thrush	Catharus ustulatus																						R	R	1177
A	Grey-cheeked Thrush	Catharus minimus																						R	R	1178
A	Veery	Catharus fuscescens																						R	R	1179
AE	Siberian Thrush	Geokichla sibirica																						R	R	1171
A	Ring Ouzel	Turdus torquatus																					RZ			1186
A	Blackbird	Turdus merula																					B.			1187
A	Eyebrowed Thrush	Turdus obscurus																						R	R	1195
A	Dusky Thrush	Turdus eunomus																						R	R	1196
A	Naumann's Thrush	Turdus naumanni																						R	R	11960
A	Black-throated Thrush	Turdus atrogularis																						R	R	1197
A	Red-throated Thrush	Turdus ruficollis																						R	R	11970
	Sub total																									

	THRUSHES cont. FLYCATCHERS, CHATS		Life list	2018	Jan	Feb	Mar	Apr	May	Jun	Jul	Aug	Sep	Oct	Nov	Dec	A	B	C	D	E	F	BTO	RBBP	BBRC	EU No
A	Fieldfare	*Turdus pilaris*																					FF	A		1198
A	Song Thrush	*Turdus philomelos*																					ST			1200
A	Redwing	*Turdus iliacus*																					RE	A		1201
A	Mistle Thrush	*Turdus viscivorus*																					M.			1202
AE	American Robin	*Turdus migratorius*																					AR		R	1203
A	Rufous Bush Chat	*Cercotrichas galactotes*																							R	1095
A	Brown Flycatcher	*Muscicapa dauurica*																							R	
A	Spotted Flycatcher	*Muscicapa striata*						✓	✓	✓	✓												SF			1335
A	Robin	*Erithacus rubecula*				✓	✓	✓	✓														R.			1099
A	Siberian Blue Robin	*Larvivora cyane*																							R	1112
A	Rufous-tailed Robin	*Larvivora sibilans*																							R	1102
A	White-throated Robin	*Irania gutturalis*																							R	1117
A	Thrush Nightingale	*Luscinia luscinia*																					FN	C	R	1103
A	Nightingale	*Luscinia megarhynchos*																					N.			1104
A	Bluethroat	*Luscinia svecica*																					BU	B		1106
A	Siberian Rubythroat	*Calliope calliope*																							R	1105
AE	Red-flanked Bluetail	*Tarsiger cyanurus*																								1113
A	Red-breasted Flycatcher	*Ficedula parva*																					FY			1343
A	Taiga Flycatcher	*Ficedula albicilla*																							R	1343
A	Collared Flycatcher	*Ficedula albicollis*																							R	1348
A	Pied Flycatcher	*Ficedula hypoleuca*																					PF			1349
A	Black Redstart	*Phoenicurus ochruros*																					BX	A		1121
A	Redstart	*Phoenicurus phoenicurus*																					RT			1122
A	Moussier's Redstart	*Phoenicurus moussieri*																							R	1127
	Sub total																									

CHATS cont. WHEATEARS, SPARROWS, WAGTAILS, PIPITS

	Common Name	Scientific Name	Life list	2018	Jan	Feb	Mar	Apr	May	Jun	Jul	Aug	Sep	Oct	Nov	Dec	A	B	C	D	E	F	BTO	RBBP	BBRC	EU No
A	Rock Thrush	*Monticola saxatilis*																					OH		R	1162
AE	Blue Rock Thrush	*Monticola solitarius*																							R	1166
A	Whinchat	*Saxicola rubetra*																					WC			1137
A	Siberian Stonechat	*Saxicola maurus*																							R	
A	Stonechat	*Saxicola rubicola*																					SC			1139
A	Wheatear	*Oenanthe oenanthe*						✓															W.			1146
A	Isabelline Wheatear	*Oenanthe isabellina*																							R	1144
A	Desert Wheatear	*Oenanthe deserti*																							R	1149
A	Black-eared Wheatear	*Oenanthe hispanica*																							R	1148
A	Pied Wheatear	*Oenanthe pleschanka*					✓	✓	✓	✓	✓												PI		R	1147
A	White-crowned Black Wheatear	*Oenanthe leucopyga*																							R	1157
A	Alpine Accentor	*Prunella collaris*																							R	1094
A	Siberian Accentor	*Prunella montanella*																							R	
A	Dunnock	*Prunella modularis*																					D.			1084
A	House Sparrow	*Passer domesticus*			✓	✓				✓													HS			1591
A	Spanish Sparrow	*Passer hispaniolensis*								✓															R	1592
A	Tree Sparrow	*Passer montanus*									✓												TS			1598
A	Rock Sparrow	*Petronia petronia*																							R	1604
A	Yellow Wagtail	*Motacilla flava*				✓			✓	✓													YW			1017
A	Citrine Wagtail	*Motacilla citreola*								✓														C	R	1018
A	Grey Wagtail	*Motacilla cinerea*						✓															GL			1019
A	Pied Wagtail	*Motacilla alba*								✓													PW			1020
A	Richard's Pipit	*Anthus richardi*									✓												PR			1002
A	Blyth's Pipit	*Anthus godlewskii*																							R	1004
	Sub total																									

PIPITS cont. FINCHES

Status	Name	Scientific name	Life list	2018	Jan	Feb	Mar	Apr	May	Jun	Jul	Aug	Sep	Oct	Nov	Dec	A	B	C	D	E	F	BTO	RBBP	BBRC	EU No
A	**Tawny Pipit**	*Anthus campestris*																					TI			1005
A	**Olive-backed Pipit**	*Anthus hodgsoni*																					OV		R	1008
A	**Tree Pipit**	*Anthus trivialis*																					TP			1009
A	**Pechora Pipit**	*Anthus gustavi*																							R	1010
A	**Meadow Pipit**	*Anthus pratensis*																					MP			1011
A	**Red-throated Pipit**	*Anthus cervinus*																					VP			1012
A	**Rock Pipit**	*Anthus petrosus*																					RC			1014
A	**Water Pipit**	*Anthus spinoletta*																					WI			1014
A	**Buff-bellied Pipit**	*Anthus rubescens*																							R	1014
A	**Brambling**	*Fringilla montifringilla*																					BL	B		1638
AE	**Chaffinch**	*Fringilla coelebs*																					CH			1636
A	**Evening Grosbeak**	*Hesperiphona vespertina*																							R	1718
A	**Hawfinch**	*Coccothraustes coccothraustes*																					HF	A		1717
A	**Common Rosefinch**	*Erythrina erythrina*																					SQ	B		1679
AE	**Pine Grosbeak**	*Pinicola enucleator*																							R	1699
A	**Bullfinch**	*Pyrrhula pyrrhula*																					BF			1710
AE	**Trumpeter Finch**	*Bucanetes githagineus*																							R	1676
AE	**Greenfinch**	*Chloris chloris*																					GR			1649
A	**Linnet**	*Linaria cannabina*																					LI			1660
A	**Twite**	*Linaria flavirostris*									✓												TW			1662
A	**Lesser Redpoll**	*Acanthis cabaret*																					LR			1663
A	**Common Redpoll**	*Acanthis flammea*																					FR	A		1663
A	**Arctic Redpoll**	*Acanthis hornemanni*																					AL			1664
A	**Two-barred Crossbill**	*Loxia leucoptera*																					PD		R	1665
	Sub total																									

FINCHES cont. BUNTINGS, NEW WORLD SPARROWS

		Life list	2018	Jan	Feb	Mar	Apr	May	Jun	Jul	Aug	Sep	Oct	Nov	Dec	A	B	C	D	E	F	BTO	RBBP	BBRC	EU No
A	**Crossbill** *Loxia curvirostra*																					CR			1666
A	**Scottish Crossbill** *Loxia scotica*																					CY			1667
A	**Parrot Crossbill** *Loxia pytyopsittacus*																					PC	A		1668
A	**Goldfinch** *Carduelis carduelis*																					GO			1653
A	**Citril Finch** *Carduelis citrinella*																							R	1644
A	**Serin** *Serinus serinus*																					NS	B		1640
A	**Siskin** *Spinus spinus*									✓												SK			1654
A	**Snow Bunting** *Plectrophenax nivalis*																					SB	A		1850
A	**Lapland Bunting** *Calcarius lapponicus*																					LA	B		1847
A	**Summer Tanager** *Piranga rubra*																							R	1786
A	**Scarlet Tanager** *Piranga olivacea*																							R	1788
A	**Rose-breasted Grosbeak** *Pheucticus ludovicianus*																							R	1887
AE	**Indigo Bunting** *Passerina cyanea*																							R	1892
A	**Eastern Towhee** *Pipilo erythrophthalmus*																							R	1798
A	**Lark Sparrow** *Chondestes grammacus*																							R	1824
A	**Savannah Sparrow** *Passerculus sandwichensis*																							R	1826
AE	**Song Sparrow** *Melospiza melodia*																							R	1835
AE	**White-crowned Sparrow** *Zonotrichia leucophrys*																							R	1839
AE	**White-throated Sparrow** *Zonotrichia albicollis*																							R	1840
AE	**Dark-eyed Junco** *Junco hyemalis*																					JU		R	1842
AE	**Black-headed Bunting** *Emberiza melanocephala*																							R	1881
A	**Corn Bunting** *Emberiza calandra*																					CB			1882
A	**Chestnut-eared Bunting** *Emberiza fucata*																							R	1869
A	**Rock Bunting** *Emberiza cia*																							R	1860
	Sub total																								

81

	BUNTINGS cont. NEW WORLD WARBLERS		Life list	2018	Jan	Feb	Mar	Apr	May	Jun	Jul	Aug	Sep	Oct	Nov	Dec	A	B	C	D	E	F	BTO	RBBP	BBRC	EU No
A	Cretzschmar's Bunting	Emberiza caesia																							R	1868
AE	Ortolan Bunting	Emberiza hortulana																					OB			1866
A	Cirl Bunting	Emberiza cirlus																					CL	A		1958
A	Yellowhammer	Emberiza citrinella																					Y.			1857
A	Pine Bunting	Emberiza leucocephalos																					EL		R	1856
A	Pallas's Reed Bunting	Emberiza pallasi																							R	1878
A	Reed Bunting	Emberiza schoeniclus																					RB			1877
A	Yellow-breasted Bunting	Emberiza aureola																						C	R	1876
A	Chestnut Bunting	Emberiza rutila																							R	
A	Yellow-browed Bunting	Emberiza chrysophrys																							R	1871
A	Little Bunting	Emberiza pusilla																					LJ			1874
A	Rustic Bunting	Emberiza rustica																								1873
AE	Black-faced Bunting	Emberiza spodocephala																							R	1853
A	Bobolink	Dolichonyx oryzivorus																							R	1897
A	Brown-headed Cowbird	Molothrus ater																							R	1899
AE	Baltimore Oriole	Icterus galbula																							R	1918
A	Ovenbird	Seiurus aurocapilla																							R	1756
A	Northern Waterthrush	Parkesia noveboracensis																							R	1757
A	Golden-winged Warbler	Vermivora chrysoptera																							R	1722
A	Black-and-white Warbler	Mniotilta varia																							R	1720
A	Tennessee Warbler	Oreothlypis peregrina																							R	1724
A	Common Yellowthroat	Geothlypis trichas																							R	1762
A	Hooded Warbler	Setophaga citrina																							R	1771
AE	American Redstart	Setophaga ruticilla																							R	1755
	Sub total																									

NEW WORLD WARBLERS

	Name	Scientific	Life list	2018	Jan	Feb	Mar	Apr	May	Jun	Jul	Aug	Sep	Oct	Nov	Dec	A	B	C	D	E	F	BTO	RBBP	BBRC	EU No
A	**Cape May Warbler**	*Setophaga tigrina*																							R	1749
AE	**Northern Parula**	*Setophaga americana*																							R	1732
AE	**Magnolia Warbler**	*Setophaga magnolia*																							R	1750
A	**Bay-breasted Warbler**	*Setophaga castanea*																							R	1754
A	**Blackburnian Warbler**	*Setophaga fusca*																							R	1747
A	**Yellow Warbler**	*Setophaga petechia*																							R	1733
A	**Chestnut-sided Warbler**	*Setophaga pensylvanica*																							R	1734
AE	**Blackpoll Warbler**	*Setophaga striata*																							R	1753
A	**Yellow-rumped Warbler**	*Setophaga coronata*																							R	1751
A	**Wilson's Warbler**	*Cardellina pusilla*																							R	1772
	Sub total																									

BRITISH BUTTERFLY CHECKLIST

SPECIES	2018 list	Life list
Chequered Skipper		
Small Skipper		
Essex Skipper		
Lulworth Skipper		
Silver-spotted Skipper		
Large Skipper		
Dingy Skipper		
Grizzled Skipper		
Swallowtail		
Wood White		
Real's Wood White		
Clouded Yellow		
Brimstone		
Large White		
Small White		
Green-veined White		
Orange-tip		
Green Hairstreak		
Brown Hairstreak		
Purple Hairstreak		
White-letter Hairstreak		
Black Hairstreak		
Small Copper		
Small Blue		
Silver-studded Blue		
Brown Argus		
Northern Brown Argus		
Common Blue		
Chalkhill Blue		
Adonis Blue		
Holly Blue		
Duke of Burgundy		
White Admiral		
Purple Emperor		
Red Admiral		

SPECIES	2018 list	Life list
Painted Lady		
Small Tortoiseshell		
Peacock		
Comma		
Small Pearl-b'dered Fritillary		
Pearl-bordered Fritillary		
High Brown Fritillary		
Dark Green Fritillary		
Silver-washed Fritillary		
Marsh Fritillary		
Glanville Fritillary		
Heath Fritillary		
Speckled Wood		
Wall		
Mountain Ringlet		
Scotch Argus		
Marbled White		
Grayling		
Gatekeeper		
Meadow Brown		
Ringlet		
Small Heath		
Large Heath		
Additional Species		
TOTAL		

BRITISH DRAGONFLY CHECKLIST

SPECIES	2018 list	Life list
Banded Demoiselle		
Beautiful Demoiselle		
Small Red Damselfly		
Northern Damselfly		
Irish Damselfly		
Southern Damselfly		
Azure Damselfly		
Variable Damselfly		
Dainty Damselfly		
Common Blue Damselfly		
Red-eyed Damselfly		
Small Red-eyed Damselfly		
Blue-tailed Damselfly		
Scarce Blue-tailed Damselfly		
Large Red Damselfly		
Southern Emerald Damselfly		
Scarce Emerald Damselfly		
Emerald Damselfly		
Willow Emerald Damselfly		
Winter Damselfly		
White-legged Damselfly		
Southern Migrant Hawker		
Azure Hawker		
Southern Hawker		
Brown Hawker		
Norfolk Hawker		
Common Hawker		
Migrant Hawker		
Vagrant Emperor		
Emperor Dragonfly		
Lesser Emperor		
Hairy Dragonfly		
Golden-ringed Dragonfly		
Downy Emerald		
Orange-spotted Emerald		

SPECIES	2018 list	Life list
Northern Emerald		
Brilliant Emerald		
Common Club-tail		
Scarlet Darter		
White-faced Darter		
Broad-bodied Chaser		
Scarce Chaser		
Four-spotted Chaser		
Black-tailed Skimmer		
Black-tailed Skimmer		
Keeled Skimmer		
Wandering Glider		
Black Darter		
Yellow-winged Darter		
Red-veined Darter		
Banded Darter		
Ruddy Darter		
Common Darter		
Additional Species		
TOTAL		

CHECKLIST NOTES

CHECKLIST NOTES

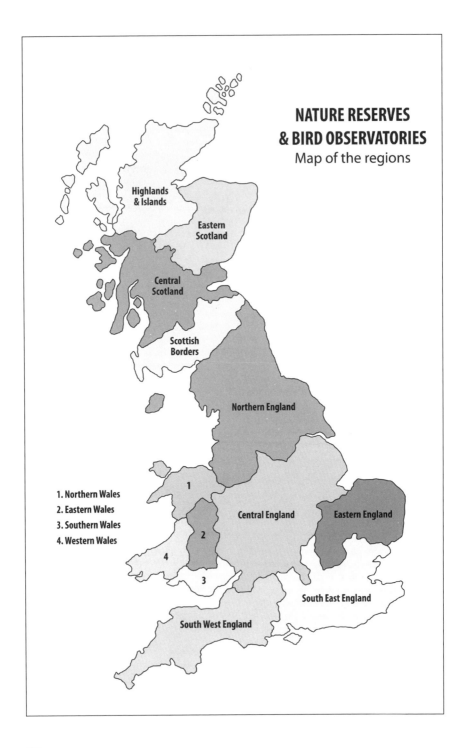

NATURE RESERVES & BIRD OBSERVATORIES
Map of the regions

Highlands & Islands

Eastern Scotland

Central Scotland

Scottish Borders

Northern England

1. Northern Wales
2. Eastern Wales
3. Southern Wales
4. Western Wales

1

2

4

3

Central England

Eastern England

South East England

South West England

RESERVES DIRECTORY

Amy Gartshore

The Northumberland Wildlife Trust's Druridge Bay Nature Reserves offer excellent birding opportunities. In early 2017, a Pacific Diver *Gavia pacifica* took up residence in the area for a few weeks... even the editor managed to see it on a trip to the county!

THE RESERVES IN this directory are listed on a regional basis (see map opposite). The selection of reserves has been chosen to give a flavour of what each county has to offer and includes many of their 'flagship' sites.

The listings cover: location~access~facilities / public transport, if practical (it is advisable to check with the bus/train providers before travelling) / habitats~key birds~other notable flora & fauna / and contact details for the reserve.

We have included postcodes, to aid sat-nav users, and map grid references - we hope these prove helpful. We welcome feedback on any way we can improve this section of The *Yearbook*. Please send any comments to the Editor (see page 6).

Central England

Derbyshire, Gloucestershire, Leicestershire & Rutland, Lincolnshire, Northamptonshire, Nottinghamshire, Oxfordshire, Shropshire, Staffordshire, Warwickshire & West Midlands, Worcestershire

Derbyshire

WITH 75% OF THE county's population living in towns, Derbyshire can offer birdwatchers many square miles of open countryside, including a large part of the Peak District National Park. Other attractions include Carsington Water, Ogston Reservoir and Willington Gravel Plts which attract large gull roosts in winter. Valleys, such as those in the Peak District, attract Redstarts, Pied Flycatchers and Wood Warblers.

1. CARR VALE NATURE RESERVE

Derbyshire Wildlife Trust.
Location: Sat nav: S44 6JX. SK 457 703. 0.75 mile W of Bolsover on A632 to Chesterfield. Turn L at roundabout (follow brown tourist signs) into Riverside Way. Use Stockley Trail car park at end of road.
Access: Open all year. Follow footpath (waymarked) around Peter Fidler reserve. Dogs only on leads.

Facilities: Car park, coach parking on approach road, good disabled access, paths, three viewing platforms.
Public transport: Stagecoach buses from Chesterfield (Stephenson Place) pass close to the reserve: nos. 82, 82A & 83 serve the roundabout on A632 and no. 83 serves Villas Road.
Habitats: Lakes, wader flashes, reedbed, sewage farm, scrub, arable fields.
Key birds: Up to 150 spp. seen annually. *Winter:* Large numbers of wildfowl inc. flocks of Wigeon and Teal, also wintering flocks of finches and buntings, Water Rail. *Spring/autumn:* Migrants inc. pipits and thrushes. In Sept, Swallows gather in the marsh in a gigantic roost of between 1,000-2,000 birds, the roost usually attract Hobbies. *Early summer:* Breeding birds, inc. Reed and Sedge Warblers, Whitethroat, Yellowhammer, Moorhen and Gadwall, plus Skylark. Long list of rarities.
Other notable flora/fauna: Dragonflies, hare, grass snake, harvest mouse, water shrew.
Contact: Derbyshire WT, T: 01773 881 188; E: enquiries@derbyshirewt.co.uk

2. CARSINGTON WATER

Severn Trent Water
Location: Sat nav: DE6 1ST. SK 241 515 (for visitor centre and main facilities). Off B5035 Ashbourne to Wirksworth road.
Access: Open all year, except Dec 25. Car parks open 7am-sunset (Apr-Oct), 7.30am-sunset in winter. Good access for wheelchairs, which can be borrowed at visitor centre, also mobility scooters for hire. Pay-and-display parking at visitor centre with reduced rates at Millfields and Sheepwash car parks.
Facilities: Visitor centre with exhibition, restaurant, four shops (inc. RSPB), play area and toilets. Four bird hides and three car parks. Cycle and boat hire.
Public transport: Yourbus, T: 01773 714 013, operates no. 110 from Matlock and no. 111 from Ashbourne.
Habitats: Open water, islands, mixed woodland, scrub and grasslands, small reedbed.
Key birds: More than 220 bird spp. recorded. *Winter:* Wildfowl and a large gull roost plus possibility of divers and rare grebes. *Spring:* Good spring passage inc. Yellow and White Wagtails, Whimbrel, Black and Arctic Terns. *Summer:* Warblers and breeding waders, inc. Little Ringed Plovers. *All year:* Tree Sparrows and Willow Tits. Ospreys often stop-off during migration.
Other notable flora/fauna: Species-rich hay meadows, ancient woodlands with bluebells, three spp. of orchid, five spp. of bat, 21 spp. of butterfly, water vole.
Contact: Carsington Water Visitor Centre, T: 01629 540 696; E: carsingtonwater@severntrent.co.uk; W: www.carsingtonbirdclub.co.uk

NATURE RESERVES - CENTRAL ENGLAND

3. DRAKELOW NATURE RESERVE

E-ON, leased to Derbyshire Wildlife Trust.
Location: Sat nav: DE14 3FG. SK 223 204. Drakelow Power Station (access via Gate C) on the outskirts of Branston, one mile NE of Walton-on-Trent, off A38, S of Burton-on-Trent.
Access: PERMIT required. Open dawn-dusk for DWT permit holders only (plus up to two guests). No dogs. Wheelchair access along main path to two main hides.
Facilities: Four main hides, car park inside former power station grounds. Nesting platforms for Ospreys erected.
Public transport: None.
Habitats: Disused flooded gravel pits with wooded islands, riverside meadows and reedbeds.
Key birds: *Summer:* Breeding Reed and Sedge Warblers. Water Rail, Hobby. *Winter:* Wildfowl (Shoveler, Goldeneye, Gadwall), Merlin, Peregrine. Rarities have inc. Great White Egret, Bittern, Spotted Crake, Ring-necked Duck and American Wigeon.
Other notable flora/fauna: Good for common species of dragonflies and butterflies.
Contact: Derbyshire WT, T: 01773 881 188;
E: enquiries@derbyshirewt.co.uk

4. GOYT VALLEY

Forestry Commission.
Location: Sat nav: SK17 6SX (Errwood Hall car park, SK 011 748) for woodland species, Derbyshire Bridge (SK 018 716) for moorland birds. From Buxton head N on A5004 (Manchester Road), then bear L on Goyt's Lane to Errwood Hall one-way system, between Errwood car park and Derbyshire Bridge.
Access: Open all year. Footpath between Errwood Hall and Goyt's Clough Quarry. Use Old Coach Road for walk between Derbyshire Bridge and Burbage.
Facilities: Toilets at Derbyshire Bridge and Bonsal Cob. Several picnic sites.
Public transport: Bowers bus services along A5004.
Habitats: Mixed conifer/broadleaf woodland, moorland, River Goyt and two reservoirs.
Key birds: *Spring/summer:* Breeding Wood Warbler, Pied and Spotted Flycatchers, Tree Pipit, Redstart and Cuckoo, Nightjar on restock areas, plus common woodland species. Long-eared Owls and Goshawks also present. Grey Wagtail and Dipper on river and Common Sandpiper on Errwood Reservoir. Ring Ouzel, Red Grouse, Curlew, Short-eared Owl and Whinchat breed on moorland areas.
Contact: Forestry Commission, T: 0300 067 4340;
E: sherwood.fdo@forestry.gsi.gov.uk

5. HILTON GRAVEL PITS

Derbyshire Wildlife Trust.
Location: Sat nav: DE65 5FN (Willowpit Lane). SK 249 315. From Derby, take A516 from Mickleover W past Etwall onto A50 junction at Hilton. Turn R at first island onto Willowpit Lane. Turn L next to a large white house and park next to the gate. Follow track along S side of the pools.
Access: Open all year. Main path and viewing screen suitable for wheelchair users. Dogs on leads only on main perimeter track.

Facilities: Tracks, boardwalks, viewing screens.
Public transport: Local Trent Barton Villager no. V1 bus to Hilton, from Derby and Burton-on-Trent.
Habitats: Ponds, lakes, scrub, woodland, fen.
Key birds: *Spring/summer:* Great Crested Grebe, Common Tern, warblers. *Winter:* Wildfowl, Siskin, Goldcrest. *All year:* All three woodpeckers, Kingfisher, tits inc. Willow Tit, Tawny Owl, Bullfinch.
Other notable flora/fauna: Dragonflies (14 spp. inc. emperor and red-eyed damselfly), great crested newt, orchids, black poplar.
Contact: Derbyshire WT, T: 01773 881 188;
E: enquiries@derbyshirewt.co.uk

6. OGSTON RESERVOIR

Severn Trent Water/Ogston Bird Club
Location: Sat nav: DE55 6FN. SK 371 603. From Matlock, take A615 E to B6014, just after Tansley. From A61 (Alfreton to Chesterfield road), at White Bear pub, Stretton turn onto B6014 towards Tansley, cross the railway, take L fork in the road and continue over the hill. The reservoir is on left after hill.
Access: View from roads. Three car parks on north, south and west banks. Public hide is accessed from west bank car park. Suitable for smaller coaches. Heronry in nearby Ogston Carr Wood (private property) viewable from Ogston new road, W of reservoir. Ogston Bird Club organises monthly guided walks (see website for details).
Facilities: One public hide is wheelchair-accessible, Ogston Bird Club members have access to three hides, (two are wheelchair-accessible) as well as the club's own two-acre Jim Mart Nature Reserve three miles north of Ogston.
Public transport: Bus - Hulleys no. 63 (Chesterfield to Clay Cross), no. 64 (Clay Cross to Matlock) - both serve N end of reservoir (not Sun).
Habitats: Open water, pasture, mixed woodland.
Key birds: All three woodpeckers, Little and Tawny Owls, Kingfisher, Grey Wagtail, warblers. *Passage:* raptors (inc. Osprey), terns and waders. *Winter:* Gull roost attracts thousands of birds, inc. regular Glaucous and Iceland Gulls. Top inland site for Bonaparte's Gull and also attracts Caspian/Herring Gull complex. Good numbers of wildfowl, tit and finch flocks.
Contact: John Parlby (Chairman), 102 Sough Road, South Normanton, Alfreton, DE55 2LE.
T: 01773 861 262 & 07767 652 036;
E: johnparlby1@gmail.com;
W: www.ogstonbirdclub.co.uk

7. PADLEY GORGE (LONGSHAW ESTATE)

National Trust (East Midlands).
Location: Sat nav: S11 7TZ (Longshaw visitor centre) SK 267 800. From Sheffield, head SW on A625. After eight miles, turn L on B6521 to Nether Padley. Grindleford Station is just off B6521 (NW of Nether Padley) and one mile NE of Grindleford village.
Access: All year, dawn-dusk. Some of the paths are rocky and are not suitable for disabled access or those unused to steep climbs. Dogs on leads only.

Facilities: Cafe, shop and toilets (inc. disabled) at Longshaw visitor centre. RADAR key needed for Hollin Bank, Hathersage toilets. Car parks, pay-and-display for non NT members.

Public transport: Bus from Sheffield to Bakewell stops at Grindleford/Nether Padley, T: 01709 566 000. Train from Sheffield to Manchester Piccadilly stops at Grindleford Station, T: 0161 228 2141.

Habitats: Steep-sided valley containing largest area of sessile oak woodland in south Pennines.

Key birds: *Spring/summer*: Pied Flycatcher, Spotted Flycatcher, Redstart, Wheatear, Whinchat, Stonechat, Ring Ouzel, Wood Warbler, Tree Pipit, plus common resident woodland species.

Contact: National Trust, High Peak Estate Office, T: 01433 637 904; E: peakdistrict@nationaltrust.org.uk

8. WILLINGTON GRAVEL PITS

Derbyshire Wildlife Trust

Location: Sat nav: DE65 6BX (Repton Road). SK 285 274. From A50 'Toyota Island' head towards Willington and Repton. Go through village towards Repton. Just before bridge over River Trent, turn R onto un-made track (Meadow Lane). Park here and walk along lane.

Access: Access only along Meadow Lane to viewing platforms all year. No access on site. Steps prevent wheelchair access to platforms.

Facilities: Viewing platforms and benches. Limited parking in lane.

Public transport: Local trains stop at Willington. Local Trent Barton Villager bus no. V3 to Willington from Derby and Burton-on-Trent.

Habitats: Open water, reedbed, shingle island, grassland.

Key birds: *Summer*: Lapwing, Redshank, Oystercatcher, Common Tern, Cetti's, Reed and Sedge Warblers, raptors inc. Peregrine, Kestrel, Hobby and Sparrowhawk. *Winter*: Bittern, waders and large flocks of wildfowl inc. Wigeon, Teal, Pochard and Shoveler. *Passage*: Large numbers of Curlew in spring, up to 20 spp. of waders in spring/autumn.

Other notable flora/fauna: Short-leaved water starwort. Several spp. of dragonfly, plus occasional otter signs, fox and other mammals.

Contact: Derbyshire WT, T: 01773 881 188; E: enquiries@derbyshirewt.co.uk

Gloucestershire

STRADDLING THE MIGHTY Severn estuary, Gloucestershire can boast a world-famous wetland site in the form of Slimbridge, but on the other side of the river, the Forest of Dean is one of the best places in Britain to see good numbers of Goshawks displaying in February/March. The county Wildlife Trust manages over 60 nature reserves.

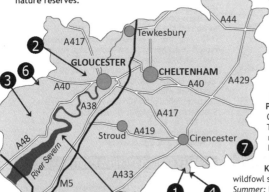

1. CLEVELAND LAKES

Cotswold Water Park Trust.

Location: Sat nav: SN6 6QW (Waterhay Car Park). Lakes 68A/B & 74, Cotswold Water Park. From A419 Cirencester to Swindon road, take B4696 towards Cotswold Water Park West. After 1.25-2 miles turn L on to Fridays Ham Lane. Follow road to Ashton Keynes village and turn L on to road to Cricklade/Leigh. Waterhay Car Park is on the left next to the River Thames (SU 059 933). Take bridleway north to kissing gate on the right. Permissive path follows southern edge of Lake 68A/B before turning north towards two hides.

Access: Open at all times, most paths firm and flat but subject to severe winter flooding. Dogs on short leads at all times.

Facilities: Toilets, refreshments, car parking and information available from Gateway Centre next to A419.

Public transport: Bus, from Kemble, Cheltenham, Cirencester and Swindon, T: 08457 090 899. Train, Kemble station four miles, T: 08457 484 950.

Habitats: Lakes with reedbed, scrapes, lagoons, marsh, ditches, islands and loafing areas.

Key birds: *Winter*: Large numbers of many wildfowl spp., plus Bittern, Water Rail, Stonechat. *Summer*: Breeding ducks, Great Crested Grebe, warblers, Hobby, Sand Martin, Reed Bunting, Little Egret, Grey Heron. Many of the above species and plenty of passage waders viewable from "Twitchers' Gate" on lane to the north of Lake 74 (SU 065 946).

Other notable flora/fauna: Otter, water vole, several spp. of dragonfllies and butterflies.

Contact: Cotswold Water Park Trust, T: 01793 752 413; W: www.waterpark.org

NATURE RESERVES - CENTRAL ENGLAND

2. HIGHNAM WOODS

RSPB (South West England Office).
Location: Sat nav: GL2 8AA. SO 778 190. Signposted on A40 three miles W of Gloucester.
Access: Open at all times, no permit required. Nature trails can be very muddy. Some limited wheelchair access. Dogs allowed on leads. Groups should book ahead.
Facilities: One nature trail (1.5 miles). One open-backed hide 150 yards from car park. Car park, usually restricted to reserve events, can be opened for groups by arrangment. No visitor centre or toilets.
Public transport: Contact Traveline, T: 0871 2002 233 between 7am-10pm daily.
Habitats: Ancient woodland in the Severn Vale with areas of coppice and scrub.
Key birds: *Spring/summer*: Up to 20 pairs of breeding Nightingale, plus common migrant warblers and Spotted Flycatcher. Resident birds inc. all three woodpeckers, Marsh Tit, Buzzard and Sparrowhawk. Ravens are frequently seen. *Winter*: Feeding site near car park good for woodland birds.
Other notable flora/fauna: Tintern spurge in late Jun-early Jul. White-letter hairstreak and white admiral butterflies seen annually.
Contact: RSPB, T: 01594 562 852;
E: highnam.woods@rspb.org.uk

3. NAGSHEAD

RSPB (South West England Office).
Location: Sat nav: GL15 4JQ. SO 606 085. In Forest of Dean, N of Lydney. Signposted immediately W of Parkend village on B4431 road to Coleford.
Access: Open at all times, no permit required. Car park open 8am-9pm or dusk if earlier. The reserve is hilly but there is limited wheelchair access. Keep dogs on leads during bird nesting season.
Facilities: Two nature trails (one mile and 2.25 miles). Information centre (with toilets) open 10am-4pm at weekends between Easter and Aug bank holiday. Two woodland hides not accessible to wheelchair users.
Public transport: Buses from Lydney Bus Station (circular) stop along B4431 signposted to Coleford. Traveline, T: 0871 2002 233.
Habitats: Much of reserve is a 200-year-old oak plantations, grazed in some areas by sheep. Rest is a mixture of open areas and conifer/mixed woodland.
Key birds: *Spring*: Pied Flycatcher, Wood Warbler and commoner warblers, Redstart. *Summer*: Nightjar. *Winter*: Siskin, Crossbill in some years. *All year*: Buzzard, Raven, Hawfinch, Woodcock, all three woodpeckers.
Other notable flora/fauna: Golden-ringed dragonfly seen annually. Silver-washed and small pearl-bordered fritillaries and white admiral butterflies present.
Contact: RSPB, T: 01594 562 852;
E: nagshead@rspb.org.uk

4. SHORNCOTE REEDBED

Thames Water / Cotswold Water Park Trust.
Location: Sat nav: GL7 5US (South Cerney car park). Lakes 84, 85A & 85B, Cotswold Water Park West. From A419 Cirencester to Swindon road, take B4696 towards Cotswold Water Park West. Turn R at crossroads (station Road) towards South Cerney. Follow road through village and park in playing fields car park after sharp R bend (SU 044 970). Take footpath through playing fields, cross road and continue on path through reedbeds to small lakes and hides.
Access: Open at all times. Floods regularly in winter, so wellies essential.
Facilities: Toilets, refreshments, car parking/information available from nearby Cotswold Country Park (entry charge may apply). Two hides. Alternative refreshments/toilets at Gateway Centre near A419 junction.
Public transport: Buses, from Kemble, Cheltenham, Cirencester and Swindon, T: 08457 090 899. Train, Kemble station four miles, T: 08457 484 950.
Habitats: Lakes with reedbed, marsh, ditches, islands and loafing areas.
Key birds: *Winter*: Common wildfowl, Water Rail, Snipe, Peregrine, Merlin, Bittern, Stonechat and Starling flocks. *Summer*: Breeding ducks, Little Grebe, warblers, Hobby, Snipe, Sand Martin, Reed Bunting.
Other notable flora/fauna: Otter, water vole, several spp. of dragonflies.
Contact: Cotswold Water Park Trust, T: 01793 752 413.

5. SLIMBRIDGE

The Wildfowl & Wetlands Trust.
Location: Sat nav: GL2 7BS. SO 723 048. On banks of River Severn, S of Gloucester. Signposted from M5 (exit Junc 13 or 14).
Access: Open daily, except Dec 25, 9.30am-5.30pm (5pm in winter). Last entry one hour before closing. Wheelchair hire (book beforehand) - all paths wheelchair accessible. Free parking. Admission charges for non-WWT members. Assistance dogs only.
Facilities: Restaurant, gift shop, gallery, cinema, discovery centre. Outdoor facilities inc. 15 hides, tropical house, worldwide collection of wildfowl species, observatory and observation tower. Plenty of family attractions inc. a pond zone, wader aviary, commentated swan feeds in the winter, Land Rover safaris and a canoe safari trail. Binoculars for hire.
Public transport: Railway stations at Cam and Dursley (4 miles). Local buses stop on A38.
Habitats: Reedbed, saltmarsh, freshwater pools, mudflats and wet grassland.
Key birds: 200+ spp. each year. *Winter*: 30,000 to 40,000 wildfowl esp. Bewick's Swan, White-fronted Goose, Wigeon, Teal, Pintail. Waders inc. Lapwing, Golden Plover, Spotted Redshank and Little Stint. Often large roosts of Starlings and gulls. *Breeding*: Kingfisher, Lapwing, Redshank, Oystercatcher, Common Tern, Reed Bunting and a good range of warblers. *Passage*: Waders, terns and gulls, inc. Mediterranean and Yellow-legged Gulls. Yellow Wagtail and large passerine movements. Hobbies now reach double figures in summer. Good list of rarities.

Other notable flora/fauna: Brown hare, otter, polecat and water vole. Scarce chaser and hairy dragonfly among 22 recorded spp.
Contact: T: 01453 891 900;
E: info.slimbridge@wwt.org.uk

6. SYMONDS YAT

RSPB/Forestry Commission England.
Location: Sat nav: HR9 6JL. SO 563 160. Hill-top site on the edge of Forest of Dean, three miles N of Coleford on B4432, signposted from Forest Enterprise car park. Also signposted from A40, S of Ross-on-Wye.
Access: Open at all times. RSPB Information Officer on site daily, Apr to Aug.
Facilities: Car park (fee payable), toilets with adapted facilities for disabled visitors, picnic area, drinks and light snacks. Environmental education programmes available.
Public transport: Very limited.
Habitats: Cliff above the River Wye and woodland.
Key birds: *Summer:* Peregrine, Buzzard, Goshawk, Raven and woodland species. Apr to Aug: Telescope is set up daily between 10am-4pm by RSPB volunteers to watch the Peregrines on the nest.
Contact: RSPB, T: 01594 562 852.

7. WHELFORD POOLS

Gloucestershire Wildlife Trust
Location: Sat nav: GL7 4EH. SU 174 995. Lakes lying in eastern section of Cotswold Water Park between Fairford and Lechlade, from minor road S of A417.
Access: Open at all times. Dogs must be on leads.
Facilities: Car park for 12 vehicles (one designated for disabled). Two bird hides.
Public transport: Cycle path from Lechlade.
Habitats: Former gravel pit workings now reverted to nature - part of SSSI. Two large lakes, plus three smaller pools for dragonflies.
Key birds: *Winter:* Wildfowl inc. Wigeon, Pochard and Tufted Ducks, plus occasional Bittern sightings. *Spring/summer:* Common Tern, Kingfisher and Nightingale, plus breeding Sedge Warbler, Reed Bunting and Great Crested Grebe. Artificial nesting bank for Sand Martins. Waders on passage.
Other notable flora/fauna: County's only site for pea mussel. Emperor, migrant hawker, black-tailed skimmer and red-eyed damselfly all breed.
Contact: Gloucestershire WT, T: 01452 383 333;
E: info@gloucestershirewildlifetrust.co.uk

Leicestershire & Rutland

AN INLAND COUNTY better known for fox hunting than its birding potential, Leicestershire can boast 33 Wildlife Trust reserves with a broad range of habitats. However, it is the adjoining county of Rutland that holds the jewel in the crown — Rutland Water with its breeding Ospreys, huge numbers of wildfowl, and good selection of passage waders — while nearby Eyebrook Reservoir is excellent for Smew, sizeable Golden Plover flocks and roosting gulls in winter.

1. EYEBROOK RESERVOIR

Corby & District Water Co.
Location: Sat nav: LE15 9JG. SP 853 964. Reservoir built 1940. S of Uppingham, from unclassified road W of A6003 at Stoke Dry.
Access: Access to 150 acres of private grounds granted to members of Leics & Rutland OS and Rutland NHS. All visitors should sign in at fishing lodge. Organised groups should contact Andy Miller, otherwise view from roadside lay-bys.
Facilities: SSSI since 1956. Three bird hides. Fishing season Mar to Nov. Toilets and visitor centre at fishing lodge.
Public transport: None.
Habitats: Open water, plantations and pasture.
Key birds: *Summer:* Good populations of breeding birds, sightings of Ospreys and Red Kite. *Passage:* waders and Black Tern. *Winter:* Wildfowl (inc. Goldeneye, Goosander, Smew) and waders. Tree Sparrow and Yellowhammer at feeding station, also Barn and Short-eared Owls can be seen hunting at dusk near Great Easton village (close to recycling centre).
Other notable flora/fauna: Otter, muntjac deer, red darter, demoiselle and blue damselfly, scalloped hazel and riband wave moths.
Contact: Eyebrook Trout Fishery, T: 01536 772 930;
E: lodge@flyfisheyebrook.co.uk;
W: www.flyfisheyebrook.co.uk

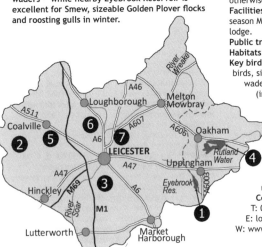

NATURE RESERVES - CENTRAL ENGLAND

2. HICKS LODGE

Forestry Commission.
Location : Sat nav: LE65 2UP. NGR SK 329 155. Within National Forest, approx 0.5 miles from Moira village. Follow brown tourist signs for National Forest Cycle Centre from Moira, Ashby-de-la-Zouch and from junc 12 of A42.
Access: Site open all year: 8am-8pm. Height barrier at main site entrance is removed when site is open, so no vehicle restrictions.
Facilities: Pay-and display car park (for approx 80 cars), with designated disabled (4) and mini-bus parking (2) bays. On-site forest centre with small cafe (open 9am-5pm), bike hire and toilets (inc. disabled and baby-changing facilities). All-ability trails and cycle trails. Most birdwatching activity occurs in front of the main centre, around the Hicks Lodge Loop and on the site ponds/lakes and open fields
Public transport: None
Habitats: New native woodland, with occasional European larch, rough grassland, open seasonally-grazed fields, lakes and ponds. Largest lake has two small islands, one of which is managed for Little Ringed Plover and other ground-nesting species.
Key birds: Raptors inc. Buzzard,Red Kite, Kestrel, Hobby, Sparrowhawk and Peregrine. Common wildfowl in winter, plus a good range of finches (inc. Crossbill), buntings, tits and summer warblers. Wader records inc. Bar-tailed Godwit, Greenshank, Ringed and Little Ringed Plovers, Common Sandpiper, Oystercatcher, Temminck's Stint, Lapwing and Golden Plover. Migrants on passage inc. Cuckoo, Wheatear, Whinchat, Stonechat, Spotted Flycatcher, hirundines and Black Tern.
Contact: Forestry Commission, T: 01889 586 593; E: info_nationalforest@forestry.gsi.gov.uk

3. NARBOROUGH BOG

Leicestershire & Rutland Wildlife Trust.
Location: Sat nav: LE19 2DB. SP 549 979. Between River Soar and M1, 5 miles S of Leicester. From city, turn L off B4114 (Leicester Road) just before going under motorway, follow track to sports club. Park near club house and walk across recreation ground to reserve entrance.
Access: Open at all times, please keep to paths. Not suitable for wheelchairs. Dogs on short leads only. Site may flood after heavy rain.
Facilities: None. Small bus/coach could park in sports field car park.
Public transport: Narborough train station. Bus nos. X5 & 140 to Narborough then 0.6 mile walk. Traveline, T: 0871 200 2233.
Habitats: Peat bog SSSI (the only substantial deposit in Leicestershire), wet woodland, reedbed, dense scrub and fen meadow.
Key birds: More than 130 spp. of birds recorded, inc. three spp. of woodpeckers, six spp. of tit, Tawny Owl, Sparrowhawk and Kingfisher.

Other notable flora/fauna: Butterflies inc. common blue, meadow brown, large and small skippers, small heath and gatekeeper. Banded demoiselles, also good for moths and beetles. Harvest mice and water voles recorded, also breeding grass snakes. Meadow saxifrage, common meadow-rue and marsh thistle.
Contact: Leics & Rutland WT HQ, T: 0116 262 9968; E: info@lrwt.org.uk

4. RUTLAND WATER

Anglian Water/Leics & Rutland Wildlife Trust
Location: Two nature reserves - 1: Egleton Reserve (Sat nav: LE15 8BT). SK 878 075, from Egleton village off A6003 or A606 S of Oakham. Hosts British Birdwatching Fair in Aug. 2: Lyndon Reserve SK 894 058, south shore E of Manton village off A6003 S of Oakham. Follow 'nature reserve' signs to car park.
Access: 1: The Anglian Water Bird Watching Centre Open daily, except Dec 25/26, 9am-5pm, (9am-4pm Nov-Jan). 2: Open daily from mid-Mar to mid-Sept (9am-5pm). Day permits available for both. Reduced admission for disabled and carers. Book a place in the badger-watching hide (contact AWBW Centre).
Facilities: 1: Birdwatching centre has toilets and disabled access, mobility scooter for hire. 28 hides (disabled access possible to 12 hides). 2: Interpretive centre toilets, inc. disabled, paths, use of a mobility scooter. Seven hides, four accessible to wheelchairs.
Public transport: Rutland Shore Link Bus runs from Oakham at 9.35am and 12.35pm.
Habitats: Ramsar-designated reservoir, lagoons, scrapes, woods, meadows, plantations, reedbeds.
Key birds: *Spring/autumn:* Outstanding wader passage, with up to 28 species recorded. Also wide range of raptors, owls, passerine flocks, terns (Black, Arctic, breeding Common, occasional Little and Sandwich). *Winter:* Up to 28 species of wildfowl (inc. internationally important numbers of Gadwall and Shoveler). Also Goldeneye, Smew, Goosander, rare grebes, all divers, Ruff. *Summer:* Ospreys among 70 breeding species.
Other notable flora/fauna: Otter, badger, fox, weasel, stoat. Up to 20 species of dragonflies/damselflies and 24 butterfly species.
Contact: Egleton, T: 01572 770 651; E: julia@rutlandwater.org.uk; Lyndon, T: 01572 737 378; W: www.rutlandwater.org.uk / www.ospreys.org.uk

5. SENCE VALLEY FOREST PARK

Forestry Commission.
Location: Sat nav: LE67 6NW. SK 404 113. Within The National Forest. 10 miles NW of Leicester and two miles SW of Coalville, between Ibstock and Ravenstone. The car park is signposted from A447 N of Ibstock.
Access: Open all year, 8am-7pm (Apr-Sept), 9am-4pm rest of year (precise times on noticeboard). Height barrier at main entrance, where there is access to wheelchair-friendly surfaced paths. A week's notice required for coach or minibus.

Facilities: Two car parks, toilets (inc. disabled and baby-changing facilities), information and recent sightings boards, hide, all-abilities trails.
Public transport: None.
Habitats: New forest (native broadleaf, mixed and pine), rough grassland, wildflower meadow, pools, wader scrape, River Sence.
Key birds: *Spring/summer:* Artificial Sand Martin nesting wall, Wheatear, Whinchat, Redstart, Common and Green Sandpipers, Ringed and Little Ringed Plovers, Redshank. Dunlin and Greenshank frequent, possible Wood Sandpiper. Reed Bunting, Meadow Pipit, Skylark, Linnet, Yellow Wagtail. Possible Quail. Kestrel and Barn Owl seen occasionally. *Winter:* Stonechat, Redpoll, Short-eared Owl, Goosander and Wigeon possible.
Contact: Forestry Commission, T: 01889 586 593;
E: info_nationalforest@forestry.gsi.gov.uk

6. SWITHLAND RESERVOIR

Severn Trent Water.
Location: Sat nav: LE7 7SB. SK 558 140. Lies S of Quorn, E of A6 (Leicester to Loughborough road). Use minor road between Swithland and Rothley for southern section. For northern section take Kinchley Lane along eastern shore to the dam.
Access: No access to water's edge: view from roads.
Facilities: None.
Public transport: None.
Habitats: Large reservoir divided by Great Central Railway line. Small area of woodland (Buddon Wood).
Key birds: Common wildfowl are regular, but site has produced seaduck such as Common Scoter, Scaup and Long-tailed Duck ans occasional divers. Black-necked Grebe seen in late summer/autumn, while Mediterranean Gulls are annual. High water levels curb wader sightings, but Kingfishers are regular and Ravens are seen daily. All three woodpeckers are in Buddon Wood, along with a range of woodland species. It is the county's best site for wintering Peregrines. Also Buzzards, Sparrowhawks and Hobbies (summer). Good track record of rarities in recent years.

Other notable flora/fauna: Buddon Wood along Kinchley Lane is good for purple hairstreak butterfly and orange underwing moth – look for the latter around silver birch.

7. WATERMEAD COUNTRY PARK

Leics County Council
Location: LE7 1AD. SK 608 108 (car park). Located off Wanlip Road, Syston (off A46 or A607), six miles N of Leicester city centre. Watermead CP (South) is managed by Leicester City Council.
Access: Open from 7am to dusk all year. Wanlip Road gives access to four car parks (fees payable). Southern entrance in Alderton Close, Thurmaston. Wheelchair access on just over five miles of surfaced tracks. RADAR key needed by mobility scooter riders to negotiate kissing gates on perimeter track.
Facilities: Four bird hides in nature reserve. Toilets, inc. disabled. Sand Martin nesting wall.
Public transport: Buses on route nos. 5/5A/6 from Leicester to Syston/East Goscote/Melton, buses every few mins in the day to/from Leicester and up to three buses/hour on Sun. Get off at Alderton Close.
Habitats: River Soar and Grand Union Canal, plus 12 lakes and pools, wildflower meadow, woodland and reedbeds (one of largest in Midlands). Park stretches nearly two miles in length. Wanlip Meadows can be viewed from Plover Hide.
Key birds: 200 spp. recorded, inc. common wildfowl, Little Egret, Kingfisher, Water Rail, Cetti's Warbler. *Winter:* Bittern, Caspian Gull, Yellow-legged Gull and Scandinavian thrushes. *Passage:* Garganey and Black Terns. Wanlip Meadows very good for waders, inc. Little Ringed Plover, and is the county's best site for Temminck's Stint.
Other notable flora/fauna: Otters now regular, but elusive. Emperor and other dragonfly spp.
Contact: T: 0116 305 5000;
E: countryparks@leics.gov.uk;
W: www.leicscountryparks.org.uk/

Lincolnshire

THIS LARGE RURAL county sits between two major bird-friendly estuaries – the Humber to the north and the Wash to the south-east – and boasts several coastal sites such as Frieston Shore and Gibraltar Point which attract migrants and wintering wildlfowl. Agriculture dominates inland, but there are reservoirs which can produce interesting birds. Lincoln Cathedral, one high point in a very flat county, has attracted breeding Peregrines.

1. ALKBOROUGH FLATS

North Lincolnshire Council.
Location: Located on S bank of Humber where Rivers Trent and Ouse meet to form the Humber. Follow brown tourism signs to Alkborough Flats from the A1077 near Winterton. Reach two car parks by following the duck signs through Alkborough village.Car park at the bottom of Prospect Lane (SE 879 221) is mainly for disabled visitors. Main car park (SE 887 224) off Whitton Road, just N of Alkborough village. Site also accessible via a permissive footpath from Julian's Bower, Back Street, Alkborough. Sat nav: DN15 9JN or SE 880 218.
Access: Open at all times, limited access for disabled visitors.
Facilities: Four bird hides, inc. a tower hide at north eastern end of site. Five miles of public footpaths (two miles wheelchair-friendly). Three bird hides are accessible by wheelchair users.

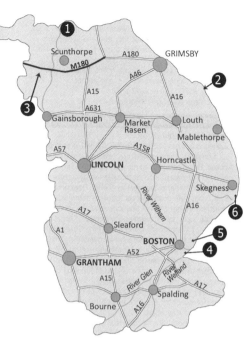

Refreshments locally at The Paddocks Tea Room, Back Street, Alkborough (SE 881 246), open Thur-Sun and bank holidays.

Public transport: Limited bus service to Alkborough from Scunthorpe. Traveline, T: 0871 200 2233.

Habitats: 440 ha managed realignment site created by breaching the river defences to protect homes from flooding. Mixture of inter-tidal mudflats, grasslands, reedbeds and arable land.

Key birds: 200 spp. recorded. Lying on a key migration route, the site attracts geese and ducks in large numbers. Long-billed Dowitcher, Lesser Yellowlegs and Marsh Sandpiper brought the site's wader total to 40 spp. *Winter:* Huge flocks of Lapwings (10,000 regularly) and Golden Plover (up to 14,000 but 5,000-10,000 regular), plus Marsh Harrier, Hen Harrier, Peregrine and Merlin, Teal, Wigeon, Black-tailed Godwit, while a large flock of Barnacle Geese can be seen at nearby Whitton Sands. *Summer:* Marsh Harriers have attempted to breed, Little Egret, Bearded Tit, Reed Warbler, Water Rail. Spoonbills are regular visitors. Avocets in autumn; passage waders in spring/autumn.

Other notable flora/fauna: Roe deer, badger, brown hare, water vole, otter, fox. Wall brown among a range of butterflies and black-tailed skimmer among the dragonflies.

Contact: Site Manager, Anna Moody
T: 01724 721 269

2. DONNA NOOK

Lincolnshire Wildlife Trust.
Location: Sat nav: LN11 7PB. TF 422 998. Several access points off the main A1031 coastal road with parking facilities at Stonebridge (TF 422 998), Howden's Pullover (TF 449 952), Sea Lane, Saltfleet (TF 456 944) and Saltfleet Haven (TF 467 935).
Access: Donna Nook beach is closed on weekdays as this is an active bombing range, but dunes remain open. Dogs on leads. Some disabled access.
Facilities: No toilets or visitor centre.
Habitats: Dunes, slacks and intertidal areas, seashore, mudflats, sandflats.
Key birds: *Summer:* Little Tern, Ringed Plover, Oystercatcher. *Winter:* Brent Goose, Shelduck, Twite, Lapland Bunting, Shorelark, Linnet.
Other notable flora/fauna: One of the largest and most accessible breeding colonies of grey seals in UK (viewing area open late Oct-Dec, LN11 7PD), plus fox, badger, stoat and weasel. Three spp. of shrew have been identified. Common lizard.
Contact: Lincolnshire WT, T: 01507 526 667;
E: info@lincstrust.co.uk

3. EPWORTH TURBARY

Lincolnshire Wildlife Trust.
Location: Sat nav: DN9 1EA. SE 758 036. SW of Scunthorpe. Take A18 W from Scunthorpe then A161 S to Epworth. Turn R on High Street, and head towards Wroot. The entrance is near bridge over Skyer's Drain. Park inside or on verge adjoining reserve, well away from corner.
Access: Open at all times. Keep to waymarked paths and use hides to avoid disturbing birds on the ponds.
Facilities: Car park, way-marked trail, two hides.
Habitats: One of the few relics of raised bog in Lincolnshire. Areas of active sphagnum bog still exist, plus reed swamp and mixed fen vegetation, also considerable area of birch woodland of varying ages.
Key birds: *Spring/summer:* Breeding birds inc. Tree Pipit, warblers, finches, Green and Great Spotted Woodpeckers and Woodcock. Greenshank, Green Sandpiper and Little Grebe are attracted to the wet area. Around Steve's Pond, occasional Hobby and Marsh Harrier, plus Teal, Little Grebe, Tree Pipit, Sparrowhawk and Buzzard. Willow Tit, Long-tailed Tit, Reed Bunting and Willow Warbler in the woodland areas. Occasionally Corn Buntings on the adjoining farmland. *Autumn/winter:* Large corvid flocks roost in reserve. At Pantry's Pond in winter occasional Hen Harrier. Other birds inc. Yellowhammer, Linnet, Jay and Magpie. Sometimes in winter Long-eared Owls can be observed roosting close to the path.
Other notable flora/fauna: 11 spp. of breeding dragonflies recorded. Wood tiger moth is well established. Plants inc. sneezewort, yellow and purple loosestrife, meadow-rue, and devil's-bit scabious.
Contact: Lincolnshire WT, T: 01507 526 667;
E: info@lincstrust.co.uk

4. FRAMPTON MARSH

RSPB (Eastern England Office).
Location: Sat nav: PE20 1AY. TF 356 392. Four miles SE of Boston. From A16 follow signs to Frampton then Frampton Marsh.
Access: Visitor centre open daily 9.30am-4pm (Nov-Feb, except Dec 25) and 9.30am-4pm weekdays, 9.30am-5pm weekends (Mar-Oct). Footpaths and hides open at all times.
Facilities: Visitor centre (inc. toilets), footpaths and three hides all suitable for wheelchairs. Hot drinks and snacks available at centre, benches, viewpoints, 60-space car park (three for disabled visitors), binocular hire, bicycle rack, free information leaflets and events programmes.
Public transport: None.
Habitats: Saltmarsh, wet grassland, freshwater scrapes and developing reedbed.
Key birds: *Summer:* Breeding Redshank, Avocet, Lapwing, Skylark, Little Ringed Plover, Ringed Plover, Sand Martin and several species of ducks plus passage waders (inc. Greenshank, Curlew Sandpiper, Wood Sandpiper, Little and Temminck's Stints, Ruff and Black-tailed Godwit), Marsh Harrier and Hobby. *Winter:* Hen Harrier, Short-eared Owl, Merlin, dark-bellied Brent Goose, Golden Plover, Twite, Lapland Bunting.
Other notable flora/fauna: Water vole, stoat. Dragonflies inc. emperor, hawkers, chasers and darters. Common butterflies plus wall brown, painted lady and speckled wood. Scarce pug, star wort and crescent striped moths on saltmarsh. Important brackish water flora and fauna inc. nationally scarce spiral tassleweed and several rare beetles.
Contact: RSPB, T: 01205 724 678;
E: lincolnshirewashreserves@rspb.org.uk

5. FREISTON SHORE

RSPB (Eastern England Office).
Location: Sat nav: PE22 0LZ. TF 398 425. Four miles E of Boston. From A52 at Haltoft End follow signs to Freiston Shore.
Access: Open at all times. Keep dogs on leads on all footpaths.
Facilities: Footpaths, two car parks, bird hide, circular wetland trail. Free leaflets on site, guided walks programme. Bicycle rack, benches, viewpoints, seawatching shelter, viewing screen and viewing platform.
Public transport: None.
Habitats: Saltmarsh, saline lagoon, mudflats, wet grassland.
Key birds: *Summer:* Breeding waders inc. Avocet, Ringed Plover and Oystercatcher, Common Tern, Corn Bunting and Tree Sparrow. *Winter:* Twite, dark-bellied Brent Goose, wildfowl, waders, Short-eared Owl and Hen Harrier. *Passage:* Waders, inc. Greenshank, Curlew Sandpiper and Little Stint. *Autumn:* Occasional seabirds inc. Arctic and Great Skuas.

Other notable flora/fauna: Water vole, muntjac and roe deer, stoat. Dragonflies inc. emperor, hawkers, chasers and darters. Common butterflies plus wall brown, painted lady and speckled wood. Scarce pug, star wort and crescent striped moths on saltmarsh. Important lagoon invertebrates and plants.
Contact: RSPB, T: 01205 724 678;
E: lincolnshirewashreserves@rspb.org.uk

6. GIBRALTAR POINT NNR & BIRD OBSERVATORY

Lincolnshire Wildlife Trust.
Location: Sat nav: PE24 4SU. TF 556 580. Three miles S of Skegness, signposted from town centre.
Access: Open dawn-dusk all year. Charges for parking. Free admission to reserve. Some access restrictions to sensitive sites at S end. Dogs on leads at all times - no dogs on beach during summer.
Facilities: Visitor centre and cafe open 10am-3pm (may stay open later during busy periods), toilets. Location of Wash Study Centre and Bird Observatory. Field centre is an ideal base for birdwatching/natural history groups in spring, summer and autumn. Public hides overlook freshwater and brackish lagoons. Wash viewpoint overlooks saltmarsh and mudflats. Four hides suitable for wheelchairs, as well as surfaced paths. Day visit groups must be booked in advance. Access for coaches. Contact Wash Study Centre for residential or day visits.
Public transport: Bus service from Skegness runs occasionally, summer service only. Otherwise taxi from Skegness. Cycle route from Skegness.
Habitats: Sand dune grassland and scrub, saltmarshes and mudflats, freshwater marsh and lagoons.
Key birds: Large scale visible migration during spring and autumn passage. Internationally important populations of non-breeding waders between Jul and Mar (peak Sep/Oct). Winter flocks of Brent Geese, Shelduck and Wigeon on flats and marshes with Hen Harrier, Merlin and Short-eared Owl often present. Red-throated Divers offshore, (peak Feb). Colonies of Little Tern and Ringed Plover in summer. More than 100 spp. can be seen in a day during May and Sept. Can be a good passage of autumn seabirds in northerly winds.
Other notable flora/fauna: Patches of pyramidal orchids. Grey and common seal colonies, with porpoises offshore in most months. Butterflies inc. brown argus and green hairstreak.
Contact: Reserve & wildlife: Kev Wilson, T: 01754 898 079; E: kwilson@lincstrust.co.uk or E: gibnnr@lincstrust.co.uk;
Vistor Centre: T: 01754 898 057; gibvc@lincstrust.co.uk
W: http://gibraltarpointblrdobservatory.blogspot.com

Northamptonshire

RED KITES WERE re-introduced in the area north-east of Corby and they, along with Buzzards, are thriving and spreading out. Blatherwycke Lake is good for Mandarins, while Thrapston and Ditchford gravel pits, Pitsford and Hollowell reservoirs are good for a range of wildfowl, especially in winter. Harrington airfield can hold good numbers of wintering Short-eared Owls and raptors.

1. DITCHFORD LAKES & MEADOWS

Beds, Cambs & Northants Wildlife Trust.
Location: Sat nav: NN8 1RL. SP 930 678. From Wellingborough, take A45 towards Rushden and Higham Ferrers. Take exit marked A5001 to Rushden. Turn L at roundabout onto Ditchford Road towards Irthlingborough/Ditchford. Small car park is 500 yards on right
Access: Rough grass paths, flat overall. Some areas soft and muddy esp. in winter. Dogs on leads.
Facilities: Car park (height restriction).
Public transport: None.
Habitats: Part of the upper Nene valley floodplain - a complex of old gravel pits, grassland, lakes surrounded by mature scrub.
Key birds: *Winter*: Common Sandpiper, Snipe, Teal, Wigeon, Gadwall, Tufted Duck. *Spring*: Redshank, Oystercatcher, Cetti's Warbler, Little Grebe, Grey Heron. *Summer*: Reed Warbler, Sedge Warbler, Swift, House Martin. *Autumn*: Snipe, Great Crested Grebe, Moorhen, Coot, Grey Heron.
Other notable flora/fauna: Hairy dragonfly, grass snake, otter. Plants inc. marsh woundwort, dropwort, great burnet.
Contact: BCN WT, T: 01604 405 285;
E: northamptonshire@wildlifebcn.org

2. PITSFORD WATER

Anglian Water/Beds, Cambs & Northants Wildlife Trust.
Location: Sat nav: NN6 9SJ. SP 786 700. Five miles N of Northampton. From A43 take turn to Holcot and Brixworth. From A508 take turn to Brixworth and Holcot.
Access: Reserve (N of causeway) open all year to permit holders. Wildlife Trust members can apply for free permit from HQ. Non-members can obtain day permits from fishing lodge, open mid-Mar to mid-Nov from 8am-dusk. Winter opening times variable, check in advance. No dogs. Disabled access from Lodge to first hide.
Facilities: Toilets available in Lodge, 15 miles of paths, nine bird hides and car parking.
Habitats: Open water (up to 120 ha), marginal vegetation and reed grasses, wet woodland, grassland and mixed woodland (40 ha).
Key birds: Typically 165-170 spp. per year with a total list of 253 spp. *Summer*: Breeding warblers, terns, grebes, herons. *Autumn*: Waders if water levels suitable. *Winter*: Up to 10,000 wildfowl, feeding station with Tree Sparrow and occasional Corn Bunting.
Other notable flora/fauna: 32 spp. of butterflies, 392 of macro moths, 21 of dragonflies, 377 of flora, 105 of bryophytes and 404 of fungi.
Contact: BCN WT, T: 01604 405 285;
E: northamptonshire@wildlifebcn.org
Pitsford Water Fishing Lodge, Brixworth Road, Holcot, Northampton, NN6 9SJ. T: 01604 781 350;
E: fishing@anglianwater.co.uk

3. STANWICK LAKES

Rockingham Forest Trust
Location: Sat nav: NN9 6GY. SP 967 715. Entrance off the A45, eight miles N of Wellingborough.
Access: Reserve open 7am-9pm (Mar-Oct); 7am-5pm (Nov-Feb), except Dec 25. Visitor centre open 10am-4pm weekdays, 10am-5pm weekends and school holidays, except Dec 25/26. Charges for car and coach parking. Disability scooter available for hire.
Facilities: All paths, visitor centre, gift shop, toilets and bird hide are wheelchair accessible.
Habitats: 750 acre countryside park inc. Ramsar-designated wetland on site of former quarry, part of Nene Valley Special Protection Area. Inc. reedbeds, hedgerows and grazed areas.
Key birds: Resident Little Egret, Kingfisher, Green and Great Spotted Woodpeckers, Grey Wagtail, Cetti's Warbler and Barn Owl. *Autumn/winter*: Wildfowl inc. Pintail, Goldeneye and Goosander. Bittern, Redpoll and Siskin. *Spring/summer*: Waders inc. Oystercatcher (breeding), Little Ringed Plover, Greenshank and Green Sandpiper. Hobby, Yellow Wagtail, hirundines and migrant warblers.
Other notable flora/fauna: Otter, grass snake, 150 spp. of moths, dragonflies.
Contact: Rockingham Forest Trust,
T: 01933 625 522; E: info@rftrust.org.uk

4. SUMMER LEYS LNR

Beds, Cambs & Northants Wildlife Trust.
Location: Sat nav: NN29 7TQ. SP 886 633. Off Hardwater Road, Great Doddington, three miles from Wellingborough, accessible from A45 and A509.
Access: Open at all times, no permits required. Dogs on leads. 40 space car park, small tarmaced circular route suitable for wheelchairs.
Facilities: Three hides, one feeding station. No toilets, nearest are at Irchester Country Park on A509 towards Wellingborough.
Public transport: Nearest train station is Wellingborough. Nearest bus services run regularly to Great Doddington (X47 - Stagecoach) about a mile away.
Habitats: Scrape, two ponds, lake, scrub, flood meadows, hedgerow.
Key birds: *All year:* Tree Sparrow. *Spring/summer:* Common Tern, Black-headed Gull, Ringed and Little Ringed Plover, Redshank and Oystercatcher all breed. Whimbrel, Turnstone, Common Sandpiper on passage. *Winter:* Large numbers of common wildfowl, plus Lapwing, Golden Plover and Ruff.
Other notable flora/fauna: 16 spp. of dragonflies recorded, inc. hairy dragonfly (check Marigold Pond). Common blue and brown argus butterflies on grassland.
Contact: BCN WT, T: 01604 405 285;
E: northamptonshire@wildlifebcn.org

5. THRAPSTON GRAVEL PITS & TITCHMARSH LNR

Natural England (Lincs & Northants Team/ BCN Wildlife Trust.
Location: Sat nav: NN14 3EE (Lowick Lane car park). TL 006 812. Seven miles E of Kettering. From A14 take A605 N. For Titchmarsh turn L at Thorpe Waterville, continue towards Aldwincle. Take first L after church (Lowick Lane) and continue to small car park on left. Take footpath to reserve.
Access: As well as the Aldwincle access point, there is a public footpath from lay-by on A605 N of Thrapston. Muddy conditions after heavy rain.
Facilities: Six hides in LNR, none on main pits.
Public transport: Bus services to Thrapston.
Habitats: Alder/birch/willow wood; old duck decoy, series of water-filled gravel pits.

Key birds: *Summer:* Breeding Grey Heron (no access to heronry), Common Tern, Little Ringed Plover; warblers. Migrants, inc. Red-necked and Slavonian Grebes, Hobby, Bittern and Marsh Harrier recorded. *Winter:* Good range of wildfowl inc. nationally important numbers of Gadwall, Wigeon and Goosander, plus gulls. Waders on passage.
Other notable flora/fauna: Banded demoiselle, red-eyed damselfly, brown, southern and migrant hawker dragonflies.
Contact: BCN WT, T: 01604 405 285;
E: northamptonshire@wildlifebcn.org

6. TOP LODGE & FINESHADE WOODS

Forestry Commission.
Location: Sat nav: NN17 3BB. SP 978 983. Off A43 between Stamford and Corby. Follow brown tourist signs to Top Lodge Fineshade Woods.
Access: Fully accessible visitor centre - open daily, except Dec 25, 10am-5pm (Mar-Oct); 10am-4pm weekdays/10am-5pm on weekends (Nov-Feb). Caravan Club site open Mar to Nov (see CC website for details). Smelter's Walk is an all-ability trail leading to the hide. Electric bikes available from Fineshade Cycling shop.
Facilities: Two pay-and-display car parks. Visitor centre, toilets, Top Lodge Cafe, events/activities throughout the year. Wildlife hide in wood. Orienteering course. Three way-marked walking trails (one is for all abilities, two are surfaced), one horse trail, one family cycle trail with skills loops, dedicated coach and horse box parking. Sensory garden.
Public transport: None.
Habitats: Ancient woodland, coniferous woodland, beech woodland, open areas, small pond.
Key birds: Centre of Northants' Red Kite reintroduction scheme. A wide range of birds of mixed woodlands. *All year:* Red Kite, Buzzard, Great Spotted Woodpecker, Goshawk, Nuthatch, Crossbill, Marsh Tit, Willow Tit. *Summer:* Turtle Dove, warblers. *Winter:* Hawfinch.
Other notable flora/fauna: Adder, grass snake, slow worm, common lizard. Fallow deer, badger. Orchids inc. greater butterfly, early purple and common spotted, other flora of ancient woodland.
Contact: Forestry Commission, Top Lodge, T: 0300 067 4340; E: northants@forestry.gsi.gov.uk

Nottinghamshire

GRAVEL PITS DOMINATE birding habitats in Nottinghamshire, though remnant pockets of heathland still hold iconic species such as Nightjar and Woodlark. The most recently developed gravel pit sites are the Idle Valley NR (formerly known as Lound) and the RSPB's new reserve at Langford Lowfields, near Newark. A raptor watchpoint at Welbeck can produce sightings of Honey Buzzard, Goshawk and Osprey and you can try for Hawfinches in winter in Clumber Park.

1. ATTENBOROUGH NATURE RESERVE

Cement UK/Nottinghamshire Wildlife Trust.
Location: Sat nav: NG9 6DY. Car park at SK 515 339. In Nottingham alongside River Trent. Signposted from A6005 between Beeston and Long Eaton.
Access: Open all year, 7am-dusk, (visitor centre open 9am-5pm, 6pm on weekends and bank holidays). Dogs on leads (guide dogs only in visitor centre). Paths suitable for disabled access. Coaches by prior appointment. Car park charge.

NATURE RESERVES - CENTRAL ENGLAND

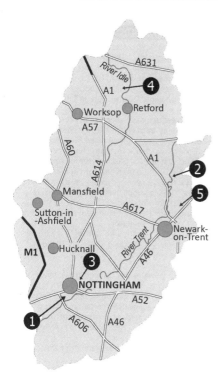

Facilities: Education and visitor centre with cafe and shop, all accessible to wheelchair users. Nature trail (leaflet from Notts WT), four bird hides inc. an elevated hide and new and innovative Sand Martin hide – a sunken bird hide within an artificial Sand Martin bank.
Public transport: Railway station at Attenborough – reserve is five mins walk away, Visitor centre a further 10 mins. Trent Barton Indigo bus service between Nottingham Broadmarsh and Derby bus station runs regularly throughout day. Alight at Chilwell Retail Park, walk 500 yards along Barton Lane.
Habitats: Designated SSSI, composed of disused, flooded gravel workings with associated marginal and wetland vegetation.
Key birds: *Spring/summer*: Breeding Common Tern (40+ pairs), Reed Warbler, Black Tern regular (bred once). *Winter*: Wildfowl, plus Bittern, Grey Heron colony, adjacent Cormorant roost.
Other notable flora/fauna: Smooth newt, dragonflies inc. four-spotted chaser and migrant hawker.
Contact: Attenborough Nature Centre,
T: 01159 721 777;
E: enquiries@attenboroughnaturecentre.co.uk;
W: www.attenboroughnaturecentre.co.uk

2. BESTHORPE NATURE RESERVE

Nottinghamshire Wildlife Trust.
Location: Sat nav: NG23 7HL. SK 817 640 and SK 813 646 (access points north and south of Trent Lane). Take A1133 N of Newark. Turn into Trent Lane S of Besthorpe village, reserve entrances second turn on L and R turn at end of lane (at River Trent).
Access: Open access to a hide, several screens (one in south section with disabled access from car park). No access to SSSI meadows. Limited access to areas grazed with sheep. Dogs on leads.
Facilities: No toilets (pubs etc. in Besthorpe village), two hides in southern section, paths, nature trail (northern part), several screens.
Public transport: Limited. Bus - Travel Wright (67) along A1133 to Besthorpe village (0.75 mile away).
Habitats: Former gravel workings with islands, SSSI neutral grasslands, hedges, reedbed, etc.
Key birds: *Spring/summer*: Breeding Grey Heron, Cormorant, Little Ringed Plover, Common Tern, Kingfisher, Grasshopper Warbler. *Winter*: Large numbers of ducks (Pochard, Tufted Duck, Pintail, Wigeon) and Peregrine. Recent re-profiling of water margins has increased the numbers of visiting waders.
Other notable flora/fauna: Nationally rare plant community in meadows.
Contact: Nottinghamshire WT, T: 01159 588 242;
E: info@nottswt.co.uk

3. COLWICK COUNTRY PARK

Nottingham City Council.
Location: Sat nav: NG4 2DW. SK 610 395. Access from Mile End Road, off A612 two miles E of Nottingham city centre. Adjacent to park-and-ride car park.
Access: Open at all times, but no vehicle access after dusk or before 7am. Best parking is in Colwick Hall access road from the racecourse.
Facilities: Nature trails. Sightings log book in Fishing Lodge.
Public transport: Nottingham City Transport Buses: no. 44 from stop Q3 on Queens Street (outside the Post Office); Park and Ride Service: Citylink2 from stop CL2 on Lower Parliament Street (outside Victoria Centre).
Habitats: Lakes, pools, woodlands, grasslands, new plantations, River Trent.
Key birds: *Summer*: 64 breeding spp. recorded, inc. warblers and Common Tern (15+ pairs). Good track record for rarities. *Winter*: Wildfowl (high concentrations of Goldeneye) and gulls. In nature reserve look for Lesser Spotted Woodpecker, Water Rail and Kingfisher. Passage migrants inc. Stonechat and Whinchat.
Other notable flora/fauna: Pool designated a SSSI for its 14 spp. of breeding dragonflies. Purple and white letter hairstreak butterflies.
Contact: Country Park, Mile End Road, Colwick, Nottingham, NG4 2DW.

4. IDLE VALLEY

Nottinghamshire Wildlife Trust/Tarmac/Private.
Location: Sat nav: DN22 8SG. SK 690 856. S end of reserve is 0.5 mile N of Retford off A638 to Barnby Moor, via entrance to Tarmac. Rural Learning Centre is on R.
Access: Open all year. Keep to walkways and public rights of way. Parking for reserve in first parking bay (large car park is for Learning Centre only). Footpath at south end is wheelchair accessible.
Facilities: Learning centre reception and toilets open (10am-4pm) all year. including cafe. Six viewing screens, two overlooking Chainbridge NR Scrape, two at Neatholme Scrape and single screens at Neatholme Fen and Neatholme Pit. Two hides in Chainbridge Wood.
Public transport: Buses from Doncaster, Gainsborough and Worksop to Retford bus station, then on Stagecoach no. 27 via Lound village crossroads (Chainbridge Lane).
Habitats: Former sand and gravel quarries, restored gravel workings, conservation grazed areas, woodland, reedbed, river valley, farmland, scrub, willow plantations, open water.
Key birds: 251 spp. recorded. *Summer:* Gulls, terns, wildfowl and waders. Passage waders, terns, passerines and raptors. *Winter:* Wildfowl, gulls, raptors. Good site for rarities, which have inc. Broad-billed Sandpiper, Great White Egret, Baird's Sandpiper and Steppe Grey Shrike in recent times.
Contacts: Idle Valley Rural Learning Centre, Great North Road, Retford, DN22 8RQ; T: 01777 858 245; E: info@nottswt.co.uk

5. LANGFORD LOWFIELDS

RSPB Midlands Office/ Lefarge Tarmac
Location: Sat nav: NG23 7RF. SK 821 601. Lies NE of Newark-on-Trent. From A1 take A46 (signposted to Lincoln) and then turn onto A1133 (to Collingham). After two miles turn L on Tarmac access road (signposted Langford Quarry). Park in Tarmac car park.
Access: Access to main working quarry restricted to reserve trails at north end of site, except for working parties and guided group walks (see RSPB website for dates). View from public footpath around perimeter (mostly not suitable for disabled visitors, except for resurfaced section from new car park on NE boundary). Cottage Lane car park open dawn-dusk.
Facilities: Viewing screen overlooking reedbed. No toilets except for work party volunteers.
Public transport: Newark-Collingham buses will stop near to footpath if requested.
Habitats: RSPB is working with Tarmac to create the East Midlands largest reedbed (currently 30 ha) at this sand and gravel quarry site. Mature woodland, lake and shallow pools.
Key birds: Large waterfowl numbers in winter, plus Starling roosts, and five owl spp. Bittern also recorded. *Summer:* Ten spp. of warbler, inc. Cetti's, Grasshopper and regionally important numbers of Reed and Sedge. Numerous Cuckoos, Turtle Doves, Marsh Harriers, Hobbies, hirundines and breeding Little Ringed Plovers and Avocets.
Other notable flora/fauna: Badgers, more than 18 spp. of butterflies.
Contact: RSPB, T: 01636 893 611 to book group visits or to enquire about work parties.

Oxfordshire

A LAND-LOCKED, LARGELY agricultural county, Oxfordshire has two outstanding birding locations: Farmoor reservoir for passage migrants, wintering wildfowl and rarities and Otmoor, where wet meadows and reedbeds are being developed by the RSPB to benefit breeding waders such as Redshank, Snipe and Lapwing in spring and Hobbies in summer. Wildfowl numbers increase in winter and Hen Harriers, Merlins, Peregrines and Short-eared Owls hunt.

1. ASTON ROWANT NNR

Natural England (Thames Team).
Location: Sat nav: HP14 3YL (for Beacon Hill car park). SU 731 966. From the M40 Lewknor interchange at Junc 6, travel NE for a short distance and turn R onto A40. After 1.5 miles at the top of hill, turn R and R again into a narrow, metalled lane. Car park is signposted from A40.
Access: Open all year. Some wheelchair access at Cowleaze Wood (contact for details).
Facilities: On-site parking at Beacon Hill and Cowleaze Wood, viewpoint, seats, interpretation panels.
Public transport: Red Rose buses between High Wycombe and Oxford stop at both Stokenchurch and Lambert Arms, Aston Rowant. Stagecoach Oxford Tube buses stop at Lewknor village, a short walk from reserve.
Habitats: Chalk grassland, chalk scrub, beech woodland.
Key birds: *Spring/summer:* Blackcap, other warblers, Turtle Dove. Passage birds inc. Ring Ouzel, Wheatear and Stonechat. *Winter:* Brambling, Siskin, winter thrushes. *All year:* Red Kite, Buzzard, Sparrowhawk, Woodcock, Tawny Owl, Green and Great Spotted Woodpeckers, Skylark, Meadow Pipit, Marsh Tit.
Other notable flora/fauna: Rich chalk grassland flora, inc. Chiltern gentian clustered bellflower, frog, bee, pyramidal and fragrant orchids. Less common butterflies inc. silver-spotted, dingy and grizzled skippers, chalkhill blue, adonis blue, green hairstreak and green fritillary.
Contact: Natural England, Aston Rowant NNR, T: 01844 351 833; E: michael.venters@naturalengland.org.uk

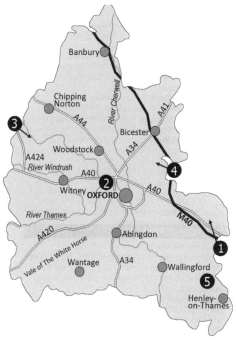

2. FARMOOR RESERVOIR

Thames Water.
Location: Sat nav: OX2 9NT. SP 452 061. Lies W of Oxford between A 40 and A420. Widely signposted by brown tourist signs. At mini-roundabout in Farmoor village, turn L and look for car park at Gate 3 (0.5 mile distance).
Access: Free car parking at Gate 3.
Facilities: Car park off B4017. Bird hide at Pinkhill Reserve, west of reservoir.
Public transport: Frequent Stagecoach no. 100 bus between Oxford and Witney stop in Farmoor village (0.5 mile walk to Gate 3).
Habitats: The county's largest body of fresh water contained in two concrete basins separated by a causeway. Shallow pools in Pinkhill Reserve. Reedbed, wet grassland and pools in the small Shrike Meadow and Buckthorne Meadow reserves.
Key birds: *Winter:* Wildfowl, grebes, divers and gulls. Snipe and Water Rail at Pinkhill. *Summer:* Breeding Little Ringed Plover, Common Tern and Black-headed Gull. Large numbers of hirundines, Hobby, Cuckoo. Attractive to passage migrants such as White and Yellow Wagtails, Wheatear, Black Tern, Little Gull, Dunlin and Little Stint, plus a long history of rarities.
Other notable flora/fauna: Dragonflies, aquatic life-forms.
Contact: E: hanna.jenkins@thameswater.co.uk

3. FOXHOLES RESERVE

Berks, Bucks & Oxon Wildlife Trust.
Location: Sat nav: OX7 6QD. SP 255 207. Travelling N on A424 from Burford, take R turn to Bruern. Continue past staggered crossroads towards Bruern for two miles then past R turn to Shipton-under-Wychwood. Park in lay-by after 200 yards and walk 600 yards down pot-holed track to reserve entrance. 4x4 vehicles can drive track to surfaced car park.
Access: Open all year. Please keep to the paths. Footpaths can be very muddy.
Facilities: Car park, 1.75 mile circular wildlife walk.
Public transport: None.
Habitats: Broad-leaved woodland, grassland.
Key birds: *Spring/summer:* Spotted Flycatcher, Marsh Tit and warblers. *Winter:* Redwing, Fieldfare, Woodcock. *All year:* Raven, Tawny Owl, Little Owl, Green and Greater Spotted Woodpeckers, common woodland species.
Other notable flora/fauna: Fantastic show of bluebells from mid-Apr and into May. Autumn fungi (200+ spp. recorded). Silver-washed fritillary among 23 spp. of butterflies recorded.
Contact: BBOWT, T: 01865 775 476;
E: info@bbowt.org.uk;

4. OTMOOR NATURE RESERVE

RSPB (Central England Office).
Location: Sat nav: OX3 9TD (Otmoor Lane). SP 570 126. Car park seven miles NE of Oxford city centre. From Junc 8 of M40, take A40 W to Wheatley, then B4027. Take turn to Horton-cum-Studley, then first L to Beckley. After 0.7 mile turn R (before the Abingdon Arms public house). After 200 yards, turn L into Otmoor Lane. Car park at the end of lane (approx one mile) - if full do not park along Otmoor Lane (emergency access).
Access: Open dawn-dusk. No entry fee. No dogs allowed on the reserve visitor trail (except public rights of way). In wet conditions, the visitor route can be muddy and wellingtons are essential.
Facilities: Limited. Small car park with cycle racks, visitor trail (three mile round trip) and two screened viewpoints. The reserve is not accessible by coach and is unsuitable for large groups.
Public transport: None.
Habitats: Wet grassland, reedbed, open water.
Key birds: *Summer:* Breeding birds inc. Cetti's and Grasshopper Warblers, Lapwing, Redshank, Curlew, Snipe, Yellow Wagtail, Shoveler, Gadwall, Pochard, Tufted Duck, Little and Great Crested Grebes. Hobby breeds locally. *Winter:* Wigeon, Teal, Shoveler, Pintail, Gadwall, Pochard, Tufted Duck, Lapwing, Golden Plover, Hen Harrier, Peregrine, Merlin. *Autumn/spring passage:* Marsh Harrier, Short-eared Owl, Greenshank, Green Sandpiper and Common Sandpipers, Spotted Redshank and occasional Black Tern.
Contact: RSPB, T: 01865 351 163.

5. WARBURG NATURE RESERVE

Berks, Bucks & Oxon Wildlife Trust.
Location: Sat nav: RG9 6BJ. SU 721 878. From the A4130 turn into Bix Village. Take a left turn into Rectory Lane. Go down the steep hill and turn left at the bottom, signposted Bix Bottom. Continue for about one mile until reaching the car park at the end of the lane on the right. The lane has some potholes so drive carefully.
Access: Open all year. Dogs on leads - in some areas, only guide dogs allowed. Mobility vehicle available – contact/book before visiting.
Facilities: Car park and toilets open at all times, Interpretation Centre (open daily 9am-5pm), two hides, one with disabled access, children's Nature Detectives Trail, nature trail, picnic benches, leaflets. Car park not suitable for coaches.

Habitats: Scrub, mixed woodland, chalk grassland, ponds.
Key birds: *All year:* Sparrowhawk, Red Kite, Treecreeper, Nuthatch, Tawny Owl. *Spring/summer:* Occasional Firecrest. Warblers inc. Whitethroat and Lesser Whitethroat. *Winter:* Redpoll, Siskin, sometimes Crossbill, Woodcock.
Other notable flora/fauna: Good for orchids (15 spp.), butterflies (inc. purple hairstreak and silver-washed fritillary) and common deer spp.
Contact: BBOWT, T: 01491 642 001;
E: info@bbowt.org.uk

Shropshire

L YING ALONG THE Welsh border, Shopshire's habitats range from upland moorland with its Red Grouse and Ring Ouzels to fertile lowland valleys, extensive farmland and mixed woodland. The cluster of waters near Ellesmere attract winter wildfowl and gulls while Venus Pools, Wood Lane and Chelmarsh are the county's chief wader-watching sites.

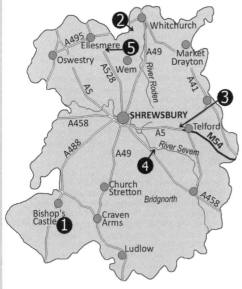

1. CLUNTON COPPICE

Shropshire Wildlife Trust.
Location: Sat nav: SY7 0HL. SO 342 806. From Craven Arms, take B4368 to Clunton village, go straight over bridge and up the hill to small car park just before reserve sign.
Access: Open at all times. Access along road and public rights of way only.
Facilities: Limited parking in small quarry entrance on right, or opposite The Crown pub.
Public transport: Buses between Craven Arms and Clun stop at Clunton. Steep one mile walk to reserve.
Habitats: One of the county's largest sessile oak woods. Good for ferns, mosses and fungi.
Key birds: Great Spotted Woodpecker, Buzzard and Raven regular. *Spring/summer:* Wide range of woodland birds, inc. Redstart, Wood Warbler, Spotted and Pied Flycatchers, Woodcock.
Other notable flora/fauna: Hairy woodrush and bromerape, sessile oak woodland plants, bluebell, bilberry.
Contact: Shropshire WT, T: 01743 284 280;
E: enquiries@shropshirewildlifetrust.org.uk

2. FENN'S WHIXALL & BETTISFIELD MOSSES

Natural England (West Midlands Team).
Location: Sat nav: SY13 3NY (Fenn's Bank). Located four miles SW of Whitchurch, to the S of A495 between Fenn's Bank, Whixall and Bettisfield. Roadside parking at entrances, car parks at Morris's Bridge, Roundthorn Bridge, World's End and a large car park at Manor House. Disabled access by prior arrangement along the railway line.
Access: Permit required except on Mosses Trail routes.
Facilities: Information panels at main entrances and leaflets are available when permits are applied for. Three interlinking Mosses Trails explore the NNR and canal from Morris's and Roundthorn bridges.
Public transport: Mon-Fri, Shropshire Link provides a demand responsive service into Whixall from Wem, Ellesmere and Whitchurch (0845 678 9068).

Habitats: 800ha of raised peatland meres and mosses.
Key birds: *Spring/summer*: Breeding Teal, Mallard, Nightjar, Hobby, Curlew, Tree Sparrow. Hobbies hunt here. *All year*: Kingfisher, Skylark, Linnet. *Winter*: Short-eared Owl.
Other notable flora/fauna: Water vole, brown hare, polecat, adder, 2,000 spp. of moths, 27 spp. of butterflies, nationally important for dragonflies, inc. white-faced darter and yellow-spot chaser.
Contact: Natural England, Manor House NNR Base, T: 01948 880 362;
E: peter.bowyer@naturalengland.org.uk

3. PRIORSLEE LAKE

Severn Trent Water/Friends of Priorslee Lake
Location: Sat nav: TF2 9CQ. SJ 724 094. In Telford between M54 and A5. Leave M54 going north (B5060) at Junc 4 and park in lay-by (100 yards from Junc 4) overlooking the lake. Alternatively park without blocking gates by Water Sports Association entrance gate at the end of Teece Drive, Priorslee, Telford. The Flash, Priorslee is a slightly smaller lake half a mile distant. Follow the stream that comes in at the western end of Priorslee Lake or head for Derwent Drive, Priorslee.
Access: Open at all times. Footpath around lake but can be muddy when wet.
Facilities: None.
Public transport: No. 24 bus from Telford town centre bus station, three miles from site, goes via train station, two miles.
Habitats: A man-made balancing lake, surrounded by woodland, rough grassland and three reedbeds on northern side.
Key birds: More than 155 spp. recorded (41 spp. breeding). *Winter*: A nearby landfill site makes Priorslee Lake a magnet for gulls and the site has a good track record for Yellow-legged, Caspian and white-winged gulls. Check the wildfowl for less common species such as Goosander and Pintail. Bittern and Snipe have been recorded in reedbeds. Finches, tits (inc. Willow), Redpoll, Siskin in woodland. *Summer*: Warblers, inc. Reed and Sedge.
Other notable flora/fauna: Wide range of butterflies, dragonflies and other insects. Southern marsh, bee and common spotted orchids.
Contact:
W: http://friendsofpriorsleelake.blogspot.co.uk/

4. VENUS POOL

Shropshire Ornithological Society.
Location: Sat nav: SY5 6JT. SJ 548 062. 6 miles SE of Shrewsbury in angle formed by A458 and minor road leading S to Pitchford. Entrance is 0.5 mile along minor road which leaves A458, 0.5 mile SE of Cross Houses.
Access: Public access inc. four hides. Please keep to footpaths shown on notice boards at both entrances. Wheelchair-friendly paths to two public hides and Lena's Hide overlooking feeding station. Dogs not allowed.

Facilities: Car park with height barrier. Five hides (two for SOS members only). Information boards.
Public transport: Shrewsbury-Bridgnorth buses stop at Cross Houses, a one mile walk from Venus Pool, partly along busy main road.
Habitats: Approx 27 ha site. Pool, several islands, open shoreline, marshy grassland, hedgerows, scrub and woodland. Species-rich meadows, field growing bird-friendly crops.
Key birds: Noted for wintering wildfowl and passage waders, plus occasional county rarities, inc. Black-necked Grebe, Purple Heron, Spoonbill, Red Kite and Woodlark. *All year*: Common ducks and waterfowl, passerines, inc. Tree Sparrow. *Apr-Jun*: Passage waders inc. Curlew, Ringed Plover, Dunlin, Redshank, Green and Common Sandpipers, and both godwits. Passage Black Tern. Breeding Oystercatcher, Little Ringed Plover, Lapwing, warblers, hirundines. *Jul-Sep*: Wader passage can inc. Little Stint, Greenshank, Green, Wood, Curlew and Common Sandpipers, and possible rarities. *Oct-Mar*: Occasional wintering Bittern. Geese inc. occasional White-fronted. Ducks inc. Wigeon, Teal, Pintail, Shoveler, Pochard, Goosander (up to 50 in evening roosts) and occasional Goldeneye. Water Rail, vagrant raptors and owls, winter thrushes and large passerine flocks inc. Lesser Redpoll, Linnet, Tree Sparrow, Reed Bunting and Yellowhammer.
Contact: W: www.shropshirebirds.com/venus-pool-reserve/

5. WOOD LANE

Shropshire Wildlife Trust.
Location: Sat nav: SY12 0HY. SJ 424 328. Take the Colemere road, off A528 at Spunhill, one mile SE of Ellesmere. Car park is 0.75 mile down on right.
Access: Open at all times. Disabled access.
Facilities: Car parks signposted. Two hides.
Habitats: Gravel pit restored by Tudor Griffiths Group.
Key birds: Over 180 spp. recorded since 1999, 40 breeding spp. *Summer*: Breeding Sand Martin (up to 500 pairs have bred), Lapwing, Little Ringed Plover, Yellowhammer and Tree Sparrow. Popular staging post for waders (inc. Redshank, Greenshank, Ruff, Dunlin, Little Stint, Green and Wood Sandpiper). *Winter*: Large flocks of Lapwing, plus Curlew and common wildfowl.
Other notable flora/fauna: Good range of dragonflies.
Contact: Shropshire WT, T: 01743 284 280;
E: enquiries@shropshirewildlifetrust.org.uk

Staffordshire

OUTSIDE ITS URBAN areas, the county can offer Red Grouse on the northern moors, as well as Lesser Spotted Woodpeckers, Pied Flycatchers and other songbirds at RSPB Coombes Valley. Cannock Chase is good for Nightjars, Woodlark and Goshawk, and often has wintering Great Grey Shrikes. Belvide, Blithfield and Croxall Lakes are the best reservoirs to work for wintering birds.

1. BELVIDE

Canal and Rivers Trust/West Midland Bird Club.
Location: Sat nav: ST19 9LX. SJ 870 098. Entrance and car park on Shutt Green Lane, Brewood, seven miles NW of Wolverhampton.
Access: Access only by permit from the West Midland Bird Club (members free, non-members charged).
Facilities: Five hides (three with wheelchair access), hard surface paths. Parking for 25-30 cars (lock combination issued to permit holders).
Public transport: Wolverhampton buses (nos. 3 & 877) and Walsall bus (no. 6) all stop at Kiddermore Green (eight mins walk to reserve).
Habitats: Reservoir with marsh, reedbeds, woodland and scrub.

Key birds: Wintering wildfowl, inc. Great Northern Diver, Bewick's Swan and Goosander. Winter gull roost sometimes inc. Glaucous or Iceland Gulls. Breeding and passage waders (up to 12 spp. in a day when conditions are right) and terns. Warblers breed in reedbeds and hedgerows. Recent scarcities inc. Sabine's Gull, White-winged and Whiskered Terns and Yellow-browed Warbler.
Other notable flora/fauna: Dragonflies/damselflies.
Contact: Mark Rickus (Secretary West Midland BC), 27 Ringmere Ave, Castle Bromwich, Birmingham, B36 9AT. T: 0121 749 5348;
E: secretary@westmidlandbirdclub.org.uk

2. BLITHFIELD RESERVOIR

South Staffs Water/West Midland Bird Club
Location: Sat nav: WS15 3NJ. SK 058 237. View from causeway on B5013 (Rugeley/Uttoxeter). Close to village of Abbots Bromley. Look for signposts to Blithfield Education Centre.
Access: For members of WMBC only or one-off group permit. Further details from the secretary.
Facilities: Free car park, toilets. Walk One has partial wheelchair access.
Public transport: None. **Habitats:** Large reservoir.
Key birds: More than 250 spp. recorded. *Winter:* Good populations of wildfowl (inc. Bewick's Swan, Goosander, Goldeneye), large gull roost (can inc. Glaucous, Iceland, Mediterrean and Caspian). Passage terns (Common, Arctic, Black) and waders, esp. in autumn (Little Stint, Curlew Sandpiper, Spotted Redshank regular).
Contact: Mark Rickus - see site 1.

3. COOMBES VALLEY

RSPB (Midlands Regional Office).
Location: Sat nav: ST13 7EU. SK 009 534. Three miles SE of Leek. From Leek take A523 towards Ashbourne. After Bradnop, turn R on minor road (cross a railway line) to Apesford and follow signs to reserve.
Access: Open daily 9am-9pm or dusk (except Dec 25), no charge. Free parking. Coach groups welcome by prior arrangement. Only guide dogs allowed off public footpaths. Most trails unsuitable for disabled visitors.
Facilities: Visitor centre (closes at 5pm), toilets and hot drinks. Two nature trails with eight benches.
Public transport: No. 108 bus from Leek to Ashbourne, twice daily stops 1.2 miles from reserve, walk towards Ashbourne then take first right, cross railway and continue to reserve.
Habitats: Steep-sided valley with sessile oak woodland, unimproved pasture and meadow.
Key birds: *Spring:* Displaying Woodcock, drumming Great Spotted Woodpeckers and common woodland species are joined by migrant Pied and Spotted Flycatchers, Redstart, Tree Pipit, Grey Wagtail and Wood Warbler. *Jan-Mar:* Displaying birds of prey. *Autumn/winter:* Lesser Redpoll, Siskin, winter thrushes.
Other notable flora/fauna: Bluebells, various butterflies, slow worm.
Contact: RSPB, T: 01538 384 017;
E: coombes.valley@rspb.org.uk

4. CROXALL LAKES

Staffordshire Wildlife Trust.
Location: Sat nav: WS13 8QX. SK 190 139. From Lichfield head N on A38, following signs for National Memorial Arboretum. At NMA entrance, continue over river bridge and turn L on second track into car park.
Access: Open at all times, except to restricted areas. Surfaced access to track, leading to hide overlooking main lake. Wheelchair ramps for both hides but woodland path is uneven. Kissing gate at entrance wide enough for wheelchairs. Restricted areas for dog walkers.
Facilities: Small car park, two bird hides.
Public transport: Bus services from Lichfield to Alrewas (1.2 miles from reserve).
Habitats: Two large lakes formed from gravel pits at the junction of Rivers Tame, Trent and Mease, plus shallow pools, wader scrapes and reedbeds.
Key birds: *Winter:* Substantial numbers of wildfowl, inc. Wigeon, Teal, Goldeneye, Shoveler and occasional Smew. Between Nov and Jan, Short-eared Owls hunt over rough ground. *Spring/summer:* Nesting species inc. grebes, plus waders such as Redshank, Oystercatcher, Ringed Plover and Lapwing. Other species on passage.
Other notable flora/fauna: Otters, water voles and harvest mice all present but dragonflies will be easier to see.
Contact: Staffordshire WT, T: 01889 880 100;
E: info@staffs-wildlife.org.uk

5. DOXEY MARSHES

Staffordshire Wildlife Trust.
Location: Sat nav: ST16 1JR. SJ 903 250. On W side of Stafford town centre, just off A513 (Eccleshall Road) from Junc 14 on the M6. Parking by play park at end of Wootton Drive/ Creswell Farm Drive.
Access: Open at all times. Most of site accessible by wheelchair. Dogs on leads in sensitive areas.
Facilities: One hide, three viewing platforms.

Warwickshire & West Midlands

WARWICKSHIRE'S RIVER VALLEYS and gravel pits are crucially important for breeding and passage birds. Tame Valley sites such as Kingsbury, Ladywalk and the Sandwell reserves attract passage waders while Brandon Marsh, HQ for the local Wildlife Trust, is important for breeding Cetti's and Grasshopper Warblers. The Warwickshire Wildlife Trust manages 56 nature reserves.

Public transport: Buses and trains to Stafford town centre, walk upstream from Sainsbury's supermarket along River Sow to reserve entrance.
Habitats: Designated SSSI for wet meadow habitats. Marsh, pools, reedbeds, hedgerows, reed sweet-grass swamp
Key birds: More than 200 spp. (80 spp. breeding) recorded. *Spring/summer:* Breeding Lapwing, Redshank, Little Ringed Plover, Oystercatcher, Shelduck, warblers, Skylark, Water Rail. *Autumn/ Winter:* Snipe, Jack Snipe, Goosander, other wildfowl, Passage waders, vagrants
Other notable flora/fauna: Otter, harvest mouse, water shrew, noctule bat, musk beetle, reed-sweet grass.
Contact: Staffordshire WT, T: 01889 880 100;
E: info@staffs-wildlife.org.uk

6. HIGHGATE COMMON

Staffordshire Wildlife Trust.
Location: Sat nav: DY7 5BS (Highgate Road). SO 836 895. From A449 at Himley take B4176 towards Bridgnorth. After approx one mile, turn L at traffic lights onto Wombourne Rd, signposted towards Swindon. Continue through Swindon, along Chasepool Rd. At the T Junction turn R onto Camp Hill Road. About one mile after Camp Farm, take 1st L then R at the T junction onto Highgate Rd. Take 1st entrance on R.
Access: Several car parks, network of paths.
Facilities: Public toilets at Warden's Office (opening hours vary but usually 9am-4.30 pm Mon-Sat).
Public transport: None.
Habitats: Lowland heath with broadleaf woodland.
Key birds: Cuckoo, Green Woodpecker, Stonechat, Tree Pipit, Skylark, Yellowhammer.
Other notable flora/fauna: More than 5,000 spp. of insect recorded, inc. several red data book species of bee and wasp, also glow worm and common lizard.
Contact: Staffordshire WT, T: 01889 880 100;
E: info@staffs-wildlife.org.uk

1. BRANDON MARSH

Warwickshire Wildlife Trust.
Location: Sat nav: CV3 3GW. SP 386 761. Three miles SE of Coventry, 200 yards SE of A45/A46 junction (Tollbar End). Turn E off A45 (just after Texaco garage) into Brandon Lane. Reserve entrance signposted 1.25 miles on right.
Access: Visitor centre open weekdays (9am-4.30pm), weekends (10am-4.30pm), closes at 4pm Oct-Mar. Only Trust members can visit site outside these hours. Entrance charge (free to WT members). Wheelchair access to nature trail and Wright hide. No dogs. Parking for two coaches, by arrangement.
Facilities: Visitor centre, toilets, tea-room (open daily 10am-4pm daily), nature trail, seven hides.
Public transport: Bus service from Coventry to Tollbar End then 1.25 miles walk.

NATURE RESERVES - CENTRAL ENGLAND

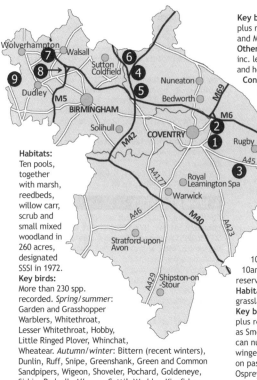

Habitats:
Ten pools, together with marsh, reedbeds, willow carr, scrub and small mixed woodland in 260 acres, designated SSSI in 1972.
Key birds:
More than 230 spp. recorded. *Spring/summer*: Garden and Grasshopper Warblers, Whitethroat, Lesser Whitethroat, Hobby, Little Ringed Plover, Whinchat, Wheatear. *Autumn/winter*: Bittern (recent winters), Dunlin, Ruff, Snipe, Greenshank, Green and Common Sandpipers, Wigeon, Shoveler, Pochard, Goldeneye, Siskin, Redpoll. *All year*: Cetti's Warbler, Kingfisher, Water Rail, Gadwall, Little Grebe, Buzzard.
Other notable flora/fauna: Badger, otter, great crested newt. More than 20 spp. of butterflies and 18 spp. of dragonflies recorded. Almost 500 plant spp. listed on W: www.brandonbirding.co.uk
Contact: Warwickshire WT, T: 024 7630 2912; E: enquiries@wkwt.org.uk

2. COOMBE COUNTRY PARK

Coventry City Council.
Location: Sat nav: CV3 2AB. SP 402 795. At Binley, five miles E of Coventry centre, on B4027 Coventry to Brinklow road.
Access: Park open daily, main car park available at all times. Visitor centre closed on Dec 25/26 & Jan 1. Entry by foot is free. Pay-and-display parking. Paths mainly hard surfaces accessible for wheelchairs. Manual wheelchairs can be hired for a returnable deposit.
Facilities: Visitor centre (10am-4pm), toilets, inc. disabled, cafe (10am-4pm), bird hide, gift shop, picnic benches and wildflower meadow (Mar-Sept).
Public transport: By rail to Coventry City Centre, 20 mins bus journey to park. Bus no. 585 Mike de Courcey Travel (for timetable T: 024 7630 2656).
Habitats: 500 acres of parkland, lake, woodland and formal gardens.

Key birds: Large heronry (50+ nests) on lake island, plus many Cormorants. Lesser Spotted Woodpecker and Marsh Tit top the list of woodland species.
Other notable flora/fauna: More than 250 spp. of plant, inc. lesser celandine, foxglove, bluebell, red campion and herb robert. Mammals inc. wood mouse, muntjac.
Contact: Coombe Country Park, T: 024 7645 3720; E: coombe.countrypark@coventry.gov.uk

3. DRAYCOTE WATER

Severn Trent Water.
Location: Sat nav: CV23 8AB. SP 460 700. Reservoir and 20 acre country park situated near Dunchurch, 3.5 miles SW of Rugby off the A426.
Access: Open all year, except Dec 25. 7.30am-8pm (Apr-Sept), 7.30pm-dusk (Oct-Mar). Access to reservoir on foot or bicycle only. Cars must stop at pay-and-display car park. Disabled parking allowed at Toft, close to bird hide. Paths good for wheelchairs. Dogs only in Country Park.
Facilities: Visitor centre, toilets, cafe open 10am-6pm (Apr-Sept), 10am-5pm (Oct, Feb,Mar), 10am-4pm (Nov-Jan). Five mile road surrounding reservoir. One bird hide.
Habitats: Very large storage reservoir, surrounded by grassland and wooded areas.
Key birds: *Winter*: A wide range of common wildfowl, plus regular sightings of less common species such as Smew, Scaup and Black-necked Grebe. Gull roost can number in excess of 50,000 birds, with white-winged gulls seen regularly. *Spring and autumn*: Birds on passage inc. waders, Black and Arctic Terns and Ospreys. Farm and woodland species in surrounding countryside all year round.
Contact: Draycote Water, Kites Hardwick, Warwickshire CV23 8AB; T: 01788 811 107; E: draycotewater@severntrent.co.uk.

4. KINGSBURY WATER PARK

Warwickshire County Council.
Location: Sat nav: B76 0DY. SP 203 960. Signposted `Water Park' from Junc 9 M42 & A4097 NE of Birmingham.
Access: Open all year, except Dec 25 (generally 8am-dusk, as early as 5.30am in Jun/Jul). Pay on entry car park or annual permits in advance online.
Facilities: Four hides, two with wheelchair access overlooking Cliff Pool nature reserve. Miles of flat surfaced footpaths, loan scheme for mobility scooters. Cafes, information centre with gift shop (opening varies depending on time of year).
Public transport: Call for advice.
Habitats: Open water; numerous small pools, some with gravel islands; gravel pits; silt beds with reedmace, reed, willow and alder; rough areas and grassland.
Key birds: 230 spp. recorded, inc. Kingfisher. *Summer*: Breeding warblers (nine spp.), Little Ringed Plover, Great Crested and Little Grebes. Shoveler, Shelduck and a thriving Common Tern colony. Passage Ospreys, Hobbies, waders (esp. spring). *Winter*: Wildfowl, Short-eared Owl.
Other notable flora/fauna: Orchids.

NATURE RESERVES - CENTRAL ENGLAND

Contact: Kingsbury Water Park, T: 01827 872 660;
E: parks@warwickshire.gov.uk;

5. LADYWALK RESERVE

E.on/West Midland Bird Club
Location: Sat nav: B46 2BS. SP 212 917. Site of old
Hams Hall power station, in Tame Valley - 10 miles
from Birmingham city centre. From Junc 9 of M42,
head S on A446 to Hams Hall Distribution Centre.
Follow Faraday Avenue to reserve. WMBC members
can use secure car park near Sainsbury's warehouse.
Access: Enter site by footbridge. Reserve open only
to WMBC members, but other groups can organise
visits with Sec. Non-members can observe site from
public footpaths east of River Tame. No easy access
on site for disabled visitors. Display permits on
dashboard if using secure car park. Dogs not allowed.
Facilities: Six bird hides, inc. elevated River Walk
Hide. Other screens for close-up viewing. Circular
footpath (1.6 miles).
Public transport: Buses for Birmingham Airport (nos.
17 & 717 from Nuneaton) and no. 777 (from Coleshill)
stop in Faraday Avenue.
Habitats: 125 acres of floodland, reedbed and
woodland within a loop of The River Tame.
Key birds: More than 200 spp. recorded. *Winter:*
Hundreds of wildfowl, inc. Wigeon, Teal, Shoveler,
Goldeneye and Goosander. Water Rail and Woodcock
regular and lots of small bird activity at the feeding
stations. Up to four Bitterns in recent years, plus
Siskin, Redpoll and winter thrushes. *Spring/summer:*
Passage waders inc. Greenshank, Curlew, godwits and
plovers, plus many hirundines and other migrants.
Other notable flora/fauna: Five spp. of orchid, inc.
the county's only known colony of marsh hellibore.
Also locally rare yellow bird's nest. Butterflies are
plentiful and 16 spp. of dragonflies recorded.
Contact: Mark Rickus (Secretary West Midland BC),
27 Ringmere Ave, Castle Bromwich, Birmingham, B36 9AT.
T: 0121 749 5348;
E: secretary@westmidlandbirdclub.org.uk;

6. MIDDLETON LAKES

RSPB (Midlands Regional Office).
Location: Sat nav: B76 9JG. SP 192 967. Reserve lies
in the Tame Valley, S of Tamworth, next to Middleton
Hall. Leave M42 at Junc 9 onto A446, then A4091 and
finally into Bodymoor Heath Road.
Access: Open dawn till dusk daily. Free for RSPB
members, parking charge for non-members. Surfaced
path from car park to Middleton Hall and heronry. Other
paths are unsurfaced but generally flat. Playmeadow
Trail has partial wheelchair access. Car park for 30, bike
racks. Dogs allowed on leads on parts of the site.
Facilities: Three viewing platforms and three viewing
screens. Lookout hide open to view northern scrapes
(see RSPB website for lock combination number).
Four trails, ranging from 500 yards to two miles in
length. Nearest toilets at Middleton Hall.
Public transport: No local bus service. Wilnecote
train station is 2.5 miles from the reserve.

Habitats: This former quarry now boasts lakes,
reedbeds, meadows and woodland areas.
Key birds: *All year:* Barn Owls are regularly seen and
Cetti's Warbler frequently heard. *Spring/summer:*
100-strong heronry, plus common migrant warblers,
Lapwing, hirundines and woodland species. *Winter:*
Lesser Spotted and Great Spotted Woodpeckers and
Willow Tit on the feeders, plus peak numbers of
wildfowl and waders. Raptors inc. Hen and
Marsh Harriers, Merlin, Peregrine and Short-eared Owl.
Other notable flora/fauna: Bluebells and spring
flowers, grass snake, common butterflies and moths.
Contact: RSPB, T: 01827 259 454;
E: middletonlakes@rspb.org.uk

7. ROUGH WOOD CHASE LNR

Walsall Council.
Location: Sat nav: WV12 5NH. SJ 984 007. Reserve
composed of six sites on W edge of Walsall Borough.
From Junc 10 of M6 head for Willenhall and A462.
Turn R into Bloxwich Road North and R again into
Hunts Lane. Car park on bend.
Access: Open all year.
Facilities: Circular nature trail linking all sites.
Public transport: Buses - no. 369 Walsall and
Willenhall, no. 364 Walsall and Coppice Farm, and
no. 341 Walsall and Willenhall.
Habitats: 70 acres of oakwood, significant for West
Midlands. Sneyd reservoir, meadows, ponds, pools,
marsh and scrubland.
Key birds: Great Crested and Little Grebes on
pools in the north end of Chase. Breeding Jay and
Sparrowhawk. Common woodland species all year and
warblers in summer.
Other notable flora/fauna: Great crested and smooth
newts, water vole, various dragonfly spp. purple
hairstreak, brimstone and small heath butterflies.
Contact: Walsall Countryside Services,
T: 01922 653 344; E: cleanandgreen@walsall.gov.uk

8. SANDWELL VALLEY COUNTRY PARK

Sandwell Metropolitan Borough Council.
Location: Sat nav: B71 4BG (Salter's Lane). Entrances
at SP 012 918 and SP 028 992. Located approx
one mile NE of West Bromwich town centre. Main
entrance off Salters Lane or Forge Lane.
Access: Car parks open 8am-sunset. Wheelchair
access to Priory Woods LNR, Forge Mill Lake LNR and
other parts of the country park.
Facilities: 1,700 acre site. Visitor centre, toilets, cafe
at Sandwell Park Farm open daily, except christmas
period, 10am-4.30pm. Good footpaths around LNRs
and much of the country park. Coach parking by
appointment. 20 acre RSPB reserve nearby (see
below).
Public transport: West Bromwich bus station and
central metro stop. (Traveline, T: 0871 200 2233).
Habitats: Pools, woodlands, grasslands, inc. three
Local Nature Reserves.

Key birds: Wintering wildfowl inc. regular flock of Goosander, small heronry. *All year:* Grey Heron, Great Crested Grebe, Lapwing, Reed Bunting, Great Spotted and Green Woodpeckers, Sparrowhawk, Kestrel. *Spring:* Little Ringed Plover, Oystercatcher, up to eight spp. of warber breeding, passage migrants. *Autumn:* Passage migrants. *Winter:* Goosander, Shoveler, Teal, Wigeon, Snipe.
Other notable flora/fauna: Common spotted and southern marsh orchid. Ringlet butterfly. Water vole, weasel.
Contact: Sandwell Valley Country Park, T: 0121 569 3070.

9. SANDWELL VALLEY RSPB

RSPB (Midlands Regional Office).
Location: Sat nav: B43 5AG. SP 035 928. Great Barr, Birmingham. Follow signs S from M6 Junc 7 via A34. Take R at 1st junction onto A4041. Take 4th L onto Hamstead Road (B4167), then R at 1st mini roundabout onto Tanhouse Avenue.
Access: 800 yards of paths accessible to assisted and powered wheelchairs with some gradients (please phone for further information). Dogs on leads. Car parks closed on Mon and Thurs.

Facilities: Visitor Centre still unavailable following fire in 2010 - toilets, refreshments and car parking at Forge Mill Farm (15 mins walk). Viewing screens. Phone centre for details on coach parking. Lakeside hide and car park are open (10.30am-1pm, Tue-Fri), (10.30am-3.30pm, Sat-Sun), at other times the reserve is open to pedestrians. More facilities are being added.
Public transport: Bus no. 16 from Corporation Street (Stand CJ), Birmingham city centre (ask for Tanhouse Avenue). Train - Hamstead Station, then no. 16 bus for one mile towards West Bromwich from Hamstead (ask for Tanhouse Avenue).
Habitats: Open water, wet grassland, reedbed, dry grassland and scrub.
Key birds: *Summer:* Lapwing, Little Ringed Plover, Reed Warbler, Whitethroat, Sedge Warbler, Willow Tit. *Passage:* Sandpipers, Yellow Wagtail, chats, Common Tern. *Winter:* Water Rail, Snipe, Jack Snipe, Goosander, Bullfinch, woodpeckers and wildfowl.
Contact: RSPB, T: 0121 357 7395;
E: sandwellvalley@rspb.org.uk

Worcestershire

THE LARGELY RURAL county has only one sizeable reservoir — Bittell — but there are excellent wetlands to explore at Upton Warren and Bredon's Hardwick. For the widest range of woodland species, the best area is the Wyre Forest west of Kidderminster, but the Wildlife Trust owns or manages more than 75 reserves covering a wide range of habitats.

1. KNAPP & PAPERMILL

Worcestershire Wildlife Trust.
Location: Sat nav: WR6 5HR. Take A4103 SW from Worcester; R at Bransford roundabout then L towards Suckley and reserve is approx three miles (do not turn off for Alfrick). Park at Bridges Stone lay-by (SO 751 522), cross road and follow path to the Knapp House.
Access: Open daily. Large parties should contact Warden in advance. Paths steep and uneven.
Facilities: Nature trail, small visitor centre with toilets, wildlife garden, Kingfisher viewing screen.
Public transport: None.
Habitats: Broadleaved woodland, unimproved grassland, fast stream, old orchard in Leigh Brook Valley.
Key birds: *Summer:* Breeding Grey Wagtail and Dipper, Nuthatch and common woodland species, Kingfisher, Spotted Flycatcher, all three woodpeckers. Buzzard, Sparrowhawk and Redstart.
Other notable flora/fauna: Otters have returned recently. Good numbers of dragonflies and butterflies (30 spp. recorded) on all three meadows inc. holly blue, purple hairstreak and white admiral. Bluebells, green-winged and spotted orchids.
Contact: Worcestershire WT T: 01905 754 919;
E: enquiries@ worcestershirewildlifetrust.org

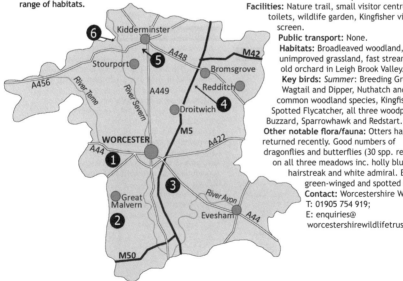

2. MALVERN HILLS

Malvern Hills Trust.
Location: Sat nav: WR13 6HR (British Camp car park). SO 756 402. An eight mile long range of hills and commons lying S and W of Great Malvern, covering approx 3,000 acres. Best birding areas inc. Castlemorton Common and Midsummer Hill.
Access: Open all year. Car parking (6am-11pm) - charges apply - annual permit available.
Facilities: Public toilets with disabled access opposite British Camp car park (A449 Worcester Road). Two easy-access trails at Earnslaw (450 yards) and Blackhill (250 yards).
Habitats: Grassland on hilltops, mixed woodland, scrub, quarries, small reservoirs and lakes.
Key birds: Raptors inc. Buzzard, Sparrowhawk, Peregrine and Hobby. Ravens nest in quarries and spring passage migrants inc. Wheatear, Ring Ouzel (best in Happy Valley between Worcestershire Beacon and North Hill) and more rarely, Dotterel. Autumn sees a good range of migrants heading south. Wooded areas hold all the expected common species, plus breeding warblers and flycatchers, all three woodpeckers and Tree Pipits on woodland edges. A few Nightingales hang on in areas of dense scrub, which also hold chats, pipits and Linnets. A winter highlight is Snow Bunting on the highest hills.
Other notable flora/fauna: Lesser horseshoe and barbastelle bats, polecat, 25 spp. of butterflies recorded, inc. high brown fritillary. Broad range of plants inc. blinks, crosswort and common spotted orchid.
Contact: Malvern Hills Trust, Manor House, Grange Road, Malvern WR14 3EY. T: 01684 892 002;
E: info@malvernhills.org.uk

3. TIDDESLEY WOOD NATURE RESERVE

Worcestershire Wildlife Trust.
Location: Sat nav: WR10 2AD. SO 929 462. Take B4084 from Pershore towards Worcester. Turn L towards Besford and Croome near town boundary just before the summit of the hill. Entrance is on left after about 0.75 mile.
Access: Open all year. Cycles and horses only allowed on the bridleway. Dogs on leads. Avoid military firing range in SW corner of wood, marked by red flags. Do not enter NE plot, which is private property. Main ride stoney, with some potholes. Small pathways difficult if wet. Coach parking by appointment.
Facilities: Information board. Circular trail around small pathways. Car park off B4084 (signposted to Besford and Croome).
Public transport: First Midland Red services.
Habitats: Ancient woodland, conifers.
Key birds: *All year:* Coal Tit, Goldcrest, Sparrowhawk, Willow Tit, Marsh Tit. *Spring:* Chiffchaff, Blackcap, Cuckoo. *Winter:* Redwing, Fieldfare.
Other notable flora/fauna: Dragonflies inc. club-tailed and white-legged damselflies. Good for butterflies, inc. white admiral, peacock and gatekeeper. Important invertebrates inc. nationally rare noble chafer beetle which has been recorded here for many years.
Contact: Worcestershire WT, T: 01905 754 919;
E: enquiries@worcestershirewildlifetrust.org

4. UPTON WARREN

Worcestershire Wildlife Trust.
Location: Sat nav: B61 7ER (Outdoor Education Centre). SO 936 677. Two miles S of Bromsgrove on A38. Leave M5 at Junc 5 and head N on A38, turning third exit and first roundabout.
Access: Christopher Cadbury Wetland Reserve consists of Moors Pools (freshwater) and Flashes Pools (saline). Open dawn-dusk but parking restrictions apply. Education centre and The Moors car parks open at all times, The Flashes car park open 9am-8pm (Apr-Sep) and 9am-4pm (Oct-Mar). A day permit is required from: Trust offices at Smite (free for Trust members), the sailing centre cafe or volunteers on site. Disabled access to hides at Moors Pools only by prior arrangement. No dogs.
Facilities: Six hides, maps at entrances, paths can be very muddy. Coach parking at sailing centre by previous booking.
Public transport: Birmingham/Worcester buses pass reserve entrance.
Habitats: Fresh and saline pools with muddy islands, some woodland and scrub.
Key birds: *Winter:* Wildfowl, Bittern, Water Rail, Snipe. *Spring/autumn:* Passage waders. *Summer:* Breeding Avocet, Redshank, Little Ringed Plover, Oystercatcher, Common Tern, Sedge, Reed, Grasshopper and Cetti's Warblers. Hobby nearby.
Other notable flora/fauna: Saltmarsh plants, dragonflies.
Contact: Worcestershire WT, T: 01905 754 919;
E: enquiries@worcestershirewildlifetrust.org

5. WILDEN MARSH

Worcestershire Wildlife Trust.
Location: Sat nav: DY13 9JT. SO 825 730. S of Kidderminster. Take A449 S from Kidderminster. At junction with A442 go straight across roundabout into Wilden Lane, a very busy road with few parking spaces, so park carefully in lay-by.
Access: Enter over stile at gated entrance next to southern lay-by. Please obey signs to leave certain areas undisturbed. No access to northern part of the site. Gated entrances are open at all times. This reserve is complex and new visitors should consult a map. Secure cattle gates at all times. Beware boggy areas, steep banks by the River Stour and deep ditches.
Facilities: None. Limited parking on Wilden Lane.
Public transport: Nearest bus stop at Wilden, 0.5 mile from reserve.
Habitats: Dry and marshy fields with small alder and willow woods, reedbeds and many drainage ditches.
Key birds: 192 spp. have been recorded since 1968 and about 70 breed, inc. Yellow Wagtail, nine spp. of warblers and Redshank. Wintering area for Water Pipits, though numbers have declined recently.
Other notable flora/fauna: Plants inc. southern marsh orchids, marsh cinquefoil, marsh arrow-grass, marsh pennywort and lesser water parsnip.
Contact: Worcestershire WT, T: 01905 754 919;
E: enquiries@worcestershirewildlifetrust.org

6. WYRE FOREST NNR

Natural England (West Midlands Team/Worcs Wildlife Trust.
Location: Sat nav: DY14 9XQ (Callow Hill).
SO 750 740. On A456 Kidderminster to Tenbury Wells
road, 3 miles west of Bewdley.
Access: Observe reserve signs and keep to paths.
Facilities: Toilets and refreshments (with disabled
access). Several waymarked trails (some suitable for
wheelchair users) as well as regular guided walks,
also family cycle routes through the reserve.
Public transport: The nearest train station is in
Kidderminster. Local bus services between Bewdley
and Kidderminster are provided by First Group,
T: 0871 200 2233.

Habitats: Oak forest, conifer areas, birch heath,
lowland grassland, stream.
Key birds: Breeding birds inc. Redstart, Pied
Flycatcher, Wood Warbler, Buzzard and Raven, with
Dipper, Grey Wagtail and Kingfisher found on the
larger streams.
Other notable flora/fauna: Mammals inc. fallow, roe
and muntjac deer, polecat, otter and mink, yellow-
neck mouse, dormouse, voles and water shrew.
Several bat spp. inc. pipistrelle and Daubenton's.
Important site for invertebrates inc. England's largest
colony of pearl-bordered fritillary butterflies.
Contact: Wyre Forest NNR, Natural England Office,
Lodge Hill Farm, Dowles Brook, Bewdley DY12 2LY;
T: 01299 400 686.

Eastern England

Bedfordshire, Cambridgeshire, Essex, Hertfordshire, Norfolk, Suffolk

Bedfordshire

THOUGH ONE OF England's smallest counties,
Bedfordshire is not devoid of birding interest.
Blows Down is one of the best southern sites in to
see Ring Ouzels on spring passage. Intense observer
coverage at the RSPB's HQ at The Lodge, Sandy, has
produced a series of excellent records. Exploring
Country Parks such as Priory and Harold-Odell is
best early in the morning before the dog-walkers
are out.

1. BLOW'S DOWNS

Beds, Cambs & Northants Wildlife Trust.
Location: Sat nav: LU5 4AE. TL 030 215. On the
outskirts of Dunstable. Take A5065 from W of Luton,
cross M1, take first exit at roundabout, park with
care on verge. Can also walk 0.5 mile from Dunstable
centre to W entrance at Half Moon Lane off A5.
Access: Open all year, not suitable for wheelchairs
due to steep slopes.
Facilities: None. Park on road verge.
Public transport: None.
Habitats: SSSI, chalk downland, scrub and grassland,
that is a traditional resting place for incoming spring
migrants.
Key birds: *Winter:* Lapwing, Meadow Pipit, Skylark.
Spring/autumn: Ring Ouzel, Wheatear, Whinchat,
Black Redstart, Stonechat, Willow Warbler.
Other notable flora/fauna: Chalkhill blue, brown
argus and marbled white butterflies. Plants inc. small
scabious, burnet-saxifrage, squinancywort, great
pignut, common spotted and bee orchids.
Contact: BCN WT, T: 01234 364 213;
E: bedfordshire@wildlifebcnp.org

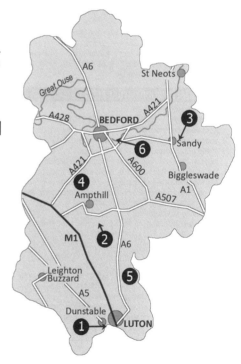

NATURE RESERVES - EASTERN ENGLAND

2. FLITWICK MOOR

Beds, Cambs & Northants Wildlife Trust.
Location: Sat nav: MK45 5BP. TL 046 354.
E of Flitwick. From Flitwick town centre (Tesco roundabout) on A5120, cross railway bridge, R at roundabout, immediately L into King's Road. After 500 yards, L into Maulden Road towards A507. After quarter mile R at Folly Farm, follow track to small car park. Also footpath to reserve from Moor Lane.
Access: Open all year.
Facilities: Car park. Please stick to public paths.
Public transport: Frequent buses (United Counties) from Bedford and Luton to Flitwick, or take train to Flitwick and then 0.75 mile walk.
Habitats: SSSI. Important wetland for the area, blend of fen, meadow, wet woodland and fragile peaty soil. Supports mosses ferns and flowers.
Key birds: *Winter*: Siskin, Water Rail, Great Spotted Woodpecker. *Spring*: Lesser Spotted Woodpecker, Willow Warbler, Blackcap. *Summer*: Water Rail, Grasshopper and Garden Warblers, Cuckoo. *Autumn*: Brambling.
Other notable flora/fauna: Good variety of butterflies and dragonflies, plus chimney sweeper moth and conehead bush cricket. Plants inc. ten spp. of sphagnum moss, marsh pennywort, black knapweed, water figwort plus fly agaric and yellow brain fungus in autumn.
Contact: BCN WT, T: 01234 364 213;
E: bedfordshire@wildlifebcnp.org

3. THE LODGE

RSPB (Central England Office).
Location: Sat nav: SG19 2DL. TL 191 485. Reserve lies one mile E of Sandy, signposted from the B1042 road to Potton.
Access: Reserve open daily 7am-9pm (or sunset when earlier); shop 9am-5pm weekdays, 10am-5pm weekends and bank holidays. Non-members: charge per vehicle. Dogs only allowed on bridleway.
Facilities: Five miles of nature trails. One bridleway (0.5 mile) and gardens are wheelchair/pushchair accessible. One hide (wheelchair accessible), 50 yards from car park. Coach parking at weekends by arrangement. Refreshments at shop. Toilets (inc. disabled).
Public transport: Buses to Sandy Market Square from Bedford, infrequent service. One mile walk or cycle from centre of Sandy or 0.5 mile from Sandy railway station, in part along trail through heathland restoration.
Habitats: This 180 ha reserve is a mixture of woodland, heathland and acid grassland and inc. the formal gardens of the RSPB's UK headquarters. New areas being restored to heathland.
Key birds: *Spring/summer*: Hobby, Spotted Flycatcher, breeding common woodland species and warblers. *All year*: Woodpeckers, woodland birds. *Winter*: Winter thrushes, woodland birds.

Other notable flora/fauna: Natterjack toads, rare heathland insects. Particularly good site for fungi, and lichens. Garden pools are good for dragonflies.
Contact: RSPB, T: 01767 693 333;
E: thelodgereserve@rspb.org.uk

4. MARSTON VALE MILLENIUM COUNTRY PARK

Marston Vale Trust.
Location: Sat nav: MK43 0PS. TL 004 417. SW of Bedford off A421 at Marston Moretaine. Only five mins from Junc 13 of M1, along A421 towards Bedford.
Access: Pedestrian access to park at any time. Forest Centre open summer 10am-6pm, winter 10am-5pm. Forest centre and car park closed Dec 25/26, Jan 1. No dogs in wetlands. Entry charge for wetland reserve. Main 5 mile trail and 1.25 mile wetland trail surfaced for wheelchair and pushchair access. Coach parking available.
Facilities: Cafe bar, gift shop, art gallery. Free parking. The 1.25 mile wetland trail is a level path with a compacted, loose stone surface inc. two hand gates with top latches.
Public transport: Trains to Millbrook and Stewartby station, 20 mins walk to forest centre.
Habitats: Millenium Country Park covers 555 acres and inc. the 210 acre Stewartby Lake which attracts birds when smaller waters are frozen. Reedbeds, woodland, hawthorn scrub, ponds and wet grassland.
Key birds: *Winter*: Bittern, Peregrine, Siskin, Redpoll, Stonechat, Snipe, gulls inc. Caspian, Yellow-legged and Mediterranean Gulls, thrushes, wildfowl (Gadwall, Shoveler, Pochard, Teal and Tufted Duck), Little and Great Crested Grebes. Rarer species can inc. divers, grebes, Common Scoter, Smew and Scaup. *Spring*: Passage waders and terns (Black, Sandwich and Arctic Terns), hirundines, Wheatear, Whinchat, Osprey and Little Gull. Yellow Wagtail and Garganey occasionally breed.
Summer: Ten species of breeding warblers, Hobby, Turtle Dove, Nightingale, Bearded Tit, Cuckoo, Barn Owl, Marsh Harrier, Water Rail, Kingfisher and common wildfowl. *Autumn*: Passage waders and terns. *Rarities*: Glossy Ibis, Laughing Gull, Caspian Gull, Manx Shearwater, Purple Heron and White Stork.
Other notable flora/fauna: Dingy and grizzled skipper butterflies, excellent for dragonflies. Also otter and brown hare, plus bee and pyramidal orchids and stoneworts.
Contact: Forest Centre, T: 01234 767 037;
E: info@marstonvale.org; W: www.marstonvale.org

5. PEGSDON HILLS RESERVE

Beds, Cambs & Northants Wildlife Trust.
Location: TL 120 295. Five miles W of Hitchin. Take B655 from Hitchin towards Barton-le-Clay. Turn R at Pegsdon then immediately L and park in lay-by. Reserve entrance across B655 via footpath.
Access: Open all year. Dropping off point for coaches only.
Facilities: None.
Public transport: Luton to Henlow buses (United Counties) stop at Pegsdon.

NATURE RESERVES - EASTERN ENGLAND

Habitats: Chalk grassland, scrub and woodland.
Key birds: *Winter*: Brambling, Stonechat, winter thrushes, raptors inc. Buzzard. *Spring*: Wheatear, Ring Ouzel, Tree Pipit, Yellowhammer. *Summer*: Turtle Dove, Grey Partridge, Lapwing, Skylark.
Other notable flora/fauna: Dark green fritillary, dingy and grizzled skippers, chalkhill blue, brown argus and small heath butterflies. Glow worms. Plants inc. pasqueflower in spring, fragrant and common spotted orchids.
Contact: BCN WT, T: 01234 364 213;
E: bedfordshire@wildlifebcnp.org

6. PRIORY COUNTRY PARK

Bedford Borough Council.
Location: Sat nav: MK41 9DJ. TL 071 495. 1.5 miles SE from Bedford town centre. Signposted from A4280 and A421. Entry point to new 'River Valley Park'
Access: Park and hides open all year round. Main car parks (free) access from Barkers Lane, open 5am-9pm. No access to fenced/gated plantations.
Facilities: Toilets and visitor centre open daytime, all-year-round disabled access on new path around lake. Hides, nature trails, labyrinth, Premier Inn for meals, accommodation.
Public transport: Stagecoach (T: 01604 676 060) 'Blue Solo 4' every 20 mins. Mon to Sat. Alight 1st stop Riverfield Drive (200 yds). Rail station at Bedford (approx 2.5 miles).

Habitats: Lakes, reedbeds, scrub and woodland, meadows adjoining Great Ouse.
Key birds: 212 spp. recorded. Good numbers/variety of winter wildfowl, varied mix of spring passage species, with breeding warblers and woodpeckers, augmented by feeding terns, hirundines and raptors lakeside. *Winter*: Grebes, Pochard, Shoveler, Gadwall, Merlin, Water Rail, gulls, thrushes, Chiffchaff, corvids, buntings. *Passage*: Raptors, waders, terns, pipits. *Summer*: Hobby, Turtle Dove, Swift, hirundines, *acrocephalus* and *sylvia* warblers. *All year*: Cormorant, Little Egret, Grey Heron, Stock Dove, woodpeckers, Kingfisher, Grey Wagtail, Treecreeper, Goldfinch, Bullfinch.
Other notable flora/fauna: 23 spp. of dragonflies, inc. small red-eyed damsel and hairy hawker. 20 spp. of butterflies. Large plant list. Fox, muntjac and otter.
Contact: Visitor Centre, Priory CP, Barkers Lane, Bedford, MK41 9SH. T: 01234 718 012;
E: prioryrangers@bedford.gov.uk

Cambridgeshire

THE NENE AND OUSE Washes are superb for wintering wildfowl, owls and raptors, with the former also offering the chance of Cranes, breeding Black-tailed Godwits, Spotted Crakes plus introduced Corncrakes in summer. Grafham Water attracts plenty of scarce species, while Paxton Pits is probably the best place in the country to actually see Nightingales.

1. FEN DRAYTON LAKES

RSPB (Eastern England Office).
Location: Sat nav: PE27 4TR. TL 341 699. NW of Cambridge. Leave A14 at Junc 28; follow signs to Swavesey. Turn L in Boxworth End (signed to Fen Drayton). Turn R onto minor road (signed to Swavesey), then L into entrance to Fen Drayton Lakes. Follow signs to car park.
Access: Open at all times. Dogs only allowed on public footpaths and bridleways. Disabled birders can get car access to one viewing screen.
Facilities: Five viewing screens, one hide and three open viewing shelters. Ten-mile network of trails. Information boards give access details. Free trail guides and events leaflets available from the Elney car park.

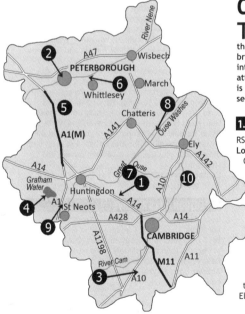

Public transport: Cambridgeshire Guided Bus service between Huntingdon and Cambridge runs every 10 mins and has a request stop in the reserve.
Habitats: A complex of lakes (former gravel workings) and traditional riverside meadows next to the River Great Ouse).
Key birds: At least 213 spp. have been recorded in the area with some 65 spp. being regular breeders, inc. Common Tern. Hobby, waders on passage. Rarities inc. Great White Egret, Purple Heron, Glossy Ibis, Common Crane, Red-Footed Falcon, Honey Buzzard and Whiskered Tern. Bitterns are now a regular sight, with Holywell Lake and Elney Lake being the favoured sites. *Winter*: Nationally important numbers of Gadwall and Coot.
Other notable flora/fauna: Good site for butterflies, dragonflies and mammals.
Contact: RSPB, T: 01954 233 260;
E: fendraytonlakes@rspb.org.uk

2. FERRY MEADOWS COUNTRY PARK

Nene Park Trust.
Location: Sat nav: PE2 5UU (Ham Lane). TL 145 975. Three miles W of Peterborough city centre and two miles E of A1. On all major routes into city, follow brown tourist signs for Nene Park or country park symbol. Also signposted on Oundle Road (A605).
Access: Open all year, 7am-dusk (summer), 8am-sunset (winter). Electric scooters and wheelchair available for loan - book in advance. Coach parking free at all times. Car parking charge apply (8am-8pm summer, 8am-5pm winter).
Facilities: Car park, visitor centre - open 10am-5pm (Nov-Mar) 10am-4pm (Nov-Mar), toilets (inc. disabled), cafe, two wheelchair-accessible hides in nature reserve area. Hard surface paths in park's central areas, but steep slopes in Bluebell Wood.
Public transport: Stagecoach no. X14 stops on A605 by Notcutts Nursery. 0.5 mile walk to park entrance. Traveline T: 0870 6082 608 or W: www. traveline.org.uk
Habitats: Lakes, meadows, scrub, broadleaved woodland and small wetland nature reserve.
Key birds: *All year*: Good selection of woodland and water birds, Kingfisher.
Spring: Terns, waders, Yellow Wagtail. *Winter*: Grebes, gulls, Siskin, Redpoll, Water Rail.
Other notable flora/fauna: Bluebell, wood anenome, wild garlic in woodland.
Contact: Nene Park Trust, T: 01733 234 193;
E: visitor.services@neneparktrust.org.uk;
W: www.neneparktrust.org.uk

3. FOWLMERE

RSPB (Eastern England Office).
Location: Sat nav: SG8 6EZ. TL 406 461. Seven miles S of Cambridge. From A10, turn towards Fowlmere at Fowlmere-Shepreth crossroads (no RSPB sign); after one mile, turn R by cemetery (RSPB sign); after another 0.6 mile, turn left into reserve.
Access: Open at all times along marked trail. Dogs only on private track on eastern boundary. Donations requested from non-RSPB members.

Facilities: 1.8 miles of trails. Three hides, toilets inc disabled. Space for one coach, prior booking essential. Wheelchair access to one hide, toilet and some of the trails.
Public transport: Shepreth railway station two miles. By bus: Dunsbridge Turnpike (outside Country Homes & Gardens), one mile. Walk towards Melbourn - after 300 yards, cross road and turn left on to single track road to Fowlmere (beware of traffic); after 0.75 mile, turn right into reserve (RSPB sign).
Habitats: Reedbeds, meres, woodland, scrub.
Key birds: *Spring/summer*: Little Grebe, Turtle Dove, ten breeding warblers. *All year*: Water Rail, Kingfisher, Reed Bunting. *Autumn*: Yellowhammer, Corn Bunting. *Winter*: Snipe, Water Rail, raptors.
Other notable flora/fauna: Healthy population of water shrews and otters. 18 spp. of dragonflies.
Contact: RSPB, T: 01767 693 013;
E: fowlmere@rspb.org.uk

4. GRAFHAM WATER

Beds, Cambs & Northants Wildlife Trust.
Location: Sat nav: PE28 0BX. TL 143 671. Follow signs for Grafham Water from A1 at Buckden or A14 at Ellington. Follow B661 road towards Perry and Staughtons to West Perry. As you leave village, Anglian Water's Mander car park is signposted on right.
Access: Open all year, except Dec 25. No dogs in wildlife garden, on leads elsewhere. Car parking £2 for day ticket.
Facilities: Six bird hides in nature reserve, three in bird sanctuary area. Two in wildlife garden accessible to wheelchairs. A further hide overlooks islands and scrapes in the settlement lagoons. Cycle track through reserve also accessible to wheelchairs. Visitor centres at Mander and Plummer car parks with restaurants, shops and toilets. Disabled parking. Use Plummer car park for lagoons and Marlow car park for dam area (good for waders and vagrants).
Public transport: None.
Habitats: Open water, lagoons, reedbeds, open water, wet mud and willow carr, ancient and plantation woodland, scrub, species-rich grassland.
Key birds: *Resident*: Common woodland birds, wildfowl. *Winter*: Waders inc. Common Sandpiper and Dunlin, Great Crested Grebe. Wildfowl inc. large flocks of common species, plus Shelduck, Goldeneye, Goosander and Smew, gulls (can be up to 30,000 roosting in mid-winter). *Spring/summer*: Breeding Nightingale, Reed, Willow and Sedge Warblers, Common and Black Terns. *Autumn*: Passage waders.
Rarities: Have inc. Wilson's Phalarope (2007), Ring-necked Duck, Great Northern Diver, Glaucous, Iceland and Mediterranean Gulls.
Other notable flora/fauna: Bee, common spotted and early purple orchids, common twayblade (in woods), cowslip. Common blue and marbled white butterflies, dragonflies inc. broad-bodied chaser, voles, grass snakes.
Contact: Grafham Water Nature Reserve,
T: 01480 811 075; E: grafham@wildlifebcn.org

NATURE RESERVES - EASTERN ENGLAND

5. THE GREAT FEN

BC&N Wildlife Trust/Natural England (East Anglia Team)/ Environment Agency/Hunts District Council
Location: Sat nav: PE26 2RS. TL 245 848 (Ramsey Heights), plus Holme Fen NNR and Woodwalton NNR (Chapel Road, Ramsey Heights), south of Peterborough, lying between the A1 in the west and Ramsey. B660 runs through the centre of Great Fen.
Access: Open access at all times to three visitor sites with views over farmland linking the reserves. Eventually Great Fen will occupy 3,700ha. No dogs allowed. Wheelchair access difficult on grassy rides.
Facilities: Countryside Centre at Ramsey Heights site. Three elevated bird hides at Woodwalton reached via steps. One bird hide at Holme Fen. Grassed paths at Woodwalton and Holme Fens. New Decoy visitor information point.
Public transport: Limited bus service between Peterborough and Ramsey stops at end of Chapel Road, 0.5 mile from Countryside Centre.
Habitats: Pools formed from clay pits at Ramsey Heights; extensive birch forest (largest in lowland Britain) and reedbed at Holme Fen; mixed woodland, open waters, fen and grassland at Woodwalton.
Key birds: Wide variety of common wildfowl, plus Kingfisher, Grey Heron, Bittern and wintering Goosander on meres. Hen Harriers visit in winter while Marsh Harriers breed in reedbed, along with Bearded Tit and Cetti's Warbler. Common Crane observed in recent years. Wet meadows at Darlow's Farm attractive to breeding Lapwing, Snipe and Redshank and wintering Whooper and Bewick's Swans.
Other notable flora/fauna: Great crested newt and rare beetles at ramsey heights. Otter, hare, deer spp., water vole. Scarce chaser dragonfly, small copper and white admiral butterflies. Wide variety of bog and heath plants.
Contact: Great Fen Team, T: 01487 710 420; E: info@greatfen.org.uk; W: www.greatfen.org.uk

6. NENE WASHES

RSPB (Eastern England Office).
Location: Sat nav: PE7 2DD. TL 318 991. Reserve is eight miles E of Peterborough, and NE of Whittlesey. Car park at end of Eldernell Lane, N off A605 east of Coates. There is currently no signposting to reserve.
Access: Open at all times along South Barrier Bank, accessed at Eldernell. Group visits along central path by arrangement. No access to fields or for wheelchairs along bank.
Facilities: Small car park - one coach max - at end of Eldernell Lane. No toilets or hide. Nene Valley Way path offers elevated views over reserve.
Public transport: Stagecoach Bus (T: 01733 554 575) runs on A605, alight at Coates, walk down Eldernell Lane.
Habitats: Wet grassland with ditches. Often flooded.
Key birds: Spring/early summer: Corncrake release scheme, plus Spotted Crake. UK's top site for breeding Black-tailed Godwit. Other breeding waders inc. Lapwing, Redshank and Snipe. Duck (inc. Garganey),

Marsh Harrier, Hobby, Yellow Wagtail and Tree Sparrow. Autumn/winter: Waterfowl in large numbers (inc. Bewick's Swan, Pintail, Shoveler), Barn and Short-eared Owls, Hen Harrier, Common Crane, roost of up to 20 Marsh Harriers.
Other notable flora/fauna: Water vole, otter, water violet, flowering rush and fringe water lily.
Contact: RSPB, T: 01733 205 140.

7. OUSE FEN

RSPB (Eastern England office)/ Hanson.
Location: Sat nav: PE27 4TA. TL 348 726. Located at Needingworth, near St Ives. Leave Junc 26 of A14 onto A1096 London Road. Go straight over three roundabouts. At the fourth take third exit (A1123). Cross over the next roundabout and take next right-hand turn onto Bluntisham Road. After 400 yards, turn left into the reserve.
Access: Open at all times. Free parking. One Blue Badge space. Guide dogs welcome.
Facilities: Two waymarked visitor trails. Two viewpoints (one screened). No visitor centre/toilets.
Public transport: Whippet Buses run from St Ives to Needingworth (nos. 21/22 - limited services Mon to Fri). From village bus stop follow Bluntisham Road east for 0.75 mile until signpost for reserve on the right. Traveline, T: 0870 6082 608.
Habitats: A working sand and gravel quarry being developed into a vast nature reserve with open water, grassland and potentially the UK's largest reedbed.
Key birds: Spring/summer: Breeding Great Crested Grebe, Skylark, Marsh Harrier, Black-headed Gull, Reed Bunting, Bearded Tit and incoming migrants such as Reed and Sedge Warblers, hirundines, Black-tailed Godwit, Ruff, Garganey, Common Tern and Hobby. Autumn: Passage waders inc. Green Sandpiper, increasing numbers of common wildfowl and incoming winter thrushes. Winter: Good numbers of Mute Swan, Gadwall, Tufted Duck, Wigeon and Pochard and regular sightings of Smew. Large numbers of Little Egret, plus flocks of tits, finches and buntings. Barn Owl and Bittern regular, plus occasional Short-eared Owl, Hen Harrier and Peregrine.
Other notable flora/fauna: Brown hare, roe and muntjac deer. Wide range of butterfly and dragonfly spp.
Contact: RSPB, T: 01954 233 260.

8. OUSE WASHES

RSPB (Eastern England Office).
Location: Sat nav: PE15 0NF. TL 471 860. Between Chatteris and March on A141, take B1093 to Manea. Reserve signposted from Manea. Reserve office and visitor centre located off Welches Dam.
Access: Access from visitor centre (open 9am-5pm daily, except Dec 25/26). Hides open at all times. Welches Dam to public hides approached by marked paths behind boundary bank. No charge. Dogs on leads. Disabled access to Welches Dam hide, 350 yards from car park. Groups welcome, but large coaches cannot traverse final bend to reserve.

Facilities: Car park (inc. two disabled bays) and toilets. Space for up to two small coaches. Ten hides overlook reserve - nearest 350 yards from visitor centre (with disabled access) up to 1.8 miles from visitor centre. Boardwalk over pond is good for dragonflies in summer.
Public transport: None to reserve entrance. Buses and trains stop at Manea, three miles from reserve.
Habitats: Lowland wet grassland – seasonally flooded. Open pool systems in front of some hides, particularly Stockdale's hide.
Key birds: *Summer*: Around 70 spp. breed inc. Black-tailed Godwit, Lapwing, Redshank, Snipe, Shoveler, Gadwall, Garganey and Spotted Crake. Also Hobby and Marsh Harrier. *Autumn*: Passage waders inc. Wood and Green Sandpipers, Spotted Redshank, Greenshank, Little Stint, plus terns and Marsh and Hen Harriers. *Winter*: Large number of wildfowl (up to 100,000 birds) inc. Bewick's and Whooper Swans, Wigeon, Teal, Shoveler, Pintail, Pochard. Tree Sparrow.
Other notable flora/fauna: Good range of dragonflies, butterflies and fenland flora.
Contact: RSPB, T: 01354 680 212;
E: ouse.washes@rspb.org.uk

9. PAXTON PITS NATURE RESERVE

Huntingdonshire District Co./Friends of Paxton Pits.
Location: Sat nav PE19 6ET. TL 196 629. Access from A1 at Little Paxton, two miles N of St Neots. Reserve signposted from edge of Little Paxton.
Access: Reserve open at all times. Subject to volunteer availability, the visitor centre/toilets are open 10am-4.30pm, except Dec 25. Dogs allowed under control. Heron trail suitable for wheelchairs during summer. Coaches and group visits by arrangement.
Facilities: Wheelchair-accessible visitor centre/toilets, sells books, bird feeders/seed etc, and light refreshments. Three hides (always open), marked nature trails.
Public transport: Buses run from St Neots and Huntingdon to Little Paxton (enquiries T: 0845 045 5200). The nearest train station is St Neots (enquiries T: 0845 748 4950).
Habitats: Grassland, scrub, lakes. the 78ha site is due to be expanded over the next 10 years, to inc. extensive reedbed.
Key birds: *Spring/summer*: Nightingale, Kingfisher, Common Tern, Sparrowhawk, Hobby, Grasshopper, Sedge and Reed Warblers, Lesser Whitethroat. Large Cormorant colony. *Winter*: Smew, Goldeneye, Goosander, Gadwall, Pochard.

Other notable flora/fauna: Wildflowers, butterflies (27 spp. recorded) and dragonflies (21 spp. regularly seen) are in abundance. Along the meadow trail there are common spotted orchids. Bee orchids are found around the car park. Otters are known to use the reserve.
Contact: The Rangers, Paxton Pits Nature Reseve, High Street, Little Paxton, St Neots, Cambs PE19 6ET. T: 01480 406 795; W: www.paxton-pits.org.uk; E: paxtonpits@huntingdonshire.gov.uk

10. WICKEN FEN NNR

The National Trust.
Location: Sat nav: CB7 5XP (Lode Lane, Wicken, Nr Ely). TL 563 705. Lies 17 miles NE of Cambridge and ten miles S of Ely. From A10 drive E along A1123.
Access: Reserve open dawn-dusk daily, except Dec 25. Entry fee for non-members of NT. Visitor centre, shop and cafe open daily (10am-5pm, or dusk in winter). Boardwalk suitable for wheelchairs, with two hides. Disabled toilets.
Facilities: Toilets, visitor centre, cafe, nine wildlife hides (three equipped for wheelchairs), boardwalk, footpaths, cycle route (NCN Route 11 passes through reserve), disabled parking in main car park and close to visitor centre, coach parking limited (parties need to pre-book). Dragonfly centre open weekends during the summer months.
Public transport: No buses to Wicken.
Habitats: A wetland of international importance, inc. open fen meadows, sedge fields, grazing marsh, partially flooded wet grassland, reedbed, scrub, woodland.
Key birds: *Spring*: Passage waders and passerines. *Summer*: Marsh Harriers, Hobbies, waders and warblers. *Winter*: Wildfowl, Hen Harriers roost on Sedge Fen, Marsh Harrier, Barn and Short-eared Owls, Bittern, Black-tailed Godwit, Cetti's Warbler.
Other notable flora/fauna: More than 9,000 spp. recorded: 21 spp. of dragonflies, 27 spp. of butterflies and 1,200+ spp. of moths. Water vole, otter.
Contact: Wicken Fen Visitor Centre, T: 01353 720 274; E: wickenfen@nationaltrust.org.uk

Essex

ESSEX WILDLIFE TRUST manages 87 nature reserves of varied habitats throughout this huge county. As well as woodland at Epping Forest, the reservoirs at Abberton and Hanningfield, and coastal marshes such as Rainham Marshes RSPB and Old Hall Marshes RSPB, are all rich in birds. Try the migration hotspots at the Naze, a bird observatory at Bradwell and even seawatching along the Thames off Southend Pier.

1. ABBERTON RESERVOIR

Essex Wildlife Trust.
Location: Sat nav: CO2 0EU. TL 962 177. Six miles SW of Colchester on B1026 (Colchester to Maldon). Follow signs from Layer-de-la-Haye or Great Wigborough.
Access: Open daily (9am-5pm), except Dec 25/26. Good viewing where roads cross reservoir. Electric wheelchair for hire.

NATURE RESERVES - EASTERN ENGLAND

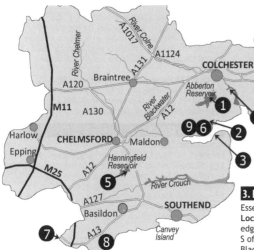

Public transport: None.
Habitats: Saltmarsh, saline lagoons, grazing marsh, farmland, woodland, freshwater lakes and ponds with Ramsar, SPA and SAC designations.
Key birds: *Winter*: Waders and wildfowl, large roost of Little Egrets. Passage migrants and summer warblers. Skylark, Grey Partridge, Corn Bunting and other farmland species
Other notable flora/fauna: Range of butterflies, reptiles, newts and water vole.
Contact: Essex WT, T: 01621 862 960;
E: admin@essexwt.org.uk

3. BRADWELL BIRD OBSERVATORY

Essex Birdwatching Society.
Location: Sat nav: CM0 7PN. TM 035 085. Located on edge of Bradwell Shell Bank nature reserve, 100 yards S of St Peter's Chapel, Bradwell-on-Sea. Mouth of Blackwater estuary, between Maldon and Foulness.
Access: Open all year. Keep to seawall in breeding season to prevent disturbance.
Habitats: Mudflats, saltmarsh, 30 acres of shellbank.
Key birds: *Winter*: Wildfowl (inc. Brent Geese, Red-throated Diver, Red-breasted Merganser), large numbers of waders (up to 20,000); small numbers of Twite, Snow Bunting and occasional Shore Lark on beaches, also Hen Harrier, Merlin and Peregrine. Good passage of migrants usual in spring and autumn. *Summer*: Small breeding population of terns and other estuarine species, plus Yellow Wagtail, Reed Bunting and Linnet.
Other notable flora/fauna: A variety of dragonflies inc. hairy dragonfly and scarce emerald damselfly.
Contact: Graham Smith (Sec), 48 The Meads, Ingatestone, Essex CM4 0AE. T: 01277 354 034;
E: silaum.silaus@tesco.co.uk

4. FINGRINGHOE WICK

Essex Wildlife Trust.
Location: Sat nav: CO5 7DN. TM 048 193. Reserve signposted from B1025 to Mersea Island, five miles S of Colchester.
Access: Open daily 9am-5pm (9am-4pm Nov-Jan), except Dec 25/26. Entry by suggested donation: for adult/child/family. Dogs on leads limited to dog walk area at edge of reserve
Facilities: Visitor centre: toilets inc. baby changing facilities, easy access toilet. One wheelchair is available. Gift shop, tearoom open 9am-4.30pm (9am-4pm, Nov-Jan), optics, observation room with displays, observatory, car park, seven bird hides, nature trails.
Public transport: None.
Habitats: Old gravel pit, large lake, many ponds, sallow/birch thickets, young scrub, reedbeds, saltmarsh, gorse heathland.

Facilities: Visitor centre inc. toilets, viewing verandah, tearoom (9.30am-4.30pm) and gift shop. Nature trails with panoramic views, two bird hides overlook water, one more in new woodland. Ample parking, inc. disabled and coach. Middleditch Wild Play Area.
Habitats: 60 acres on edge of expanding 1,200 acre reservoir. Concrete edges now replaced by wader-friendly muddy margins.
Key birds: *Winter*: Nationally important for Coot, Mallard, Teal, Wigeon, Shoveler, Gadwall, Pochard, Tufted Duck, Goldeneye. Smew, Bittern and Goosander regular. Golden Plover and Lapwing flocks on surrounding fields. *Spring*: Passage waders, terns, birds of prey. *Summer*: Tree-nesting Cormorant colony; raft-nesting Common Tern. Hobby, Yellow Wagtail, warblers, Nightingale, Turtle Dove, Skylark, Corn Bunting. *Autumn*: Red-crested Pochard, waders, rarities.
Other notable flora/fauna: Dragonflies inc. broad-bodied chaser, small red-eyed damselfly. Butterflies inc. brown argus and purple hairstreak. Roesel's bush-cricket. Brown hare, smooth newt, wasp spider.
Contact: Essex WT, T: 01206 738 172;
E: abberton@essexwt.org.uk

2. ABBOTT'S HALL FARM

Essex Wildlife Trust.
Location: Sat nav: CO5 7RZ. TL 963 146. On Blackwater estuary, seven miles SW from Colchester. Turn E off B1026 (Colchester-Maldon road) towards Peldon. Entrance, near Great Wigborough, is 0.5 mile on right.
Access: Weekdays (9am-5pm). Two hides with wheelchair ramps. Dogs only in designated area. Wildlife Trust HQ. Working farm, so please take care.
Facilities: Toilets, three hides, guided walks, factsheets, information boards. Many footpaths through active farmland areas.

Key birds: Up to 200 spp. recorded. *Autumn/winter*: Brent Goose, waders, Hen Harrier, Little Egret. *Spring*: 40+ male Nightingales. Good variety of warblers in scrub, thickets, and Turtle Dove, Green/ Great Spotted Woodpeckers. *Winter*: Little Grebe, Mute Swan, Teal, Wigeon, Shoveler, Gadwall on lake. **Other notable flora/fauna:** Swathes of sea lavender in summer among 350 plant spp. on site. Numerous spp. of dragonflies and butterflies.
Contact: Fingringhoe Wick Visitor Centre, T: 01206 729 678; E: fingringhoe@essexwt.org.uk

5. HANNINGFIELD RESERVOIR

Essex Wildlife Trust.
Location: Sat nav: CM11 1WT. TQ 725 971. Three miles N of Wickford. Exit off Southend Road (Old A130) at Rettendon onto South Hanningfield Road. Follow this for two miles until reaching the T-junction with Hawkswood Road. Turn R and the entrance to the visitor centre and reserve is one mile on the right.
Access: Open daily 9am-5pm (9am-4pm Nov-Jan), except Dec 25/26. Voluntary entrance donation. Disabled parking, toilets, adapted hide. No dogs. No cycling.
Facilities: Visitor centre, gift shop, optics, refreshments, toilets, four bird hides, nature trails, picnic area, coach parking, education room.
Public transport: Chelmsford to Wickford bus no. 14 to Downham village and walk 0.5 mile down Crowsheath Lane.
Habitats: Mixed woodland (110 acres) with grassy glades and rides, adjoining 870 acre Hanningfield Reservoir, designated an SSSI due to its high numbers of wildfowl.
Key birds: *Spring*: Good numbers and mix of woodland warblers. *Summer*: Vast numbers of Swifts, Swallows and martins feeding over the water. Hobby and Osprey. *Winter*: Good numbers and mix of waterfowl. Large gull roost.
Other notable flora/fauna: Spectacular displays of bluebells in spring. Dragonflies around ponds. Grass snakes, common lizards sometimes bask in rides.
Contact: Hanningfield Reservoir Visitor Centre, T: 01268 711 001; E: hanningfield@essexwt.org.uk

6. OLD HALL MARSHES

RSPB (Eastern England Office).
Location: Sat nav: CM9 8TP. TL 959 122. Overlooks River Blackwater, SW of Colchester. From the A12 take the B1023, via Tiptree to Tolleshunt D'Arcy. Turn L at village maypole then R into Chapel Road (back road to Tollesbury). After approx 1 mile, turn L into Old Hall Lane. Continue up Old Hall Lane, through iron gates, then follow signs straight ahead to car park.
Access: Open 9am-5pm (or dusk if earlier) when car park gates are locked. No wheelchair access or facilities. No coaches. Dogs under control allowed on footpaths.
Facilities: Two trails - one of three miles and one of 6.5 miles. Viewing screens overlooking saline lagoon area at E end of reserve. No visitor centre or toilets (nearest are in Tiptree, six miles away).

Public transport: Limited bus service to Tollesbury (two miles away). Train to Kelvedon followed by bus to Tollesbury or cycle.
Habitats: 1,560 acres of coastal grazing marsh, reedbed, open water, saline lagoon, saltmarsh and mudflat.
Key birds: *Summer*: Breeding Avocet, Redshank, Lapwing, Pochard, Shoveler, Gadwall, Marsh Harrier, Bearded Tit and Barn Owl. *Winter*: Large assemblies of wintering wildfowl: Brent Goose (approx 4,000), Wigeon, Teal, Shoveler, Goldeneye, Red-breasted Merganser, all the expected waders, Hen Harrier, Merlin, Short-eared Owl and Twite. *Passage*: All expected waders inc. Spotted Redshank, Green Sandpiper and Whimbrel. Yellow Wagtail, Whinchat and Wheatear.
Other notable flora/fauna: Brown hare, water vole, hairy dragonfly, scarce emerald damselfly, ground lackey moth, cream spot tiger, white letter hairstreak among 24 spp. of butterflies recorded, yellow meadow ant.
Contact: RSPB, T: 01621 869 015; E: oldhallmarshes@rspb.org.uk

7. RAINHAM MARSHES

RSPB (Eastern England office)
Location: Sat nav: RM19 1SZ. TQ 552 792. Off New Tank Hill Road (A1090) in Purfleet, just off the A1306 between Rainham and Lakeside. This is accessible from the Aveley, Wennington and Purfleet junction of A13 and Junc 30/31 of M25.
Access: Open Nov-Jan 9.30am-4.30pm, Feb-Oct 9.30am-5pm. Closed Dec 25/26. Entry fee for non-RSPB members. Guided walks - check RSPB website for details. Approx 2.5 miles of boardwalks suitable for wheelchairs and pushchairs. Dogs allowed only on Thames riverside path.
Facilities: Award-winning visitor centre, disabled toilets, car park (seven Blue Badge spaces) on site, picnic area, shop, wildlife garden and children's playground. Cafe open 10am-to 30 mins before reserve closes. Two bird hides. Entry charges for non-RSPB members.
Public transport: No.44 (Ensignbus, T: 01708 865 656) runs daily between Grays and Lakeside via Purfleet. Nearest train station is Purfleet. Reserve is 15 mins walk.
Habitats: Former MoD shooting range, largest remaining area of lowland wetland along the Thames.
Key birds: *Spring*: Marsh Harrier, Hobby, Wheatear, hirundines and other migrants. *Summer/autumn*: Many waders, inc. Black-tailed Godwit, Whimbrel, Greenshank, Snipe, Lapwing, Avocet. Yellow-legged Gull. Hunting Merlin and Peregrine. *Winter*: Waders, wildfowl, Water Pipit, Short-eared Owl, Little Egret and Penduline Tit most winters.
Other notable flora/fauna: 21 spp. of dragonfly, inc. hairy hawker, scarce emerald and small red-eyed damselfly. Marsh frog, water vole, water shrew, fox, stoat, weasel, 32 spp. of butterfly, and 13 spp. of orthoptera. Deadly nightshade, flowering rush.
Contact: RSPB, T: 01708 899 840; E: rainham.marshes@rspb.org.uk

8. THURROCK THAMESIDE NATURE PARK

Essex Wildlife Trust/Cory Environmental Trust.
Location: Sat nav: SS17 0RN. TQ 696 806. From Basildon head SW on A13 towards Stanford-le-Hope. Take A1014 exit and follow signs for Walton Hall Farm Museum. Past the museum entrance turn R into Mucking Wharf Road and take single lane entrance road to visitor centre.
Access: Open daily 9am-5pm (9am-4pm Nov-Jan), except Dec 25/26. Good access for wheelchair users to visitor centre, toilet and paths. Dogs must be on leads.
Facilities: Visitor centre with rooftop viewing platform, café, gift shop, toilets (inc. disabled). Bird hide overlooks mudflats.
Public transport: No trains or buses within three miles of reserve.
Habitats: Reclaimed landfill site covering 120 acres overlooking Mucking Flats SSSI and the Ramsar-designated Thames estuary. Features saltmarsh, grassland, woodland, ponds and reedbed.
Key birds: Internationally important numbers of Ringed Plover and Avocet and nationally significant numbers of Grey Plover, Dunlin, Redshank and godwits. Also look for wildfowl, Kingfisher, Barn Owl, Reed Bunting, Bearded Tit, Cetti's Warbler and Skylark.
Other notable fauna: Water vole, harvest mouse, shrill carder bee, great crested newt, adder.
Contact: Essex WT, T: 01375 643 342; E: ttnp@essexwt.org.uk

9. TOLLESBURY WICK MARSHES

Essex Wildlife Trust.
Location: Sat nav: CM9 8RJ. TL 970 103. On Blackwater Estuary eight miles E of Maldon. Follow B1023 to Tollesbury via Tiptree, leaving A12 at Kelvedon. Then follow Woodrolfe Road S towards the marina. Use small public car park at Woodrolfe Green (TL 964 107), 500 yards before reserve entrance on sea wall. Car park suitable for mini-buses and small coaches.
Access: Open all times along exposed sea wall footpath. Motorised wheelchair access possible to Block House Bay.
Facilities: Bird hide. Public toilets at Woodrolfe Green car park.

Public transport: Hedingham bus services run to Tollesbury from Maldon, Colchester and Witham - T: 01621 869 778 for information.
Habitats: Estuary with fringing saltmarsh and mudflats with some shingle. Extensive freshwater grazing marsh, brackish borrowdyke and small reedbeds.
Key birds: *Winter*: Large numbers of wintering wildfowl and waders, particularly Brent Geese and Wigeon, Lapwing and Golden Plover. Short-eared Owl, Hen Harrier and, increasingly, Marsh Harrier. *Summer*: Breeding Avocet, Redshank, Lapwing, Little Tern, Reed and Sedge Warblers, Reed Bunting, Barn Owl. *Passage*: Whimbrel, Spotted Redshank, Green Sandpiper.
Other notable flora/fauna: Plants inc. spiny restharrow, grass vetchling, yellow horned-poppy, slender hare's-ear. Hairy dragonfly, Roesel's and great green bush-crickets. Brown hares. Occasional common seals can be seen from the sea wall.
Contact: Essex WT, T: 01621 862 960; E: admin@essexwt.org.uk

10. WRABNESS NATURE RESERVE & MARSH

Essex Wildlife Trust.
Location: Sat nav: CO11 2TD. TM 167 315. Lies of southern bank of Stour estuary. From B1352 between Bradfield and Wrabness turn down Whitesheaf Lane to reach reserve. Car park is on left just beyond railway bridge.
Access: Open all year. Hard-surfaced path around site suitable for wheelchairs.
Facilities: Car park, footpath, bird hide.
Public transport: Wrabness railway station is a mile walk from reserve on public footpath. Bus service from Colchester to Harwich runs along the B1352.
Habitats: 60 acre site of grazed grassland and open scrub overlooking wader and wildfowl feeding grounds in Jacques Bay.
Key birds: *Winter*: Internationally important species such as Brent Goose, Shelduck, Wigeon, Pintail, Black-tailed Godwit, Grey Plover, Dunlin, Turnstone and Curlew. Short-eared and Barn Owls hunt over grassland. *Spring/summer*: Nightingale, Whitethroat, Turtle Dove, Bullfinch, Yellowhammer.
Other notable flora/fauna: Wildflowers, plus good range of butterflies and dragonflies.
Contact: Essex WT, T: 01621 862 960; E: admin@essexwt.org.uk

Hertfordshire

WITH MORE THAN 40 nature reserves under its control, the Herts & Middlesex Wildlife Trust can offer residents of the urbanised Home Counties a welcome taste of the countryside. Gravel pits such as those at Amwell and Tring are the best places to watch for birds, the latter holding a special place in the history of British birding as the site where Little Ringed Plover first bred in the UK.

1. AMWELL NATURE RESERVE

Herts & Middlesex Wildlife Trust.
Location: Sat nav: SG12 9SS. TL 376 127. In Lee Valley near Ware. From A10, leave at junction signposted A414 to Harlow. At first roundabout, take B181 to St Margarets and Stanstead Abbotts. On entering St Margarets, just before railway, turn L on Amwell Lane. Reserve is on the right (signposted).
Access: Open all year. Dragonfly Trail is open May to Sept.
Facilities: Three hides, several viewing areas and Dragonfly Trail boardwalk.

NATURE RESERVES - EASTERN ENGLAND

Public transport: St Mary's Church, Hoddesdon Road, St Margarets (nos. 310, 311, C4) five mins walk from railway station. Rail: St Margarets (0.75 mile). From station walk E along B181 to footpath of River Lee Navigation, then walk N for 0.5 mile to reserve.
Habitats: Disused gravel pit with reedbeds and woodland.

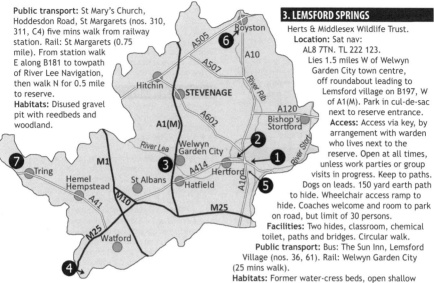

Key birds: *Spring/summer*: Ringed Plover, Little Ringed Plover. *Winter*: Smew, other ducks, Bittern. SSSI for wintering Gadwall and Shoveler.
Other notable flora/fauna: Best county site for dragonflies (19 spp. recorded), otter, nationally scarce marsh dock, plus early and southern marsh orchids.
Contact: Herts & Middlesex WT, T: 01727 858 901; E: info@hmwt.org

2. KINGS MEAD

Herts & Middlesex Wildlife Trust.
Location: Sat nav: SG12 9XD. TL 349 136. From Ware head SE on A1170 High Street, turn R into Burgage Lane shortly after Ware Museum. Park in public car park. From here pedestrian access is via the River Lee, go over the bridge, turn R and walk 250 yards. Turn left into the reserve.
Access: Open all year.
Facilities: None.
Public transport: Bus stops on Hertford Road (A119). Trains to Ware station (five mins walk to reserve).
Habitats: Largest remaining area of grazed riverside flood meadow in Hertfordshire.
Key birds: 119 spp. recorded. *Summer*: Skylark, Reed Warbler, Reed Bunting, seven species of breeding warblers, Yellow Wagtail. *Winter/spring*: Gadwall, Shoveler, Wigeon, Teal, Snipe, gulls, waders.
Other notable flora/fauna: 265 spp. of wildflowers, 18 spp. of dragonflies. Significant population of short-winged conehead.
Contact: Herts & Middlesex WT, T: 01727 858 901; E: info@hmwt.org

3. LEMSFORD SPRINGS

Herts & Middlesex Wildlife Trust.
Location: Sat nav: AL8 7TN. TL 222 123. Lies 1.5 miles W of Welwyn Garden City town centre, off roundabout leading to Lemsford village on B197, W of A1(M). Park in cul-de-sac next to reserve entrance.
Access: Access via key, by arrangement with warden who lives next to the reserve. Open at all times, unless work parties or group visits in progress. Keep to paths. Dogs on leads. 150 yard earth path to hide. Wheelchair access ramp to hide. Coaches welcome and room to park on road, but limit of 30 persons.
Facilities: Two hides, classroom, chemical toilet, paths and bridges. Circular walk.
Public transport: Bus: The Sun Inn, Lemsford Village (nos. 36, 61). Rail: Welwyn Garden City (25 mins walk).
Habitats: Former water-cress beds, open shallow lagoons. Stretch of the River Lea, marsh, hedgerows. Nine acres.
Key birds: *Spring/summer*: Breeding warblers, Grey Wagtail, Kestrel, Green Woodpecker. *Autumn/winter*: Green Sandpiper, Water Rail, Snipe, Siskin, Little Egret, occasional Jack Snipe. *All year*: Mandarin Duck, Kingfisher, Grey Heron, Sparrowhawk.
Other notable flora/fauna: Muntjac, fox and stoat. Common butterflies and damselflies in summer.
Contact: Herts & Middlesex WT, T: 01727 858 901; E: info@hmwt.org;
Warden (for key): Barry Trevis, T: 01707 335 517

4. MAPLE LODGE

Thames Water/Maple Lodge Conservation Society
Location: Sat nav: WD3 9SF. TQ 036 925. S of Rickmansworth, close to village of Maple Cross. From M25 Junc 17 drive towards Denham/Uxbridge, turn L at traffic lights. Drive down Maple Lodge Close and park in social club car park on right.
Access: Restricted to members of MLCS. Visits by non-members and groups can be arranged in advance. Site can be boggy - keep to designated paths.
Facilities: Information centre, toilets. Nine bird hides - two wheelchair-friendly (plus two more when ground is dry). Winter feeding stations.
Public transport: Bus services are available from Rickmansworth train station to Maple Cross.
Habitats: A man-made wetland habitat formed from two gravel pits and a sludge settlement area. Two lakes and a reedbed. Mixed broadleaf plantation on eastern side.

Key birds: Wildfowl throughout year, numbers building in winter. All three woodpeckers, plus variety of finches, thrushes and woodland species. Nesting species inc. Kingfisher, Tawny Owl, Water Rail and migrant warblers. Snipe, Green and Common Sandpipers on passage. Birds of prey inc. Sparrowhawk, Hobby, Red Kite and Common Buzzard.
Other notable flora/fauna: 250 spp. of moths, plus many butterflies and aquatic insects. 125 spp. of wildflowers. Seven of the nine bat spp. found in Herts.
Contact: Maple Lodge Conservation Society,
T: 07580 535 986; Keith Pursall, Chairman
E: keith@maplelodge.org; W: www.maplelodge.org

5. RYE MEADS

RSPB/Herts & Middlesex Wildlife Trust.
Location: SG12 8JS. TL 389 103. Take Hoddesdon turn off A10 and follow brown duck signs. Near Rye House railway station.
Access: Open daily, 9am-5pm (or dusk if earlier), except Dec 25/26. Gates are locked when the reserve is closed. No dogs allowed, except guide dogs.
Facilities: Visitor centre, toilets & trails have disabled access. Drinks machine, staffed reception, classrooms, picnic area, car park (charge for non-members), bird feeding area. Nature trails, 10 hides. RSPB reserve has close-circuit TV on Kingfisher and Common Tern nests in summer.
Public transport: Rail (Rye House) 400 yards, bus (no. 310) stops 600 yards from entrance.
Habitats: Marsh, willow scrub, pools, scrapes, lagoons and reedbed.
Key birds: *Summer:* Breeding Water Rail, Tufted Duck, Gadwall, Common Tern, Kestrel, Kingfisher, Little Ringed Plover, nine species of warblers. Hobby. *Winter:* Bittern, Shoveler, Goldeneye, Teal, Water Rail, Snipe, Jack Snipe, Redpoll and Siskin. *Autumn:* Birds on passage inc. Green Sandpiper, Teal and Snipe, plus occasional rarities.
Other notable flora/fauna: Fen vegetation, invertebrates and reptiles.
Contact: RSPB, T: 01992 708 383;
E: rye.meads@rspb.org.uk
Herts & Middlesex WT, T: 01727 858 901;
E: info@hmwt.org

6. THERFIELD HEATH LNR

Conservators of Therfield Heath.
Location: Sat nav: SG8 5GB. TL 335 400. Common land SSSI lies west and south of Royston and is accessed from A505 (Baldock Road).
Access: Open at all times.
Facilities: Open downland walks, golf course and sports fields.
Public transport: Royston railway station a two minute walk from heath.
Habitats: Natural chalk/grass downland.
Key birds: Noted stop-off site for migrants such as Ring Ouzel and Wheatear. *Spring/summer:* Breeding Skylark, Meadow Pipit, Willow Warbler, Whitethroat, Lesser Whitethroat and Grey Partridge. Good selection of raptors seen regularly.

Other notable flora/fauna: 26 spp. of butterflies recorded, inc. increasingly rare chalkhill blue. Several orchid spp., plus pasque flower and wide variety of chalk grassland flowers.
Contact: Conservators of Therfield Heath,
E: clerk.conservators.therfield@gmail.com
W: www.conservators-of-therfield-heath.org.uk/

7. TRING RESERVOIRS

Canals & Rivers Trust/Herts & Middlesex Wildlife Trust [water treatment works lagoon – Thames Water]
Location: Sat nav: HP23 4NW (Wilstone Res.)
SP 903 134. Other reservoirs SP 920 135.
WTW Lagoon SP 923 134, adjacent to Marsworth Res. Reservoirs 1.5 miles due N of Tring, all accessible from B489 which crosses A41 Aston Clinton by-pass. NB: exit from by-pass only southbound.
Access: Reservoirs open at all times. Coaches can only drop off and pick up, contact for advice. Wilstone Res. has restricted height barrier. Disabled access available for Startops and Marsworth Reservoirs from car park, as well as Lagoon Hide.
Facilities: Cafe and pubs adjacent to Startops Res. car park, safe parking for cycles. Wilstone Res: Pub 0.5 mile away in village. Cafe and farm shop 0.25 mile from car park. Hides on all reservoirs.
Public transport: Buses from Aylesbury and Tring inc. a weekend service, T: 0871 200 2233. Tring Station is 2.5 miles away via canal towpath.
Habitats: Four reservoirs with surrounding woodland, scrub and meadows. Two of the reservoirs have extensive reedbeds. WTW Lagoon with islands and dragonfly scrape, surrounding hedgerows and scrub.
Key birds: *Spring/summer:* Breeding water birds Common Terns and heronry. Regular Black Terns and Red Kite, warblers inc. Cetti's. Occasional Marsh Harrier, Osprey. *Autumn/winter passage:* Waders, occasional White-winged Black Tern. *Winter:* Gull roost, large wildfowl flocks, bunting roosts, Bittern.
Other notable flora/fauna: Black poplar trees, some locally rare plants in damp areas. 18 spp. of dragonfly inc. black-tailed skimmer, ruddy darter and emerald damselfly. Holly blue and speckled wood butterflies. Chinese water deer, Daubenton's, Natterer's and both pipistrelle bats.
Contact: Herts & Middlesex WT, T: 01727 858 901;
E: info@hmwt.org

Norfolk

ITS EAST COAST location and largely unspoilt coastline, and many iconic nature reserves, ensures Norfolk's reputation as our finest birding county. Whatever the season you can be guaranteed a wide variety of birds, including many vagrants, out-and-out rarities and thousands of over-wintering geese, ducks and waders.

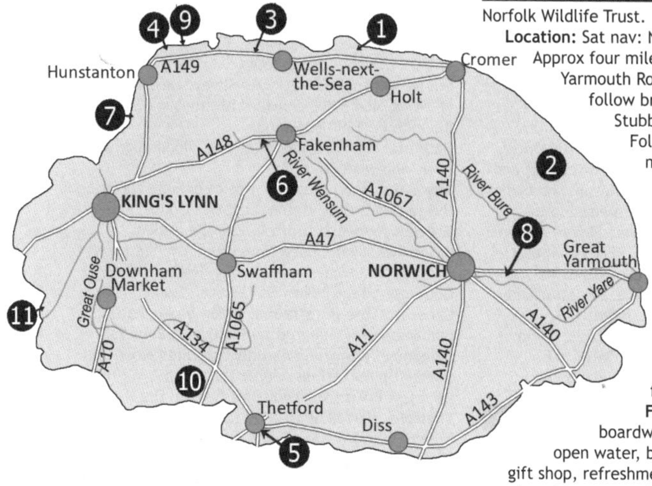

Key birds: Avocet, Marsh Harrier, Spoonbill, Bearded Tit and large numbers of wintering wildfowl, inc. Wigeon, Teal, Pintail and Brent Goose. Migrating waders such as Ruff and Temminck's Stint. Many rarities.
Contact: NWT Cley Marshes Visitor Centre, T: 01263 740 008;
Norfolk WT, T: 01603 625540;
E: info@norfolkwildlifetrust.org.uk

2. HICKLING BROAD NNR

Norfolk Wildlife Trust.
Location: Sat nav: NR12 0BW. TG 428 222. Approx four miles SE of Stalham, just off A149 Yarmouth Road. From Hickling village, follow brown badger tourist signs into Stubb Road at the Greyhound Inn. Follow Stubb Road for another mile and turn R at the end for nature reserve.
Access: Reserve open all year (dawn-dusk). Visitor centre open Easter to Sept (10am-5pm daily) / Oct - weekends & half term only. Entrance fee charged for the reserve, children under 16 and NWT members free. Dogs only allowed on Weaver's Way footpath.
Facilities: Visitor centre, boardwalk trail through reedbeds to open water, birdwatching hides, wildlife gift shop, refreshments, picnic site, toilets, coach parking, car parking, disabled access to broad, boardwalk and toilets. Groups welcome. Water trail boat trips May to Sept (additional charge - booking essential).
Public transport: Morning bus service only Mon to Fri from Norwich (Neaves Coaches) Cromer to North Walsham (Sanders). Buses stop in Hickling village, a 25 minute walk away.
Habitats: Hickling is the largest and wildest of the Norfolk Broad with reedbeds, grazing marshes and wide open skies.
Key birds: Marsh Harrier, Bittern, warblers. From Nov to Feb the raptor roost at Stubb Mill, provides excellent views of raptors flying in to roost. Likely birds inc. Marsh and Hen Harriers, Merlin, Crane and Pink-footed Goose. *Autumn/winter:* Shoveler, Teal and Goldeneye. *All year:* Bittern, Pochard, Water Rail, Cetti's Warbler, Bearded Tit.
Other notable flora/fauna: Swallowtail butterfly, Norfolk hawker dragonfly, marsh orchid.
Contact: Hickling Broad Visitor Centre, T: 01692 598 276;
Norfolk WT, T: 01603 625540;
E: info@norfolkwildlifetrust.org.uk

[Map of Norfolk showing locations: Hunstanton, Wells-next-the-Sea, Holt, Cromer, Fakenham, King's Lynn, Downham Market, Swaffham, Norwich, Great Yarmouth, Thetford, Diss, with roads A149, A148, A1067, A47, A10, A134, A1065, A11, A140, A143 and Rivers Wensum, Bure, Yare, Great Ouse. Numbered markers 1-11 shown.]

1. CLEY MARSHES NNR

Norfolk Wildlife Trust.
Location: Sat nav: NR25 7SA. TG 054 440. Situated four miles N of Holt on A149 coast road, 0.5 mile E of Cley-next-the-Sea. Visitor centre and car park on inland side of road.
Access: Reserve open dawn-dusk. Visitor Centre open daily, except Dec 24/25 (Mar-Oct 10am-5pm, Nov-Feb 10am-4.30pm). Cafe closes 30 mins before the centre. Free admission to visitor centre, entrance fee charged for the reserve. NWT members and children are free. No dogs.
Facilities: Environmentally-friendly visitor centre (wheelchair accessible) incorporates an observation area, interactive interpretation, inc. remote controllable wildlife camera, cafe and sales area. Five hides (three with excellent wheelchair access). Audio trail. Wildlife detective bumbags for children, free to hire. Boardwalk and information boards. Reserve leaflet. Regular events.
Public transport: Coasthopper bus service frequently stops outside. Connections for train and bus services at Sheringham.
Habitats: Reedbeds, salt and freshwater marshes, scrapes and shingle ridge with international reputation as one of the finest birdwatching sites in Britain.

3. HOLKHAM NNR

Natural England (East Anglia Team).
Location: Sat nav: NR23 1RH. TF 890 450. Three miles W of Wells on A149. From Holkham village turn down Lady Ann's Drive (opposite entrance to Holkham Hall) to park. More parking at end of Wells Beach Road in Wells and at Burnham Overy.
Access: Unrestricted, keep to paths and off grazing marshes and farmland. Pay-and-display parking.
Facilities: Two hides. Disabled access.
Public transport: Coasthopper bus service every 30 mins in summer. Norbic Norfolk bus information line T: 0845 3006 116.
Habitats: 4,000 ha of sandflats, dunes, marshes, pinewoods, reclaimed saltmarsh.
Key birds: *Passage:* Migrants, inc. Yellow Wagtail, Wheatear, Cuckoo and many unusual species. *Winter:* Wildfowl, inc. Brent (7,000), Pink-footed (20,000) and White-fronted Geese, up to 13,000 Wigeon. Shorelark, Twite and Snow Bunting. *Summer:* Breeding Little Tern, Snipe, Oystercatcher and Ringed Plover. *All year:* Marsh Harrier, Grey Heron, Lapwing, Barn Owl, Kestrel.
Other notable flora/fauna: Seablite bushes, attractive to incoming migrant birds, sea aster and sea lavender. Antlion recently recorded.
Contact: Natural England, Hill Farm Offices, Main Road, Holkham, Wells-next-the-Sea, NR23 1AB. T: 01328 800 730; E: s.henderson@holkham.co.uk

4. HOLME OBSERVATORY

Norfolk Ornithologists' Association (NOA).
Location: Sat nav: PE36 6LQ. TF 717 450. E of Hunstanton, signposted from A149. Access from Broadwater Road, Holme. Reserve and visitors centre are beyond the White House at the end of the track.
Access: Open daily to members dawn-dusk; non-members (9am-5pm) by permit from the Observatory. Parties by prior arrangement. Dogs on leads.
Facilities: Accredited Bird Observatory operating all year for bird ringing, MV moth trapping and other scientific monitoring. Visitor centre, car park and several hides (seawatch hide reserved for NOA members), together with access to beach and coastal path.
Public transport: Coastal bus service (Hunstanton to Sheringham) roughly every 30 mins in summer. Norfolk Green Bus, T: 01553 776 980.
Habitats: In ten acres of diverse Habitats: sand dunes, Corsican pines, scrub and reed-fringed lagoon make this a migration hotspot.
Key birds: Species list over 320, over 150 spp. ringed. Recent rarities have inc. Red Kite, Common Crane, Osprey, Red-flanked Bluetail, Yellow-browed, Pallas's, Arctic and Barred Warblers.
Other notable flora/fauna: Moth trap run Mar-Oct, migrant moths and butterflies recorded yearly.
Contact: Sophie Barker, Holme Bird Observatory, Broadwater Road, Holme, Hunstanton, Norfolk PE36 6LQ. T: 01485 525 406; E: info@noa.org.uk; W: www.noa.org.uk

5. NUNNERY LAKES

British Trust for Ornithology.
Location: TL 873 815. On the S edge of Thetford, adjacent to the BTO's headquarters at The Nunnery. Main access point is via Nun's Bridges car park, across pedestrian bridge at TL 874 821.
Access: Open dawn-dusk. Public access along permissive paths. Keep dogs on leads at all times. Call reception in advance to arrange wheelchair access to lakes and hide.
Facilities: Waymarked paths, information panels, bird hide, boardwalk through wet woodland. Pre-booked coaches can park in grounds. Toilets on Nunnery Place at back of BTO - office hours only.
Public transport: Thetford railway station one mile (T: 0845 7484 950). Thetford bus terminal approx 0.5 mile (T: 0870 6082 608).
Habitats: Flood meadows, scrape, flooded gravel pits, scrub and woodland.
Key birds: Wide range of species present throughout the year inc. Grey Heron, Egyptian Goose, Kingfisher, Green Woodpecker. *Spring:* Passage waders, hirundines, Swift, passerines. *Summer:* Warblers, Cuckoo, Oystercatcher, Lapwing, Hobby. *Winter:* Goosander, Teal, Water Rail, Snipe, Siskin.
Other notable flora/fauna: Otter, brown hare, muntjac, grass snake, common lizard. Emperor dragonfly, red-eyed damselfly. Speckled wood and orange tip butterflies. Mossy stonecrop.
Contact: British Trust for Ornithology, The Nunnery, Thetford, Norfolk IP24 2PU. T: 01842 750 050; E: info@bto.org

6. SCULTHORPE MOOR

Hawk and Owl Trust.
Location: Sat nav: NR21 9GN. TF 900 305. In Wensum Valley, just W of Fakenham, on A148 to King's Lynn. Nature reserve signposted opposite village of Sculthorpe. Follow Turf Moor Road to visitor centre.
Access: Open daily inc. bank holidays, except Dec 25, Apr-Oct (8am-6pm), Nov-Mar: (8am-4pm). Entrance by suggested donation for adult visitors - children and members free. Guide dogs only.
Facilities: Visitor centre open daily 9am-5pm (4pm in winter), with adapted toilets, hot drinks, interpretive displays and live CCTV coverage from around the reserve. Reserve and two hides accessible to wheelchairs and buggies via a mile of boardwalk. Bark chipping path to other hides. Coach parking available.
Public transport: Norfolk Green (T: 01553 776 980; W: www.norfolkgreen.co.uk) bus no. X8 Fakenham to King's Lynn stops at end of Turf Moor Road. Sustrans No.1 cycle route runs within 200 yards of Turf Moor Road. Bike racks on site.
Habitats: Wetland reserve, fen containing saw sedge (a European priority habitat), reedbed, wet woodland, pools, ditches and riverbank.
Key birds: 90 spp. recorded, inc. breeding Marsh Harrier, Barn Owl and Tawny Owl, visiting Buzzard, Goshawk, Hobby, Kestrel, Osprey, Sparrowhawk, also Water Rail, Kingfisher, Marsh Tit, Lesser Spotted Woodpecker and Willow Tit.

NATURE RESERVES - EASTERN ENGLAND

Other notable flora/fauna: Otter, water vole, roe deer, 19 spp. of dragonflies, butterflies inc. white admiral. Glow-worms.
Contact: The Hawk and Owl Trust, Turf Moor Road, Sculthorpe, Fakenham NR21 9GN. T: 01328 856 788; E: sculthorpe@hawkandowl.org; W: www.hawkandowl.org/sculthorpe/about-sculthorpe

7. SNETTISHAM

RSPB (Eastern England Office).
Location: Sat nav: PE31 7PS. TF 650 328. Car park two miles along Beach Road, signposted off A149 S of Hunstanton, opposite Snettisham village.
Access: Open at all times, free entry - donation welcomed. Dogs on lead please.
Facilities: Car park, three trails, two hides (one storm damaged, to be replaced), leaflet, walks.
Habitats: Intertidal mudflats, saltmarsh, shingle beach, brackish lagoons, and unimproved grassland/scrub. Highest tides best for good views of waders.
Key birds: *Autumn/winter/spring:* Waders (particularly Knot, Bar and Black-tailed Godwits, Dunlin, Grey Plover), wildfowl (particularly Pink-footed and Brent Geese, Wigeon, Gadwall, Goldeneye), Peregrine, Hen Harrier, Merlin, owls. Migrants in season. *Summer:* Breeding Mediterranean Gull, Ringed Plover, Redshank, Avocet, Common Tern. Marsh Harrier regular.
Other notable flora/fauna: Yellow horned poppies and other shingle flora along the beach.
Contact: RSPB, T: 01485 210 779; E: snettisham@rspb.org.uk

8. STRUMPSHAW FEN

RSPB (Eastern England Office).
Location: Sat nav: NR13 4HS. TG 341 065. Near Brundell, seven miles ESE of Norwich. Follow signposts. Entrance across level-crossing from car park, reached by turning sharp R and R again into Low Road from Brundall, off A47 to Great Yarmouth.
Access: Open dawn-dusk (except Dec 25). Entry fee for non-RSPB members. Guide dogs only. Limited wheelchair access - phone for advice.
Facilities: Toilets, reception hide (open 9am-5pm Apr-Sept, 10am-4pm Oct-Mar), two other hides, two walks, five miles of trails.
Public transport: Brundall train station ca.1.5 miles from reserve. First Eastern Counties Bus no.15 &15A from Acle/Lingwood-Wymondham stops 0.5 mile from reserve.
Habitats: Reedbed/reedfen, wet grassland, woodland.
Key birds: *Summer:* Bittern, Little Egret, Bearded Tit, Marsh Harrier, Hobby, Kingfisher, Cetti's Warbler and other reedbed birds. *Winter:* Bittern, wildfowl, Marsh and Hen Harrier.
Other notable flora/fauna: Rich fen flora - six spp. of orchid, inc. marsh helleborine and narrow-leaved marsh orchid. Otter, Chinese water deer and water vole. Swallowtail, white admiral and small heath butterflies, Norfolk hawker, scarce chaser and variable damselfly among 20 dragonfly spp.
Contact: RSPB, T: 01603 715 191; E: strumpshaw@rspb.org.uk

9. TITCHWELL MARSH

RSPB (Eastern England Office).
Location: Sat nav: PE31 8BB. TF 750 438. E of Hunstanton, signposted off A149.
Access: Reserve and hides open at all times. Wheelchairs available (no charge). All trails suitable for wheelchairs, but beach not accessible due to collapse of boardwalk. Coach parking - pre-booking essential. Car park charge for non-RSPB members. Dogs allowed only on west bank path.
Facilities: Visitor centre, shop with large selection of optics, birdfood and books, open daily 10am-5pm (Nov-Feb, 10am-4pm). Cafe open 10am-4.30pm daily (Nov-Feb, 9.30am-4pm). Visitor centre/cafe closed Dec 25/26. Three large hides.
Public transport: Traveline East Anglia, T: 0871 200 2233 for times of Stagecoach Norfolk or Coasthopper buses stopping in Titchwell.
Habitats: Freshwater reedbed and fresh water lagoons, extensive salt marsh, dunes, sandy beach with associated exposed peat beds.
Key birds: Diverse range of breeding reedbed and wetland birds with good numbers of passage waders during late summer/autumn. *Spring/summer:* Breeding Avocet, Bearded Tit, Bittern, Marsh Harrier, Reed Sedge and Cetti's Warbler, Redshank, Ringed Plover and Common Tern. *Summer/autumn:* Passage waders inc. Knot, Wood and Green Sandpiper, Little Stint, Spotted Redshank, Curlew Sandpiper and many more. *Winter:* Brent Goose, Hen/Marsh Harrier roost, Snow Bunting. Offshore Common and Velvet Scoter, Long-tailed Duck, Great Northern and Red-throated Divers.
Other notable flora/fauna: 25 spp. of butterflies, inc. all the common species, plus Essex skipper and annual clouded yellow. 21 spp. of dragonflies, inc. small red-eyed damselfly. Good diversity of saltmarsh plants inc. shrubby sea-blite and three spp. of sea lavender.
Contact: RSPB, T: 01485 210 779; E: titchwell@rspb.org.uk

10. WEETING HEATH

Norfolk Wildlife Trust.
Location: Sat nav: IP26 4NQ. TL 757 881. Weeting Heath is signposted from the Weeting-Hockwold road, two miles W of Weeting near to Brandon in Suffolk. Nature reserve can be reached via B1112 at Hockwold or B1106 at Weeting.
Access: Open daily from late-Mar-Jul (7am to dusk) - extended into Aug if Stone Curlews still nesting due to replacement nests. Entrance charge, NWT members and children free. Disabled access to visitor centre and hides.
Facilities: Visitor centre open daily end-Mar-Jul (9.30am-4.30pm) - extended into Aug if Stone Curlews still nesting due to replacement nests, birdwatching hides, wildlife gift shop, refreshments, toilets, coach parking, car park, groups welcome (book first).
Public transport: Train services to Brandon and bus connections (limited) from Brandon High Street.
Habitats: Breckland, grass heath.

Key birds: Stone Curlew (main attraction), migrant passerines, Wood Lark, Spotted Flycatcher.
Contact: Weeting Heath Visitor Centre,
T: 01842 827 615;
Norfolk WT, T: 01603 625540;
E: info@norfolkwildlifetrust.org.uk

11. WELNEY WETLAND CENTRE

The Wildfowl & Wetlands Trust.
Location: Sat nav: PE14 9TN. TL 546 944. Hundred Foot Bank, ten miles N of Ely, signposted from A10 and A1101. Check if A1101 is flooded in winter before setting off.
Access: Open daily, except Dec 25. Summer: Mar-Oct (9.30am-5pm); Winter: Nov-Feb (Mon to Wed, 10am-5pm & Thurs to Sun, 10am-8pm) - last asmissions 4.30pm, 4.30pm & 6.30pmn respectively. Entrance fee - free admission to WWT members. Wheelchair accessible. Access roads and paths to remote hides may be flooded so check before visiting. No dogs allowed.
Facilities: Visitor centre (wheelchair-friendly). Cafe opening times, Summer: 10am-4.00pm daily, Winter: Nov-Feb (Mon to Wed, 10am-4.30pm & Thurs to Sun, 10am-6pm). Large, heated observatory, additional five hides. Free parking and coach parking. Blue Badge parking, wheelchairs for hire (one electric scooter and two manual chairs), lifts, disabled toilets, ramps.

Public transport: None.
Habitats: 1,000 acres of washland reserve, spring damp meadows, winter wildfowl marsh (SPA, Ramsar site, SSSI, SAC). Additional 200 acres of recently created wetland habitat next to visitor centre.
Key birds: Large numbers of wintering wildfowl are replaced by breeding waders, terns and warblers. Local Cranes regularly seen, esp. post-breeding birds. *Winter:* Bewick's and Whooper Swans, wintering wildfowl e.g. Wigeon. *Spring/summer:* Common Tern, Avocet, Lapwing, Black-tailed Godwit, House Martin, occasional rarities. *Autumn:* waders inc Little Stint, Ruff and Curlew Sandpiper.
Other notable flora/fauna: Purple loosestrife, meadow rue, mixed grasses. Dragonflies inc. scarce chaser, emperor, banded demoiselle, small red-eyed damselfly. Approx. 400 spp. of moths inc. goat moth. Butterflies inc. brown argus.
Contact: WWT Welney, T: 01353 860 711;
E: info.welney@wwt.org.uk;

Suffolk

SUFFOLK HOSTS MORE Breckland sites than neighbouring Norfolk and there are other inland locations good for birds among the Wildlife Trust's 53 reserves. However, it is the coastal hotspots such as Minsmere, Landguard Bird Observatory, Walberswick and Dunwich Heath that tend to get most attention from visiting birders.

1. BENACRE BROAD NNR

Natural England (East Anglia Team)
Location: Sat nav: NR34 7JW (Covehithe).
TM 528 827. On coast S of Kessingland. From A12 take minor road to Covehithe at Wrentham. Park near Covehithe church.
Access: Open at all times on permissive paths. Clifftop from Covehithe unstable, so walk with care. If sea has breached sandbar it is not possible to reach bird hide from the north. Telescope needed for best views. Dogs on lead.
Facilities: Elevated bird hide on southern edge of Broad.
Public transport: None.
Habitats: Coastal woodland, saline lagoons, reedbeds and heathland covering 393ha.
Key birds: 100 spp. of breeding birds, inc. Marsh Harrier, Bearded Tits, Water Rail and wildfowl. Bittern breeds irregularly. Woodlark, Hobby and Wheatear breed on heathland areas and Little Terns fish off the coast. *Winter:* Shorelark possible on cliff-top areas, winter thrushes.

Map of Suffolk showing numbered reserve locations, towns (Lowestoft, Southwold, Diss, Newmarket, Bury St Edmunds, Stowmarket, Woodbridge, Ipswich, Sudbury, Felixstowe, Aldeburgh, Saxmundham), rivers and major roads.

Other notable flora/fauna: Lagoon shrimp, starlet sea-anemone, yellow-horned poppy, grey hair grass.
Contact: Natural England, T: 01502 676 171

2. BOYTON & HOLLESLEY MARSHES

RSPB (Eastern England Office).
Location: Sat nav: IP12 3LR. TM 387 475. Two grazing marshes in lower reaches of Alde-Ore Estuary, approx. seven miles E of Woodbridge. Follow B1084 to Butley. Turn R and follow to Capel St. Andrew before turning L towards Boyton village. Approx 0.25 mile before village, bear L down concrete track on sharp right-hand turn.
Access: Open at all times. Entrance free but donations welcome. Public footpath on site not suited to wheelchair use. Dogs only on public footpaths.
Facilities: Car park at Boyton (eight spaces only). For Hollesley park at Shingle Street. No toilets or hides at either site. Information boards at both sites.
Public transport: No. 160 (Ipswich-Bealings-Woodbridge-Orford)/bus stops at Boyton village. Reserve is located 0.5 mile NE of village.
Habitats: 57 ha of coastal grazing marsh and saltmarsh on the lower Alde-Ore estuary.
Key birds: *Spring:* Breeding waders and wildfowl, such as Lapwing, Avocet, Shoveler and Gadwall. Spring migrants inc. Yellow Wagtail and Whitethroat. Barn and Little Owls. *Autumn:* Wintering wildfowl such as Teal and Wigeon. Migrating waders inc. Whimbrel, Black-tailed Godwit and Greenshank. *Winter:* Wintering wildfowl and wading birds, inc. Wigeon, Teal, Curlew, Dunlin and Redshank.
Other notable flora/fauna: Grassland butterflies such as skippers, wall and meadow browns and dragonflies.
Contact: RSPB, T: 01394 450 732;
E: havergate.island@rspb.org.uk

3. CARLTON MARSHES

Suffolk Wildlife Trust.
Location: TM 508 920. NR33 8HU. SW of Lowestoft, at W end of Oulton Broad. From Lowestoft, take A146 towards Beccles and turn R after Tesco garage.
Access: Open dawn-dusk. Keep to marked paths. Dogs allowed in some areas, on leads at all times. Car park suitable for coaches.
Facilities: Education centre with disabled toilet. Firm path around part of the marsh, inc. easy access gates. Disabled access route along the river wall from Oulton Broad to Carlton Marshes. Free car park.
Public transport: Bus and train in walking distance.
Habitats: 120 acres of grazing marsh, peat pools, fen.
Key birds: Over 150 spp. recorded inc. a wide range of wetland and Broadland birds, inc. Reed, Sedge and Cetti's Warblers, Bearded Tit, Hobby and Marsh Harrier.
Other notable flora/fauna: Water vole, 15 spp. of dragonflies inc. Norfolk hawker, rare water soldier and fen raft spider. Plants inc. common spotted and southern marsh orchids.
Contact: Suffolk WT, T: 01502 564 250;
E: info@suffolkwildlifetrust.org

4. DINGLE MARSHES

Suffolk Wildlife Trust/RSPB (Eastern England Office)/ Natural England (East Anglia Team).
Location: Sat nav: IP17 3DZ TM 479 708 (Dunwich beach car park). Eight miles from Saxmundham. Follow brown signs from A12 to Minsmere and continue to Dunwich. Forest car park (hide) TM 467 710. The reserve forms part of the Suffolk Coast NNR.
Access: Open at all times. Access via public rights of way and permissive path along beach. Dogs on lead in breeding season. Coaches can park on beach car park.
Facilities: Toilets at beach car park, Dunwich. Hide in Dunwich Forest overlooking reedbed, accessed via Forest car park. Circular trail marked from car park.
Public transport: Book in advance - Via Coastlink, Dial-a-ride service from Leiston/Saxmundham area to Dingle (T: 01728 833 526) - links to buses and trains.
Habitats: Grazing marsh, reedbed, shingle beach, fresh and saline lagoons with forest and heath.
Key birds: *All year:* In reedbed, breeding Bittern, Marsh Harrier, Bearded Tit. *Winter:* Hen Harrier, White-fronted Goose, Wigeon, Snipe, Teal on grazing marsh, Twite. *Summer:* Lapwing, Avocet, Snipe, Black-tailed Godwit, Hobby. Good for passage waders.
Other notable flora/fauna: Site is internationally important for starlet sea anemone — the rarest sea anemone in Britain. Otter and water vole.
Contact: Suffolk WT; T: 01502 478 788;
E: info@suffolkwildlifetrust.org;
RSPB, T: 01728 648 780; E: minsmere@rspb.org.uk

5. HAVERGATE ISLAND

RSPB (Eastern England Office).
Location: Sat nav: IP12 2NU (Orford quay). TM 425 495. Part of the Orfordness-Havergate Island NNR on the Alde/Ore estuary. Orford is 10.5 miles NE of Woodbridge, signposted off the A12.
Access: Pre-booked boat crossings from Orford Quay at 10am on first Sat of the month (except May-July), plus special event weekends (see website). Book in advance through Minsmere RSPB visitor centre, (T: 01728 648 281; E: minsmere@rspb.org.uk), reduced charge for RSPB. Park in Orford's pay-and-display car park next to quay. Guide dogs only.
Facilities: Toilets, picnic area, four birdwatching hides, one viewing screen, visitor trail (approx 1.25 miles).
Public transport: Local bus (no. 160) from Ipswich to Orford. For timetable info, T: 0870 608 2608. Bus stop is 0.25 mile from quay.
Habitats: Shallow brackish water, lagoons with islands, Mudflats, saltmarsh.
Key birds: *Summer:* Breeding gulls, terns, Avocet, Shelduck and Oystercatcher. A flock of Spoonbills is present from mid-Jul onwards. *Winter:* Wildfowl and waders inc. Wigeon, Teal, Pintail, Shoveler, Avocet, Lapwing and Black-tailed Godwit. Also, Short-eared Owl, Marsh Harrier and Barn Owl.
Other notable flora/fauna: Brown hare.
Contact: RSPB, T: 01394 450 732;
E: havergate.island@rspb.org.uk

6. HEN REEDBED NNR

Suffolk Wildlife Trust.
Location: Sat nav: IP18 6SH. TM 471 771. Three miles from Southwold. Turn off A12 at Blythburgh and follow A1095 for two miles to signposted car park. The reserve forms part of the Suffolk Coast NNR.
Access: Open at all times. No dogs in hides.
Facilities: Two hides overlook Wolsey Creek marsh and two viewing platforms on waymarked trails.
Public transport: Bus service between Halesworth and Southwold.
Habitats: Reedbed, grazing marsh, scrape and estuary.
Key birds: *Spring/summer:* Marsh Harrier, Bittern, Bearded Tit, Hobby, Lapwing, Snipe, Avocet, Black-tailed and Bar-tailed Godwits, Reed and Sedge warblers. *Passage:* Wood and Green Sandpipers. *Winter:* Large flocks of waders on estuary, inc Golden and Grey Plovers, Bar and Black-tailed Godwits, Avocet and Dunlin.
Other notable flora/fauna: Otters and water voles frequently seen. Four-spot chaser and hairy dragonfly, occasional Norfolk hawker. Brown argus butterfly colony close to car park.
Contact: Suffolk WT; T: 01502 478 788;
E: info@suffolkwildlifetrust.org

7. LACKFORD LAKES NATURE RESERVE

Suffolk Wildlife Trust.
Location: Sat nav: IP28 6HX. TL 803 708. Via track off N side of A1101 (Bury St Edmunds to Mildenhall road), between Lackford and Flempton. Five miles from Bury.
Access: Reserve and hides open dawn-dusk daily. Visitor centre open Tues-Sun, 10am-5pm (open Mon school and bank holidays).
Facilities: Visitor centre with viewing area upstairs, coffee shop, toilets. Visitor centre, Kingfisher Trail and four hides good for wheelchair access. Eight hides. Coaches should pre-book.
Public transport: Bus to Lackford village (Bury St Edmunds to Mildenhall service) - walk from church.
Habitats: Restored gravel pit with open water, lagoons, islands, willow scrub, reedbeds.
Key birds: *Winter:* Bittern, Water Rail, Bearded Tit. Large gull roost (20,000+). Wide range of waders and wildfowl (inc. Goosander, Pochard, Tufted Duck, Shoveler). *Spring/autumn:* Migrants, inc. raptors. Breeding Shelduck, Little Ringed Plover and reedbed warblers. Nightingale, Turtle Dove, Hobby in summer and Osprey on passage.
Other notable flora/fauna: Otter. 17 spp. of dragonflies inc. hairy and emperor. Early marsh and southern orchid.
Contact: Lackford Lakes Visitor Centre,
T: 01284 728 706; E: info@suffolkwildlifetrust.org

8. LAKENHEATH FEN

RSPB (Eastern England Office).
Location: Sat nav: IP27 9AD. TL 722 864. W of Thetford, straddling the Norfolk/Suffolk border. From A11, head N on B1112 to Lakenheath and then two miles further. Entrance is 200 yards after level crossing.

Access: Reserve open daily dawn-dusk. Visitor centre and toilets open 9am-5pm daily (closed Dec 25-26, limited opening 24 Dec & 27 Dec-2 Jan). Group bookings welcome. Visitor centre accessible to wheelchair users and a few points on the reserve. Car park fee for non-RSPB members. Dogs restricted to public footpaths.Coaches must book.
Facilities: Visitor centre, toilets (inc. disabled). Four nature trails of varied terrain, but most OK for wheelchairs. Viewpoints. Picnic area with tables. Events programme.
Public transport: On-demand Brecks Bus (Mon to Fri) reaches the reserve from Brandon and Thetford. To book, Brecks Bus T: 01638 664 304 by noon the weekday before travel. Weekend-only trains on Norwich-Ely service stop in Lakenheath.
Habitats: Reedbed, riverside pools, poplar woods.
Key birds: Principally a site for nesting migrants but ducks and some wild swans in winter. *Spring/summer:* Bittern, Marsh Harrier, Turtle Dove, limited numbers of Golden Oriole, Hobby (up to 40), Grasshopper, Reed and Sedge Warblers. *Autumn:* Harriers, Bearded Tit. *Winter:* Ducks, swans, Common Crane, Peregrine, Barn Owl, Kingfisher.
Other notable flora/fauna: More than 15 spp. of dragonflies and damselflies, inc. hairy dragonfly and scarce chaser. Range of fenland plants inc. water violet, common meadow rue and fen ragwort. Roe deer, otter and water vole.
Contact: RSPB, T: 01842 863 400;
E: lakenheath@rspb.org.uk

9. LANDGUARD BIRD OBSERVATORY

Landguard Conservation Trust.
Location: Sat nav: IP11 3TW. TM 283 317. On Landguard peninsula, off View Point Road S of Felixstowe town centre. Housed in wartime emplacements alongside Languard Fort.
Access: Visiting by appointment, e-mail well in advance to check a volunteer will be available.
Facilities: Migration watch point and ringing station.
Public transport: Buses and trains to Felixstowe centre (1.5 miles away).
Habitats: Adjoining Local Nature Reserve, composed of close grazed turf, raised banks with holm oak, tamarisk, etc.
Key birds: Unusual species and common migrants, esp. in spring and autumn. Mediterranean Gull regular on beach. In summer and autumn check for seabird and wildfowl movements offshore.
Other notable flora/fauna: 18 spp. of dragonflies and 29 spp. of butterflies have been recorded on the site. Several small mammal spp. plus sightings of cetaceans and seals off-shore. Nationally rare stinking goosefoot.
Contact: Landguard Bird Observatory, View Point Road, Felixstowe, IP11 3TW. T: 01394 673 782;
E: enquiries@lbo.org.uk (general enquiries)
E: landguardbo@yahoo.co.uk (to arrange a visit);
W: www.lbo.org.uk

10. MINSMERE

RSPB (Eastern England Office).
Location: Sat nav: IP17 3BY. TM 473 672. Six miles NE of Saxmundham. From A12 at Yoxford or Blythburgh. Follow brown tourist signs via Westleton village. Car park is two miles from village.
Access: Car park and hides open dawn-dusk daily, except Dec 25/26. Visitor centre/shop open 9am-5pm (9am-4pm Nov-Jan). Cafe open 9.30am-4.45pm (Feb-Oct) /10am-3.30pm (Nov-Jan). Entry fee to visit the reserve (adults/under-19s), RSPB members free. Free entry to visitor centre.
Facilities: Car park, hides, toilets (inc. disabled and nappy changing), visitor centre with RSPB shop and cafe. Volunteer guides. Guided walks and family events (see website for details). Coaches by appointment only.
Public transport: Train to Saxmundham or Darsham (five miles) then Suffolk Coastlink bus (book in advance, T: 01728 833 526.
Habitats: Coastal lagoons, 'the scrape', freshwater reedbed, grazing marsh, vegetated dunes, heathland, arable reversion and woodland.
Key birds: *All year:* Marsh Harrier, Bearded Tit, Bittern, Cetti's and Dartford Warblers, Little Egret, Green and Great Spotted Woodpeckers. *Summer:* Breeding Hobby, Avocet, Lapwing, Redshank, Common, Sandwich and Little Terns, Mediterranean Gull, Sand Martin, warblers, Nightingale, Nightjar, Woodlark, Stone Curlew (sometimes visible). *Winter:* Wildfowl inc. White-fronted Goose, Bewick's Swan, Smew, Hen Harrier (scarce), Water Pipit, Siskin. *Autumn/spring:* Passage waders inc. Black-tailed Godwit, Spotted Redshank, Ruff. Regular Wryneck, Red-backed Shrike, Yellow-browed Warbler.
Other notable flora/fauna: Red and muntjac deer, otter, water vole, badger. Dragonflies inc. emperor, Norfolk hawker and small red-eyed damselfly. 27 spp. of butterflies inc. purple and green hairstreaks and brown argus. Adder. Antlion. Marsh mallow, southern marsh orchid.
Contact: RSPB, T: 01728 648 281;
E: minsmere@rspb.org.uk

11. NORTH WARREN

RSPB (Eastern England Office).
Location: Sat nav: IP15 5BH. TM 467 576. Directly N of Aldeburgh on Suffolk coast. Take A1094 to Aldebugh then follow Thorpe Road towards Thorpeness. Use signposted main car park on beach.
Access: Open at all times. Pay-and-display car park on Thorpe Road. Dogs only allowed on public footpaths/bridleways. Beach area suitable for disabled.
Facilities: Three nature trails, leaflet available from Minsmere RSPB. Toilets in Aldeburgh and Thorpeness. Three spaces for coaches at Thorpeness beach car park.
Public transport: Bus service to Aldeburgh. First Eastern Counties (T: 08456 020 121). Nearest train station is Saxmundham (six miles away).
Habitats: Grazing marsh, lowland heath, reedbed, woodland.

Key birds: *Winter:* White-fronted Goose, Tundra Bean Goose, Wigeon, Shoveler, Teal, Gadwall, Pintail, Snow Bunting. *Spring/summer:* Breeding Bittern, Marsh Harrier, Hobby, Nightjar, Woodlark, Nightingale, Dartford Warbler.
Other notable flora/fauna: Hairy dragonfly, Norfolk hawker and red-eyed damselfly, green and purple hairstreak butterflies and southern marsh orchid.
Contact: RSPB, T: 01728 648 281;
E: minsmere@rspb.org.uk

12. REDGRAVE & LOPHAM FENS

Suffolk Wildlife Trust.
Location: Sat nav: IP22 2HX. TM 052 803. Five miles from Diss, signposted and easily accessed from A1066 and A143.
Access: Reserve open all year (10am-5pm summer, 10am-4pm winter). Dogs on short leads. Visitor centre is fully accessible. Five waymarked circular trails (wheelchair-accessible gates on 'spider' trail). Trails can be muddy after heavy rain (not wheelchair accessible).
Facilities: Education centre with café, gift shop and light refreshments, toilets, inc. disabled, car park with coach space. Bike parking area, boardwalk and viewing platform/short boardwalk.
Public transport: Buses and trains to Diss - Coaches to local villages of Redgrave and South Lopham from Diss. Simonds Coaches T: 01379 647 300 and Galloway Coaches T: 01449 766 323.
Habitats: Calcareous fen with open water areas, wet acid heath, river corridor, scrub and woodland.
Key birds: *All year:* Water Rail, Snipe, Teal, Shelduck, Gadwall, Woodcock, Sparrowhawk, Kestrel, Great Spotted and Green Woodpeckers, Tawny, Little and Barn Owls, Kingfisher, Reed Bunting, Bearded Tit, Willow and Marsh Tits, Linnet. *Summer:* Hobby, Blackcap, Chiffchaff, Willow, Reed, Sedge and Grasshopper Warblers, Spotted Flycatcher, Whitethroat, Hobby plus large Swallow and Starling roosts. *Winter/ occcasionals on passage:* Marsh Harrier, Greenshank, Green Sandpiper, Shoveler, Pintail, Garganey, Jack Snipe, Bittern, Little Ringed Plover, Oystercatcher, Wheatear, Stonechat and Whinchat.
Other notable flora/fauna: Otter, water vole, roe, muntjac and Chinese water deer, stoat, pipistrelle and Natterer's bats. Great crested newt, grass snake, adder, slow worm, common lizard. More than 300 spp. flowering plants. 27 spp. of butterflies inc. purple and green hairstreaks and brown argus. More than 20 spp. of dragonfly inc. emperor, hairy dragonfly, black-tailed skimmer and scarce emerald damselfly. Fen raft spider population on site.
Contact: Suffolk WT, T: 01379 687 618;
E: info@suffolkwildlifetrust.org

Northern England

Cheshire & Wirral, Cumbria, Durham, Lancashire & North Merseyside, Manchester (Greater), Northumberland, Yorkshire (East Riding), Yorkshire (North), Yorkshire (South & West)

Cheshire

FROM THE FELLS and forests bordering the Peak District to the wader-rich coastal sites along the Dee and Mersey estuaries, Cheshire has much to interest birdwatchers, while the Wildlife Trust's 40-plus reserves cover a broad range of habitats of value to flora and fauna.

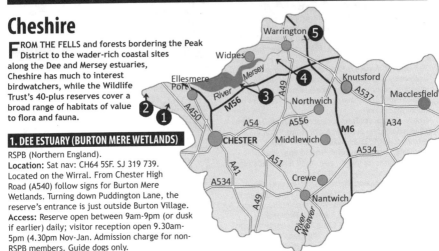

1. DEE ESTUARY (BURTON MERE WETLANDS)

RSPB (Northern England).

Location: Sat nav: CH64 5SF. SJ 319 739. Located on the Wirral. From Chester High Road (A540) follow signs for Burton Mere Wetlands. Turning down Puddington Lane, the reserve's entrance is just outside Burton Village.

Access: Reserve open between 9am-9pm (or dusk if earlier) daily; visitor reception open 9.30am-5pm (4.30pm Nov-Jan. Admission charge for non-RSPB members. Guide dogs only.

Facilities: Reception centre and cafe. Large car park, not suitable for coaches (groups should ring for advice). Two major hides (one in reception building) overlooking pools and wetland area, plus viewing screens. Wheelchair access to footpaths and hides. Toilets inc. disabled facilities. Picnic tables. Guided walks and binocular hire available.

Public transport: Nearest bus stop at Ness Botanic Gardens, 1.5 miles from reserve. Traveline, T: 0871 200 2233.

Habitats: Former farm and fishery now converted to wetland and meadow habitats.

Key birds: *All year:* Little Egret. Great Spotted and Green Woodpecker. *Spring/summer:* Avocet, Grasshopper Warbler, Lesser Whitethroat and other commoner warblers, passage Black-tailed Godwit, Spotted Redshank and regular Mediterranean Gull. Hobby, Marsh Harrier, Spoonbill. *Autumn:* Passage waders (inc. Little Stint, Ruff, Spotted Redshank, Green, Curlew and Wood Sandpipers). *Winter:* Linnet, Brambling, Fieldfare, Redwing, Whooper and Bewick's Swans, Teal, Water Rail, Hen Harrier.

Other notable flora/fauna: Extensive butterfly list. Pipistrelle, noctule, Daubenton's bats, water vole, wide array of orchids. Red-eyed damselfly.

Contact: RSPB, T: 0151 353 8478; E: deeestuary@rspb.org.uk

& Wirral

NORTH-WESTERLY GALES in autumn bring Leach's Petrels to the tip of the Wirral peninsula, probably the best place in Britain to see them away from their breeding sites.

2. DEE ESTUARY (PARKGATE)

RSPB (Northern England).
Location: Sat nav: CH64 6RL. SJ 273 789. On W side of Wirral, S of Birkenhead. View high tide activity from Old Baths car park near Boathouse pub, Parkgate, off B5135.
Access: Open at all times. Viewing from public footpaths and car parks. Don't walk on saltmarsh - the tides are dangerous and nesting birds should not be disturbed. Dogs allowed only on footpaths.
Facilities: Shared car park (closes at 5pm in winter and 8pm in summer), picnic area, group bookings, guided walks, special events, wheelchair access. Toilets at Parkgate village opposite the Square.
Public transport: Bus to Parkgate every hour. Rail station at Neston, two miles from reserve.
Habitats: Estuary, saltmarsh, pools, mud, sand.
Key birds: *Spring/summer/autumn:* Little Egret, Greenshank, Spotted Redshank, Curlew Sandpiper, Skylark, Reed Bunting. *Winter:* Pink-footed Goose, Shelduck, Teal, Wigeon, Pintail, Grey Plover, Black-tailed Godwit, Curlew, Redshank, Merlin, Peregrine, Water Rail, Short-eared Owl, Hen Harrier.
Other notable flora/fauna: On very high tides, the incoming water displaces several mammal spp. inc. pygmy shrew, water shrew, harvest mouse, weasel and stoat.
Contact: RSPB, T: 0151 336 7681;
E: deeestuary@rspb.org.uk

3. FRODSHAM MARSH

Manchester Ship Canal Company.
Location: Sat nav: WA6 7BN. SJ 512 779 (Marsh Lane), SJ 520 785 (Weaver Bend/Ship Street). Large area of mixed habitat lying alongside Manchester Ship Canal, SW of Runcorn. Follow Marsh Lane from Frodsham town centre under M56 motorway until it becomes a dirt track. Follow for three miles to small concrete bridge crossing Hoole Pool Gutter.
Access: Open at all times. Park just before concrete bridge and walk along grassy track to barrier gates and then towards vantage points overlooking Rivers Mersey and Weaver. Wheelchair access difficult.
Facilities: None.
Public transport: None.
Habitats: Saltmarsh, mudflats, embanked tanks to hold river dredgings, reedbeds, farmland and river.
Key birds: More than 20 spp. of wader recorded, inc. large flocks of Black-tailed Godwit, Dunlin and Redshank. *Winter:* Wildfowl, inc. Whooper Swan, Pinkfeet, Shelduck, Pochard, Pintail, Wigeon and other common species, Raven, Short-eared Owl, Hen Harrier, Peregrine. Passage migrants inc. wagtails, pipits, terns, Garganey, Wheatear and Whinchat. *Summer:* Breeding Oystercatcher, Ringed and Little Ringed Plovers, Grasshopper, Sedge and Reed Warblers. Hobbies hunt in autumn.
Contact: None.

4. MOORE NATURE RESERVE

FCC Environment.
Location: Sat nav: WA4 6XE. SJ 577 854. SW of Warrington, via A56 Warrington-to-Chester road. At traffic lights at Higher Walton, follow signs for Moore. Take Moore Lane over swing bridge to reserve.
Access: Open all year. One hide suitable for wheelchairs, other parts of site unsurfaced or gravel paths.
Facilities: Car park, coaches by prior arrangement. Paths, ten bird hides, bird feeding area. Guided walks available on request. See website for wildlife events throughout the year.
Public transport: Nos. 62 & 66 buses from Warrington and Runcorn stop in Moore village, less than 0.75 mile from reserve. T: 0870 608 2608 for times.
Habitats: Almost 200 acres of wetland, woodland, grasslands, five pools.
Key birds: More than 130 spp. every year, inc. occasional rarities. *Spring/summer:* Breeding wildfowl and waders, warblers. *Autumn/winter:* Wide variety of wildfowl, Bittern. Also good for gulls, woodpeckers, owls (all five UK spp. recorded) and raptors. See website for list and latest sightings.
Other notable flora/fauna: Wildfowers inc. some rarities. Great crested newt.
Contact: Moore Nature Reserve, T: 01925 444 689;
W: www.fccenvironment.co.uk/moorenaturereserve

5. WOOLSTON EYES

Woolston Eyes Conservation Group.
Location: SJ 654 888. E of Warrington between the River Mersey and Manchester Ship Canal. Off Manchester Road down Weir Lane or from Latchford to end of Thelwall Lane. Do not park at the bottom end of Weir Lane.
Access: Open all year. Permits required - contact via website for details.
Facilities: Toilets located at No.3 bed.
Public transport: Buses along A57 nearest stop to Weir Lane, or Thelwell Lane, Latchford. The bus to Weir Lane, Martinscroft (to access reserve from the N) is no.3 from Central Station, Warrington. To access reserve from S take either no.1 or no.2 bus to Westy, Whitley Avenue and walk to the East end of Thelwall Lane. For further info W: www.networkwarrington.co.uk
Habitats: Wetland, marsh, scrubland, wildflower meadow areas.
Key birds: Breeding Black-necked Grebe, warblers (inc. Grasshopper Warbler), all raptors (Merlin, Peregrine, Marsh Harrier). SSSI for wintering wildfowl, many duck spp. breed.
Other notable flora/fauna: 19 mammal spp. recorded, plus 241 spp. of lepidoptera, four spp. of bat. Wide variety of butterflies and 22 spp. of dragonflies. Notable plants inc. marsh and bee orchids, helleborine, snakeshead fritillary and cowslip.
Contact: E: via website; W: www.woolstoneyes.com

Wirral

1. DEE ESTUARY

Metropolitan Borough of Wirral.
Location: Sat nav: CH60 9JS. SJ 255 815. Leave A540 Chester to Hoylake road at Heswall and head downhill (one mile) to the free car park at the shore end of Banks Road. Heswall is 30 mins from South Liverpool and Chester by car.
Access: Open at all times. Best viewpoint 600 yards along shore N of Banks Road. No disabled access along shore, but good birdwatching from bottom of Banks Road. Arrive 2.5 hours before high tide. Coach parking available.
Facilities: Information board. No toilets in car park. Sheldrakes Restaurant, at the end of Banks Road, has an outside terrace overlooking the foreshore. Wirral Country Park Visitor Centre open 10am-4.45pm), except Dec 25, located three miles N, off A540, has toilets, hide, cafe, kiosk (all accessible to wheelchairs).
Public transport: Bus service to Banks Road car park from Heswall bus station, or bus to Irby village, then walk one mile. Mersey Travel, T: 0151 236 7676.
Habitats: Saltmarsh and mudflats.
Key birds: *Autumn/winter:* Large passage and winter wader roosts - Redshank, Curlew, Black-tailed Godwit, Oystercatcher, Golden Plover, Knot, Shelduck, Teal, Red-breasted Merganser, Peregrine, Merlin, Hen Harrier, Short-eared Owl. Smaller numbers of Pintail, Wigeon, Bar-tailed Godwit, Greenshank, Spotted Redshank, Grey and Ringed Plovers, Whimbrel, Curlew Sandpiper, Little Stint, occasional Scaup and Little Egret.
Contact: Wirral Country Park Visitor Centre, Station Road, Thurstaston, Wirral CH61 0HN. T: 0151 648 4371; E: wcp@wirral.gov.uk

2. HILBRE ISLAND LNR

Metropolitan Borough of Wirral.
Location: Sat nav: CH48 0QA (Dee Lane, West Kirby). SJ 184 880. Three tidal islands in the mouth of the Dee Estuary. Park in West Kirby on A540 Chester-to-Hoylake road, 30 mins from Liverpool, 45 mins from Chester. Follow the brown Marine Lake signs to Dee Lane pay & display car park or free parking along the promenade. Coach parking available at West Kirby.
Access: Two mile walk across sands from Dee Lane slipway - DO NOT cross either way within 3.5 hours of high water - tide times and suggested safe route on noticeboard at slipway. No disabled access. Permit required for groups of six and above (apply to Wirral Country Park Visitor Centre).
Facilities: Hilbre Bird Observatory by prior appointment only. Composting toilets on the main island (Hilbre) and at Wirral Sailing Centre (end of Dee Lane, West Kirby). Leaflets and tide times from Thurstaston Visitor Centre.
Public transport: Bus and train station (from Liverpool) within 0.5 mile of Dee Lane slipway. Contact Mersey Travel, T: 0151 236 7676.
Habitats: Sandflats, rocky shore and open sea.

Key birds: *Late summer/autumn:* Seabird passage inc. Gannets, terns, skuas, shearwaters and after NW gales good numbers of Leach's Petrel. *Winter:* Wader roosts at high tide, Purple Sandpiper, Turnstone, sea ducks, divers, grebes. Passage migrants.
Other notable flora/fauna: Nationally scarce rock sea-lavender and sea spleenwort. Field vole, grey seal. Whales and dolphins seen offshore.
Contact: Wirral Country Park Visitor Centre, Station Road, Thustaston, Wirral CH61 0HN. T: 0151 648 4371; E: wcp@wirral.gov.uk
Hilbre Island Bird Obs, Chris Williams (Chair & Ringer in Charge), E: chris@islandelec.com; W: http://hilbrebirdobs.blogspot.co.uk

3. NORTH WIRRAL COASTAL PARK

Metropolitan Borough of Wirral.
Location: Sat nav: CH46 4TA. SJ 241 909. Located between the outer Dee and Mersey Estuaries. From Moreton take A553 E. then A551 N. Turn L onto Tarran Way South then R onto Lingham Lane. Parking available by lighthouse. Foreshore can be viewed from footpath which runs alongside.
Access: Open at all times.
Facilities: Visitor centre, eight car parks, three toilet blocks (one summer only), extensive footpath network and public bridleways, four picnic areas.
Public transport: The area being served by Grove Road (Wallasey), Leasowe, Moreton, and Meols Merseyrail Stations, and with bus routes along Leasowe Road, Pasture Road and Harrison Drive.
Habitats: Saltmarsh.
Key birds: Important as a feeding and roosting site for passage and wintering flocks of waders, wildfowl, terns and gulls. Wintering populations of Knot (20,000+), Bar-tailed Godwit (2,000+) and Dunlin (10,000). Redshank (1,000+) and Turnstone (500+) feed on the rocky shore at Perch Rock and on the rocky sea walls. Oystercatcher (500+), Curlew, Grey Plover and Black-tailed Godwit also regularly roost here in relatively high numbers. Small populations of wildfowl, inc. Common Scoter, Scaup and Goldeneye, Red-throated Divers and Great Crested Grebes also frequently winter on this site.
Other notable flora/fauna: Sea holly, marram grass, storksbill, burnet rose and rarities like the Isle of Man cabbage can be found. One of two known sites in the world for the very rare British sub-species of the belted beauty moth.
Contact: Wirral Country Park Visitor Centre, Station Road, Thustaston, Wirral CH61 0HN. T: 0151 648 4371; E: wcp@wirral.gov.uk

Cumbria

SITES ALONG THE SOLWAY coast tend to hog the limelight when it comes to bird sightings, but the Lake District can still offer a typical range of upland birds and an Osprey watchpoint at Lake Bassenthwaite. In all, the county's Wildlife Trust manages 44 reserves, of which 38 are open to visitors.

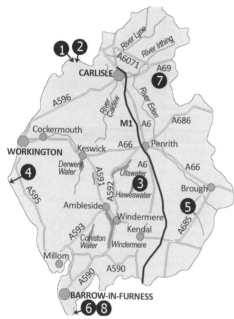

Spring/summer: Breeding Lapwing, Curlew, Redshank, Snipe, Tree Sparrow and warblers. *Spring and autumn*: Passage waders such as Black-tailed Godwit, Whimbrel. Look for Pomarine, Arctic, Great and Long-tailed Skuas over the Solway. *Autumn/winter*: Up to 10,000 Oystercatchers among large roosting wader flocks. Hen Harrier.
Other notable flora/fauna: Roe deer, brown hare. Bog rosemary, bog asphodel, sundews and cotton grass. Large numbers of dragonflies (inc. azure and emerald damselflies and four-spotted chaser).
Contact: RSPB, T: 01697 351 330;
E: campfield.marsh@rspb.org.uk

2. DRUMBURGH MOSS NNR

Cumbria Wildlife Trust.
Location: Sat nav: CA7 5DW. NY 255 586. From Carlisle city centre, head W on B5307 to Kirkbride. After about one mile, turn R to Burgh by Sands. Follow road for 7.5 miles to Drumburgh village. Turn L by post box, continue down track and park on right past Moss Cottage.
Access: Open all year. Difficult terrain, so it is best to walk on paths or waymarked routes.
Facilities: None.
Public transport: Bus service between Carlisle and Bowness-on-Solway stops in Drumburgh.
Habitats: One of four raised bogs south of Solway (rated the best in England), woodland, wet heath, grassland.
Key birds: *Summer*: Curlew, Redshank and Grasshopper Warbler all breed. *Winter*: Geese from the Solway, plus Short-eared Owl.
Other notable flora/fauna: Large heath butterfly, emperor moth, adder and lizards, roe deer, brown hare. Specialist plants inc. 13 spp. of sphagnum moss, sundews, cotton grass and bog rosemary.
Contact: Cumbria WT, 01228 829 570;
E: mail@cumbriawildlifetrust.org.uk

3. HAWESWATER

RSPB (Northern England)/United Utilities.
Location: Sat nav: CA10 2QT (Haweswater car park). NY 469 108. For the old eagle viewpoint, go to Bampton village, 10 miles S of Penrith and five miles NW of Shap. From Bampton, head S towards Haweswater reservoir. Drive down unclassified road alongside Haweswater reservoir, the road ends at a car park. You'll need to walk from here.
Access: The vast majority of the site is open access.
Facilities: Since the last Golden Eagle disappeared from the site there is no longer a manned viewpoint.
Habitats: Fells with rocky streams, steep oak and birch woodlands.
Key birds: *Upland breeders*: Peregrine, Raven, Ring Ouzel, Curlew, Redshank, Snipe. *Woodlands*: Pied Flycatcher, Wood Warbler, Tree Pipit, Redstart, Buzzard, Sparrowhawk. Breeding Goosander and Dipper around the lake. Large gull roost in winter.
Other notable flora/fauna: Red deer, red squirrel.
Contact: RSPB, T: 01931 713 376;
E: haweswater@rspb.org.uk

1. CAMPFIELD MARSH

RSPB (Northern England).
Location: Sat nav: CA7 5AG. NY 197 615. At North Plain Farm, on S shore of Solway estuary, W of Bowness-on-Solway. Signposted on unclassified coast road from B5307 from Carlisle.
Access: Open at all times, no charge. Car park at North Plain Farm. Disabled visitors can drive to wheelchair-friendly hide to view high-tide roosts. Grassed paths can be muddy.
Facilities: Small visitor centre at North Plain (open 10am-4pm). One hide overlooking wetland areas, four viewing screens along nature trail (three miles). Three lay-bys over wader roosts on saltmarsh.
Public transport: Bus no. 93 from Carlisle terminates at reserve's eastern end - 1.5 miles walk to North Plain Farm.
Habitats: Saltmarsh/intertidal areas, open water, peat bog, wet grassland.
Key birds: *Winter*: Waders and wildfowl inc. Barnacle and Pinkfooted Geese, Shoveler, Scaup, Grey Plover.

NATURE RESERVES - NORTHERN ENGLAND

4. ST BEES HEAD

RSPB (Northern England).
Location: Sat nav: CA27 0ET. NX 959 118. S of Whitehaven via the B3545 road to St Bees village. Car park at end of Beach Road.
Access: Open at all times, no charge. Access via coast-to-coast footpath. The walk to the viewpoints is long and steep in parts. Dogs only on public footpaths.
Facilities: Copeland Borough Council pay-and-display car park, toilets next to reserve. Three viewpoints overlooking seabird colony, three mile cliff-top path.
Public transport: Nearest trains at St Bees (0.5 mile). No bus services.
Habitats: Three miles of sandstone cliffs up to 300 feet high.
Key birds: *Summer:* Largest seabird colony on W coast of England: Guillemot, Razorbill, Puffin, Kittiwake, Fulmar and England's only breeding pairs of Black Guillemot (around Fleswick Bay). Linnet, Stonechat, Whitethroat and Rock Pipit in cliff-top heath areas.
Contact: RSPB, T: 01697 351 330;
E: stbees.head@rspb.org.uk

5. SMARDALE GILL NNR

Cumbria Wildlife Trust.
Location: Sat nav: CA17 4HG. NY 727 070. NNR occupies a 3.75 miles stretch of the disused railway between Tebay and Darlington. Approx 2.5 miles NE of Ravenstonedale on A685 or 0.5 mile S of Kirkby Stephen station. Take turning signed to Smardale. Cross over railway and turn L to junction, ignoring turn to Waitby. Cross over railway and turn L at junction ignoring sign for Smardale. Cross disused railway, turn L immediately and L again to car park.
Access: Railway line is open to all, non-members should obtain a permit before visiting other parts of the reserve.
Facilities: None.
Public transport: Train: nearest station Kirkby Stephen. Buses from here to Kendal, Brough and Sedburgh.
Habitats: Limestone grassland, river, ancient semi-natural woodland, quarry.
Key birds: *Summer:* Redstart, Pied Flycatcher and commoner woodland species. *All year:* Usual woodland birds, Buzzard, Sparrowhawk, Raven, Green Woodpecker and Dipper.
Other notable flora/fauna: Scotch argus, northern brown argus, common blue and dark green fritillary butterflies. Fragrant orchid, common rockrose, bluebell and bloody cranesbill. Red squirrel.
Contact: Cumbria WT, 01539 816 300;
E: mail@cumbriawildlifetrust.org.uk

6. SOUTH WALNEY

Cumbria Wildlife Trust.
Location: Sat nav: LA14 3YQ. SD 225 620. Six miles S of Barrow-in-Furness. From Barrow, cross Jubilee Bridge onto Walney Island, turn L at lights. Continue through Biggar village to South End Caravan Park. Follow road for one mile to reserve.
Access: Open daily (10am-5pm, 4pm in winter). No dogs except assistance dogs. Day permits required, adult/child rates. Cumbria Wildlife Trust members free.
Facilities: Toilets, nature trails, eight hides (two are wheelchair accessible), 200 yard boardwalk. Electric wheelchair for hire. Coach parking available.
Public transport: Bus service as far as Biggar.
Habitats: Shingle, lagoon, sand dune, saltmarsh.
Key birds: *Spring/autumn:* Passage migrants inc. Wheatear, Redstart, Goldcrest and Willow Warbler. *Summer:* 14,000 breeding pairs of Herring, Greater and Lesser Black-backed Gulls, Shelduck, Eider. *Winter:* Teal, Wigeon, Goldeneye, Redshank, Greenshank, Curlew, Oystercatcher, Knot, Dunlin, Merlin, Short-eared Owl, Twite.
Other notable flora/fauna: 450 spp. of flowering plants. Natterjack toad at North Walney.
Contact: Cumbria WT, T: 01229 471 066;
E: mail@cumbriawildlifetrust.org.uk

7. TALKIN TARN COUNTRY PARK

Carlisle City Council
Location: Sat nav: CA3 8QW. NY 544 591. Twelve miles E of Carlisle. From A69 E at Brampton, head S on B6413 for two miles. Talkin Tarn is on E just after level crossing.
Access: All year. Wheelchair access around tarn, Tearoom has lift. Coaches welcome.
Facilities: Carpark (charges). Tearoom open 10.30am-4pm daily from easter to Oct half term and Sat/Sun + school holidays from end Oct half-term to easter. Dogs allowed on outdoor balcony. Toilet facilities. Angling by day permit (with closed season). Watersport activities have made it harder to see water birds.
Public transport: Bus: infrequent, T: 0870 608 2608. Train: nearest station is Brampton Junction, T: 0845 748 4950. One mile away by footpath.
Habitats: Natural glacial tarn, mature oak/beech woodland, orchid meadow (traditionally managed), wet mire and farmland.
Key birds: *Spring/summer:* Spotted Flycatcher, Redstart, Chiffchaff, Wood Warbler. *Winter:* Grebes, Smew, Long-tailed Duck, Goosander, Gadwall, Wigeon, Brambling, swans.
Other notable flora/fauna: Common blue damselfly, common darter, small copper butterfly, otter, red squirrel.
Contact: Talkin Tarn Country Park, Tarn Road, Brampton, Cumbria, CA8 1HN; T: 01228 817 200;
E: talkintarn@carlisle.gov.uk
W: www.carlisle.gov.uk/talkintarn/

8. WALNEY BIRD OBSERVATORY

Location: Sat nav: LA14 3YQ. Walney Island, S of Barrow-in-Furness.
Access: Several areas, notably the golf course/ airfield, are restricted but the island's narrow width means most sites are viewable from the road or footpaths.
Facilities: Monitoring and ringing of breeding and migrant, with ringing opportunities for qualified visitors. For availability contact Walney Bird Obs.

Public transport: Barrow-in-Furness connects to the rail network and local bus routes serve Walney Island. Nos. 1 & 1A cover the central area while nos. 6 & 6A cover the north end of the island. No bus route to southern end.
Habitats: Estuarine, maritime, dunes, freshwater and brackish pools, scrub and farmland.
Key birds: Renowned Eider and gull colonies at south end. The winter months provide a wildfowl and wader spectacular across the island. Migrants aplenty appear during both passage periods – the island has a proven pedigree for attracting rare and unusual species.

Other notable flora/fauna: Famed for Walney geranium, but also important for coastal shingle species such as sea holly, sea rocket and sea kale. More than 500 spp. of moth recorded, inc. sand dune specialities such as coast dart and sand dart.
Contact: Walney Bird Observatory, Coastguard Cottages, Walney Island, Barrow-in-Furness, Cumbria LA14 3YQ.
E: walneyobs@gmail.com;
W: http://walneybo.blogspot.co.uk

Durham

WHILE COASTAL SITES such as Hartlepool Headland pull in rarities and regular migrants, there are many rewards in the unspoiled inland areas too.

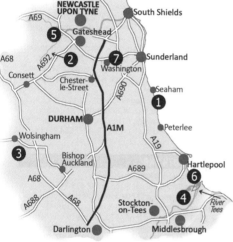

Habitats: Extensive area of semi-natural habitat situated on magnesian limestone escarpment. Steep-sided ravine woodland and limestone grassland.
Key birds: *Summer:* Skylark (important conservation site), Twite, Linnet, Yellowhammer, Goldfinch, Whitethroat, Blackcap, Wren, Long-tailed Tit, Grasshopper Warbler, Reed Bunting, Green Woodpecker, Kestrel, Sparrowhawk. *Winter:* Wide variety of waders inc. Turnstone, Purple Sandpiper, Redshank, Curlew, Oystercatcher. Seabirds inc. Red-throated Diver, Common Scoter, Guillemot, Cormorant and Great Crested Grebe. *Passage:* Wheatear, Fieldfare, Redwing, Waxwing, Buzzard, Ringed Plover, Dunlin, Knot, Lapwing.
Other notable flora/fauna: Good variety of butterflies. Snowdrops, bluebells and numerous spp. of orchid, inc. early purple, bird's nest, lesser butterfly and bee. Roe deer, badger and brown hare.
Contact: Durham WT, T: 0191 584 3112;
E: mail@durhamwt.co.uk

2. DERWENT WALK COUNTRY PARK & DERWENTHAUGH PARK

Gateshead Council.
Location: Sat nav: NE39 1AU (Thornley Woodlands Centre). NZ 178 604. Along River Derwent, four miles SW of Newcastle and Gateshead. Several car parks along A694. Derwent Walk follows old railtrack bed for 11 miles from Swalwell to Consett.
Access: Site open all times. Thornley visitor centre near Rowlands Gill open Mon-Fri (10am-3pm), weekends (10pm-4pm). Keys for hides from Thornley Woodlands Centre. Swalwell visitor centre open 10am-3pm, Mon-Fri only. Both centres are closed on bank holidays and between Christmas and New Year. Derwent Walk and Derwenthaugh Parks both accessible to wheelchairs from Swalwell centre. Shopmobility scooters can be hired here.
Facilities: Toilets at Thornley and Swalwell visitor centres. Hides at Far Pasture Ponds and Thornley feeding station.
Public transport: Bus nos. 45, 46, 46A, 47/47A/47B from Newcastle/Gateshead to Swalwell/Rowlands Gill. Bus stop Thornley Woodlands Centre. (Regular bus service from Newcastle). Details - Nexus Travel Information, T: 0191 203 3333; W: www.nexus.org.uk
Habitats: Mixed woodland, river, ponds, meadows.

1. BEACON HILL & HAWTHORN DENE MEADOW

Durham Wildlife Trust/National Trust.
Location: Sat nav: SR7 8SH. NZ 424 459. Hawthorn Dene and Meadow located between Easington and Seaham on Durham coast. Leave A19 at Easington or Seaham and join B1432 to Hawthorn village. From N end of village, follow minor road E, signposted 'Quarry Traffic'. After 0.25 mile, road ends at two metal gates. Park on grass verge on opposite side to cottage. Access is by foot taking the right-hand path. Access to Beacon Hill (NZ 440 455) is along Coastal Footpath or through southern end of Hawthorn Dene.
Access: Open all year, dogs on leads in spring.
Facilities: Information point. Footpaths.
Public transport: Regular bus services from Durham to Hawthorn.

Key birds: *Summer:* Red Kite, Grasshopper Warbler, Lesser Whitethroat, Kingfisher, Dipper, Great Spotted and Green Woodpeckers, Blackcap, Garden Warbler, Nuthatch. *Winter:* Teal, Tufted Duck, Brambling, Marsh Tit, Bullfinch, Siskin, Great Spotted Woodpecker, Nuthatch, Goosander, Kingfisher.
Other notable flora/fauna: Otter, roe deer, badger, woodland flowers.
Contact: Thornley Woodlands Centre, T: 01207 545 212; Swalwelll Visitor Centre, T: 0191 414 2106
E: countryside@gateshead.gov.uk

3. HAMSTERLEY FOREST

Forestry Commission.
Location: Sat nav: DL13 5NL (Forest Drive car park). NZ 091 312. Ten miles W of Bishop Auckland. Main entrance is five miles from A68, S of Witton-le-Wear and signposted through Hamsterley village and Bedburn.
Access: Open all year. Daily toll charge (higher on bank holiday weekends). Forest drive and car park open 8am-8pm (5pm in winter). Information point open daily (9am-5pm, 4pm Nov-Feb) and cafe open Apr-Oct (10am-5pm) and weekends Nov & Jan-Mar (11am-4pm). Visitors should not enter fenced farmland.
Facilities: Visitor centre, tea-room, toilets, shop, access for disabled. Cycles for hire.
Public transport: None.
Habitats: Commercial woodland, mixed and broadleaved trees.
Key birds: *Spring/summer:* Willow Warbler, Chiffchaff, Wood Warbler, Redstart, Pied Flycatcher. *Winter:* Crossbill, Redwing, Fieldfare. *All year:* Jay, Dipper, Green Woodpecker.
Other notable flora/fauna: Hay meadows have wide variety of plants inc. globe flower.
Contact: Forestry Commission, T: 01388 488 312; E: enquiries.hamsterley@forestry.gsi.gov.uk

4. SALTHOLME

RSPB (Northern England).
Location: Sat nav: TS2 1TU. NZ 506 231. N of River Tees between Middlesbrough and Billingham. From A19, take A689 north of Stockton and then A1185. After four miles join A178 at mini roundabout. Take third exit and reserve is 250 yards on right.
Access: Open daily, except Dec 25. Car Park charge for non-members. RSPB members, users of public transport and cyclists free. Opening hours: Apr-Oct (9.30am-5pm), Nov-Mar (9.30am-4pm). Dogs only allowed in small exercise area.
Facilities: Award-winning visitor centre with tea-room (open 9.30am-4pm daily) and shop, large car park, inc.Blue Badge spaces and coach parking. Toilets (inc. disabled), picnic area. Bound gravel surfaces to four nature trails - wheelchair users may need assistance to reach the three bird hides. Walled garden designed by TV gardener Chris Beardshaw.
Public transport: Stagecoach no. 1 from Hartlepool stops outside reserve.
Habitats: Wet grasslands, reedbeds, pools with tern islands, wader scrapes.

Key birds: *All year:* Lapwing, Peregrine, Water Rail. *Spring/summer:* Breeding Great Crested Grebe, common wildfowl, hirundines, Snipe, Skylark, Yellow Wagtail, large colony of Common Terns. *Autumn:* Varied waders inc. Black-tailed Godwits and Green Sandpipers, occasional rarer species. *Winter:* Large numbers of wildfowl and waders, inc. impressive flocks of Golden Plover and Lapwing.
Contact: RSPB, T: 01642 546 625;
E: saltholme@rspb.org.uk

5. SHIBDON POND

Durham Wildlife Trust/Gateshead Council.
Location: Sat nav: NE21 5LU. NZ 192 628. E of Blaydon, S of Scotswood Bridge, close to A1. Car park at Blaydon swimming baths. Open access from B6317 (Shibdon Road).
Access: Open at all times. Disabled access to hide.
Facilities: Hide in SW corner of pond.
Public transport: At least six buses per hour from Newcastle/Gateshead to Blaydon (bus stop Shibdon Road). Nexus Travel Line, T: 0191 232 5325.
Habitats: Pond, marsh, scrub and damp grassland.
Key birds: *Winter:* Large numbers of wildfowl, Water Rail, occasional white-winged gulls. *Summer:* Reed Warbler, Sedge Warbler, Lesser Whitethroat, Grasshopper Warbler, Water Rail. Roosts of terns and Cormorants. *Autumn:* Passage waders and wildfowl, Kingfisher.
Other notable flora/fauna: 17 spp. of butterfly, inc. dingy skipper. Nine spp. of dragonflies inc. ruddy darter, migrant hawker. Otter, great crested newt.
Contact: Contact: Durham WT, T: 0191 584 3112; E: mail@durhamwt.co.uk

6. TEESMOUTH NNR

Natural England (North East Team).
Location: Two areas, centred on NZ 535 276 and NZ 530 260, three and five miles S of Hartlepool, E of A178. Access to northern area from car park at NZ 533 282, 0.5 mile E of A178. Access to southern area from A178 bridge over Greatham Creek at NZ 509 254. Car park adjacent to A178 at NZ 508 251. Both car parks can accommodate coaches.
Access: Open at all times. In northern area, no restrictions over most of dunes and North Gare Sands (avoid golf course, dogs must be kept under close control). In southern area, easy-access path to public hides at NZ 516 255 and NZ 516 252 (no other access).
Facilities: Nearest toilets at Seaton Carew, one mile to the N and RSPB Saltholme (one mile to S). Easy-access path and hides, interpretive panels and leaflet. Teesmouth Field Centre, T: 01429 853 847.
Public transport: Half-hourly bus service, no. 1 operates Mon-Sat between Middlesbrough and Hartlepool (hourly on Sun), along A178, Stagecoach Hartlepool, T: 01429 267 082. Seaton Carew train station is 1.25 miles from North Gare car park.
Habitats: Grazing marsh, dunes, intertidal flats.

Key birds: Passage and winter wildfowl and waders. Passage terns and skuas in late summer. Scarce passerine migrants and rarities. *Spring/summer:* Breeding Ringed Plover, Lapwing, Oysterctacher, Redshank and Snipe. *Winter:* Internationally important numbers of waterbirds, inc. waders and Shelduck. Merlin, Peregrine, Snow Bunting, Twite, divers, grebes.
Other notable flora/fauna: Northern area has large marsh orchid populations in damp dune grassland. Colony of 100 common seals at Seal Sands (pups born in late-Jun).
Contact: Natural England,
T: 01429 853 325 or 07803 228 394;
E: northumbria.hub@naturalengland.org.uk

7. WASHINGTON

The Wildfowl & Wetlands Trust.
Location: Sat nav: NE38 8QU. NZ 329 560. On N bank of River Wear, four miles E of A1(M), sign-posted from A195, A19, A182 and A1231.

Access: Open all year, except Dec 25, 9.30am-5.30pm (Apr-Oct), 9.30am-4.30pm (Nov-Mar) - last admission one hour before closing. Admission charge for non-members, free to WWT members.Guide dogs only. Good disabled access.
Facilities: Visitor centre, toilets, parent and baby room, range of hides. Shop and cafe (open 10am).
Public transport: Buses from Sunderland, Newcastle, Durham and South Shields to Waterview Park (short walk to centre).
Habitats: Wetlands, woodland and meadows.
Key birds: *Spring/summer:* Nesting colony of Grey Heron, other breeders inc. Common Tern, Avocet, Oystercatcher, Lapwing. *Winter:* Bird-feeding station visited by Great Spotted Woodpecker, Bullfinch, Jay and Sparrowhawk. Goldeneye and other ducks.
Other notable flora/fauna: Wildflower meadows hold cuckoo flower, bee orchid and yellow rattle. Dragonfly and amphibian ponds.
Contact: Washington Wetland Centre,
T: 0191 416 5454; info.washington@wwt.org.uk

Lancashire

THE COUNTY'S MOSSES attract huge numbers of wintering Pink-footed Geese, Bewick's and Whooper Swans, while tens of thousands of waders winter in Morecambe Bay. A series of estuaries are attractive to wildfowl and waders and Seaforth Docks has a good reputation for rare gulls. Inland, Pendle Hill attracts regular Dotterel on spring passage.

& North Merseyside

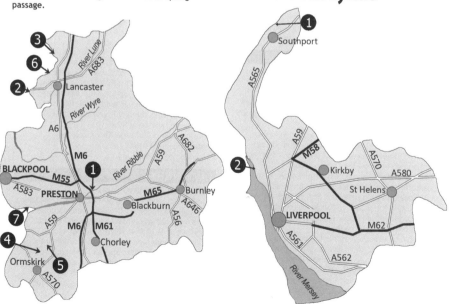

NATURE RESERVES - NORTHERN ENGLAND

1. BROCKHOLES

Wildlife Trust for Lancashire, Manchester & N. Merseyside
Location: Sat nav: PR5 0AG. SD 589 309. Site in Preston New Road, Samlesbury, opened in 2011, is adjacent to Junc 31 of M6. From S take A59 towards Blackburn and then first exit, signposted to reserve, and follow under the southbound slip road north of River Ribble.
Access: Open daily (Apr-Oct, 6am-9pm and Nov-Mar 6am-7pm). Most paths are surfaced and wheelchair-friendly - a refundable deposit required for keys to access gates bypassing kissing gates. Car park charges, but free coach parking. Guided tours need to be booked. No dogs.
Facilities: Floating World is a cluster of buildings made from sustainable materials and housing a village store and gift shop, restaurant, and adapted toilets - open daily, except Dec 25/26, 10am-5pm (Apr-Oct), Tues-Sun 4pm for rest of year. Bird hides.
Public transport: Buses - Stagecoach no.59 or Transdev Lancashire United nos. X80/280 between Preston-Blackburn-Accrington, stop at Tickled Trout Motel by M6.
Habitats: Created from disused gravel pits, the site alongside the River Ribble now features open water, reedbeds, wet grassland and woodland.
Key birds: *Spring/summer:* Breeding Great Crested Grebe, Lapwing, Redshank, Reed and Sedge Warblers, Reed Bunting, Skylark. *Winter:* Good for wildfowl, inc. Pochard, Pintail, Goldeneye and Teal. Passage waders inc. Turnstone, Grey Plover, Greenshank, Whimbrel, Curlew, Wood, Green and Curlew Sandpipers and Black-tailed Godwit.
Other notable flora/fauna: Brown hawker and emperor dragonflies.
Contact: WT for Lancashire, Manchester & N. Merseyside; T: 01772 872 000; E: info@brockholes.org

2. HEYSHAM NR & BIRD OBSERVATORY

Wildlife Trust for Lancashire, Manchester & N. Merseyside /EDF Energy Estates.
Location: Sat nav: LA3 2UP (Duke of Rothesay pub). SD 407 601 W of Lancaster. Take A683 to Heysham port. Turn L at traffic lights by Duke of Rothesay pub, then first R after 300 yards.
Access: Gate to reserve car park open 9am-6pm (dusk in winter). Pedestrian access at all times. Limited disabled access. Dogs barred on main reserve but an extensive off-lead area nearby.
Facilities: Map giving access details at the reserve car park. No manned visitor centre or toilet access, but someone usually in reserve office, next to the main car park, in the morning. Check out the observatory's blogpot for virtually daily updates, plus detailed map at the bottom of the page.
http://heyshamobservatory.blogspot.co.uk/
Public transport: Train services connect with nearby Isle of Man ferry terminal. Plenty of buses to Lancaster from various Heysham sites within walking distance (ask for nearest stop to the harbour).
Habitats: Varied: wetland, acid grassland, alkaline grassland, foreshore.
Key birds: Passerine migrants in the correct conditions. Good passage of seabirds in spring, especially Arctic Tern. Storm Petrel and Leach's Petrel during strong onshore (SW-WNW) winds in mid-summer and autumn respectively. Good variety of breeding birds (inc. eight spp. of warbler on the reserve itself). Two-three scarce land-birds each year, most frequent being Yellow-browed Warbler.
Other notable flora/fauna: Notable area for dragonflies: red-veined darter has bred for several years at nearby Middleton Community Woodland main pond SD 418 592 (mid-Jun to mid-Jul). Bee orchid.
Contact: WT for Lancashire, Manchester & N. Merseyside; Reserve Warden, Heysham Nature Reserve, T: 07979 652 138; E: rneville@lancswt.org.uk

3. LEIGHTON MOSS

RSPB (Northern England).
Location: Sat nav: LA5 0SW. SD 478 750. Four miles NW of Carnforth, Lancs. Leave M6 at Junc 35. Take the A6 N towards Kendal and follow brown signs for Leighton Moss off A6.
Access: Reserve open daily dawn-dusk. Visitor centre and cafe open 9.30am-5pm (4.30pm Dec-Jan, except Dec 25). Free for RSPB members or those arriving by public transport or bike. Entry fee for non-RSPB members (adult, concession, child rates). Dogs restricted to Causeway public footpath.
Facilities: Visitor centre, shop, cafe, toilets, disabled toilet. Nature trails and seven hides (four have wheelchair access), plus two hides at saltmarsh pools. Stairlift to cafe for those with mobility issues. Binoculars for hire.
Public transport: Silverdale train station (on Manchester Airport to Barrow line) is 250 yards from reserve. **Habitats:** Reedbed, shallow meres and woodland. Saltmarsh pools approx one mile.
Key birds: *All year:* Bittern, Bearded Tit, Water Rail, Shoveler, Gadwall, Marsh Tit, Little Egret. *Summer:* Breeding Marsh Harrier, Reed and Sedge Warbler. Avocet at saltmarsh pools. *Passage:* Good numbers of Black-tailed Godwits in spring with Greenshank, Ruff and godwits in autumn. *Winter:* Large flocks of Starlings roosting, hunting Peregrine and Merlin terrorise overwintering wildfowl.
Other notable flora/fauna: Otter, red deer.
Contact: RSPB, T: 01524 701 601; E: leighton.moss@rspb.org.uk

4. MARTIN MERE

The Wildfowl & Wetlands Trust.
Location: Sat nav: L40 0TA. SD 428 145. Off Fish Lane, Burscough, six miles N of Ormskirk via Burscough Bridge (A59). 20 miles from Liverpool and Preston.
Access: Open 9.30am-4.30pm (Nov-Mar, closed Dec 25); 9.30am-6pm (Apr-Oct) - last admission one hour before closing time. Special dawn and evening events. Guide dogs only. Admission charge for non-WWT members. Special rates for coach parties. Fully accessible to disabled, all hides suitable for wheelchairs. Coach park available.

Facilities: Visitor centre, toilets, gift shop, cafe, education centre, play area, nature reserve/nature trails, hides, waterfowl collection, sustainable garden.
Public transport: Train to Burscough Bridge or New Lane Stations (both 1.5 miles from reserve).
Habitats: Open water, wet grassland, moss, copses, reedbed, parkland.
Key birds: *Winter*: Whooper and Bewick's Swans, Pink-footed Goose, various ducks, Ruff, Black-tailed Godwit, Peregrine, Hen Harrier, Tree Sparrow. *Spring*: Ruff, Shelduck, Little Ringed and Ringed Plovers, Lapwing, Redshank. *Summer*: Marsh Harrier, Garganey, hirundines, Tree Sparrow. Breeding Avocet, Lapwing, Redshank, Shelduck. *Autumn*: Pink-footed Goose, waders on passage.
Other notable flora/fauna: Whorled caraway, golden dock, tubular dropwort, 300 spp. of moth.
Contact: WWT Martin Mere Wetland Centre, T: 01704 895 181; E: info.martinmere@wwt.org.uk

5. MERE SANDS WOOD

Wildlife Trust for Lancashire, Manchester & N. Merseyside
Location: Sat nav: L40 1TL. SD 447 157. 12 miles by road from Southport, 0.5 mile off A59 Preston to Liverpool road, in Rufford along B5246 (Holmeswood Road).
Access: Public footpaths open at all times. Car park open 9am-8pm summer, 9am-5pm winter (charge for non-members). Three miles of wheelchair-accessible footpaths. All hides accessible to wheelchairs.
Facilities: Visitor centre with toilets (inc. disabled), open Tues-Sun and bank-hol Mons, 9.30am-4.30pm, six viewing hides, three trails, exhibition room, latest sightings board. Feeding stations. Guided walks for bird/wildlife groups can be arranged. Booking essential for two motorised buggies.
Public transport: Bus: Southport-Chorley no. 347 and Preston-Ormskirk no. 2B stop in Rufford, 0.5 mile walk. Train: Preston-Ormskirk train stops at Rufford station, one mile walk.
Habitats: 40 ha inc. freshwater lakes, mixed woodland, sandy grassland/heath.
Key birds: 170 spp. recorded, with 60 known to have bred. *Winter*: Regionally important for Teal and Gadwall, good range of waterfowl inc. Mandarin and Goosander, Kingfisher. Feeding stations attract Tree Sparrow, Bullfinch, Reed Bunting, Water Rail. *Woodland*: Lesser Spotted Woodpecker, Willow Tit, Treecreeper, Nuthatch. *Summer*: Kingfisher. *Passage*: Most years, Osprey, Crossbill, Green Sandpiper, Greenshank.
Other notable flora/fauna: 18 spp. of dragonflies recorded annually, broad bucker fern, 200+ spp. of fungi.
Contact: WT for Lancashire, Manchester & N. Merseyside; Reserve Manager, Mere Sands Wood NR, T: 01704 821 809; E: lbeaton@lancswt.org.uk

6. MORECAMBE BAY (HEST BANK)

RSPB (Northern England).
Location: Sat nav: LA2 6HN. SD 467 666. Two miles N of Morecambe at Hest Bank. Access car park from Hest Bank level crossing off A5105.
Access: Open at all times. Do not go onto saltmarsh or intertidal area: dangerous channels and quicksands. Paths from car park too rough for wheelchairs. Dogs allowed.

Facilities: Viewpoint and toilets at local council car park. Guided walks programme.
Public transport: No. 5 bus runs between Carnforth and Morecambe. T: 0870 608 2608. Nearest rail station is Morecambe (three miles from reserve).
Habitats: Saltmarsh, estuary.
Key birds: 250,000 waders and wildfowl spend winter on Britain's second-most important estuary site. *Winter*: Wildfowl (Pintail, Shelduck, Wigeon) and waders. This is an important high tide roost for Oystercatcher, Curlew, Redshank, Dunlin and Bar-tailed Godwit.
Contact: RSPB, T: 01524 701 601; E: leighton.moss@rspb.org.uk

7. RIBBLE ESTUARY

Natural England (Greater Manchester, Merseyside & Cheshire Team).
Location: SD 380 240. Lies approx 4.5 miles W of Preston, stretching on both sides of River Ribble as far as Lytham and Crossens. Take A584 and minor roads for north bank and A59 and minor roads for the southern side.
Access: Public footpaths open at all times, but no access to saltmarsh itself.
Facilities: No formal visiting facilities. Ribble Discovery Centre is at Fairhaven Lake (3.2 miles of Lytham). RSPB Marshside, adjacent to NNR, has hides, parking and information boards.
Public transport: For bus service information - W: www.stagecoachbus.com
Habitats: Ramsar and SPA designation for one of England's largest areas of saltmarsh, and mudflats.
Key birds: High water wader roosts of Knot, Dunlin, Black-tailed Godwit, Oystercatcher and Grey Plover are best viewed from Southport, Marshside, Lytham and St Annes. Pink-footed Geese and wintering swans are present in large numbers from Oct-Feb on Banks Marsh and along River Douglas respectively. Banks Marsh can be viewed from the public footpath which runs along the sea defence embankment from Crossens Pumping Station to Hundred End. The large flocks of Wigeon, for which the site is renowned, can be seen on high tides from Marshside but feed on saltmarsh areas at night. Good numbers of raptors also present in winter.
Contact: Natural England, T: 01704 578 774; E: dave.mercer@naturalengland.org.uk

North Merseyside

1. MARSHSIDE

RSPB (Northern England).
Location: Sat nav: PR9 9PJ. SD 353 205. From Southport, follow minor coast road Marine Drive N (1.5 miles from Southport Pier) to small car park by sand works.
Access: Open all year 8.30am-5pm (dusk in winter). Guide dogs only. Coach parties please book in advance. No charges, donations welcomed. Park in Sefton Council car park along Marine Drive.
Facilities: Visitor centre, toilets (inc. disabled), two hides (one heated) and trails accessible to wheelchairs. Two viewing screens and a viewing platform.

Public transport: Bus service to Elswick Road/ Marshside Road half-hourly, bus no. 44, from Lord Street. Traveline, T: 0870 608 2608.
Habitats: Coastal grazing marsh and lagoons.
Key birds: *Winter:* Pink-footed Goose, wildfowl, waders, raptors inc. Peregrine, Merlin, Sparrowhawk and Kestrel. *Spring:* Breeding waders, inc. Avocet and wildfowl, Garganey, migrants. *Autumn:* Migrants. *All year:* Black-tailed Godwit.
Other notable flora/fauna: Hares, various plants inc. marsh orchid, migrant hawker dragonfly.
Contact: RSPB, T: 01704 211 690.

2. SEAFORTH NATURE RESERVE

Wildlife Trust for Lancs, Manchester and N Merseyside.
Location: Sat nav: L21 1JD. SJ 318 971. Five miles from Liverpool city centre. From M57/M58 take A5036 to docks. Enter via Liverpool Freeport entrance in Crosby Road South.
Access: Open at all times. Permit required - Trust members can apply for permits from the Trust but must pick them up in person from Port Police (visitor pass and vehicle pass required). Organised groups must contact reserve office (see below) at least seven days in advance of their planned trip. Coaches welcome.

Facilities: Toilets at visitor centre when open, three hides.
Public transport: Train to Waterloo or Seaforth stations from Liverpool. Buses to dock gates from Liverpool.
Habitats: Saltwater and freshwater lagoons, scrub grassland and small reedbed.
Key birds: Major roosting site for waders and Seabirds. Noted for Little Gull on passage (Apr), plus Roseate, Little and Black Terns. Breeding and passage: Common Tern (Apr-Sep). Passage and winter: waders and gulls – 15 spp. of gulls recorded, with Ring-billed annual and Mediterranean seen almost daily. Passage passerines, especially White Wagtail, pipits and Wheatear, plus a sprinkling of vagrants.
Contact: Seaforth Nature Reserve, T: 0151 920 3769; E: seaforth@lancswt.org.uk

Manchester (Greater)

FOR A LARGELY urban area, there are good places for birdwatching. Pennington Flash is the area's best all-round birding site, while Peregrines and Black Redstarts breed in the city centre and urban regeneration has cleaned up the water to such an extent that increasing numbers of ducks are wintering in Salford Docks. Etherow CP holds Dipper, Grey Wagtail, Pied Flycatcher and all three woodpeckers.

1. BROAD EES DOLE (SALE WATER PARK)

Mersey Valley Countryside Warden Service
Location: Sat nav: M32 9UP. SJ 799 933. Local Nature Reserve located close to visitor centre in Sale Water Park, Trafford. Access from Junc 6 of M60, following signs for Trafford Water Sports Centre.
Access: No paths within the reserve, so view from perimeter paths. Sale Water Park visitor centre car park off Rifle Road. Walk to reserve by following track behind visitor centre.
Facilities: Small concrete bird hide overlooks site.
Habitats: Wetland site with water levels managed to provide feeding and breeding opportunities for a variety of birds such as herons, Kingfisher, Little Ringed Plover and Lapwing.
Key birds: Important site for migratory species and waders inc. Snipe and Jack Snipe. Winter wildfowl inc. Mallard, Gadwall, Teal, Coot, Moorhen in LNR, wider variety on main lake of Water Park.
Other notable flora/fauna: Spotted orchid, smooth and great crested newts. Variety of fish on main lake in Sale Water Park.
Contact: MVCWS, T: 0161 881 5639; E: info@merseyvalley.org.uk;

2. ETHEROW COUNTRY PARK

Stockport Metropolitan Borough Council.
Location: Sat nav: SK6 5JD. SJ 965 908. Site lies at the halfway point on the 12-mile Valley Way Footpath which links Stockport and Woolley Bridge. Situated at Compstall on B6104 near Romiley, Stockport.

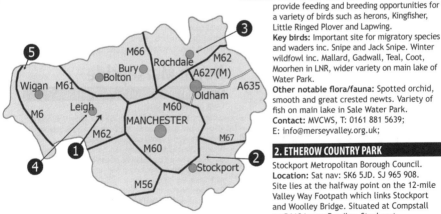

Access: Park land open at all times; permit required for conservation area. Keep to paths.
Facilities: Reserve area has SSSI status. One bird hide, nature trail, visitor centre (11am-4pm, when possible), cafe and toilets, scooters for disabled. Check opening times for facilities prior to arrival, T: 0161 427 6937. Good parking but charges are in operation.
Public transport: There is a good bus service from Stockport, one route coming through Romiley and one coming through Marple - bus nos. 383 & 384. Nearest train stations are at Romiley and Marple Bridge.
Habitats: River Etherow, woodlands, marshy area, ponds and surrounding moorland.
Key birds: More than 100 spp. recorded, inc. Sparrowhawk, Buzzard, Dipper, all three woodpeckers, Pied Flycatcher, warblers. *Winter*: Brambling, Siskin, Water Rail. Frequent sightings of Merlin and Raven over hills.
Other notable flora/fauna: 200 spp. of plant.
Contact: Etherow Country Park Visitor Centre, T: 0161 427 6937

3. HOLLINGWORTH LAKE

Hollingworth Lake/Rochdale MBC.
Location: Sat nav: OL15 0AQ. SD 939 153 (visitor centre). On outskirts of Littleborough, four miles NE of Rochdale, signposted from A58 Halifax Road and Junc 21 of M62 (B6225 to Littleborough).
Access: Open access to lake and surroundings.
Facilities: Cafes, hide, trails and education service, car parks, coach park by prior arrangement. Free wheelchair hire, disabled toilets and baby changing facilities, fishing. Visitor centre open 10am-3pm, Fri to Tues. Toilets and cafe open at 9.30am.
Public transport: Bus nos. 452, 455 & 456 Train to Littleborough or Smithy Bridge.
Habitats: Lake (116 acres, inc. 20 acre nature reserve), woodland, streams, marsh, willow scrub.
Key birds: *All year*: Great Crested Grebe, Kingfisher, Lapwing, Little Owl, Bullfinch, Cormorant. Occasional Peregrine, Sedge Warbler, Water Rail, Snipe. *Spring/ autumn*: Passage waders, wildfowl, Kittiwake. *Summer*: Reed Bunting, Dipper, Common Sandpiper, Curlew, Oystercatcher, Black Tern, 'Commic' Tern, Grey Partridge, Blackcap. *Winter*: Goosander, Goldeneye, Siskin, Redpoll, Golden Plover.
Contact: Hollingworth Lake Country Park and Visitor Centre, T: 01706 373 421

4. PENNINGTON FLASH COUNTRY PARK

Wigan Leisure and Culture Trust.
Location: Sat nav: WN7 3PA. SJ 640 990. One mile from Leigh town centre and well signposted from A580 East Lancashire Road. Main entrance on A572 (St Helens Road).
Access: Park is permanently open. Five largest hides, toilets and information point open 9am-dusk (except Dec 25). Main paths flat and suitable for disabled. Main car park pay & display with coach parking available if booked in advance.

Facilities: Toilets (inc. disabled) and information point. Total of eight bird hides. Site leaflet available and Rangers based on site. Group visits welcome but please book in advance.
Public transport: Only one mile from Leigh bus station. Several services stop on St Helens Road near entrance to park. T: 01942 883 501 for more details.
Habitats: Lowland lake, ponds and scrapes, fringed with reeds, rough grassland and young woodland.
Key birds: Waterfowl all year, waders (14+ spp.) and terns (4+ spp.) mainly on passage in both spring and autumn. Breeding birds inc. nine spp. of warbler. Feeding station attracts Willow Tit, Stock Dove and up to 40 Bullfinches all year. Large gull roost in winter. More than 240 spp. recorded, inc. seven county firsts in the last decade alone.
Other notable flora/fauna: Several spp. of orchid, inc. bee orchid. Wide variety of butterflies and dragonflies.
Contact: Pennington Flash Country Park, T: 01942 605 253

5. WIGAN FLASHES

Wildlife Trust for Lancs, Manchester and N Merseyside/ Wigan Council.
Location: Sat nav: WN3 5NY (Hawkley Hall school). SD 585 030. Leave M6 at J25 head N on A49, turn R on to Poolstock Lane (B5238). There are several entrances to the site; at end of Carr Lane near Hawkley Hall School; one off Poolstock Lane; two on Warrington Road (A573). Also accessible from banks of Leeds and Liverpool Canal.
Access: Free access, open at all times. Areas suitable for wheelchairs. Paths (6.25 miles in total) being upgraded. Access for coaches: contact reserve manager for details.
Facilities: Six hide screens. Poolstock Lane car park has 300 spaces.
Public transport: Diamond Bus North West, no.610 bus (Hawkley Hall Circular).
Habitats: Open water (eight flashes) with reedbed, wet woodland and rough grassland.
Key birds: More than 200 spp. recorded. Black Tern on migration. *Summer*: Nationally important for Reed Warbler and breeding Common Tern. Willow Tit, Cetti's and Grasshopper Warblers, Kingfisher. *Winter*: Wildfowl, especially diving duck and Gadwall. Bittern (esp.winter).
Other notable flora/fauna: Interesting orchids, with the six spp. inc. marsh and dune helleborine. One of the UK's largest feeding assemblage of noctule bats. Water vole. Eighteen spp. of dragonflies which has inc. red-veined darter.
Contact: WT for Lancashire, Manchester & N. Merseyside; T: 01942 233 976; E: mchampion@lancswt.org.uk

Northumberland

THIS IS A STUNNING county, with a fantastic range of habitats. The seabird colonies on the Farne Islands are world famous, while Holy Island (Lindisfarne) attracts a range of migrants in spring and autumn, plus huge numbers of wintering birds. Kielder Forest is good for Crossbills and raptors, including Goshawk. The nearby moors hold a good selection of upland species.

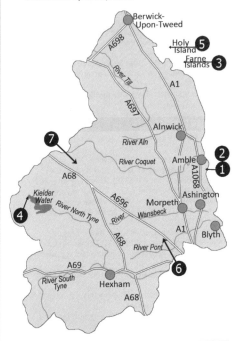

1. DRURIDGE POOLS & CRESSWELL POND

Northumberland Wildlife Trust.
Location: Two sites lying on coast between Newbiggin and Amble, off A1068. 1: Sat nav: NE61 5EG for Druridge Pools (NZ 275 963). Roadside parking next to NT's Druridge Links site. 2: Cresswell Pond (NZ 283 944). Park at bottom of track to Blakemoor Farm. 0.5 mile N of Cresswell.
Access: 1: Access along public footpath or short path to screen. 2: Access along short path from farm track. Wheelchair users can view northern part of Cresswell Pond from public footpath or roadside. Dogs on leads.
Facilities: 1: Three hides; 2: Hide.
Public transport: 1: Arriva no. X18 to Widdrington village (two miles). 2: Arriva no.1 to Cresswell village.
Habitats: 1: Deep lake and two wet meadows with pools behind dunes. 2: Shallow brackish lagoon behind dunes fringed by saltmarsh and reedbed, some mudflats.

Key birds: 1: Especially good in spring. Winter and breeding wildfowl (mostly Wigeon and Teal); passage and breeding waders. 2: Good for waders, esp. on passage. Most northly recorded breeding Avocets in 2011. Pinkfooted Geese in winter, plus wildfowl.
Other notable flora/fauna: The sheltered sunny banks are good for a range of butterflies and dragonflies in summer at Druridge Pools. Otters often seen by the lakes.
Contact: Northumberland WT, T: 0191 284 6884; E: mail@northwt.org.uk

2. EAST CHEVINGTON

Northumberland Wildlife Trust.
Location: Sat nav: NE61 5BX. NZ 270 990. Near Red Row, overlooking Druridge Bay, off A 1068 between Hauxley and Cresswell.
Access: Main access from overflow car park at Druridge Bay Country Park (signpost from main road).
Facilities: Four public hides, cafe and information at Country Park (County Council). ID boards for coastal plants.
Public transport: Arriva X18 to Red Row (one mile).
Habitats: Ponds and reedbeds created from former open cast coal mine. Areas of scrub and grassland.
Key birds: Large numbers of wildfowl, inc. Greylag and Pinkfooted Geese in winter. Breeding Skylark, Stonechat, Reed Bunting, plus Reed, Sedge and Grasshopper Warblers. Capable of attracting rarities at any time of year. Marsh Harriers bred in 2009 (first county record for 130 years).
Other notable flora/fauna: Coastal wildflowers and in grassland, dyer's greenweed.
Contact: Northumberland WT, T: 0191 284 6884; E: mail@northwt.org.uk

3. FARNE ISLANDS

The National Trust.
Location: Sat nav: NE68 7SS (Seahouses). NU 230 370. Access by boat from Seahouses Harbour, which is reached from A1.
Access: Apr, Aug-Oct: Inner Farne 10.30am-6pm and May-Jul: Staple Island 10.30am-1.30pm and Inner Farne: 1.30pm-5pm. Disabled access possible on Inner Farne, phone Property Manager for details. Four boat companies run boats from Seahouses. Dogs allowed on boats but not on islands. NT fees for visiting islands (free to members) DO NOT include boatmens' fees.
Facilities: Toilets on Inner Farne.
Public transport: Nearest rail stations at Alnmouth and Berwick. Hourly Travelsure buses between Budle and Beadnell Bays (Mon to Sat); T: 01665 720 955.
Habitats: Maritime islands - between 15-28 depending on height of tide.
Key birds: 23 breeding spp., 100,000 pairs of seabirds - four spp. of tern (inc. Roseate), Puffin, Razorbill, Guillemot, Kittiwake, Eider, Shag. Shearwaters, skuas offshore. Rarities often turn up - but usually difficult to see as a visitor.
Other notable flora/fauna: Large grey seal population, breed late-Oct to early Dec.
Contact: The Farne Islands, Seahouses, NE68 7SR. T: 01289 389 244; E: farneislands@nationaltrust.org.uk

4. KIELDER WATER & FOREST PARK

Forestry Commission.
Location: Sat nav: NE48 1ER (Kielder Castle).
NY 632 934. Kielder Castle is situated at N end of Kielder Water, NW of Bellingham, 30 miles from Hexham.
Access: Forest open all year. Toll charge for the 12-mile forest drive (rough surface). Forest drive is closed from Nov to end-Apr due to weather conditions and lack of mobile phone signal throughout. Car parking facilities at Kielder Castle and overflow behind the Angler's Arms pub - 24-hour parking ticket required. Ticket transferable for all car parks on south shore of Kielder Reservoir.
Facilities: Kielder Castle Information Centre, free exhibition, licensed Kielder Castle Cafe with live wildlife viewing screens, access for disabled and toilets inc. baby changing facilities. Kielder Cycle Centre and bike wash, post office/local shop, Angler's Arms pub, youth hostel, camp site, No 27 B&B and 24 hour (pay by card) garage. The one mile multi-access Duke's Trail inc. an arboretum and hide where red squirrels can usually be viewed. Nature reserve and dipping pond at Bakethin Nature Reserve. Many walking and mountain biking trails start from Kielder Castle, ask staff at the Information Centre for more info.
Public transport: Bus nos. 880 & 714: Check with local transport operators before travel - Snaith's Travel and Tyne Valley Coaches.
Habitats: Commercial woodland, coniferous and broadleaved trees.
Key birds: Successful Osprey breeding programme since 2009. *Spring/summer*: Goshawk, Raven, Chiffchaff, Willow Warbler, Redstart, Siskin. *Winter*: Crossbill, Siskin and winter thrushes. *Resident*: Jay, Nuthatch, Dipper, Great Spotted Woodpecker, Green Woodpecker, Tawny Owl, Song Thrush, Goldcrest.
Other notable flora/fauna: Impressive display of northern marsh orchids at entrance to Kielder Castle. Red squirrel, badger, otter, roe deer, seven bat spp.
Contact: Forestry Commission, T: 01434 250 209; E: kieldercastle@forestry.gsi.gov.uk
W: www.forestry.gov.uk/kielder

5. LINDISFARNE NATIONAL NATURE RESERVE

Natural England (North East Team).
Location: Sat nav: TD15 2SS. NU 090 430. Island access lies two miles E of A1 at Beal, signposted to Holy Island, 10 miles S of Berwick-on-Tweed.
Access: Causeway floods at high tide, so check when it is safe to cross. Some restricted access (bird refuges). Coach parking available on Holy Island.
Facilities: Toilets, visitor centre in village. Hide on island (new hide with disabled access at Fenham-le-Moor). Self-guided trail on island.
Public transport: Irregular bus service to Holy Island, mainly in summer. Main bus route follows mainland boundary of site north-south.
Habitats: Dunes, sand, mudflats and saltmarsh, rocky shore and open water.
Key birds: *Passage and winter*: Wildfowl and waders, inc. Pale-bellied Brent Goose, Long-tailed Duck and Whooper Swan. Rare migrants.

Other notable flora/fauna: Butterflies inc. dark green fritillary (Jul) and grayling (Aug). Guided walks advertised for nine spp. of orchid inc. coralroot and Lindisfarne helleborine.
Contact: Natural England, T: 01289 381 470.

6. PRESTWICK CARR

Northumberland Wildlife Trust.
Location: Sat nav: NE20 9UD (Prestwick). NZ 192 733. Seven miles NW of Newcastle city centre between Dinnington and Ponteland. Take A696 from A1 western bypass for three miles and take minor road to Prestwick hamlet. Park on minor roads north of Prestwick and Dinnington.
Access: Restricted to minor roads and a bridleway across the carr. No access to northern section when military firing range between Prestwick Mill Farm and Berwick Hill is in use.
Facilities: Viewing platform and interpretation.
Habitats: SSSI designation for section of lowland raised mire, woodland, farmland.
Public transport: Bus no. 45 runs between Newcastle Haymarket and Dinnington (0.75 mile walk to carr's eastern end).
Key birds: A noted raptor watchpoint: 2010's White-tailed Eagle became 14th bird of prey species recorded since 1990s. Hen Harriers are regular between Oct and Jan, along with Merlin and Peregrine. Barn, Little, Tawny and Long-eared Owls all nest and Short-eared Owls hunt in winter. Waders occur in large numbers at passage times if carr is flooded. Water Rail, Kingfisher, Stonechat, Whinchat and Willow Tit are resident with a good range of summer migrants, inc. Grasshopper Warbler.
Contact: Northumberland WT, T: 0191 284 6884; E: mail@northwt.org.uk

7. WHITELEE MOOR

Northumberland Wildlife Trust.
Location: Sat nav: TD8 6PT (Carter Bar). NT 700 040. Reserve located at head of Redesdale, S of A68 Newcastle to Jedburgh road where it crosses Scottish Border at Carter Bar.
Access: Park at tourist car park at Carter Bar and on lay-bys on forest track at reservoir end. A public footpath along old track to Whitelee Limeworks and then southwards extends to site's southern boundary and eastwards to link up with a bridleway from White Kielder Burn to Chattlehope Burn. Additional access on foot via Forestry road near eastern corner of reserve. Reserve is remote and wild, so hill-walking experience needed if attempting long walks.
Facilities: Car park and lay-bys.
Habitats: Active blanket bog and heather heath.
Key birds: The River Rede and its tributaries add to the habitat and bird diversity. Notable breeding birds inc. Merlin and Stonechat. Black Grouse, Skylark, Meadow Pipit, Dunlin, Curlew, Golden Plover, Grey Wagtail, Dipper and Ring Ouzel regularly visit the reserve.
Other notable flora/fauna: Otters often hunt along the Rede and a herd of feral goats may be seen.
Contact: Northumberland WT, T: 0191 284 6884; E: mail@northwt.org.uk

Yorkshire (East Riding)

COASTAL BIRDING DOMINATES here: Bempton Cliffs is probably the best seabird colony in England, with Puffins in front of your face and a Gannetry to boot. Two headlands — Flamborough Head and Spurn Point — attract migrants, including scarce vagrants, in autumn. Book a boat trip from Bridlington to see shearwaters and skuas in autumn.

1. BEMPTON CLIFFS

RSPB (Northern England).
Location: Sat nav: YO15 1JF. TA 197 738. Near Bridlington. Take Cliff Lane N from Bempton village off B1229 to car park and visitor centre.
Access: The Yorkshire Seabird Centre open year round (9.30am-5pm Mar-Oct, 9.30am-4pm Nov-Feb). Car parking fee for non-RSPB members - rates for cars, minibuses coaches). Cliff-top public footpath with two observation points accessible for wheelchair users. Dogs on leads.
Facilities: Visitor centre, toilets inc. disabled, light refreshments, five cliff-top observation points, picnic area, limited coach parking. Four miles of stunning chalk cliffs, highest in county. Short farmland footpath. Binoculars for hire.
Public transport: Bempton railway station (limited service) 1.5 miles — irregular bus service to village 1.25 miles from reserve.
Habitats: Seabird nesting cliffs, farmland, grassland, coastal scrub.
Key birds: Largest mainland seabird colony in UK; only Gannet colony in England. Birds present Jan to Oct with numbers peaking in excess of 200,000 between Apr and Jun inc. Kittiwake, Gannet, Puffin, Guillemot, Razorbill and Fulmar. Nesting Tree Sparrow and Corn Bunting.
Other notable flora/fauna: Harbour porpoise and grey seal regularly offshore. Bee and northern marsh orchids.
Contact: RSPB, T: 01262 422 212;
E: bempton.cliffs@rspb.org.uk

2. BLACKTOFT SANDS

RSPB (Northern England).
Location: Sat nav: DN14 8HL. SE 843 232. Eight miles E of Goole. Follow brown tourist signs on minor road between Ousefleet and Adlingfleet.
Access: Reserve open 9am-9pm or dusk if earlier daily (except Dec 25). Reception hide open daily 9am-5pm (Apr-Sept) and at weekends 10am-4pm (Oct-Mar). RSPB members free, permit required for non-members (adult, child, concessionary and family rates available). Guide dogs only.
Facilities: Car park, toilets, visitor centre, six hides with wheelchair spaces, one viewing screen, footpaths suitable for wheelchairs. Binoculars for hire.
Public transport: No. 360/361 bus from Goole stops at the reserve entrance (Busline T: 01482 592 929 or W: www.eyms.co.uk for details.
Habitats: Second largest tidal reedbed in UK, saline lagoons, lowland wet grassland, willow scrub.
Key birds: 270 species recorded. *Summer:* Breeding Avocet (up to 40 pairs), Tree Sparrows (ca. 30 pairs), Marsh Harrier, Bittern, Bearded Tit, passage waders (exceptional list inc. many rarities), up to 350 pairs of Reed Warblers, 250 pairs of Sedge Warblers. *Winter:* Hen Harrier, Merlin, Peregrine, wildfowl.
Other notable flora/fauna: Good place to see water vole. Small number of dragonflies and damselflies inc. black-tailed skimmer, four-spotted chaser, large red damselfly. Marsh sow thistle easily seen from footpaths in summer. Rare brown-veined wainscot moth.
Contact: RSPB, T: 01405 704 665;
E: blacktoft.sands@rspb.org.uk

3. FLAMBOROUGH CLIFFS

Yorkshire Wildlife Trust.
Location: Sat nav: YO15 1BJ. TA 239 720. The reserve is part of Flamborough headland, approx four miles NE of Bridlington. From Bridlington take B1255 to Flamborough and follow the signs for the North Landing.
Access: Open all year. Pay & display car park at North Landing gives access to both parts of the reserve. Paths not suitable for wheelchairs.
Facilities: Car park, trails, refreshments available at cafe at North Landing (open Apr-Oct, 10am-5pm), toilets.
Public transport: Flamborough is served by buses from Bridlington and Bempton. T: 01482 222 222 for details.
Habitats: Coastal cliffs, species-rich rough grassland and scrub, farmland. Spectacular views of this chalk coastline and living seas beyond.

144

Key birds: *Summer:* Nesting Puffin, Guillemot, Razorbill, Kittiwake, Shag, Fulmar, Skylark, Meadow Pipit, Linnet, Whitethroat, Yellowhammer, Tree Sparrow, occasional Corn Bunting. Thornwick reedbeds hold Reed and Sedge Warblers and Reed Buntings. *Passage migrants:* Fieldfare, Redwing and occasional rarities such as Wryneck and Red-backed Shrike. *Autumn:* Passage divers, grebes and seaduck.
Other notable flora/fauna: Pyramidal and northern marsh orchids, harebell, thrift on cliff tops. Migrant butterflies such as small skipper and painted lady.
Contact: Yorkshire WT, T: 01904 659 570; E: info@ywt.org.uk

4. HORNSEA MERE

Wassand Hall.
Location: Sat nav: HU18 1AX. Hornsea lies 12 miles E of Beverley on B1244. Enter town, onto Southgate then take signposted road to car park at Kirkholme Point.
Access: The Mere is owned by the nearby Wassand Hall estate, which opens to the public on selected days throughout the year. Mere footpath open all year during the day (see notices for closing times). View from footpath along southern edge. Dogs on leads.
Facilities: Cafe on site (limited winter opening), toilets.
Habitats: Yorkshire's largest body of freshwater, located 0.6 mile inland from the coast. Edged by reedbeds and woodland.
Key birds: Common wildfowl throughout the year, but in winter there is always the chance of divers, grebes, Long-tailed Duck, Goosander and Pintail. *Spring and autumn passage:* Marsh Harrier, Osprey, Little Gull, terns, White and Yellow Wagtails, Wheatear, plus rarer species.
Contact: Warden, T: 01964 532 251 or 07972 05841; W: www.wassand.co.uk
W: https://hornseamere.wordpress.com/

5. LOWER DERWENT VALLEY NNR

Natural England (Yorkshire Team)/ Yorkshire Wildlife Trust/Carstairs Countryside Trust.
Location: Sat nav: YO19 6FE (Bank Island). Six miles SE of York, stretching 12 miles S along River Derwent from Newton-on-Derwent to Wressle and along Pocklington Canal. Visitor facilities at Bank Island (SE 691 448), Wheldrake Ings YWT (SE 691 444 see separate entry - page 146), Thorganby (SE 692 418) and North Duffield Carrs (SE 697 367).
Access: Open all year. No dogs. Disabled access at North Duffield Carrs.
Facilities: Bank Island - two hides, viewing tower. Wheldrake Ings - four hides. Thorganby - viewing platform. North Duffield Carrs - two hides and wheelchair access. Car parks at all sites. Bicycle stands in car parks at Bank Island and North Duffield Carrs.
Public transport: Bus from York/Selby - contact First (T: 01904 622 992). Train station at Wressle.
Habitats: SPA and Ramsar site composed of flood and hay meadows, swamp, open water and alder/willow woodland.

Key birds: More than 80 spp. recorded in recent times. *Spring/summer:* Breeding wildfowl and waders, inc. Garganey, Snipe and Ruff, plus Corncrake and Spotted Crake. Barn Owl and warblers. *Winter/spring:* Bittern, 20,000-plus waterfowl inc. Whooper Swan, wild geese, Teal and Wigeon. Large gull roost, inc. white-winged gulls. Also passage waders, inc. Whimbrel.
Other notable flora/fauna: Pocklington Canal is particularly good for a wide range of aquatic plants and animals. Noctule, Daubenton's and pipistrelle bats regularly recorded. Water vole, pygmy shrew and brown hare.
Contact: Natural England, T: 07917 088 021; E: craig.ralston@naturalengland.org.uk

6. NORTH CAVE WETLANDS

Yorkshire Wildlife Trust.
Location: Sat nav: HU15 2LY. SE 886 328. NW of North Cave village, approx 10 miles W of Hull. From Junc 28 of M62, follow signs to North Cave on B1230. In village, turn L and follow road to next crossroads, then go L, then and park in Dryham Lane.
Access: Open all year with car parking on Dryham Lane. Part of circular footpath is suitable for all abilities. No dogs in reserve.
Facilities: Five bird-viewing hides inc. unique straw bale constructions, four are accessible to wheelchair users. Portaloo available on site and Wild Bird Cafe open each day on Dryham Lane, adjacent to reserve.
Public transport: Buses serve North Cave from Hull and Goole, T: 01482 222 222 for details.
Habitats: Former gravel pits have been converted into various lagoons for wetland birds, inc. one reedbed. There are scrub and hedgerows, and since 2010 a large area of wet grassland.
Key birds: More than 200 spp. recorded. Breeding birds inc. Great Crested Grebe, Gadwall, Pochard, Sparrowhawk, Avocet, Little Ringed and Ringed Plover, Oystercatcher, Sedge Warbler and Reed Bunting. Large numbers of Sand Martins feed over reserve in summer. Wintering wildfowl and waders inc. Golden Plover, Dunlin, Ruff and Redshank. Tree Sparrow.
Other notable flora/fauna: Water vole, dragonflies, several butterfly spp. inc. small colony of brown argus.
Contact: Yorkshire WT, T: 01904 659 570; E: info@ywt.org.uk

NATURE RESERVES - NORTHERN ENGLAND

7. SPURN NNR

Yorkshire Wildlife Trust.
Location: Sat nav HU12 0UH. Entrance Gate
TA 419 149. 26 miles from Hull. Take A1033 from Hull
to Patrington then B1445 from Patrington to Easington
and unclassified roads on to Kilnsea and Spurn Point.
Access: Normally open at all times. Vehicle admission
fee. No charge for pedestrians. No dogs allowed
under any circumstances, not even in cars. Coaches
by permit only (must be in advance).
Facilities: Reserve open all year. Blue Bell cafe open
10.30am-4pm daily. Spurn Discovery Centre under
construction, three hides. Public toilets in Blue Bell
car park.
Public transport: Nearest bus service is at Easington
(3.5 miles away). Sun service to the Point, hail and
ride, Easter to last weekend of Oct.
Habitats: Sand dunes with marram and sea buckthorn
scrub. Mudflats around Humber Estuary.
Key birds: *Spring:* Many migrants on passage
and often rare birds such as Red-backed Shrike,
Bluethroat etc. *Summer:* Little Terns feed offshore.
Autumn: Passage migrants and rarities such as
Wryneck, Pallas's Warbler. *Winter:* Large numbers of
waders, Shelduck and Brent Geese, plus Merlin and
Peregrine.
Other notable flora/fauna: Unique habitats and
geographical position makes Spurn a very interesting
site in Yorkshire for butterflies (25 spp. recorded) and
moths.
Contact: Yorkshire WT, T: 01964 650 313;
E: info@ywt.org.uk

8. TOPHILL LOW NATURE RESERVE

Yorkshire Water.
Location: Sat nav: YO25 9RH. TA 071 482. Located
SE of Driffield and signposted from village of Watton
on A164.
Access: Open daily (9am-6pm), outside of these
hours by reserve membership only. Entrance fee,
concessions available. No dogs. Provision for disabled
visitors (paths, ramps, hides, toilet etc). Coaches
welcome.
Facilities: Toilets open daily. 12 hides (eight with
wheelchair access), paths and sightings board.
Public transport: None.
Habitats: Open water (two reservoirs), marshes, wet
grassland, wader scrapes, woodland and thorn scrub.
Key birds: 160 spp. annually. *Winter:* SSSI for
wildfowl, plus one of the UK's largest Black-headed
and Common Gull roosts. Regular wintering Bittern
and Smew. Active feeding station with Marsh and
Willow Tit. *Spring/early summer:* Hirundines, Black
Tern and Black-necked Grebe. Breeding Little Ringed
Plover, Common Tern, Kingfisher and Barn Owl with
variety of warblers. *Late summer/autumn:* Up to 20
spp. of passage wader.
Other notable flora/fauna: 400+ spp. flora, 365+ spp.
fungi, 16 spp. odonata inc. hairy hawker. Grass snake,
otter, water vole, great crested newt and roe deer.

Contact: Richard Hampshire, Tophill Low Nature
Reserve, Hutton Cranswick, Driffield, East Yorkshire
YO25 9RH. T: 01377 270 690.
E: richard.hampshire@yorkshirewater.co.uk;
W: www.tophilllow.blogspot.com

9. WHELDRAKE INGS

Yorkshire Wildlife Trust.
Location: Sat nav: YO19 6FE (Ings Lane car park).
SE 694 444. From York by-pass (A64) head S on A19
towards Selby for 1.2 miles, then turn L on Wheldrake
Lane. Drive through Wheldrake village and turn sharp
R to reach Natural England's Bank Island car park.
Access: Open at all times, but entrance road to YWT
Wheldrake car park (Ings Lane) can be flooded in
winter. Free admission and parking. Paths and hides
not suitable for wheelchairs. No dogs allowed.
Facilities: Four hides. Sightings board in Bank Island
car park. RADAR key toilets at Bank Island car park.
Public transport: York to Selby buses stop 25 yards
from entrance road on Thorganby Road.
Habitats: Flooded meadows and pools, riverside
vegetation.
Key birds: A noted site for large numbers of wintering
wildfowl, inc. Shelduck, Pintail and Goldeneye among
the commoner species. Records of Hen Harrier,
Whooper and Bewick's Swans, Little Egret. *Spring
passage:* Garganey, Little Gull, terns and Wheatear.
Summer: Breeding waders, plus Turtle Dove, Yellow
Wagtail, hirundines and migrant warblers. *Autumn:*
Passage waders, Hobby and wildfowl. Kingfisher,
Little and Barn Owl are among a long list of resident
species.
Other notable flora/fauna: Internationally important
community of meadow plants.
Contact: Yorkshire WT, T: 01904 659 570;
E: info@ywt.org.uk

Yorkshire (North)

SEAWATCHING IN AUTUMN from Filey Brigg can produce a range of skuas and shearwaters, with divers and grebes becoming more noticeable as the season progresses. The North York Moors hold breeding waders, chats, raptors and Red Grouse. There are several areas to explore in the Lower Derwent Valley, with first class birding throughout the year.

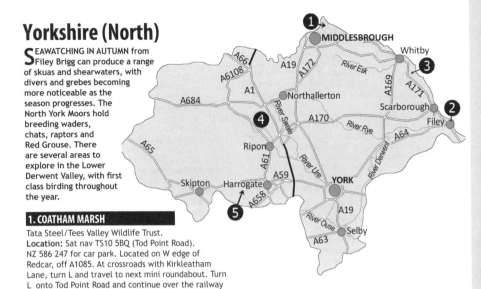

1. COATHAM MARSH

Tata Steel/Tees Valley Wildlife Trust.
Location: Sat nav TS10 5BQ (Tod Point Road). NZ 586 247 for car park. Located on W edge of Redcar, off A1085. At crossroads with Kirkleatham Lane, turn L and travel to next mini roundabout. Turn L onto Tod Point Road and continue over the railway bridge. The reserve is on the left.
Access: Reserve is open throughout daylight hours. Please keep to permissive footpaths only.
Facilities: Good footpaths around site, but section along The Fleet prone to winter flooding. Nearest toilets on Redcar seafront.
Public transport: Frequent buses between Redcar and Middlesbrough. Nearest stops are in Coatham 0.25 mile from reserve. Arriva T: 0871 200 2233. Redcar Central Station one mile from site. Frequent trains from Middlesbrough and Darlington.
Habitats: 54 ha of freshwater pools, lakes, reedswamp.
Key birds: *Spring/autumn*: Wader passage (inc. Wood Sandpiper and Greenshank). *Summer*: Passerines (inc. Sedge Warbler, Yellow Wagtail). *Winter*: Large numbers of common ducks (plus Smew). *Occasional rarities*: Water Rail, Great White Egret, Avocet, Bearded Tit and Bittern.
Other notable flora/fauna: Lime-rich soil good for wildflowers, inc. northern marsh orchid. Insects inc. migrant hawker dragonfly.
Contact: Tees Valley WT, T: 01287 636 382; E: info@teeswildlife.org

2. FILEY BRIGG BIRD OBSERVATORY & THE DAMS

FBOG/Yorkshire Wildlife Trust (The Dams).
Location: Sat nav: YO14 0DG (The Dams). TA 106 807. Two access roads into Filey from A165 (Scarborough to Bridlington road). Filey Dams is a nature reserve within the Observatory's recording area.
Access: Opening times - no restrictions. Dogs only in Parish Wood and The Old Tip (on lead). Coaches welcome. Park at the end of Wharfedale Road (Dams), Sycamore Avenue (Parish Wood/Tip) or in North Cliff Country Park (Brigg).

Facilities: Wheelchair access to the Main Hide (dams). Two open-access hides at The Dams, one on The Brigg (for FBOG members only). Toilets in Country Park (Apr-Oct) and town centre. Nature trails at The Dams, Parish Wood/Old Tip. Cliff top walk for seabirds along Cleveland Way.
Public transport: All areas are within a mile of Filey railway station.
Habitats: The Dams - two freshwater lakes, fringed with some tree cover and small reedbeds. Parish Wood - a newly planted wood which leads to the Old Tip, the latter has been fenced (for stock and crop strips) though there is a public trail. Carr Naze has a pond and can produce newly arrived migrants.
Key birds: *The Dams:* Breeding and wintering water birds, breeding Sedge Warbler, Reed Warbler and Tree Sparrow. *The Tip:* Important for breeding Skylark, Meadow Pipit, common warblers and Grey Partridge. *Winter:* Buntings, inc. Lapland. *Seawatch Hide (Jul-Oct):* All four skuas, shearwaters, terns. *Winter:* Divers and grebes. *Rocket Pole Field:* A new project should encourage breeding species and wintering larks, buntings etc. Many sub-rare/rare migrants possible at all sites.
Contact: E: secretary@fbog.co.uk; W: www.fbog.co.uk
Yorkshire WT, T: 01904 659 570; E: info@ywt.org.uk

3. FYLINGDALES MOOR CONSERVATION AREA

Hawk and Owl Trust/Strickland Estate/
Fylingdales Moor ESS Co Ltd.
Location: Sat nav: YO22 4UL (car park). NZ 947 003.
Conservation area covers 6,800 acres within National
Park off A171 S of Whitby, stretching between Sneaton
High Moor (Newton House Plantation) and the coast
at Ravenscar.
Access: Open access. Parking (inc. coaches) available
at Jugger Howe lay-by (NZ 947 003) on A171.
Facilities: Numerous footpaths inc. Jugger Howe Nature
Trail, Lyke Wake Walk and Robin Hood's Bay Road.
Public transport: Half-hourly Arriva buses (nos. 93 &
X93) between Scarborough and Whitby, nearest stop
at Flask Inn (approx one mile N of Jugger Howe lay-
by). T: 0191 281 1313 for timetable information or
W: www.arrivabus.co.uk
Habitats: Heather moorland (former grouse moor),
with scattered trees, wooded valleys and gulleys.
Managed exclusively for wildlife and archaeological
remains, the moor is an SSSI and SPA (Merlin and
Golden Plover) and a Special Area of Conservation.
Key birds: More than 80 common bird species, plus
rare and endangered breeding birds such as harriers,
Merlin, Golden Plover, Red Grouse, Curlew, Wheatear,
Stonechat, Whinchat, Skylark, Marsh Tit, Willow Tit,
Linnet, Bullfinch, Reed Bunting and Yellowhammer.
The moor is also home to Kestrel, Lapwing, Snipe,
Cuckoo, Meadow Pipit, Grey Wagtail and Wood
Warbler and visited by Peregrine.
Other notable flora/fauna: Otter, roe deer, brown
hare, stoat, weasel and badger. Important for water
vole. Three spp. of heather, plus cranberry, cowberry,
moonwort and, in wetter parts, bog myrtle, lesser
twayblade, bog asphodel, butterwort, marsh helleborine,
and sundews can be found. Also rare orchids and sedges.
Insect spp. inc. large heath and small pearl-bordered
fritillary butterflies and emperor moth.
Contact: Chris Hansell, The Hawk and Owl Trust
T: 07591 567 338; E: cathansell85@hotmail.co.uk;
W: www.hawkandowl.org

4. NOSTERFIELD LNR

Lower Ure Conservation Trust.
Location: Sat nav: DL8 2QZ. SE 278 795. Six miles
N of Ripon, between West Tanfield and Nosterfield
E of A6108 (Ripon to Masham road) and approx four
miles W of A1.
Access: Open all year. Lower viewing area beyond car
park permits viewing from cars only. Footpath (approx
one mile) is fully wheelchair-friendly. Dogs (on short
leads) on most of footpath network. Coaches - book
in advance.
Facilities: Two disabled-friendly hides, interpretation
panels (main hide), comfortable 'woolly' seats,
lowered windows for wheelchair users. No other on-
site facilities.
Public transport: Irregular buses from Ripon and
Masham stop at West Tanfield (0.5 mile walk to
reserve).

Habitats: Wetland grassland and open water. Also
Magnesian limestone grassland, gravel banks,
hedgerows and scrub.
Key species: 150 spp. recorded annually - more than
225 spp. recorded overall (inc. rarities). *Spring/
autumn:* Up to 30 wader spp. recorded annually,
also terns. *Summer:* Breeding spp. inc. Redshank,
Lapwing, Avocet, Oystercatcher, Curlew, Ringed
Plover, Mediterranean Gull, Shoveler, Gadwall, Barn
Owl, Skylark, Lesser Whitethroat, Tree Sparrow,
Linnet, Reed Bunting. *Autumn:* Passage waders inc.
regular Pectoral Sandpiper. *Winter:* Wildfowl (Wigeon,
Teal, Greylag and rarer geese), waders (Golden
Plover, Lapwing, Curlew) and Peregrine.
Other notable flora/fauna: Specialist grassland and
wetland flora, inc. seven spp. of orchid, mudwort,
yellow rattle, golden dock. Butterflies inc. white-
letter hairstreak, brown argus, wall and large colony
of common blue. Dragonflies inc. emperor, black-
tailed skimmer, red-veined darter (has bred). At least
480 spp. of moths have now been recorded. Also,
brown hare and water shrew.
Contact: Warden, E: simon.warwick@luct.org.uk;
W: www.luct.org.uk

5. TIMBLE INGS

Yorkshire Water.
Location: Sat nav: LS21 2PP. SE 170 542 (parking
opposite Anchor Farm). Large area of upland
woodland west of Harrogate, north of Otley. Off the
A59 south of Blubberhouses, near Timble village.
Access: Open at all times, all year.
Facilities: Toilets, cafes, pubs, coach parking all
nearby. Hard forest tracks.
Public transport: None.
Habitats: Pine, larch and spruce woodland and nearby
reservoir. SW corner of wood a good place to observe
visible migration in autumn.
Key birds: Bradford Ornithological Group spp. list
stands at 134. Habitat management work by Yorkshire
Water makes site attractive to Long-eared and Tawny
Owls, Nightjars and Tree Pipits. Buzzards now nest
and Red Kites seen regularly. Goshawk numbers in
decline. *Summer:* Breeding species inc. Redpoll,
Siskin, Crossbill, Woodcock, Redstart and Grasshopper
Warbler. Short-eared Owls hunt adjacent moorland.
Winter: Fieldfare, Redwing, Brambling, occasional
Waxwings and Hawfinches.
Other notable flora/fauna: Roe deer, badger, brown
hare, shrew, vole and mouse spp. (all detected from
owl pellets). Ponds attractive to amphibians and
dragonflies, inc. broad-bodied chaser, emperor and
black darter.
Contact: Recreation Officer, Yorkshire Water,
E: Geoff.D.Lomas@yorkshirewater.co.uk

Yorkshire (South & West)

CONSIDERING THE NUMBER of industrial towns in the area, such as Sheffield, Barnsley and Doncaster, South Yorkshire still manages to offer birdwatchers a surprising number of interesting wildlife sites. Places such as RSPB Fairburn Ings (right next to the A1), Potteric Carr, RSPB Old Moor reserve and its near neighbour, Bolton Ings, all have year-round interest.

1. BOLTON INGS (DEARNE VALLEY)

RSPB (Northern England).
Location: Sat nav: S73 0YF. SE 425 020. Park at RSPB Old Moor and walk east along Trans-Pennine Trail to Bolton Ings. By car, Old Moor is just off Manvers Way (A633). From the M1, take Junc 36 then follow the A6195. From the A1M, take Junc 37 then follow the A635 towards the A6195.
Access: Open all year round. Dearne Way footpath and Trans-Pennine Trail open at all times, but not suitable for wheelchair users. Dogs only on public footpaths.
Facilities: Cormorant View hide. More facilities at RSPB Old Moor.
Public transport: Wombwell and Swinton train stations approx three miles from reserve. Buses run to Old Moor reserve from Barnsley, Doncaster and Meadowhall — Traveline, T: 01709 515 151 for details. Trans-Pennine Trail runs along southern edge of reserve.
Habitats: 43 ha of reedbed and scrub. Excellent warbler habitat.
Key birds: *All year:* Kingfisher, Grey Heron. *Winter:* Stonechat. *Spring/summer:* Reed Bunting. breeding waders and warblers, Cuckoo, Garganey. Avocets and Spoonbills also recorded. *Autumn:* Passage waders inc.Greenshank, Green Sandpiper, Golden Plover.

Winter: Wildfowl, inc. Goosander, Wigeon and Teal.
Other notable flora/fauna: Dragonflies inc. banded demoiselle, brown hare.
Contact: RSPB, T: 01226 751 593;
E: old.moor@rspb.org.uk

2. DENABY INGS

Yorkshire Wildlife Trust.
Location: Sat nav: S64 0JJ (Pastures Rd, off A6023 near Mexborough). SE 496 008. Proceed along Pastures Road for 0.5 mile and watch for a sign on R marking entrance to car park. Climb flight of concrete steps to enter reserve.
Access: Open all year. Dogs on leads.
Facilities: Car park, two hides, interpretation panels, circular trail.
Public transport: None.
Habitats: Hay meadows, open water, deciduous woodland, marsh, willows.
Key birds: *Spring/summer:* Waterfowl, Barn Owl, Tawny Owl, Sand Martin, Swallow, Whinchat, Grasshopper Warbler, Lesser Whitethroat, Whitethroat, other warblers, Kingfisher. *Passage:* Waders, Common, Arctic and Black Terns, Redstart, Wheatear. *Winter:* Whooper Swan, wildfowl, Jack Snipe and other waders, Grey Wagtail, Fieldfare, Redwing, Brambling, Siskin. *All year:* Corn Bunting, Yellowhammer, all three woodpeckers, common woodland birds, possible Willow Tit.
Contact: Yorkshire WT, T: 01904 659 570;
E: info@ywt.org.uk

3. FAIRBURN INGS

RSPB (Northern England).
Location: Sat nav: WF10 2BH. SE 451 277. 12 miles from Leeds, six miles from Pontefract, three miles from Castleford. Next to A1246 from Junc 42 of A1.
Access: Reserve and hides open daily, except Dec 25/26. Centre and shop open 9am-5pm Mar-Oct (car park shuts at 8pm), 4pm for rest of year (car park shuts at 4pm). Dogs on leads welcome. Boardwalks leading to Pickup Pool, feeding station and Kingfisher viewpoint all wheelchair-friendly. Car parking free for RSPB members and disabled drivers. Dogs on leads welcome.
Facilities: Five hides open at all times. Two public trails (one accessible to wheelchairs). Toilets open 9am-5pm. Disabled toilets and baby-changing facilities. Hot and cold drinks, snacks available. Wildlife garden, pond-dipping and mini beast areas, plus duck feeding platform. Coach parking for club visits.
Public transport: Nearest train stations are Castleford, Micklefield and Garforth. Imfrequent bus service to Fairburn and Ledstone villages.
Habitats: Open water, wet grassland, marshand fen scrub, reedbed, reclaimed colliery spoil heaps.

Key birds: *All year:* Tree Sparrow, Kingfisher, Willow Tit, Green Woodpecker, Bullfinch. *Winter:* Smew, Goldeneye, Goosander, Wigeon, Peregrine. *Spring:* Osprey, Little Gull, Wheatear, five species of tern inc. annual Black Tern, Garganey, Little Ringed Plover. *Summer:* Nine species of breeding warbler, Grey Heron, Gadwall, Little Ringed Plover. *Autumn:* Thousands of waders on passage inc Green Sandpiper, Little Ringed Plover and Black-tailed Godwit.
Other notable flora/fauna: Brown hare, harvest mouse, roe deer, Leisler's and Daubenton's bats, 28 spp. of butterflies and 20 spp. of dragonflies.
Contact: RSPB, T: 01977 628 191;
E: fairburnings@rspb.org.uk

4. HARDCASTLE CRAGS

National Trust.
Location: Sat nav: HX7 7AA (Midgehole car park) or HX7 7AZ (Clough Hole car park). SD 988 291. From Hebden Bridge follow National Trust signs to A6033 Keighley Road. Follow for 0.75 mile. Turn L at the National Trust sign to car parks. Alternate pay-and-display car park at Clough Hole on Widdop Road, Heptonstall.
Access: Open all year. NT car park charges. Admission: no charge for NT members and disabled badge holders. Charge for non-members (adult, child and family rates).
Facilities: Two small car parks, cycle racks and several way-marked trails. Gibson Mill visitor centre has toilets, cafe, exhibitions. **Public transport:** Trains to Hebden Bridge from Manchester or Leeds every 30 mins. T: 08457 484 950. Weekday buses every 30 mins to Keighley Road, then one mile walk to Midgehole. Summer weekend bus no. 906 Widdop-Hardcastle Crags, T: 0113 245 7676.
Habitats: 400 acres of unspoilt wooded valleys, ravines, streams, hay meadows and moorland edge.
Key birds: *Spring/summer:* Cuckoo, Redstart, Lesser Whitethroat, Garden Warbler, Blackcap, Wood Warbler, Chiffchaff, Spotted Flycatcher, Pied Flycatcher, Curlew, Lapwing, Meadow Pipit. *All year:* Sparrowhawk, Kestrel, Green, Greater Spotted and Lesser Spotted Woodpeckers, Tawny Owl, Barn Owl, Little Owl, Jay, Coal Tit, Dipper, Grey Wagtail and other woodland species. Goshawk in Crimsworth Dean.
Other notable flora/fauna: Northern hairy wood ant, moss carder bee, tree bumble bee, killarney fern, brittle bladder fern, roe deer, eight spp. of bat.
Contact: National Trust, Hardcastle Crags, T: 01422 846 236;
E: hardcastlecrags@nationaltrust.org.uk

5. INGBIRCHWORTH RESERVOIR

Yorkshire Water.
Location: Sat nav: S36 7GN. SE 217 058. Leave M1 at Junc 37 and take A628 towards Manchester. After five miles turn R at roundabout onto A629 Huddersfield road. Drive 2.5 miles to Ingbirchworth and at The Fountain Inn, turn L, then bear L to cross the dam, proceed straight forward onto the track leading to the car park.
Access: Open all year. One of the few reservoirs in the area with footpath access.
Facilities: Car park, picnic tables.
Public transport: None.
Habitats: Reservoir, small strip of deciduous woodland.
Key birds: *Spring/summer:* Whinchat, warblers, woodland birds, House Martin. *Spring/autumn passage:* Little Ringed Plover, Ringed Plover, Dotterel, other waders, Common Tern, Arctic Tern, Black Tern, Yellow Wagtail, Wheatear. *Winter:* Wildfowl, Golden Plover, waders, occasional rare gull such as Iceland or Glaucous, Grey Wagtail, Fieldfare, Redwing, Brambling, Redpoll.
Other notable flora/fauna: Woodland wildflowers, inc bluebells.
Contact: Recreation Officer, Yorkshire Water, E: Geoff.D.Lomas@yorkshirewater.co.uk

6. OLD MOOR (DEARNE VALLEY)

RSPB (Northern England).
Location: Sat nav: S73 0YF. SE 422 022. By car, Old Moor is just off Manvers Way (A633). From the M1, take Junc 36 then follow the A1M. From the A1M, take Junc 37 then follow the A635 towards the A6195.
Access: Reserve open until 8pm from Apr-Oct. Visitor centre open daily, except Dec 25/26 (9.30am-5pm, Feb-Oct and 9.30am-4pm, Nov-Jan). Cafe open 9.30am-4.30pm, Mar-Oct and 9.30am-4pm, Nov-Feb RSPB Members free, adult non-members (adult, child, concession and family rates). Guide dogs only.
Facilities: Visitor centre, cafe, shop, education and meeting rooms. Accessible toilets. Two trails with seven hides, all suitable for wheelchair users. Two viewing screens. Mobility scooter for hire.
Public transport: Buses run to Old Moor reserve from Barnsley, Doncaster and Meadowhall - Traveline, T: 01709 515 151.
Habitats: Lakes and flood meadows, wader scrape and reedbeds.
Key birds: *All year:* Kingfisher, Little Owl. *Winter:* Large numbers of wildfowl, spectacular flocks of Lapwing and Golden Plover (up to 8,000 birds), Peregrine, Tree Sparrow in garden feeding area. *Summer:* Breeding Bittern, Sand Martin waders, inc. Little Ringed Plover and drumming Snipe, migrant warblers and wildfowl.
Other notable flora/fauna: Water vole, brown hare, weasel, pygmy shrew, wildflowers inc. orchids and adders tongue fern.
Contact: RSPB, T: 01226 751 593;
E: old.moor@rspb.org.uk

7. POTTERIC CARR

Yorkshire Wildlife Trust.
Location: Sat nav: DN4 8DB. SE 589 007. From M18, Junc 3 take A6182 (Doncaster) and at first traffic lights turn R. Entrance and car park are on right after 50 yards.
Access: Open daily, 9am-5pm. Entrance fee to visit reserve, members free. Adult, child, concession and family (up to two adults/four children) rates for non-members. Groups of ten or more should book in advance. Guide dogs only.
Facilities: Around five miles of paths (3.2 miles accessible to wheelchairs, unassisted), 14 viewing hides (10 suitable for disabled). Tearooms open daily (10am-4pm). Toilets at entrance reception, in tea-rooms (during opening times) and outside.
Public transport: Nearest railway station is Doncaster. From Frenchgate Interchange, bus nos. 72 & 75, and alight at B&Q on Woodfield Way. Cross White Rose Way, walk down Mallard Way. Cross car park to reserve entrance in Sedum House.
Habitats: Flood plain of River Tome, with reed fen, subsidence ponds, artificial pools, grassland, woodland.
Key birds: 102 of recorded 230 spp. have bred on site. Nesting waterfowl (inc. Shoveler, Gadwall, Pochard), Water Rail, Kingfisher, all three woodpeckers, Lesser Whitethroat, Reed and Sedge Warblers, Willow Tit. *Passage/winter*: Bittern, Marsh Harrier, Black Tern, waders, wildfowl.

Other notable flora/fauna: 20 spp. of dragonfly recorded, 28 spp. of butterfly inc. purple hairstreak and dingy skipper. Palmate and great crested newt. Common spotted and bee orchids.
Contact: Potteric Carr Nature Reserve, T: 01302 570 077; E: potteric.carr@ywt.org.uk

8. SPROTBOROUGH FLASH & DON GORGE

Yorkshire Wildlife Trust.
Location: Sat nav: DN5 7NB (postcode for Boat Inn). SE 534 006. Leave A1(M) at Junc 36 onto A630 towards Rotherham. After 0.5 mile, turn R at traffic lights to Sprotborough. After approx two miles the road drops down into Don Gorge. Cross a bridge over river, then another over a canal, turn immediately L. Public car park on left next to toll house in Nursery Lane.
Access: Open all year.
Facilities: Three hides (two accessible to wheelchairs), footpaths, interpretation panels.
Public transport: River bus from Doncaster in summer months. Bus service from Doncaster to Sprotbrough village (10 mins walk to reserve).
Habitats: Limestone gorge, woodland, limestone grassland on plateau and open water.
Key birds: *Summer*: Hirundines, Lesser Whitethroat, Whitethroat, Garden Warbler, Blackcap, Chiffchaff, Willow Warbler, Cuckoo. *Spring/autumn passage*: Little Ringed Plover, Dunlin, Greenshank, Green Sandpiper, waders, Yellow Wagtail. *Winter/all year*: Wildfowl, Water Rail, Snipe, Little Owl, Tawny Owl, all three woodpeckers, thrushes, Siskin, possible Corn Bunting.
Contact: Yorkshire WT, T: 01904 659 570; E: info@ywt.org.uk

South East England

Berkshire, Buckinghamshire, Hampshire, Kent, London (Greater), Surrey, Sussex (East), Sussex (West)

Berkshire

DESPITE ITS PROXIMITY to London, Berkshire offers a surprisingly wide range of habitats including heathland and downland. It is the gravel pits that attract the widest range of bird species though, including good numbers of wintering Smew. Increasingly wide areas along the Thames are good for Ring-necked Parakeets.

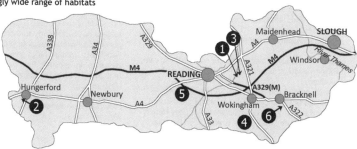

NATURE RESERVES - SOUTH EAST ENGLAND

1. DINTON PASTURES

Wokingham Borough Council.
Location: Sat nav: RG10 0TH. SU 784 718.
From Junc 10 of M4 head towards Reading, then follow sign to Winnersh on A329. Park is signposted off B3030 between Hurst and Winnersh.
Access: Open all year, dawn to dusk. Car parking charges apply 6am-10pm daily. Dogs allowed. Electric buggies available for disabled visitors.
Facilities: Three hides (one adapted for wheelchairs), information centre, car park, cafe open daily 8.30am-5pm (4pm in winter), toilets (suitable for wheelchairs). Electric buggies for hire. Various trails between one and three miles. Walks leaflet at cafe.
Public transport: Courtney Bus nos. 126, 128 & 129 between Reading and Wokingham stop near main entrance, approx one/hour. Winnersh rail station is 15 min walk.
Habitats: 335 acres of mature gravel pits and banks of River Loddon. Sandford Lake managed for wildfowl, Lavell's Lake (see below) best for waders and scrub species.
Key birds: *All year:* Kingfisher, Water Rail, Barn Owl. *Spring/summer:* Hobby, Little Ringed Plover, Common **Key birds:** *All year:* Kingfisher, Water Rail, Barn Owl. *Spring/summer:* Hobby, Little Ringed Plover, Common Tern, Nightingale, common warblers. *Winter:* Bittern, wildfowl (inc. Goldeneye, Wigeon, Teal, Gadwall), thrushes. Waders inc. Green and Common Sandpipers, Snipe, Redshank.
Other notable flora/fauna: Water vole, harvest mouse, great crested newt, Loddon pondweed and Loddon lily. 18 spp. of dragonflies inc. emperor, black-tailed skimmer, migrant hawker, white-legged and banded agrion damselfies.
Contact: Dinton Pastures Country Park, T: 0118 974 6343; E: countryside@wokingham.gov.uk; W: www.dinton-pastures.co.uk

2. HUNGERFORD MARSH

Town and Manor of Hungerford
Location: Sat nav: RG17 0JB. SU 333 687. On W side of Hungerford, beside the Kennet and Avon Canal. From town centre, go along Church Street past the town hall. Turn R under the railway. Follow public footpath over swing bridge on the canal near the church. The reserve is separated from Freeman's Marsh by a line of willows and bushes.
Access: Open all year. Please keep to the footpath. Dogs on leads please.
Facilities: Car park.
Public transport: Hungerford railway station half mile from reserve.
Habitats: An idyllic waterside site with chalk stream, water meadows, unimproved rough grazing and reedbed.
Key birds: 120 spp. recorded. *Spring/summer:* Reed and Grasshopper Warblers. *Winter:* Siskin and Water Rail. *All year:* Common wildfowl, Grey Heron, Kingfisher, Mute Swan, Little Grebe, Reed Bunting, Bullfinch.

Other notable flora/fauna: Water vole, otter and grass snake. Southern marsh orchid, fen bedstraw.
Contact: Clerk to T&M of H, T: 01488 685 081; E: admin@townandmanor.co.uk; W: www.hungerfordtownandmanor.co.uk

3. LAVELL'S LAKE

Wokingham Borough Council.
Location: SU 785 727. Via Sandford Lane off B3030 between Hurst and Winnersh, E of Reading or from Dinton Pastures.
Access: Dawn to dusk. No permit required. Dogs on leads all year.
Facilities: Car park (open 9am-5pm), two public hides, one with disabled access, one members-only hide (see below), viewing screen.
Public transport: Thames Travel bus nos. 128 & 129 run between Reading and Wokingham, stopping outside Dinton Pastures main entrance. Nearest train services are at either Winnersh, or Winnersh Triangle.
Habitats: 10 ha site composed of gravel pits, two wader scrapes, reed beds, rough grassland, marshy area, sand martin banks, between River Loddon and Emm Brook. To north of Lavell's Lake, gravel pits are being restored to attract birds. The lake at Lea Farm is viewable walking N along the River Loddon from Lavell's Lake over small green bridge. It is on R and can be seen through a viewing screen and a members only hide for Friends of Lavell's Lake (www.foll.org.uk). No access.
Key birds: *All year:* Great Crested Grebe, Gadwall, Sparrowhawk, Kingfisher, Red Kite, Buzzard, Cetti's Warbler. *Summer:* Common Tern, Redshank, Lapwing, Hobby, warblers inc. Reed, Sedge, Whitethroat. *Passage:* Garganey, Little Ringed Plover, Common and Green Sandpiper and Greenshank. *Winter:* Water Rail, Bittern, Little Egret, Teal, Shoveler, Pochard, Goldeneye, occasional Smew and Goosander. Along River Loddon - Siskin, Lesser Redpoll, Fieldfare and Redwing.
Contact: Dinton Pastures Country Park, T: 0118 974 6343; E: countryside@wokingham.gov.uk

4. MOOR GREEN LAKES

Lakes Group Moor Green/Blackwater Valley Countryside Partnership
Location: Sat nav: RG40 3TF (free car park in Lower Sandhurst Road, Finchampstead (open 8am-dusk). SU 805 628. Alternatively, Horseshoe Lakes free car park in Mill Lane, Sandhurst (SU 820 620).
Access: Reserve closed to all, but can be viewed from footpaths bordering eastern, southern and westerns sides. Paths can be used by wheelchairs, though surface not particularly suitable. Southern path forms part of Blackwater Valley long distance footpath.
Facilities: Two bird hides open to MGLG members (see map on website), four viewing screens available to public. Feeding station viewable from bench on western path.
Public transport: Nearest railway station, Crowthorne on Reading to Gatwick line (First Great Western Trains).

Habitats: 36 ha in total. Three lakes with gravel islands, beaches and scrapes. River Blackwater, grassland, surrounded by willow, ash, hazel and thorn hedgerows. **Key birds:** More than 200 spp. recorded, with 60 breeding on a regular basis. *Spring/summer:* Little Ringed Plover, Reed Warbler and Hobby. Also Whitethroat, Sedge Warbler, Common Sandpiper. Mandarin Duck, Common Tern and Barn Owl breed on site. Dunlin and Green Sandpiper on passage. *Winter:* Wigeon, Teal, Gadwall and of particular interest, a roost of Goosander on Grove Lake. Little Egret regular, Snipe, Lapwing and Green Sandpiper. Gull roost on adjacent Manor Farm workings inc. up to 1,000 Lesser Black-backed. **Other notable flora/fauna:** 31 spp. of butterflies and 15 spp. of dragonflies have been recorded. See website for more details. **Contact:** Moor Green Lakes Group, E: chairman@mglg.ork.uk; W: www.mglg.org.uk Blackwater Valley Countryside Partnership, T: 01252 331 353; E: blackwater.valley@hants.gov.uk

5. THEALE GRAVEL PITS

Theale Area Bird Conservation Group.
Location: Sat nav: RG7 4AP. SU 656 703 (Main Pit). Group of pits situated between Juncs 11 & 12 of the M4, south of Reading. Inc. Hosehill Lake LNR (SU 648 696). From Theale town centre head S on Station Road and Hanger Road and park in lay-bys in Dean Copse Road. **Access:** Open at all times. Parking for a few vehicles in lay-bys near Fox & Hounds pub. **Facilities:** Tern rafts, Sand Martin bank and wildflower meadow in Hosehill Lake LNR, together with information boards and benches on a mile-long circular walk. **Public transport:** Theale railway station within walking distance of nearest pits. **Habitats:** Flooded fields, Kennet & Avon Canal, scrub and worked-out gravel pits. **Key birds:** *Spring/summer:* Migrant warblers, breeding Nightingale and Common Tern, passage Arctic and Black Terns, large number of hirundines, resident Peregrine favours pylon area. *Autumn:* Dunlin, Common Sandpiper and other waders on passage. Little Gulls recorded, along with terns on passage, plus Osprey.

Winter: Large numbers of wildfowl, inc. Goldeneye and Goosander. Thousands of gulls on nearby Moatlands pit. Bitterns sometimes recorded in Hosehill Lake LNR reedbed. **Other notable flora/fauna:** Good range of dragonflies and butterflies. Grass vetchling worthy of note. **Contact:** TABCC Sec, Cathy McEwan T: 01189 415 792; E: tabcgsec@yahoo.com

6. WILDMOOR HEATH

Berks, Bucks & Oxon Wildlife Trust.
Location: Sat nav: RG45 7PW. SU 838 630. Between Bracknell and Sandhurst. From Sandhurst shopping area, take the A321 NW towards Wokingham. Turn E at the mini-roundabout on to Crowthorne Road. Continue for about one mile through one set of traffic lights. Car park is on the right at the bottom of the hill. **Access:** Open all year. No access to woodland N of Rackstraw Road at Broadmoor Bottom. Dogs on a lead. Not suitable for wheelchairs due to slope of site and muddy, uneven terrain. **Facilities:** Car park. **Public transport:** The reserve is one mile north of Sandhurst railway station. **Habitats:** 99 ha of wet and dry lowland heath, bog, mixed woodland and mature Scots pine plantation. **Key birds:** *Spring/summer:* Wood Lark, Tree Pipit, Nightjar, Dartford Warbler, Hobby, Reed Bunting and Stonechat among 55 spp. recorded at this site. **Other notable flora/fauna:** Dragonflies (20 spp. recorded), silver-studded blue butterfly, slow worm, adder, grass snake, common lizard, roe deer. Bog plants inc. sundews. **Contact:** BBOWT, T: 01628 829 574; E: info@bbowt.org.uk;

Buckinghamshire

BORDERED BY THE River Thames to the south and River Ouse to the north, Buckinghamshire offers a good selection of woods, lakes and gravel pits. The high ground of the Chiltern escarpment is an excellent place to watch Red Kites. There is a good breeding population of Firecrests in the county.

1. BURNHAM BEECHES NNR

City of London Corporation.
Location: Sat nav: SL2 3PS. SU 950 850. 2.5 miles N of Slough and on W side of A355, running between Junc 2 of M40 and Junc 6 of M4. Entry from A355 via

Beeches Road. Also smaller parking areas in Hawthorn Lane and Pumpkin Hill to the S and Park Lane to the W. **Access:** Open all year, except Dec 25. Main Lord Mayor's Drive open from 8am-dusk. Beeches Cafe, public toilets and information point open 10am-5pm. Motorised buggy available for hire. Network of wheelchair accessible roads and paths. **Facilities:** Car parks, toilets, cafe, visitor information centre. Easy access path network, suitable for wheelchairs, most start at Victory Cross. Coach parking. **Public transport:** Train, nearest station is Slough on main line from Paddington. Arriva, First and Jason Tours, bus nos. 74 & 40, T: 0871 200 2233. **Habitats:** Ancient woodland, streams, pools, heathland (Stoke Common), grassland, scrub.

NATURE RESERVES - SOUTH EAST ENGLAND

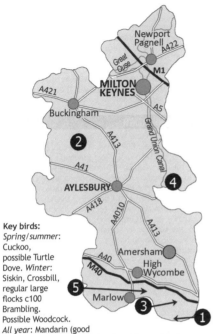

Key birds:
Spring/summer:
Cuckoo,
possible Turtle
Dove. *Winter*:
Siskin, Crossbill,
regular large
flocks c100
Brambling.
Possible Woodcock.
All year: Mandarin (good
population), all three woodpeckers, Sparrowhawk,
Marsh Tit, possible Willow Tit, Red Kite and Buzzard.
Other notable flora/fauna: Ancient beech and oak
pollards with associated wildlife. Rich array of fungi.
Contact: Burnham Beeches Office, Hawthorn Lane,
Farnham Common, SL2 3TE. T: 01753 647 358;
E: burnham.beeches@cityoflondon.gov.uk;
W: www.cityoflondon.gov.uk

2. CALVERT JUBILEE

Berks, Bucks & Oxon Wildlife Trust.
Location: Sat nav: OX27 0BG. SP 682 252. Near
Steeple Claydon, 6.5 miles E of Bicester. Park
opposite Greatmoor Sailing Club.
Access: Please keep to network of paths. Surfaced
path to bird hide. Guide dogs only.
Facilities: Two hides, small car park.
Public transport: None.
Habitats: Ex-clay pit, railway and landfill site. Now
with deep lake, marginal reedbed and scrub habitat.
Key birds: *Summer*: Nesting Common Tern on rafts,
Kingfisher, Hobby, warblers and Cuckoo. *Passage
migrants*: Black Tern and fly-over waders. *Winter*:
Over-wintering wildfowl. Bittern, Water Rail and
large gull roost with occasional Glaucous and Iceland
Gulls. Rarer birds turn up regularly.
Other notable flora/fauna: Rare butterflies, inc.
dingy and grizzled skippers and black hairstreak. Bee
and common spotted orchids.
Contact: BBOWT, T: 01442 826 774:
E: info@bbowt.org.uk

3. CHURCH WOOD

RSPB (Midlands Regional Office).
Location: Sat nav: SL2 3XB. SU 971 872. Reserve lies
three miles from Junc 2 of M40 in Hedgerley. Park in
village, walk down small track beside pond for approx
200 yards. Reserve entrance is on left.
Access: Open all year, dawn-dusk. Not suitable for
wheelchairs. Please keep dogs on leads (Apr-Jun).
Facilities: Two marked paths with some inclines. No
toilets or car park on site.
Public transport: Bus no. 40 from Slough to
Hedgerley or no. 74 from Slough to Farnham
Common.
Habitats: Mixed woodland.
Key birds: *Spring/summer*: Red Kite, Buzzard,
Blackcap, Garden Warbler, Swallow. *Winter*: Redpoll,
Siskin. *All year*: Marsh Tit, Willow Tit, Nuthatch,
Treecreeper, Great Spotted and Green Woodpeckers.
Other notable flora/fauna: Wood anenome,
wood sorrel, bluebell and other woodland plants.
Brimstone, comma, white admiral and peacock
butterflies. Good range of fungi spp.
Contact: RSPB, T: 01865 351 163

4. COLLEGE LAKE

Berks, Bucks & Oxon Wildlife Trust.
Location: Sat nav: HP23 5QG. SP 926 138. Two miles
N of Tring on B488, 0.25 mile N of canal bridge at
Bulbourne turn L into gated entrance. Marked with
brown tourist signs.
Access: Open daily, 9.30am-5pm (4pm in winter).
Wheelchair access to some hides and disabled toilets.
Electric tramper available for disabled visitors -
phone to book.
Facilities: Large car park, coach park, 11 bird hides,
interactive interpretation. Network of wheelchair-
friendly paths, visitor centre/gift shop, toilets. Cafe
open 10am-4pm (Feb to Oct) and 10am-3pm for rest
of year. Closed 24-31 Dec.
Public transport: Tring railway station, two miles
walk mostly on canal towpath.
Habitats: Deep lake in former chalk pit, shallow
pools, chalk and rough grasslands, woodlands, scrub.
Key birds: *Spring/summer*: Breeding Lapwing,
Redshank and Little Ringed Plover. Sand Martin,
Hobby, Common Tern, Skylark and Shelduck. *Winter*:
Wildfowl (Wigeon, Shoveler, Teal, Gadwall), waders,
inc. Snipe, Peregrine Falcon. Rarer birds turn up
regularly.
Other notable flora/fauna: Chalk grassland flowers.
Arable Weed Project inc. displays of cornfield flowers
in Jun/Jul. Butterflies inc. small blue and green
hairstreak. Good numbers of dragonflies (16 spp.).
Brown hare.
Contact: BBOWT, T: 01442 826 774;
E: collegelake@bbowt.org.uk;

5. LITTLE MARLOW GRAVEL PITS

Lefarge Aggregates/private ownership.
Location: Sat nav: SL8 5PS. SU 880 880. NE of Marlow from Junc 4 of M40. Use permissive path from Coldmoorholm Lane to Little Marlow village. Follow path over a wooden bridge to N end of lake. Permissive path ends just past the cottages where it joins a concrete road to sewage treatment works. Be careful at all times when walking round the lake.
Access: Open all year. Do not enter the gravel works and watch for heavy traffic when crossing site's entrance road.

Facilities: Permissive footpath.
Habitats: Gravel pit with sand spit (best viewed from west bank), lake, scrub.
Key birds: *Spring*: Passage migrants inc. Whimbrel, Wheatear, Whinchat, Sand Martin, Garganey, Hobby. *Summer*: Reedbed warblers, Kingfisher, wildfowl. *Autumn*: Passage migrants. *Winter*: Wildfowl, possible Smew, Goldeneye, Water Rail, Yellow-legged Gull among large gull flocks, Lapwing, Snipe.
Contact: Little Marlow Lakes Country Park Community Partnership,
E: littlemarlowlakescountrypark@hotmail.co.uk

Hampshire

DOMINATED BY THE New Forest, this huge county holds many scarce breeding birds including Honey Buzzard, Goshawk, Red Kite (north of the county), Firecrest, Hawfinch, Dartford Warbler and Nightjar, with Great Grey Shrikes regular in winter. Keyhaven and Farlington Marshes are the best sites for migrants. Blashford Lakes holds a good selection of waterbirds including wintering Bitterns.

1. BLASHFORD LAKES

Hampshire & Isle of Wight Wildlife Trust/ Wessex Water.
Location: Sat nav: BH24 3PJ. SU 151 083. From Ringwood take A338 for two miles towards Fordingbridge/Salisbury, pass Ivy Lane R and take next R at Ellingham Cross, into Ellingham Drove. The main car park for hides is first left after 400 yards - entrance shared with Hanson works.
Access: Car park, hides and visitor centre (with toilets) open daily, except Dec 25, 9am-4.30pm. Paths open outside these hours but no vehicle access. Dogs not allowed. Groups should book in advance. RADAR keys needed to open kissing gates for wheelchairs.
Facilities: Education centre, with toilets. Parking, footpaths, six hides, viewing screens, toilets and information inc. recent sightings board, webcams. Coach parking by arrangement.
Public transport: No. X3 Bournemouth-Salisbury bus service stops at Ellingham Cross, 500 yards W of the main reserve entrance.
Habitats: Flooded gravel pits, areas of wet ancient woodland, also dry grassland and lichen heath.
Key birds: *Winter*: Up to 5,000 over-wintering wildfowl, inc. internationally important numbers of Gadwall. Grey Heron, Little Egret and Bittern. Also a large gull roost on Ibsley Water. *Spring/ summer*: Breeding birds inc. Common Tern, Sand Martin (in artificial bank), Lapwing, Redshank, Oystercatcher, Kingfisher, Garden Warblers are esp. common. *Autumn*: Waders on migration inc. Green and Common Sandpipers and Greenshank, also Hobby, Black Tern and passerines.

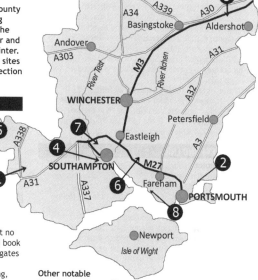

Other notable flora/fauna: Dragonflies (25 spp. recorded) inc. brown hawker, scarce chaser and large and small red-eyed damselfly. Roe deer, badgers, otters, foxes, reptiles inc. adders and grass snakes.
Contact: Hampshire & Isle of Wight WT, T: 01425 472 760; E: BlashfordLakes@hiwwt.org.uk

2. FARLINGTON MARSHES

Hampshire & Isle of Wight Wildlife Trust.
Location: Sat nav: PO6 1RN. SU 685 045. N of Langstone Harbour. Main entrance off roundabout junction A2030/ A27 is a small lane between the A27 westbound and the A2030 leading to Portsmouth.
Access: Open at all times, no charge or permits, but donations welcome. Dogs on leads at all times. Wheelchair access via RADAR gates. Short slopes up to sea wall. Paths mostly level but main track along the sea wall is uneven in places and muddy in wet weather.

155

Facilities: 2.5 miles circular walk around sea wall with benches every 300 yards. Information at entrance and shelter. No toilets. Height barriers on car parks.

Public transport: No. 21 service from Portsmouth Harbour to Havant stops by Farlington Sainsbury's (north of A27), a 15+ mins walk to the reserve. Contact First bus service, T: 023 8058 4321. By train: Hilsea station is 1.5 miles from reserve. Contact South West Trains, T: 0845 6000 650.

Habitats: Coastal grazing marsh with pools and reedbed within reserve. Views over intertidal mudflats/saltmarshes of Langstone Harbour.

Key birds: *Summer:* Breeding waders and wildfowl (inc. Lapwing, Redshank and Shelduck) also breeding Cetti's, Sedge and Reed Warbler, Bearded Tit. *Late summer:* Passage migrants (Yellow Wagtail, Whimbrel, etc) and returning waders, chance of rarities such as Spotted Crake, Curlew Sandpiper, stints. *Autumn/winter:* Waders and wildfowl, good numbers of Teal, Wigeon, Pintail, Marsh Harrier, Short-eared Owl regular visitors. Internationally-important numbers of Dark-bellied Brent Goose and Bar-tailed Godwit. Important high tide roost site best viewed over spring high tide.

Other notable flora/fauna: Corky fruited waterdropwort, slender hares-ear, southern marsh and early marsh orchids. Water vole in ditches.

Contact: Hampshire & Isle of Wight Wildlife Trust, T: 01489 774 429; feedback@hiwwt.org.uk

3. FLEET POND LNR

Hart District Council Service/Fleet Pond Society.

Location: Sat nav: GU51 2RR. SU 822 551. Located in Fleet, W of Farnborough. The main site car park, which is free, is off Cove Road B3013/A327 (follow brown duck signs).

Access: Open all year. Additional free parking is available in Wellington Avenue and Chestnut Grove but limited to two hours. Kenilworth Road and Westover Road offer unlimited free parking.

Facilities: Some surfaced paths, boardwalks in wet areas.

Public transport: Fleet railway station lies N of site.

Habitats: Largest freshwater lake in Hampshire, marshes, reedbeds, heathland, wet and dry woodland.

Key birds: Up to 180 spp. recorded. *Spring/autumn:* Migrant waders inc. Little Ringed Plover, Dunlin, Greenshank, Little Gull, Lesser Spotted Woodpecker, occasional Kittiwake, terns, Wood Lark, Skylark, occasional Ring Ouzel, Firecrest, Pied Flycatcher. *Summer:* Hobby, Common Tern, Tree Pipit, occasional Red Kite and Osprey. *Winter:* Bittern, wildfowl, occasional Smew, Snipe, occasional Jack Snipe, Siskin, Redpoll.

Other notable flora/fauna: Dragonflies in wet areas of marshes and heathlands (21 spp. recorded). Butterflies (26 spp. recorded), roe deer. More than 400 plant spp. inc. ling and bell heather, phragmites reeds.

Contact: Hart District Council, T: 01252 623 443; E: enquiries@hart.gov.uk; W: www.hart.gov.uk/fleet-pond

4. LOWER TEST MARSHES

Hampshire & Isle of Wight Wildlife Trust.

Location: Sat nav: SO40 3BR. SU 365 145. Area bounded by M27, M271 and A35 W of Southampton. Limited on-road parking near Salmon Leap pub, Testwood Lane, Totton.

Access: Open at all times. No coach parking facilities. Disabled access limited. Dogs allowed only on Test Way footpath.

Facilities: One hide and two screens, all accessible on foot from Compton Road. Hide open 9am-4pm daily, screens open at all times. Boardwalk over wetter areas of site. Another viewpoint at Old Redbridges, an unsurfaced lay-by off A36.

Public transport: Totton train station and bus stops within easy walking distance. T: 01983 827 005 for bus details.

Habitats: Saltmarsh, brackish grassland, wet meadows, reedbed, scrapes, meres, estuary.

Key birds: *Summer/breeding:* Kingfisher, Oystercatcher, Reed Warbler, Cetti's Warbler, Sedge Warbler, Reed Bunting. *Autumn/winter waders:* Green Sandpiper, Common Sandpiper, Oystercatcher, Redshank, Curlew, Black-tailed Godwit, Lapwing. *Winter wildfowl:* Wigeon, Teal, Mallard, Shelduck. *Other notable species:* Peregrine, Water Pipit. *On passage:* Osprey, Marsh Harrier, Wood Sandpiper, Garganey.

Other notable flora/fauna: Good range of common butterflies. Dragonflies inc. scarce chaser, emperor and migrant hawker. Early marsh, green-winged, southern marsh orchids and green-flowered helleborine.

Contact: Hampshire & Isle of Wight Wildlife Trust, T: 02380 424 206; feedback@hiwwt.org.uk

5. MARTIN DOWN

Natural England (Wessex Team).

Location: Sat nav: SP6 3LS. SU 060 201. Fourteen miles SW of Salisbury, 0.6 mile W of Martin village. The N part of the site is crossed by the A354. Main car park is on the A354 and another at the end of Sillens Lane, a minor road from Martin village.

Access: Open access, but organised groups of 10+ should book in advance. Main car park height barrier (7ft 6 ins). Coaches only by prior arrangement. Hard flat track from A354 car park suitable for wheelchairs.

Facilities: Two car parks, interpretative boards.

Public transport: One bus Salisbury/Blandford, T: 01722 336 855 or visit www.wdbus.co.uk

Habitats: Unimproved chalk downland and scrub.

Key birds: Spring/summer: Grey Partridge, Turtle Dove, Nightingale (all now scarce), Cuckoo, plus warblers. Winter: Occasional Merlin, Hen Harrier. All year: Yellowhammer, Skylark.

Other notable flora/fauna: Species-rich chalk downland with a variety of orchids, plus pasqueflower and milkwort. More than 20 spp. of butterflies.

Contact: Natural England, T: 0300 060 6000, E: enquiries@naturalengland.org.uk

6. SWANWICK LAKES NATURE RESERVE

Hampshire & Isle of Wight Wildlife Trust.
Location: Sat nav: SO31 7AY. SU 507 099. SE from Southampton. About two miles from Bursledon and seven miles from Fareham. From Junc 8 of M27, follow signs to A3024 Southampton and Hamble and then Park Gate A27. At lights by The Navigator pub turn L onto Swanwick Lane. Cross motorway then L onto Sopwith Way. Turn R at mini roundabout by security gates. From Junc 9 follow signs for Southampton A27 up to Park Gate. Take road to Botley. At Elm Tree pub turn L onto Swanwick Lane. After about a mile, turn R onto Sopwith Way. Turn R at mini roundabout by security gates.
Access: Some surfaced paths for wheelchairs, plenty of benches. Groups should contact reserve before visiting. Dogs welcome.
Facilities: Network of surfaced and unsurfaced paths, three waymarked trails of varying lengths, frequent benches, fantastic viewpoints, reserve leaflet inc. a trail guide available. Toilets available when study centre is open.
Public transport: By train - about 30 mins walk from Swanwick. From station turn R at end of access road then continue to Elm Tree Pub. Turn L onto Swanwick Lane then continue as above. By bus - several First Group buses stop on A27, at the bottom of Swanwick Lane. W: www.firstgroup.com/ukbus/hampshire
Habitats: Mixed woodland, flower-rich meadows and deep lakes.
Key birds: Good range of birds inc. Little Grebe, Gadwall, Buzzard, Kingfisher, Great Spotted and Green Woodpecker, Nuthatch, Treecreeper, finches and tits.
Other notable flora/fauna: Common butterflies, with occasional silver-washed fritillary and purple emperor, common dragonflies and other insects inc. mining bees. Great crested newts. Common spotted orchid. Rich variety of different fungi. Roe deer.
Contact: Hampshire & Isle of Wight Wildlife Trust, T: 01489 570 240; SwanwickLakes@hiwwt.org.uk

7. TESTWOOD LAKES

Southern Water /
Hampshire & Isle of Wight Wildlife Trust.
Location: Sat nav: SO40 3WX. SU 347 155. Take M271 West Junc 2 towards Totton. L at first roundabout, then left onto A36. L at next roundabout onto Brunel Rd. Entrance on left after 0.25 mile.
Access: Car parks open 8am-5pm summer and 8am-5pm winter. Surfaced paths around lakes and to hides are relatively flat. RADAR key (available at centre) needed for wheelchair users to get through gates. Mobility vehicle available (please book in advance).

Facilities: Testwood Lakes Centre open 9am-4pm (Mon-Fri) and Sun 1pm-4pm (summer), 12pm-3pm (winter). Weekday access may not be possible if school groups are in attendance. Two hides and two screens. Hides open 10am-4pm daily. Disabled toilet in Education Centre.
Public transport: Totton rail station is 1.5 miles from the reserve. Bluestar and Wilts & Dorset buses stop 0.25 mile from entrance, T: 01983 827 005.
Habitats: Flooded gravel pits, scrapes, wet and dry grasslands, woodland and hedgerows.
Key birds: Winter: Various wildfowl (inc. Tufted Duck, Wigeon, Pochard, Teal, Gadwall, Goosander), Siskin, Hawfinch, Meadow Pipit, Common Sandpiper, Green Sandpiper, Pochard, Redwing, Fieldfare. Spring: Shelduck, Sand Martin, Little Ringed Plover, Willow Warbler. Summer: Swift, Swallow, Blackcap, Whitethroat. Autumn: Wheatear, Yellow Wagtail, Goldfinch.
Other notable flora/fauna: Good range of butterflies. Dragonflies inc. emperor, scarce chaser, southern and migrant hawker and golden ringed.
Contact: Hampshire & Isle of Wight Wildlife Trust, T: 02380 424 206; T: 02380 667929 (Education Centre); E: TestwoodLakes@hiwwt.org.uk

8. TITCHFIELD HAVEN NNR

Hampshire County Council.
Location: Sat nav: PO14 3JT. SU 535 025. Located on Cliff Road, Hill Head in Fareham. Reach from A27 and B3334 W of Fareham. Car park adjacent to Hill Head Sailing Club (free for blue badge holders).
Access: Free admission to visitor centre, charge applied for reserve. Open daily all year 9.30am-5pm (Apr-Oct) 9.30am-4pm (Nov-Mar, except Dec 25/26). Public footpath follows derelict canal along W of reserve and road skirts S edge. Guide dogs only.
Facilities: Centre has information desk, toilets, tea room and shop. All six hides are accessible to wheelchair users. Guided walks.
Public transport: Bus stop in Solent Road is within 200 yards of reserve.
Habitats: Covers 369 acres of Lower Meon valley. Shoreline, reedbeds, freshwater scrapes, wet grazing meadows.
Key birds: More than 200 spp. recorded. Spring/ summer: Waders (inc. Avocet and Black-tailed Godwit), wildfowl, Common Tern, breeding Cetti's Warbler, Water Rail. Autumn/winter: Bittern, Kingfisher, Bearded Tit, Brent Geese, Wigeon, Teal, Shoveler and Snipe.
Other notable flora/fauna: Six spp. of nationally rare plant, roe deer, badger and pipistrelle bat. Water voles released in 2013. Dragonflies (19 spp. recorded) and more than 30 spp. of butterflies.
Contact: Titchfield Haven, T: 01329 662 145; E: titchfield.enquiries@hants.gov.uk

Kent

THIS IS A FABULOUS county for birders. Being so close to France, the shingle spit at Dungeness offers excellent seawatching, an RSPB reserve and bird observatory. There is another observatory at Sandwich Bay, marshes all along the north coast and reedbeds at Stodmarsh. The Isle of Sheppey holds a wide selection of birds of prey in winter.

1. BOUGH BEECH RESERVOIR

Kent Wildlife Trust.
Location: Sat nav: TN14 6LD. TQ 496 494. Lying SW of Sevenoaks, Bough Beech is situated 3.5 miles S of Ide Hill, signposted off B2042.
Access: Visitor centre in Winkhurst Green, Ide Hill open on Tues, Wed, Sat & Sun and all bank holidays between 11am-6pm. Dogs on leads at all times. Roadside parking.
Facilities: Visitor centre offers hot/cold drinks and light snacks, gift shop, picnic facilities, toilets (inc. disabled). Paths are uneven and can be muddy. Hide overlooks wader scrape.
Public transport: Rail service to Penshurst Station (two miles south).
Habitats: Reserve occupies northern end of the reservoir and adjacent woodland and farmland.
Key birds: Approx 60 spp. breed annually in and around the reserve, with Tufted Duck, Mandarin and Great Crested Grebe notable among the waterfowl. Little Ringed Plover nest most years. *Autumn:* Good for numbers of waders like Green and Common Sandpipers and Greenshank. Many rarities have been recorded. Ospreys recorded most years. Winter wildfowl numbers are much higher than summer and inc. Goldeneye and Goosander.

Other notable flora/fauna: Great crested newt, toad, dragonflies (black-tailed skimmer, ruddy darter, emperor, southern aeshna, migrant hawker, red-eyed damselfly), common lizard, Roesel's bush cricket, long-winged conehead, dormouse, water shrew, white admiral butterfly, glow-worm, bats (pipistrelle, Daubenton, noctule, brown long-eared).
Contact: Kent WT, T: 01732 750 624;
E: info@kentwildlife.org.uk

2. CLIFFE POOLS

RSPB (South East Region Office).
Location: Sat nav: ME3 7SU (Salt Lane, Cliffe). TQ 722 757. From coastbound A2, take A289 near Strood. From A289 follow signs for Wainscott and Cliffe onto B2000. At T-junction turn L to Cliffe. At crossroads, turn L to Higham. Before you enter Cliffe, take 2nd L after Cliffe sign. Turn L at next T-junction and L again into Salt Road. Car park is on left just past a sharp right-hand bend.
Access: Car park (free) open daily from 9am-5pm, except over xmas period. Monthly guided walks available. Dogs only on public footpaths. Group bookings welcome.
Facilities: Six viewing points. Public rights of way encircle reserve and bisect it. Pushchair friendly.
Public transport: No. 133 bus from Chatham, Rochester and Strood stops at Six Bells pub in Cliffe (1.5 miles from reserve).
Habitats: A mix of saline lagoons, freshwater pools, grassland, saltmarsh and scrub.
Key birds: Massed flocks of waders in winter (more than 9,000 Black-tailed Godwits reported in winter 2013), up to 10,000 Dunlin plus a wide range of wildfowl. A great variety of passage birds in spring and autumn. Breeding species inc. Lapwing, Redshank, Avocet, Ringed Plover, Shelduck. Also look out for Nightingale, Hobby, Mediterranean Gull and Turtle Dove.
Other notable flora/fauna: Good range of insects (rare bees inc. shrill carder bee, brown-banded carder bee). Butterflies, inc. marbled white, common blue, Essex skipper and the migrant clouded yellow, grasshoppers and bush crickets, inc. Roesel's.
Contact: RSPB, T: 01634 222 480;
E: northkentmarshes@rspb.org.uk

3. DUNGENESS NNR

RSPB (South East Region Office).
Location: Sat nav: TN29 9PN. TR 062 197. One mile out of Lydd on the Dungeness Road, turn R for main site. Visitor centre and car park are one mile along entrance track. Entrance to Hanson ARC site and car park is opposite main reserve entrance on left of Dungeness Road.

NATURE RESERVES - SOUTH EAST ENGLAND

Access: Open daily (9am-9pm, sunset when earlier) - closed Dec 25/26. Visitor centre open (10am-5pm, or 4pm Nov-Feb). Parties over 12 by prior arrangement. Entry fee for non-RSPB members (adult, child and concession rates). Only guide dogs allowed on site.
Facilities: Visitor centre, toilets (inc. disabled access), six hides (all wheelchair-accessible), viewing screen, two nature trails. Fully equipped classroom/meeting room. Coach parking available. Hide and viewing screen at Hanson ARC site.
Public transport: Limited service. Bus no. 11 from Ashford stops at reserve entrance on request - one mile walk to visitor centre.
Habitats: Shingle, 90 flooded gravel pits, sallow scrub, newly-extended reedbed on Denge Marsh, wet grassland.
Key birds: *All year:* Bittern, Marsh Harrier, Bearded Tit, Cetti's Warbler *Spring:* Garganey, Little Ringed Plover over a wide variety of waders, Wheatear, Yellow Wagtail, Lesser Whitethroat, Black Redstart. *Autumn:* Migrant waders and passerines, inc. large flocks of swallows and martins. *Winter:* Smew, Goldeneye, Black-necked and Slavonian Grebes, Wigeon, Goosander, Bewick's Swan, Marsh and Hen Harriers, plus other raptors.
Other notable flora/fauna: Jersey cudweed, Nottingham catchfly, endemic leafhopper.
Contact: RSPB, T: 01797 320 588;
E: dungeness@rspb.org.uk

4. DUNGENESS BIRD OBSERVATORY

Dungeness Bird Observatory Trust.
Location: Sat nav: TN29 9NA. TR 085 173. Three miles SE of Lydd. Turn south off Dungeness Road at TR 087 185 and continue to end of road, past two lighthouses.
Access: Observatory open throughout the year. Wardens on site between Mar and Nov. No wheelchair access.
Facilities: Accommodation for up to nine people (reduced charges for Friends). Apply in writing to the warden or by phone. Bring own sleeping bag/sheets and toiletries. Shared facilities inc. a fully-equipped kitchen. Coach parking available at railway station.
Public transport: Bus service between Rye and Folkestone, nos. 11 & 12. Alight at the Pilot Inn, Lydd-on-Sea, a short walk from Observatory. Stagecoach East Kent, T: 01227 472 082.
Habitats: Shingle promontory with scrub and gravel pits.
Key birds: Breeding birds inc. Raven, Wheatear and Black Redstart and seabirds on RSPB Reserve. Important migration site with regular overshoots such as Bee-eater, Purple Heron and Red-rumped Swallow. Excellent seawatching when weather conditions are suitable. Power station outfall, 'The Patch' good for terns and gulls, inc Mediterranean and Yellow-legged.
Other notable flora/fauna: Long Pits are excellent for dragonflies, inc. small red-eyed damselfly. Moth trapping throughout the year.
Contact: Dungeness Bird Observatory, 11 RNSSS Cottages, Dungeness, Romney Marsh, Kent TN29 9NA.
T: 01797 321 309; E: dungenessobs@vfast.co.uk;
W: www.dungenessbirdobs.org.uk

5. ELMLEY MARSHES NNR

Private.
Location: Sat nav: ME12 3RW. TQ 924 698. From Junc 5 of M2, follow A249 towards Sheerness. Reserve signposted from the exit for Iwade and Ridham Dock, immediately before the Sheppey bridge. At the roundabout, take second exit onto the old road bridge. On the Isle of Sheppey, after 1.25 miles, turn R following reserve sign. Follow the rough track for approx two miles to the car park at Kingshill Farm.
Access: Open daily (9am-7pm, dusk if earlier) - closed Tues & Dec 25/26. Honesty box in car park for parking fees. Guide dogs only allowed on reserve. Less mobile visitors may drive closer to the hides.
Facilities: Five hides. Disabled access to Wellmarsh hide. Toilets located in car park 1.25 miles from hides. Pushchair friendly. Guide dogs only.
Public transport: Swale Halt nearest railway station on Sittingbourne to Sheerness line. From there is a three mile walk to reserve.
Habitats: 3,000 acres of coastal grazing marsh, ditches and pools alongside the Swale Estuary with extensive intertidal mudflats and saltmarsh.
Key birds: *Spring/summer:* Breeding waders — Redshank, Lapwing, Avocet, Yellow Wagtail, passage waders, Hobby. *Autumn:* Passage waders. *Winter:* Spectacular numbers of wildfowl, especially Wigeon and White-fronted Goose. Waders. Hunting raptors — Peregrine, Merlin, Hen Harrier and Short-eared Owl.
Other notable flora/fauna: Water vole.
Contact: T: 07930 847 520;
E: info@ www.elmleynaturereserve.co.uk;
W: www.elmleynaturereserve.co.uk

6. NORTHWARD HILL

RSPB (South East Region Office).
Location: Sat nav: ME3 8DS. TQ 768 765. Leave M2 at Junc 1 and join A228, signposted to Grain. Reserve is in Cooling Road, adjacent to High Halstow, approx four miles NE of Rochester.
Access: Open at all times, free access, trails in public area of wood joining Saxon Shoreway link to grazing marsh. Dogs only allowed on Saxon Shoreway. Trails often steep and not suitable for wheelchair users.
Facilities: Four trails vary in length from 0.3 to 2.5 miles. The Toddler trail is surfaced and suitable for 'off-road' push-chairs. Four viewpoints with benches. Rough surface in car park, where toilets are located.
Public transport: difficult, contact reserve for more info.
Habitats: Ancient and scrub woodland (approx 130 acres), grazing marsh (approx 350 acres).
Key birds: *Spring/summer:* Wood holds UK's largest heronry, with c100 pairs of Grey Heron and c50 pairs of Little Egret, breeding Nightingale (1% of UK population), Turtle Dove, scrub warblers and woodpeckers. Marshes — breeding Lapwing, Redshank, Avocet, Marsh Harrier, Shoveler, Pochard. *Winter:* Wigeon, Teal, Shoveler. Passage waders, inc.Black-tailed Godwit, raptors, Corn Bunting. Long-eared Owl.

Other notable flora/fauna: Good range of dragonflies over the marsh, white-letter hairstreak butterfly in the woods.
Contact: RSPB, T: 01634 222 480;
E: northkentmarshes@rspb.org.uk

7. OARE MARSHES LNR

Kent Wildlife Trust.
Location: Sat nav: ME13 0QA. TR 013 647 (car park). Off Church Road, Oare, two miles N of Faversham. From A2 follow signs to Oare and Harty Ferry.
Access: Open at all times. Car parking opposite the Watch House near seawall. Disabled-only car park 300 yards from East Flood hide. Access along marked paths only. Dogs on leads.
Facilities: Three hides. Roadside viewpoint of East Hide accessible to wheelchair users. Those with pneumatic tyres can reach seawall path and hide. Small car park, restricted turning space, not suitable for coaches.
Public transport: No. 333 bus from Feversham, Sittingbourne and Maidstone to Oare Village, one mile from reserve. Arriva service (Mon to Sat), Jaycrest (Sun). Traveline, T: 0870 608 2608. Train: Faversham (two miles away).
Habitats: Ramsar, SPA and SSSI designated site with grazing marsh, freshwater dykes, open water scrapes, reedbed, mudflats/Swale Sea Channel.
Key birds: *All year:* Waders and wildfowl, Little Egret, Marsh Harrier, Water Rail, Barn and Little Owls. *Winter:* Brent Goose, Red-breasted Merganser, Hen Harrier, Merlin, Peregrine, Short-eared Owl, Bittern, Stonechat. Divers, grebes and sea ducks on Swale. *Spring/summer:* Avocet, Garganey, Green, Wood and Curlew Sandpipers, Little Stint, Black-tailed Godwit, Little Tern. Site has a good record for attracting rarities.
Contact: Kent WT, T: 01622 662 012;
E: info@kentwildlife.org.uk

8. SANDWICH BAY BIRD OBSERVATORY

Sandwich Bay Bird Observatory Trust.
Location: Sat nav: CT13 9PF. TR 355 575. 2.5 miles from Sandwich, five miles from Deal. A256 to Sandwich from Dover or Ramsgate. Follow signs to Sandwich Station and then Sandwich Bay.
Access: Open daily. Disabled access.
Facilities: New Field Study Centre. Visitor centre, toilets, refreshments, hostel-type accommodation, plus self-contained flat.
Public transport: Sandwich train station two miles from Observatory.
Habitats: Coastal, dune land, farmland, marsh, two small scrapes.
Key birds: *Spring/autumn passage:* Good variety of migrants and waders, especially Corn Bunting. Annual Golden Oriole. Firecrest and Yellow-browed Warbler occur in The Elms. *Winter:* Golden Plover. Breeding residents inc. Grey Partridge, Stonechat, Stock Dove, Little Owl, Oystercatcher, Littled Ringed Plover.
Other notable flora/fauna: Sand dune plants such as lady's bedstraw and sand sedge. Small heath butterfly, red-veined darter.

Contact:, Sandwich Bay Bird Obs, Guildford Road, Sandwich, CT13 9PF; T: 01304 617 341;
E: sbbot@talk21.co.uk; W: www.sbbot.co.uk

9. STODMARSH NNR

Natural England (Kent, S.London & E.Sussex Team).
Location: Sat nav: CT3 4BA (Red Lion, Stodmarsh). TR 222 618. Lies alongside River Stour and A28, five miles NE of Canterbury. Car park in Stodmarsh village.
Access: Open at all times. Keep to paths. No dogs.
Facilities: Fully accessible toilets at the Stodmarsh entrance car park. Five hides (one fully accessible), easy access nature trail, footpaths and information panels. Car park, picnic area and toilets adjoining the Grove Ferry entrance with easily accessible path, viewing mound and two wheelchair-accessible hides.
Public transport: There is a regular Stagecoach East Kent bus service from Canterbury to Margate/ Ramsgate. Alight at Upstreet for Grove Ferry. Hourly on Sun.
Habitats: Internationally-important mix of open water, reedbed (largest in SE England), wet meadows, dry meadows, woodland.
Key birds: *Spring/summer:* Breeding Marsh Harrier, Bearded Tit, Cetti's Warbler, Garganey, Reed, Sedge and Willow Warblers, Nightingale. Migrant Black Tern, Hobby, Osprey, Little Egret. *Autumn:* Large roosts of Swallows, martins and Starlings. *Winter:* Wildfowl, Hen Harrier, Bittern.
Other notable flora/fauna: Nationally rare plants and invertebrates, inc. shining ram's horn snail.
Contact: Natural England, T: 07767 321 053;
E: Stephen.Etherington@naturalengland.org.uk

London (Greater)

PEREGRINES ARE HAPPILY colonising tall city structures such as Tate Modern, Battersea Power Station and the O2 Arena to name but a few. Black Redstarts are present too. Recent attention has been devoted to impressive visible migration over the city. There are many parks to explore and Common Terns now fish along the cleaned-up Thames.

1. BEDFONT LAKES COUNTRY PARK

London Borough of Hounslow.
Location: Sat nav: TW14 8QA (Clockhouse Lane). TQ 080 728. From M25 take Junc 13 (A30) towards central London. Continue through Crooked Billet traffic light complex, past Ashford Hospital and take B3003 (Clockhouse Lane) from the Clockhouse roundabout.
Access: Park open daily except Dec 25 (8am-4pm /4.30pm). Disabled friendly. Dogs on leads. Main nature reserve only open Sun (2pm-4pm). Keyholder membership available (BLCP, annual fee payable) to access reserve at any time.
Facilities: Toilets, information centre, several hides, nature trail, free parking, up-to-date information.
Public transport: Train to Feltham and Ashford. Bus no. H26 (Feltham to Hatton Cross) and no. 116 from Hounslow to Ashford Hospital.
Habitats: North side nature reserve consists of 180 acres of lakes, reedbed, wildflower meadows, wet woodland, scrub.
Key birds: 140 spp. recorded. *Winter:* Water Rail, Bittern, Smew and other wildfowl, Meadow Pipit. *Summer:* Common Tern, Willow, Garden, Reed and Sedge Warblers, Whitethroat, Lesser Whitethroat, hirundines, Hobby, Blackcap, Chiffchaff, Skylark. *Passage:* Wheatear, Wood Warbler, Spotted Flycatcher, Ring Ouzel, Redstart, Yellow Wagtail.
Other notable flora/fauna: 140 plant spp. inc. bee and pyramidal orchid. Nathusius pipistrelle bat, emperor dragonfly plus other butterflies and dragonflies.
Contact: Bedfont Lakes Country Park LNR; T: 0845 456 2796; E: hounslow-info@carillionservices.co.uk Friends of BLCP: E: info@bedfontlakes.co.uk; W: www.bedfontlakes.co.uk

2. BRENT (WELSH HARP) RESERVOIR

Canal & River Trust.
Location: Sat nav: NW9 7BH. In NW london close to Junc 1 of M1. A5 (Edgeware Road) runs along eastern edge of site. From A5 turn into Cool Oak Lane and park just behind the bridge separating northern and eastern marshes.
Access: Open access at all times. Park in Birchen Grove to access Welsh Harp Open Space nature reserve.
Facilities: Raised viewing platform and permanently open public hide overlooks northern marsh. Circular walk.

Public transport: Hendon station (Thameslink) is a short walk away take Station Road and West Hendon Broadway to Cool Oak Lane.
Habitats: Reservoir surrounded by marshland, woodland, unimproved grassland and playing fields.
Key birds: More than 250 spp. recorded. *Spring/ summer:* Breeding Great Crested Grebe, Gadwall, Shoveler, Pochard, Common Tern, woodland species and up to eight spp. of warbler. A long history of rare birds inc. London's first Great White Egret in 1997 and the UK's first Iberian Chiffchaff in 1972. *Winter:* A wide range of wildfowl and gull spp.
Other notable flora/fauna: 28 spp. of butterflies recorded, inc.marbled white and ringlet, plus 15 spp. of dragonflies. A noted site for bat spp.
Contact: WHCG, T: 0208 4471 810.

3. DAGENHAM CHASE LNR

London Borough of Barking & Dagenham.
Location: Sat nav: RM7 0SS (Millenium Centre). TQ 515 860. Lies in the Dagenham Corridor, an area of green belt between the London Boroughs of Barking & Dagenham and Havering.
Access: Open throughout the year and at all times. Reserve not suitable for wheelchair access. Eastbrookend Country Park which borders The Chase LNR has surfaced footpaths for wheelchair use.
Facilities: Millennium visitor centre in Eastbrookend CP, toilets, ample car parking, Timberland Trail walk.
Public transport: Rail: Dagenham East (District Line) 15 mins walk. Bus: no. 174 from Romford or Dagenham five mins walk.
Habitats: Shallow wetlands, reedbeds, horse-grazed pasture, scrub and wetland. These harbour an impressive range of animals and plants, inc. the nationally rare black poplar tree.
Key birds: A haven for birds, with approx 190 spp. recorded. *Summer:* Breeding Reed Warbler, Lapwing, Water Rail, Lesser Whitethroat, Little Ringed Plover, Kingfisher, Reed Bunting. *Winter:* Significant numbers of Teal, Shoveler, Redwing, Fieldfare and Snipe dominate the scene. *Spring/autumn migration:* Yellow Wagtail, Wheatear, Ruff, Wood Sandpiper, Sand Martin, Ring Ouzel, Black Redstart and Hobby regularly seen.
Other notable flora/fauna: 140 plant spp., wasp spider, butterflies and dragonflies.
Contact: LBB&D, T: 020 8227 2332; W: www.dagenhamchaselnr.org.uk

4. LONDON WETLAND CENTRE

The Wildfowl & Wetlands Trust.
Location: Sat nav: SW13 9WT. TQ 228 770. In Queen Elizabeth's Walk, Barnes, less than one mile from South Circular (A205). In London Zone 2/3, one mile from Hammersmith.
Access: Open 9.30am-5.30pm (Mar-Oct), 9.30am-4.30pm (Nov-Feb), last admission one hour before closing. Charge for admission for non-WWT members. Coach parking by arrangement.

Facilities: Visitor centre, hides, nature trails, discovery centre and children's adventure area, restaurant (hot/cold food), cinema, shop, observatory building, six hides (all wheelchair accessible), sustainable gardens, interactive pond zone, three interpretative buildings.

Public transport: Train: Barnes. Tube: Hammersmith then bus no. 283 (comes into centre). Other buses from Hammersmith nos. 33, 72, 209; from Richmond no. 33.

Habitats: Main lake, reedbeds, wader scrape, open water lakes, wet woodland, grazing marsh.

Key birds: Nationally important numbers of wintering waterfowl, inc. Gadwall and Shoveler. Important numbers of wetland breeding birds, inc. grebes, swans, a range of duck spp. such as Pochard, plus Lapwing, Little Ringed Plover, Redshank, warblers, Reed Bunting and Bittern. Cetti's Warblers remain on site all year round and bred for the first time in 2010. Artifical nesting bank for Sand Martins and rafts for nesting terns. Peregrines which nest on Charing Cross Hospital sighted regularly.

Other notable flora/fauna: Water voles, slow worm, grass snake, common lizard. Seven spp.of bat, 22 spp. of dragonflies and 25 spp. of butterflies. Notable plants inc. snake's head fritillaries, cowslip, pyramidal and bee orchids.

Contact: London Wetland Centre, T: 020 8409 4400; E: info.london@wwt.org.uk;

5. SYDENHAM HILL WOOD

London Wildlife Trust.

Location: Sat nav: SE26 6RU. TQ 344 725. Forest Hill, SE London, SE26, between Forest Hill and Crystal Palace, just off South Circular (A205). Entrances at Crescent Wood Road and Coxs Walk.

Access: Open at all times, no permits required. Some steep slopes, so wheelchair access is difficult.

Facilities: Nature trail, information boards. No toilets.

Public transport: Train stations: Forest Hill (from London Bridge) or Sydenham Hill (from Victoria). Bus nos. 363, 202, 356, 185, 312, 176, P4. Transport for London for details, T: 0207 5657 299.

Habitats: Ancient woodland, reclaimed Victorian gardens, meadow and small pond.

Key birds: Woodland and gardens species all year round. *All year*: All three woodpeckers, Tawny Owl, Kestrel, Sparrowhawk, Goldcrest, Nuthatch, Treecreeper, Stock Dove. *Summer*: Blackcap, Chiffchaff, Willow Warbler. *Winter*: Fieldfare, Redwing.

Other notable flora/fauna: Five spp. of bat, inc. noctule and brown long-eared. Bluebell, wood anemone, dog violet and primrose. Oak and hornbeam. Speckled wood, comma, painted lady and orange-tip butterflies.

Contact: London WT, T: 020 7252 9186; E: dgreenwood@wildlondon.org.uk

Surrey

LONDON'S URBAN SPRAWL has now enveloped much of northern Surrey, but reservoirs and the sewage farm at Beddington offer opportunities for birders. To the west of the county, heathland at Thursley Common and around Frensham are good for the likes of Nightjar, Hobby, Woodlark and Dartford Warbler.

1. CHOBHAM COMMON NNR

Surrey Wildlife Trust.

Location: Sat nav: GU24 8TU. SU 971 647 (Staple Hill car park). From Junc 3 of M3 head N on A322 and A30 in direction of Sunningdale. Car park in Staple Hill Road leading off from B383 Windsor Road.

Access: Open at all times.

Facilities: Three self-guided trails, six car parks with information boards. Site leaflet available from rangers.

Public transport: Hourly buses from Woking to Chobham, stopping in Bowling Green Road, just S of Common. Also services to Sunningdale from Ascot, Windsor, Camberley and Staines. Sunningdale railway station is 600 yards from NW corner of Common.

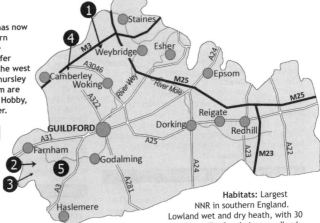

Habitats: Largest NNR in southern England. Lowland wet and dry heath, with 30 pools, mixed broadleaf and pine woodlands.

Key birds: More than 115 spp. recorded, inc. Dartford Warbler, Hobby and Nightjar. Other notable birds inc. Yellowhammer, Stonechat, Linnet and Skylark.

Other notable flora/fauna: More than 350 spp. flowering plants, 25 spp. of mammal, 29 spp. of butterflies inc. silver-studded blue and 22 spp. of dragonflies recorded.

Contact: Surrey WT, T: 01483 795 440; E: info@surreywt.org.uk

NATURE RESERVES - SOUTH EAST ENGLAND

2. FARNHAM HEATH

RSPB (South East Region Office).
Location: Sat nav: GU10 2DL. SU 859 433. Take B3001 SE from Farnham. Take the R hand fork, signposted Tilford, immediately past level crossing. Keep to that road. Just outside Tilford village look for sign to the Rural Life Centre. Entrance is on right after 0.5 mile.
Access: Reserve open at all times. Adjacent Rural Life Centre car park can be used: open Wed-Fri & Sun all year, and Sat from Apr-Sept at 9.30 am weekdays, 10.30am weekends (closed over christmas period). Tea room there opens at 11 am.
Facilities: Large grass car park, shared with Rural Life Centre. No height barrier, but gates may be locked outside opening hours. No bike racks. Toilets (inc. disabled), picnic area, refreshments. Group bookings accepted, guided walks available. Good for walking, pushchair friendly. Three way-marked trails.
Public transport: Bus no. 19 (Farnham to Hindhead service) stops in Millbridge village, outside entrance to Pierrepont House. Reserve is a mile away, along Reeds Road (follow signs to the Rural Life Centre).
Habitats: Heathland and pine woodland.
Key birds: *Spring:* Blackcap, Tree Pipit, Woodcock, Woodlark. *Summer:* Woodcock and Nightjar, woodland birds, inc. Stock Dove, Green and Great Spotted Woodpeckers. *Winter:* Crossbills in pine woods, winter finches, inc. Brambling around the feeders, winter thrushes.
Other notable flora/fauna: Fungi - more than 150 spp. Bats in summer. Sand lizard, plus a range of butterflies inc. grayling.
Contact: RSPB, T: 01252 795 632;
E: farnham.heath@rspb.org.uk

3. FRENSHAM COMMON & COUNTRY PARK

Waverley Borough Council/National Trust.
Location: Sat nav: GU10 3BT (Frensham main car park SU 856 418) or Bacon Lane car park, Churt (GU10 2QB, SU 843 403). Common (1,000 acres in area) lies on either side of A287 between Farnham and Hindhead.
Access: Open at all times. Car park (9am-9pm). Keep to paths. Dogs on leads during breeding season.
Facilities: Car parks at Great and Little Ponds (free on weekdays). Information rooms, toilets (inc. disabled) and refreshment kiosk at Great Pond.
Public transport: Stagecoach bus no. 19 from Farnham to Haslemere stops at Frensham Pond Lane (not Sun).
Habitats: Dry and humid heath, woodland, two large ponds, reedbeds.
Key birds: *Summer:* Dartford Warbler, Woodlark, Hobby, Nightjar, Common Tern, Stonechat, Spotted Flycatcher, Sedge and Reed Warblers, Reed Bunting. *Winter:* Wildfowl (inc. occasional Smew), Bittern, Great Grey Shrike.
Other notable flora/fauna: Tiger beetle, purple hairstreak and silver-studded blue butterflies, sand lizard, smooth snake.
Contact: Rangers Office, T: 01483 523 394 or 01252 792 416;
E: parks&countryside@waverley.gov.uk

4. LIGHTWATER COUNTRY PARK

Surrey Heath Borough Council.
Location: Sat nav: GU18 5RG.
SU 921 622. From Junc 3 of M3, take the A322 and follow brown Country Park signs. From Guildford Road in Lightwater, turn into The Avenue. Entrance to the park is at the bottom of the road.
Access: Open all year, dawn-dusk.
Facilities: Car park, toilets, waymarked trails with leaflets available. Cafe & information poibnt open daily, 10am-4.30pm.
Public transport: Train: Bagshot two miles. SW Trains, T: 0845 6000 650. Arriva Bus: no. 34 stops at Lightwater village, T: 01483 306 397.
Habitats: Heathland, woodland, three ponds and meadows.
Key birds: *All year:* All three woodpeckers, Goldcrest in woods, Coot, Moorhen, Grey Heron and Kingfisher on ponds. *Summer:* Nightjar, Willow Warbler, Chiffchaff, Blackcap, Whitethroat. *Winter:* Fieldfare, Redwing, Siskin.
Other notable flora/fauna: Ox-eye daisies, knapweed and common spotted orchid in meadow, heathers and gorse species on heath. Wood ant nests in woodlands. Range of dragonflies and butterflies.
Contact: Surrey Heath BC, T: 01276 707 100;
E: business.services@surreyheath.gov.uk;

5. THURSLEY COMMON NNR

Natural England (Thames Team).
Location: Sat nav: GU8 6LN. SU 900 417. From Guildford, take A3 SW to B3001 (Elstead/Churt road). Use the Moat car park, S of Elstead village.
Access: Open access. Parties must obtain prior permission.
Facilities: Boardwalk in wetter areas along the Heath Trail (2.25 miles in length).
Public transport: None.
Habitats: Wet and dry heathland, woodland, bog.
Key birds: *Winter:* Hen/Marsh Harriers, Great Grey Shrike and passage/migrant waders such as Redshank, Greenshank, Wood and Common Sandpipers. *Summer:* Hobby, Woodlark, Lapwing, Stonechat, Curlew, Snipe, Nightjar, Spotted Flycatcher, Redstart, Crossbill.
Other notable flora/fauna: Large populations of silver-studded blue, grayling and purple emperor butterflies can be seen here, alongside 26 recorded dragonfly spp. Sandier sites on the reserve provide homes for many spp. of solitary bees and wasps and tiger beetles. Damp areas support carnivorous sundews and a large population (in the thousands) of early marsh orchid.
Contact: Natural England, T: 01428 685 675;
E: james.giles@naturalengland.org.uk

Sussex (East)

THE AREA AROUND Rye Harbour and nearby Pett Level guarantees a good day's birdwatching, with an interesting mix of wildfowl, waders, raptors, terns and Bitterns, depending on the season. If you enjoy finding your own migrants, then a spring or autumn visit to Beachy Head is a must. Ashdown Forest offers a fine mix of woodland and heathland birds.

1. CASTLE WATER, RYE HARBOUR

Sussex Wildlife Trust.
Location: Sat nav: TN31 7TX. TQ 942 189. Local Nature Reserve is one mile SE of Rye along Harbour Road. The Trust manages 88 ha around Castle Water, while the Environment Agency is responsible for the Beach reserve and Rye Harbour Farm.
Access: Open at all times, entry is free. Information centre at Limekiln Cottage open daily 10am-5pm (4pm Oct-Mar) when volunteers are available. Site is flat with some wheelchair access to all four hides, although there are stiles where the sheep are grazing the fields.
Facilities: Information centre, large car park at Rye Harbour with nearby toilets. Replacement wader pool hide now open.
Habitats: Large area of intertidal saltmarsh, marsh, drainage ditches, shingle ridges, pits, sand, scrub, woodland.
Key birds: Many birds occur here in nationally important numbers, such as Shoveler and Sanderling in the winter and breeding Little Tern and Mediterranean Gull. Nesting Black-headed Gull colony, Common and Sandwich Terns and a good range of waders and ducks. Barn and Short-eared Owls.
Other notable flora/fauna: The saltmarsh supports such unusual plants as sea-heath and marsh mallow, and even highly specialised insects inc. the star-wort moth and saltmarsh bee.
Contact: Sussex WT, T: 01273 492 630; E: enquiries@sussexwt.org.uk

2. LULLINGTON HEATH NNR

Natural England (Kent, S.London & E. Sussex Team).
Location: Sat nav: BN26 5RH. TQ 525 026. Seven miles NW of Eastbourne, between Jevington and Litlington, on northern edge of Friston Forest.
Access: Via footpaths and bridleways. Site open for access on foot.
Facilities: None. Nearest toilets/refreshments at pubs in Jevington, Litlington or Seven Sisters CP, 1.25 miles to S.
Public transport: Nearest bus stop is Seven Sisters Country Park. Brighton & Hove services, T: 01273 886 200; E: info@buses.co.uk;
Habitats: Grazed chalk downland/heath, mixed scrub/gorse.

Key birds: *Summer:* Breeding Nightingale, Turtle Dove, Nightjar and diverse range of grassland/scrub-nesting species. Passage migrants inc. Wheatear, Redstart, Ring Ouzel. *Winter:* Raptors (inc. Hen Harrier), Woodcock.
Other notable flora/fauna: Bell heather, ling and gorse on chalk heath; orchid species in grassland.
Contact: Natural England, T: 07825 386 620

3. OLD LODGE RESERVE

Sussex Wildlife Trust.
Location: Sat nav: TN22 3JD. TQ 469 306. A Local Nature Reserve within the much larger Ashdown Forest on W side of B2026 between Maresfield and Hartfield, about 0.75 mile N of junction with B2188 at Kings Standing.
Access: Open all year on well-marked nature trail leading from car park. Dogs must be kept on leads between Jan-Sept and when livestock is present.
Facilities: Car park, well-marked nature trail. Steep paths.
Public transport: None.
Habitats: Heath, pine and deciduous woodlands covering 76 ha.
Key birds: *All year:* Heathland specialists inc. Dartford Warbler. *Spring/summer:* Breeding Nightjar, Woodcock, Redstart, Woodlark, Tree Pipit, Stonechat. *Autumn/winter:* Raven, Crossbill.
Other notable flora/fauna: Good for dragonflies inc. black darter, golden ringed and small red damselfly. Small colony of silver-studded blue butterflies.
Contact: Sussex WT, T: 01273 492 630; E: enquiries@sussexwt.org.uk

4. RYE HARBOUR

Sussex Wildlife Trust.
Location: Sat nav: TN31 7TU. TQ 942 189. One mile from Rye off A259 signed Rye Harbour. From Junc 10 of M20 take A2070 until it joins A259.
Access: Open at all times by footpaths. Organised groups please book.
Facilities: Car park in Rye Harbour village. Information kiosk in car park. Shop, two pubs, toilets and disabled facilities near car park, four hides (wheelchair access), Lime Kiln Cottage Information Centre open most days (10am-4pm) by volunteers.
Public transport: Train stations at Rye and Winchelsea (T: 08457 484 950), bus (T: 0870 608 2608)
Habitats: Sea, sand, shingle, pits, saltmarsh and grassland.

Key birds: Seventy of the 279 recorded spp. have bred on the reserve. *Spring:* Passage waders, especially roosting Whimbrel. *Summer:* Turtle Dove, Breeding terns (three spp), waders (seven spp), gulls (six spp. inc Mediterranean), Garganey, Shoveler, Cetti's Warbler, Bearded Tit, Wheatear. *Winter:* Wildfowl, inc. Smew and nationally important numbers of Shoveler, Water Rail, Bittern.
Other notable flora/fauna: Good shingle flora inc. endangered least lettuce and stinging hawksbeard. Excellent range of dragonflies inc. breeding red-veined darter and scarce emerald damselfly.
Contact: Lime Kiln Cottage Info Centre, T: 07884 494 982;
W: sussexwildlifetrust.org.uk/visit/rye-harbour

Sussex (West)

PAGHAM HARBOUR IS worth a visit at any time of year. Nearby Selsey Bill is good for migrants and there is a noticeable skua passage in the spring. The WWT reserve at Arundel is good for Mandarins and Cetti's Warblers, while further inland, RSPB Pulborough Brooks holds important numbers of wintering wildfowl including the chance of Bewick's Swans.

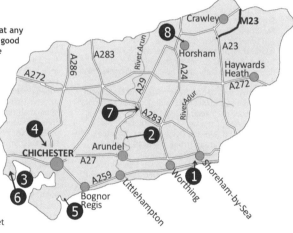

1. ADUR ESTUARY

RSPB (South East Region Office).
Location: Sat nav: BN43 5EE. TQ 215 049. On W side of Shoreham-on-Sea: view from Coronation Green, situated near town centre or footbridge linking High Street and Riverside Road.
Access: No direct access to reserve areas, but good views from riverside paths between footbridge in Shoreham town centre and A259 Norfolk bridge (car park). Free public car park at the Council's recreational field on N side of A259.
Facilities: None.
Public transport: Trains: Shoreham-by-Sea. Bus: Shoreham-by-Sea town centre. Brighton and Hove buses, T: 01273 886 200, less than one mile away.
Habitats: Mudflats and saltmarsh.
Key birds: A small area but a haven for waders and wildfowl. *Spring/summer:* Little Egret, Turnstone, Ringed Plover, Dunlin, Redshank, Common and Sandwich terns. *All year:* Oystercatcher. *Winter:* Good range of gulls, Kingfisher and several wader species.
Contact: RSPB, T: 01273 775 333

2. ARUNDEL WETLAND CENTRE

Wildfowl and Wetland Trust.
Location: Sat nav: BN18 9PB. TQ 020 081. Centre on Mill Road clearly signed from Arundel, just N of A27.
Access: Open daily, closed Dec 25, 9.30am-5.30pm (summer), 9.30am-4.30pm (winter), last admissions 30mins before closing. Approx 1.5 miles of level footpaths, suitable for wheelchairs. Guide dogs only. Admission charges for non-WWT members.
Facilities: Visitor centre, restaurant, shop, hides, picnic area, seasonal nature trails. Eye of The Wind Wildlife Gallery. Corporate hire facilities. Electric boat safaris. Manual wheelchairs available.
Public transport: Arundel station, 15-20 mins walk. T: 01903 882 131. Buses from Brighton and Worthing (no. 700) to Arundel (one mile walk to reserve).
Habitats: Site covers 65 acres with lakes, wader scrapes, reedbed.

Key birds: *All year*: All three woodpeckers, Kingfisher. *Summer*: Nesting Redshank, Lapwing, Oystercatcher, Common Tern, Sedge, Reed and Cetti's Warblers, Peregrine, Hobby. *Winter*: Teal, Wigeon, Reed Bunting, Water Rail, Cetti's Warbler and occasionally roosting Bewick's Swan.
Other notable flora/fauna: Bee orchid, water shrew, palmate and smooth newt, grass snake, six spp. of bat.
Contact: Arundel Wetland Centre, T: 01903 883 355; E: info.arundel@wwt.org.uk

3. CHICHESTER HARBOUR

Chichester Harbour Conservancy.
Location: West of Chichester, with various viewing points along 47 miles of coastline to Hayling Island. East Head/ West Wittering good places for birding from A27 S of Chichester, follow brown signs for West Wittering Beach. Sandy Point Nature Reserve occupies the SE corner of Hayling Island but can only be visited on guided walks.
Access: Five paths suitable for wheelchairs: Cobnor Point/ Itchenor/ Prinsted/ North Common, Northney/ Sandy Point, Hayling Island.
Facilities: Wheelchair-accessible viewing platform and toilet at Itchenor. RADAR-key toilet at Dell Quay.
Public transport: Contact Stagecoach South, T: 0871 200 2233 for information on services.
Habitats: Deep saltwater channels, mud banks, sand dunes and shingle.
Key birds: Internationally-important for birds, with an estimated 55,000 birds residing or passing through the harbour each year. *Autumn/winter*: Waders inc. Golden Plover, Lapwing, Curlew, Whimbrel, Black- and Bar-tailed Godwits, Oystercatcher, Turnstone, Snipe, Dunlin and Sanderling. Up to 10,000 Brent Geese, Red-breasted Merganser and common wildfowl species. Kingfisher, Short-eared owl, Hen Harrier, Linnet and Skylark. *Spring/summer*: Little, Sandwich and Common Terns all breed. Dartford Warbler breeds at Sandy Point NR.
Other notable flora/fauna: Harbour seal, water vole, stoat, marsh samphire, sea purslane, sea lavender and sea aster.
Contact: Harbour Office (inc Friends of Chichester Hbr, Itchenor, T: 01243 512 301;
E: info@conservancy.co.uk W: www.conservancy.co.uk
E: info@friendsch.org; W: www.friendsch.org

4. KINGLEY VALE NNR

Natural England (Solent & Downs Team).
Location: Part of South Downs National Park. Sat nav: PO18 9BN for the local church. Continue west past church to reserve car park 100 yards down the hill. SU 825 088 (West Stoke car park, 0.6 mile from reserve entrance). Approx five miles NW of Chichester town centre (as the crow flies). Travel N from Chichester on A286 to Lavant, then turn L by the church on to Downs Road, follow to West Stoke. Turn R at junction after the church to West Stoke car park.
Access: Via a footpath from reserve car park, bridleway access is via Woodend. No permits required, no disabled access. All dogs on a lead to protect grazing stock, nesting birds and other sensitive wildlife.

Facilities: Nature trail (posts 1-24) and an unmanned information centre, leaflets and nature trail guides. No toilets.
Public transport: Nearest railway station Chichester, three miles away.
Habitats: Greatest yew forest in western Europe (more than 30,000 yew trees). Chalk grassland, mixed oak/ash woodland and scrub. Chalk heath.
Key birds: *Spring/summer*: Nightingale, Whitethroat, Blackcap, Lesser Whitethroat. *Autumn/winter*: Hen Harrier on migration, Buzzard, Hobby on migration, Red Kite, Barn and Tawny Owls, Hawfinch, Ravens, Goldcrest, Firecrest, Redwing, Fieldfare, Osprey (passing over on migration), Green Woodpecker, Nuthatch, Bullfinch, Treecreeper, Woodcock.
Other notable flora/fauna: Ancient yew trees, yellow meadow ant, 39 recorded spp. of butterflies inc. brown argus and chalkhill blue, 11 spp. of orchid, brown hare, dormice, bats.
Contact: Natural England, T: 0300 060 6000; E: enquiries@naturalengland.org.uk

5. PAGHAM HARBOUR

West Sussex County Council/RSPB.
Location: Sat nav: PO20 7NE. SZ 857 966. Five miles S of Chichester on B2145 towards Selsey. After 0.5 mile turn R at first roundabout still following Selsey. Look for entrance just after leaving Sidlesham after speed limit increases to 50mph.
Access: Sidlesham Ferry and Church Norton car parks open at all times. Dogs must be on leads. Disabled trail with accessible hide. All groups and coach parties must book in advance.
Facilities: Visitor centre open throughout the year, closed Dec 25/26, 10am-4pm. Toilets (inc. disabled), three hides (only Ferry Pool hide accessible to wheelchairs) and several other viewpoints, one nature trail.
Public transport: Bus no. 51 (Chichester to Selsey) stops by visitor centre.
Habitats: Mudflats, intertidal saltmarsh, shingle beaches, lagoons and farmland.
Key birds: *Spring*: Passage migrants (warblers, hirundines, Wheatear). *Summer*: Breeding Little and Common Terns. *Autumn*: Passage waders inc Curlew Sandpiper, Ruff and Little Stint, other migrants, inc. Pied and Spotted Flycatchers, incoming wildfowl species. *Winter*: 20,000 birds inc. Brent Goose, Slavonian Grebe, wildfowl and waders. *All year*: Little Egret.
Other notable flora/fauna: Common and grey seals (winter). Wide range of grasses, butterflies and dragonflies (inc. emperor, broad-bodied chaser and hairy dragonfly).
Contact: RSPB, T: 01243 641 508; E: pagham.harbour@rspb.org.uk

NATURE RESERVES - SOUTH EAST ENGLAND

6. PILSEY & THORNEY ISLANDS

RSPB (South East Region Office).
Location: Sat nav. PO10 8HS. SU 766 051.
W of Chichester. Take A259 and park in Prinstead, near Emsworth. Walk over sea walls to view both Thorney and Pilsey islands.
Access: No vehicle access to Thorney Island, viewing from footpaths only. Pilsey Island can also be viewed from 5.5 mile coastal path (the Sussex Border Path) that runs around the Thorney Island MoD base. Long, exposed walk.
Facilities: None.
Habitats: Intertidal sandflats and mudflats, fore dunes and yellow dunes, bare and vegetated shingle and saltmarsh.
Key birds: The reserve, together with the adjacent area of Pilsey Sand, forms one of the most important pre-roost and roost site for passage and wintering waders in the area. Brent Geese in winter, plus Merlin and Peregrine possible. *Summer:* Breeding Sandwich and Common Terns. Ringed Plovers and Osprey possible. *Autumn:* Passage wader numbers increase and Brent Geese return in Oct.
Contact: RSPB, T: 01798 875 851;
E: pilsey.island@rspb.org.uk

7. PULBOROUGH BROOKS

RSPB (South East Region Office).
Location: Sat nav: RH20 2EL. TQ 058 164.
Part of South Downs National Park, signposted on A283 between Pulborough (via A29) and Storrington (via A24). Two miles SE of Pulborough.
Access: Visitor centre open daily (9.30am-5pm), except Dec 25/26. Nature trail and hides (sunrise-sunset), closed Dec 25. Admission fee for nature trail (adult and child rates, free to RSPB members). No dogs. All hides accessible to wheelchair users, though strong helper is needed.
Facilities: Visitor centre (inc. RSPB shop, tea room with terrace (9.30am-4.30pm), displays, toilets). Nature trail, four hides and three viewpoints. Large car park inc. coach area. Play and picnic areas. An electric buggy is available for free hire.
Public transport: Two miles from Pulborough train station. Connecting bus service regularly passes reserve entrance (a request stop) - Compass Travel bus no. 100 Burgess Hill to Horsham, T: 01903 690 025. Cycle stands.
Habitats: Lowland wet grassland (wet meadows and ditches). Restored heathland, hedgerows, scrub and woodland.
Key birds: *Winter:* Thousands of wintering wildfowl and waterbirds, Bewick's Swan. Peregrine, Hen Harrier, Merlin and Short-eared Owl hunt regularly. *Spring/summer:* Breeding wading birds and songbirds (inc. Lapwing and Nightingale), Hobby, Nightjar, Woodlark, Lesser-spotted Woodpecker, Barn Owl. *Autumn:* Passage wading birds, Redstart, Whinchat, Yellow Wagtail, incoming wildfowl species.
Other notable flora/fauna: Good range of butterflies and dragonflies (inc. emperor, four-spotted chaser and downy emerald).
Contact: RSPB, T: 01798 875 851;
E: pulborough.brooks@rspb.org.uk

8. WARNHAM LNR

Horsham District Council.
Location: Sat nav: RH12 2RA. TQ 167 324. One mile NW from Horsham town centre on B2237, just off A24 'Robin Hood' roundabout.
Access: Open all year, except Dec25/26), 10am-6pm Mar-Oct, 10am-5pm Nov-Feb. Day permit charge for adults, children under 16 free. Annual permits also available. No dogs or cycling allowed. Good wheelchair access over most of the Reserve.
Facilities: Free access to visitor centre and cafe. Large car park - coaches by request. Toilets (inc. disabled), four hides, reserve leaflets, millpond nature trail, bird feeding station, wader scrapes, boardwalks, benches and hardstanding paths.
Public transport: One mile from Horsham Railway Station, along Hurst Road, with a R turn onto Warnham Road. Buses from 'CarFax' in Horsham Centre stop within 150 yards of the reserve. Travelline, T: 0870 608 2608.
Habitats: Site of 92 acres inc. 17 acre millpond, reedbeds, marsh, meadow and woodland (deciduous and coniferous).
Key birds: *Summer:* Common Tern, Kingfisher, woodpeckers, Mandarin Duck, Marsh Tit, Goldcrest, hirundines, Hobby, warblers. *Winter:* Cormorant, gulls, Little Grebe, Water Rail, Brambling, Siskin, Lesser Redpoll, thrushes and wildfowl. *Passage:* Waders, pipits, terns and hirundines.
Other notable flora/fauna: Extensive invertebrate interest, inc. 33 spp. of butterflies and 25 spp. of dragonfly. Mammals inc. harvest mouse, water shrew and badger. More than 450 spp. of plant, inc. broad-leaved helleborine and common spotted orchid.
Contact: Horsham DC, T: 01403 256 890;
E: parks@horsham.gov.uk

South West England

Cornwall, Devon, Dorset, Somerset, Wiltshire

Cornwall

LOCATION, LOCATION, LOCATION.... Cornwall is ideally placed to attract overflying migrants in both spring and, particularly, autumn including migrant hotspots near Land's End such as Cot and Nanquidno Valleys. Headlands at St Ives and Porthgwarra are ideal for autumn seawatching, while Choughs are recolonizing the Lizard.

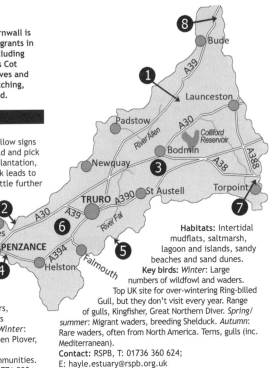

1. CROWDY RESERVOIR

South West Lakes Trust.
Location: Sat nav. PL32 9XJ. SX 13 834. Follow signs from A39 at Camelford to Davidstow Airfield and pick up signs to reservoir. On edge of forestry plantation, park in pull-in spot near cattle grid. A track leads to a hide via stiles. Main car park located a little further down the lane.
Access: Open all year. No wheelchair access on tracks.
Facilities: Hide accessed from car park along rough track.
Public transport: None.
Habitats: Reservoir, bog, moorland, forestry.
Key birds: *Spring*: Passage migrants, inc. Wheatear, Whimbrel, Ruff. *Summer*: Black-headed Gull, Grasshopper, Reed and Sedge Warblers, returning waders. *Autumn*: Waders, raptors possible inc. Peregrine, Goshawk, Merlin. *Winter*: Wild swans, wildfowl, possible Smew. Golden Plover, Woodcock, Fieldfare, Redwing.
Other notable flora/fauna: Mire floral communities.
Contact: South West Lakes Trust, T: 01566 771 930; E: info@swlakestrust.org.uk; W: www.swlakestrust.org.uk

2. HAYLE ESTUARY

RSPB (South West England Office).
Location: Sat nav: TR27 6JF. SW 551 364. In town of Hayle. Follow signs to Hayle from A30. Take B3301 through Hayle past the Tempest factory, turn L into Chenells Rd and right into Ryans Field. See website for access to other points on the reserve.
Access: Open at all times. No permits required. No admission charges. Not suitable for wheelchair users. Dogs on leads restricted to public footpaths. No coaches.
Facilities: Eric Grace Memorial Hide overlooks Ryan's Field, but birds here only at high tide. Nearest toilets in town of Hayle. No visitor centre but information board at hide. Circular walk around Ryan's Field and public footpath around Carnsew Pool.
Public transport: Western Greyhound bus services no. 501 (summer only, not Sat) or no. 515 (not Sun). Nearest bus stop for Carnsew Pool is in Foundry Square, Hayle (450 yards away). T: 0871 200 2233 for details. Nearest rail station at St Erth (one mile away).

3. HELMAN TOR NATURE RESERVE

Cornwall Wildlife Trust.
Location: Sat nav: PL30 5DU. SX 062 615 (The Barn, Lower Gurtla). Large wetland complex incorporating Breney Common and Red Moor Memorial Reserve. 2.5 miles S of Bodmin. From A30/A391 (Innis Downs) roundabout south of Bodmin, turn N to Lanivet and take first R under A30 bridge. For Breney Common entrance, turn R at Reperry Cross, then L fork to Trebell Green and on towards Gurtla. The entrance track is on the L in Gurtla, after the Methodist church, opposite The Barn.
Access: Open at all times but please keep to paths. Disabled access from small car park at Breney. Small car park at Helman Tor. Wilderness Trail can be very muddy after heavy rain.
Facilities: Wilderness trail from Helman Tor. Boardwalk sections the only suitable surface for wheelchairs, but can be slippery when wet.
Public transport: None.
Habitats: Huge site (536 acres) inc. wetland, grassland, heath and scrub.
Key birds: Willow Tit, Nightjar, Tree Pipit, Sparrowhawk, Lesser Whitethroat, Curlew.

Habitats: Intertidal mudflats, saltmarsh, lagoon and islands, sandy beaches and sand dunes.
Key birds: *Winter*: Large numbers of wildfowl and waders. Top UK site for over-wintering Ring-billed Gull, but they don't visit every year. Range of gulls, Kingfisher, Great Northern Diver. *Spring/summer*: Migrant waders, breeding Shelduck. *Autumn*: Rare waders, often from North America. Terns, gulls (inc. Mediterranean).
Contact: RSPB, T: 01736 360 624; E: hayle.estuary@rspb.org.uk

Other notable flora/fauna: Royal fern, sundews and other bog plants. Butterflies (inc. marsh and small pearl-bordered fritillaries, silver-studded blue).
Contact: Cornwall WT, T: 01872 273 939;
E: sean.ohea@cornwallwildlifetrust.org.uk

4. MARAZION MARSH

RSPB (South West England Office).
Location: Sat nav: TR17 0AA. SW 510 312. Reserve is one mile E of Penzance, 500 yards W of Marazion. Entrance off seafront road near Marazion.
Access: Open at all times. Park in privately operated car parks within walking distance. Free admission. Not suitable for wheelchair users. Dogs on leads please. No coaches.
Facilities: No toilets or visitor centre. Viewing bay on seafront pavement overlooks pools and reedbeds of the sanctuary area. Nearest toilets in Marazion and seafront car park.
Public transport: First Group buses run from Penzance bus station to Marazion, and from St Ives in teh summer. T: 0871 200 2233 for details.
Habitats: Wet reedbed, willow carr.
Key birds: More than 250 spp. recorded. *Winter*: Wildfowl, Snipe, occasional Bittern, impressive pre-roost flocks of Starlings up to New year attract Buzzards and Sparrowhawks. *Spring/summer*: Breeding Reed, Sedge and Cetti's Warblers, herons, swans. *Autumn*: Large roost of Swallows and martins in reedbeds, migrant warblers and Water Rail.
Other notable flora/fauna: Up to 22 spp. of dragonflies, plus 500 spp. of vascular plants, inc. lawn camomile and yellow flag.
Contact: RSPB, 01736 360 624;
E: marazion.marsh@rspb.org.uk

5. NARE HEAD

National Trust.
Location: Part of the NT's Roseland estate. Sat nav: TR2 5PH. SW 92 2 379 (Nare Head car park). Approx ten miles SE of Truro. from A390 head S on A307 to two miles S of Tregony just past the garage. Follow signs to Veryan then L signposted to Carne. Go straight over at crossroad, following Carne and Pendower. Turn L on a bend following NT signs for Nare Head. Bearing R, cross over a cattle grid to the car park. From the garage, Nare Head is about four miles.
Access: Open all year. Approach cliff edges with care as they are unstable.
Facilities: Car park.
Habitats: Headland, open sea.
Key birds: *Spring/summer*: Razorbill, Guillemot, Shag, Sandwich, Common and Arctic Terns, possible Whimbrel, Fulmar, occasional Chough. *Winter*: Black-throated and Great Northern Divers, and Red-throated Diver possible. Common Scoter, Velvet Scoter, Slavonian, Black-necked and Red-necked Grebes.
Contact: National Trust, T: 01872 580 553;
E: roseland@nationaltrust.org.uk

6. STITHIANS RESERVOIR

South West Lakes Trust.
Location: Sat nav: TR16 6NW (Golden Lion Inn). SS 715 365. Signposted from B3297 S of Redruth.
Access: Good viewing from causeway.
Facilities: Hide near main centre (opposite Golden Lion Inn) open to all. Two other hides for members of CBWPS. Toilets, cafe. Footpath around reservoir.
Habitats: Open water, marshland.
Key birds: County's best open water site for winter wildfowl. Winter gull flocks inc. Mediterranean. Good for waders such as Common, Green and Wood Sandpipers. Passage birds can inc. Osprey, Black Tern, Garganey. Good track record for rarities inc. Pied-billed Grebe, Pectoral, White-rumped and Semipalmated Sandpipers, Lesser Yellowlegs, Wilson's Phalarope, Caspian Tern and Black Kite.
Contact: Stithians Activity Centre, T: 01209 860 301;
E: stithiansOA@swlakestrust.org.uk;
W: www.swlakestrust.org.uk

7. TAMAR ESTUARY

Cornwall Wildlife Trust.
Location: Sat nav: PL12 6LJ (China Fleet Club). SX 431 614 (Landulph section). SX 436 627 (Cargreen). From Plymouth head W on A38. Access parking at Cargreen and Landulph from minor roads off A388.
Access: Open at all times. Footpath from Cargreen to Landulph. Access two bird hides from China Fleet Club car park, Saltash. Follow path alongside golf course - do not walk on course itself. Combination number for hide locks available at club reception.
Facilities: Two hides on foreshore, first (0.25 mile from car park) overlooks estuary, second (0.5 mile) has excellent views across Kingsmill Lake.
Habitats: 269 acres of tidal mudflat with some saltmarsh.
Key birds: *Winter*: Large number of Avocet (Oct to Mar), Snipe, Black-tailed Godwit, Redshank, Dunlin, Curlew, Whimbrel, Spotted Redshank, Green Sandpiper, Golden Plover, Kingfisher. *Spring/summer*: Breeding Shelduck.
Contact: Cornwall WT, T: 01872 273 939;
E: peter.kent@cornwallwildlifetrust.org.uk

8. TAMAR LAKES

South West Lakes Trust.
Location: Sat nav: EX23 9SB. SS 295 115. Site lies E of A39, N of Bude. Follow brown tourist signs from Holsworthy or Kilkhampton.
Access: Open all year. Limited wheelchair access. Pay-and-display car parks. Sailing and other watersports means Upper Lake is limited for birding. Nature reserve is located on Lower lake.
Facilities: Bird hides at both lakes. Cafe (limited opening) at Upper Tamar. Toilets at Upper open all year, those at Lower only open in summer. Trail leaflet available from cafe.
Public transport: None.
Habitats: Two freshwater lakes, plus swamp, scrub and grassland.

Key birds: *All year*: Great Crested Grebe, Black-headed Gull, Kingfisher, Willow Tit, Reed Bunting. *Spring*: Black Tern. *Summer*: Breeding Sedge, Reed and Willow Warblers and House Martin. *Winter*: Moderate numbers of wildfowl, inc. Wigeon and Teal and gulls.
Other notable flora/fauna: Badger, roe deer, otter, southern marsh orchid, wood white butterfly, grass snake.

Contact: Upper Tamar Lakes Activity Centre, T: 01288 321712; E: TamarOA@swlakestrust.org.uk; W: www.swlakestrust.org.uk

Devon

EXMOOR, WITH WONDERFUL wooded valleys attractive to birds, is the prettier of the county's two National Parks, whereas Dartmoor is much bleaker. Red-backed Shrikes are attempting to re-establish themselves on Dartmoor. The island of Lundy in the Bristol Channel is good for vagrants. Look for waders around Exminster Marshes while the southern coast holds localised but increasing pockets of Cirl Buntings.

1. AYLESBEARE COMMON

RSPB (South West England Office).
Location: Sat nav: EX10 0DF. SY 057 898. Five miles E of Junc 30 of M5 at Exeter, 0.5 mile past Halfway Inn on B3052. Turn R to Hawkerland, car park on left. The reserve is on the opposite side of the main road.
Access: Open all year. One track suitable for wheelchairs and pushchairs. Dogs only on public footpaths.

Facilities: Car park, two nature trails, picnic area, group bookings, guided walks and special events. Disabled access via metalled track to private farm. No toilets or viewing facilities.
Public transport: Stagecoach Buses T: 01392 427 711 - Exeter to Seaton/Honiton, nos. 9 and 9A, request stop at Joneys Cross (reserve entrance).
Habitats: Heathland, wood fringes, streams and ponds.
Key birds: *All year*: Dartford Warbler, Buzzard, Yellowhammer. *Spring/summer*: Hobby, Nightjar, Tree Pipit, Stonechat. *Winter*: Possible Hen Harrier.
Other notable flora/fauna: Good range of dragonflies (inc Southern Damselfly) and butterflies.
Contact: RSPB, T: 01395 233 655; E: aylesbeare.common@rspb.org.uk

2. BERRY HEAD NNR

Torbay Coast & Countryside Trust.
Location: Sat nav: TQ5 9AP (Berry Head car park). SX 940 561. Signposted from Brixham on minor roads from A3022 and A379. Located at end of Gillard Road, past Landscove Holiday Village.
Access: Open all year. Guardhouse visitor centre open easter-Oct (Tues-Sun, 10am-4pm and Mon 1pm-4pm), Oct-easter Sat/Sun only, 10am-4pm. Wheelchair-friendly 300 yards path from car park to visitor centre and cafe.
Facilities: Pay-and-display car park. Visitor centre (CCTV images of nesting seabirds), cafe and toilets. Two mobility vehicles for hire (pre-book). Bird hide overlooking cliffs.
Public transport: Bus no. 17 from Brixham to Victoria Road (0.5 mile walk to Berry Head: some steep sections). Torbay Coastpath runs from Torquay.
Habitats: Limestone cliffs (200ft), grassland, quarry.
Key birds: *All year*: Cirl Buntings (in flocks in autumn), Peregrine (hunting in quarry area), Fulmar. *Spring/summer*: Up to 1,200 nesting Guillemots on cliffs below Southern Fort. Well known as a migrant watchpoint.
Other notable flora/fauna: Limestone flora inc. eight spp. of orchid, small hare's-ear. Harbour porpoise, common dolphin, greater and lesser horseshoe bats (walks arranged), bloody nose beetle and range of butterflies.
Contact: Berry Head NNR, T: 01803 882 619; E: berryhead@countryside-trust.org.uk, W: www.countryside-trust.org.uk/berryhead

NATURE RESERVES - SOUTH WEST ENGLAND

3. BOVEY HEATHFIELD

Devon Wildlife Trust.
Location: Sat nav: TQ12 6TU. SX 824 765. On the outskirts of Bovey Tracey on SE edge of Dartmoor. From A382 Bovey Straight take Battle Road into Heathfield Industrial estate. Turn L into Cavalier Road, then Dragoon Close – the reserve is along a gravel path.
Access: Open all year. Dogs allowed on leads. Please keep to paths. Rough paths not suitable for wheelchairs. No coach access.
Facilities: Information hut open when warden is on site. Circular way-marked path and viewpoint.
Public transport: Exeter to Plymouth buses stop at Drum Bridge, a 20 mins walk to reserve.
Habitats: Mix of wet and dry lowland heath, surrounding by secondary woodland covering 58 acres. Contains numerous ponds.
Key birds: Breeding Nightjar, Tree Pipit, Stonechat and Dartford Warbler, plus commoner species such as Skylark, Linnet and Yellowhammer.
Other notable flora/fauna: Heathers, wet and dry heathland plants, more than 60 endangered insect spp., plus grayling and green hairstreak butterflies, slow worm, adder and grass snake.
Contact: Devon WT, T: 01392 279 244;
E: contactus@devonwildlife trust.org

4. BOWLING GREEN MARSH

RSPB (South West England Office).
Location: Sat nav: EX3 0EN (Holman Rd car park). SX 971 875. On the E side of River Exe, four miles SE of Exeter in Bowling Green Road, Topsham.
Access: Open at all times. Park at the Holman Way or The Quay public car parks in Topsham village, not in the lane by the reserve. Blue Badge parking space near hide.
Facilities: RSPB shop at Darts Farm (EX3 0QH), one mile from reserve, east of Topsham across River Clyst. Weekly guided walks from Darts Farm. Nearest RADAR toilets at The Quay car park. Wheelchair-friendly bird hide and viewing platform.
Public transport: Exeter to Exmouth railway has regular (every 30 mins) service to Topsham station (one mile from reserve). Stagecoach Devon no. 57 (Mon-Sat every 12 mins, Sun every half-hour) from Exeter to Topsham stops at Elm Grove Road (0.6 mile from reserve). Call Traveline, T: 0871 200 2233.
Habitats: Coastal grassland, open water/marsh.
Key birds: *Winter*: Large numbers of Wigeon, Shoveler, Teal, Black-tailed Godwit, Curlew, Golden Plover. Also Avocet and Brent Geese. *Spring*: Shelduck, passage waders inc. Ringed Plover, Little Stint, Ruff and sandpipers, Whimbrel, passage Garganey and Yellow Wagtail. *Summer*: Gull/tern roosts, high tide wader roosts contain many passage birds. *Autumn*: Wildfowl, Peregrine, wader roosts.
Other notable flora/fauna: Hairy dragonfly, wasp spider.
Contact: RSPB (Darts Farm), T: 01392 879 438 or (the Reserve), T: 01392 833 311

5. BURRATOR RESERVOIR

South West Lakes Trust.
Location: Sat nav: PL20 6PE. SX 568 689. On south side of Dartmoor, 10 miles NE of Plymouth, off A386 (Tavistock road). At Yelverton take B3212 towards Princeton. Turn R at Burrator Inn and follow signs to reservoir.
Access: Open all year. Free parking areas around reservoir. Main route, though suitable for disabled, is also used by motorists and cyclists. There are about 25 stiles on minor routes.
Facilities: Visitor centre (opening times/days vary depending on time of year), toilets (inc disabled). Snacks and ice-creams available during summer.
Public transport: Bus daily from Plymouth to Dousland (a short walk from the reservoir) - no. 82 Western National or no. 48 (Sun). T: 01752 402 060. Train: nearest station is Plymouth. T: 08457 484 950.
Habitats: Pine forests, wooded streams, open moorland scrub.
Key birds: *Winter*: Goosander, Dipper, Grey Wagtail, Green Sandpiper, Brambling, Crossbill, Siskin, Redpoll. *All year*: All three woodpeckers, Buzzard, Sparrowhawk, Kestrel, Barn Owl, Tree Sparrow.
Other notable flora/fauna: Marsh fritillary butterfly, dragonflies, esp. in arboretum, bats, otter.
Contact: Burrator Discovery Centre,
T: 01822 855 700; E: heritage@swlakestrust.org.uk;
W: www.swlakestrust.org.uk

6. DAWLISH WARREN NNR

Teignbridge District Council.
Location: Sat nav: EX7 0NF. SX 983 788. At Dawlish Warren on S side of Exe estuary mouth. Turn off A379 at sign to Warren Golf Club, between Cockwood and Dawlish. Turn into car park adjacent to Lea Cliff Holiday Park. Pass under tunnel and turn L away from amusements. Park at far end of car park and pass through two pedestrian gates.
Access: Open public access, but avoid mudflats. Also avoid beach beyond groyne nine around high tide due to roosting birds. Parking charges. No dogs on beach or dunes between ninth groyne at any time (inc. the hide).
Facilities: Visitor centre open most days Apr-Sept, weekends Oct-Mar (10.30am-5pm, closed 1pm-2pm) -also closed if in use by groups or wardens out on site. Toilets at entrance tunnel and in resort area only. Bird hide one mile NE of visitor centre open at all times – best around high tide.
Public transport: Train station at site, also regular bus service operated by Stagecoach.
Habitats: High tide roost site for wildfowl and waders of Exe estuary on mudflats and shore. Dunes, dune grassland, woodland, scrub, ponds.
Key birds: *Winter*: Waders and wildfowl in large numbers. Also good for divers and Slavonian Grebe offshore. *Summer*: Particularly good for terns. Excellent variety of birds all year, esp. on migration.
Contact: Visitor Centre, T: 01626 863 980.
W: www.dawlishwarren.co.uk

7. EAST DARTMOOR WOODS & HEATHS NNR

Natural England (Devon, Cornwall & Isles of Scilly Team).
Location: Sat nav: TQ13 9LJ (Yarner Wood).
SX 778 788. The NNR is two miles from Bovey Tracey
on road to Becky Falls and Manaton. Road continues
across Trendlebere Down, where there are roadside
car parks and adjacent paths.
Access: Yarner Wood car park open 8.30am-7pm or
dusk if earlier. Outside these hours, access on foot from
Trendlebere Down. Dogs welcome under close control.
Facilities: Information/interpretation display and
self-guided trails available in Yarner Wood car park
also hide with feeding station (Nov-Mar).
Public transport: Carmel Coaches no. 671
(Okehampton to Newton Abbot) stops at Manaton.
Habitats: The reserve consists of three connected
sites (Yarner Wood, Trendlebere Down and Bovey
Valley Woodlands), a total of 365 ha of upland
oakwood and heathland.
Key birds: *All year*: Raven, Buzzard, Goshawk,
Sparrowhawk, Lesser Spotted, Great Spotted and
Green Woodpeckers, Grey Wagtail and Dartford
Warbler (on Trendlebere Down). *Spring/summer*:
Pied Flycatcher, Wood Warbler, Redstart, Tree Pipit,
Linnet, Stonechat, Cuckoo, Whitethroat, Skylark and
Nightjar on heaths. *Autumn/winter*: Good range of
birds with feeding at hide, inc. Siskin, Redpoll, plus
Hen Harrier on Trendlebere Down.
Other notable flora/fauna: Good range of butterflies,
inc. fritilleries and grayling.
Contact: Natural England, Yarner Wood,
T: 01626 832 330.

8. EXMINSTER & POWDERHAM MARSHES

RSPB (South West England Office).
Location: Sat nav: EX6 8DZ (Swan's Nest Inn).
SX 954 872. Five miles S of Exeter on W bank of River
Exe. Marshes lie between Exminster and the estuary.
Powderham Marsh accessed from car park behind
Swan's Nest Inn (A379).
Access: Open at all times (except permissive path at
Powderham). No dogs at Powderham Marshes.
Facilities: No toilets or visitor centre at either site -
refreshments and toilets at Swans Nest Inn and Turf
pub. Information in RSPB car park (Exminster site)
and marked footpaths across reserve. Exminster
circular walk takes 90 mins.
Public transport: Exeter to Newton Abbot no. 2 bus
stop at Swan's Nest roundabout is 400 yards from
reserve car park. Traveline, T: 0871 200 2233.
Habitats: Coastal grazing marsh with freshwater
ditches and pools, reeds, scrub-covered canal banks,
winter stubbles/crops managed for farmland birds.
Key birds: *Winter*: Hundreds of Brent Geese and
Wigeon, plus smaller numbers of other common ducks,
Water Rail, Short-eared Owl. *Spring*: Redshank and
wildfowl breed, Cetti's Warbler on canal banks. Devon's
final breeding site for Lapwing. *Summer*: Gull roosts,
passage waders, hirundines, Hobby. *Autumn*: Peregrine,
Short-eared Owl, winter wildfowl, finch flocks. There
are also records of Cirl Bunting and Woodlark.

Other notable flora/fauna: 23 spp. of dragonfly, inc.
hairy and scarce chaser.
Contact: RSPB, T: 01392 833 311.

9. ROADFORD LAKE COUNTRY PARK

South West Lakes Trust.
Location: Sat nav: PL16 0JL. SX 421 900. Reservoir
lies eight miles E of Launceston, signposted from A30.
Access: Two bird hides, several walks and cycleway.
For disabled access to Bill Oddie Hide park in lay-by
at SX 435 929.
Facilities: Visitor centre, cafe and toilets. Two bird
hides. Pay-and-display car parks.
Public transport: Carmel Coaches' Fri-only
service from Halwill Junction to Tavistock stops as
Broadwoodwidger (short walk to lake).
Habitats: Reservoir of 295 ha (northern third
designated Special Protection Zone to benefit birds),
surrounded by marsh, scrub and fields.
Key birds: County's top inland site for wildfowl (up
to 2,000 birds in winter). Small wader passage in
autumn depending on water levels. Internationally
important site for Lesser Black-backed Gulls. Good
record of attracting rarities.
Other notable flora/fauna: Hazel dormouse, various
bat spp.
Contact: Roadford Lake Activity Centre,
T: 01409 211 507; E: roadfordOA@swlakestrust.org.uk;
W: www.swlakestrust.org.uk

10. SLAPTON LEY NNR

Field Studies Council/Natural England
Location: Sat nav: TQ7 2QP (field centre).
SX 825 440. The largest freshwater lake in SW
England, which lies S of Dartmouth on the south
coast, is separated from Start Bay by a shingle bank
which carries A379.
Access: Pay-and-display car parks off A379 at
Torcross and Slapton Sands. Higher Ley is closed to
the public, but can be viewed from public footpath.
Facilities: Hides overlooking Torcross and Stokely
Bay areas of the lagoon and surrounding backdrops.
Slapton Field Centre offers residential courses.
Public transport: Stagecoach no. 3 bus from
Plymouth to Slapton stops outside field centre.
Habitats: Freshwater lake, reedbeds, marsh and
woodland.
Key birds: Good seawatching in favourable conditions
in spring and autumn, plus migrants on passage.
Large gathering of Swallows in autumn roosts.
Winter: Divers and grebes on sea, Bittern at Higher
Ley. Diving ducks and grebes on Lower Ley. *Spring/
summer*: Migrant warblers. *All year*: Up to four pairs
of Cirl Bunting, Cetti's Warbler (around 40 singing
males each year). Most south-westerly population of
Great Crested Grebe.
Other notable flora/fauna: UK's only site for
strapwort. Badger, otter, dormouse.
Contact: T: 01548 580 466;
E: enquiries.sl@field-studies-council.org;
W: www.slnnr.org.uk

Dorset

DORSET IS WELL ESTABLISHED as one of England's top birding counties. Weymouth makes a splendid base, with two RSPB reserves – Lodmoor and Radipole – in the town itself. From there you can visit the bird observatory and migration hotspot of Portland and The Fleet and Jurassic coast to the west. Heathland, such as Arne RSPB, is good for Dartford Warblers and Nightjars. Studland Bay holds all three divers and five grebe species in winter.

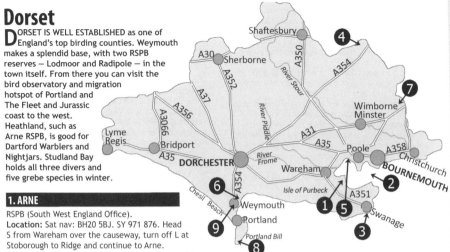

1. ARNE

RSPB (South West England Office).
Location: Sat nav: BH20 5BJ. SY 971 876. Head S from Wareham over the causeway, turn off L at Stoborough to Ridge and continue to Arne.
Access: Trails open at all times. Pay & display car park open 8.30am-dusk. (free for RSPB members) at beginning of Arne village. Shipstal Point and Coombe Trails open all year - screen & hide on Coombe Trail overlooks the Middlebere Channel. Open all year, except Dec 25/26. Limited wheelchair access on trails. Coaches and escorted parties by prior arrangement.
Facilities: Shop 9.30am-5pm/cafe 9.30am-4.30pm (opposite car park), small info centre & toilets in car park. Five signposted trails for different abilities. Two hides, one viewpoint and two viewing screens.
Public transport: None to reserve. Nearest train station is Wareham (four miles from reserve), but 10% discount on cycle hire for RSPB members (Purbeck Cycle Hire, based at railway station, T: 01929 556 601).
Habitats: Lowland heath, woodland, reedbed and saltmarsh, extensive mudflats of Poole Harbour.
Key birds: *All year*: Little Egret, Spoonbill, Marsh Harrier (brred in harbour), Dartford Warbler, Stonechat. *Winter*: 30,000 waders/wildfowl use Poole Harbour, many seen from Arne inc. grebes, divers, Brent Goose, Black-tailed Godwit, Avocet, plus occasional Long-tailed Duck, Eider and Scaup. Hen Harrier, winter thrushes and finches. *Summer*: Nightjar, Sandwich and Common Terns, Barn Owl, hirundines, warblers. *Passage*: Osprey, Hobby, Spotted Redshank, Whimbrel, Greenshank.
A five-year Osprey re-introduction programmed started in Poole Harbour in 2017.
Other notable flora/fauna: Sika deer, all six spp. of UK reptile, silver-studded blue and 32 spp. other butterflies, 23 spp. dragonflies, 850 spp. moths and 500 spp. flowering plants.
Contact: RSPB, T: 01929 553 360;
E: arne@rspb.org.uk

2. BROWNSEA ISLAND NATURE RESERVE

Dorset Wildlife Trust/National Trust.
Location: Sat nav: PH15 1HP (Poole Quay).
SZ 028 878. Half hour boat rides from Poole Quay with Greenslade Pleasure Boats (T: 01202 669 955) and Brownsea Island Ferries (T: 01929 462 383). 10 mins from Sandbanks Quay (next to Studland chain-ferry).
Access: Open late-Mar to late-Oct (10am-5pm). Landing fee, free for NT members. Free admission to nature reserve for DWT members (show card to NT staff), but landing fee must be paid if visiting rest of island. Assistance dogs only.
Facilities: Toilets, information centre, cafe, gift shop, five hides, nature trail.
Public transport: Poole rail/bus station for access to Poole Quay/boats. Wilts & Dorset bus T: 01202 673 555.
Habitats: Saline lagoon, reedbed, lakes, coniferous and mixed woodland covering 101 ha.
Key birds: *Winter/Spring*: Avocet, Black-tailed Godwit, Spotted Redshank and other waders, Water Rail, gulls and wildfowl. *Summer*: Common and Sandwich Terns, Yellow-legged Gull, Little Egret, Little Grebe, Golden Pheasant. *Autumn*: Curlew Sandpiper, Little Stint and rarities often turn up on the DWT Lagoon. Spoonbill now all year round.
Other notable flora/fauna: Red squirrel (up to 200 on island), water vole, Bechstein's bat found 2007. Good range of butterflies and dragonflies.
Contact: Dorset WT, T: 01202 709 445.

3. DURLSTON NNR & COUNTRY PARK

Dorset County Council.
Location: Sat nav: BH19 2JL. SZ 032 774. Lighthouse Road, Swanage, one mile S of town centre (signposted).
Access: Open between sunrise-sunset. Visitor centre and cafe open daily, except Dec 25/26. Pay-&-display parking.

Facilities: Visitor centre (10am-5pm Apr-Oct, 10am-4pm Nov-Mar) located in Durlston Castle which also features cafe (9.30am-5pm & Fri/Sat evenings Apr-mid Oct), toilets, exhibitions, art displays and shop. Dolphin watchpoint hide, waymarked trails. Guided walks, events.
Public transport: Durlston shuttle bus runs between end-May and end-Sept (half-hourly from Swanage railway station and pier).
Habitats: 280 acres of sea cliffs, woodland, grassland, hedges, cliff, meadows and downland.
Key birds: Cliff-nesting seabird colonies inc. Fulmar, Guillemot, Razorbill and Shag; good variety of scrub and woodland breeding spp.; spring and autumn migrants (esp. important location for visible migration in autumn). Also can be good for seabirds on passage - seawatching esp. Apr/May and Aug/Nov.
All year: Peregrine, Kestrel, Raven, woodland species.
Other notable flora/fauna: 34 spp. of butterflies inc. Lulworth skipper, 800 spp. of moths and 500+ spp. of flowering plants, inc. nine spp. of orchid. Bottle-nose dolphin.
Contact: The Ranger, Durlston CP, T: 01929 424 443; E: info@durlston.co.uk; W: www.durlston.co.uk

4. GARSTON WOOD

RSPB (South West England Office).
Location: Sat nav: SP5 5PA (postcode for Dean Lane). SU 003 194. SW from Salisbury. From A354 take turn to Sixpenny Handley then take Bowerchalke road (Dean Lane). Proceed for approximately 1.5 miles on single-track road (with passing places). Garston Wood car park on left side of road.
Access: Open at all times - many tracks. Two trails accessible to pushchairs but terrain is best in dry conditions. Dogs on leads only on public footpaths and bridleways.
Facilities: Car park, reserve leaflet, picnic area, group bookings accepted, guided walks available, remote location, good for walking, pushchair friendly. No toilets or catering facilities.
Public transport: From Salisbury bus station, take Wilts & Dorset no. 184 to Sixpenny Handley (Roebuck Inn). One mile walk to reserve.
Habitats: Actively-managed ancient woodland includes large area of coppiced hazel and maple. Other habitats inc. oak woodland, scrub and mixed plantation, with important features such as glades, rides and dead wood.
Key birds: Common woodland birds plus and migrant warblers inc. Blackcap, Willow Warbler, Garden Warbler, Spotted Flycatcher. Raptors inc. Buzzard, Sparrowhawk and (occasional) Goshawk. Winter thrushes. Turtle Dove and Nightingale have bred in the past.
Other notable flora/fauna: Bluebells and spring flowers. Butterflies, inc. silver-washed fritillary and elusive white admiral. Adders can be seen on the rides. Good range of fungi. Fallow deer.
Contact: RSPB, T: 01929 553 360; E: arne@rspb.org.uk

5. HAM COMMON LNR

Poole Borough Council.
Location: Sat nav: BH15 4LR (for Hamworthy Pier). SY 980 902. W of Poole. In Hamworthy, take the Blandford Road S along Lake Road, W along Lake Drive and Napier Road, leading to Rockley Park. Park in the beach car park by Hamworthy Pier or Rockley Viewpoint car park, off Napier Road, opposite the entrance to Gorse Hill Central Park.
Access: Open all year. Not suitable for coaches.
Facilities: Toilets at Lake Drive car park near Hamworthy Pier at eastern end of reserve.
Habitats: 32-acre LNR consisting of damp and dry heathland, scrub, reedbeds, freshwater lake. Views over Wareham Channel and Poole Harbour.
Key birds: *Spring/summer:* Stonechat, Dartford Warbler. *Winter:* Brent Goose, Red-breasted Merganser, occasional divers, rarer grebes, Scaup. Waders inc. Whimbrel, Greenshank and Common Sandpiper. *All year:* Little Egret.
Other notable flora/fauna: Up to 34 spp. of butterflies, 25 spp. of dragonflies, and all six British reptile spp.
Contact: Poole Borough Council, T: 01202 265 265;

6. LODMOOR NATURE RESERVE

RSPB (South West England Office).
Location: Sat nav: DT4 7SX (Country Park). SY 688 809. Adjacent Lodmoor Country Park, NE of Weymouth, off A353 to Wareham.
Access: Free entry at all times.
Facilities: One viewing shelter, Three nature trails mostly accessible to wheelchairs. No visitor centre or toilets. Three pay-and-display car parks nearby. Blue Badge spaces at Country Park.
Public transport: Nearest bus stop (without shelter) Preston Beach Road, 300 yards away. Bus nos. 4, 4B, 31 & X53. Details from First Buses, T: 0870 0106 022.
Habitats: Marsh, shallow pools, large reedbed and scrub, remnant saltmarsh.
Key birds: *All year:* Little Egret, Marsh Harrier (breeding), Kingfisher, Cetti's Warbler, Bearded Tit. *Spring/summer:* Common Tern colony, warblers (inc. Reed, Sedge, Lesser Whitethroat, occassionally Grasshopper), Hobby. *Winter:* Wildfowl, waders, Bittern. *Passage:* Waders (inc. Black-tailed Godwit, Green and Wood Sandpipers) and other migrants and rarities regularly turn up.
Contact: RSPB, T: 01305 778 313; E: weymouth.reserves@rspb.org.uk

7. MOORS VALLEY CP & RINGWOOD FOREST

East Dorset Council/Forestry Commission.
Location: Sat nav: BH24 2ET. On Horton Road, Ashley Heath. Two miles W of Ringwood, well-signposted from Ashley Heath roundabout (junction of A31 and A338) between Ringwood and St Leonards.
Access: Open daily (except Dec 25) 8am. Closes 5pm Sept-Mar, 6pm Apr-May, 7pm Jun-Aug. Visitor centre open 9am-4.30pm daily. Many trails wheelchair friendly.

Facilities: Visitor centre, toilets, tea-room, country shop. Coach parking. Way-marked trails are in good condition. Pay-and-display car parks (free for Blue Badge holders).
Public transport: Wilts & Dorset no. 38 bus stops at Castleman Trailway entrance, one mile to visitor centre. Traveline SW T: 0845 0727 093 or W: www.travelinesw.com/
Habitats: River, wet meadow, lakes, scrub, broad-leaved woodland, large coniferous forest, golf course.
Key birds: *Spring/summer:* Cuckoo, Nightjar, Sand Martin, Tree Pipit, Whitethroat. Occasional Woodlark, Sedge Warbler. *Winter:* Teal, Pochard, Gadwall, Snipe, Redpoll. Occasional Brambling, Goosander. *Passage:* Whimbrel, Common Sandpiper, waders. *All year:* Buzzard, Lapwing, Woodcock, Little Owl, Grey Wagtail, Kingfisher, Dartford Warbler, Crossbill, usual woodland species.
Other notable flora/fauna: 20 spp. of dragonfly. Good numbers of butterflies and other invertebrates. Roe deer, muntjac, badger, fox, rabbit, grey squirrel, adder, slow worm.
Contact: Moors Valley Country Park, T: 01425 470 721, W: rangers@moors-valley; W: www.moors-valley.co.uk; Forestry Commission T: 0300 067 4601

8. PORTLAND BIRD OBSERVATORY

Portland Bird Observatory (registered charity).
Location: Sat nav: DT5 2JT. SY 681 690. Six miles S of Weymouth beside the road to Portland Bill.
Access: Open at all times. Parking only for members of Portland Bird Observatory. Self-catering accommodation for up to 20. Take own towels, sheets, sleeping bags.
Facilities: Displays and information, toilets, natural history bookshop, equipped kitchen.
Public transport: Bus service from Weymouth (First Dorset Transit Route no. 1).
Habitats: World famous migration watchpoint. Scrub, quarries, open fields.

Key birds: *Spring/autumn:* Most of the regular common and scarce migrants recorded annually. National rarities often found. Good selection of seabird species on passage inc. Pomarine Skua, Balearic Shearwater, Arctic Tern. *Summer:* Breeding Razorbill and Guillemot, Fulmar, Shag, Little Tern (Ferrybridge). Puffin (occasionally seen at the Bill). *Winter:* Large concentration of Mediterranean Gulls at Ferrybridge, Over 355 spp. recorded on Portland.
Contact: Martin Cade (Warden PBO), T: 01305 820 553; E: obs@btinternet.com; W: http://portlandbirdobs.blogspot.co.uk/

9. RADIPOLE LAKE

RSPB (South West England Office).
Location: Sat nav: DT4 7TZ. SY 671 804. In Radipole Park Drive, Weymouth. Enter from Swannery car park (pay-and-display) on footpaths.
Access: Public footpaths open at all times through the reserve. Access to the northern part of site from (8.30am-4.30pm). Visitor centre open daily, except 24-26 Dec, summer (9am-5pm), winter (9am-4pm). Dogs on leads.
Facilities: Network of paths, north hide replaced with a viewing screen, one viewing shelter (both wheelchair-friendly). Information centre contains cafe and disabled toilets.
Public transport: Reserve is 400 yards from train station serving London and Bristol.
Habitats: Lake, reedbeds.
Key birds: *Winter:* Wildfowl (many Pochard), Water Rail, Bittern, pre-roost gatherings of Pied Wagtails. *Spring/summer:* Hirundines arrive. Breeding reedbed warblers (inc. Cetti's), Bearded Tit, passage waders and other migrants. Garganey regular in spring while Hobbies hunt later in season. Marsh Harrier, breeding and now seen all year round. Good for rarer gulls and other rarities.
Contact: RSPB, T: 01305 778 313; E: weymouth.reserves@rspb.org.uk

---

Somerset

EXTENSIVE HABITAT RESTORATION work since the 1980s has boosted bird breeding success in the Somerset Levels (including Bittern) and Common Cranes, hatched at Slimbridge, have been released and are breeding in the area. Somerset is attractive to wildfowl and waders in autumn and winter thanks to a mild climate and its link to the Bristol Channel.

1. BREAN DOWN

National Trust.
Location: Sat nav: TA8 2RS. ST 290 590. 300ft high promontory jutting into Bristol Channel five miles N of Burnham-on-Sea. From junc 22 of M5, head for Weston-super-Mare on A370 and then head for Brean at Lympsham.

Access: Open all year (free of charge). Dogs on lead. Steep slope not recommended for wheelchair-users.
Facilities: Pay & display car park, members free, cafe/shop (9am-5pm) at bottom of Brean Down. Toilet (disabled) at cafe.
Public transport: Highbridge to Weston-super-Mare, via Brean - 1.75 miles.
Habitats: Extension of the Mendips' hard limestone, featuring calcareous grassland, scrub and steep cliffs.
Key birds: *All year:* Peregrine, Raven. *Summer:* Blackcap, Garden Warbler, Whitethroat, Stonechat. *Winter:* Curlew, Shelduck, Dunlin on mudflats. *Passage:* Skuas, shearwaters, divers, Gannet, gulls, waders and passerines.
Other notable flora/fauna: Chalkhill blue, marbled white and other butterflies. Extremely rare white rock rose in Jun. Somerset hair grass, dwarf sedge.
Contact: National Trust, T: 01278 751 874; E: breandown@nationaltrust.org.uk

2. BRIDGWATER BAY NNR

Natural England (Wessex Team).
Location: ST 270 470. 3.25 miles N of Bridgwater
and extends to Burnham-on-Sea. Take Junc 23 or 24
of M5. Turn N off A39 at Cannington and take minor
roads to car park at Steart.
Access: Hides open daily, except Dec 25.
Permits needed for Steart
Island (by boat only).
Dogs on leads. Disabled
access to hides only
by arrangement, other
areas accessible.
Facilities: Car park,
interpretive panels and
leaflet dispenser at Steart -
follow footpath approx 0.5 mile to
tower hide and five other hides at mouth
of River Parrett. No toilets within reserve.
Public transport: Train and bus stations in
Bridgwater. First Group buses on A39 stop at
Stockland Bristol, 1.25 miles SW of Steart -
W: www.firstgroup.com.
Habitats: Parrett River estuary, intertidal mudflats,
saltmarsh totalling 2,559ha.
Key birds: *All year:* Approx 200 spp. recorded on this
Ramsar and SPA site. Wildfowl inc. large population
of Shelduck (Europe's second largest moulting ground
with up to 2,000 birds in Jul) and nationally important
numbers of Wigeon. Internationally important numbers
of Whimbrel and Black-tailed Godwit. Resident Curlews,
Avocets and Oystercatchers joined by many other
waders on passage. Good for birds of prey. *Spring/
autumn:* Passage migrants, inc. occasional vagrants.
Winter: Raptors inc. Peregrine, harriers and Short-
eared Owls. Large numbers of waders and wildfowl.
Other notable flora/fauna: Saltmarsh flora. Rare
invertebrates inc. great silver water beetle, aquatic
snail and hairy dragonfly.
Contact: Natural England, T: 01458 860 120;
E: somersetavonandwiltshire@naturalengland.org.uk

3. CATCOTT COMPLEX NATURE RESERVES

Somerset Wildlife Trust.
Location: Five reserves - Catcott Lows, North, Heath,
South and Fen - now managed together. ST 400 415
(Catcott Lows). Access from Catcott Broad Drove
(Sat nav TA7 8NQ), approx one mile N of Catcott
village (off A39 from Junc 23 of M5).
Access: Open at all times.
Facilities: Car park at reserve entrance. River Parrett
Trail passes through reserve. Two hides at Catcott
Lows (one wheelchair-accessible).
Public transport: None.
Habitats: Wet meadows with winter flooding and
summer grazing.
Key birds: *Winter:* Wigeon, Teal, Pintail, Shoveler,
Gadwall, Bewick's Swan, Peregrine and other raptors.
Siskins and Redpolls in alders. *Spring:* Nationally
important numbers of roosting Whimbrels, plus
passage Greenshank, Ruff and Black-tailed Godwits.

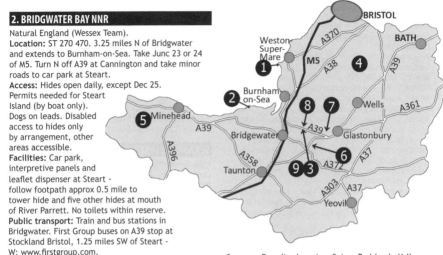

Summer: Breeding Lapwing, Snipe, Redshank, Yellow
Wagtail, warblers. *All year:* Little Egret, Kingfisher,
Cetti's Warbler, Reed Bunting.
Other notable flora/fauna: Otter, roe deer, great
crested newt, rare dragonflies, threatened saw
sedge.
Contact: Somerset WT, T: 01823 652 400;
E: enquires@somersetwildlife.org

4. CHEW VALLEY LAKE

Avon Wildlife Trust/Bristol Water Plc.
Location: Sat nav: BS40 6HN (AWT reserve at
Herriott's Pool). ST 570 600. Nine miles S of Bristol. Take
B3114 south from Chew Stoke, bear L for West Harptree
and head NE on A368. View reserve from causeway at
Herriott's Bridge where there is car parking.
Access: Roadside viewing at Herons Green Bay.
Permit required for access to hides (five at Chew, two
at Blagdon) - apply to Bristol Water (see contact).
Parking for coaches available.
Facilities: Grebe Trail (0.75 mile long) has hard surface
suitable for wheelchairs. Unsurfaced Bittern Trail (one
mile) leads to hide but can be muddy. No dogs on this
section. Chew tea-shop open 10.30am-5.30pm
(mid-Mar to Oct), 4.30pm rest of year.
Public transport: Traveline, T: 0870 6082 608.
Habitats: Largest artificial lake in SW England with
important reedbed.
Key birds: More than 270 spp. recorded - often
attracts rarities. *Winter and passage:* Wildfowl inc.
important numbers of Shoveler, Gadwall, Teal and
Tufted Duck. Large numbers of Goosander, Great
Crested Grebe and Cormorant, with the grebe
numbers often the highest in Britain in autumn.
Plus Bewick's Swan, Goldeneye, Smew, Ruddy Duck.
Huge winter gull roost (up to 50,000+), mostly Black-
headed, Common and Mediterranean Gull. *Summer:*
Breeding Great Crested and Little Grebes, Gadwall,
Tufted Duck, Shoveler, Pochard, Reed Warbler.

Hobbies hunt in late summer. When the water level is low, mud can attract waders such as Dunlin, Ringed Plover and Green Sandpiper.
Other notable flora/fauna: Ruddy darter and migrant hawker dragonflies.
Contact: Avon WT, T: 0117 917 7270;
E: mail@avonwildlifetrust.org.uk;
Bristol Water, Woodford Lodge, Chew Stoke, Bristol BS18 8SH. T: 01275 332 339.

5. DUNKERY & HORNER WOOD NNR

National Trust.
Location: Sat nav: TA24 8HY. SS 920 469 (Horner Wood). On northern boundary of Exmoor, 4.5 miles S of Minehead. Take A39 W to minor road 0.5 mile E of Porlock signposted to Horner. Park in village car park.
Access: Open all year. Car parking in Horner village, West Luccombe and Webber's Post, 150 miles of footpaths. Webber's Post circular walk suitable for wheelchairs. Rugged terrain to reach Dunkery Beacon.
Facilities: Tearoom and toilets. Walks leaflets available from Selworthy shop on Selworthy Green. Interpretation boards in car parks.
Public transport: First Group bus between Porlock and Minehead passes close to reserve.
Habitats: Ancient oak woodland, moorland covering 1,604ha. Part of the 4,800ha NT Holnicote Estate.
Key birds: *Spring/summer:* Wood Warbler, Pied Flycatcher, Redstart, Stonechat, Whinchat, Tree Pipit, Dartford Warbler possible. *All year:* Dipper, Grey Wagtail, woodpeckers, Buzzard, Sparrowhawk.
Other notable flora/fauna: Holnicote estate holds 15 of the UK's spp. of bat. Silver-washed and heath fritillary butterflies. Red deer.
Contact: National Trust, T: 01643 862 542;
E: holnicote@nationaltrust.org.uk

6. GREYLAKE

RSPB (South West England Office).
Location: Sat nav: TA7 0JD
(Othery). ST 399 346. Off A361 Taunton to Glastonbury road, between Othery and Greinton.
Access: Open all year, dawn-dusk, free admission. Guide-dogs only. Wheelchair users can access a 750 yard-long boardwalk and viewing hide.
Facilities: Information centre, but no toilets or catering facilities. Two nature trails (only one surfaced), interpretive signs. Hide on easy-access trail, viewing screen on reedbed loop trail. No toilets.
Public transport: First Group Taunton-Glastonbury bus no. 29 stops in Greinton, by phone box, or in Othery (by London Inn) - driver may stop at reserve on request otherwise there is a two mile walk along A361 from either stop.
Habitats: A large wet grassland reserve, formerly arable farmland.
Key birds: *Spring/summer:* Kingfisher, Grey Heron, Little Egret and breeding Garganey, Snipe, Lapwing, Redshank, Skylark, Meadow Pipit, Yellow Wagtail. *Autumn:* Green Sandpiper, waders on passage. *Winter:* Waders, wildfowl (inc. Lapwing, Golden Plover, Shoveler, Pintail, Teal and Wigeon). Peregrine, Hen Harrier.

Other notable flora/fauna: Roe deer, water vole, stoat, otter, dragonflies inc. four-spotted chaser.
Contact: RSPB, T: 01458 252 805;
E: greylake@rspb.org.uk

7. HAM WALL

RSPB (South West England Office).
Location: Sat nav: BA6 9SX. ST 449 397.
W of Glastonbury. From A39 turn N in Ashcott and follow road onto the moor. After three miles pass Church Farm Horticultural building. Shortly after, at metal bridge, reserve is opposite side of road to Shapwick Heath NNR.
Access: Reserve open all year but car park (2m height restriction) controlled by automatic gates open 7am-6.30pm (Oct-Jan), 7am-8pm (Feb-Mar), 6am-10pm (Apr-Sep), parking charge to non-members). Also Height-restricted car park in Ashcott Road (shared with Natural England) - open outside of these hours. Coach parking available at Avalon Marshes Centre, Shapwick Road. Dogs only on public footpaths and disued railway line. Wheelchair users can access viewing areas from main track (use RADAR key). Other rougher tracks cover 3.8 miles.
Facilities: Welcome building, toilets, drink machine. Two open-air viewing platforms, five roofed viewing screens and one raised hide. Two nature trails.
Public transport: Bus to St Mary's Road, Meare (approx 1.2 miles from reserve entrance).
Habitats: 200+ ha wetland, inc. SW's largest reedbed.
Key birds: *All year:* Bittern, Great and Little Egret, Cetti's Warbler, Water Rail, Barn Owl. *Spring/summer:* Migrant warblers, hirundines, Hobby, Whimbrel, sandpipers. *Autumn:* Migrant thrushes, Lesser Redpoll, Siskin, Kingfisher, Bearded Tit. *Winter:* Million-plus Starling roost, plus large flocks of ducks, Peregrine, Merlin, Short-eared Owl. Cranes re-introduced in to the area sometimes seen.
Other notable flora/fauna: Otter, roe deer, water vole, dragonflies, butterflies.
Contact: RSPB, T: 01458 860 494;
E: ham.wall@rspb.org.uk

8. SHAPWICK MOOR

Hawk and Owl Trust.
Location: Sat nav: BA6 9TT (Peat Moors Centre). ST 417 401. On Somerset Levels. From Junc 23 of M5 take A39 towards Glastonbury, after six miles turn N onto minor road, signed Shapwick. Continue straight over crossroads, through Shapwick village, towards Westhay, turn L at T-junction following signs for Peat Moors Centre, park here. Reserve is about half way between centre and Shapwick village.
Access: Open all year (except Dec 25). Access only along public footpaths and permissive path. Dogs on leads only.
Facilities: Information panels. Public toilets at nearby Avalon Marshes Centre (ST 425 414), none on site.
Public transport: Train to Bridgwater, then First Bus, T: 01278 434 574, no. 375 Bridgwater-Glastonbury, to Shapwick village.

Habitats: A wet grassland reserve covering 134 acres. Grazing pasture, hay meadows with rough grass edges, fen, open ditches, pollard willows and hedges. **Key birds:** *Spring/summer:* Hobby, Barn Owl, Reed Bunting and Cetti's Warbler. Whimbrel and other waders on passage. Passerines such as Skylark, Bullfinch, Greenfinch and Yellowhammer. *Autumn/ winter:* Flocks of finches, Snipe, Shoveler, Gadwall, Stonechat, Brambling. Peregrine and harriers may fly over. *All year:* Buzzard, Kestrel, Sparrowhawk, Kingfisher, Lapwing, Grey Heron, Mute Swan. **Other notable flora/fauna:** Roe deer, brown hare, stoat, badger, otter and water vole. **Contact:** Hawk and Owl Trust, T: 01328 850 590; E: enquiries@hawkandowl.org; www.hawkandowl.org

9. SWELL WOOD

RSPB (South West England Office). **Location:** Sat nav: TA3 6PX. ST 360 238. Reserve lies 11 mile E of Taunton. From A378 Langport road, take minor road one mile E of Fivehead. **Access:** Swell Wood car park and heronry hide open all year (dawn-dusk). Coach parking in lay-by across main road. Heronry hide and part of woodland trail are wheelchair accessible. **Facilities:** Heronry hide, two nature trails: Scarp Trail (only path accessible to dogs) links to public footpaths, disabled parking area.

Public transport: First Group Somerset & Avon no. 54 bus from Taunton stops at Swell - take Scarp Trail to reserve. WebberBus nos. 37 & 38 accessible to wheelchairs and will make request stop. **Habitats:** Semi-natural ancient oak woodland and views across wet grassland from woodland trails. Part of the Somerset Levels and Moors. **Key birds:** Largest heronry in SW England with up to 100 pairs of Grey Herons and small number of Little Egrets. *Spring/summer:* Breeding Buzzard, Bullfinch, Spotted Flycatcher, Song Thrush, warblers such as Chiffchaff, Blackcap and Garden Warbler. *On escorted walks:* Curlew, Snipe, Sedge Warbler, Yellow Wagtail, Skylark, Nightingale. *Autumn:* Green Woodpecker, Robin, Wren, Coal Tit. *Winter:* Long-tailed Tit, Treecreeper, Great Spotted Woodpecker, Nuthatch. **Other notable flora/fauna:** Roe deer, dormouse, woodland flora such as bluebells, wood anemone, lesser celandine, plus dragonflies and butterflies. **Contact:** RSPB, T: 01458 252 805; E: swell.wood@rspb.org.uk

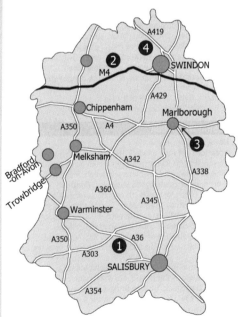

Wiltshire

WILTSHIRE'S POSITION AWAY from the coast limits its range of birds but the Wildlife Trust maintains more than 40 reserves throughout the county. The chalk downlands of Marlborough Downs and the extensive Salisbury Plain are internationally threatened habitats. The Army's use of Salisbury Plain limits human access which helps birds, and for this reason the area has been selected for the experiment to re-introduce Great Bustards to Britain.

1. LANGFORD LAKE

Wiltshire Wildlife Trust. **Location:** Sat nav: SP3 4PA. SU 037 370. Nr Steeple Langford, S of A36, approx eight miles W of Salisbury. In centre of village, turn S into Duck Street, signposted Hanging Langford. Langford Lakes is first left just after a small bridge. **Access:** Main gates open during the day. Advance notice required for coaches. No dogs. **Facilities:** Visitor centre, toilets, education centre. Four hides, all accessible to wheelchairs. Cycle stands provided (250 yards from Wiltshire Cycleway between Great Wishford and Hanging Langford). **Public transport:** Nearest bus stop 500 yard - no. 265 service between Salisbury and Bath.

NATURE RESERVES - SOUTH WEST ENGLAND

Habitats: Four former gravel pits, with newly created islands and developing reed fringes. 12 ha of open water; also wet woodland, scrub, chalk river. Great Meadow wetland opened in 2012.
Key birds: More than 150 spp. recorded. *Summer:* Breeding Coot, Moorhen, Tufted Duck, Pochard, Gadwall, Little Grebe, Great Crested Grebe. Also Kingfisher, Common Sandpiper, Grey Wagtail, warblers (eight spp.). *Winter:* Common wildfowl - Wigeon, Shoveler, Teal, Water Rail, Little Egret, also sometimes Bittern. *Passage:* Sand Martin, Green Sandpiper and other waders, Black Tern.
Other notable flora/fauna: Otter, water vole, water shrew. Spawning salmon and trout in river.
Contact: Wiltshire WT, T: 01380 725 670;
E: info@wiltshirewildlife.org

2. RAVENSROOST WOOD COMPLEX

Wiltshire Wildlife Trust.
Location: Sat nav: SN16 9RL. SU 241 877 (Ravensroost Wood car park). NW of Swindon. Take B4696 Ashton Keynes road N from Wootton Bassett. After two miles take second turn L to Minety. Go straight on when main road turns R. Go straight over next crossroads and car park is on right after 0.25 mile.
Access: Wood connects to Ravensroost and Avis Meadows, Distillery and Warbler Meadows and all sites are open at all times.
Facilities: Small car park, small shelter.
Habitats: Woodland, both coppice and high oak forest, and ponds. Surrounding meadows rich in wildflowers.
Key birds: Breeding Willow Warbler, Blackcap, Chiffchaff and Garden Warbler. In winter mixed flocks of Nuthatches, tits and Treecreepers move noisily through the wood and Woodcock can be flushed from wet, muddy areas.
Other notable flora/fauna: Butterflies inc. silver-washed fritillary and white admiral. Good display of spring bluebells, wood anemone, wood sorrel, sanicle, violet and primrose. In summer, common spotted, early purple and greater butterfly orchids, hemp agrimony and betony.
Contact: Wiltshire WT, T: 01380 725 670;
E: info@wiltshirewildlife.org

3. SAVERNAKE FOREST

Savernake Estate.
Location: Sat nav: SN8 3HP. From Marlborough the A4 Hungerford road runs along side of forest. Two pillars mark Forest Hill entrance, 1.5 mile E of A346/A4 junction. The Grand Avenue leads straight through the middle of the woodland to join a minor road from Stibb.
Access: Privately owned but open all year to public. Visitors can drive along main avenues, but all roads are closed on one day a year - usually the first working day of the year.
Facilities: Car park, picnic site at NW end by A346. Only enter fenced-off areas if there is a footpath.

Habitats: Ancient woodland, with one of the largest collections of veteran trees in Britain. Beech avenue (four miles in length) longest in UK. Designated SSSI for its lichens and fungi.
Key birds: *Spring/summer:* Garden Warbler, Blackcap, Willow Warbler, Chiffchaff, Wood Warbler, Redstart, occasional Nightingale, Tree Pipit, Spotted Flycatcher. *Winter:* Finch flocks possibly inc. Siskin, Redpoll, Brambling and Hawfinch. *All year:* Sparrowhawk, Buzzard, Red Kite, Woodcock, owls, all three woodpeckers, Marsh Tit, Willow Tit, Jay and other woodland birds.
Other notable flora/fauna: Rare lichens and fungi, all main deer spp., badgers, foxes.
Contact: Savernake Estate, T: 01672 512 161;
E: savernakeestate1@gmail.com ;
W: www.savernakeestate.co.uk

4. SWILLBROOK LAKES

Lower Mill Estate/Wiltshire Wildlife Trust
Location: Sat nav: SN16 9QA. SU 018 934. NW of Swindon. Also known as Lakes 46 & 48 of Cotswold Water Park. From A419 Swindon to Cirencester road, turn L onto Cotswold Water Park Spine Road. Cross B4696 South Cerney/Ashton Keynes road, take next L, Minety Lane, after about 1.5 miles. Park in gateway either side of road, after about 0.5 mile. Swillbrook Lakes nature reserve and information board is on east side of road.
Access: Open at all times. Adjacent to Clattinger Farm, a Wiltshire Wildlife Trust reserve.
Facilities: Footpath along N and E sides of lakes. Nearest toilets in Keynes Country Park.
Habitats: Gravel pits with shallow pools, rough grassland and scrub around edges.
Key birds: *Winter:* Wildfowl (inc. Gadwall, Pochard, Smew, Goosander, Goldeneye). *Summer:* Breeding Nightingale, Garden, Reed and Sedge Warblers, Blackcap, Cetti's Warbler, Sand and House Martins, Swallow. One of the best sites for Hobby and Nightingale in Cotswold WP.
Other notable flora/fauna: 13 spp. of dragonflies inc. downy emerald and lesser emperor in recent years.
Contact: Cotswold Water Park Trust, T: 01793 752 413;
W: www.waterpark.org

Scottish Borders

Borders

OFTEN OVERLOOKED AS BIRDERS head for the Highlands, counties in the Borders have many good sites for birds. St Abb's Head holds a large summer seabird colony, while migrants move past in spring and autumn. Ospreys have recently moved into the area and can often be seen fishing at Duns Castle. Water Rails breed at Yetholm Loch, which is also good for wildfowl.

1. BEMERSYDE MOSS

Scottish Wildlife Trust.
Location: NT 614 340.
Located eight miles E of Melrose. From here head S on A48 to St Boswells, then take B6404 across the Tweed into minor road to Maidenhall. At T-junction turn right and reserve is 0.5 mile ahead.
Access: Open at all times. Limited parking in lay-by on southern edge of loch.
Facilities: Boardwalk leads to wheelchair-friendly bird hide.
Habitats: Long narrow strip of marsh, willow scrub and open water.
Key birds: Breeding birds inc. Black-necked Grebe, Lapwing, Curlew, Spotted Flycatcher, Tree Sparrow, Yellowhammer, Reed Bunting, Grasshopper Warbler and up to 15,000 pairs of Black-headed Gulls. Good range of wintering wildfowl inc. large numbers of Wigeon and Greylag Goose.
Other notable flora/fauna: Otter, water vole.
Contact: Scottish WT, T: 0131 312 7765.

2. DUNS CASTLE RESERVE

Scottish Wildlife Trust.
Location: Sat nav: TD11 3NW. NT 778 550. Duns lies W of Berwick-upon-Tweed. From town centre head N on Castle Street and North Castle Street. Alternatively drive N on A6112 for one mile and turn L on B6365 to car park on northern edge of reserve.
Access: Reserve covering 190 acres open all year.
Facilities: Network of well-marked paths, some suitable for wheelchair access.
Habitats: Two man-made lochs (Hen Poo and Mill Dam) and woodland.
Key birds: Woodland birds such as Green and Great Spotted Woodpeckers, Goldcrest and Redstart (summer), waterfowl.
Other notable flora/fauna: Red squirrel, roe deer, occasional otter. Woodland rich in wild flowers.
Contact: Scottish WT, T: 0131 312 7765.

3. ETTRICK MARSHES

Location: Sat nav: TD7 5HU (Honey Cottage caravan park). Sited in Ettrick Valley, off B7009, approx 16 miles SW from Selkirk.
Access: Open at all times. Best access from Honey Cottage car park.
Facilities: Three car parks, network of footpaths and board walk. Can be flooded after heavy rain.
Habitats: Floodplain mosaic of woodland, wetland, grass and open water of national conservation importance covering 125 ha.
Key birds: 80 spp. recorded. Goosander, Kingfisher, Buzzard, Crossbill and Dipper seen all year, with occasional Goshawk and Osprey. *Summer:* inc. Redstart, Sedge Warbler and Sand Martin.
Other notable flora/fauna: Red squirrel, otter. Moths and plants at northern edge of range.

4. GUNKNOWE LOCH & PARK

Scottish Borders Council.
Location: Sat nav: TD1 3RP. NT 518 345. At Tweedbank, two miles from Galashiels on the A6091. Park at Gunknowe Loch or Abbotsford House visitor centre.
Access: Open all year. Surfaced paths suitable for wheelchair use.
Facilities: Car park, information boards, paths in park. Visitor centre, cafe and toilets at Abbotsford House.
Public transport: Tweedbank is on the Melrose-to-Peebles bus route.
Habitats: River, man-made loch, parkland, scrub, woodland.

Key birds: *Spring/summer:* Grey Wagtail, Kingfisher, Sand Martin, Blackcap, Sedge and Grasshopper Warblers. *Passage:* Yellow Wagtail, Whinchat, Wheatear. *Winter:* Thrushes, Brambling, Wigeon, Tufted Duck, Pochard, Goldeneye. *All year:* Great Spotted and Green Woodpeckers, Redpoll, Goosander, possible Marsh Tit.
Contact: Ranger Service, T: 01835 825 060; W: www.scotborders.gov.uk

5. ST ABBS HEAD

National Trust for Scotland.
Location: Sat nav: TD14 5QF. NT 913 674 for car park and bus stop. Lies five miles N of Eyemouth. Follow A1107 from A1.
Access: Reserve open all year. All-ability path to viewpoint at Starney Bay. Well behaved dogs welcome - please ensure droppings are taken home. Coach parking at Northfield Farm by prior arrangement.
Facilities: Visitor centre open daily, mainly unmanned, (Easter)/1st Apr-Oct (10am-5pm), public toilets (inc. disabled).
Public transport: Nearest rail station is Berwick-upon-Tweed, bus service from Berwick.
Habitats: Cliffs, coastal grasslands and freshwater loch.
Key birds: *Apr-Aug:* Seabird colonies with large numbers of Guillemot and Kittiwake; also Shag, Razorbill, Fulmar. *Apr-May & Sept-Oct:* Good autumn seawatching.
Other notable flora/fauna: Common rock-rose, purple milk-vetch, spring sandwort. Northern brown argus butterfly.
Contact: Ranger's Office, T: 01890 771 443

Dumfries & Galloway

THE SOLWAY HOLDS nationally important numbers of wintering Barnacle Geese, with WWT Caerlaverock and RSPB Mersehead being prime sites. Ospreys and Red Kites are colonising and there is a chance of a Golden Eagle over upland areas or Hen Harrier on moorland. The Mull of Galloway has fine seabird cliffs, while the Ken/Dee Marshes hold Willow Tit and Nuthatch.

6. CAERLAVEROCK WETLAND CENTRE

The Wildfowl & Wetlands Trust.
Location: Sat nav: DG1 4RS. NY 051 656. Overlooks the Solway. From St Michael's church in Dumfries take B725 towards Bankend, following tourist signs. Also signposted from A75 W of Annan.
Access: Open daily, except Dec 25, 10am-5pm. Charge for non-WWT members. Assistance dogs only.
Facilities: 20 hides, heated observatory, four towers, Salcot Merse Observatory, sheltered picnic area. Self-catering accommodation and camping facilities. Nature trails in summer. Old Granary visitor building; coffee shop serving light meals and snacks; bookshop; optics for sale. Theatre/conference room. Binoculars for hire. Parking for coaches.

Public transport: Bus no. D6A from Dumfries stops one mile from reserve. Stagecoach, T: 01387 253 496.
Habitats: Saltmarsh, grassland, wetland.
Key birds: *Winter:* Wildfowl esp. Barnacle Geese (max 40,000), Pink-footed Geese and Whooper Swans. *Summer:* Osprey (web-cam on nest), Barn Owl, Skylark, Tree Sparrow, migrant warblers.
Other notable flora/fauna: Natterjack toad, badger, tadpole shrimp, bats. Northern marsh, common spotted and twayblade orchids.
Contact: WWT Caerlaverock, T: 01387 770 200; E: info.caerlaverock@wwt.org.uk

7. CROOK OF BALDOON

RSPB (South & West Scotland).
Location: NX 442 530. Four miles S of Wigtown. From Wigtown, head S along the A714. Go through Bladnoch, then take the minor road to the L (at the Penkiln Sawmill sign); follow this road straight down to the Crook of Baldoon car park – ignore left hand turns along this road.
Access: Open at all times. Dogs under close control. Site not currently suitable for disabled access.
Facilities: Car park and picnic tables.
Public transport: None.
Habitats: Saltmarsh, wet grassland (other wetland features under development).
Key birds: *Winter:* Pink-footed and Barnacle Geese, Whooper Swan, Golden Plover, Curlew, Lapwing, Hen Harrier, Peregrine, Merlin, Twite. *Summer:* Lapwing, Redshank, Skylark, Osprey, Linnet, Wheatear.
Other notable flora/fauna: Thrift, sea-lavender.
Contact: RSPB, T: 01988 402 130; E: crookofbaldoon@rspb.org.uk

8. KEN-DEE MARSHES

RSPB (South & West Scotland).
Location: Sat nav: DG7 2NJ. NX 699 684. Six miles from Castle Douglas. Off the A762 (N of Laurieston) or B795 (at Glenlochar), parking at the Mains of Duchrae.
Access: From car park at entrance to Mains of Duchrae farm. Open during daylight hours. Dogs must be under close control.
Facilities: Two hides (one is wheelchair-accessible), viewing platform, nature trails. Three miles of trails available, limited parking for elderly and disabled next to first hide. Part of Red Kite trail.
Public transport: None.
Habitats: Marshes, woodlands, open water.
Key birds: *All year:* Mallard, Grey Heron, Buzzard, Nuthatch, Willow Tit. *Spring/summer:* Lapwing and Curlew nest on farmland. Pied Flycatcher, Redstart, Tree Pipit, Sedge Warbler. *Winter:* Greenland White-fronted and Greylag Geese, raptors (Hen Harrier, Peregrine, Merlin, Red Kite).
Other notable flora/fauna: Red squirrel, roe deer, otter.
Contact: RSPB, T: 01556 670 464; W: www.gallowaykitetrail.com

9. MERSEHEAD

RSPB (South & West Scotland).
Location: Sat nav: DG2 8AH. NX 928 566. From Dumfries take A710 S for about 16 miles. Reserve is signposted from New Abbey and then on L just before Caulkerbush village. Single track road with passing places runs for a mile to car park, adjacent to visitor centre. From Castle Douglas, take A745, then A711 to Dalbeattie. Follow signs from Dalbeattie before joining A710.
Access: Dawn-dusk daily. Wheelchair-friendly hides and trails open at all times.
Facilities: Visitor centre with viewing room, toilets and refreshments (open 10am-5pm) - may close earlier in winter. Blue Badge parking spaces within 400 yards of hides and 20 yards from visitor centre.
Public transport: None.
Habitats: Wet grassland, arable farmland, saltmarsh, inter-tidal mudflats.
Key birds: *Winter*: Whooper Swan, up to 9,500 Barnacle Geese, 4,000 Teal, 2,000 Wigeon, 1,000 Pintail, waders (inc. Dunlin, Knot, Oystercatcher), Hen Harrier. *Summer*: Breeding birds inc. Lapwing, Redshank, Skylark.
Other notable flora/fauna: Natterjack toad, otter.
Contact: RSPB, T: 01387 780 579;
E: mersehead@rspb.org.uk

10. MULL OF GALLOWAY

RSPB (Scotland).
Location: Sat nav: DG9 9HP. NX 156 305. Most southerly tip of Scotland - follow brown signs for five miles from village of Drummore, S of Stranraer.
Access: Open at all times. Blue Badge parking by centre. No wheelchair access to foghorn viewing platform overlooking seabird colonies or circular trail. Centre open between Easter and Oct.
Facilities: Visitor centre, toilets, nature trails, CCTV on cliffs. Small shop at neighbouring Gallie Craig cafe (not RSPB).
Public transport: None.
Habitats: Sea cliffs, coastal heath.

Key birds: *Spring/summer*: Fulmar, Kittiwake, Guillemot, Razorbill, Black Guillemot, Puffin, Raven, Wheatear, Rock Pipit, Twite. Migrating Manx Shearwater. *All year*: Peregrine.
Contact: RSPB, T: 01988 402 130;
E: mullofgalloway@rspb.org.uk

11. WIGTOWN BAY LNR

Dumfries & Galloway Council.
Location: Sat nav: DG8 9JH. NX 560 460. Between Wigtown and Creetown, S of Newton Stewart. The A75 runs along E side, with A714 S to Wigtown and B7004 providing superb views of the LNR.
Access: Reserve open at all times. The hide is disabled-friendly. Main accesses: Roadside lay-bys on A75 near Creetown and parking at Martyr's Stake and Wigtown Harbour. All suitable for coaches. Visitor Centre in Wigtown County Building has coach parking plus full disabled access, inc. lift and toilets.
Facilities: Hide at Wigtown Harbour overlooking River Bladnoch, saltmarsh and fresh water wetland has disabled access from harbour car park. Another hide at Martyr's Stake car park. CCTV of Ospreys breeding in Galloway during summer and wetland birds in winter. Open Mon to Sat 10am-5pm (later some days), Sun 2pm-5pm.
Public transport: Bus nos. 400 or X75 to travel from Dumfries and Stranraer to Creetown and Newton Stewart and the 415 from Newton Stewart to Wigtown.
Habitats: The largest LNR in Britain at 2,845 ha features an estuary with extensive saltmarsh/merse and mudflats plus a freshwater wetland at Wigtown Harbour.
Key birds: *Winter*: Internationally important for Pink-footed Goose, nationally important for Curlew, Whooper Swan and Pintail, with major gull roost and other migratory coastal birds. Small Twite flock. *Summer*: Breeding Osprey, Peregrine, waders and duck.
Other notable flora/fauna: Fish inc. smelt and shad. Lax-flowered sea-lavender, sea aster.
Contact: Visitor Centre, T: 01988 402 673.
Keith Kirk, Countryside Ranger, T: 0303 333 3000 or 07850 157 661; E: keith.kirk@dumgal.gov.uk

Central Scotland

Argyll, Ayrshire, Clyde, Fife, Forth, Lothian

Argyll

TWO ISLANDS TAKE the birding honours for this region. Islay is renowned for its wintering wildfowl, including huge numbers of Barnacle and White-fronted Geese. Choughs, raptors and Corncrakes are other island specialities. The island of Mull is home to the highest breeding densities of Golden Eagle and White-tailed Eagles in Britain.

1. COLL RESERVE

RSPB (South & West Scotland).
Location: Sat nav: PA78 6TB, NM 167 563. By ferry from Oban to island of Coll. Take the B8070 W from Arinagour for five miles. Turn R at Arileod. Continue for about one mile. Park at end of the road. Reception point at Totronald.
Access: Open all year. A natural site with unimproved paths not suitable for wheelchairs. Avoid walking through fields and crops.

NATURE RESERVES - CENTRAL SCOTLAND

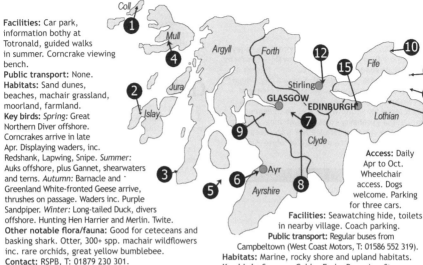

Facilities: Car park, information bothy at Totronald, guided walks in summer. Corncrake viewing bench.
Public transport: None.
Habitats: Sand dunes, beaches, machair grassland, moorland, farmland.
Key birds: *Spring:* Great Northern Diver offshore. Corncrakes arrive in late Apr. Displaying waders, inc. Redshank, Lapwing, Snipe. *Summer:* Auks offshore, plus Gannet, shearwaters and terns. *Autumn:* Barnacle and Greenland White-fronted Geese arrive, thrushes on passage. Waders inc. Purple Sandpiper. *Winter:* Long-tailed Duck, divers offshore. Hunting Hen Harrier and Merlin. Twite.
Other notable flora/fauna: Good for cetaceans and basking shark. Otter, 300+ spp. machair wildflowers inc. rare orchids, great yellow bumblebee.
Contact: RSPB, T: 01879 230 301.

2. LOCH GRUINART, ISLAY

RSPB (South & West Scotland).
Location: Sat nav: PA44 7PR. NR 275 672. Sea loch on N coast of Islay, seven miles NW from Bridgend.
Access: Two hides and trails with viewpoints open at all times. Visitor centre open daily 10am-5pm, except christmas/new year. Disabled access to south hide, viewing area and toilets. Assistance required for wheelchair users. Car parking at centre and start of trails. Coach parking at visitor centre only. No dogs in hides, on trails must be kept under close control.
Facilities: Toilets (inc. disabled), visitor centre (offers hot drinks), two hides, two trails. Trails car park, opposite the viewpoint, is level and made from rolled stone. Group bookings accepted. Weekly guided walks Apr to Oct.
Public transport: Nearest bus stops three miles.
Habitats: Lowland wet grasslands, sea loch, farmland, moorland.
Key birds: *Oct-Apr:* Large numbers of Barnacle and White-fronted Geese, plus other wildfowl and waders. *May-Aug:* Breeding and displaying waders and Corncrake. *Sept-Nov:* Many passage migrants and arriving wildfowl. Birds of prey are present all year, esp Hen Harrier and Peregrine, while Chough can be seen feeding in nearby fields. *Spring:* Displaying Snipe, Lapwing, Curlew and Redshank.
Other notable flora/fauna: Otter, red and roe deer. Marsh fritillary butterflies during May and Jun.
Contact: RSPB, T: 01496 850 505:
E: loch.gruinart@rspb.org.uk;

3. MACHRIHANISH SEABIRD/WILDLIFE OBSERVATORY

Eddie Maguire (sponsored by SNH).
Location: Sat nav: PA28 6PZ. NR 628 209. Southwest Kintyre, Argyll. Six miles W of Campbeltown on A83, then B843.

Access: Daily Apr to Oct. Wheelchair access. Dogs welcome. Parking for three cars.
Facilities: Seawatching hide, toilets in nearby village. Coach parking.
Public transport: Regular buses from Campbeltown (West Coast Motors, T: 01586 552 319).
Habitats: Marine, rocky shore and upland habitats.
Key birds: *Summer:* Golden Eagle, Peregrine, Storm Petrel and Twite. *Autumn:* Passage seabirds and waders. On-shore gales/squalls often produce inshore movements of Leach's Petrel and other scarce seabirds, inc. Balearic Shearwater, Sabine's Gull and Grey Phalarope. *Winter:* Great Northern Diver, Purple Sandpiper, Ruddy Turnstone with occasional Glaucous and Iceland Gulls.
Other notable flora/fauna: Grey and common seals, bottle-nosed dolphin, otter, wild goat.
Contact: Eddie Maguire, Warden, T: 07919 660 292;
E: msbowarden@gmail.com;
W: www.machrihanishbirdobservatory.org.uk/

4. MULL (WHITE-TAILED) EAGLE WATCH

RSPB (South & West Scotland)/Forestry Commission Scotland/SNH/MICT/Police Scotland.
Location: 1) Glen Seilisdeir (SW Mull) - meeting point just off the B8035 road in Glen Seilisdeir, NM 480 302. 2) West Ardhu (NW Mull) - turn off the B8073 Dervaig-Calgary road at the sign for The Old Byre/Torloisk and keep on that road until you see the signs for Mull Eaglewatch, NM 428 505.
Access: Ranger led trips run seven days a week (10am and 1pm, late-Mar to autumn) between the two viewing hides. Booking places on trips is essential - charges apply.
Facilities: Purpose-built hides for observing nesting White-tailed Eagles. No toilet facilities.
Habitats: Large sea loch with tidal mudflats at its head (Loch Beg).
Key birds: Apart from the White-tailed Eagles, other raptors in the area inc. ⬚ and Buzzard. In winter a⬚ to see three species of d⬚ Red-breasted Merganser⬚ be seen on muddy areas⬚
Other notable flora/fau⬚ common here.
Contact: Booking throu⬚ Information Centre at C⬚

Ayrshire

A RUGGED coastline, combined with river valleys and inland woodland means Ayrshire has many potentially good birding opportunities, though its best known site is the island of Ailsa Craig, which boasts a huge gannetry, together with plenty of other breeding seabirds. Don't miss Martnaham Loch (good for wildfowl and a range of common species) or Turnberry Point (seawatching, plus Twite). The shore at Barassie and Troon sees a large build-up of waders in autumn, plus white-winged gulls in winter.

5. AILSA CRAIG

RSPB (South & West Scotland).
Location: NX 020 998. Island is nine miles offshore, nearest town on mainland is Girvan.
Access: No formal arrangements. Accessible (viewing) only by boat: MFV Glorious (T: 01465 713 219) or Kintyre Express (T: 01294 270 160) from Girvan during summer. Also from Campbeltown by Mull of Kintyre Seatours' fast rib (T: 07785 542 811).
Facilities: None.
Public transport: None.
Habitats: Volcanic plug (350ft high) provides nest sites for seabirds.
Key birds: Ailsa Craig hosts the third largest gannetry in the UK and supports 73,000 breeding seabirds, inc. Guillemont, Razorbill, Puffin, Black Guillemot, Kittiwake and up to 36,000 pairs of Gannets. Twite can also be found here.
Other notable flora/fauna: Slow worm.
Contact: RSPB, T: 0141 331 0993;
E: glasgow@rspb.org.uk

6. CULZEAN CASTLE COUNTRY PARK

National Trust for Scotland.
Location: Sat nav: KA19 8LE. NS 234 103. 12 miles SW of Ayr on A719.
Access: Country Park open all year 9am-dusk. Access leaflet available. Admission charges for Country Park.
Facilities: Car park, visitor centre/restaurant/shops open daily (closed mid-Dec to early Jan), children's playground, picnic areas, 21 miles of footpath and estate tracks, ranging from unsurfaced woodland paths to metalled roads.
Public transport: Stagecoach bus no. 60 (Ayr to Girvan) stops at site entrance. One mile walk downhill to visitor centre and castle.
Habitats: Shoreline, parkland, woodland, gardens, streams, ponds.
Key birds: *All year:* Good populations of common woodland species, inc. Jay, Great Spotted Woodpecker and thrushes. *Spring/summer:* Arriving migrants, esp. Blackcap, Chiffchaff and Willow Warbler. Nesting Raven and Gannet on cliffs, Gannet d terns offshore. *Autumn/winter:* Regular flocks of ng and Fieldfare, Waxwing, crossbills. Wildfowl inc. Little Grebe, Tufted Duck, Goldeneye. vers and Eider.

Other notable flora/fauna: Roe deer, otter, water vole, several spp. of bat. Shoreline SSSI rich in rock pool life.
Contact: Culzean Ranger Service, T: 01655 884 455;
E: culzean@nts.org.uk

Clyde

THE FALLS OF CLYDE Scottish Wildlife Trust reserve has a well-known Peregrine watchpoint, with Dippers and Kingfishers along the river. Whinchats and several species of warbler breed at Baron's Haugh, with a good autumn passage of waders there. RSPB Lochwinnoch offers a good selection of commoner species throughout the year.

7. BARON'S HAUGH

RSPB (South & West Scotland).
Location: Sat nav: ML1 2SG. NS 756 553. On SW edge of Motherwell, overlooking River Clyde. Use Adele Street, then lane off North Lodge Avenue.
Access: Open all year. Most paths suitable for wheelchairs, except circular nature trail, which has some steep sections.
Facilities: Four hides, information board in car park. Disabled access along some of the Clyde walkway but it is difficult due to erosion - phone for details.
Public transport: Airbles train station, with frequent services from Glasgow Central is about 15 mins walk. Bus nos 2 & 245 from Motherwell stop in Adele Street (0.5 mile from reserve).
Habitats: Marshland, flooded areas, woodland, parkland, meadows, scrub, river.
Key birds: *Summer:* Breeding Gadwall, warblers (inc. Garden, Grasshopper); Whinchat, Common Sandpiper, Kingfisher, Sand Martin. *Autumn:* Excellent for waders (22 species). *Winter:* Whooper Swan, Pochard, Wigeon, Sparrowhawk.
Contact: RSPB, T: 0141 331 0993;
E: baronshaugh@rspb.org.uk

8. FALLS OF CLYDE

Scottish Wildlife Trust.
Location: Sat nav: ML11 9DB (visitor centre). NS 881 423. Reserve covers both sides of Clyde Gorge from New Lanark to Bonnington Weir, approx one mile S of Lanark. From Glasgow travel S on M74 until Junc 7, then along A72, following brown signs for New Lanark.
Access: Reserve open daily. From New Lanark car park, walk into village, through the iron gates and down steps to the right of the New Lanark Visitor Centre. Follow road to the Falls of Clyde Visitor Centre. Reserve terrain too steep for wheelchairs, but visitor centre is wheelchair friendly, inc. toilet facilities.
Facilities: Visitor centre open daily 10am-4pm. Admission charge for non-SWT members. Peregrine watch site open from Mar-Jun. Woodland trails and a range of guided walks inc self-guided, wildflower trail and badger watches.
Public transport: Scotrail trains run to Lanark. Local bus service from Lanark to New Lanark stops near reserve.

NATURE RESERVES - CENTRAL SCOTLAND

Habitats: Reserve stretches along both sides of an ancient gorge, with waterfalls, meadow and wet woodland.
Key birds: Over 100 spp. of birds, unrivalled views of breeding Peregrines. Others inc. Kingfisher, Dipper, Jay, Spotted Flycatcher and Goosander.
Other notable flora/fauna: Badgers, otters, bats and wildflowers.
Contact: Falls of Clyde Visitor Centre, T: 01555 665 262; E: fallsofclyde@scottishwildlifetrust.co.uk

9. LOCHWINNOCH

RSPB (Scotland).
Location: Sat nav: PA12 4JF. NS 358 582. 18 miles SW of Glasgow, adjacent to A760 Largs Road, off the A737 (Irvine Road). Leave M8 at Junc 28A.
Access: Reserve open at all times (charge for non-members). Visitor centre open daily (10am-5pm), except Dec 25/26, Jan 1/2.
Facilities: Visitor centre, tea-room, shop, binocular hire. Two trails, one two hides and toilets all accessible to disabled visitors.
Public transport: Rail station adjacent, bus services on A737 more than 0.5 mile from reserve.
Habitats: Shallow lochs, marsh, mixed woodland.
Key birds: *Winter:* Wildfowl (esp. Whooper Swan, Wigeon, Goosander, Goldeneye and occasional Smew). Hen Harrier and Kingfisher regular. *Passage:* Occasional migrants inc. Whimbrel, Greenshank. *Summer:* Breeding Great Crested Grebe, Water Rail, Sedge and Grasshopper Warblers, Reed Bunting.
Other notable flora/fauna: Possible otters, roe deer, small mammals, butterflies, moths and dragonflies.
Contact: RSPB, T: 01505 842 663; E: lochwinnoch@rspb.org.uk

Fife

WINTERING FLOCKS OF seaducks off Ruddons Point often hold a few Surf Scoters among the more numerous Common and Velvet Scoters, while Fife Ness is good for seawatching and autumn migrants. The Eden Estuary holds good numbers of wildfowl and waders throughout the year but especially in winter. Tentsmuir offers an unusual mix of woodland and coastal habitats.

10. EDEN ESTUARY LNR

Fife Coast and Countryside Trust.
Location: Sat nav: KY16 0UG. NO 450 192 (Eden Estuary Centre). Reserve centre off main street in Guardbridge, two miles from St Andrews on A91, and from Leuchars via Tentsmuir Forest off A919 (four miles). Use Outhead at St Andrews, off West Sands beach, to access Balgove Bay.
Access: Eden Estuary Centre, Guardbridge (keypad number available from ranger service) open 9am-5pm daily except Dec 25/26, 31 & Jan 1. Evans Hide: at GR 483 183, parking at Pilmuir Links golf course car park. Combination number required from ranger service.
Facilities: Visitor centre at Guardbridge. Viewing platform and picnic area at Outhead. Evans Hide at Balgove Bay (access number from Ranger Service).

Public transport: Leuchars train station (1.5 miles), regular bus service from Cupar and Dundee, T: 08457 484 950.
Habitats: Intertidal mudflats, saltmarsh, river, reed, sand dunes and wetland covering 891 ha.
Key birds: *Winter and passage:* Significant numbers of waders and wildfowl. Outer estuary good for seaduck such as scoters, Eider and Long-tailed Duck, plus Gannet, terns and skuas. Mudflats ideal for godwits, plovers, sandpipers, Redshank and Shelduck. River good for Kingfisher, Common Sandpiper and Goosander. Surrounding area attracts Short and Long-eared Owls, Peregrine, Marsh Harrier, White-tailed Eagle and Merlin. Osprey are regular visitors.
Other notable flora/fauna: Northern marsh orchid, dune grasses and herbs. Harbour and grey seal, bottle-nosed dolphin, porpoise, brown hare, stoat and otter. Butterflies inc. comma, grayling, small pearl-bordered, dark green fritilliary, painted lady and orange tip.
Contact: Ranald Strachan, Fife Ranger Service, T: 07985 707 593; E: Ranald.Strachan@fifecountryside.co.uk

11. ISLE OF MAY NNR

Scottish Natural Heritage.
Location: NT 655 995. Small island lying six miles off Fife Ness in the Firth of Forth.
Access: Boats run from Anstruther and North Berwick (4-5 hour round trip, weather dependent). Contact SNH for details or visit W: www.nnr-scotland.org.uk/isle-of-may/visiting/. Keep to paths. Those using Obs accommodation should note delays are possible, both arriving/leaving, because of weather.
Facilities: No dogs; no camping; no fires. Prior permission required if scientific work, photography or filming is to be carried out.
Public transport: Regular bus service to Anstruther and North Berwick harbour.
Habitats: Sea cliffs, rocky shoreline.
Key birds: *Early summer:* Breeding auks, gulls and terns, Kittiwake, Shag, Eider, Fulmar. Over 45,000 pairs of Puffins. *Autumn/spring:* Weather-related migrations inc. rarities each year.
Contact: Accomodation Bookings Secretary: Mark Newell. T: 07909 707 971; E: bookings@isleofmaybirdobs.org; W: www.isleofmaybirdobs.org
Other enquiries: SNH, T: 01334 654 038; W: www.nnr-scotland.org

Forth

CAMBUS POOLS ATTRACTS passage waders and winter wildfowl, while high tide at Kinneil produces good numbers of waders in spring and autumn. The RSPB reserve at Inversnaid is good for Black Grouse, Twite, Redstart, Wood Warbler and Pied Flycatcher. There are large movements of finches and thrushes in autumn. A Red Kite feeding station at Argaty provides visitors with close-up views.

12. CAMBUS POOLS

Scottish Wildlife Trust.
Location: Sat nav: FK10 2PG. NS 846 937. From Stirling, take A907 east towards Alloa. From a roundabout drive 0.6 mile to where the B9096 leads off to Tullibody. Take the minor road (Station Road) R to the small village of Cambus.
Access: Cross River Devon by bridge at NS 853 940 and walk down stream on R bank past bonded warehouses. Open all year. Best viewing around high tide.
Facilities: Bench on S side of western pool.
Public transport: None.
Habitats: Wet grazed grassland, reedbeds and two salty pools.
Key birds: Used extensively by migrants in spring and autumn, inc. wildfowl (Mute and Whooper Swans, Goldeneye, Teal, Shelduck) and waders such as Black-tailed Godwit, Oystercatcher and Greenshank. Gadwall have bred here and Kingfisher is seen regularly. Small birds inc. Yellowhammer and Reed Bunting.
Other notable flora/fauna: Brown hare, stoat, short-tailed vole, 115 spp. of vascular plants. Harbour porpoise seen in Forth.
Contact: Contact: Scottish WT, T: 0131 312 7765.

Lothian

THOUGH COASTAL LOCATIONS usually grab the headlines, the Lammermuir Hills hold a range of upland species. More than 250 species have been recorded at Aberlady Bay, including many thousands of geese in winter. The Seabird Centre at North Berwick is a great place to interest young children, or take a boat out to the gannetry at Bass Rock, while Ferny Ness sees a build-up of Red-necked Grebes in late summer.

13. ABERLADY BAY LNR

East Lothian Council.
Location: Sat nav: EH32 0QB. NT 472 806. From Edinburgh take A198 E to Aberlady. Reserve car park is 1.5 miles E of Aberlady village.
Access: Britain's first Local Nature Reserve is open at all times. Stay on footpaths to avoid disturbance. Disabled access from reserve car park. No dogs.
Facilities: Small car park and toilets. Notice board with recent sightings at end of footbridge. The Scottish Ornithologists' Club (SOC) HQ, Waterston House, is located W of Aberlady village (open daily 10am-4pm) inc. shop, library, gallery, hot/cold drinks.
Public transport: East Coast Buses (Edinburgh to N Berwick service nos. 124, X24 passes the reserve (ask to be dropped nearby). Nearest train station four miles away at Longniddry.
Habitats: Tidal mudflats, saltmarsh, freshwater marsh, dune grassland, scrub, open sea.
Key birds: *Summer*: Breeding birds inc. Shelduck, Eider, Reed Bunting and up to eight spp. of warbler. Passage waders inc. Green, Wood and Curlew Sandpipers, Little Stint, Greenshank, Whimbrel, Black-tailed Godwit. *Winter*: Divers (esp. Red-throated), Red-necked and Slavonian Grebes and geese (up to 15,000 Pinkfeet roost); sea-ducks, waders.
Contact: Countryside Officer, T: 01620 827 459; E: dpriddle@eastlothian.gov.uk

14. BASS ROCK/ SCOTTISH SEABIRD CENTRE

Location: NT 605 875. Island NE of North Berwick. Scottish Seabird Centre is located in North Berwick Harbour (EH39 4SS).
Access: Bass Rock is private property. Regular sailings from N Berwick or Dunbar around Rock between Apr-Sept; local boatman has owner's permission to carry individuals or parties by prior arrangement (three hours on island). Cheaper non-landing trips by boat or RIB (rigid inflatable) around Bass Rock and Craigleath run from late-Mar to Oct. Contact The Seabird Centre/check their website for full details of boat trips in the area.
Facilities: Cafe, shop, aquaria, telescope deck and toilets at Seabird Centre. No facilities on Bass Rock.
Habitats: Sea cliffs.
Key birds: The spectacular cliffs hold a massive Gannet colony, (with up to 150,000 birds it's the largest in the world), plus Puffin, Guillemot, Razorbill, Kittiwake, Shag, Common Tern and Fulmar.
Contact: The Scottish Seabird Centre, T: 01620 890 202; E: info@seabird.org; W: www.seabird.org

15. BAWSINCH RESERVE & DUDDINGSTON LOCH

Scottish Wildlife Trust.
Location: Sat nav: EH15 3PX. NT 284 725. Two miles from centre of Edinburgh, below Arthur's Seat. Use car park on Duddingston Road West and Holyrood Park Gate.
Access: Open access to north shore of loch and cavalry ground to SE - best views from Hangman's Rock. Remainder of site and hide only open by prior arrangement with SWT.
Facilities: Hide (SWT members only), bird/plant lists.
Habitats: Edinburgh's only natural freshwater loch. Reedbed, marsh, ponds, mixed woodland, flower meadow and scrub. Bawsinch reserve developed from former industrial wasteland.
Key birds: Heronry. Important site for breeding swans, geese, ducks, grebes and Water Rail. *Summer*: Migrants, inc. Spotted Flycatcher, hirundines, warblers, inc. occasional Grasshopper Warbler. *Winter*: Roosting wildfowl, gulls and Bittern.
Other notable flora/fauna: Fox, water vole and otter. Dragonflies, four spp. of amphibian.
Contact: Scottish WT, T: 0131 312 7765.

Eastern Scotland

Angus & Dundee, Moray & Nairn, NE Scotland, Perth & Kinross

Angus & Dundee

THE ANGUS GLENS hold a typical range of upland species, including Ring Ouzel, grouse, chats and Golden Eagle. Ospreys fish regularly at RSPB Loch of Kinnordy, while Montreathmont Forest is a mix of coniferous and broadleaved woodland. Montrose Basin is a flagship Scottish Wildlife Trust reserve, with a good selection of wildfowl ever present and waders on passage.

1. LOCH OF LINTRATHEN

Scottish Water/Scottish Wildlife Trust.
Location: Sat nav: DD8 5JH. NO 278 550. Located next to Bridgend of Lintrathen, seven miles W of Kirriemuir. Take B951 and choose circular route on unclassified roads round loch.
Access: Two public hides (one on eastern side of loch is wheelchair-accessible) open 24 hours a day. Rest of reserve is private, but good views possible from unclassified roads.
Facilities: Viewpoint can accommodate five cars. Roadside parking at NO 276 557 off a minor road W of loch. Forest track leads to hide. Second hide (wheelchair accessible) on E side of loch.
Public transport: None.
Habitats: Oligotrophic-mesotrophic loch designated a Ramsar site and SPA because of its value to waterbirds. Surrounded by mainly coniferous woodland in the foothills of Braes of Angus.
Key birds: *Summer*: Grey Heron, Great Crested Grebe and other water birds. Osprey seen occasionally. *Winter*: Internationally-important numbers of Icelandic Greylag Geese (up to 3,000), plus Pink-footed Goose, Goosander, Whooper Swan, Wigeon, Teal and other wildfowl. Birds feed on surrounding farmland during day.
Other notable flora/fauna: Red squirrel, pipistrelle.
Contact: Scottish WT, T: 0131 312 7765.

2. MONTROSE BASIN LNR

Scottish Wildlife Trust/Angus Council.
Location: Sat nav: DD10 9TA. NO 702 565 (SWT Wildlife Centre on A92). 1.5 miles from centre of Montrose. Main car park for western end at the Old Mill, Mains of Dun (NN 669 591).
Access: Pick up site map at Visitor Centre, open daily Mid-Feb to Oct (10.30am-5pm) and from Nov to mid-Feb (10.30am-4pm, Fri-Mon), closed Dec 25/26 & Jan 1/2. Admission: adult, concessions and family rates available, SWT members free. Several hides open at all times.

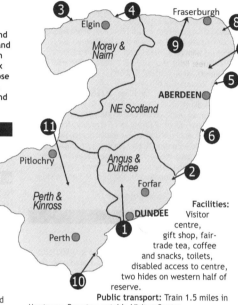

Facilities: Visitor centre, gift shop, fair-trade tea, coffee and snacks, toilets, disabled access to centre, two hides on western half of reserve.
Public transport: Train 1.5 miles in Montrose. Bus stop outside Visitor Centre.
Habitats: Estuary, saltmarsh, reedbeds, farmland.
Key birds: Internationally important for Pink-footed Goose (up to 40,000 arrive Oct), Knot and Redshank. Wintering wildfowl and waders (Curlews at peak numbers in Aug, Dunlin in Feb). Breeding terns, gulls, Shelduck, Goldeneye, Eider (up to 2,000), Grey Partridge in surrounding fields. Nationally important moulting site for Mute Swan (approx 300 birds).
Contact: Montrose Basin Wildlife Centre, T: 01674 676 336;
E: montrosebasin@scottishwildlifetrust.org.uk

Moray & Nairn

YEAR-ROUND VARIETY IS on offer here, with Lochindorb the best area of moorland to explore, with grouse, raptors, divers and waders all breeding. Roseisle F̶ opens out onto Burghea̶ winter for seaducks, di̶ can be explored from e̶ attracts passage wader̶ and wildfowl.

3. CULBIN SANDS

RSPB (East Scotland).
Location: Sat nav: IV12 5LF. NH 900 576. Approx 1.5 miles NE of Nairn, overlooking Moray Firth. Use East Beach car park, signed off A96. Follow road through Maggot Road caravan park.
Access: Open at all times. 800 yards path to Minster's Pool suitable for all abilities.
Facilities: Toilets (inc. disabled) and bike racks at car park. Track along dunes and saltmarsh.
Public transport: Buses stop in St Ninian's Road, Nairn, one mile W of site - Rapsons, T: 0870 608 2608 or Stagecoach, T: 01862 892 683. Train station in Nairn 1.5 miles W of reserve.
Habitats: Saltmarsh, sandflats, dunes.
Key birds: *Winter*: Common Scoter (large number), Long-tailed Duck, Red-breasted Merganser, Knot, Bar-tailed Godwit. Raptors inc. Peregrine, Merlin and Hen Harrier attracted by wader flocks. Roosting geese, Snow Bunting flocks. *Spring*: Tern flock, esp. Sandwich, passage waders. *Summer*: Breeding Eider, Ringed Plover, Oystercatcher. Osprey on passage.
Other notable flora/fauna: Dolphins in Firth. Otters sometimes seen.
Contact: RSPB, T: 01463 715 000

4. SPEY BAY

Scottish Wildlife Trust.
Location: Sat nav: IV32 7NW. NJ 325 657. Eight miles NE of Elgin. From Elgin take A96 and B9015 to Kingston. Reserve is immediately east of village. Car parks at Kingston and Tugnet.
Access: Open all year.
Facilities: Car park, info board. Circular walk at Tugnet.
Public transport: None.
Habitats: Shingle, rivermouth and coastal habitats.
Key birds: *Summer*: Osprey, waders, wildfowl. *Winter*: Seaduck and divers offshore, esp. Long-tailed Duck, Common and Velvet Scoters, Red-throated Diver.
Other notable flora/fauna: Otter, plus dolphin offshore. Good range of dragonflies.
Contact: Contact: Scottish WT, T: 0131 312 7765.

NE Scotland

SCOTLAND'S ONLY MAINLAND gannetry is at Troup Head, while RSPB Loch of Strathbeg is the main UK arrival point for Pink-footed Geese and Whooper Swans every autumn. The Ythan Estuary is good for breeding terns, Eiders, and passage and wintering waders. The interior holds typical Highlands species, with the notable exception of Crested Tit.

5. FORVIE NNR

Scottish Natural Heritage.
Location: Sat nav: AB41 8RU (Forvie visitor centre). NK 034 289. Inc. the Ythan Estuary, 12 miles N of Aberdeen. Waterside car park (NK004271 – AB41 6AB) [...] mile N of Newburgh; visitor centre three miles [...]burgh at Collieston.

Access: Reserve open at all times but ternery closed Apr to end-Aug. Stevenson Forvie Centre open daily (Apr-Oct). Centre, short trail and hide are wheelchair-accessible.
Facilities: Interpretive display and toilets at Stevenson Forvie Centre. Bird hide, waymarked trails. Coach parking at Waterside car park and Stevenson Forvie Centre.
Public transport: Bluebird no. 63 to Cruden Bay. Ask for the Newburgh or Collieston Crossroads stop. T: 01224 591 381.
Habitats: Estuary, dunes, coastal heath.
Key birds: *Spring/summer*: Breeding Eider and terns. Migrant waders and seabirds offshore. *Autumn*: Pink-footed Goose, migrant seabirds, waders and passerines inc. occasional scarce species or rarity. *Winter*: Waders and wildfowl, inc. Whooper Swan, Long-tailed Duck and Golden Plover.
Other notable flora/fauna: Occasional ceteceans offshore, esp. in summer.
Contact: Reserve Manager, T: 01358 751 330; E: nnr@snh.gov.uk; W: www.nnr-scotland.org

6. FOWLSHEUGH

RSPB (East Scotland).
Location: Sat nav: AB39 2TP. NO 879 808. Reserve is three miles S of Stonehaven. From A92 take minor road signposted Crawton. Car park just before end of road.
Access: Unrestricted. Not suitable for wheelchair users. Only assistance dogs allowed.
Facilities: Car park with 12 spaces, 200 yards from reserve. Stone-built viewing shelter at end of footpath. Nearest toilets in Stonehaven.
Public transport: Request bus stop (Stonehaven to Johnshaven route). One mile walk to reserve entrance. **Habitats:** Sea cliffs.
Key birds: Spectacular 130,000 strong seabird colony, mainly Kittiwake and Guillemot plus Razorbill, Fulmar and Puffin. Gannet, Eider and skuas offshore, Peregrine regular throughout year. *Autumn*: Red-throated Diver on sea, terns on passage.
Other notable flora/fauna: Grey and common seals, bottle-nosed dolphin regular, white-beaked dolphin and minke whale occasional in summer. Spring flowers, common butterflies and moths.
Contact: RSPB, T: 01346 532 017; E: strathbeg@rspb.org.uk

7. HADDO COUNTRY PARK

Aberdeenshire Council.
Location: Sat nav: AB41 7EQ. NJ 875 345. On the A90 Aberdeen-Peterhead road. After Bridge of Don, turn on to the B999. Continue to Tarves for about 12.5 miles and pick up signs for Haddo House.
Access: Grounds open dawn-dusk all year. Car park free, donation welcomed - id busy do not park on road verges.
Facilities: Car parks, display boards, more than 3.2 miles of surfaced paths, toilets open all year (inc. disabled) and bird hides with wheelchair access. Coach parking. Tearoom, visitor centre connected to the house.

Public transport: None.
Habitats: Parkland, woodland, wetland, loch, ponds.
Key birds: *Spring/summer:* Osprey, Sedge Warbler, Blackcap, Chiffchaff, Lapwing. *Winter:* Canada and Greylag Geese, Teal, Wigeon, Goldeneye, Goosander, Brambling. *All year:* Buzzard, Sparrowhawk, Grey Partridge, Great Spotted Woodpecker, Goosander, Grey Wagtail, Tawny Owl, herons, Cormorant.
Other notable flora/fauna: Meadow brown, ringlet and common blue butterflies. Red squirrels, otters and pipistrelle and Daubenton's bats.
Contact: Haddo House & Country Park,
T: 01651 851 041; E: haddo@visithaddo.com

8. LOCH OF STRATHBEG

RSPB (East Scotland).
Location: Sat nav: AB43 8QN. NK 055 577. Near Crimond on the A90, nine miles S of Fraserburgh. Reserve signposted from village.
Access: Visitor Centre open daily 9am-5pm, dusk if earlier.
Facilities: Visitor centre (inc observation room), with toilets and coffee machine. Tower Pool hide offers panoramic views, open dawn-dusk - 700 yards from visitor centre. Two hides overlooking loch accessed via drive to airfield. Wildlife garden, indoor children's area. Long beach walks from St Combs.
Public transport: Access to whole reserve difficult without vehicle. Buses from Fraserburgh and Peterhead to Crimond, one mile from centre. Details W: www.travelinescotland.com
Habitats: Britain's largest Dune loch, with surrounding marshes, reedbeds, grasslands and dunes.
Key birds: Breeding wetland species, passage waders, internationally important numbers of wintering wildfowl. Scarcities year round. *Winter:* Pink-footed and Barnacle Geese, Whooper Swan, large numbers of duck. Snow Goose and Smew annual. Raptors inc. Hen and Marsh Harriers. Great Northern Diver offshore. *Summer:* Common Tern, Water Rail, Corn Bunting. *Spring/autumn:* Spoonbill, Avocet, Marsh Harrier, Garganey, Little Gull, regular Pectoral Sandpiper. Osprey (seen almost daily), Common Crane (now annual on reserve).
Other notable flora/fauna: Otter, badger, stoat, roe deer. Early purple, butterfly and northern marsh orchids, dark green fritillary butterfly.
Contact: RSPB, T: 01346 532 017;
E: strathbeg@rspb.org.uk

9. TROUP HEAD

RSPB (East Scotland).
Location: Sat nav: AB45 3JN. NJ 822 665. Troup Head is between Pennan and Gardenstown on B9031, E along coast from Macduff. It is signposted off B9031. Look for small RSPB signs which direct you to car park past the farm buildings.
Access: Unrestricted, but unsuitable for wheelchairs.
Facilities: Parking for small number of cars. Not suitable for coaches. Live pictures are beamed from the reserve to the Macduff Marine Aquarium during the summer.
Public transport: None.

Habitats: Sea cliffs, farmland.
Key birds: Spectacular seabird colony, inc. Scotland's only mainland nesting Gannets. Bonxies linger in summer. Migrants occur during spring/autumn.
Other notable flora/fauna: Impressive common flower assemblage in spring. Cetaceans possible offshore in summer inc. minke whale. Brown hare common.
Contact: RSPB, T: 01346 532 017;
E: strathbeg@rspb.org.uk

Perth & Kinross

RSPB LOCH LEVEN (formerly known as Vane Farm) is the region's best known reserve and holds huge numbers of wintering geese, ducks and swans. Ospreys fish there too but the well-known watchpoint of Loch of the Lowes offers better views of birds on the nest than RSPB Loch Garten. The Hermitage at Dunkeld is good for woodland species, Dippers and raptors, possibly including Goshawk.

10. LOCH LEVEN (VANE FARM)

RSPB (East Scotland).
Location: Sat nav: KY13 9LX. NT 160 990. Part of Loch Leven NNR. Seven miles from Cowdenbeath, signposted two miles E Junc 5 of M90 onto B9097. Drive for approx two miles. Car park on right.
Access: Reserve trails open at all times. Visitor centre open daily (10am-5pm) except Dec 25/26, Jan 1/2. Entry fee for non-RSPB members (adult, child, concession and family rates). Disabled access to shop, coffee shop, observation room area and toilets. Coach parking available. Free car parking. Assistance dogs only.
Facilities: Shop, cafe (open 10am-4pm) and observation room with four telescopes overlooking Loch Leven and the reserve. There is a 1.25 miles hill trail through woodland and moorland. Wetland trail with three observation hides. Toilets, inc. disabled. Binoculars can be hired from shop. Eight-mile cycle path around loch.
Public transport: Limited bus service, Stagecoach Fife no. 2043 runs to the reserve from Kinross (four miles) on Sun. Stagecoach Fife, T: 01592 610 686.
Habitats: Wet grassland and flooded areas by Loch Leven. Arable farmland. Native woodland and heath moorland.
Key birds: *Spring/summer:* Breeding and passage waders (inc. Lapwing, Redshank, Snipe, Curlew), hirundines, Great Crested Grebe, Osprey. Farmland birds (inc. Skylark and Yellowhammer), Tree Pipit. *Autumn:* Migrating waders on exposed mud. *Winter:* Major fuelling stop for Pink-footed Geese (around 20,000 in late autmn). Also Whooper Swan (6% of Scotland's wintering population), Bewick's Swan, White-tailed Eagle, finch and tit flocks.
Other notable flora/fauna: 237 spp. butterflies and moths, 25 spp. mammal spp. inc. pipstrelle bat and roe deer.
Contact: RSPB, T: 01577 862 355;
E: lochleven@rspb.co.uk

11. LOCH OF THE LOWES

Scottish Wildlife Trust.
Location: Sat nav: PH8 0HH. NO 041 435. Sixteen miles N of Perth, two miles NE of Dunkeld, just off A923 (signposted).
Access: Admission charge for non-members of SWT. Visitor Centre open daily Mar-Oct (10am-5pm) and Fri to Sun for rest of year (10.30am-4pm). Observation hide open all year during daylight hours. Crannog hide accessible during visitor centre opening hours. No dogs allowed. Full access for wheelchairs.
Facilities: Visitor Centre with exhibition, shop and toilets. Two hides overlooking loch.

Public transport: Railway station at Birnam and Dunkeld, three miles from reserve. Buses to Dunkeld, two miles from reserve.
Habitats: Freshwater loch fringed by areas of fen, reedbeds and semi-natural woodland.
Key birds: Breeding Ospreys (Apr to end Aug) nest 200 yards from hide. Wildfowl and woodland birds.
Other notable flora/fauna: Red squirrels.
Contact: Loch of the Lowes Visitor Centre, T: 01350 727 337; E: lochofthelowes@scottishwildlifetrust.org.uk

Highlands & Islands

Highlands
Orkney
Outer Hebrides
Shetland

HABITATS FOUND NOWHERE else in Britain hold a range of scarce species: Dotterel, Ptarmigan and Snow Buntings on the tops, plus Crested Tit, the endemic Scottish Crossbill and Capercaillie are in the Caledonian pine forests. The boggy Flow Country of Caithness and Sutherland attracts breeding Greenshank, Common Scoter and Red- and Black-throated Divers.

THE ISLANDS OF Orkney and Shetland hold spectacular concentrations of seabirds, the Outer Hebrides offer the best chance of finding Corncrake in the UK and regular sightings of White-tailed Eagle. Rarities can turn up anywhere... particularly on Fair Isle (mid-way between Orkney and Shetland).

NATURE RESERVES - HIGHLANDS & ISLANDS

1. BEINN EIGHE & LOCH MAREE ISLANDS NNR

Scottish Natural Heritage.
Location: NH 019 630. IV22 2PD. Complex mountain massif by Kinlochewe, Wester Ross, 50 miles from Inverness and 20 miles from Gairloch on A832.
Access: Reserve (UK's oldest NNR) open at all times, no charge. Visitor centre just outside Kinlochewe.
Facilities: Visitor centre open Mar-Oct (9am-5pm), T: 01445 760 258, toilets, woodland, rhyming and mountain trails (self-guided with leaflets from visitor centre). Two trails suitable for all abilities.
Public transport: Very limited bus service from Inverness to Kinlochewe.
Habitats: Caledonian pine forest, dwarf shrub heath, mountain tops, freshwater loch shore.
Key birds: *All year*: Golden Eagle, Scottish Crossbill, Ptarmigan, Red Grouse, Siskin. *Summer*: Black-throated Diver, Redwing, Snow Bunting. Golden Plover breed on moorland.
Other notable flora/fauna: Wide range of dragonflies, inc. northern emerald, golden ringed and common hawker. Red deer, pine marten, mountain hare.
Contact: SNH, T: 01445 760 254; E: nnr@snh.gov.uk

2. CORRIMONY

RSPB (North Scotland).
Location: Sat nav: IV63 6TW (Corrimony village). NH 384 302 (car park). Lies 22 miles SW of Inverness between Glen Affric and Loch Ness, off A 831. Park in Corrimony Cairns car park.
Access: Open at all times. Waymarked trail suitable for wheelchairs. Unimproved paths, so terrain may not be suitable for disabled visitors.
Facilities: Way-marked trail (8.5 miles long) passes through farm - please leave gates as you find them. Guided minibus safaris to see Black Grouse leks in Apr and May.
Public transport: No. 17 bus from Inverness to Cannich stops 1.5 miles from reserve (request stop).
Habitats: 1,531 ha of pine woodland, moorland, blanket bog.
Key birds: Black Grouse (more than 30 displaying males), Crested Tit, crossbill spp., occasional Golden Eagle and Osprey. Breeding Greenshank, Red Grouse, Red-throated Diver. *Spring/summer*: Tree Pipit, Whinchat, Goosander. *Autumn*: Whooper Swan, Pinkfooted Goose, Woodcock.
Other notable flora/fauna: Red deer, pine marten. Many orchids in Jul.
Contact: RSPB, T: 01463 715 000; E: nsro@rspb.org.uk

3. FORSINARD FLOWS

RSPB (North Scotland).
Location: NC 891 425. 30 miles SW of Thurso on A897. From S turn off at Helmsdale (24 miles) or from N coast road (A836) turn two miles E of Melvich (14 miles).
Access: Open at all times. Contact reserve office during breeding season (mid-Apr to end-Jul) and during deerstalking season (Jul 1 to Feb 15) for advice. Families welcome. Two self-guided trails open all year, disabled viewpoint accessed via farm track on Forsinain Trail. No dogs on Dubh Lochan Trail during breeding season Apr-Aug.

Facilities: Visitor centre situated in Forsinard station open daily Easter to Oct (9am-5pm). Hen Harrier nest CCTV. Wheelchair access to centre and toilet. Guided walks Tues/Thur afternoons, May-Aug. Accommodation available locally. Viewpoint on Lochan Trail (not wheelchair accessible).
Public transport: Trains between Inverness and Thurso stop at Forsinard three times a day. Scotrail - T: 08457 484 950.
Habitats: Blanket bog, upland hill farm.
Key birds: The best time to visit for birds is May-Jul. Join a guided walk for the best chance of views of Red-throated Diver, Golden Plover, Greenshank, Dunlin, Hen Harrier, Merlin, Short-eared Owl, Dipper. Few birds between Sept and Feb apart from Red Grouse, Golden Eagle, Raven and Buzzard.
Other notable flora/fauna: Red deer, otter,, water vole, azure hawker dragonfly, emperor moth, bog plants inc. sundews.
Contact: RSPB, T: 01641 571 225; E: forsinard@rspb.org.uk

4. HANDA

Scourie Estate/Scottish Wildlife Trust.
Location: NC 138 480. Island accessible by boat from Tarbet, near Scourie - follow A894 N from Ullapool for 40 miles. Continue another three miles, turn L down single track road another three miles to Tarbet.
Access: Open Apr-Aug inc. No Sun sailings. Ferry runs 9.30am-16.45pm (last boat to island at 2pm). Ferry tickets, include % of the price going to SWT. Not suitable for disabled due to uneven terrain. No dogs.
Facilities: Three mile circular path, visitor shelter, compost toilet. Visitors are given introductory talk and a leaflet with map on arrival.
Public transport: Post bus to Scourie,T: 01549 402 357 Lairg Post Office. Train to Lairg. No connecting public transport between Scourie and Tarbet.
Habitats: Sea cliffs, blanket bog and heath, small sandy beaches and coastal grassland.
Key birds: *Spring/summer*: Biggest Guillemot and Razorbill colony in Britain and Ireland. Also nationally important for Kittiwake, Arctic and Great Skuas. Puffin, Shag, Fulmar and Common and Arctic Terns also present.
Contact: Handa Ranger (Apr-Aug), T: 07920 468 572; E: handaranger@scottishwildlifetrust.org.uk; Ferry operator: Roger Tebay, T: 07780 967 800; E: info@handa-ferry.com.

5. INSH MARSHES

RSPB (North Scotland).
Location: Sat nav: PH21 1NS. NN 775 998. In Spey Valley. From A9 take exit to Kingussie. Follow B970 S from village and then beyond Ruthven Barracks. Entrance to reserve is 0.6 mile further on. Parking close to viewpoint and opposite entrances to Lynachlaggan and Loch Insh Wood trails.
Access: Open at all times. Disabled access to the information viewpoint. Coach parking available at car park.

Facilities: Unmanned information viewpoint, two hides, three nature trails. No toilets.
Public transport: Nearest rail station and bus stop at Kingussie (one mile).
Habitats: More than 1,000 ha of marshes, woodland, river, open water.
Key birds: *Spring/summer:* Waders (Lapwing, Curlew, Redshank, Snipe), wildfowl (inc. Goldeneye and Wigeon), Osprey, Wood Warbler, Redstart, Tree Pipit. *Winter:* Hen Harrier, Whooper Swan, Greylag Goose, Teal, Wigeon, other wildfowl.
Other notable flora/fauna: Black darter dragonflies along Invertromie trail plus northern brown argus butterflies. Five spp. of orchid in Tromie Meadow. Roe deer.
Contact: RSPB, T: 01540 661 518; E: insh@rspb.org.uk

6. LOCH GARTEN & ABERNETHY FOREST

RSPB (North Scotland).
Location: Sat nav: PH25 3HA. NH 978 183. 2.5 miles from Boat of Garten, eight miles from Aviemore. Off B970, follow 'RSPB Ospreys' road signs (between Apr and Aug only).
Access: Osprey Centre open daily 10am-6pm (Apr to first sunday Sept). Disabled access. Guide dogs only. RSPB members free. Non-members: adult, concession, under-16 and family tickets available. Additional fee for Caper-watch, 05.30am-8am, (reduced for RSPB members). Dogs on leads please.
Facilities: Osprey Centre overlooking nesting Ospreys, toilets, optics and CCTV live pictures, shop, toilets. Three way-marked trails.
Public transport: Rapsons no. 34 bus service to Boat of Garten from Aviemore, (ask for Raebreck Junction stop), then a 2.5 mile footpath to Osprey Centre. Steam railway to Boat of Garten from Aviemore.
Habitats: Caledonian pine wood.
Key birds: *Spring/summer:* Ospreys nesting from Apr to Aug, Crested Tit, Redstart, Spotted Flycatcher, Tree Pipit, crossbills. Possible views of lekking Capercaillies from the Osprey Centre (Apr to mid-May). On loch look for Goldeneye, Wigeon and Common Sandpiper. *Autumn/winter:* Pink-footed and Greylag Geese roost on loch, Whooper Swan and various duck spp.
Other notable flora/fauna: Red squirrel, roe deer, otter, woodland plants and fungi.
Contact: RSPB, T: 01479 831 476;
E: abernethy@rspb.co.uk

7. UDALE BAY

RSPB (Scotland).
Location: Sat nav: IV7 8LU. NH 712 651. On the Black Isle, one mile W of Jemimaville on the B9163.
Access: Open all year. View wader roost from lay-by.
Facilities: Wheelchair-accessible hide (no dogs here), large lay-by. No coach parking. Nearest adapted unisex toilet in Allen Square, Cromarty (five miles away).
Public transport: No. 26 bus stops in Jemimaville six times a day (approx 5 mins walk). Contact Rapsons, T: 0870 608 2608 or Stagecoach, T: 01862 892 683.

Habitats: Mudflat, saltmarsh and wet grassland.
Key birds: *Spring/summer:* 10,000 Pinkfeet on passage each year, other wildfowl, Oystercatcher, Redshank, waders. Possible Osprey. *Autumn/winter:* Large flocks of wildfowl (approx 10,000 Wigeon), geese, waders (Oystercatcher, Knot, Bar-tailed Godwit and Dunlin join commoner species), Peregrine.
Contact: RSPB, T: 01463 715 000; E: nsro@rspb.org.uk

Orkney

A LACK OF MANAGED grouse moors means that Hen Harriers breed here in excellent numbers. Other scarce breeders include Whimbrels, Great and Arctic Skuas and Red-throated Divers. There are excellent seabird colonies such as the one at Marwick Head. North Ronaldsay attracts good numbers of migrants.

8. HOBBISTER

RSPB (East Scotland).
Location: Sat nav: KW17 2RA. HY 395 069 (car park) or HY 382 068 (Waukmill Bay). Overlooking Scarpa Flow 3.2 miles W of Kirkwall on A964.
Access: Open access between A964 and the sea. Dogs on leads. Stout footwear recommended when trails are muddy.
Facilities: A council-maintained footpath to Waulkmill Bay, two car parks. New circular walk from RSPB car park along cliff top and Scapa Flow.
Public transport: Buses along A964 run five times a day. Contact Visit Orkney, T: 01856 872 856 for timetables.
Habitats: Orkney moorland, bog, fen, saltmarsh, coastal cliffs, scrub.
Key birds: *Summer:* Breeding Hen Harrier, Merlin, Short-eared Owl, Red Grouse, Red-throated Diver, Eider, Red-breasted Merganser, Black Guillemot, Twite. Wildfowl and waders at Waulkmill Bay. *Autumn/winter:* Waulkmill for sea ducks, divers, auks and grebes (Long-tailed Duck, Red-throated, Black-throated and Great Northern Divers, Slavonian Grebe).
Other notable flora/fauna: Otter occasionally seen from Scapa trail. Grey and common seal both possible from footpath looking towards Scapa Flow.
Contact: RSPB, T: 01856 850 176;
E: orkney@rspb.org.uk

9. MARWICK HEAD

RSPB (East Scotland).
Location: Sat nav: KW17 2NB. HY 229 240. Orkney's largest cliffside seabird colony lies four miles N of Skara Brae on W coast of mainland Orkney, near Dounby. Path N from Marwick Bay, or from council car park at Cumlaquoy at HY 232 252 (best for Kitchener Memorial).
Access: Open all year. Rough terrain not suitable for wheelchairs.
Facilities: Cliff top path. Information board in Marwick car park.

Public transport: OCTO bus, T: 01856 871 536 operates a 'by request' service to all parts of the west mainland of Orkney.
Habitats: Rocky bay, sandstone cliffs. The Choin low-tide lagoon good for waders and ducks.
Key birds: May to Jul best for up to 25,000 seabirds. Huge numbers of Kittiwakes and auks, inc. Puffins, also nesting Fulmar, Rock Dove, Raven, Rock Pipit, Short-eared owl.
Other notable flora/fauna: Cetaceans are a possibility from Marwick with porpoise and minke whale occasionally seen. Beach path good place for great yellow bumblebee in Aug.
Contact: RSPB, T: 01856 850 176; E: orkney@rspb.org.uk

10. NORTH HILL, PAPA WESTRAY

RSPB (East Scotland).
Location: Sat nav: KW17 2BU. HY 495 538. From pier or airfield travel N along main road. From shop/hostel, take road N to junction at Holland Farm and turn R onto main road. Continue past Rose Cottage to reserve entrance.
Access: Access at all times. During breeding season report the Warden at Rose Cottage, 650 yards S of reserve entrance or use trail guide (available in hide).
Facilities: Nature trail (three miles) around Mull Head, hide/info hut. Limited parking. Not suitable for wheelchairs or pushchairs.
Public transport: Orkney Ferries, T: 01856 872 044, Loganair, T: 1856 872 494.
Habitats: Sea cliffs, maritime heath (large by European standards).
Key birds: Summer: Close views of Puffin, Guillemot, Razorbill and Kittiwake. Black Guillemot nest under flagstones around reserve's coastline. One of UK's largest colonies of Arctic Tern, also Arctic and Great Skuas. Breeding Lapwing, Redshank and Snipe in grazed areas. Winter: Gannet, Fulmar, Eider and winter thrushes.
Other notable flora/fauna: One of the best areas to see Scottish primrose (*primula scotica*), with two flowering periods that just overlap (May to Aug). Orcas and whales on migration in autumn. Grey and common seals in winter.
Contact: RSPB, T: 01856 850 176; E: orkney@rspb.org.uk

11. NORTH RONALDSAY BIRD OBSERVATORY

Location: Sat nav: KW17 2BE. HY 64 52. 35 miles from Kirkwall, Orkney mainland.
Access: Open all year except Christmas.
Facilities: Guest house and hostel accommodation, restaurant, cafe, fully licenced, croft walk.
Public transport: Daily subsidised Loganair flights from Kirkwall from Mainland Orkney to North Ronaldsay. 15 mins flight gives stunning views of several islands. Loganair website (www.loganair.co.uk/reservations/) for full information.
Habitats: Crofting island with a number of eutrophic and oligotrophic wetlands. Coastline has sandy bays and rocky shores. Walled gardens concentrate passerines.

Key birds: *Spring/autumn:* Prime migration site inc. regular BBRC species. Wide variety of breeding seabirds, wildfowl and waders. *Winter:* Waders and wildfowl inc. Whooper Swan and hard weather movements occur.
Contact: North Ronaldsay Bird Observatory, T: 01857 633 200; E: alison@nrbo.prestel.co.uk; W: www.nrbo.co.uk

Outer Hebrides

THESE ISLANDS ARE THE Corncrake stronghold of Britain, though having large numbers of birds doesn't make them any easier to see! There is a strong passage of Long-tailed and Pomarine Skuas past RSPB Balranald in May. The area's ability to attract rare migrants is only just being discovered with recent autumnal trips to Barra turning up trumps.

12. BALRANALD

RSPB (North Scotland).
Location: Sat nav: HS6 5DL. NF 706 707. On W coast of North Uist, three miles N of Bayhead. From Skye take ferry to Lochmaddy, North Uist. Drive W on A865 for 20 miles to reserve. Turn off main road at signpost to Houghharry.
Access: Reserve open at all times, no charge. Visitor centre open Apr-Aug (9am-6pm). Dogs on leads. Circular walk not suitable for wheelchairs.
Facilities: Visitor centre and toilets (disabled access). Marked circular nature trail (three miles). Group bookings welcome.
Public transport: Post bus service, T: 01876 560 244. Caledonian MacBrayne ferries, T: 08705 650 000.
Habitats: Freshwater loch, machair, coast and crofts.
Key birds: *Spring:* Skuas and divers at sea, Purple Sandpiper, Turnstone, Dunlin and other waders on shore. Dotterel. *Summer:* Corncrake, Corn Bunting, Lapwing, Oystercatcher, Dunlin, Ringed Plover, Redshank, Snipe, terns. *Autumn:* Hen Harrier, Peregrine, Greylag Goose. *Winter:* Twite, Snow Bunting, Whooper Swan, Greylag Goose, Wigeon, Teal, Shoveler, sightings of Golden and White-tailed Eagles becoming commoner. *Passage:* Barnacle Goose, Pomarine Skua, Long-tailed Skua.
Other notable flora/fauna: Blanket bog and machair plants reach their peak in Jul. Look for rare great yellow bumblebee on wildflowers. Otters in freshwater lochs.
Contact: RSPB, T: 01463 715 000; E: nsro@rspb.org.uk

13. LOCH DRUIDIBEG NNR

Scottish Natural Heritage.
Location: Sat nav: HS8 5RS. NF 782 378. Lies just N of Kildonan on South Uist. Turn off A865 in Stillgarry at B890 road for Loch Sgioport. Track is 1.5 miles further on - park at side of road.

Access: Open all year. Several tracks and one walk covering a range of habitats - most not suitable for wheelchairs. Stout footwear essential. Observe Scottish Outdoor Access Code in all areas with livestock. View E part of reserve from public roads but parking and turning areas for coaches is limited.
Facilities: None.
Public transport: Buses Lochmaddy to Lochboisdale stop at reserve. Hebridean Coaches, T: 01870 620 345, MacDonald Coaches, T: 01870 620 288.
Habitats: Covering 1,677 ha, the NNR contains freshwater lochs, marshes, machair, coast, moorland.
Key birds: *Summer:* Breeding waders, Corncrake, Black-throated Diver, Greylag Goose, wildfowl, terns and raptors. *Spring and autumn:* Migrant waders and wildfowl. *Winter:* Waders, wildfowl and raptors inc. Golden Eagle and Hen Harrier.
Contact: SNH, T: 01870 620 238; E: E: nnr@snh.gov.uk

Shetland

BRITAIN'S MOST NORTHERLY archipelago is always going to attract large numbers of vagrants, with the observatory on Fair Isle boasting a phenomenal list of species. Seabird colonies here are spectacular and include such unusual species as Leach's Petrels; an overnight stay on Mousa is the best way to catch up with this largely nocturnal species.

14. FAIR ISLE BIRD OBSERVATORY

Fair Isle Bird Observatory.
Location: HZ 2172. Famous island for rarities located SE of mainland Shetland.
Access: Open from end-Apr to end-Oct. No access restrictions.
Facilities: Public toilets at airstrip and Stackhoull Stores (shop). Accommodation at Fair Isle Bird Observatory inc. one room with wheelchair access (phone/e-mail for brochure/details). Guests can join in observatory work and see birds in the hand. Slide shows, guided walks through Ranger Service.
Public transport: Regular flights to Sumburgh, Shetland or ferry from Aberdeen to Lerwick. To Fair Isle: Airtask services from Tingwell (nr Lerwick) - contact for details, T: 01595 840 246. Alternatively, Good Shepherd ferry (12 passangers) from Grutness, Shetland on Tues, Thurs, Sat, May-Sept). Contact for details T: 01595 760 363.
Habitats: Heather moor and lowland pasture/crofting land. Cliffs.
Key birds: Large breeding seabird colonies (auks, Gannet, Arctic Tern, Kittiwake, Shag, Arctic Skua and Great Skua). Many common and rare migrants Apr to early-Jun and late-Aug to Nov.
Other notable flora/fauna: Northern marsh, heath spotted and frog orchid, lesser twayblade, small adders tongue, oyster plant. Orca, minke whale, white-backed, white-sided and Risso's dolphins. Endemic field mouse.
Contact: Fair Isle Bird Obs, T: 01595 760 258; E: fibo@btconnect.com; W: www.fairislebirdobs.co.uk

15. FETLAR

RSPB (East Scotland).
Location: HU 603 917. Small island lying E of Yell. Take car ferry from Gutcher on Yell to Hamarsness, then drive 6 miles E. Ferry booking advised, T: 01957 722 259.
Access: Apart from the footpath to Hjaltadance circle, Vord Hill, the Special Protection Area is closed mid-May to end-Jul by arrangement with warden. Rest of site open at all times. Loch of Funzie can be observed from road.
Facilities: Hide at Mires of Funzie open Apr to Nov. Toilets and payphone at ferry terminal, interpretive centre at Houbie, campsite, shop.
Public transport: None.
Habitats: Serpentine heath, rough hill lane, upland mire.
Key birds: *Summer:* Breeding Red-throated Diver, Eider, Shag, Whimbrel, Golden Plover, Dunlin, Arctic and Great Skuas, Manx Shearwater, Storm Petrel. Red-necked Phalarope on Loch of Funzie (HU 655 899) viewed from road or RSPB hide overlooking Mires of Funzie.
Other notable flora/fauna: Heath spotted orchid and autumn gentian. Otters are common, harbour and grey seals breed.
Contact: RSPB, T: 01957 733 246; E: fetlar@rspb.org.uk

16. NOSS NNR

Scottish Natural Heritage.
Location: HU 531 410. Take car ferry to Bressay from Lerwick and follow signs for Noss (3.2 miles). At end of road walk to shore (600 yards) where inflatable ferry (passenger only) to island will collect you. If red flag is flying, island is closed due to sea conditions.
Access: Access by zodiac inflatable - Noss Ferry Line - 0800 107 7818 - updated daily by 9am. Open (subject to weather) Tue/Wed, Fri to Sun (10am-5pm) between late-Apr and end-Aug. No dogs on ferry. Steep rough track down to ferry. Commercial boat trips around island - contact the tourist office, T: 01595 693 434.
Facilities: Visitor centre, toilets. Bike rack/car park on Bressay side. Parking for small coaches.
Habitats: Dune and coastal grassland, moorland, heath, blanket bog, sea cliffs.
Key birds: *Spring/summer:* Breeding Fulmar, Shag, Gannet, Arctic Tern, Kittiwake, Herring and Great Black-backed Gull, Great Skua, Arctic Skua, Guillemot, Razorbill, Puffin, Black Guillemot, Eider, Lapwing, Dunlin, Snipe, Wheatear, Twite plus migrants.
Other notable flora/fauna: Grey and common seals, otter, porpoise regularly seen, killer whales annual.
Contact: SNH, T: 01595 693 345; E: nnr@snh.gov.uk

Eastern Wales

Breconshire, Montgomeryshire, Radnorshire

POWYS, FORMED FROM the old counties of Breconshire, Radnorshire and Montgomeryshire, is a largely upland rural area with a limited but interesting community of birds. Raptors are prominent, with Hen Harrier, Merlin, Red Kite and Peregrine all well established, while Cors Dyfi has become a successful breeding site for Ospreys.

1. BRECHFA POOL

Location: Sat nav: LD3 0NL (Llyswen). SO 118 377. Travelling NE from Brecon look for lane off A470, 1.5 miles SW of Llyswen; on Brechfa Common, pool is on right after cattle grid.
Access: Open dawn-dusk. Road runs around three-quarters of the pool, giving good access.
Facilities: None.
Public transport: None.
Habitats: Marshy grassland, large shallow lake located at a height of 900ft.

Key birds: Good numbers of wintering wildfowl are replaced by breeding gulls and commoner waterfowl. Species recorded inc. Teal, Gadwall, Tufted Duck, Shoveler, Wigeon, Little Grebe, Black-headed Gull, Lapwing, Dunlin, Redshank, Kestrel.
Other notable flora/fauna: Rare pillwort around pond margins, crowfoot, penny royal and orange foxtail.

2. CORS DYFI NATURE RESERVE

Montgomeryshire Wildlife Trust.
Location: Sat nav: SY20 8SR. SN701 985. Lies 3.5 miles SW of Machynlleth on the A487 Abersytwyth road. Approx 2.5 miles S of Derwenlas, turn R after caravan park.
Access: Open 10am-6pm, Apr-Sept and weekends for rest of year. Programme of special events in winter. Donations welcome to help fund reserve and Dyfi Osprey Project. Site is wheelchair-accessible apart from elevated bird hide.
Facilities: Visitor centre, toilets (inc. disabled), small cafe, elevated hide, 360 degree observatory. Extensive boardwalk.
Public transport: Nearest bus stop at Llyfnant Valley Bridge 0.5 mile from reserve.
Habitats: Bog, wet woodland and scrub.
Key birds: Site sprang to national prominence when Ospreys first bred in 2011. Spring/summer: Osprey, Nightjar, Grasshopper, Sedge and Reed Warblers, Snipe, Stonechat, Reed Bunting.
Other notable flora/fauna: Common lizard, four-spotted chaser dragonfly.
Contact: Montgomeryshire WT, T: 01938 555 654; E: info@montwt.co.uk
Osprey Project (Mar-Aug) T: 01654 781 414; E: enquiries@dyfiospreyproject.com; W: www.dyfiospreyproject.com/

3. ELAN VALLEY

Elan Valley Trust/Welsh Water.
Location: Sat nav: LD6 5HP. SN 928 646 (visitor centre). Three miles SW of Rhayader, off B4518.
Access: Mostly open access. Pay-and-display car park with Blue Badge spaces.
Facilities: Visitor centre, cafe and toilets (open daily, except Dec 25). 9.30am-5pm. Nature trails all year and hide at SN 905 617.
Public transport: None.
Habitats: 45,000 acres of moorland, woodland, river and reservoir.
Key birds: Spring/summer: Upland birds inc. Golden Plover and Dunlin. Red Kite, Buzzard, Sparrowhawk, Peregrine, Raven, Green Woodpecker, Grey Wagtail and Marsh Tit are joined in the summer by Pied Flycatcher, Spotted Flycatcher, Wood Warbler, Redstart, Tree Pipit and Cuckoo. Autumn/winter: Fieldfare, Redwing, Ring Ouzel, woodpeckers and woodland species.
Other notable flora/fauna: Internationally important oak woodlands. 3,000+ spp. of flora and fauna recorded.
Contact: Visitor Centre, Rangers Office
T: 01597 810 880; W: www.elanvalley.org.uk

NATURE RESERVES - EASTERN WALES

4. GIGRIN FARM

Location: Sat nav: LD6 5BL. SN 978 676. Farm lies 0.5 mile south of Rhayader, Powys off A470.
Access: Open for kite feeding sessions Tues-Sun and bank holiday/school holiday Mons, from end-Dec to Nov (12.30pm-5pm). Feeding times: 2pm (winter) and 3pm (summer). No booking required. See website for admission charges. Dogs on leads welcome.
Facilities: Red Kite Shop, five hides (three with disabled access), plus specialist photography hides. Brilliant views of Red Kites. For the past 20 years, Gigrin has been the official Red Kite feeding station for Wales, helping young birds survive in winter. By attracting large numbers of birdwatchers it relieves pressure on other nest sites in summer.
Habitats: 200 acre upland sheep farm rising to 1,200 feet above sea level.
Key birds: Daily feeds attract a wide range of species inc. Carrion Crow, Raven, Jackdaw, Buzzard and Red Kite. Kite numbers vary from a few dozen to around 400 when weather is bad. Other feeding stations attract smaller birds such as Brambling, Yellowhammer and Siskin. A 1.5 mile trail links to the RSPB Dyffryn reserve while a wetland area attracts wild ducks, Grey Heron and wagtails.
Contact: Chris Powell, Gigrin Farm, South Street, Rhayader, Powys LD6 5BL. T: 01597 810 243; E: chris@gigrin.co.uk; W: www.gigrin.co.uk

5. GILFACH FARM RESERVE

Radnorshire Wildlife Trust.
Location: Sat nav: LD6 5LF (visitor centre). SN 967 717. Gilfach is just off the A470, seven miles from Llangurig. Follow the brown Nature Reserve signs. The visitor centre is one mile across the Reserve. Parking at Marteg Bridge, three miles N of Rhayader.
Access: Open daily, all year. Disabled access possible to centre, toilets and purpose-built trail.
Facilities: Visitor centre open Easter-Sept, subject to availability of volunteers. Circular nature trail, short easy-access trail. Wye Valley Walk and Gwastedyn Church Trail also pass through reserve.
Public transport: None.
Habitats: Working organic hill farm covering 410 acres, river, oak woods, meadows, hill-land.
Key birds: 73 spp. recorded, 55 breed regularly, inc. Common Sandpiper, Dipper, Grey Wagtail, Pied and Spotted Flycatchers, Redstart, Wood Warbler, Tree Pipit, Whinchat, Stonechat, Linnet, Yellowhammer, Siskin, Redpoll, Marsh and Willow Tits, Stock Dove, Wheatear, Barn Owl, Raven. Other visitors inc. Curlew, Merlin, Red Kite, Goshawk, Sparrowhawk, Peregrine, Goosander, Kingfisher, Reed Bunting.
Other notable flora/fauna: Green hairstreak, wall brown and ringlet butterflies, mountain pansy, bloody-nosed beetle. Welsh clearwing moth first record for Radnorshire.
Contact: Radnorshire WT, T: 01597 823 298; E: info@rwtwales.org

6. LAKE VYRNWY

Severn Trent/RSPB (Wales HQ).
Location: SJ 020 193. Located WSW of Oswestry. Nearest village is Llanfyllin on A490. Take B4393 to Llanwddyn and at dam, turn L and L again.
Access: Reserve open all year.
Facilities: Toilets, visitor centre open, except Dec 24/27 & Jan 1, 10.30am-5pm Apr-Oct, 10.30pm-4pm rest of year), RSPB shop, coffee shop, craft workshops, five colour-coded nature trails. Three bird hides, one accessible to wheelchair users.
Public transport: Infrequent bus service to dam.
Habitats: Heather moorland, woodland, meadows, rocky streams and large reservoir.
Key birds: *All year:* Siskin, Great Spotted Woodpecker, Buzzard, Raven. *Spring/summer:* Hen Harrier, Curlew, Cuckoo, Whinchat, Dipper, Kingfisher, Pied Flycatcher, Wood Warbler, Redstart, hirundines, Peregrine and Hobby.
Other notable flora/fauna: Mammals inc. otter, polecat, brown hare. Golden-ringed dragonflies frequent in summer.
Contact: RSPB, T: 01691 870 278; E: vyrnwy@rspb.org.uk

7. PWLL-Y-WRACH

Brecknock Wildlife Trust.
Location: Sat nav: LD3 0DS (Talgarth). SO 165 326. From Talgarth town centre cross over River Enig, then take Bell Street and Hospital Road. After 1.5 miles, reserve is on the right.
Access: Reserve open all year. Please keep to footpaths. Level, wheelchair-friendly path runs halfway into site. Elsewhere paths can be muddy and there are steps. Dogs allowed on leads
Facilities: Information panel in car park.
Public transport: No local services.
Habitats: 17.5 ha of ancient woodland, river and spectacular Witches Pool waterfall.
Key birds: Large variety of resident woodland birds, with migrant boost in spring. Dipper, Kingfisher, Pied Wagtail, Great Spotted Woodpecker, Chiffchaff, Wood Warbler, Pied Flycatcher, Mistle and Song Thrushes, Nuthatch.
Other notable flora/fauna: Otter, dormouse, bats, common lizard. Early purple and birds' nest orchids, herb paris, bluebell, wood anemone.
Contact: Brecknock WT, T: 01874 625 708; E: enquiries@brecknockwildlifetrust.org.uk

8. ROUNDTON HILL NNR

Montgomeryshire Wildlife Trust.
Location: Sat nav: SY15 6EL. SO 293 946. SE of Montgomery. Follow brown duck signs from Churchstoke on A489, taking minor road towards Old Churchstoke. After one mile turn R at phone box, then first right.
Access: Open access. Tracks rough in places. Dogs on lead at all times. Uneven tracks not suitable for wheelchairs.
Facilities: Car park. Waymarked trails.
Public transport: Buses to Old Churchstoke, 600 yards from reserve.

Habitats: Ancient hill grassland, woodland, streamside wet flushes, scree, rock outcrops.
Key birds: *All year:* Buzzard, Red Kite, Raven, all three woodpeckers, Tawny Owl, Linnet, Goldfinch. *Spring/summer:* Wheatear, Redstart, Whitethroat.

Contact: Montgomeryshire WT, T: 01938 555 654; E info@montwt.co.uk

Northern Wales

Anglesey, Caernarfonshire, Denbighshire, Flintshire, Merioneth

HIGHLIGHTS ON ANGLESEY include a seabird colony and Choughs at South Stack, terns at Cemlyn Bay and waders at Malltraeth. RSPB Valley Lakes and Newborough Warren are all worth exploring too, while Conwy is one of the RSPB's flagship reserves. Smaller inland sites offer a good range of birds.

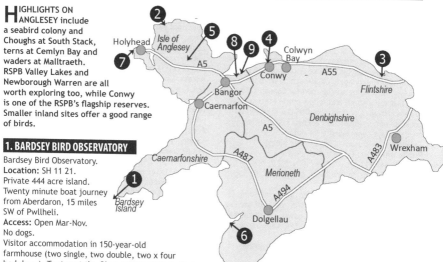

1. BARDSEY BIRD OBSERVATORY

Bardsey Bird Observatory.
Location: SH 11 21.
Private 444 acre island.
Twenty minute boat journey from Aberdaron, 15 miles SW of Pwllheli.
Access: Open Mar-Nov.
No dogs.
Visitor accommodation in 150-year-old farmhouse (two single, two double, two x four bed dorm). To stay at the Observatory contact Alicia Normand, T: 01626 773 908; E: stay@bbfo.org.uk Day visitors by Bardsey Ferries, T: 07971 769 895.
Facilities: Public toilets available for day visitors. Three hides, one on small bay, two seawatching. Gift shops and payphone.
Public transport: Trains from Birmingham to Pwllheli, bus from Bangor to Pwllheli.
Habitats: Sea-birds cliffs viewable from boat only. Farm and scrubland, spruce plantation, willow copses and gorse-covered hillside.
Key birds: All year: Chough, Peregrine. Spring/summer: Night walks to see Manx Shearwaters (20,000 pairs). Other seabirds. Migrant warblers, chats, Redstart, thrushes. Autumn: Masses of common migrants, plus many rarities (inc. Eye-browed Thrush, Lanceolated Warbler, American Robin, Yellowthroat, Summer Tanager).
Other notable flora/fauna: Autumn ladies' tresses.
Contact: Steven Stansfield (Warden), T: 07855 264 151; E: info@bbfo.org.uk; W: www.bbfo.org.uk

2. CEMLYN

North Wales Wildlife Trust.
Location: Sat Nav: LL67 0EA. Cemlyn on north coast of Anglesey is signposted from Tregele on A5025 between Valley and Amlwch.
Access: Open all year. Dogs on leads. No wheelchair access. During summer months walk on seaward side of ridge and follow signs.
Facilities: Car parks SH 336 932 & SH 329 936 at either end of reserve.
Public transport: None within a mile.
Habitats: Brackish lagoon, shingle ridge, salt marsh, mixed scrub.
Key birds: Wintering wildfowl and waders, breeding terns, gulls and warblers, pipits and passing migrants. *Spring:* Wheatear, Whitethroat, Sedge Warbler, Manx Shearwater, Whimbrel, Dunlin, Knot and Black-tailed Godwit. *Summer:* Breeding Arctic, Common and Sandwich Terns, Black-headed Gull, Oystercatcher and Ringed Plover. *Autumn:* Golden Plover, Lapwing, Curlew, Manx Shearwater, Gannet, Kittiwake, Guillemot.

Winter: Little and Great Crested Grebes, Shoveler, Shelduck, Wigeon, Red-breasted Merganser, Coot, Turnstone, Purple Sandpiper.
Other notable flora/fauna: 20 spp. of butterflies recorded. Sea kale, yellow horned poppy, sea purslane, sea beet, glasswort. Grey seal, harbour porpoise, bottlenose dolphin.
Contact: North Wales WT, T: 01248 351 541;
E: nwwt@wildlifetrustswales.org

3. CONNAH'S QUAY POWER STATION RESERVE

EON/Deeside Naturalists Society.
Location: Sat nav: CH5 4BP. SJ 275 715. Travel W to end of M56 which then becomes A494. Follow signposts for Flint. Take first slip road to left which joins a large roundabout and turn right onto A548. Continue straight on this road (there are several roundabouts) After crossing the River Dee take first slip road and turn R at the first roundabout and then straight on at second roundabout. Follow the signs for the power station: the reserve entrance is on the left at the next roundabout.If approaching from the west follow A548, exiting on slip road for Connah's Quay. Turn L at roundabout and follow power station signs.
Access: Advance permit from DNS required (group bookings only). Wheelchair access. Public welcome on open days - see website for details.
Facilities: Field studies centre, five hides.
Public transport: Contact Arriva Cymru,
T: 01745 343 492.
Habitats: Saltmarsh, mudflats, grassland scrub, open water, wetland meadow.
Key birds: *Summer:* Small roosts of non-breeding estuarine birds. *Winter:* High water roosts of waders and wildfowl inc. Black-tailed Godwit, Oystercatcher, Redshank, Spotted Redshank, Curlew, Lapwing, Teal, Pintail and Wigeon.
Other notable flora/fauna: 17 spp. of butterflies.
Contact: Secretary, T: 01244 313 404;
E: secretary@deesidenaturalists.org.uk;

4. CONWY

RSPB (North Wales).
Location: Sat nav: LL31 9XZ. SH 797 773. On E bank of Conwy Estuary. Access from A55 at exit 18 signposted to Conwy and Deganwy. Footpath and cycleway accessed from Conway Cob.
Access: Open daily (9.30am-5pm) except Dec 25. Ample parking for coaches. Toilets, buildings and trails to pushchairs and wheelchairs.
Facilities: Visitor centre, gift shop, coffee shop (10am-4pm), toilets inc. disabled. Three hides (accessible to wheelchairs) and three viewing screens. Three trails firm and level, though a little rough in places and wet in winter.
Public transport: Train service to Llandudno Junction, 10 mins walk. Bus service to Tesco supermarket, Llandudno Junction five mins walk, T: 0871 200 2233.
Habitats: Lagoons, islands, reedbed, scrub, estuary.

Key birds: Wildfowl and waders in winter, warblers and wetland breeding birds in summer. *Spring:* Passage waders, hirundines and wagtails. *Summer:* Lapwing, waterbirds and warblers. *Autumn:* Black-tailed Godwit and other passage waders. *Winter:* Kingfisher, Goldeneye, Water Rail, Red-breasted Merganser, wildfowl, huge Starling roost.
Other notable flora/fauna: Common butterflies through summer, esp. common blues. Great display of cowslips in Mar, bee orchids in summer. Otters seen early mornings.
Contact: RSPB, T: 01492 584 091; for events
T: 01492 581025; E: conwy@rspb.org.uk

5. LLYN CEFNI

Welsh Water/ Hamdden Ltd.
Location: Sat nav: LL77 7RQ (Rhosmeirch car park). A reservoir located two miles NW of Llangefni, in central Anglesey. NE section of reservoir managed as nature reserve - entrance at Rhosmeirch SH 451 783. Follow B5111 or B5109 from the village.
Access: Open at all times. Dogs allowed except in sanctuary area. Good footpath (wheelchair accessible) for most of the site, bridges over streams. Walkers can reach reservoir from Dingle nature reserve, Llangefni, on boardwalks and cycle route (one mile).
Facilities: Two picnic sites, good footpath, coach parking at Rhosmeirch car park.
Public transport: Bus nos. 4 & 32 (44 Sun only, 52 Thur only), T: 0871 200 2233 for information.
Habitats: Large area of open water, reedy bays, coniferous woodland, scrub, carr.
Key birds: *Summer:* Sedge and Grasshopper Warblers, Whitethroat, Buzzard, Tawny Owl, Little Grebe, Gadwall, Shoveler, Kingfisher. *Winter:* Waterfowl (Whooper Swan, Goldeneye), Crossbill, Redpoll, Siskin, Redwing. *All year:* Stonechat, Treecreeper, Song Thrush.
Other notable flora/fauna: Northern marsh orchid, rustyback fern, needle spikerush. Banded demoiselle, migrant hawker, golden ringed dragonfly, emerald damselfly. Ringlet, gatekeeper, clouded yellow and wall butterflies. Bloody nose beetle.
Contact: Welsh Water, T: 01443 452 350.

6. MAWDDACH VALLEY

RSPB (North Wales).
Location: 1: Coed Garth Gell sat nav: LL40 2TU (village of Bontddu). On north side of Mawddach Estuary, the footpath to the reserve entrance goes from the Fiddler's Elbow carpark at SH 678 189. 2: Arthog Bog (SH 630 138) is off Dolgellau-to-Tywyn road (A493) west of Arthog. Park at Morfa Mawddach station.
Access: Nature trails are open at all times. Dogs on leads.
Facilities: Nature trails at both sites in Mawddach Valley, plus information boards.
Public transport: Nearest bus stop is Taicynhaeaf on Dolgellau to Barmouth no. X94. 0.5 mile walk to Coed Garth Gell.
Habitats: Oak woodland, bracken and heathland at Coed Garth Gell. Willow and alder scrub and raised bog at Arthog Bog.

NATURE RESERVES - NORTHERN WALES

Key birds: *At Coed Garth Gell:* Buzzard, Sparrowhawk, Peregrine, Raven, Lesser Spotted Woodpecker, Grey Wagtail, Dipper and Hawfinch are joined in the summer by Pied Flycatcher, Spotted Flycatcher, Wood Warbler, Redstart, Tree Pipit and Cuckoo. *At Arthog Bog:* Buzzard, Sparrowhawk, Peregrine, Raven are seen all year round. Summer migrants inc. Tree Pipit, Grasshopper Warbler and Cuckoo. In winter flocks of Redpoll and Siskin are common and Red-breasted Merganser, Pintail and Little Egret are on the nearby estuary.
Other notable flora/fauna: Coed Garth Gell has Tunbridge filmy and beech ferns and a wide variety of butterflies. Golden-ringed dragonfly is regular.
Contact: RSPB, T: 01654 700 222;
E: mawddach@rspb.org.uk

7. SOUTH STACK CLIFFS

RSPB (North Wales).
Location: Sat nav: LL65 1YH. RSPB visitor centre SH 218 818, Ellin's Tower information centre SH 206 820. Follow A55 to W end in Holyhead, proceed straight on at roundabout, continue straight on through traffic lights. After another 0.5 mile turn L and follow the brown tourist signs for RSPB South Stack.
Access: RSPB car park (no charge) with Blue Badge parking. 'Access for all' track to viewing area overlooking the lighthouse. Access to Ellin's Tower Seabird Centre gained via staircase. Reserve covered by an extensive network of paths, some of which are not accessible via wheelchair.
Facilities: Visitor centre open daily 10am-5pm, except Dec 25. Ellin's Tower which has windows overlooking main auk colony open daily (10am-5pm Easter to Sept). Network of footpaths over coastal and heathland terrain.
Public transport: None.
Habitats: Sea cliffs, maritime grassland, maritime heath, lowland heath.
Key birds: Peregrine, Chough, Fulmar, Puffin, Guillemot, Razorbill, Rock Pipit, Skylark, Stonechat, Linnet, Shag, migrant warblers and passage seabirds.
Other notable flora/fauna: Spathulate fleawort, endemic to South Stack, adders, lizards, porpoise.
Contact: RSPB, T: 01407 762 100;
E: south.stack@rspb.org.uk

8. SPINNIES ABER OGWEN

North Wales Wildlife Trust.
Location: Sat nav: LL57 3YH. SH 613 721. From Bangor follow the Tal-y-Bont road from roundabout on A5122 near Penrhyn Castle entrance. Road to reserve is signposted on L after 0.6 mile. Reserve can also be approached from a road at junction 12 off A55. Minor road leads to car park where reserve entrance is signposted
Access: Open all year. Dogs on leads. Keep to the paths. Wheelchair accessible to the main hide.
Facilities: Two hides clearly signposted from the car park, main hide is wheelchair accessible and offers views of Traeth Lafan sands and the Spinnies lagoon. There is a drop-off point at the main entrance. Footpaths are good throughout

Public transport: No. 5 or no. 5X bus from Bangor or Llandudno.
Habitats: Woodland, scrub, grassland, shingle beach mudflats, reed swamp and open water.
Key birds: *Autumn/winter:* Large numbers of wintering wildfowl and waders such as Redshank, Greenshank, Wigeon and Teal. Kingfisher can be seen from Sep to Mar. *Spring/summer:* Red-breasted Merganser, Sandwich Tern, large numbers of Mute Swans, Little Grebe, Blackcap and Sedge Warbler.
Other notable flora/fauna: Broad-leaved helleborine, dog's mercury, bluebells. Red admiral, speckled wood, holly blue, orange tip and small copper butterflies.
Contact: North Wales WT, T: 01248 351 541;
E: nwwt@wildlifetrustswales.org

9. TRAETH LAFAN LNR

Gwynedd Council.
Location: NE of Bangor, stretching six miles to Llanfairfechan. 1: For Traeth Lafan, take minor road from old A55 near Tal-y-Bont (SH 610 710) to Aberogwen car park by coast (SH 614 723). 2: For nearby Morfa Aber Reserve (SH 646 731) follow brown signs from junction 13 of A55. 3: Access to Morfa Madryn Reserve is on foot one mile W from Llanfairfechan promenade (SH 679 754).
Access: Open access from 1, 2,& 3. All sites are wheelchair accessible.
Facilities: Public paths. 1: Car park, hides 200 yards away at Spinnies Reserve. 2: Car park and hide. 3: Car and coach park with toilets and cafe, hides at reserve.
Public transport: For local bus and train timetables, T: 0870 60 82 608 or W: www.gwynedd.gov.uk
Habitats: Intertidal sands and mudflats (2,500 ha), wetlands, streams. SPA SAC SSSI and LNR.
Key birds: Third most important area in Wales for wintering waders; of national importance for moulting Great Crested Grebe and Red-breasted Merganser; internationally important for Oystercatcher and Curlew; passage waders; winter concentrations of Goldeneye and Greenshank, and of regional significance for wintering populations of Black-throated, Red-throated and Great Northern Divers and Black-necked and Slavonian Grebes and breeding Lapwings at Morfa Madryn.
Contact: Gwynedd Council, T: 01766 771 000.

Southern Wales

Glamorgan, Gower, Gwent

SUMMER ALONG THE GOWER coastline will produce breeding seabirds, Peregrines and thousands of Manx Shearwaters offshore. Cardiff Bay is good for passage and wintering waders. The best wetlands are Kenfig Pools — half way between and Cardiff and Swanse a — and the Newport Wetlands Reserve. Both are worth visiting at any time of year.

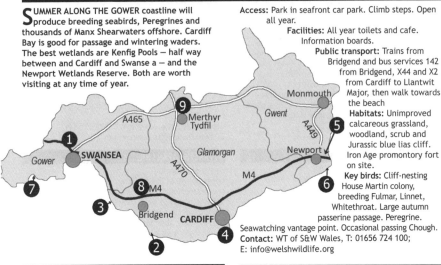

Access: Park in seafront car park. Climb steps. Open all year.

Facilities: All year toilets and cafe. Information boards.

Public transport: Trains from Bridgend and bus services 142 from Bridgend, X44 and X2 from Cardiff to Llantwit Major, then walk towards the beach

Habitats: Unimproved calcareous grassland, woodland, scrub and Jurassic blue lias cliff. Iron Age promontory fort on site.

Key birds: Cliff-nesting House Martin colony, breeding Fulmar, Linnet, Whitethroat. Large autumn passerine passage. Peregrine. Seawatching vantage point. Occasional passing Chough.

Contact: WT of S&W Wales, T: 01656 724 100;
E: info@welshwildlife.org

1. CWM CLYDACH

RSPB (Wales HQ).

Location: Sat nav: SA6 5TL. SN 684 026. N of Swansea. Three miles N of Junc 45 of M4, through the village of Clydach on B4291, follow the signs for Craig-cefn-Parc. Car park is close to the New Inn pub.

Access: Open at all times along public footpaths and waymarked trails. Not suitable for wheelchairs. Coach parking not available. Dogs on leads.

Facilities: Two nature trails link to network of public footpaths, car park, information boards.

Public transport: Hourly buses from Swansea to Craig Cefn Parc stop at reserve entrance.

Habitats: Oak and beech woodland on steep slopes along the banks of the fast-flowing Lower Clydach River.

Key birds: Red Kite, Sparrowhawk, Buzzard, Raven, Green Woodpecker, Dipper and Grey Wagtail are joined in the summer by Spotted Flycatcher, Garden Warbler, Wood Warbler and Cuckoo. In winter Siskin, Lesser Redpoll and Woodcock are regular.

Other notable flora/fauna: Fungi, wood sorrel, silver-washed fritillary and speckled wood butterflies.

Contact: RSPB, T: 029 2035 3000;
E: cymru@rspb.org.uk

2. CWM COL-HUW

The Wildlife Trust of South and West Wales.

Location: Sat nav: CF61 1RF (Cwm Col-Huw car park). SS 960 674. SE from Bridgend, site inc. Iron Age fort, overlooking Bristol Channel. From Bridgend take B4265 S to Llanwit Major. Follow beach road from village.

3. KENFIG NNR

Bridgend County Borough Council.

Location: Sat nav: CF33 4PT. SS 802 811. Seven miles W of Bridgend. From Junc 37 of M4, drive towards Porthcawl, then North Cornelly, then follow signs.

Access: Open at all times. Unsurfaced sandy paths, not suitable for wheelchairs. Flooding possible in winter and spring. Coach parking available.

Facilities: Toilets, hides, free car parking and signposted paths.

Public transport: Local bus service stops at reserve. Traveline Cymru, T: 0871 200 2233.

Habitats: 1,300 acre sand dune system, freshwater lake with reeds, numerous wet dune slacks, sandy coastline with some rocky outcrops.

Key birds: *Summer:* Warblers inc. Cetti's, Sedge, Reed, Grasshopper and Willow Warbler, Blackcap and Whitethroat. *Winter:* Wildfowl, Water Rail, Bittern, grebes.

Other notable flora/fauna: 16 spp. of orchid, hairy dragonfly, red-veined and ruddy darters, small blue, dark green fritillary, grayling, brown argus butterflies.

Contact: Kenfig NNR, T: 01656 815 070.

4. LAVERNOCK POINT

The Wildlife Trust of South and West Wales.

Location: Sat nav: CF64 5XQ. ST 181 681 (main entrance). five miles S of Cardiff. Access is from B4267 via Fort Road, signposted Lavernock Point. Limited parking by gate or in public car park at the end of Fort Road.

Access: Not suitable for wheelchairs as access is via a stile.

Facilities: Info boards.

Public Transport: Bus no. 94 from Cardiff to Lavernock.

Habitats: Sea, coastal calcareous grassland and scrub.

Key birds: Important site for watching bird migrations. In autumn large flocks of Swallow, thrushes and finches. Breeding birds inc. Whitethroat, Lesser Whitethroat, Bullfinch and Chiffchaff.
Other notable flora/fauna: Butterflies, wild flowers.
Contact: WT of S&W Wales, T: 01656 724 100;
E: info@welshwildlife.org

5. MAGOR MARSH

Gwent Wildlife Trust.
Location: Sat nav: NP26 3DD (Redwick Road).
ST 428 866. Reserve lies to S of Magor. Leave M4 at Junc 23, turning R onto B4245. Follow signs for Redwick in Magor village. Take first L after railway bridge. Reserve entrance is 0.5 mile further on right.
Access: Open all year. Keep to path. Wheelchair access to bird hide. No dogs please.
Facilities: Hide. Car park, footpaths and boardwalks.
Public transport: Bus no. 61 from Newport stops outside reserve.
Habitats: 90 acres of sedge fen, reedswamp, willow carr, damp hay meadows and open water.
Key birds: Important for wetland birds. *Spring*: Reed, Sedge and Grasshopper Warblers, occasional Garganey and Green Sandpiper on passage, Hobby. *Winter*: Teal, Peregrine, Jack Snipe, Snipe, occasional Shoveler and Gadwall, Bittern records in two recent years. *All year*: Little Egret, Little Grebe, Reed Bunting, Cetti's Warbler and Water Rail.
Contact: Gwent WT, T: 01600 740 600;
E: info@gwentwildlife.org

6. NEWPORT WETLANDS NNR

NRW/ RSPB (Wales HQ)/ Newport City Council.
Location: Sat nav: NP18 2BZ. ST 334 834. SW of Newport. Reserve car park on West Nash Road, just before entrance to Uskmouth power station. From Junc 24 of M4, take the A48 to Newport Retail Park, turn towards steelworks and follow brown 'duck' signs to the reserve car park.
Access: Visitor Centre open daily 9am-5pm except Dec 25. Six disabled parking bays. Nature trails are accessible by wheelchair. Dogs only on perimeter footpath.
Facilities: Information centre, tea-room (10am-4pm), shop, toilets (inc. disabled), viewing screens.
Public transport: No.63 bus runs from Newport Bus Station to the reserve daily (exc. bank holidays).
Habitats: 438 ha of wet meadows, saline lagoons, reedbed, scrub and mudflats on Severn estuary.
Key birds: *Spring/summer*: Breeding waders such as Lapwing and Oystercatcher, Bearded Tit, Cetti's Warbler, Cuckoo and regular migrants on passage. *Autumn*: Large numbers of migrating wildfowl and waders arrive at the reserve — regulars inc. Curlew, Dunlin, Ringed Plover, Shoveler. *Winter*: Massive Starling roost (up to 50,000 birds). Bittern, nationally important numbers of Black-tailed Godwit, Shoveler and Dunlin.
Other notable flora/fauna: Badger, wood mouse, otter. Great crested newt. Orchids in spring, 16 spp. of dragonflies, 23 spp. of butterflies and ca. 200 spp. of moths.
Contact: Newport Wetlands Reserve (NRW)
RSPB Visitor Centre, T: 01633 636 363;
E: newport-wetlands@rspb.org.uk

7. OXWICH NNR

NRW (Swansea Office).
Location: Sat nav: SA3 1LS. SS 501 865. From Swansea take A4118 Gower road towards Killay, Parkmill and continue through Nicholaston Oxwich village.
Access: Most of NNR open at all times. Groups can visit some restricted areas by arrangement. No permit required for access to foreshore, dunes, woodlands and facilities.
Facilities: Private car park and toilets, Apr-Oct only, charge. Marsh boardwalk and marsh lookout. No visitor centre, no facilities for disabled visitors.
Public transport: Bus service Swansea/Oxwich. First Cymru, T: 01792 580 580.
Habitats: Freshwater marsh, saltmarsh, foreshore, dunes, woodlands.
Key birds: *Summer*: Breeding Reed, Sedge and Cetti's Warblers, Treecreeper, Nuthatch, woodpeckers. *Winter*: Wildfowl.
Contact: NRW, T: 0300 065 3000;
E: enquiries@naturalresourceswales.gov.uk

8. PARC SLIP NATURE PARK

The Wildlife Trust of South and West Wales.
Location: Sat nav: CF32 0EH. SS 880 840. 0.6 mile W of Aberkenfig. From Junc 36 of M4 take A4063 towards Maesteg, then B4281 (signposted Aberkenfig and Pyle) and follow brown signs to visitor centre in Fountain Road.
Access: Open dawn-dusk. Space for coach parking.
Facilities: Visitor centre with coffee shop (open 10am-4pm daily, except Mon & christmas period). Five hides, regular events, interpretation centre. Free car park off Fountain Road. Good access for wheelchairs throughout the site.
Public transport: Bus no. 63 from Bridgend bus station stops outside the Fountain Inn at the bottom of Fountain Road. Train station at Tondu.
Habitats: Restored opencast mining site, wader scrape, lagoons, grassland, woodland.
Key birds: *Summer*: Breeding Tufted Duck, Lapwing, Skylark. Migrant waders (inc. Little Ringed Plover). Kingfisher, Green Woodpecker. *Winter*: Snipe, Water Rail, Shoveler.
Other notable flora/fauna: 20 spp. of dragonflies recorded, inc. emperor and scarce blue-tailed damselfly. Seven spp. of orchid, twayblade and broad-leaved helleborine. Great crested newt, harvest mouse, reptiles.
Contact: WT of S&W Wales, T: 01656 724 100;
E: info@welshwildlife.org

9 . TAF FECHAN

The Wildlife Trust of South and West Wales.
Location: Sat nav: CF48 2HH. SO 033 084, SO 037 076 and SO 045 097 (main entrances). Two miles N of Merthyr Tydfil centre. Several entrances along Taff Trail and footpath from Cyfarthfa Park.
Access: Open all year. Not accessible to wheelchairs due to steep terrain and steps.
Facilities: Information boards.

Public Transport: Train station at Merthyr Tydfil then bus nos. 25 & 26 to Cefn Coed y Cymmer or nos. 40, 33 & 24 to Pontsarn.
Habitats: Ancient broadleaved woodland, calcareous grasslands, river gorge and cliffs.
Key birds: Pied Flycatcher, Tawny Owl, Dipper, Kingfisher, Grey Wagtail, Peregrine, Woodcock.

Other notable flora/fauna: Otter, migrating salmon.
Contact: WT of S&W Wales, T: 01656 724 100;
E: info@welshwildlife.org

Western Wales

Carmarthenshire, Ceredigion, Pembrokeshire

A SUMMER BOAT trip to either Skomer or Skokholm to see the huge seabird colonies, is a must-do outing in summer, but inland, steep wooded valleys are good for Redstarts, Pied Flycatchers, Wood Warblers and Red Kites in spring and summer. For good winter birds head for the National Wetland Centre for Wales in Llanelli.

1. CASTLE WOODS

The Wildlife Trust of South and West Wales.
Location: Sat nav: SA19 6RT (Dinefwr Park). SN 614 218. About 60 acres of woodland overlooking River Tywi, 1.25 miles W of Llandeilo town centre, adjacent to Dinefwr Park.
Access: Open all year by footpath from Tywi Bridge, Llandeilo (SN 627 221) or park next to fire station off A40 and walk down Dinefwr Park Drive.
Facilities: Footpaths, mostly too steep for wheelchairs. Bird hide.
Public transport: Bus no. X13 from Swansea and nos. 280 from Carmarthen to Llandovery. Train station in Llandeilo.
Habitats: Old mixed deciduous woodlands, castle.
Key birds: All three woodpeckers, Buzzard, Raven, Sparrowhawk. *Summer:* Pied and Spotted Flycatchers, Redstart, Wood Warbler. *Winter:* On water meadows look for Teal, Wigeon, Goosander, Shoveler, Tufted Duck and Pochard.
Other notable flora/fauna: Fallow deer, badger, butterflies inc. silver-washed fritillary.
Contact: WT of S&W Wales, T: 01656 724 100; E: info@welshwildlife.org

2. CORS CARON NNR

NRW (Mid Wales Area).
Location: Sat nav: SY25 6JF (car park). SN 692 625. On B4343 two miles N of Tregaron, Ceredigion, NE of Lampeter.
Access: Open access from new car park on B4343. Circular four mile Riverside Walk, shut at times due to flooding/management requirements. Dogs under control on Old Railway Walk, on leads on boardwalk, but not allowed on Riverside Walk.

Facilities: Coach accessible car park with toilets and picnic space. Bird hide on boardwalk, 2nd hide on Old Railway Walk 1.5 miles from car park. Footpath through reserve part of Ystwyth Trail.
Public transport: Infrequent buses (nos. 585 & 588) stop iin Tregaron.
Habitats: Raised bog, river, fen, wet grassland, willow woodland, reedbed.
Key birds: *Summer:* Lapwing, Redshank, Curlew, Red Kite, Hobby, Grasshopper Warbler, Whinchat, Redpoll, Reed Bunting. *Winter:* Teal, Wigeon, Whooper Swan, Hen Harrier, Red Kite.
Other notable flora/fauna: Small red damselfy among the abundant dragonflies which can be seen from boardwalk. Also adder and common lizard.
Contact: NRW, T: 0300 065 3000;
W: www.naturalresourceswales.gov.uk

NATURE RESERVES - WESTERN WALES

3. DYFI NNR

NRW (Mid Wales Area).
Location: Sat nav: SY24 5JZ (Ynyslas visitor centre).
SN 640 955. Extensive reserve midway between
Machynlleth and Aberystwyth and seaward side of
A487, incorporating part of Dyfi estuary, Ynyslas
dunes and Borth Bog.
Access: Ynyslas dunes and the estuary have unrestricted
access. No access to Borth Bog (Cors Fochno) for casual
birdwatching; permit required for study and research
purposes. Good views over the bog and Aberleri marshes
from W bank of Afon Leri. Public footpaths off A493 E
of Aberdyfi, and off B4353 (S of river); minor road from
B4353 at Ynyslas to dunes and parking area.
Facilities: NRW visitor centre/shop/toilets at
Ynyslas (open 9am-5pm from Easter to end-Sept). No
refreshments. Public hide overlooking marshes beside
footpath at SN 611 911.
Public transport: Aberystwyth to Tre'r-ddol bus
service stops at Borth and Ynyslas.
Habitats: Sandflats, mudflats, saltmarsh, creeks,
dunes, raised bog, grazing marsh.
Key birds: *Winter:* Greenland White-fronted Goose,
wildfowl, waders and raptors. *Summer:* Breeding
wildfowl and waders (inc. Teal, Shoveler, Merganser,
Lapwing, Curlew, Redshank).
Contact: NRW, T: 0300 065 3000;
W: www.naturalresourceswales.gov.uk

4. GWENFFRWD-DINAS

RSPB (Wales HQ).
Location: SN 788 471. North of Llandovery. From
A483 take B road signposted to Llyn Brianne Reservoir
and then follow signs to reserve, which lies between
Cynghordy and Llanwrda.
Access: Public nature trail at Dinas open dawn to
dusk. Donation for parking appreciated.
Facilities: Nature trail inc. a boardwalk and four
benches. Other parts of the trail are rugged. Car park
and information board at start of trail. Coach parking
can be arranged.
Public transport: None.
Habitats: Hillside oak woods, streams and bracken
slopes. Spectacular upland scenery.
Key birds: Upland species such as Red Kite, Buzzard,
Peregrine, Raven, Goosander, Dipper and Grey
Wagtail are joined in the summer by Pied Flycatcher,
Spotted Flycatcher, Wood Warbler, Redstart, Tree
Pipit, Common Sandpiper and Cuckoo. Marsh Tit and
all three woodpecker species are present.
Other notable flora/fauna: Golden-ringed dragonfly,
purple hairstreak, silver-washed fritillary and Wilson's
filmy fern.
Contact: RSPB, T: 01654 700 222;
E: gwenffrwd.dinas@rspb.org.uk

5. LLANELLI WETLAND CENTRE

The Wildfowl & Wetlands Trust.
Location: Sat nav: SA14 9SH. SS 533 984. Overlooks
the Burry Inlet near Llanelli. Leave M4 at Junc 48.
Signposted from A484, E of Llanelli.
Access: Open daily 9.30am-5pm, except Dec 24/25.
Grounds open until 6pm in summer. Centre is fully
accessible with disabled toilets. Mobility scooters and
wheelchairs are free to hire.
Facilities: Visitor centre with toilets, hides,
restaurant, shop, education facilities, free car and
coach parking. The centre has level access and hard-
surfaced paths.
Public transport: Llanelli 'Dial a Ride' bus service
operates between the Llanelli bus station, railway
station and the centre - book on T: 0845 634 0661
Mon-Fri 9.30am-12pm up to teh day before travel
(bookings for Sat & Mon must be made by Fri before).
Habitats: Inter-tidal mudflats, reedbeds, pools,
marsh, waterfowl collection.
Key birds: Large flocks of Curlew, Oystercatcher,
Redshank on saltmarsh. *Winter:* Up to 50,000
waterbirds, inc. Pintail, Wigeon, Teal. Also Little
Egret, Short-eared Owl, Barn Owl, Peregrine.
Other notable flora/fauna: Bee and southern marsh
orchids, yellow bartisa. Dragonflies, water voles, otters.
Contact: WWT Llanelli Wetland Centre,
T: 01554 741 087; E: info.llanelli@wwt.org.uk

6. RAMSEY ISLAND

RSPB (Wales HQ).
Location: Sat nav: SA62 6PY (mainland). SM 706 237.
One mile offshore from lifeboat station at St Justinians,
two miles west of St Davids, Pembrokeshire.
Access: Open daily, weather permitting, Apr 1st (or
easter if earlier) to Oct, 10am-4pm. RSPB landing
fees for non-members, in addition to boat fare.
No wheelchair access. Coach and car parking at
St Justinians. For boat bookings (sailings from the
lifeboat station at 10am and 12 noon), contact:
Thousand Island Expeditions, T: 01437 721 721;
E: sales@thousandislands.co.uk
Facilities: Small RSPB visitor centre/shop selling snacks
and hot and cold drinks on island. Toilets a five minute
walk uphill from harbour. A 3.5 mile self-guiding circular
trail on island (rugged in parts) with introduction from
resident wardens. Guided walks are also available.
Public transport: Trains to Haverfordwest Station.
Hourly buses from Haverfordwest to St Davids and
then Celtic Coaster shuttle bus to boat embarkation
point (T: 01348 840 539).
Habitats: Acid grassland, maritime heath, seacliffs.
Key birds: *Spring/summer:* Cliff-nesting auks
(Guillemot, Razorbill), Kittiwake, Fulmar, Shag,
Stonechat, Wheatear, Skylark, Linnet, Little Owl,
plus passage migrants. *All year:* Peregrine, Raven,
Chough.
Other notable flora/fauna: Largest grey seal colony
in south-west Britain, red deer, harbour porpoise.
Contact: RSPB, T: 07836 535 733;
E: ramsey.island@rspb.org.uk;

7. SKOKHOLM NNR

The Wildlife Trust of South and West Wales.
Location: Sat nav: SA62 3BJ (Marloes). SM 735 050.
Island lying S of Skomer. Boats embark from Martin's
Haven.
Access: No day visitors - residential stays available Apr
to Sept. Bookings open in the autumn for the following
season. Boat fare paid directly to the boatman in cash.
Facilities: Recently given Bird Observatory status
and welcomes visting ringers. Upgraded self-catering
accommodation for up to 20 people. Small shop
selling basic foodstuffs.
Public transport: None.
Habitats: Cliffs, bays and inlets.
Key birds: *Spring:* Manx Shearwaters arrive at end
of Mar. *Summer:* Internationally important colonies
of Razorbill, Puffin, Guillemot, Storm Petrel, Lesser
Black-backed Gull. Migrants inc. rare species.
Other notable flora/fauna: Grey seals, harbour
porpoise, occasional common, bottlenose and Risso's
dolphins, nationally rare moths.
Contact: Main Office & Island Bookings
(Mon-Fri 9am-5pm), T: 01656 724 100;
E: islands@welshwildlife.org

8. SKOMER

The Wildlife Trust of South and West Wales.
Location: Sat nav: SA62 3BJ (Marloes). SM 725 095.
15 miles from Haverfordwest. Take B4327 turn-off for
Marloes, embarkation point at Martin's Haven, two
miles past village. National Trust car park at Martin's
Haven.
Access: National Trust operates a car park in Martin's
Haven at SA62 3BJ. Island open from Apr-Sept (or
easter if earlier). Not suitable for infirm (steep
landing steps and rough ground). Day visitors: Boats
sail from 10am, 11am and 12pm daily, not Mons,
except bank holidays. T: 01646 636 800 to see if boats
running. Boat fare paid on the boat (applies to all),
island landing fees (non-members) payable at Lockley
Lodge visitor centre (present membership card for
free landing). Visitors staying overnight depart at 9am
- booking essential (bookings open in the autumn for
the following season)/length of stay conditions apply.
Facilities: Information centre, toilets, two hides,
booklets, guides, nature trails. Visitors need to take
water/food.
Public transport: None.
Habitats: Maritime cliff, bluebells, red campion,
freshwater ponds.
Key birds: Largest colony of Manx Shearwater in the
world. Puffin, Guillemot, Razorbill (Apr to end-Jul).
Kittiwake (until end-Aug), Fulmar, Short-eared Owl,
Chough, Peregrine, Buzzard (all year), migrants (inc.
rare spp.)
Contact: Main Office & Island Bookings
(Mon-Fri 9am-5pm), T: 01656 724 100;
E: islands@welshwildlife.org

9. WELSH WILDLIFE CENTRE

The Wildlife Trust of South and West Wales.
Location: Sat nav: SA43 2TB. SN 188 451. Centre
based in Teifi Marshes Nature Reserve, Cilgerran,
two miles SE of Cardigan. River Teifi is N boundary.
Signposted from A478 Cardigan to Fishguard road.
Access: Nature reserve open all year. Free parking
for members, charge for non-members. Dogs on leads
welcome. Disabled access to visitor centre, paths,
four hides.
Facilities: Visitor centre/cafe (open 10am-5pm
Easter-Oct, 4pm Nov-Mar, closed christmas week),
network of four nature trails and seven hides.
Binoculars for hire.
Public transport: Bus nos 430 & 390 between
Cardigan and Cilgerran, then walk to centre.
Habitats: Wetlands, marsh, swamp, reedbed, open
water, creek (tidal), river, saltmarsh, woodland.
Key birds: Extensive flooding in winter attracts large
numbers of wildfowl, notably Teal, Wigeon and Mallard.
Other winter regulars are Water Rail, Curlew, Snipe,
Lapwing and Peregrine. Breeding birds inc. Cetti's
Warbler, Kingfisher, Greater Spotted Woodpecker, gulls,
Sand Martin, Redstart. Occasional Bittern and Red Kite.
Other notable flora/fauna: Otter, water shrew, sika
and red deer, good range of dragonflies.
Contact: Welsh Wildlife Centre, T: 01239 621 600;
E: wwc@welshwildlife.org

10. YNYS-HIR

RSPB (Wales HQ).
Location: Sat nav: SY20 8TA. SN 682 961. Car park is
one mile from Eglwys-fach village, off A487, six miles
SW of Machynlleth.
Access: Open daily (dawn-dusk). Visitor centre open
daily Apr-Oct (9am-5pm) and Nov-Mar (10am-4pm),
except the christmas period. Coaches welcome but
call for parking information. No dogs allowed.
Facilities: Visitor centre and toilets. Two main
circular trails (not suitable for wheelchairs), five
hides, two viewpoints, drinks machine.
Public transport: Bus service to Eglwys-fach from
either Machynlleth or Aberystwyth, T. 01970 617 951.
Rail service to Machynlleth.
Habitats: Estuary, freshwater pools, woodland and
wet grassland.
Key birds: Large numbers of wintering waders,
wildfowl and birds of prey on the estuary are replaced
with breeding woodland birds in spring and summer.
All year: Red Kite, Buzzard, Little Egret, Lapwing,
Teal. *Spring:* Wood Warbler, Redstart, Pied Flycatcher,
nine spp. of warbler. *Winter:* Greenland White-fronted
Goose, Barnacle Goose, Wigeon, Hen Harrier.
Other notable flora/fauna: Sixteen spp. of
dragonflies inc. small red damselfly and golden-
ringed dragonfly. Butterflies inc. dark green fritillary,
brimstone and speckled wood. Otters (rarely seen)
and brown hares are resident.
Contact: RSPB, T: 01654 700 222;
E: ynyshir@rspb.org.uk

DIRECTORY OF WILDLIFE LECTURERS, PHOTOGRAPHERS & ARTISTS

Neil Gartshore

The magnificent Steller's Sea Eagle (*Haliaeetus pelagicus*) has to be one of the world's most stunning birds of prey for photographers to capture on film.

WILDLIFE LECTURERS & PHOTOGRAPHERS

THIS DIRECTORY LISTS a number of individuals who offer lectures covering a wide variety of wildlife related subjects. In addition, a number of them also offer a range of photographic products/services.

Each listing indicates whether the individual offer lectures (L) and/or photographic product/services (P) followed by a short biography.

Under *'Lectures'* there is an indication of the talks that are available but bear in mind that this is probably not the full list of what may be available.
- Fee: this will inevitably vary due to the travel distances involved but will give an idea of what is charged.
- Distance: how far lecturers are willing to travel/any restrictions are noted here.
- Time: when lecturers are available/any restrictions are noted here.

If any of the listings offer photographic products/services they are described under *'Photography'*.

If you are an organiser of a group looking to book a speaker for your meetings or would like further information about the photographic products/services offered please contact the individuals directly via the details at the end of their listing - please mention *'The Birdwatcher's Yearbook'* when making an enquiry.

ALMOND, Jim L, P

A very active birder, bird photographer and experienced lecturer with additional interest in Butterflies/Odonata.

Lectures: See website for full descriptive details and titles, inc. Wild Peregrines; Birding in Shropshire/ Venus Pool; Scilly Pelagics; North Norfolk; New England; Vancouver; Bird & Nature Photography; Bird identification; other wildlife inc. butterflies & dragonflies. All talks are digitally presented in an entertaining style with audio-visual finale. All levels of interest catered for.

Fee: £95 for standard lecture and fuel at 30p per mile. **Distance:** Any. **Time:** Any.

Photography: All UK birds, special interest in wild Peregrines. See website for main interests, gallery and portfolio. **Products & services:** Images for publication, lectures and workshops / individual tuition available. Vast library of images. Available for commissions, lectures / tours. Competitive terms for larger projects.

Contact: 5 Coolock Close, St Peters Park, Shrewsbury, SY3 9QD; T: 07940 678 719; E: shropshirebirder@gmail.com; W: www.shropshirebirder.co.uk

BELL, Graham L, P

A professional ornithologist, cruise lecturer worldwide (covering all seven continents), photographer, author, former BBRC member.

Lectures: Arctic; Antarctic; Siberia; Australia; Iceland; Seychelles; UK - identification, behaviour, seabirds, garden birds, entertaining bird sound imitations, birds in myth & fact, bird names, taking better photos, etc.

Fee: £20 donation to BirdLife International plus travel and B&B (if required). **Distance:** Any. **Time:** Any.

Photography: Birds, animals, flowers, landscapes, all seven continents from Arctic to Antarctic. **Products & services:** Original slides for sale, £2.00 ea.; Photographic lecture available - Taking Better Photos.

Contact: Ros View, South Yearle, Wooler, Northumberland NE71 6RB; T: 01668 281 310; E: seabirdsdgb@hotmail.com

BOND, Terry L

An ex-company chairman, international consultant, bank director. Conference speaker worldwide, photographer, group field leader, lecturer on birds for more than 30 years.

Lectures: Six talks - inc. Scilly Isles; Southern Europe; North America; Scandinavia; Birdwatching Identification - a New Approach (an audience participation evening).

Fee: By arrangement (usually only expenses). **Distance:** Most of UK. **Time:** Evenings.

Contact: 3 Lapwing Crescent, Chippenham, Wiltshire SN14 6YF; T: 01249 462 674; E: terryebond@btopenworld.com

BOWDEN, Paul L

Birdwatcher and nature photographer (4K-Video and DSLR photos of birds and other wildlife) for 30+ years (serious amateur). Founder member and current Chairman of Glamorgan Wildlife Photographic Club. Member of local and national organisations (Glamorgan Birds, RSPB and WWT). Provide own HD Projector, HD Laptop, amplifier and speakers.

Lectures: Birds of Europe (Austria, Belarus, Bulgaria, Estonia, Finland, Germany, Greece (Lesvos), Hungary, Italy, Portugal & Madeira, Spain & Balearic and Canary Islands, Sweden & UK); Egypt; Libya; Morocco; Oman; Azerbaijan; India; Hong Kong; Japan; Australia; Panama; Brazil; USA (nine States: AZ, CA, FL, HI, IL, MO, OR, TX, WA) & Canada. Also Butterflies and Dragonflies from UK, Europe and Overseas. Presentations as HD Video Movie and/or Powerpoint.

Fee: £60 plus reasonable travelling expenses (with overnight accommodation for longer trips). **Distance:** Any. **Time:** Any by arrangement.

Contact: 4 Patmore Close, Gwaelod-y-Garth, Cardiff, CF15 9SU; T: 029 2081 3044 or 07771 664 819; E: bowden_pe@hotmail.com

WILDLIFE LECTURERS & PHOTOGRAPHERS

BROADBENT, David L, P
A professional photographer.

Lectures: UK birds & wild places; In praise of natural places, travel and photography.

Fee: £85 locally. **Distance:** 30 miles without travel costs, anywhere with travel costs - using your AV equipment. **Time:** Any.

Photography: UK birds and wild places, travel and photography. **Products & services:** Images for editorial use, lecturer in wild life and general photography, owns Forest of Dean School of Photography offering courses in the UK south-west and fine art print sales.

Contact: based in the Forest of Dean;
T: 07771 664 973; E: info@davidbroadbent.com;
W: www.davidbroadbent.com

BROOKS, Richard L, P
Wildlife photographer, writer, lecturer, birding guide.

Lectures: Over a dozen talks, including Lemnos; Lesvos; Evros Delta; Kerkini; Poland; Spain; Israel; Canaries; Oman; plus East Anglia; Wales; Scotland and Western Isles (Uist, Mull and Islay).

Fee: £80 plus petrol. **Distance:** Any if accommodation provided. **Time:** Any.

Photography: Owls (especially Barn), raptors, Kingfisher and a variety of European birds (especially Lemnos, Lesvos) and landscapes. **Products & services:** Guided birding and wildlife photography in Norfolk, by arrangement - owls a speciality (Barn & Tawny on site, Little nearby), 20+ years experience of siting Barn Owl boxes in North Norfolk.Mounted and unmounted computer prints (6x4, A3+ size), framed pictures, A5 greetings cards, surplus slides for sale. Norfolk bird calendar available (see website).

Contact: 24 Croxton Hamlet, Fulmodeston, Fakenham, Norfolk NR21 0NP; T: 01328 878 632;
E: email@richard-brooks.co.uk
or r.brooks662@btinternet.com;
W: www.richard-brooks.co.uk

Eider / Neil Gartshore

BUCKINGHAM, John L, P
Long-standing and popular lecturer, worldwide bird and wildlife photographer, tour leader.

Lectures: 60+ titles covering birds, wildlife, botany, ecology and habitats in UK, Europe, Africa, Australia, Indian sub-continent, North-South and Central America. Includes favourites such as How Birds Work; The Natural History of Birds; Wonders of Bird Migration.

Fee: £100 plus expenses. **Distance:** Any. **Time:** Any.

Photography: Huge range of birds, botany and wildlife from UK, Europe, Africa, Americas, Australia, Asia and worldwide. **Products & services:** Digital images available for publication and purchase plus original slides for lectures and personal use.

Contact: 10 Courtlands, Kingsdown Road, Kingsdown, Walmer, CT14 8BW; T: 01304 364 231;
E: john.birdtalk@btinternet.com

CLEAVE, Andrew MBE L
Wildlife photographer, author, lecturer and tour leader.

Lectures: More than 30 talks (incl. Canadian Rockies; New Zealand seabirds and endemics; India; Southern Sweden; Belarus; Bermuda; Mediterranean birds and wildlife; Isles of Scilly; Lundy; Shetland; Ancient Woodlands; Dormice; Coastal Birds: Life Between the Tides. Full list available.

Fee: £70 plus petrol. **Distance:** Approx. 60 miles without accommodation. **Time:** Afternoons and evenings, not school holidays.

Contact: 31 Petersfield Close, Chineham, Basingstoke, Hampshire RG24 8WP; T: 01256 320 050 & 07785 767 263;
E: andrew@bramleyfrith.co.uk;
W: http://andrewcleave.co.uk/

COLLINS, Chris L
Wildwings tour leader, Neotropical Bird Club council member & treasurer, experienced lecturer and wildlife photographer.

Lectures: In search of the Spoon-billed Sandpiper/ Birds of the Russian Far East; Finding a new species: the New Caledonian Storm-petrel; Pacific Odyssey: New Zealand to Japan; Birds of Antarctica and the Southern Ocean Islands; Birds of Guyana; South America: The Bird Continent; Amazing Birds; Around the World in 80 minutes.

Fee: £105 + travel expenses. **Distance:** Four hours from Surrey/London or overnight accommodation. **Time:** Any by prior agreement.

Contact: 9 Pound Close, Long Ditton, Surbiton, Surrey KT6 5JW; T: 020 8398 1742;
E: chris@birdsandwildlife.com;
W: www.birdsandwildlife.com/lectures

WILDLIFE LECTURERS & PHOTOGRAPHERS

COUZENS, Dominic [L]

Full-time birdwatcher, tour leader (UK /overseas), writer and lecturer.

Lectures: The Secret Lives of Garden Birds; Birding a Local Patch; Mammal Watching in Britain; Encounters with Remarkable Birds; Have Wings Will Travel (the marvel of bird migration).

Fee: £100 plus travel. **Distance:** London/south. **Time:** Any.

Contact: 61 Felton Road, Poole, Dorset BH14 0QR; T: 01202 743 819 or 07721 918 174; E: dominic.couzens@btinternet.com; W: www.birdwords.co.uk

DAVIES, Alan & MILLER, Ruth [L]

Alan and Ruth both worked for the RSPB before giving up their jobs to travel the world birding for a whole year in 2008. They now run their own birdwatching tour/talks company called BirdwatchingTrips with The Biggest Twitch based in North Wales, offering small-group birdwatching tours in the UK, Europe and further afield.

Lectures: A wide range of illustrated talks, the most popular include: The Biggest Twitch, around the world in 4,000 birds - the entertaining warts-and-all story of their big birding year; Land of the Midnight Sun: Finland and Norway; Quetzals and More: Costa Rica; A Spoonful of Thailand; Merlin and More: magical year-round birdwatching in North Wales! We are continuously adding to our range of talks.

Fee: £80 plus fuel cost. **Distance:** Any considered, but overnight accommodation may be required. **Time:** Very flexible all year apart from Mar-Jun and Sep/Oct when we are away guiding. Please e-mail to check availability.

Contact: 12 Ormeside Court, 19 Church Walks, Llandudno, LL30 2HG; T: 01492 872 407; E: info@birdwatchingtrips.co.uk; W: www.birdwatchingtrips.co.uk

ELSOM, Stuart ACIEEM LRPS [L]

Tour leader, professional ecologist and wildlife photographer with Royal Photographic Society distinction.

Lectures: Currently offers around a dozen talks covering a wide range of birding destinations across six continents.

Fee: £70 plus 40p per mile travel expenses. **Distance:** Willing to travel up to 100 miles. **Time:** Daytime and evening. Travelling for approx 5 months of the year normally with several weeks in between so reasonable notice (6+ months) required if booking talks.

Contact:
E: stuartelsom@btinternet.com
(note: delayed response could be due to tour-leading commitments, definitely not due to lack of interest);
W: www.stuartelsom.co.uk;
Facebook: www.facebook.com/stu.elsom
Flickr: https://www.flickr.com/photos/126819682@N04/sets/

EYRE, John [L]

Author, photographer, ornithological consultant.

Lectures: Many talks covering birding around the world (Europe, Africa, Asia, Australasia and the Americas), plus special Hampshire subjects. Examples include: New Zealand - Seabird Feast, Land Bird Famine; California Birds - Sea, Sage and Spotted Owls; Birds of Wallacea - Where Continents Collide; Family Quest - In search of all the worlds' bird families; Gilbert White's Birds; The Secret Lives of Heathland Birds; The Hampshire Bird Atlas. Several others, so please call/ e-mail to discuss options.

Fee: £80 plus travel. **Distance:** Negotiable. **Time:** Any.

Contact: 3 Dunmow Hill, Fleet, Hampshire GU51 3AN; T: 01252 677 850; E: John.Eyre@ntlworld.com

FORGHAM, Jonathan [L]

Primary school teacher for 30 years, now running science enhancement company and professional bird guide. Has given over 100 illustrated talks to bird groups in last three years in south east of England and occasionally, further afield. Visited most of Europe and parts of Asia and Australia, too. Life-long birder and all round naturalist, recording all aspects of nature within the parish of Little Hadham, East Hertfordshire. References available, all excellent. See website for recent bookings.

Lectures: The Birds of the North Norfolk Coastal Footpath; The Birds of The Camargue; The Birds of The Algarve and Baixa Alentejo; The Birds of southern Sri Lanka; The Bird Reserves of Kent; The Whole Natural History of an East Hertfordshire Parish; The Walk to Hel (a 50-mile walk around Gdansk Bay, Poland); Moths of Hertfordshire. (Will provide own laptop, cables, and projector).

Fee: £100 in total for 150 mile round trip. £125 in total for in excess of 150 mile round trip. In excess of 200 mile round trip, fee negotiable. **Distance:** Live in Herts so easy access to motorways, no restrictions under around 200 mile round trip. **Time:** Available evenings, daytime too (if early booking).

Contact: 6 Chapel Lane, Little Hadham, Ware, Herts SG11 2AA; T: 01279 776 112 (eves) or 07805 571 551 (day/texts); E: jforgham@hotmail.com; W: http://littlehadhambirding.blogspot.co.uk

GALLOP, Brian [L]

Speaker, photographer.

Lectures: 35 talks covering UK, Africa, India, Galapagos, South America and Europe (all natural history subjects). Made-to-measure talks available on request. 24hr emergency service.

Fee: £50 plus travel expenses. **Distance:** Any, but overnight accommodation if over 100 mls. **Time:** Any.

Contact: 13 Orchard Drive, Tonbridge, Kent TN10 4LT; T: 01732 361 892; E: brian_gallop@hotmail.co.uk

WILDLIFE LECTURERS & PHOTOGRAPHERS

GALVIN, Chris L, P
A birding photographer with passion for wildlife for more than 30 years.

Lectures: Northwest Year; Around the World in 80 Birds; Bee-eaters & Kingfishers: an intro to the Birds of Goa; Birding by Camera; Birding on the Doorstep; Just Add Water; Kenya – More than just Birds.

Fee: £90 to £150 depending on distance travelled. *Distance:* 150 miles radius from home. *Time:* Any.

Photography: Birds. **Products & services:** Images for publication, prints, mounted prints, commissions considered.

Contact: 17 Henley Rd, Allerton, Liverpool, Merseyside L18 2DN; T: 0151 729 0123 or 07802 428 385; E: chris@chrisgalvinphoto.com; W: www.chrisgalvinphoto.com

GARNER, Jackie L
Professional wildlife artist, author & illustrator of *The Wildlife Artist's Handbook*.

Lectures: Birds/Nature in Art; Focus on the Falklands; Wildlife of Ancient Egypt; Wildlife Artist's World; The Making of a Wildlife Art Book; Lifting the Lid on Lundy.

Fee: £130 + expenses. *Distance:* Any. *Time:* Any.

Contact: The Old Cider House Studio, Humphries End, Randwick, Stroud, Glos GL6 6EW; T: 01453 847 420 or 07800 804 847; E: artist@jackiegarner.co.uk; W: www.jackiegarner.co.uk

GARTSHORE, Neil L
Author of '*Best Birdwatching Sites in Dorset*'. Spent 23-years working in the nature conservation field with National Trust; Percy FitzPatrick Institute of African Ornithology/Cape Town, South Africa; RSPB. Now a freelance bird surveyor, natural history book seller, tour guide, writer, lecturer and is the editor/publisher of '*The Birdwatcher's Yearbook*'.

Lectures: Dorset's Best Birdwatching Sites; Poole Harbour and its Birds; Japan - birding in the land of the rising sun; Birding in Spain - marshes, mountain and migration; A Sub-Antarctic Experience - the Prince Edward Islands; Wildlife Wanderings in South Africa; The Farne Islands - Northumberland's seabird city; Dorset's Heathlands - their wildlife and management; Lesvos - Jewel in the Aegean. Ask for a list/details.

Fee: Variable, depending on distance travelled. *Distance:* Any considered. *Time:* Flexible - sometimes available at short notice.

Contact: Moor Edge, 2 Bere Road, Wareham, Dorset BH20 4DD; T: 01929 552 560 or 07986 434 375; E: neilgartshore@btinternet.com; W: www.dorsetbirdingandwildlife.co.uk

GLENN, Neil L
Author of *Best Birdwatching Sites in Norfolk* and *Best Birdwatching Sites in Yorkshire*; regular contributor to *Bird Watching* magazine; bird tour leader for Avian Adventures. UK Rep for South Texas Nature and also a Patron for Birding For All.

Lectures: Wildlife of the Lower Rio Grande Valley, Texas; Birding the Arctic Circle; Moroccan Spice: from The Sahara to the Atlas Mountains; Warbler Wonderland: Spring Migration in Ohio and Michigan; more to follow!

Fee: Negotiable. *Distance:* Any. *Time:* Any.

Contact: 13 Gladstone Avenue, Gotham, Nottingham NG11 0HN; T: 0115 983 0946; E: n.glenn@ntlworld.com

GROVE, Ashley L, P
Professional photographer and tour leader, with a specialism in wildlife. A list of available lectures is below. References on request if required. Recommended speaker by the RSPB and Royal Horticultural Society.

Lectures: Shetland to Scilly, Birds of the British Isles; Jewels of the Gambia, Kingfishers, Bee-eaters & Rollers; Great British Birds; Lammergeiers of the Spanish Pyrenees; Trinidad & Tobago, Home of the Hummingbird; Wonderful Winter Wildlife; A Beginners Guide to Birdwatching. More talks under construction.

Fee: £80 plus 25p per mile expenses (may be negotiable if you're able to recommend a nearby group to speak to on an adjacent evening). *Distance:* Any within reason. *Time:* Any.

Photography: Tours - Ashley arranges and leads very reasonably priced tours for wildlife photographers and birdwatchers. Tours to The Gambia, The Spanish Pyrenees and Trinidad & Tobago are run annually, with more destinations coming soon. Visit Ashley's website for more information on the tours and for a selection of images gathered on these trips.

Contact: 16 Lint Meadow, Wythall, Worcestershire B47 5PH; T: 07704 189 835; E: birdergrove@gmail.com; W: www.ashleygrovewildimages.co.uk

LINGARD, David L, P
Photographer, retired from RAF, now UK delegate to LIPU (BirdLife in Italy).

Lectures: Choice of talks on birding but primarily on Birdwatching in Italy and the work of LIPU.

Fee: Donation to LIPU, plus petrol costs. *Distance:* Any. *Time:* Any.

Photography: Birds and views of places visited around the world. **Products & services:** 35mm transparencies (last Century) but now, exclusively digital images.

Contact: Fernwood, Doddington Road, Whisby, Lincs LN6 9BX; T: 01522 689 030; E: mail@lipu-uk.org; W: www.lipu-uk.org

WILDLIFE LECTURERS & PHOTOGRAPHERS

LOVELL, Stephen [L]

Naturalist, RSPB, cruise ship and guest lecturer, photographer, adult education teacher.

Lectures: Available on a wide range of European destinations including Lesvos, Majorca, Extremadura and Britain. Other talks available on a wide variety of destinations around the world including Costa Rica, Trinidad and Tobago, Nepal, Sri Lanka, India, New Zealand, Australia, Tanzania, St Lucia, Borneo, Iceland and whale watching in Mexico. I have a wide variety of talks covering garden related topics such as Encouraging Wildlife into the Garden. There is also a talk on The Miracle of Migration.

Fee: £70 to £90 + travel (negotiable according to distance travelled). **Distance:** Any considered. **Time:** Any.

Contact: 6 Abingdon Close, Doddington Park, Lincoln, LN6 3UH; T: 01522 689 456 or 07957 618 684; E: stephenlovell58@btinternet.com; W: www.stevelovellgreenspaces.co.uk

LOWEN, James [L, P]

Author of five books (plus another four out in 2018!) making wildlife accessible to the non-specialist: 'Antarctic wildlife', 'Pantanal wildlife' the acclaimed '52 wildlife weekends: a year of British wildlife-watching breaks' and 'A summer of British wildlife: 100 great days out watching wildlife', and 'Badgers'. Columnist in Bird Watching magazine, and regular feature-writer for BBC Wildlife among other publications. Professional photographer, represented by FLPA. His Bird Fair lectures routinely pack marquees each year, including in the Author's Forum!

Lectures: Many talks, e.g. Antarctic wildlife; Pantanal wildlife; 52 European wildlife weekends; Gaucho birding in Argentina; Chile birds; Japan - the world's best winter birding?; A summer of British wildlife; Britain's top wildlife weekends; Butterfly Britain; Britain's dragonflies; Britain's amazing orchids; Wildlife photography made easy; Getting into moths.

Fee: £80 plus 25p per mile plus £10 per hour travel time over two hours total. **Limits:** Negotiable, overnight accommodation may be needed. **Time:** Any.

Photography: All wildlife, from UK, Argentina, Brazil, Antarctica, Japan, various European countries. **Products & services:** digital images, prints, lectures, commissioned photography.

Contact: Norwich, Norfolk. T: 07523 000 490. E: lowen.james@gmail.com; W: http://jameslowen.com; W: www.pbase.com/james_lowen; Twitter: @JLowenWildlife

MAYER, Edward [L]

Founder of Swift Conservation advice service, formerly Head of Gallery Management at the Tate Gallery.

Lectures: Swifts, Their Lives and Conservation, also Urban Biodiversity Awareness, Strategies and Techniques for the Built Environment; Talks and training sessions for enthusiasts, ornithologists, architects, developers, planners, biodiversity and facilities staff. Talks from 30 minutes to two hours, training from one hour to one day.

Fee: From £85, depending on type and length of talk, or collection/donation, plus travel expenses. **Distance:** UK/Europe. **Time:** Any.

Contact: 28 Yale Court, Honeybourne Road, London NW6 1JG; T: 020 7794 2098; E: mail@swift-conservation.org; W: www.swift-conservation.org

MILES, John [L]

Former warden for RSPB, tour guide, consultant, journalist and author of *Best Birdwatching Sites: The Solway, [co-author] of Best Birdwatching Sites: Yorkshire, Hadrian's Birds, Exploring Lakeland Wildlife, Pharoah's Birds, Hadrian's Wildlife*. Series of children's books growing evey year.

Lectures: The Solway - the whole of Cumbria and Dumfries & Galloway; Hadrian's Wildlife - History of birds back to Roman times + many present day locations to visit; Death on the Nile - looks at the history of birds from Ancient Egypt to present time birds while cruising the Nile; Mull: Not just Eagles! - year round look at this island; Go Birding - follows John around Britain in search of articles in 'Go Birding' in Bird Watching magazine; British Bee-eaters - Will they ever BEE Every Year!; Caithness - the forgotten part of Scotland!; Islay - Not just Geese!; Yorkshire - Not just a White Rose!

Fee: Prices on request. **Distance:** Anywhere in UK. **Time:** Evenings best.

Contact: Jockey Shield, Castle Carrock, Carlisle, Cumbria CA4 9NF; T: 01228 670 205; E: john@chickbooks.co.uk; W: chickbooks.co.uk

NEWTON, Ian [L, P]

Photographer (ARPS) and lecturer, former Chairman York Ornithological Club.

Lectures: 16 talks, all digital, mainly birds and other wildlife of North, Central and South America, Europe and UK.

Fee: £70 plus petrol. **Distance:** Any. **Time:** Any.

Photography: **Products & services:** Prints, canvas & board mounted images etc.

Contact: 5 Fairfields Drive, Skelton, York, YO30 1YP; T: 01904 471 446 or 07976 849 832; E: iannewton@acsemail.co.uk; W: www.iannewtonphotography.com

WILDLIFE LECTURERS & PHOTOGRAPHERS

OFFORD, Keith [L]

Photographer, lecturer, course & workshop tutor, tour leader, conservationist.

Lectures: 16 talks covering raptors (biology and identification), flight, uplands, gardens, migration, woodland wildlife, Texas, Spain, Sri Lanka, Estonia, Morocco, Iceland, Costa Rica, Namibia, Western Cape.

Fee: £100 (pro-rota to travel distance per mile after 100 miles) plus travel costs. **Distance:** Any. **Time:** Sept to Apr.

Contact: Yew Tree Farmhouse, Craignant, Selattyn, Nr Oswestry, Shropshire SY10 7NP; T: 01691 718 740; E: keith@keithofford.co.uk; W: www.keithofford.co.uk

PATERSON, Scott [L]

Worked in the conservation field for over 20 years - on the Farne Islands, at St Abbs Head, Vane Farm, Loch of Strathbeg and Minsmere. Currently County Recorder for Perth and Kinross and a self-employed ornithological surveyor and guide, Scott enjoys giving talks, leading events and training courses in Scotland and northern England, particularly bird identification courses.

Lectures: Birds of Perth and Kinross; Look Again at Garden Birds; Wildlife in Your Garden; Bird Identification; Learn Bird Songs and Calls.

Fee: Variable depending on talk and location. **Distance:** Scotland. **Time:** Flexible, including weekends.

Contact: Kinross Ecology, 12 Ochil View, Kinross, KY13 8TN; T: 01577 864 248 or 07501 640 518; E: scott@kinrossecology.co.uk; W: www..kinrossecology.co.uk

RSPB Weymouth Reserves - urban birding at its best / Neil Gartshore

READ, Mike [L, P]

Photographer (wildlife/landscapes), tour leader, writer.

Lectures: 12 talks featuring British and foreign subjects (list available on receipt of sae or see website).

Fee: £70 plus travel. **Distance:** 80 miles from Ringwood. **Time:** Available Sept to Mar.

Photography: Birds, mammals, plants, landscapes, and some insects. UK, France, USA, Ecuador (inc. Galapagos) plus many more. Behaviour, action, portraits, artistic pictures available for publication. More than 100,000 images in stock. **Products & services:** Extensive stock photo library. Canvas and giclee prints, greetings cards, books.

Contact: Claremont, Redwood Close, Ringwood, Hampshire BH24 1PR; T: 01425 475 008; E: mike@mikeread.co.uk; W: www.mikeread.co.uk

REDMAN, Nigel [L]

Author, editor and tour leader.

Lectures: Mostly birds, inc. Ethiopia; Somaliland; Eritrea; Kenya; Morocco; Russia (and former Soviet Union); the Caucasus; Antarctica; Arctic (North-west Passage/Svalbard); New Zealand; Mexico.

Fee: Negotiable. **Distance:** Any (but overnight accommodation may be required). **Time:** Any.

Contact: Hollyhocks, Edgefield Road, Briston, Norfolk NR24 2HX; T: 01263 862 866 or 07734 886 515; E: nigelredman28@hotmail.com

ROTHERHAM, Prof Ian [L]

Former local authority ecologist, environmental campaigner, researcher, lecturer, writer and broadcaster.

Lectures: Numerous illustrated talks on all aspects of conservation inc.: the Lost Fens; Yorkshire's Forgotten Fenlands; Shadow Woods - a search for lost ladscapes; Wild woods and woodland heritage; Wildlife and history of moors, heaths and bogs; Urban Wildlife; Gardening for Wildlife; Alien and invasive species; Wild Peak District; Eco-history; Wilding Nature ; Wilder Visions - re-constructing nature for the 21st century; Eco-fusion - our hybrid future; Loving the aliens?; Understanding the ancient woods; Sherwood Forest - wildlife, history & heritage; Wildlife & Heritage - Yorkshire's Viking Coast.

Fee: £85, plus petrol 50p per mile. **Distance:** Prepared to travel if expenses are covered. **Time:** Any by arrangement.

Contact: 42 School Lane, Norton, Sheffield, S8 8BL; T: 07751 089 499; E: i.d.rotherham@shu.ac.uk; W: www.ukeconet.org; Blog: http://ianswalkonthewildside.wordpress.com/

WILDLIFE LECTURERS & PHOTOGRAPHERS

SCOTT, Ann [L]

Retired. Formerly Senior Wildlife Adviser for RSPB, lecturer and teacher of ornithology.

Lectures: Various talks on UK & abroad. Latest talk: Kenya, Cuckoos, Coastal Forest & Conservation Concerns. Modern technology has revealed a secret about cuckoos and migration. It gives yet more reasons for conserving the Coastal Forest of Kenya and enlarging the Kirosa Scott Reserve. Learn more at: http://www.whytsbirds.org or from www.justgiving.com/ann-scott1/

Fee: £70 plus expenses (negotiable). **Distance:** Normally 2 hours drive from Huntingdon but willing to discuss. **Time:** Available mid-Mar to mid-Nov.

Contact: 17 Springfield Close, Buckden, Huntingdon, Cambs PE19 5UR; T: 01480 811 848; E: abscott@buckdencambs.co.uk

SIMPSON, Rick and Elis [L]

Joint founders of Wader Quest, birders, wader enthusiasts, fundraisers and conservationists. Rick: speaker, writer, artist, Elis: team photographer.

Lectures: Wader Quest (stories and facts about waders and their conservation); Confessions of a Bird Guide (guiding in Brazil); many other titles, mainly concerned with the waders of the world... full list on application.

Fee: £80, plus up to £20 contribution towards fuel costs. **Distance:** Any considered. **Time:** Any, often available at short notice.

Contact: 20 Windsor Avenue, Newport Pagnell, Bucks, MK16 8HA. T: 07484 186 443; E: rick@rick-simpson.com; W: www.waderquest.org; Blog: www.rick@rick-simpson.com

SMART, Oliver [L, P]

Photographer, lecturer and ornithologist.

Lectures: A Voyage to the South Atlantic; The Science & Beauty of Birds; Exploring Ethiopia; Butterfly Britain; From 60 Degrees North; Cameras and Creatures - from Cumbria to Canada; Cuba: A Flicker of Interest; Birds of Lesvos; RAW Nature: Images Uncovered; Grizzly Bears of Alaska.

Fee: £80 plus 25p per mile plus £10 per hour above two hours total travel time. **Distance:** Any, can also provide own accommodation. **Time:** Any.

Photography: All wildlife subjects, UK based, also Alaska, Antarctica, California, Canada, Colombia, Cuba, Ecuador & the Galapagos Islands, Ethiopia, Europe, Falkland Islands, Ghana, India, Kenya, Madagascar, Nepal, New Zealand, Patagonia, Seychelles, South Georgia, and The Gambia. **Products & services:** Acrylic prints, aluminium prints, aluminescent prints, bean bags, canvas prints, desk calendars, digital image library, digital slideshow lectures, greeting cards, mounted prints (to A2 size), photographic tours, workshops and puzzles.

Contact: 78 Aspen Park Road, Weston-Super-Mare, Somerset BS22 8ER; T: 07802 417 810; E: oliver@smartimages.co.uk; W: www.smartimages.co.uk

SUMMERFIELD, Saffron [L]

Lifelong Birdwatcher and Professional Musician/ Composer and Sound Recordist. Artist in Residence at Rye Harbour Nature Reserve in 2008.

Lecture: WHEN BIRDS SING
Just why does a small bird (Marsh Warbler) 'collect' up to 250 other bird songs and calls on its migratory path from Africa to Northern Europe?

How many composers have been inspired by listening to bird song?

Why does the Dawn Chorus have such an emotional and calming effect on some Humans?

This fascinating, entertaining and extensively researched Talk is digitally presented with many of her own field recordings, photos and music and all levels of interest catered for.

Fee: Variable, depending on distance travelled. **Distance:** Any. **Time:** Any.

Contact: 15 Pond Gate, Redhouse Park, Bucks MK14 5FB. T: 01908 613 334 or 07941 932 543; E: saffronsummerfield@icloud.com; W: see videos and sound recordings at www.motherearthmusic.co.uk

TODD, Ralph [L]

Lecturer & photographer, former tour leader and course tutor.

Lectures: Galapagos - The Enchanted Isles; On the Trail of the Crane – parts 1 and 2; Polar Odyssey; Operation Osprey; Natural Wonders and Wildlife of Iceland; Man & Birds-Travels through time; Where Yeehaa meets Ole; Birds in the Land of Disney; Antarctic Adventure; Springtime in Lesvos.

Fee: £75 plus expenses. **Distance:** Any. **Time:** Any - also short notice.

Contact: 9 Horsham Road, Bexleyheath, Kent DA6 7HU; T: 01322 528 335; E: rbtodd@btinternet.com

Sand Lizard - not just birds / Neil Gartshore

WILDLIFE LECTURERS & PHOTOGRAPHERS

van GROUW, Katrina [L]

A graduate of the Royal College of Art, expert on historical bird art, a qualified bird ringer, and former curator of the Natural History Museum's bird collections, Katrina is best known as the author and illustrator of the bestselling book 'The Unfeathered Bird', voted third place in the BTO/British Birds Bird Book of the Year, and featured on BBC TV Springwatch Unsprung.

Katrina currently offers two lectures:

A Very Fine Swan Indeed: Art, Science & The Unfeathered Bird. An entertaining and inspiring lecture on the making of The Unfeathered Bird. The talk follows the author through her 25-year journey to make her dream a reality.

Unnatural Selection: A talk about her new book of the same title; about Darwin, evolution, and why domesticated animals deserve a second look.

"Katrina is a dazzling speaker. Her talk will enthral anyone interested in birds."

"One of the most interesting and entertaining talks we had heard for a long time. This talk is really not to be missed!"

Fee: Variable, depending on distance travelled. Distance: Any. Time: Flexible - sometimes available at short notice.

Contact: 36 Northern Road, Aylesbury, Bucks HP19 9QY; T: 01296 398 571 & 07503 038 687; E: katrinavangrouw@aol.co.uk; W: www.unfeatheredbird.com

WREN, Graham J. ARPS [L]

Wildlife photographer & lecturer.

Lectures: 25 talks - UK: Bird Nesting Habitats - Past, Present and Future; Nest-boxes (over 40 years of Monitoring); 40 Years on The Farne Islands (new). Detailed information package supplied on request.

Fee: £50-80 plus petrol. **Distance:** Any. **Time:** Any.

Contact: The Kiln House, Great Doward, Whitchurch, Ross-on-Wye, Herefordshire HR9 6DU; T: 01600 890 488; E: susanjhampshire@aol.com

213

WILDLIFE LECTURERS & PHOTOGRAPHERS

BTO SPEAKERS

THIS DIRECTORY HAS been compiled to help Bird Clubs and similar organisations in finding speakers from the BTO for indoor meetings. Each entry consists of an individual speaker, a list of talks/lectures available, details of fees and expenses required and travel distance limitations. If you are interested in any of the speakers, please contact Ieuan Evans (ieuan.evans@bto.org). Alternatively, contact the BTO on 01842 750 050.

Austin, Dr Graham (Senior Research Ecologist, Wetland & Marine Research)
Subjects: Wetland Bird Survey. Fee: £40. Distance: Travel by agreement.

Baillie, Dr Stephen (Senior Research Fellow)
Subjects: BirdTrack; Population Monitoring. Fee: £40. Distance: Travel by agreement.

Baker, Jeff (Head of Marketing)
Subjects: Little Brown Jobs - Warblers & How to Identify Them; The Work of the BTO; Garden Birds & Feeding. Fee: £40. Distance: Dependent on expenses.

Balmer, Dawn (Head of Surveys & National Survey Co-ordinator)
Subjects: Bird Atlas 2007-11; House Martins; Surveys. Fees: £40. Distance: 100 mile radius of Thetford, further by agreement.

Barimore, Carl (Nest Records Organiser)
Subjects: Nest Records Scheme. Fee: £40. Distance: By agreement.

Blackburn, Jez (Ringing Licensing and Sales Manager)
Subjects: Demography Team Bird Moult (suitable for ringers); Ringing for Conservation; Sule Skerry Seabirds. Fee: £40 (£70 for private talks). Distance: East Anglia. *Unavailable until Jan 2018.*

Calbrade, Neil (WeBS Low Tide Count Organiser)
Subjects: BTO/JNCC/RSPB Wetland Bird Survey (WeBS). Fee: £40. Distance: By agreement.

Clark, Jacquie (Head of Demography & Head of Ringing Scheme)
Subjects: Waders & Severe Weather; Ringing for Conservation; Why Ring Birds? Fee: £40. Distance: 100 mile radius of Thetford.

Conway, Greg (Research Ecologist, Land-use Research)
Subjects: Nightjars; Woodlarks; Dartford Warblers; Wintering Warblers in the UK; Firecrests. Fee: £40. Distance: 100 mile radius of Thetford.

Dadam, Dr Daria (Reseach Ecologist, Demography)
Subjects: Bird Disease; Marsh Tits; House Sparrow Ecology and Decline. Fees: £40. Distance: By agreement.

Darvill, Ben (Development & Engagement Manager, Scotland)
Subjects: Upland Birds; Ecology, Conservation and How You Can Help; Cuckoos and Other Long-distance Migrants; Birding With Your Eyes Shut; Fascinating Facts About Our Feathered Friends Found Through Technology, Tags and Tracks.
Fee: Negotiable. Distance: Negotiable.

Evans, Ieuan (Associate Director, Communications (Engagement))
Subjects: Unravelling the Mysteries of Bird Migration. Fee: Negotiable. Distance: Negotiable.

Franks, Samantha (Research Ecologist, Population Ecology)
Subjects: Bird Migration; North American Waders; Alaska; Wildlife of British Columbia and the Pacific Northwest. Fee: Negotiable. Distance: Negotiable.

Frost, Dr Teresa (Wetland Bird Survey National Organiser)
Subjects: BTO/JNCC/RSPB Wetland Bird Survey (WeBS). Fee: £40. Distance: By agreement.

Gillings, Dr Simon (Head of Population Ecology and Modelling)
Subjects: Atlas 2007-11; Winter Golden Plovers & Lapwings; Waders; Knot Migration. Fee: £40. Distance: Negotiable.

Harris, Sarah (Breeding Bird Survey National Organiser)
Subjects: BTO/JNCC/RSPB Breeding Birds Survey. Fee: £40. Distance: By agreement.

Henderson, Dr Ian (Senior Research Ecologist, International Research)
Subjects: Arable Farming and Birds; Nightjars. Fee: £40. Distance: By agreement.

Johnson, Dr Alison (Ecological Statistician, Population Ecology & Modelling)
Subjects: Climate Change and Birds. Fee: £40. Distance: East Anglia.

Jones, Kelvin (BTO Cymru Development Officer)
Subjects: Work of the BTO, other subjects by agreement i.e. Hawfinch and Twite in North Wales; Ringing in Aras Turkey. Fee: £40. Distance: By agreement.

McAvoy, Stephen (BirdTrack Support Officer)
Subjects: Mapping Migration with BirdTrack. Fee: £40. Distance: By agreement.

Moran, Nick (BirdTrack Organiser)
Subjects: What BirdTrack Can Do For You; Better Birding; Birds and Birding in Arabia. Fee: £40. Distance: By agreement.

Musgrove, Dr Andy (Head of Monitoring)
Subjects: Ornithology: How Can Birdwatchers Contribute to Recordiing Other Wildlife. Fee: £40. Distance: By agreement.

Noble, Dr David (Principal Ecologist, Monitoring)
Subjects: Developing Bird Indicators; Population Trends. Fee: £40. Distance: By agreement.

BTO SPEAKERS

Pearce-Higgins, Dr James (Director, Science)
Subjects: Birds and Climate Change; Upland Birds; A Year in the Life of a Golden Plover. **Fee:** £40. **Distance:** By agreement.

Risely, Kate (Garden BirdWatch Organiser)
Subjects: Garden Birds and Wildlife. **Fee:** £40. **Distance:** By agreement.

Robinson, Dr Rob (Associate Director, Research)
Subjects: Farming & Birds; Conservation Value of Ringing. **Fee:** £40. **Distance:** By agreement.

Ross-Smith, Dr Viola (Science Communications Manager)
Subjects: Gulls, Seabirds, Tracking Studies (General). **Fee:** £40. **Distance:** By agreement.

Siriwardena, Dr Gavin (Head of Land-Use Research)
Subjects: Research Farmland Birds (General); Marsh & Willow Tits; Quantifying Migratory Strategies; Winter Feeding of Farmland Birds. **Fee:** £40. **Distance:** Negotiable.

Stancliffe, Paul (Press Officer)
Subjects: Atlas 2007-11; Homes to Let – Nestboxes; Birds, Birders and the Work of the BTO; Tracking African Migrants. **Fee:** £40. **Distance:** Negotiable.

Toms, Mike (Associate Director, Communications (Science))
Subjects: Are Gardens Good for Birds or Birdwatchers?; Owls and Man - a cultural History; **Fee:** Negotiable. **Distance:** Negotiable.

Wernham, Dr Chris (Associate Director, Country Offices)
Subjects: The Work of BTO Scotland; Breeding Bird Survey in Scotland; BirdTrack in Scotland. **Fee:** £40. **Distance:** Travel Scotland and NE England.

WILDLIFE ART GALLERIES

BIRDSCAPES GALLERY
Manor Farm Barns, Glandford, Holt, Norfolk NR25 7JP; T: 01263 741 742; E: art@birdscapes.co.uk; W: www.birdscapesgallery.co.uk
Opening times: All year, daily 11am to 5pm, but may close for part of the day before a new exhibition.

DAVID SHEPHERD WILDLIFE FOUNDATION
7 Kings Road, Shalford, Guildford, Surrey GU4 8JU. T: 01483 272 323; E: dswf@davidshepherd.org; W: www.davidshepherd.org
Opening times: Mon - Fri, 9am to 5pm.

CHENG KIM LOKE GALLERY, SLIMBRIDGE
Wildfowl & Wetland Trust, Slimbridge, Gloucestershire GL2 7BT; T: 01453 891 900; E: info.slimbridge@wwt.org.uk; W: www.wwt.org.uk
Opening times: All year, daily except Dec 25, 9.30am to 5.30pm/last admission at 4.30pm [5pm/4pm winter]. Admission charge for non-WWT members.

GORDALE (host of EXHIBITION OF WILDLIFE ART)
Gordale Garden and Home Centre, Chester High Road, Burton, South Wirral, Cheshire CH64 8TF; T: 0151 336 2116; E: admin@gordale.co.uk; W: www.gordale.co.uk & www.ewa-uk.com
Opening times: Stages an Exhibition of Wildlife Art in late July. Daily 9.30am to 6pm (11am-5pm Sunday). Free admission.

HOUSE OF BRUAR (WILDLIFE ART GALLARY)
By Blair Atholl, Perthshire PH18 5TW; T: 0345 136 0111; E: mailorder@houseofbruar.com; W: www.houseofbruar.com
Opening times: All year, daily except Dec 25 & Jan 1. 9.30am to 6pm (May to Nov); 10am to 5pm rest of year. Free admission.

MALL GALLERIES
The Mall, London SW1; T: 0207 930 6844; E: info@mallgalleries.com; W: www.mallgalleries.org.uk
Opening times: Stages British Wildlife Photography Awards and the Society of Wildlife Artists' annual exhibition around Oct/Nov (10am to 5pm). Admission charge.

NATURE IN ART
Wallsworth Hall, Twigworth, Gloucester GL2 9PA; T: 01452 731 422; E: via website; W: www.nature-in-art.org.uk
Opening times: Closed Mondays (exc. Bank Holidays) and Dec 24 to 26. Otherwise open daily 10am to 5pm. Admission charge.

PINKFOOT GALLERY
High Street, Cley-next-the-Sea, Norfolk NR25 7RB; T: 01263 740 947; E: info@pinkfootgallery.co.uk; W: www.pinkfootgallery.co.uk
Opening times: All year, **daily** 10.00am to 5.00pm (Mon to Sat), 11am to 4pm (Sun). Free admission.

WATERSTON HOUSE
Donald Watson Gallery, The SOC, Waterston House, Aberlady, East Lothian EH32 0PY; T: 01875 871 330; E: mail@the-soc.org.uk; W: www.the-soc.org.uk
Opening times: All year, daily 10.00am to 4.00pm. Free entry.

THE WILDLIFE ART GALLERY
98-99 High St, Lavenham, Sudbury, Suffolk CO10 9PZ; T: 01787 248 562; E: info@wildlifeartgallery.com; W: https://wildlifeartgallery.com
Opening times: All year, Wed to Sun 11am to 4pm, closed Mon & Tues.

WILDLIFE ARTISTS

Looking for some artwork? The artists below offer work for sale - check them out to see if there is anything you like.

AKROYD, Carry
E: carry@carryakroyd.co.uk;
W: www.carryakroyd.co.uk

ALLEN, Richard
T: 01206 826 753; E: richardallenart@btinternet.com;
W: www.richardallenillustrator.com

ANGUS, Max
T: 07766 277 915; E: max@maxangus.co.uk;
W: www.maxangus.co.uk

APLIN, Roy
T: 01929 553 742; E: aplin4664@btinternet.com;
W: www.royaplin.iclwebdesign.co.uk

ARTINGSTALL, Nigel
T: 01204 412 531; E: the-artist@ntlworld.com;
W: www.nigelartingstall.com

ATKINSON, Kim
Ty'n Gamdda, Uwchmynydd, Aberdaron, Pwllheli,
Gwynedd LL53 8DA.

BARTLETT, Paul
T: 01382 698 346; E: pauljbartlett@hotmail.com;
W: www.naturalselectiongallery.co.uk

BENNETT, David
16 Pearl Street, Starbeck, Harrogate, N. Yorks, HGJ 4QW

BROCKIE, Keith
T: 01887 830 609; E: kbrockie@btinternet.com;
W: www.keithbrockie.co.uk

BROWN, Diana
Shannel Ballogie, Aboyne, Aberdeenshire, AB34 5DR

BURN, Hilary
E: hilaryburn@fireflyuk.net

BURTON, P.K.J.
High Kelton, Doctors Commons Rd, Berkhampstead, HB4 3DH.

COOK, Robert
T: 01253 884 849; E: info@robcookart.com;
W: www.robcookart.com

DALY, Dave
W: www.davedalyartist.com

DAVIS, John
E: wildlife@tiscali.co.uk;

DAY, Nick
T: 07763 109 020; E: birdmanday@yahoo.com;
W: www.nick-day-wildlife-artist.co.uk

DEMAIN, Michael
T: 01254 406 230; E: mdemainwildart@aol.com;
W: www.michaeldemainwildlifeart.co.uk

EDWARDS, Brin
T: 01787 211 162; E: studio@brin-edwards.com;
W: www.brin-edwards.com

EDWARDS, Victoria
403 London Road, Ditton, Aylesford, Kent ME20 6DB.
E: vedwards74@hotmail.co.uk

FINNEY, David
T: 01270 876 789; E: dave@davidfinney.com;
W: www.davidfinney.co.uk

FOKER, John
E: jffoker.com; W: www.bearparkartists.co.uk

FULLER, Robert
T: 01759 368 355; E: mail@robertefuller.com;
W: www.robertefuller.com

GALE, John
T: 01392 832 026; E: johngaleartist@outlook.com;
W: www.galleryofbirds.co.uk

GARNER, Jackie
T: 01453 847 420; E: artist@jackiegarner.co.uk;
W: www.jackiegarner.co.uk

GILLMOR, Robert
North Light, Hilltop, Cley-next-the-Sea, Holt,
Norfolk NR25 7SE.

GREENHALF, Robert
W: www.robertgreenhalf.co.uk

GRIFFITHS, Ian
T: 07971 678 464; E: mail@artbygriff.com;
W: www.artbygriff.com

HAMPTON, Michael
E: greatcrestedgrebes@googlemail.com
W: www.michael-hampton.com

HASLEN, Andrew
W: http://andrewhaslen.com/

HEWITT, Angela
T: 01983 296 110; E: angela.hewitt@btclick.com;
W: www.angelahewitt.co.uk

HESELDEN, Russ
E: heselden860@btinternet.com;
W: www.russheselden.co.uk

HODGES, Gary
T: 0207 096 0653; E: gary@garyhodges-wildlife-art.com;
W: www.garyhodges-wildlife-art.com

HOWEY, Paul
W: www.paulhowey.co.uk

INGRAM, Alison
T: 01403 263 179; E: alison@alisoningram.co.uk;
W: www.alisoningram.co.uk

WILDLIFE ARTISTS

JOHNSON, Richard
E: rjohnson.birdart@gmail.com

KEMP, Carolyn
T: 07719 367 223; E: carolyn@carolynkemp.co.uk;
W: www.carolynkemp.co.uk

KOSTER, David
5 East Cliff Gardens, Folkestone, Kent CT19 6AR.

LANGMAN, Mike
T: 01803 528 008; E: mikelangman@blueyonder.co.uk;
W: www.mikelangman.co.uk

LEAHY, Ernest
E: ernest.leahy@ntlworld.com;
W: www.flickr.com/photos/ernsbirdart

LEWINGTON, Ian
T: 01235 819 792: E: lewbirder@btinternet.com;
W: www.ian-lewington.co.uk

LEWINGTON, Richard
T: 01235 848 451: E: enquiries@richardlewington.co.uk;
W: www.richardlewington.co.uk

LOCKWOOD, Rachel
T: 01263 740 947; E: rachel@rachellockwoodartist.com;
W: www.rachellockwoodartist.co.uk/

McCALLUM, James
E: email@jamesmccallum.co.uk;
W: www.jamesmccallum.co.uk

MESSAGE, Steve
T: 07909 585 988; E: messagewildlifeart@btinternet.com;
W: www.message-wildlife-art.co.uk

MICHEL, Sally
30 Woodland Way, Bidborough, Tunbridge Wells, TN4 OUY.

MILLER, David
T: 01994 453 545; E: david@davidmillerart.co.uk;
W: www.davidmillerart.co.uk

NEILL, William
W: william-neill.co.uk

NEWELL, Kerry
T: 07752 325 031; E: kerrynewell1@gmail.com;
W: www.kerrynewell.com

PAIGE, John
T: 01780 470 247; E: paiges@oldbrewerystudios.co.uk;
W: www.oldbrewerystudios.co.uk

PALMER, John
T: 07900 934 145; E: sales@johnpalmerfineart.co.uk;
W: www.johnpalmerfineart.co.uk

PARRY, David
T: 01672 563 708; E: davidparryart@gmail.com;
W: www.davidparryart.com

PARTINGTON, Peter
T: 07966 579 592; E: p.n.partington@gmail.com;

PAUL, Jeremy
T: 01624 832 980; E: jpaul@manx.net;
W: www.jeremypaulwildlifeartist.co.uk

PEARSON, Bruce
T: 07710 229 428; E: bepartist@gmail.com;
W: www.brucepearson.net

PENDLETON, Chris
T: 01280 702 462; E: chris@pendleton.co.uk;
W: www.pendleton.co.uk

PHILLIPS, Antonia
T: 01308 420 423; W: www.antoniaphillips.co.uk

POMROY, Jonathan
T: 01439 788 014; E: jonathan@pomroy.plus.com;
W: www.jonathanpomroy.co.uk

POOLE, Greg
E: greg@gregpoole.co.uk; W: www.gregpoole.co.uk

POWELL, Dan and Rosie
T: 01329 668 465; E: danpowell11@btinternet.com;
W: www.powellwildlifeart.com

PROUD, Alastair
Plas Bach, Newchurch, Carmarthen, Dyfed SA33 6EJ.
W: www.alastairproud.co.uk

REANEY, John
1 Buxton Road, Brighton, East Sussex BNJ 5DE.

REES, Darren
T: 01786 870 538; E: darrenreesart@btinternet.com;
W: www.darrenrees.com

RIDLEY, Martin
T: 01764 670 695; E: art@martinridley.com;
W: www.martinridley.com

ROSE, Chris
T: 01835 822 547; E: chris@chrisrose-artist.co.uk;
W: www.chrisrose-artist.co.uk

SCOTT, Dafila
E: dafilascott@yahoo.co.uk; W: www.dafilascott.co.uk

SINDEN, Chris
T: 01594 829 903; E: chrissinden@btinternet.com;
W: www.sindencox-art.co.uk

STOCK, Andrew
E: andrew@andrewstock.co.uk;
W: www.andrewstock.co.uk

SYKES, Thelma
T: 01244 880 209; E: thelmasykes@tiscali.co.uk

WILDLIFE ARTISTS

TRADE DIRECTORY

Neil Gartshore

Chesil Beach and the gateway to Portland (Dorset) - some tour companies offer local UK -based tours as an alternative to overseas destinations.

BIRD GARDEN SUPPLIERS

IN THIS SECTION you'll find a comprehensive guide to UK-based companies offering products or services of particular interest to active birdwatchers and wildlife enthusiasts. Our aim is to make this directory as up-to-date and comprehensive as possible so if we've overlooked any companies that you feel should be included in future editions, please contact us (see page 6) with the relevant details.

If you contact any of these companies please mention *'The Birdwatchers' Yearbook'*.

BIRD GARDEN SUPPLIERS

ARK WILDLIFE LTD
Dog Kennel Farm, Charlton Road, Nr Hitchin, Herts SG5 2AB; T: 0800 085 4865;
E: via website; W: www.arkwildlife.co.uk

BAMFORDS TOP FLIGHT
Globe Mill, Midge Hall, Leyland, Lancashire PR26 6TN; T: 01772 456 300;
E: sales@bamfords.co.uk;
W: www.bamfords.co.uk

BRINVALE BIRD FOODS
Brinvale Farm, Broughton Lane, Long Clawson, Melton Mowbray, Leics LE14 4NB;
T: 01664 823 230; E: via website;
W: www.brinvale.com

CHERISH WILD BIRD FOOD
Wildlife Habits Ltd, 5 Moorlands Way, Cramlington, Northumberland NE23 1WE;
E: info@cherishwildbirdfood.uk;
W: www.cherishwildbirdfood.uk

CJ WILDBIRD FOODS LTD
The Rea, Upton Magna, Shrewsbury, Shropshire SY4 4UR; T: 0800 731 2820;
E: sales@birdfood.co.uk;
W: www.birdfood.co.uk

EYEBROOK WILD BIRD FEEDS
Rectory Farm, Great Easton, Market Harborough, Leics LE16 8SN; T: 01536 770 771;
E: rectoryfarm@eyebrookbirdfeeds.co.uk;
W: www.eyebrookwildbirdfeeds.co.uk

GARDENATURE
801 Fowler Road, Oakwood Business Park North, Clacton on Sea, Essex CO15 4AA;
T: 01255 514 451; E: via website;
W: www.gardennature.co.uk

JACOBI JAYNE & CO
Wealden Forest Park, Herne Bay; Kent CT6 7LQ;
T: 0800 072 0130;
E: enquiries@livingwithbirds.com;
W: www.livingwithbirds.com

KENNEDY WILD BIRD FOODS LTD
The Warehouse, 74 Station Rd, Deeping St James, Peterborough, PE6 8RQ; T: 01778 342 665;
E: info@kennedywildbirdfood.uk.com;
W: www.kennedywildbirdfood.uk.com

NATURE CAMERAS
3B Bonegate Rd, Brighouse, W. Yorks HD6 1TQ;
T: 01484 720 220;
E: enquiries@naturecameras.co.uk;
W: www.naturecameras.co.uk

NUTBAGS
7 Hampton Close, Blackfield, Southampton, SO45 1WQ; T: 02380 894 132; E: via website;
W: www.nutbags.co.uk

THE NESTBOX COMPANY
Eastcote House, Barston Lane, Eastcote, Solihull, B92 0HS; T: 01675 442 299;
E: mail@nestbox.co.uk;
W: www.nestbox.co.uk

THE OWL BOX
Tyddyn Waen, Nr Llangaffo, Isle of Anglesey LL60 6LP; T: 01248 421 091;
E: info@theowlbox.co.uk;
W: www.theowlbox.co.uk

SOAR MILL SEEDS
Globe Mill, Midge Hall, Leyland, Lancs PR26 6TN; T: 01772 456 317;
E: gareth.roberts@soarmillseeds.co.uk;
W: www.soarmillseeds.co.uk

VINE HOUSE FARM BIRD FOODS
Vine House Farm, Deeping St Nicholas, Spalding, Lincs PE11 3DG; T: 01775 630 208;
E: birdseed@vinehousefarm.co.uk;
W: www.vinehousefarm.co.uk

WALTER HARRISON & SONS
Pedigree House, Ambleside, Gamston, Nottingham, NG2 6NQ; T: 0115 982 3900;
E: via website; W: www.walterharrisons.com

BIRD & WILDLIFE PUBLICATIONS, BOOK PUBLISHERS, BOOK SELLERS

BIRD & WILDLIFE PUBLICATIONS

ATROPOS
The Boat House, Church Cove, Lizard,
Nr Helston, Cornwall TR12 7PH;
T: 01326 290 287; E: books@atropos.info;
W: www.atropos.info

BBC WILDLIFE
Subscriptions: BBC Wildlife Magazine,
FREEPOST LON16059, Sittingbourne, Kent ME9 8DF;
T: 0844 844 0251; E: wildlife@servicehelpline.co.uk;
W: www.discoverwildlife.com

BIRDWATCH
The Chocolate Factory, 5 Clarendon Road,
London N22 6XJ; T: 0208 881 0550;
E: editorial@birdwatch.co.uk;
W: www.birdwatch.co.uk

BIRD WATCHING
Bauer Media, Media House, Lynch Wood,
Peterborough, PE2 6EA; T: 01733 468 000;
E: birdwatching@bauermedia.co.uk;
W: www.birdwatching.co.uk

BRITISH BIRDS
4 Harlequin Gardens, St Leonards-on-Sea,
East Sussex TN37 7PF; T: 01424 755 155;
E: subscriptions@britishbirds.co.uk;
W: www.britishbirds.co.uk

BRITISH WILDLIFE PUBLISHING (now part of NHBS Ltd)
1-6 The Stables, Ford Road, Totnes, Devon
TQ9 5LE; T: 01803 467 166;
E: enquiries@britishwildlife.com;
W: www.britishwildlife.com

BOOK PUBLISHERS

BLOOMSBURY PUBLISHING
(Helm, Poyser, New Holland)
50 Bedford Square, London WC1B 3DP;
T: 0207 631 5600; E: contact@bloomsbury.com;
W: www.bloomsbury.com/uk/non-fiction/
natural-history/

BRADT TRAVEL GUIDES LTD
1st Floor IDC House, The Vale, Chalfont St
Peter, Bucks SL9 9RZ; T: 01753 893 444;
E: info@bradtguides.com;
W: www.bradtguides.com

BUCKINGHAM PRESS LTD
55 Thorpe Park Road, Peterborough PE3 6LJ;
T: 01733 561 739; E: admin@buckinghampress.co.uk;
W: www.buckinghampress.co.uk

COXTON PUBLICATIONS LTD
3 Home Farm, Saunders Lane, Walkington,
Beverley, HU17 8TX; T: 01482 881 833;
E: info@coxton.alchemica.co.uk;
W: www.coxton.alchemica.co.uk

HARPER COLLINS PUBLISHERS
The News Building, 1 London Bridge Street,
London SE1 9GF; T: 0208 741 7070;
E: enquiries@harpercollins.co.uk;
W: www.harpercollins.co.uk

THE LANGFORD PRESS
32 Eastfields, Narborough, Norfolk PE32 1SS;
T: 01760 338 415; E: sales@langford-press.co.uk;
W: www.langford-press.co.uk

PRINCETON/WILDGUIDES LTD
Princeton University Press, 6 Oxford Street,
Woodstock, Oxfordshire OX20 1TR.
T: 0800 243 407; E: customer@wiley.com;
W: www.press.princeton.edu/wildguides

THE SOUND APPROACH
12 Market Street, Poole, Dorset BH15 1NF;
T: 01202 641 004; E: info@soundapproach.co.uk;
W: www.soundapproach.co.uk

BOOK SELLERS

CALLUNA BOOKS
Moor Edge, 2 Bere Road, Wareham, Dorset
BH20 4DD; T: 01929 552 560;
E: enquiries@callunabooks.co.uk;
W: www.callunabooks.co.uk

GARRICK BOOKS
T: 0161 612 5236

SUE LOWELL NATURAL HISTORY & TRAVEL BOOKS
101 Cambridge Gardens, London W10 6JE;
T: 0208 960 4382; E: sue4382@aol.com

KEN MULLINS BOOKS
16 Heath Close, Tarvin, Chester, Cheshire
CH3 8LT; T: 07866 479 010;
E: kendonago@hotmail.com

NHBS (Natural History Book Service + equipment)
1-6 The Stables, Ford Road, Totnes, Devon
TQ9 5XN; T: 01803 865 913;
E: customer.service@nhbs.com;
W: www.nhbs.com

PANDION BOOKS
10 Carr Close, Rainton, Thirsk, North Yorkshire
YO7 3QE; T: 01237 459 731;
E: pandionbks@aol.com

BOOK SELLERS, CLOTHING SUPPLIERS, EQUIPMENT SUPPLIERS, HOLIDAY COMPANIES

PICTURE BOOK
6 Stanley Street, Leek, Staffs ST13 5HG;
T: 01538 399 033; E: info@leekbooks.co.uk;
W: www.leekbooks.co.uk

SECOND NATURE
Knapton Bookbarn, Back Lane, Knapton, York,
YO26 6QJ; T: 01904 795 489;
E: secondnatureyork@aol.com

STEVE HOLLIDAY (Bird Reports/Journals)
2 Larriston Pl, Cramlington, Northumberland
NE23 8ER; T: 01670 731 963 (eves/w.ends);
E: birdreports@hotmail.co.uk

SUBBUTEO NATURAL HISTORY BOOKS
The Rea, Upton Magna, Shrewsbury, Shropshire
SY4 4UR; T: 01743 709 420;
E: info@wildlifebooks.com;
W: www.wildlifebooks.com

WILDSIDE BOOKS
29 Kings Avenue, Eastbourne, East Sussex
BN21 2PE; T: 01323 416 211;
E: wildsidebooks@hotmail.com

WILD SOUNDS & BOOKS (+ equipment)
Cross Street, Salthouse, Norfolk NR25 7XH;
T: 01263 741 100; E: isales@wildsounds.com;
W: www.wildsounds.com

CLOTHING SUPPLIERS

COUNTRY INNOVATION
1 Broad Street, Congresbury, North Somerset
BS49 5DG; T: 01934 877 333;
E: sales@countryinnovation.com;
W: www.countryinnovation.com

PARAMO DIRECTIONAL CLOTHING SYSTEMS LTD
Unit F, Durgates Industrial Estate, Wadhurst,
East Sussex TN5 6DF; T: 01892 786 444;
W: www.paramo-clothing.com

ROHAN
30 Maryland Road, Tongwell, Milton Keynes,
Bucks MK15 8HN; T: 0800 840 1411;
E: post@rohan.co.uk; W: www.rohan.co.uk

ROYAL ROBBINS
16 Mill Street, Oakham, Rutland LE15 6EA;
T: 01572 772 475; E: via website;
W: www.royalrobbins.co.uk

TILLEY ENDURABLES
6 Tresprison Court, Helston, Cornwall TR13 0QD;
T: 01326 574 402; E: info@tilley-uk.com;
W: www.tilley.com

EQUIPMENT SUPPLIERS

LOWEPRO
DayMen International Limited, Suite 1,
Ground Floor, St. David's Court, Union Street,
Wolverhampton, WV10 9TJ; T: 0845 250 0790;
E: via website; W: www.lowepro.com

(THE) BIRDERS STORE
Unit 7 King Charles Place, St Johns, Worcester,
WR2 5AJ; T: 01905 312 877;
E: sales@birders-store.co.uk;
W: www.birders-store.co.uk

(THE) ONE STOP NATURE SHOP
9 Dalegate Market, Burnham Deepdale,
Norfolk PE31 8FB; T: 01485 211 223;
E: sales@onestopnature.co.uk;
W: www.onestopnature.co.uk

OUTDOOR PHOTOGRAPHY GEAR
73 Manchester Road, Warrington, Cheshire
WA1 4AE; T: 01925 555 727;
E: sales@outdoorphotographygear.co.uk;
W: www.outdoorphotographygear.co.uk

SCOPAC
T: 07810 560 916; E: enquiries@scopac.co.uk;
W: www.scopac.co.uk

WILDLIFE WATCHING SUPPLIES
Tiverton Way, Tiverton Business Park, Tiverton,
Devon EX16 6TG; T: 01884 254 191;
E: enquiries@wildlifewatchingsupplies.co.uk;
W: www.wildlifewatchingsupplies.co.uk

HOLIDAY COMPANIES

AIGAS FIELD CENTRE
Beauly, Inverness-shire IV4 7AD; T: 01463 782 443;
E: info@aigas.co.uk; W: www.aigas.co.uk

ART SAFARI
Harbourmaster's Office, Ferry Quay, Woodbridge,
Suffolk IP12 1BW; T: 01394 382 235;
E: info@artsafari.co.uk; W: www.artsafari.co.uk

AVIAN ADVENTURES
49 Sandy Road, Norton, Stourbridge, Worcs
DY8 3AJ; T: 01384 372 013;
E: avianadventures@btinternet.com;
W: www.avianadventures.co.uk

BIRDFINDERS
Westbank, Cheselbourne, Dorset DT2 7NW;
T: 01258 839 066; E: birdfinders@aol.co.uk;
W: www.birdfinders.co.uk

HOLIDAY COMPANIES

BIRD HOLIDAYS LTD
10 Ivegate, Yeadon, Leeds, LS19 7RE;
T: 0113 3910 510; E: info@birdholidays.co.uk;
W: www.birdholidays.co.uk

(THE) BIRD ID COMPANY
Church Farm House, Church Lane,
Hindolveston, Norfolk NR20 5BT;
T: 01263 861 892; E: info@birdtour.co.uk;
W: www.birdtour.co.uk

BIRDWATCHING BREAKS
Cygnus House, Gordon's Mill, Balblair,
Ross-shire IV7 8LQ; T: 01381 610 495;
E: enquiries@birdwatchingbreaks.com;
W: www.birdwatchingbreaks.com

BIRD WATCHING & WILDLIFE CLUB
Grant Arms Hotel, 25 The Square,
Grantown-on-Spey, Highlands PH26 3HF;
T: 0800 043 8585; E: booking@bwwc.co.uk;
W: www.bwwc.co.uk

BIRDWATCHING TRIPS WITH THE BIGGEST TWITCH
Alan Davies & Ruth Miller, 12 Ormeside Court,
19 Church Walks, Llandudno, LL30 2HG;
T: 01492 872 407;
E: info@birdwatchingtrips.co.uk;
W: www.birdwatchingtrips.co.uk

BIRDQUEST LTD
Two Jays, Kemple End, Stonyhurst, Clitheroe,
Lancashire BB7 9QY; T: 01254 826 317;
E: birders@birdquest-tours.com;
W: www.birdquest-tours.com

BRITISH-BULGARIAN SOCIETY
Balkania Travel Ltd, Avanta Harrow, 79 College Rd,
Harrow, Middx HA1 1BD; T: 020 7536 9400;
E: ognian@balkaniatravel.com;
W: www.bulgariatours.co.uk

BUTEO WILDLIFE
14 Coolgardie Avenue, London E4 9HP;
T: 07527 454 683; E: info@buteowildlife.co.uk;
W: www.buteowildlife.co.uk

CAMBRIAN BIRD HOLIDAYS
Rhydlewis, Llandysul, Ceredigion SA44 5SP;
T: 01239 851 758;
E: info@cambrianbirdholidays.co.uk;
W: www.cambrianbirdholidays.co.uk

CLASSIC JOURNEYS
Danewood, Upper Holloway, Matlock,
Derbyshire DE4 5AW; T: 07858 410 677;
E: via website; W: www.classicjourneys.co.uk

(THE) DORSET BIRDING AND WILDLIFE EXPERIENCE
Moor Edge, 2 Bere Road, Wareham, Dorset
BH20 4DD; T: 01929 552 560;
E: enquiries@dorsetbirdingandwildlife.co.uk;
W: www.dorsetbirdingandwildlife.co.uk

DUNGENESS & ROMNEY MARSH BIRD TOURS
Paul Trodd, Plovers, 1 Toby Road, Lydd-on-Sea,
Romney Marsh, Kent TN29 9PG;
T: 01797 366 935; E: troddy@plovers.co.uk;
W: www.plovers.co.uk

EXPERIENCE NATURE
16 Lint Meadow, Wythall, Worcestershire B47 5PH;
T: 07704 189 835; E: birdergrove@gmail.com;
W: www.experiencenature.co.uk

GLENLOY WILDLIFE
Glenloy Lodge, Banavie, Fort William,
Highlands PH33 7PD; T: 01397 712 700;
E: info@glenloywildlife.co.uk;
W: www.glenloywildlife.co.uk

GREENTOURS LTD
Flat 2, Southbank, 36 Devonshire Rd, Buxton,
Derbyshire SK17 6RZ; T: 01298 83563;
E: enquiries@greentours.co.uk;
W: www.greentours.co.uk

HEATHERLEA LTD
The Mountview Hotel, Nethy Bridge,
Inverness-shire PH25 3EB; T: 01479 821 248;
E: info@heatherlea.co.uk;
W: www.heatherlea.co.uk

LIMOSA HOLIDAYS
West End Farmhouse, Chapelfield, Stalham,
Norfolk NR12 9EJ; T: 01692 580 623;
E: enquiries@limosaholidays.co.uk;
W: www.limosaholidays.co.uk

NATURETREK
Mingledown Barn, Wolf's Lane, Chawton,
Alton, Hampshire GU34 3HJ; T: 01962 733 051;
E: info@naturetrek.co.uk;
W: www.naturetrek.co.uk

NATURES IMAGES
4 Deer Park Drive, Newport, Shropshire
TF10 7HB; T: 01952 411 436;
E: mark@natures-images.co.uk;
W: www.natures-images.co.uk

NORTH WEST BIRDS
Mike Robinson, Barn Close, Beetham, Cumbria
LA7 7AL; T: 01539 563 191;
E: mike@nwbirds.co.uk; W: www.nwbirds.co.uk

HOLIDAY COMPANIES, OPTICAL DEALERS

ORCADIAN WILDLIFE
Gerraquoy St. Margaret's Hope, South Ronaldsay, Orkney KW17 2TH; T: 01856 831 240; E: via website; W: www.orcadianwildlife.co.uk

ORIOLE BIRDING
8 Newcastle Hill, Bridgend, Glamorgan CF31 4EY; T: 01656 711 152; E: oriolebirding@gmail.com; W: www.oriolebirding.com

ORNITHOLIDAYS
29 Straight Mile, Romsey, Hampshire S51 9BB; T: 01794 519 445; E: info@ornitholidays.co.uk; W: www.ornitholidays.co.uk

SARUS BIRD TOURS
12 Walton Drive, Bury, Lancashire BL9 5JU; T: 0161 761 7279; E: sarus@sarusbirdtours.co.uk; W: www.sarusbirdtours.co.uk

SHETLAND NATURE
c/o Burkle, Fair Isle, Shetland ZE2 9JU; T: 01595 760 333; E: info@shetlandnature.net; W: www.shetlandnature.net

SHETLAND WILDLIFE
Windy Stacks, Quendale, Shetland ZE2 9JD; T: 01950 460 939; E: info@shetlandwildlife.co.uk; W: www.shetlandwildlife.co.uk

SPEYSIDE WILDLIFE
Wester Camerorie, Ballieward, Grantown-on-Spey, Highlands PH26 3PR; T: 01479 812 498; E: enquiries@speysidewildlife.co.uk; W: www.speysidewildlife.co.uk

SUNBIRD
26B The Market Square, Potton, Sandy, Beds SG19 2NP; T: 01767 262 522; E: sunbird@sunbirdtours.co.uk; W: www.sunbirdtours.co.uk

THINK GALAPAGOS
Millcote, Mill Lane, Bishop Burton, HU17 8QT; T: 01964 552 292; E: info@thinkgalapagos.com; W: www.thinkgalapagos.com

(THE) TRAVELLING NATURALIST
Long Barn South, Sutton Manor Farm, Bishop's Sutton, Alresford, Hampshire SO24 0AA; T: 01305 267 994; E: sales@thetravellingnaturalist.com; W: www.naturalist.co.uk

WILD ABOUT TRAVEL
25 Sapley Road, Hartford, Huntingdon, Cambs PE29 1YG; T: 01480 370 593; E: info@wildabouttravel.co.uk; W: www.wildabouttravel.co.uk

WILD INSIGHTS
Yew Tree Farmhouse, Craignant, Selattyn, Oswestry, Shropshire SY10 7NP; T: 01691 718 740; E: keith@keithofford.co.uk; W: www.wildinsights.co.uk

WILDFOOT TRAVEL
Travel House, 133 Gravel Lane, Wilmslow, Cheshire SK9 6EG; T: 0800 195 3385; E: via website; W: www.wildfoottravel.com

WILDLIFE TRAVEL
The Manor House, Broad St, Great Cambourne, Cambridge, CB23 6DH; T: 01954 713 575; E: via website; W: www.wildlife-travel.co.uk

WILDLIFE WORLDWIDE
Long Barn South, Sutton Manor Farm, Bishop's Sutton, Alresford, Hampshire SO24 0AA; T: 01962 302 086; E: reservations@wildlifeworldwide.com; W: www.wildlifeworldwide.com

WILDWINGS
Davis House, Lodge Causeway, Bristol, BS16 3JB; T: 0117 9658 333; E: via website; W: www.wildwings.co.uk

WISE BIRDING HOLIDAYS
3 Moormead, Budleigh Salterton, Devon EX9 6QA; T: 07973 483 227; E: chris@wisebirding.co.uk; W: www.wisebirding.co.uk

YORKSHIRE COAST NATURE
T: 01723 865 498; E: via website; W: www.yorkshirecoastnature.co.uk

OPTICAL DEALERS

ACE OPTICS
16 Green St, Bath, BA1 2JZ; T: 01225 466 364; E: via website; W: www.aceoptics.co.uk

BIRDNET OPTICS LTD
5 Trenchard Drive, Harpur Hill, Buxton, Derbyshire SK17 9JY; T: 01298 71844; E: paulflint@birdnet.co.uk; W: www.birdnet.co.uk

CLEY SPY
Manor Farm Barns, Glandford, Holt, Norfolk NR25 7JP; T: 01263 740 088; E: via website; W: www.cleyspy.co.uk

CLIFTON CAMERAS
28 Parsonage Street, Dursley, Gloucestershire GL11 4AA; T: 01453 548 128; E: sales@cliftoncameras.co.uk; W: www.cliftoncameras.co.uk

OPTICAL DEALERS

FOCALPOINT OPTICS
Marbury House Farm, Bentleys Farm Lane,
Higher Whitley, Warrington, WA4 4QW;
T: 01925 730 399; E: focalpoint@dial.pipex.com;
W: www.fpoint.co.uk

FOCUS OPTICS
Church Lane, Corley, Coventry, CV7 8BA;
T: 01676 540 501; E: enquiries@focusoptics.eu;
W: www.focusoptics.eu

H.A.BAKER (LEWES) LTD
44 High Street, Lewes, Sussex BN7 2DD;
T: 01273 476 479; E: sales@habaker.co.uk;
W: www.habakerltd.co.uk

IN FOCUS
E: enquiries@infocusoptics.co.uk;
W: www.at-infocus.co.uk

Gloucestershire: The Wildfowl & Wetlands
Trust, Slimbridge, Gloucestershire GL2 7BT;
T: 01453 890 978

Hertfordshire: Willows Farm Village, Coursers
Road, London Colney, Hertfordshire AL2 1BB;
T: 01727 827 799

Lancashire: The Wildfowl & Wetlands Trust,
Martin Mere, Burscough, Ormskirk, Lancashire
L40 0TA; T: 01704 897 020

London, South West: The Wildfowl & Wetlands
Trust, London Wetland Centre, Queen Elizabeth's
Walk, Barnes, London SW13 9WT; T: 0208 409 4433

Norfolk: Main Street, Titchwell, Nr. King's
Lynn, Norfolk PE31 8BB; T: 01485 210 101

Rutland: Anglian Water Birdwatching Centre,
Egleton Reserve, Rutland Water, Rutland
LE15 8BT; T: 01572 770 656

Yorkshire: Westleigh House Office Estate,
Wakefield Road, Denby Dale, West Yorkshire
HD8 8QJ; T: 01484 864 729

LONDON CAMERA EXCHANGE
T: 01962 670 007 (online orders);
E: shops via website; W: www.lcegroup.co.uk

Bath: 13 Cheap Street, Bath, Avon BA1 1NB;
T: 01225 462 234

Bath (Lakeside Optics): Picnic Area no.1,
Chew Valley Lake, Walley Lane, Chew Stoke,
BS40 8XS; T: 01275 332 042

Bristol (Baldwin Street): 3 Alliance House,
Bristol, BS1 1SA; T: 0117 929 1935

Bristol (Broadmead): 53 The Horsefair,
Bristol, BS1 3JP; T: 0117 927 6185

Cheltenham: 10-12 The Promenade,
Cheltenham, GL50 1LR; T: 01242 519 851

Chester: 9 Bridge Street Row, Chester,
CH1 1NW; T: 01244 326 531

*Chichester: 17 Eastgate Square, Chichester,
PO19 1JL;* T: 01243 531 536

Colchester: 12 Eld Lane, Colchester, Essex
CO1 1LS; T: 01206 573 444

Derby: 17 Sadler Gate, Derby, Derbyshire
DE1 3NH; T: 01332 348 644

Exeter: 174 Fore Street, Exeter, Devon
EX4 3AX; T: 01392 279 024

Gloucester: 12 Southgate Street, Gloucester,
GL1 2DH; T: 01452 304 513

Guildford: 8/9 Tunsgate, Guildford, Surrey
GU1 3QT; T: 01483 504 040

Hereford: 16 Widemarsh Street, Hereford,
HR4 9EW; T: 01432 272 655

Leamington: 4C Lunn Poly House, Clarendon
Avenue, Royal Leamington Spa, CV32 5PP;
T: 01926 886 166

Lincoln (High Street): 155 High Street,
Lincoln, LN5 7AA; T: 01522 528 577

Lincoln (Silver Street): 6 Silver Street,
Lincoln, LN2 1DY; T: 01522 514 131

London (Strand): 98 Strand, London
WC2R 0EW; T: 0207 379 0200

Manchester: 16 Cross Street, Manchester,
M2 7AE; T: 0161 834 7500

Newcastle: 76 High Street, Gosforth,
Newcastle Upon Tyne, NE3 1HB;
T: 0191 213 0060

Norwich: 12 Timber Hill, Norwich, Norfolk
NR1 3LB; T: 01603 612 537

Nottingham: 7 Pelham Street, Nottingham,
NG1 2EH; T: 0115 941 7486

Plymouth: 10 Frankfort Gate, Plymouth,
Devon PL1 1QD; T: 01752 664 894

Portsmouth: Kingswell Path, Cascades
Shopping Centre, Portsmouth, PO1 4RR;
T: 023 9283 9933

Reading: 7 Station Road, Reading, Berkshire
RG1 1LG; T: 0118 959 2149

Salisbury: 6 Queen Street, Salisbury, Wiltshire
SP1 1EY; T: 01722 335 436

Southampton (Civic Centre): 11 Civic Centre
Road, Southampton, Hants SO14 7FJ;
T: 023 8033 1720

225

OPTICAL DEALERS, OPTICAL IMPORTERS & MANUFACTURERS

Southampton (High Street): 10 High Street, Southampton, Hants SO14 2DH; T: 023 8022 1597

Taunton: 6 North Street, Taunton, Somerset TA1 1LH; T: 01823 259 955

Winchester: 15 The Square, Winchester, Hampshire SO23 9ES; T: 01962 866 203

Worcester: 8 Pump Street, Worcester WR1 2QT; T: 01905 22314

PARK CAMERAS
T: 01444 237 070; E: sales@parkcameras.com; W: www.parkcameras.com

Burgess Hill: York Road, Burgess Hill, West Sussex RH15 9TT

London: 53-54 Rathbone Place, London W1T 1JR

SHERWOODS
The Arden Centre, Little Alne, Wootton Wawen, Henley-in-Arden, Warwickshire B95 6HW; T: 01789 488 880; E: sales@sherwoods-photo.com; W: www.sherwoods-photo.com

SOUTH WEST OPTICS
22 River Street, Truro, Cornwall TR1 2SJ; T: 01872 263 444; E: internet@swoptics.com; W: www.swoptics.co.uk

UTTINGS
PO Box 672 Norwich, Norfolk NR3 2ZR; T: 01603 619 811; E: via website; W: www.uttings.co.uk

WEX PHOTOGRAPHIC
Unit B, Frenbury Estate, Drayton High Road, Norwich, Norfolk NR6 5DP; T: 01603 486 413; E: via website;W: www.wexphotographic.com

WILKINSON CAMERAS
Main address: see Preston; T: 01772 252 188; E: sales@wilkinson.co.uk; W: www.wilkinson.co.uk

Burnley: 95 James Street, Burnley, Lancs BB11 1PY; T: 01282 424 524

Bury: 61 The Rock, Bury, Greater Manchester, BL9 0NB; T: 0161 764 3402

Carlisle: 13 Grapes Lane, The Lanes Centre, Carlisle, Cumbria CA3 8NH; T: 01228 538 583

Kendal: Unit 19A, The Westmorland Centre, Stricklandgate, Kendal, Cumbria LA9 4LR; T: 01539 735 055

Lancaster: 6 James Street, Lancaster, Lancs LA1 1UP; T: 01524 380 510

Liverpool: 51 Lord Street, Liverpool, L2 6PB; T: 0151 255 0345

Preston: 27 Friargate, St George's Centre, Preston, Lancs PR1 2NQ; T: 01772 556 250

Southport: 38 Eastbank Street, Southport, Merseyside PR8 1ET; T: 01704 534 534

Warrington: 10 The Mall, The Golden Square, Warrington, WA1 1QE; T: 01925 638 290

OPTICAL IMPORTERS & MANUFACTURERS

ALPHA OPTICAL DISTRIBUTION LTD (Kite Optics)
The Old Stables, Hendal Farm, Groombridge, East Sussex; T: 07725 081 436; E: via website: www.alphaodl.co.uk; W: www.kiteoptics.com

BUSHNELL PERFORMANCE OPTICS UK LTD
Unit C83 Barwell Business Park, Leatherhead Rd, Chessington, Surrey KT9 2NY; T: 0208 391 4700; E: sales@bushnell-uk.co.uk; W: www.bushnell.eu/uk

CANON UK LTD
Canon Support. T: 0207 660 0186; E: via website; W: www.canon.co.uk

CARL ZEISS LTD
509 Coldhams Lane, Cambridge, CB1 3JS; T: 01223 401 520; E: info.uk@zeiss.com; W: www.zeiss.co.uk

HAWKE
Avocet House, Wilford Bridge Rd, Melton, Woodbridge, Suffolk IP12 1RB; T: 01394 387 762; E: uk@hawkeoptics.co.uk; W: www.hawkeoptics.co.uk

DAVID HINDS LTD (Celestron Optics)
Unit R, Cherrycourt Way, Leighton Buzzard, Bedfordshire LU7 4UH; T: 01525 852 696; E: astro@dhinds.co.uk; W: www.celestron.uk.com

INTRO 2020 (Steiner binos, Velbon & Slik tripods & more)
Unit 1, Priors Way, Maidenhead, Berks SL6 2HP; T: 01628 674 411; E: sales@intro2020.co.uk; W: www.intro2020.co.uk

KOWA OPTIMED EUROPE LTD
E: via website; W: www.kowaproducts.com

LEICA CAMERA LTD
34 Bruton Place, Mayfair, London W1J 6NQ; T: 0207 629 1351; E: customercar.uk@leica-camera.com; W: www.leica-camera.com

MANFROTTO DISTRIBUTION (Manfrotto & Gitzo Tripods)
Resolution Rd, Ashby-de-la-Zouch,
Leicestershire LE65 1DW; T: 01530 566 090;
E: via website; W: www.manfrotto.co.uk

MARCHWOOD UK (Meopta, Forest & Bresser Optics)
Unit 4.06 Cannock Chase Enterprise Centre,
Walkers Rise, Hednesford, Staffordshire
WS12 0QU; T: 01543 424 255;
E: sales@marchwooduk.co.uk;
W: www.marchwooduk.co.uk

MONK OPTICS LTD (Fujinon Binoculars)
Wye Valley Observatory, The Old School,
Brockweir, Chepstow, NP16 7NW;
T: 01291 689 858; E: msales@monkoptics.co.uk;
W: www.monkoptics.co.uk

NEWPRO UK LTD (Vortex Optics, PhoneSkope Cases)
3 Radcot Estate, Park Rd, Faringdon,
Oxfordshire SN7 7BP; T: 01367 242 411;
E: sales@newprouk.co.uk; W: www.newprouk.co.uk

NIKON UK LTD:
380 Richmond Road, Kingston-upon-Thames,
Surrey KT2 5PR; T: 0330 123 0932;
E: via website; W: www.nikon.co.uk

OPTICAL VISION LTD (Barr & Stoud & Acuter Optics)
Unit 3, Woolpit Business Park, Woolpit,
Bury St Edmunds, Suffolk IP30 9UP;
E: info:opticalvision.co.uk;
W: www.opticalvision.co.uk

OPTICRON
Unit 21, Titan Court, Laporte way, Luton,
Befordshire LU4 8EF; T: 01582 726 522;
E: sales@opticron.co.uk;
W: www.opticron.co.uk

SWAROVSKI OPTIK
Unit 11, Tarbot House, Perrywood Business
Park, Salfords, Surrey RH1 5JQ;
T: 01737 856 812;
Customer Service (Austria) T: 00800 3242 5056;
E: customerservice@swarovskioptik.com;
W: www.swarovskioptik.com

VANGUARD WORLD UK LTD
Unit 73, Basepoint Business Centre,
Enterprise Close, Aviation Business Park,
Christchurch, Dorset, BH23 6NX;
T: 01202 651 281; E: via website;
W: www.vanguardworld.co.uk

VIKING OPTICAL LTD (Viking & RSPB Optics)
Blyth Road, Halesworth, Suffolk IP19 8EN;
T: 01986 875 315; E: sales@vikingoptical.co.uk;
W: www.vikingoptical.co.uk

OPTICAL REPAIRS & SERVICING

ACTION OPTICS
18 Butts Ash Gardens, Hythe, Southampton,
SO45 3BL; T: 023 8084 2801;
E: ActionOptics@mail.com;
W: www.actionoptics.co.uk

FIXATION UK LTD (Nikon/Canon repairs & servicing)
Unit C, 250 Kennington Lane, Lambeth,
London SE11 5RD; T: 0207 582 3294;
E: admin@fixationuk.com;
W: www.fixationuk.com

INTRASIGHTS
2 The Waggon Shed, Flaxdrayton Farm,
South Petherton, Somerset TA13 5LR;
T: 01460 929 291; E: intrasights@gmail.com;
W: www.intrasights.com

OPTREP OPTICAL REPAIRS
16 Wheatfield Rd, Selsey, W. Sussex PO20 0NY;
T: 01243 601 365; E: info@opticalrepairs.com;
W: www.opticalrepairs.com

VIKING SERVICE & REPAIR CENTRE
Blyth Road, Halesworth, Suffolk IP19 8EN;
T: 01986 875 315; E: viking@vikingoptical.co.uk;
W: www.vikingoptical.co.uk

TECHNOLOGY PRODUCTS

BIRD IMAGES (DVDS)
Paul Doherty, 28 Carousel Walk, Sherburn-in-
Elmet, North Yorkshire LS25 6LP;
T: 01977 684 666; E: paul@birdvideodvd.com;
W: www.birdvideodvd.com

BIRD JOURNAL (BLUEBIRD TECHNOLOGY)
1 Turnbridge Court, Swavesey, Cambridge,
CB24 4GH; W: www.birdjournal.com

BIRDGUIDES LTD
Warners Group Publications, The Chocolate
Factory, 5 Clarendon Road, London N22 6XJ;
T: 0208 826 0934; E: contact@birdguides.com;
W: www.birdguides.com

EASYBIRDER DVDS
Dave Gosney, Valley View Cottage, 15 Low Rd,
Sheffield, S6 5FY; T: 0114 285 3712;
E: dave@easybirder.co.uk;
W: www.easybirder.co.uk

ISABELLINE FILMS
Steve Evans, 9 Milverton Close, Halesowen,
West Midlands B63 3QL; E: steve@isabelline.co.uk;
W: www.isabelline.co.uk

TRADE DIRECTORY

County Bird Reports

Check out the 'County Directory' listings to see where to purchase the latest bird reports...

COUNTY DIRECTORY

Neil Gartshore

The Buzzard *Buteo buteo* has spread into many counties in recent years and has become a common sight in areas where it was once a scarce bird.

COUNTY DIRECTORY

COUNTY DIRECTORY - EXPLANATION OF HEADINGS

THE INFORMATION IN this directory has been obtained from a number of sources - including the persons listed and the relevant national body. In some cases, where it has not proved possible to verify the details directly, alternative responsible sources have been used. When no satisfactory source was available, previously included entries have sometimes had to be deleted. Readers are requested to advise the editor of any errors, omissions or changes (see page 6).

(*Note:* for completeness, n/a has been used where information is not available or has been withheld).

Bird Atlas/Avifauna
The more recent county publications are listed here. Many of these titles should still be available to buy new but if out of print try the second hand market - check out the booksellers listed in the Trade Directory.

Bird Recorder
The County Bird Recorder is the key point of contact in the area to deal with all aspects of bird records including rarities & rare breeding birds.

Bird Report
The annual county bird report is usually, but not exclusively, published by the county bird club. In some counties, annual reports are also published covering smaller recording areas. The *(date-)* refers to the start of the current title or, in some cases, its predecessor. In the first instance, contact the relevant person/ club for the current report (& back issues). Check out the booksellers listed in the Trade Directory to look for 'out of print' reports.

BTO Regional Representative
Your local BTO Rep is the first point of contact if you wish to help with national bird surveys in your county - get involved, make a difference!

Club
Many counties have their own independent county-wide bird/natural history clubs & some have smaller clubs based on particular areas of the county. Contact details are provided here along with information about indoor meetings: get in touch/check out the club website for membership information, to confirm meeting dates/venues & for details about field trips & other club activities.

Ringing Group/Bird Observatory
For more information about becoming a licenced ringer, contact the BTO (see National Directory). Active groups of ringers are well represented around the counties - if you are interested in becoming a ringer it may be possible to join a trainer from one of these groups. If you find a ringed bird, contact the BTO/details will be on the ring.

RSPB Local Group
Groups are active in most counties offering an excellent programme of talks & field trips through the year - check out your local group to see what they have to offer. Details are provided here about the indoor meetings: get in touch/check out the group website to confirm dates/venues & for details about the field trips & other activities the group offers to members.

Wetland Bird Survey (WeBS) Organiser
Get involved with your local monthly wetland bird counts - for details of how to help contact your local organiser or contact the WeBS Office, BTO, The Nunnery, Thetford, Norfolk IP24 2PU. T: 01842 750 050; E: webs@bto.org

Wildlife Trust
Don't forget to check out your local Wildlife Trust who organise/run many talks, walks, events & other activites. The network of 47 independent Wildlife Trusts also manage a wide range of nature reserves providing valuable habitats for birds & other wildlife.

ENGLAND

BEDFORDSHIRE

Bird Atlas/Avifauna
An Atlas of the Breeding Birds of Bedfordshire 1988-92. RA Dazley & P Trodd (Bedfordshire Natural History Society, 1994).

The Birds of Bedfordshire. P Trodd & D Kramer (Castlemead Publications, 1991).

Bird Recorder
Steve Blain, 9 Devon Drive, Biggleswade, SG18 0FJ. T: 07979 606 300;
E: recorder@bedsbirdclub.org.uk

Bird Report
BEDFORDSHIRE BIRD REPORT (1946-), from Mary Sheridan, 28 Chestnut Hill, Linslade, Leighton Buzzard, LU7 2TR.
E: membership@bnhs.org.uk

BTO Regional Representative
Roger Hicks. T: 01462 816 028;
E: rogerkhicks@hotmail.com

Judith Knight (Regional Development Officer).
T: n/a; E: judithknight@waitrose.com

Club
BEDFORDSHIRE BIRD CLUB. (1992; 300).
Sheila Alliez (Hon Sec), Flat 61 Adamson Court, Adamson Walk, Kempston, Bedford, MK42 8QZ.
T: 01234 855 227; E: sjalliez12@btinternet.com;
W: www.bedsbirdclub.org.uk
Meetings: 8.00pm, last Tuesday of the month (Sep-Mar). Maulden Village Hall, Maulden, MK45 2DA.

Ringing Group/Bird Observatory
RSPB. Mr W Kirby. T: 01767 680 551;
E: will.kirby@rspb.org.uk

RSPB Local Group
BEDFORD. (1970; 80).
Carolyn Hawkes. T: 01234 768 136;
E: BedfordRSPBlocalgroup@gmail.com;
W: www.rspb.org.uk/groups/bedford
Meetings: 7.30pm, 3rd Thursday of the month (Sep-May). Aircraft Research Association, The Sports & Social Club, Manton Lane, Bedford, MK41 7PF.

Wetland Bird Survey (WeBS) Organiser
BEDFORDSHIRE. Mr RI Bashford.
T: via WeBS Office.
E: richard.bashford@rspb.org.uk

Wildlife Trust. See Cambridgeshire.

BERKSHIRE

Bird Atlas/Avifauna
The Birds of Berkshire. Neil Bucknell, Brian Clews, Renton Righelato & Chris Robinson (Birds of Berkshire Atlas Group, 2nd ed 2013).

Bird Recorder
Richard Burness, 20 Burlsdon Way, Bracknell, RG12 2PH. T: 07708 094 899; E: records@berksoc.org.uk

Bird Report
NEWBURY DISTRICT BIRD REPORT: Covers a 10-mile radius from Newbury Museum incl. parts of north Hants, south Oxon (1960-), from Lesley Staves, Hell Corner Farm, Kintbury, Hungerford, RG17 9SX. T: 01488 668 482;
E: glsdroversdale@tesco.net

THE BIRDS OF BERKSHIRE (1974-), from Sally Wearing, 9 Deans Farm, The Causeway, Reading, RG4 5JZ. E: secretary@berksoc.org.uk

BTO Regional Representative
Ken & Sarah White. T: 01635 268 442;
E: btoberks.ken.sarah@googlemail.com

Club
BERKSHIRE ORNITHOLOGICAL CLUB. (1947; 320). Iain Oldcorn (Membership Sec), 28 Huntsman Meadow, Ascot, SL5 7PF. T: 01344 625 883;

E: membership@berksoc.org.uk;
W: www.berksoc.org.uk
Meetings: 8pm, (usually) alternate Wednesdays (Sep-Apr). Room 109, Palmer Building, University of Reading, RG6 6UR.

NEWBURY DISTRICT ORNITHOLOGICAL CLUB. (1959; 90). Mrs Lesley Staves (Sec).
Address: n/a; T: 01488 682 301;
E: enquiries@newburybirders.co.uk;
W: www.newburybirders.co.uk
Meetings: 7.30pm, monthly on a Thursday (Oct-Mar). Greenham Church Hall, New Road, Greenham, Newbury, RG19 8RZ.

THEALE AREA BIRD CONSERVATION GROUP. (1988; 75). Catherine McEwan (Club Sec). Address: n/a.
T: 0118 9415 792; E: tabcgsec@yahoo.com;
W: www.tabcg.webs.com/
Meetings: 8pm, 1st Tuesday of the month (all year). Englefield Social Club, The Street, Englefield, Reading, RG7 5ES.

Ringing Group/Bird Observatory
BERKSHIRE DOWNS RG. Mr J Swallow.
T: 07909 118 825; E: jls_birding@mybtinternet.com;
W: http://berksdownsringing.blogspot.co.uk

ENGLAND

NEWBURY RG. Mr D Long. T: n/a;
E: duncanflong@aol.com; W: www.newburyrg.co.uk

RUNNYMEDE RG. Mr D Harris. T: n/a;
E: daveharris1040@gmail.com;
W: www.runnymedering.uk

RSPB Local Group
EAST BERKSHIRE. (1974; 170).
Ken Cottam. T: 01628 620 473;
E: k.s.cottam@btinternet.com;
W: www.eastberksrspb.org.uk
Meetings: 7.30pm, 3rd Thursday of the month
(Sep-May). Methodist Church Hall, King Street,
Maidenhead, SL6 1EA.

READING. (1986; 130).
Carl Feltham. T: 0118 941 1713;
E: Info@reading-RSPB.org;
W: www.reading-rspb.org;
Meetings: 8.00 pm, 2nd Tuesday of the month
(Sep-Jun). Pangbourne Village Hall, Station Road,
Pangbourne, Reading, RG8 7DY.

WOKINGHAM & BRACKNELL. (1979; 140).
Alan Moore. T: 07789 589 298;
E: RSPBwandb@gmail.com;
W: www.rspb.org.uk/groups/wokinghamandbracknell
Meetings: 7.45pm, 2nd Thursday of the month
(Sep-Jun). Finchampstead Memorial Hall,
The Village, Finchampstead, Wokingham, RG40 4JU.

Wetland Bird Survey (WeBS) Organiser
BERKSHIRE. Mr & Mrs White. T: via WeBS Office;
E: white.zoothera@gmail.com

Wildlife Trust. See Oxfordshire.

BUCKINGHAMSHIRE

BirdAtlas/Avifauna
The Birds of Buckinghamshire. David Ferguson
(Buckingham Bird Club, 2nd ed 2012).

Bird Recorder
Andy Harding, 93 Deanshanger Road,
Old Stratford, Milton Keynes, MK19 6AX.
T: 01908 565 896; E: Recorder@bucksbirdclub.co.uk

Bird Report
BUCKINGHAMSHIRE BIRD REPORT
(1980-), from Steve Marley,
51 Lower Icknield Way, Tring,
HP23 4LW.
E: FieldMeetings@
bucksbirdclub.co.uk.

BTO Regional Representative
Phil Tizzard. T: 01280 812 427;
E: phil.tizzard@care4free.net

Club
AMERSHAM BIRDWATCHING CLUB. (n/a; n/a).
Alistair McKenzie (Sec). Address: n/a.
T: 01494 717 426;
E: secretary@amershambirdwatchingclub.co.uk;
W: www.amershambirdwatchingclub.co.uk
Meetings: 7.45pm, 3rd Friday of the month
(Sep-May). Barn Hall Community Centre, Chiltern
Avenue, Amersham, HP6 5AH.

BUCKINGHAMSHIRE BIRD CLUB. (1981; 340).
Bill Parker (Sec). Address: n/a;
E: Secretary@bucksbirdclub.co.uk;
W: www.bucksbirdclub.co.uk
Meetings: 7.30pm, 1st Thursday of the month
(Oct-Dec/Feb-Apr). Wendover Memorial Hall,
Wharf Road, Wendover, HP22 6HF.

Ringing Group/Bird Observatory
COLNE VALLEY RG. Mrs D Lamsdell. T: n/a;
E: deniselamsdell@rocketmail.com

HUGHENDEN RG. Mr P Edwards. T: n/a;
E: peteandlynne73@gmail.com

RUNNYMEDE RG. See Berkshire.

RSPB Local Group
AYLESBURY. (1981; 160).
Alan Mitchener. T: 01844 208 893;
E: awmitchener@btinternet.com;
W: www.rspb.org.uk/groups/aylesbury
Meetings: 7.30pm, last Monday of the month
(Sep-May). Prebendal Farm Community Centre,
Fowler Road, Aylesbury, HP19 7QW.

NORTH BUCKS. (1976; 540).
George Conchie. T: 01908 640 097;
E: georgeconchie@cooptel.net;
W: www.rspb.org.uk/groups/northbucks
Meetings: 7.45pm, 2nd Thursday of the month
(Sep-May). Cruck Barn, City Discovery Centre,
Alston Drive, Bradwell Abbey, Milton Keynes,
MK13 9AP.

Wetland Bird Survey (WeBS) Organiser
BUCKINGHAMSHIRE (NORTH). Mr CG Coppock.
T: 07729 774 922;
E: christophercoppock@live.co.uk

BUCKINGHAMSHIRE (SOUTH). Vacant - contact
WeBS Office.

Wildlife Trust. See Oxfordshire.

CAMBRIDGESHIRE

BirdAtlas/Avifauna
Cambridgeshire Bird Atlas 2007-2011.
Louise Bacon, Alison Cooper & Hugh Venables
(Cambridge Bird Club, 2013).

ENGLAND

The Birds of Cambridgeshire. PMM Bircham (Cambridge University Press, 1989/pbk ed 2009).

Bird Recorder
Louise Bacon. Address: n/a. T: n/a;
E: recorder@cambridgebirdclub.org.uk

Bird Report
CAMBRIDGESHIRE BIRD REPORT (1927-), from Bruce Martin, 178 Nuns Way, Cambridge, CB4 2NS.
E: bruce.s.martin@btinternet.com

BTO Regional Representative
CAMBRIDGESHIRE: Rob Pople. T: n/a;
E: robgpople@hotmail.com

HUNTINGDON & PETERBOROUGH.
Derek Langslow. T: 01733 232 153;
E: drldrl49@outlook.com

Club
CAMBRIDGESHIRE BIRD CLUB. (1925; 350+).
Michael Holdsworth (Sec),
4a Cavendish Ave, Cambridge, CB1 7US. T: n/a;
E: secretary@cambridgebirdclub.org.uk;
W: www.cambridgebirdclub.org.uk
Meetings: 8pm, 2nd Friday of the month (Sep-May). Either at St John's Church Hall, Hills Road, Cambridge CB2 8RN or Cottenham Village College, High Street, Cottenham, Cambridge, CB24 8UA.

PETERBOROUGH BIRD CLUB. (1998; 185).
David Cromack, 55 Thorpe Park Road, Peterborough, PE3 6LJ. T: 01733 566 815;
E: cromackd@gmail.com;
W: www.peterboroughbirdclub.com
Meetings: 7.30pm, last Tuesday of the month (Sep-Nov, Jan-Apr). PO Social Club, Bourges Boulevard, Peterborough, PE1 2AU.

Ringing Group/Bird Observatory
KINGFISHER BRIDGE RG. Mr T Bagworth. T: n/a;
E: tim.bagworth@btinternet.com

UPPER CAM RG. Mrs R Vallance. T: 01799 550 474;
E: robynvallance2@gmail.com

WICKEN FEN RG. Dr C Thorne. T: 01954 210 566;
E: cjrt@cam.ac.uk

RSPB Local Group
CAMBRIDGE. (1977; 80).
Andrew Law. T: 01799 501 790;
E: andylaw1954@gmail.com;
W: www.rspb.org.uk/groups/cambridge
Meetings: 7.30pm, 3rd Wednesday of the month (Sep-Nov/Jan-May). Wilkinson Room, St John's the Evangelist, Hills Road, Cambridge, CB2 8RN.

HUNTINGDONSHIRE. (1982; 100).
Mervyn Vickery. T: 01480 492 519;
E: mfvickery52@outlook.com;
W: www.rspb.org.uk/groups/huntingdonshire
Meetings: 7.30pm, last Wednesday of the month (Sep-Apr, Dec may be earlier in month). The Free Church, St Ives, Market Hill, St Ives, PE27 5AL.

Wetland Bird Survey (WeBS) Organiser
CAMBRIDGESHIRE (incl. HUNTINGDONSHIRE).
Mr BS Martin. T: 01223 700 656 & 07977 381 625;
E: brucemartin@virginmedia.com

NENE WASHES. Mr CEF Kitchin. T: 01733 205 140 & 07711 157 859; E: charlie.kitchin@rspb.org.uk

OUSE WASHES. Mr P Harrington.
T: via WeBS Office; E: paul.harrington@rspb.org.uk

Wildlife Trust
THE WILDLIFE TRUST FOR BEDFORDSHIRE, CAMBRIDGESHIRE AND NORTHAMPTONSHIRE. (1994; 35,000).
The Manor House, Broad Street, Great Cambourne, Cambs CB23 6DH.
T: 01954 713 500, (fax) 01954 710 051;
E: cambridgeshire@wildlifebcn.org;
W: www.wildlifebcn.org

CHESHIRE & WIRRAL

BirdAtlas/Avifauna
Birds in Cheshire and Wirral: A Breeding and Wintering Atlas. David Norman (Liverpool University Press, 2008).

Bird Recorder
CHESHIRE & WIRRAL. Hugh Pulsford, 6 Buttermere Drive, Great Warford, Alderley Edge, SK9 7WA.
T: 01565 880 171; E: countyrec@cawos.org
[also the Secretary of Association of County Recorders and Editors (ARCE)]

Bird Report
CHESHIRE & WIRRAL BIRD REPORT (1964), from David Cogger, 71 Parkgate, Knutsford, WA16 8HF.
E: davidcogger@cawos.org

BTO Regional Representative
MID. Paul Miller. T: 01928 787 535;
E: paulandhilarymiller@live.co.uk

NORTH & EAST.
Hugh Pulsford. T: 01565 880 171;
E: ahugh.pulford@btinternet.com

John Headon (Assistant Representaive).
T: 0161 439 8557; E: johnheadon@hotmail.com

SOUTH. Hugh Pulsford - see above.

THE WIRRAL. Paul Miller - see above.

Club
CHESHIRE & WIRRAL
ORNITHOLOGICAL SOCIETY.
(1988; 310). Ted Lock (Sec),
2 Bourne Street, Wilmslow,
SK9 5HD. T: 01625 540 466;
E: info@cawos.org;
W: www.cawos.org

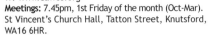

CAWOS

Meetings: 7.45pm, 1st Friday of the month (Oct-Mar).
St Vincent's Church Hall, Tatton Street, Knutsford,
WA16 6HR.

CHESTER & DISTRICT ORNITHOLOGICAL SOCIETY.
(1967; 50). David King, 13 Bennett Close,
Willaston, Neston, Cheshire CH64 2XF.
T: 0151 327 7212;
E: davidking623@btinternet.com; W: n/a
Meetings: 7.30pm, 1st Thursday of the month
(Oct-Mar). Caldy Valley Community Centre,
Caldy Valley Road, Boughton, Chester, CH3 5PR.

KNUTSFORD ORNITHOLOGICAL SOCIETY. (1974; 45).
Derek Pike (Sec). Address: n/a. T: 01565 653 811;
Press Officer/Website - E: tony@10x50.com;
W: www.10x50.com
Meetings: 8pm, 4th Friday of the month (Sept-Apr).
Jubilee Hall, Stanley Road, Knutsford, WA16 0GP.

LANCASHIRE & CHESHIRE FAUNA SOCIETY.
See Lancashire.

MID-CHESHIRE ORNITHOLOGICAL SOCIETY. (1962; 80).
John Drake (Sec), 17 Wisenholme Close,
Beechwood West, Runcorn, Cheshire WA7 2RU.
T: 01928 561 133; E: contact@midcheshireos.co.uk;
W: www.midcheshireos.co.uk
Meetings: 7:45pm, 2nd Friday of the month
(Oct-Apr). Cuddington and Sandiway Village Hall,
Norley Road, Cuddington, CW8 2LB.

NANTWICH NATURAL HISTORY SOCIETY. (1979; 40).
Mike Holmes. Address: n/a. T: n/a;
E: mabj@nantnats.fsnet.co.uk; W: n/a
Meetings: No indoor meetings but regular social
evenings relating to field work and surveys,
usually in The Vine Pub, 42 Hospital Street,
Nantwich, CW5 5RP.

SOUTH EAST CHESHIRE
ORNITHOLOGICAL SOCIETY. (1964; 130).
Derek Owen (Chairman).
Address: n/a. T: n/a;
E: derek_owen07@tiscali.co.uk;
W: www.secos.org.uk
Meetings: 7.30pm, 2nd Friday
of the month (Sep-Apr). Ettiley
Heath Church Community
Centre, Elton Road, Ettiley
Heath, Sandbach, CW11 3NE.

SECOS

WILMSLOW GUILD BIRDWATCHING GROUP. (1965; 65).
All members of the WGBG are required to be
members of the Wilmslow Guild.
T: 01625 523 903. E: via website;
W: www.wilmslowguild.org
Brian Dyke (Chairman WGBG). T: 01625 525 936;
W: http://wgbwcopy.wikidot.com/wgbg
Meetings: 7.30pm, usually last Friday of the month -
but not always - (Sep-Apr). Wilmslow Guild, 1 Bourne
Street, Wilmslow, SK9 5HD.

WIRRAL BIRD CLUB. (1977; 65).
Bill Wonderley. Address: n/a. T: 07795 148 140;
E: wirralbirdclub@gmail.com;
W: www.wirralbirdclub.com
Meetings: 8pm, 4th Thursday of the month
(Sep-Nov & Jan-Jul). Kingsmead School Hall,
Bertram Drive, Hoylake, CH47 0LL.

Ringing Group/Bird Observatory
CHESHIRE SWAN GROUP. Mr D Cookson.
T: 01270 567 526; E: Cheshireswans@aol.com;
W: http://cheshireswanstudygroup.wordpress.com

HILBRE BIRD OBSERVATORY.
Chris Williams (Chair & Ringer in Charge),
54 Park Road, Meols, Wirral CH47 7BQ.
T: n/a; E: chris@islandelec.com;
W: http://hilbrebirdobs.blogspot.co.uk

SOUTH MANCHESTER RG. Mr M Miles.
T: n/a; E: michaelmiles50@hotmail.com

RSPB Local Group
CHESTER. (1988; 220).
Norman Sadler. T: 01244 335 670;
E: rspbchester@googlegroups.com;
W: www.rspb.org.uk/groups/chester
Meetings: 7.30pm, 3rd Wednesday of the month
(Sep-Apr). Christleton Parish Hall, Village Road,
Christleton, CH3 7AS.

MACCLESFIELD. (1979; 200).
Daryll Bailey. T: 01625 430 311;
E: Secretary@macclesfieldRSPB.org.uk;
W: www.rspb.org.uk/groups/macclesfield
Meetings: 7.45pm, 2nd Tuesday of the month
(Sep-May). Macclesfield Methodist Church,
Westminster Road, Macclesfield, SK10 1BX.

NORTH CHESHIRE. (1976; 80).
Paul Grimmett. T: 01925 268 770;
E: paulwtwitcher@hotmail.com;
W: www.rspb.org.uk/groups/north_cheshire
Meetings: 7.30pm, 3rd Friday of the month
(Sep-Nov/Jan-Apr). Appleton Parish Hall, Dudlow
Green Road, Appleton, Warrington, WA4 5EQ.

ENGLAND

WIRRAL. (1982; 120).
Jeremy Bradshaw. T: 07769 673 018;
E: via the "contact us" page of website;
W: www.rspb.org.uk/groups/wirral
Meetings: 7.30pm, 1st Thursday of the month
(Sep-Jun). Bromborough Civic Centre, 2 Allport
Lane, Wirral, CH62 7HR.

Wetland Bird Survey (WeBS) Organiser
CHESHIRE (NORTH). Mr K Brides.
T: 07720 907 725; E: kane.brides@wwt.org.uk

CHESHIRE (SOUTH). Mr DA Cookson.
T: 01270 567 526 & 07976 725 031;
E: cheshireswans@aol.com

Wildlife Trust
CHESHIRE WILDLIFE TRUST. (1962; 13,000).
Bickley Hall Farm, Bickley, Malpas, SY14 8EF.
T: 01948 820 728, (fax) 0709 2888 469;
E: info@cheshirewt.org.uk;
W: www.cheshirewildlifetrust.org.uk

CORNWALL & ISLES OF SCILLY

Bird Atlas/Avifauna
The Essential Guide to Birds of The Isles of Scilly.
Bob L Flood, N Hudson & B Thomas (privately
published, 2007).

The Birds of the Isles of Scilly.
Peter Robinson
(Christopher Helm, 2003).

*The Birds of Cornwall and the
Isles of Scilly.* RD Penhallurick
(Browsers Bookshop, 1978).

Bird Recorder
CORNWALL. Dave Parker, 2
Boslevan, Green Lane, Marizion, TR17 0HQ.
T: 07932 354 711; E: recorder@cbwps.org.uk

ISLES OF SCILLY.
John Headon, Hivernia, Jackson's Hill, St Mary's,
Isles of Scilly TR21 0JZ. T: 01720 423 540;
E: recorder@scilly-birding.co.uk

Bird Report
BIRDS IN CORNWALL (1931-), from the Secretary,
CBWPS. E: secretary@cbwps.org.uk

*ISLES OF SCILLY BIRD REPORT and NATURAL
HISTORY REVIEW (1969-)*, from Carole Cilia,
Hivemia, Jackson's Hill, St Mary's, Isles of Scilly
TR21 0JZ. E: carole.cilia@btinternet.com
BTO Regional Representative
CORNWALL. Vacant - contact Dawn Balmer, BTO
T: 01842 750 050

ISLES OF SCILLY. Will Wagstaff. T: 01720 422 212;
E: will@islandwildlifetours.co.uk

Club
CORNWALL BIRD WATCHING
& PRESERVATION SOC. (1931; 1100).
Phil McVey (Sec), Little Boslymon, Bodmin,
PL30 5AP. T: 07740 923 385;
E: secretary@cbwps.org.uk; W: www.cbwps.org.uk
Meetings: see website for details.

ISLES OF SCILLY BIRD GROUP.
(2000; 375). Carole Cilia,
(Membership Sec), Hivemia,
Jackson's Hill, St Mary's,
Isles of Scilly TR21 0JZ.
T: 01720 423 540;
E: carole.cilia@btinternet.com;
W: www.scilly-birding.co.uk

Ringing Group/Bird Observatory
DEVON & CORNWALL WADER GROUP. See Devon.

WEST CORNWALL RG. Mr M Grantham. T: n/a;
E: markyjee@googlemail.com;
W: http://cornishringing.blogspot.co.uk/

RSPB Local Group
CORNWALL. (1972; 260).
Roger Hooper. T: 01209 820 610;
E: rogerwhooper@btinternet.com;
W: www.rspb.org.uk/groups/cornwall
Meetings: On a Friday, (Sep-Apr). Chacewater
Village Hall, Church Hill, nr Truro, TR4 8PZ -
contact/see website for details.

Wetland Bird Survey (WeBS) Organiser
CORNWALL (excl. TAMAR COMPLEX).
Mr P Roseveare. T: 07955 216 836;
E: peterroseveare@yahoo.com

TAMAR COMPLEX. Ms GD Grant.
T: via WeBS Office; E: gladysgrant@talktalk.net

Wildlife Trust
CORNWALL WILDLIFE TRUST. (1962; 17,000).
Five Acres, Allet, Truro, TR4 9DJ.
T: 01872 273 939, (fax) 01872 225 476;
E: info@cornwallwildlifetrust.org.uk;
W: www.cornwallwildlifetrust.org.uk

THE ISLES OF SCILLY WILDLIFE TRUST. (1984).
Trenoweth, St Marys, Isles of Scilly TR21 0NS.
T/fax: 01720 422 153;
E: enquiries@ios-wildlifetrust.org.uk;
W: www.ios-wildlifetrust.org.uk

CUMBRIA

BirdAtlas/Avifauna
*The Breeding Birds of Cumbria: A Tetrad Atlas
1997-2001.* M Stott, J Callion, I Kinley, C Raven &
J Roberts (Cumbria Bird Club, 2002).

ENGLAND

Bird Recorder
Chris Hind, 2 Old School House, Hallbankgate,
Brampton, CA8 2NW. T: 01697 746 379;
E: chris.m.hind@gmail.com

Regional Recorder
ALLERDALE & COPELAND. Nick Franklin.
Address: n/a. T: 01228 810 413;
E: nickbirder66@gmail.com

BARROW & SOUTH LAKELAND.
Ronnie Irving, 24 Birchwood Close, Vicarage Road,
Kendal, LA9 5BJ. T: 01539 727 523;
E: ronnieirving2017@gmail.com

CARLISLE & EDEN. Chris Hind - see bird recorder.

Bird Report
BIRDS AND WILDLIFE IN CUMBRIA (1970-), from
Dave Piercy - see Cumbria Bird Club.

WALNEY BIRD OBSERVATORY REPORT (1964-), from
Keith Parkes, 77 Dalton Lane, Barrow-in-Furness,
LA14 4LB. E: keith.parkes5@btopenworld.com

BTO Regional Representative
Colin Gay. T: 01229 773 820;
E: colinathodbarrow@btinternet.com

Dave Piercy (Assistant Representative).
T: 01768 773 201; E: daveandkathypiercy@tiscali.co.uk

Stephen Westerberg (Assistant Representative).
T: 01697 742 652; E: stephen.westerberg@rspb.org.uk

Peter Hearn (Regional Development Officer).
E: biarmicus@live.co.uk

Club
ARNSIDE & DISTRICT NATURAL HISTORY SOCIETY.
(1960's; 200). Gail Armstrong (Sec), 1 Bottoms Lane,
Silverdale, LA5 0TN. T: 01524 701 316;
E: info@arnsideanddistrictnhs.co.uk;
W: www.arnsideanddistrictnhs.co.uk
Meetings: 7.30pm, 2nd Thursday of the month
(Sep-Mar). WI Hall, Orchard Rd, Arnside, LA5 0DP.

CUMBRIA BIRD CLUB. (1989; 330).
Dave Piercy (Sec), 64 The Headlands, Keswick,
CA12 5EJ. T: 01768 773 201;
E: daveandkathypiercy@tiscali.co.uk;
W: www.cumbriabirdclub.org.uk
Meetings: Various evenings
and venues (Oct-Mar) -
contact/see website for
details.

**Ringing Group/
Bird Observatory**
EDEN RG. Mr G Longrigg.
T: n/a; E: longrigg977@btinternet.com

MORECAMBE BAY WADER RG. Mr J Sheldon.
T: 01229 813 458; E: christie1947@hotmail.co.uk

WALNEY BIRD OBSERVATORY.
Colin Raven (Ringing Trainer/Warden),
18 Seathwaite Road, Barrow-in-Furness, LA14 4LX.
T: 01229 830 517; E: walneyobs@gmail.com;
W: http://walneybo.blogspot.co.uk

WATCHTREE RG. Mr F Mawby. T: 01697 351 301
& 07970 206 164; E: fjmawby@redshank.org.uk;
W: www.watchtree.co.uk

RSPB Local Group
NORTH CUMBRIA. (1974; 400).
Richard Dixon. T: 01697 473 544;
E: sunzeco@hotmail.co.uk;
W: www.rspb.org.uk/groups/carlisle
Meetings: 7.30pm, usually 2nd Wednesday
(Sep-Mar). Tithe Barn, (Behind Marks &
Spencer's), West Walls, Carlisle, CA3 8UF.

SOUTH LAKELAND. (1973; 200).
Richard Evans. T: 01539 722 221;
E: RSPBsouthlakelandlocalgroup@gmail.com;
W: www.rspb.org.uk/groups/southlakeland
Meetings: 7.15pm, various locations in Kendal or
Ambleside - contact/see website for details.

WEST CUMBRIA. (1986; 135).
Dave Smith. T: 01900 85347; E: smida@talktalk.net;
W: www.rspb.org.uk/groups/westcumbria
Meetings: 7.30pm, 1st Tuesday of the month
(Sep-Apr). United Reformed Church, Main St,
Cockermouth, CA13 9LU.

Wetland Bird Survey (WeBS) Organiser
CUMBRIA (excl. ESTUARIES). Mr D Shackleton.
T: 01931 713 693;
E: d.shackleton@btinternet.com

DUDDON ESTUARY. Mr C Gay.
T: 01229 773 820 & 07896 520 351;
E: colinathodbarrow@btinternet.com

IRT/MITE/ESK ESTUARIES. Mr P Jones.
T: via WeBS Office; E: via WeBS Office

MORECAMBE BAY (NORTH).
Vacant - contact WeBS Office.

SOLWAY ESTUARY (INNER SOUTH).
Mr D Blackledge. T: via WeBS Office;
E: daveblackledge@rspb.org.uk

SOLWAY ESTUARY (NORTH). See Dumfries & Galloway.

SOLWAY ESTUARY (OUTER SOUTH).
Mr D Shackleton - see above.

Wildlife Trust
CUMBRIA WILDLIFE TRUST. (1962; 15,000).
Plumgarths, Crook Road, Kendal, LA8 8LX.
T: 01539 816 300, (fax) 01539 816 301;
E: mail@cumbriawildlifetrust.org.uk;
W: www.cumbriawildlifetrust.org.uk

ENGLAND

DERBYSHIRE

BirdAtlas/Avifauna
The Birds of Derbyshire. RA Frost & Steve Shaw (Liverpool University Press, 2014).

Bird Recorder
Joint Recorder. Roy Frost, 66 St Lawrence Road, North Wingfield, Chesterfield, S42 5LL;
T: 01246 850 037; E: frostra66@btinternet.com

Joint Recorder. Syd Garton. Address: n/a.
T: n/a; E: tonygarton13@sky.com

Recorder (Rarities). Rodney Key, 3 Farningham Close, Spondon, Derby DE21 7DZ.
T: 01332 678 571; E: r_key@sky.com

Bird Report
CARSINGTON BIRD CLUB ANNUAL REPORT (1992-), from Paul Hickling (Sec), 12 Beaurepaire Crescent, Belper, DE5 1HR.

DERBYSHIRE BIRD REPORT (1955-), from Bryan Barnacle, Mays, Malthouse Lane, Froggatt, Hope Valley, S32 3ZA. E: barney@mays1.demon.co.uk

OGSTON BIRD CLUB REPORT (1970-), records now published online. W: www.ogstonbirdclub.co.uk

BTO Regional Representative
NORTH DERBYSHIRE. Dave Budworth.
T: 01283 215 188; E: dbud01@aol.com

SOUTH DERBYSHIRE. Dave Budworth - see above.

Club
BAKEWELL BIRD STUDY GROUP. (1987; 70).
Cheryl Starr (Sec). Address: n/a.
T: 01298 79997; E: cheryl.starr@sky.com;
W: www.bakewellbirdstudygroup.org.uk
Meetings: 7.30pm, 2nd Monday of the month (Sep-May). Friends Meeting House, Chapel Lane, Bakewell, DE45 1EL.

BUXTON FIELD CLUB. (1946; 50).
Rosemary Furness. Address: n/a. T: n/a;
E: rosemary.furness@virgin.net; W: n/a
Meetings: 7.30pm, usually fortnightly on a Saturday (Oct-Mar). Buxton Methodist Church, Chapel Street, Buxton, SK17 6HX.

CARSINGTON BIRD CLUB. (1992; 250).
Paul Hicking (Sec), 12 Beaurepaire Crescent, Belper, DE5 1HR. T: 01773 827 727;
E: paulandsteph@hicking.plus.com;
W: www.carsingtonbirdclub.co.uk
Meetings: 7.30pm, 3rd Tuesday of the month (Sep-Mar). The Henmore Room, Carsington Water, Big Lane, Ashbourne, DE6 1ST.

DERBYSHIRE ORNITHOLOGICAL SOCIETY. (1954; 550).
Steve Shaw (Sec), 84 Moorland View Road, Walton, Chesterfield, S40 3DF. T: 01246 236 090;
E: steveshaw84mvr@btinternet.com;
W: www.derbyshireos.org.uk
Meetings: 7.30pm, usually last Friday of the month (Sep-Mar), various venues - contact/see website for details.

Derbyshire Ornithological Society

OGSTON BIRD CLUB. (1969; 125).
John Parlby (Chairman), 102 Sough Road, South Normanton, Alfreton, DE55 2LE. T: 01773 861 262 & 07767 652 036; E: johnparlby1@gmail.com;
W: www.ogstonbirdclub.co.uk
Meetings: Currently only an AGM is held - contact/see website for details.

Ringing Group/Bird Observatory
SORBY-BRECK RG. See Yorkshire.

SOUDER RG. Mr D Budworth. T: 01283 215 188;
E: dbud01@aol.com

RSPB Local Group
CHESTERFIELD. (1987; 275).
Stephen Williams. T: 01246 206 700;
E: stephen150williams@btinternet.com;
W: www.rspb.org.uk/groups/chesterfield
Meetings: 7.15pm, (usually) 3rd Monday of the month. Eastwood Hall, Rose Hill, Chesterfield, S40 1LW.

DERBY. (1974; 270).
Max Maughan. T: 01332 511 825;
E: RSPBlocalgroupderby@gmail.com;
W: www.rspb.org.uk/groups/derby
Meetings: 7.30pm, 2nd Wednesday of the month (Sep-Apr). The Grange Banqueting Suite, 457 Burton Rd, Littleover, Derby, DE23 6XX.

Wetland Bird Survey (WeBS) Organiser
DERBYSHIRE. Vacant - contact WeBS Office.

Wildlife Trust
DERBYSHIRE WILDLIFE TRUST. (1962; 14,000).
Sandy Hill, Main Street, Middleton, Matlock, DE4 4LR.
T: 01773 881 188, (fax) 01773 821 826;
E: enquiries@derbyshirewt.co.uk;
W: www.derbyshirewildlifetrust.org.uk

DEVON

BirdAtlas/Avifauna
Devon Bird Atlas 2007-2013. Stella D Beavan & Mike Lock (Devon Birdwatching & Preservation Society, 2016).

The Birds of Devon. Michael Tyler (Devon Birdwatching & Preservation Society, 2010).

The Birds of Lundy. Tim Davis & Tim Jones (Harpers Mill Publishing, 2007).

Bird Recorder
Kevin Rylands. Address: n/a.
T: n/a; E: recorder@devonbirds.org

Bird Report
DEVON BIRDS (1929-), from Mike Daniels (Sec), Devon Birds, 16 Erme Drive, Ivybridge, PL21 9BN.
T: 01752 690 278; E: info@devonbirds.org

LUNDY FIELD SOCIETY ANNUAL REPORT (1947-) from Michael Williams, LFS Hon. Sec, 5 School Place, Oxford, OX1 4RG. E: secretary@lundy.org.uk

BTO Regional Representative
Stella Beavan. T: 07710 879 277;
E: stellabeavan@outlook.com

Club
DEVON BIRDS. (1928; 1200).
Mike Daniels (Sec, Devon Birds), 16 Erme Drive, Ivybridge, PL21 9BN. T: 01752 690 278;
E: secretary@devonbirds.org; W: www.devonbirds.org

Branches
East Devon: Geoffrey Green. T: 01404 813 127;
E: gdgreen@talktalk.net

Mid Devon: Annabelle Strickland. T: 01392 439 685 & 07557 736 456; E: jfajstrickland@outlook.com

Plymouth: Liz Harris. T: 01752 789 594;
E: elizmharris@yahoo.com
Meetings: 7.30pm, Spugeon Hall, Mutley Baptist Church, Mutley Plain, Plymouth, PL4 6LB for programme see W: www.devonbirds.co.uk

South Devon: Mike Goss. T: 01364 72539.
E: mrgandjng@tiscali.co.uk
Meetings: 7.30pm, 3rd Monday of the month (Jan-Nov). Court Farm Inn, Abbotskerswell, TQ12 5PG

Taw & Torridge: John Towers. T: 01598 710 273.
E: johndtowers@googlemail.com
Meetings: 7.30pm, 2nd Tuesday of the month (Sep-Apr). The Castle Centre, 25 Castle Street, Barnstaple, EX31 1DR.

KINGSBRIDGE & DISTRICT NATURAL HISTORY SOCIETY. (1989; 80). Chris Klee (Chairman), The Old School House, 2 Ebrington Street, Kingsbridge, TQ7 1DF.
T: 01548 288 397; E: jcklee@pobroadband.co.uk;
W: www.knhs.org.uk
Meeting: 7.30pm, 4th Monday of the month (Sep-Apr). West Charleton Village Hall, West Charleton, Kingsbridge, TQ7 2AJ.

LUNDY FIELD SOCIETY. (1946; 500).
Michael Williams (Sec), 5 School Pl, Oxford, OX1 4RG.
T: n/a; E: secretary@lundy.org.uk;
W: www.lundy.org.uk
Meeting: AGM, 2nd Saturday of Mar in Crediton.

TOPSHAM BIRDWATCHING & NATURALISTS' SOCIETY. (1969; 115). Keith Chester (Membership Sec).
Address: n/a. T: 01392 877 817;
E: topshambns@gmail.com;
W: http://topshambns.blogspot.co.uk/
Meetings: 7.30pm, 2nd Friday of the month (Sep-Apr). Matthews Hall, Fore Street, Topsham, Exeter, EX3 0HF.

Ringing Group/Bird Observatory
AXE ESTUARY RG. Mr I Stanbridge.
T: n/a; E: stan@thestanbridges.com;
W: http://axeestuaryringinggroup.blogspot.co.uk

DEVON & CORNWALL WADER GROUP. Mr R Swinfen.
T: n/a; E: roger@swinfen5.freeserve.co.uk

LUNDY FIELD SOCIETY. Mr Tony Taylor.
T: 01258 857336; E: ammataylor@yahoo.co.uk

SLAPTON BIRD OBSERVATORY RG.
Mr K Grant. T: n/a;
E: k.grant198@btinternet.com

RSPB Local Group
EXETER & DISTRICT. (1974; 400).
Roger Tucker. T: 01392 860 518;
E: r.345tucker@btinternet.com;
W: www.rspb.org.uk/groups/exeter
Meetings: 7.30 pm, 1st or 2nd Tuesday of the month, (Sep-Apr). Southernhay United Reformed Church Rooms, Dix's Field, Exeter, EX1 1QA

PLYMOUTH. (1974; 200).
Vince Bedford. T: 01752 785 240;
E: vincebedford@live.co.uk; W: n/a
Meetings: (Sep-Mar). Trinity United Reform Church, Tor Lane, Plymouth PL3 5NY.

TORBAY & SOUTH DEVON TEAM. (n/a; n/a).
John Allan. T: 01626 821 344;
E: johnmartinallan@icloud.com
W: www.rspb.org.uk/groups/torbayandsouthdevon
Meetings: Held at various locations in the area - contact/see website for details.

Wetland Bird Survey (WeBS) Organiser
DEVON (OTHER SITES). Mr PJ Reay.
T: 01364 73293; E: peter.p.j.reay@btinternet.com

EXE ESTUARY. Ms P Avant. T: 01647 252 333 & 07792 614 680; E: penavant@yahoo.co.uk

TAMAR COMPLEX. See Cornwall

TAW/TORRIDGE. Mr T Davis. T: via WeBS Office;
E: via WeBS Office

ENGLAND

Wildlife Trust
DEVON WILDLIFE TRUST. (1962; 31,000).
Cricklepit Mill, Commercial Road, Exeter, EX2 4AB.
T: 01392 279 244, (fax) 01392 433 221;
E: contactus@devonwildlifetrust.org;
W: www.devonwildlifetrust.org

DORSET

Bird Atlas/Avifauna
The Birds of Dorset. George Green (Christopher Helm, 2004)

Bird Recorder
Marcus Lawson. Address: n/a.
T: 01202 244 805;
E: recorder@dorsetbirds.org.uk

Bird Report
DORSET BIRDS (1977-), from
Neil Gartshore,
Moor Edge, 2 Bere Road,
Wareham, BH20 4DD.
T: 01929 552 560;
E: enquiries@callunabooks.co.uk

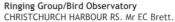
Dorset Bird Report 2015

PORTLAND BIRD OBSERVATORY REPORT (1963-),
from Martin Cade, The Old Lower Light,
Portland Bill, DT5 2JT. T: 01305 820 553;
E: obs@btinternet.com

THE BIRDS OF CHRISTCHURCH HARBOUR (1956-),
from Ian Southworth, 1 Bodowen Road, Burton,
Christchurch, BH23 7JL. E: ianbirder@aol.com

BTO Regional Representative
Claire Young. T: 07740 457992;
E: dorsetbto@gmail.com

Club
CHRISTCHURCH HARBOUR ORNITHOLOGICAL GROUP.
(1956; 300). Dave Taylor (Gen Sec), Dairy Cottage,
Sopley, Hampshire BH23 7AZ. T: 01425 672318;
E: david.dhtaylor@gmail.com; W: www.chog.org.uk
Meetings: 7.30pm, (usually) 2nd Wednesday of
the month (Oct-Mar). St Nicholas Church Hall, The
Broadway, Hengistbury Head, Christchurch, BH6 4EP.

DORSET BIRD CLUB. (1987; 450).
Mrs Diana Dyer (Membership Sec),
The Cedars, 3 Osmay Road, Swanage, BH19 2JQ.
T: 01929 421 402; E: membership@dorsetbirds.org.uk;
W: www.dorsetbirds.org.uk
Meetings: Irregular indoor meetings/AGM in Mar.

DORSET NATURAL HISTORY & ARCHAEOLOGICAL
SOCIETY. (1845; 2000). Catherine Frost
(Membership Sec), Dorset County Museum, High
West Street, Dorchester, DT1 1XA. T: 01305 262 735;
E: membership@dorsetcountymuseum.org;
W: www.dorsetcountymuseum.org

Ringing Group/Bird Observatory
CHRISTCHURCH HARBOUR RS. Mr EC Brett.
T: n/a; E: ed_brett@lineone.net

PORTLAND BIRD OBSERVATORY.
Martin Cade (Warden), The Old Lower Light,
Portland, DT5 2JT. T: 01305 820 553;
E: obs@btinternet.com;
W: www.portlandbirdobs.blogspot.co.uk

RADIPOLE RG. Mr TJ Coombs. T: 07976 710 866;
E: franchecomte11@gmail.com

STOUR RG. Mr R Gifford. T: n/a;
E: robertgifford56@gmail.com

RSPB Local Group
SOUTH DORSET. (1976; 420).
Mary Robins. T: 01305 773 502;
E: Tomlinson_nick@yahoo.com;
W: www.rspb.org.uk/groups/southdorset
Meetings: 7.30pm, 3rd Thursday of each month
(Sep-Apr). St. Georges Church Hall, Fordington,
Dorchester, DT1 1LB.

Wetland Bird Survey (WeBS) Organiser
DORSET (excl. ESTUARIES). Mr M Balmer.
T: via WeBS Office;
E: malcolm.balmer@btinternet.com

POOLE HARBOUR. Mr P Morton.
T: via WeBS Office; E: paulolua@yahoo.co.uk

RADIPOLE & LODMOOR. Mr T Branston.
T: via WeBS Office; E: toby.branston@rspb.org.uk

THE FLEET & PORTLAND HARBOUR. Mr S Groves.
T: 01305 871 562 & 07543 194 894;
E: cygnusolor@yahoo.co.uk

Wildlife Trust
DORSET WILDLIFE TRUST. (1961; 25,000).
Brooklands Farm, Forston, Dorchester, DT2 7AA.
T: 01305 264 620, (fax) 01305 251 120;
E: enquiries@dorsetwildlifetrust.org.uk;
W: www.dorsetwildlifetrust.org.uk

DURHAM

Bird Atlas/Avifauna
The Birds of Durham.
Keith Bowey & Mark Newsome
(Durham Bird Club, 2012).

Birds of Cleveland.
Martin Blick (Tees Valley
Wildlife Trust, 2009).

*The Breeding Birds of
Cleveland: A Tetrad Atlas
1999-2006.* Graeme Joynt,
James Fairbrother & Ted Parker
(Teesmouth Bird Club, 2008).

Birds of Cleveland

ENGLAND

A Summer Atlas of Breeding Birds of County Durham. Stephen Westerberg & Keith Bowey (Durham Bird Club, 2000).

Bird Recorder
CLEVELAND. Tom Francis. Address: n/a. T: n/a; E: mot.francis@ntlworld.com

DURHAM. Recorder. Andrew Kinghorn. Address: n/a; T: n/a; E: dbc.records@hotmail.co.uk

Assistant Recorder (Rarities). Chris Bell, 50 Windermere Court, Darlington, DL1 4YW. T: 01325 358 545; E: bellchris76@gmail.com

Bird Report
CLEVELAND BIRD REPORT (1974-), from John Fletcher, 43 Glaisdale Avenue, Tollesby, Middlesbrough, TS5 7PF. T: 01642 818 825; E: j.fletcher666@btinternet.com

BIRDS IN DURHAM (1970-), from D Sowerbutts, 9 Prebends Fields, Gilesgate Moor, Durham, DH1 1HH. E: david.sowerbutts@dunelm.org.uk

BTO Regional Representative
CLEVELAND. Vic Fairbrother. T: 01287 633 744; E: vic.fairbrother@ntlworld.com

DURHAM. David Sowerbutts. T: 0191 386 7201; E: david.sowerbutts@dunelm.org.uk

Club
DURHAM BIRD CLUB. (1974; 350). Contact: n/a. T: n/a; E: durhambirdclub@gmail.com; W: www.durhambirdclub.org
Meetings: Contact/see website for details.

NORTHUMBERLAND & TYNESIDE BIRD CLUB. NATURAL HISTORY SOCIETY OF NORTHUMBRIA. - See Nothumberland

TEESMOUTH BIRD CLUB. (1960; 425). Chris Sharp (Sec), 6 Maritime Avenue, Hartlepool, TS24 0XF. T: 01429 865 163; E: chrisandlucia@ntlworld.com; W: www.teesmouthbc.com
Meetings: 7.30pm, 1st Monday of the month (Sep-Apr). Stockton Library, Church Road, Stockton, TS18 1TU.

Ringing Group/Bird Observatory
DURHAM DALES RG. Mr J Hawes. T: 01388 746 280; E: jrhawes34@hotmail.com

SOUTH CLEVELAND RG. Mr W Norman. T: 01947 896 665; E: wilfgros@btinternet.com

TEES RG. Mr A Snape. T: n/a; E: allan.snape@talktalk.net

WHITBURN RG. Mr J Brown. T: 07825 767 016; E: john.brown3@networkrail.co.uk

RSPB Local Group
CLEVELAND. (1974; 100). Terry Reeve. T: 01642 512 693; E: ClevelandRSPB02@gmail.com; W: www.rspb.org.uk/groups/cleveland
Meetings: 7.30pm, 2nd Monday of the month (Sep-May). Middlesbrough Rugby Club, Green Lane, Middlesbrough, TS5 7SL.

DARLINGTON. (2005; 40). Clifford Evans. T: 01325 466 471; E: cgevans1@virginmedia.com; W: www.rspb.org/groups/darlington
Meetings: 7.30pm, 2nd Thursday of the month (except Aug). Cockerton Methodist Church, Cockerton Green, Darlington, DL3 9EG.

DURHAM. (1974; 125). Richard Cowen. T: 0191 377 2061; E: richard.cowen313@gmail.com; W: www.rspb.org.uk/groups/durham
Meetings: 7.30pm, 2nd Tuesday of the month (Oct-Apr). Laurel Avenue Children's Centre, The Woodlands, Gilesgate, Durham, DH1 2EY

Wetland Bird Survey (WeBS) Organiser
CLEVELAND (excl. TEES ESTUARY). Mr C Sharp. T: 01429 865 163; E: chrisandlucia@ntlworld.com

DURHAM. Vacant - contact WeBS Office.

TEES ESTUARY. Mr A Jones. T: via WeBS Office; E: via WeBS Office

Wildlife Trust
DURHAM WILDLIFE TRUST. (1971; 8,000). Rainton Meadows, Chilton Moor, Houghton-le-Spring, Tyne & Wear DH4 6PU. T: 0191 584 3112, (fax) 0191 584 3934; E: mail@durhamwt.co.uk; W: www.durhamwt.com

TEES VALLEY WILDLIFE TRUST. (1979; 5,000). Margrove Heritage Centre, Margrove Park, Boosbeck, Saltburn, TS12 3BZ. T: 01287 636 382, (fax) 01287 636 383; E: info@teeswildlife.org; W: www.teeswildlife.org

ESSEX

Bird Atlas/Avifauna
The Birds of Essex. Simon Wood (Christopher Helm, 2007).

Tetrad Atlas of the Breeding Birds of Essex. MK Dennis (Essex Birdwatching Society, 1996).

Bird Recorder
Michael Tracey, Robins, Hayhouse Rd, Earls Colne, Colchester, CO6 2PD. T: 07500 866 335; E: micktrac@aol.com

ENGLAND

Bird Report
ESSEX BIRD REPORT (1949/50-),
from Peter Dwyer, EBWS, 48 Churchill Avenue,
Halstead, CO9 2BE. T: 01787 476 524;
E: petedwyer@petedwyer.plus.com

BTO Regional Representative
NORTH-EAST. Rod Bleach. T: n/a;
E: rod.bleach@sesl.eu

NORTH-WEST. Graham Smith. T: 01277 354 034;
E: silaum.silaus@tiscali.co.uk

SOUTH. Vacant - contact Dawn Balmer, BTO
T: 01842 750 050

Club
ESSEX BIRDWATCHING SOCIETY. (1949; 525).
Lesley Collins (Sec), 37 Springham Drive,
Colchester, CO4 5FN. T: 07515 338 999;
E: essexbirdwatchingsociety@gmail.com;
W: www.ebws.org.uk
Meetings: 8pm, 1st Friday
of the month (Sep-Apr).
Quaker Meeting House,
82 Rainsford Road,
Chelmsford, CM1 2QL.

The ESSEX BIRDWATCHING SOCIETY

Ringing Group/
Bird Observatory
BRADWELL BIRD OBSERVATORY RG.
Mr C Harris. T: 01621 772 336;
E: christopher.phillip.harris@gmail.com

NORTH THAMES GULL GROUP. Mr P Roper.
T: n/a; E: ntgg_sightings@hotmail.com;
W: www.ntgg.org.uk

RSPB Local Group
CHELMSFORD & CENTRAL ESSEX. (1976; 1200).
Sue McClellan. T: 01245 471 576;
E: suem@idnet.com;
W: www.rspb.org.uk/groups/chelmsford
Meetings: 8pm, normally 2nd Thursday of the month
(Sep-Apr). Writtle University College, Northumberland
Theatre, Lordship Road, Writtle, CM1 3RP.

COLCHESTER. (1981; 220).
Ron Firmin. T: 07714 210 746;
E: ron.firmin@btinternet.com;
W: www.rspb.org.uk/groups/colchester
Meetings: 7.45pm, 2nd Thursday of the month
(Sep-Apr). Shrub End Social Centre, Shrub End
Road, Colchester, CO3 4SA.

SOUTH EAST ESSEX. (1983; 200).
Graham Mee. T: 01702 525 152;
E: grahamm@southendrspb.co.uk;
W: www.southendrspb.co.uk
Meetings: 8.00pm, 1st Wednesday of the month
(Sep-May). The EWT Belfairs Woodland Centre,
Eastwood Road North, Leigh-on-Sea, SS9 4LR.

Wetland Bird Survey (WeBS) Organiser
CROUCH/ROACH ESTUARY and SOUTH DENGIE.
Mr S Spicer. T: via WeBS Office;
E: stephenspicer4@gmail.com

ESSEX (OTHER SITES). Vacant - contact WeBS Office.

HAMFORD WATER. Mr J Novorol.
T: 01255 880 552; E: via WeBS Office

LEE VALLEY. See Hertfordshire.

NORTH BLACKWATER. Mr J Thorogood.
T: 01206 768 771; E: via WeBS Office

SOUTH BLACKWATER AND NORTH DENGIE.
Mr AG Harbott. T: 01992 575 213;
E: anthonyharbott@gmail.com

STOUR ESTUARY. Mr R Vonk. T: 01206 391 153 &
07711 129 149; E: rick.vonk@rspb.org.uk

SWALE, MEDWAY & NORTH KENT MARSHES.
See Kent.

THAMES ESTUARY (FOULNESS). Dr CPM Lewis.
T: via WeBS Office. E: cpm.lewis@gmail.com

Wildlife Trust
ESSEX WILDLIFE TRUST. (1959; 34,000).
Abbots Hall Farm, Maldon Road, Great Wigborough,
Colchester, CO5 7RZ.
T: 01621 862 960, (fax) 01621 862 990;
E: admin@essexwt.org.uk;
W: www.essexwt.org.uk

GLOUCESTERSHIRE

Bird Atlas/Avifauna
The Birds of Gloucestershire.
Gordon Kirk & John Phillips
(Liverpool University Press,
2013).

*Birds of The Cotswolds:
A New Breeding Atlas.*
Iain Main, Dave Pearce &
Tim Hutton (Liverpool
University Press 2009).

Bird Recorder
Richard Baatsen. Address: n/a. T: 07879 850 196;
E: Richard.Baatsen@gmail.com
(excl. S.Gloucs = Avon)

Bird Report
GLOUCESTERSHIRE BIRD REPORT (1948-),from
Andrew Bluett, 50 KIngsmead, Abbymead,
Gloucester, GL4 5DY.
E: gnsmembership@btinternet.com

BTO Regional Representative
Gordon Kirk. 01452 741 724; E: GordonKirk@aol.com

ENGLAND

Club
CHELTENHAM BIRD CLUB. (1976; 100).
Membership Sec. Address: n/a. T: 01242 690 660;
E: via website; W: www.cheltenhambirdclub.org.uk
Meetings: 7.15pm, most Mondays (Oct-Mar),
Bournside School, Warden Hill Road, Cheltenham,
GL51 3EF.

DURSLEY BIRDWATCHING
& PRESERVATION SOCIETY. (1953; 240).
Brenda Usher (Sec). Address: n/a.
T: 01452 721 863; E: dbwps@yahoo.com;
W: www.dursleybirdwatchers.btik.com
Meetings: 7.45pm, 2nd and last Mondays of the
month (Sep-Apr). Dursley Community Centre,
Rednock Drive, Dursley, GL11 4BX.

GLOUCESTERSHIRE NATURALISTS' SOCIETY.
(1948; 500). Andrew Bluett (Membership Sec),
50 KIngsmead, Abbymead, Gloucester, GL4 5DY.
T: 01452 610 085; E: gnsmembership@btinternet.
com;
W: www.glosnats.org
Meetings: 7.30pm, 2nd Friday of the month (Oct-
Apr). Watermoor Church Hall, Watermoor Road,
Cirencester, GL7 1JR.

NORTH COTSWOLD
ORNITHOLOGICAL SOCIETY. (1983; 75).
E: info@ncosbirds.org.uk; W: www.ncosbirds.org.uk
Meetings: AGM in April. This is a small surveying
and recording group based in Cheltenham and the
Cotswolds.

Ringing Group/Bird Observatory
COTSWOLD WATER PARK RG. Mr J Wells.
T: 01452 523 393; E: john.wells2@btinternet.com

SEVERN ESTUARY GULL GROUP. Mr M Durham.
T: 01452 741 312. E: mauriceedurham@gmail.com

WILDFOWL & WETLANDS TRUST. Mr K Brides.
T: n/a; E: kane.brides@wwt.org.uk

RSPB Local Group
GLOUCESTERSHIRE. (1972; 400).
David Cramp. T: 01242 620 281;
E: djcramp@btinternet.com;
W: www.rspb.org.uk/groups/gloucestershire
Meetings: 7.30pm, 3rd Tuesday of the month
(Sep-Nov, Jan-Mar). The Gala Club, Fairmile
Gardens, Longford, Gloucester, GL2 9EB.

Wetland Bird Survey (WeBS) Organiser
GLOUCESTERSHIRE (inc. SEVERN ESTUARY,
excl. COTSWOLD WATER PARK).
Mr M Smart. T: 01452 421 131 & 07816 140 513;
E: smartmike143@gmail.com

COTSWOLD WATER PARK. Mr GO Harris.
T: 07868 427 916; E: gharris_doh@hotmail.com

Wildlife Trust
GLOUCESTERSHIRE WILDLIFE TRUST. (1961; 27,000).
Conservation Centre, Robinswood Hill Country Park,
Reservoir Road, Gloucester, GL4 6SX.
T: 01452 383 333, (fax) 01452 383 334;
E: info@gloucestershirewildlifetrust.co.uk;
W: www.gloucestershirewildlifetrust.co.uk

HAMPSHIRE

Bird Atlas/Avifauna
Hampshire Bird Atlas 2007-2012. John Eyre (Ed).
(HOS, 2015).

Birds of Hampshire. JM Clark & JA Eyre
(Hampshire Ornithological Society, 1993).

Bird Recorder
Keith Betton, 8 Dukes Close, Folly Hill, Farnham,
Surrey GU9 0DR. T: 01252 724 068;
E: keithbetton@hotmail.com

Bird Report
HAMPSHIRE BIRD REPORT (1978-), from Bryan &
Sandy Coates, 8 Gardner Way, Chandler's Ford,
SO53 1JL. E: sandyandbryan@tiscali.co.uk

BTO Regional Representative
Glynne Evans. T: 01264 860 697;
E: hantsbto@hotmail.com

Brian Sharkey (Assistant Representative).
T: 01189 814 751; E: briansharkeyuk@yahoo.co.uk

John Shillitoe (Assistant Representative).
T: 01329 833 086; E: jshillitoe.googlemail.com

Club
HAMPSHIRE ORNITHOLOGICAL SOCIETY.
(1979; 1,500).

John Shillitoe (Sec), Westerly,
Hundred Acres Road, Wickham,
PO17 6HY. T: 01329 833 086;
E: jshillitoe@googlemail.com;
W: www.hos.org.uk
Meetings: Open Day/AGM at
the end of March.
John Stripe Theatre, University
of Winchester, Sparkford Road,
Winchester, SO22 4NR.

Ringing Group/Bird Observatory
FARLINGTON RG. Mr DA Bell. T: 07900 366 024;
E: duncan.bell5@ntlworld.com

ITCHEN RG. Mr W Simcox. T: n/a;
E: wilfsimcox@gmx.com

TITCHFIELD HAVEN RG. Mr BS Duffin.
T: n/a; E: b_duffin@hotmail.com

ENGLAND

RSPB Local Group

BASINGSTOKE. (1979; 60).
Peter Hutchins. T: 01256 770 831 & 07895 388 378; E: RSPBbasingstoke@gmail.com;
W: www.rspb.org.uk/groups/basingstoke
Meetings: 7.45pm, 3rd Wednesday of the month (Sep-May). The Barn, St Michael's Cottage, Church Cottage, St Michael's Church, Church Square, Basingstoke, RG21 7QW.

NEW FOREST. (2000; 175).
Tony Bates. T: 023 8084 7046;
E: enquiries@nfRSPB.org.uk;
W: www.rspb.org.uk/groups/newforest
W: www.nfrspb.org
Meetings: 7.30pm, 2nd Wednesday of the month (Sep-Jun). Lyndhurst Community Centre, High Street, Lyndhurst, SO43 7NY.

NORTH EAST HANTS. (1976; 175).
Marion Smith. T: 01252 724 093;
E: via contact page on website;
W: www.northeasthantsrspb.org.uk
Meetings: 7.30pm, in halls in Church Crookham and Fleet (Sep-Apr) - contact/see website for details.

PORTSMOUTH. (1974; 210).
Gordon Humby. T: 02392 353 949;
E: PortsmouthRSPB@gmail.com;
W: www.rspb.org.uk/groups/portsmouth
Meetings: 7.30pm, 4th Saturday of the month (Jan-Nov). St Andrews Church Hall, Havant Road, Farlington, Portsmouth, PO6 1AA.

WINCHESTER (1974; 90).
Pam Symes. T: 01962 851 821;
E: psymes033@gmail.com;
W: www.rspb.org.uk/groups/winchester
Meetings: 7.45pm, 1st Wednesday of the month (not Jan or Aug). Shawford Parish Hall, Pearson Lane, Shawford, Winchester, SO21 2AA.

Wetland Bird Survey (WeBS) Organiser

AVON VALLEY. Mr JM Clark. T: via WeBS Office;
E: johnclark50@sky.com

HAMPSHIRE (ESTUARIES/COASTAL).
Mr JRD Shillitoe. T: via WeBS Office;
E: jshillitoe.googlemail.com

HAMPSHIRE (INLAND - excl. AVON VALLEY).
Mr K Wills. T: via WeBS Office;
E: kwills57@btinternet.com

Wildlife Trust

HAMPSHIRE & ISLE OF WIGHT WILDLIFE TRUST. (1960; 27,000).
Beechcroft, Vicarage Lane, Curdridge, SO32 2DP.
T: 01489 774 400, (fax) 01489 774 401;
E: feedback@hiwwt.org.uk; W: www.hiwwt.org.uk

Bird Atlas/Avifauna

The Birds of Herefordshire 2007-2012: An Atlas of Their Breeding and Wintering Distributions.
Mervyn Davies, Peter Eldridge, Chris Robinson, Nich Smith & Gerald Wells (Liverpool University Press, 2014).

Bird Recorder

Mick Colquhoun, Old Gore House, Old Gore, Ross on Wye, HR9 7QT. T: 07587 151 627;
E: mickcolquhoun@gmail.com

Bird Report

THE BIRDS OF HEREFORDSHIRE (1951-), from Jim Wilkinson, Coughton Forge, Coughton, Ross-on-Wye, HR9 5SF. T: 01989 763 182;
E: m.jim.wilkinson@gmail.com

BTO Regional Representative

Chris Robinson. T: 01981 510 360;
E: herefordbtorep@btinternet.com

Club

HEREFORDSHIRE ORNITHOLOGICAL CLUB. (1950; 400+). Una Morgan (Sec), 5 Abercrombie Close, Ledbury, HR8 2UR. T: 01531 631 347;
E: unarmorgan@gmail.com;
W: www.herefordshirebirds.org
Meetings: 7.30pm, 2nd Thursday of the month (Sep-Mar), Holmer Parish Centre, Holmer, Hereford, HR4 9RG.

Ringing Group/Bird Observatory

LLANCILLO RG. Dr G Geen. T: 07919 880 281;
E: grahamgeen@btinternet.com

Wetland Bird Survey (WeBS) Organiser

HEREFORDSHIRE. Mr CM Robinson.
T: 01981 510 360 & 07717 831 577;
E: herefordbtorep@btinternet.com

Wildlife Trust

HEREFORDSHIRE NATURE TRUST. (1962; 3,000).
Lower House Farm, Ledbury Road, Tupsley, Hereford, HR1 1UT.
T: 01432 356 872, (fax) 01432 275 489;
E: enquiries@herefordshirewt.co.uk;
W: www.herefordshirewt.org

Bird Atlas/Avifauna

Birds of Hertfordshire. Ken W Smith, Chris W Dee, Jack D Fearnside & Mike Ilett (Herts NHS, 2015).

Bird Recorder

Alan Gardiner, 199 Watford Rd, St Albans AL2 3HH.
T: 01727 863 945; E: birdrecorder@hnhs.org

Bird Report
HERTFORDSHIRE BIRD REPORT (1980-), from David Utting (Sec), 250 Sandridge Road, St Albans, AL1 4AL. T: 01727 762 855; E: secretary@hnhs.org

BTO Regional Representative
Martin Ketcher. T: n/a; E: martinketcher@gmail.com

Club
HERTFORDSHIRE BIRD CLUB. (1971) part of HERTFORDSHIRE NATURAL HISTORY SOCIETY. (1875; 420) Chris Beach (Sec). Address: n/a. T: n/a; E: birdclubsecretary@hnhs.org; W: www.hnhs.org/birds
Meetings: Annual Herts Bird Conference - contact/see website for details.

Ringing Group/Bird Observatory
MAPLE CROSS RG. Mr R Cripps. T: n/a; E: bob.cripps@btinternet.com

RUNNYMEDE RG. See Berkshire.

RYE MEADS RG. Mrs J Swan. T: n/a; E: pigletswan@hotmail.com; W: www.rmrg.org.uk

TRING RG. Mrs L Lambert. T: n/a; E: lynne.lambert728@gmail.com; W: www.tringringinggroup.org.uk https://tringringinggroup.blogspot.co.uk/

RSPB Local Group
CHORLEYWOOD & DISTRICT. (1976; 120). Carol Smith. T: 01923 897 885; E: carolsmithuk@hotmail.com; W: www.rspb.org.uk/groups/chorleywood
Meetings: 8.00pm, 3rd Thursday of the month (Sep-May). The Russell School, Brushwood Drive, Chorleywood, Rickmansworth, WD3 5RR.
HARPENDEN. (1974; 100).
Geoff Horn. T: 01582 765 443; E: geoffrhorn@yahoo.co.uk; W: www.rspb.org.uk/groups/harpenden
Meetings: 8.00pm, 2nd Thursday of the month (Sep-Apr). All Saint's Church Hall, Station Road, Harpenden, AL5 4UU.

HEMEL HEMPSTEAD. (1972; 100).
Ian Wilson. T: 01442 265 022; E: ian.aeronautics@gmail.com; W: www.rspb.org.uk/groups/hemelhempstead
Meetings: 8.00pm, 1st Monday of the month (Sep-Jun). The Cavendish School, Warners End Road, Hemel Hempstead, HP1 3DW.

HITCHIN & LETCHWORTH. (1972; 95).
Martin Johnson. T: 01763 249 459; E: martinrjspc@hotmail.com; W: www.rspb.org.uk/groups/hitchinandletchworth
Meetings: 7.30pm, 1st Friday of the month (Sep-May). Letchworth Settlement, 229 Nevells Rd, Letchworth, SG6 4UB.

POTTERS BAR & BARNETS. (1977; 1400/area). Ian Sharp. T: 01707 662 914; E: ianrsharp@hotmail.com; W: www.rspb.org.uk/groups/pottersbarandbarnet
Meetings: 2.00pm, one Wednesday of the month (most months). St Johns URC Hall, Mowbray Rd, Barnet, EN5 1RH & 7.45pm, one Friday of the month (most months), Tilbury Hall, United Reform Church, Darkes Lane, Potters Bar, EN6 1BZ - contact/see website for details.

SOUTH EAST HERTFORDSHIRE. (1971; 2,400/area). Ron Hodgson. T: 01279 793 790; E: helenandron@greenbee.net; W: www.rspb.org.uk/groups/southeasthertfordshire
Meetings: 8.00pm, last Tuesday of the month (Sep-Jun). United Reformed Church, Mill Lane, Broxbourne, EN10 7BQ.

ST ALBANS. (1979; 240).
Colin Rose, T: 01727 767 282; E: colin.rose20@ntlworld.com; W: www.rspb.org.uk/groups/stalbans
Meetings: Occasional indoor meetings held, mainly run outdoor meetings - contact/see website for details.

STEVENAGE. (1982; 1300/area).
Ann Collis. T: 01438 861 547; E: p.collis672@btinternet.com; W: www.rspb.org.uk/groups/stevenage
Meetings: 7.30pm, 3rd Tuesday of the month (Sep-May). Friends Meeting House, Cutty's Lane, Stevenage, SG1 1UP.

STORT VALLEY. (2009; 40).
Simon Hurwitz. T: 01799 500 996; E: simon.hurwitz@ntlworld.com; W: www.rspb.org.uk/groups/stortvalley
Meetings: 7.30pm, 2nd Tuesday of the month (Sep-Jun). Bishops Park Community Centre, 2 Lancaster Way, Bishop's Stortford, SM23 4DA.

WATFORD. (1974; 590).
Janet Reynolds. T: 01923 249 647; E: janet.reynolds@whht.nhs.uk; W: www.rspb.org.uk/groups/watford
Meetings: 7.30pm, 2nd Wednesday of the month (Sep-Jun). The Stanborough Centre, 609 St Albans Road, Watford, WD25 9JL.

Wetland Bird Survey (WeBS) Organiser
HERTFORDSHIRE (excl. LEE VALLEY).
Mr JH Terry. T: 02089 051 461; E: jimjoypaddy@virginmedia.com

LEE VALLEY (GREATER LONDON/ESSEX/ HERTFORDSHIRE). Miss C Patrick. T: 01992 709 882 & 07717 449 341; E: cpatrick@leevalleypark.org.uk

ENGLAND

Wildlife Trust
HERTFORDSHIRE & MIDDLESEX WILDLIFE TRUST.
(1964; 21,000).
Grebe House, St Michael's Street, St Albans, Herts,
AL3 4SN. T: 01727 858 901, (fax) 01727 854 542;
E: info@hmwt.org; W: www.hertswildlifetrust.org.uk

ISLE OF MAN

Bird Atlas/Avifauna
*Manx Bird Atlas: An Atlas of Breeding and
Wintering Birds on the Isle of Man.*
Chris Sharpe (Liverpool University Press, 2007).

Bird Recorder
Allen Moore, Lyndale', Derby Road, Peel, IOM IM5
1HH. T: n/a; E: allen.gobbag@manx.net

Bird Report
CALF OF MAN BIRD OBSERVATORY, from Alison Crellin,
Manx National Museum, Kingswood Grove, Douglas,
IM1 3LY. T: 01624 648 033; E: alison.crellin@gov.im

MANX BIRD REPORT (1972-), from S Moore,
'Lyndale', Derby Road, Peel, IOM IM5 1HH.
E: allen.gobbag@manx.net

BTO Regional Representative
Pat Cullen. T: 01624 623 308; E: bridgeen@mcb.net

Club
MANX BIRDLIFE.
Laxey & Lanan Commissioners Offices, 35 New Road,
Laxey, Isle of Man IM4 7BG. T: 01624 861 130;
E: enquiries@manxbirdlife.im; W: http://manxbirdlife.im

MANX ORNITHOLOGICAL SOCIETY. (1997; 150).
Janet Thompson (Sec), Cott ny Greiney, Beach Road,
Port St Mary, IM9 5NF. T: 01624 835 524;
E: jthompson@manx.net;
W: http://manxbirdlife.im/manx-ornithological-society
Meetings: 7.30pm, 1st Tuesday of the month
(Oct-Mar). Union Mills Methodist Chapel,
Strang Road, Union Mills IM4 4NL.

Ringing Group/Bird Observatory
CALF OF MAN BIRD OBSERVATORY.
c/o Mr J Clague, Kionslieu, Plantation Hill,
Port St Mary, IOM. T: 07624 462 858;
W: http://manxbirdlife.im/info/the-calf-of-man/

MANX RG. Mr K Scott. T: n/a; E: manxrg@gmail.com

Wetland Bird Survey (WeBS) Organiser
ISLE OF MAN. Dr JP Cullen. T: 01624 676 774 (day)
& 01624 623 308 (eve); E: bridgeen@mcb.net

Wildlife Trust
MANX WILDLIFE TRUST. (1973; 1000).
7-8 Market Place, Peel, Isle of Man IM5 1AB.
T: 01624 844 432, (fax) 01624 842 317;
E: enquiries@manxwt.org.uk; W: www.manxwt.org.uk

ISLE OF WIGHT

Bird Recorder
Robin Attrill, 17 Waterhouse Moor, Harlow, Essex
CM18 6BA. T: 01279 423 467;
E: robinpattrill@gmail.com

Bird Report
ISLE OF WIGHT BIRD REPORT (1996-), from Dave
Hunnybun, 40 Church Hill Road, Cowes, IoW
PO31 8HH. E: davehunnybun@hotmail.com

BTO Regional Representative
Jim Baldwin. T: 01983 721 137 & 07528 586 683;
E: wightbto@hotmail.com

Club
ISLE OF WIGHT NATURAL HISTORY &
ARCHAEOLOGICAL SOCIETY.
(1919; 350).
The Secretary, Unit 16, Prospect
Business Centre, Prospect
Business Centre, West Cowes,
IoW PO31 7HD. T: 01983 282 596;
E: iwnhas@iwnhas.org; W: www.iwnhas.org
Meetings: Contact/see website for details.

ISLE OF WIGHT ORNITHOLOGICAL GROUP. (1986; 155).
Dave Hunnybun (Sec), 40 Churchill Road, Cowes,
IoW PO31 8HH. T: 01983 292 880;
E: davehunnybun@hotmail.com;
W: http://iowbirds.awardspace.com/IWOG.htm
Meetings: Only held occasionally - contact/see
website for details.

Ringing Group/Bird Observatory
ISLE OF WIGHT RG. Dr George Rowing. T: n/a;
E: iwringinggroup@gmail.com

Wetland Bird Survey (WeBS) Organiser
ISLE OF WIGHT. Mr JR Baldwin. T: 01983 202 223 (day),
01983 721 137 (eve) & 07528 586 683;
E: wightbto@hotmail.com

Wildlife Trust. See Hampshire.

KENT

Bird Atlas/Avifauna
Kent Breeding Bird Atlas 2008-13. Rob Clements,
Murray Orchard, Norman McCanch & Stephen
Wood (Kent Ornithological Society, 2015).

*The Birds of Kent: A Review of Their Status and
Distribution.* DW Taylor (Meresborough Books,
2nd ed 1984).

Bird Recorder
Barry Wright, 6 Hatton Close, Northfleet,
DA11 8SD. T: 01474 320 918;
E: umbrellabirds66@gmail.com

ENGLAND

Stephen Wood (RBBP Species), 4 Jubilee Cottages, Throwley Forstal, Faversham, ME13 0PJ.
T: 01795 890 485; E: doctorstevewood@gmail.com

Bird Report

DUNGENESS BIRD OBSERVATORY REPORT (1989-), from David Walker, Dungeness BO, 11 RNSSS Cottages, Dungeness, Romney Marsh, TN29 9NA.
T: 01797 321 309; E: dungeness.obs@vfast.co.uk

KENT BIRD REPORT (1952-), from Chris Roome, Rowland House, Station Road, Staplehurst, TN12 0PY. E: chrisgk.roome@btinternet.com

SANDWICH BAY BIRD OBSERVATORY REPORT (1962-), from SBBOT, Guildford Road, Sandwich Bay, Sandwich, CT13 9PF. T: 01304 617 341;
E: sbbotmail@gmail.com

BTO Regional Representative

Geoff Orton. T: 07788 102 238;
E: geofforton@hotmail.com

Club

 KENT ORNITHOLOGICAL SOCIETY. (1952; 650). Stephen Wood (Sec), 4 Jubilee Cottages, Throwley Forstal, Faversham, ME13 0PJ. T: 01795 890 485; E: doctorstevewood@gmail.com; W: www.kentos.org.uk

Meetings: Currently on hold and under review - contact/see website for details.

Ringing Group/Bird Observatory

DARTFORD RG. Mrs M Lockwood.
T: n/a; E: RandMLockwood@aol.com

DUNGENESS BIRD OBSERVATORY.
David Walker (Warden), Dungeness Bird Observatory, 11 RNSSS Cottages, Dungeness, Romney Marsh, TN29 9NA. T: 01797 321 309;
E: dungenessobs@vfast.co.uk;
W: www.dungenessbirdobs.org.uk

EAST KENT WILDLIFE GROUP (birding, ringing, recording, nestboxes). Mr J Pell. T: n/a;
E: EastKent.WildlifeGroup@virginmedia.com;
W: www.ekwg.org

RECULVER RG. Mr C Hindle. T: n/a;
E: christopherhindle@hotmail.com

SANDWICH BAY BIRD OBSERVATORY.
Ian Hodgson (Warden), Sandwich Bay Bird Observatory, Guildford Road, Sandwich, CT13 9PF.
T: 01304 617 341; E: info@sbbo.co.uk;
W: www.sbbot.org.uk

SWALE WADER GROUP. Mr N Tardivel.
T: n/a; E: nicktardivel@yahoo.com;
W: www.swalewaders.co.uk

RSPB Local Group

CANTERBURY. (1973; 170).
Babs Golding. T: 01227 470 151;
E: babs@squirrels.plus.com;
W: www.rspb.org.uk/groups/canterbury
Meetings: 8.00pm, 2nd Tuesday of the month (Sep-Apr). St Stephen's Community Centre, Tenterden Drive, Canterbury, CT2 7BN.

GRAVESEND. (1977; 200).
Paul Yetman. T: 01474 332 417;
E: Groupleader@RSPBgravesend.org.uk;
W: www.rspbgravesend.org.uk
Meetings: 7.30pm, 2nd Thursday of the month (Sep-May). Northfleet School for Girls, Hall Road, Northfleet, Gravesend, DA11 8AQ
& 2.00pm, 4th Tuesday of the month (Sep-Nov, Jan-Mar). Masonic Hall, 25 Wrotham Road, Gravesend, DA11 0PA.

MAIDSTONE. (1973; 250).
James Downer. T: 01622 739 475;
E: maidstoneRSPB@gmail.com;
W: www.rspb.org.uk/groups/maidstone
Meetings: 7.30pm, 3rd Thursday of the month (not Aug). Grove Green Community Hall, Penhurst Close, Grove Green, Bearsted, Maidstone, ME14 5BT.

MEDWAY. (1974; 165).
Wendy Brownrigg. T: 07831 751 256;
E: medwayrspb.leader@outlook.com;
W: www.rspb.org.uk/groups/medway
Meetings: 7.30pm, 3rd Tuesday of the month (not Aug). Parkwood Community Centre, Parkwood Green, Gillingham, ME8 9PN.

SEVENOAKS. (1974; 180).
Anne Chapman. T: 01732 456 459;
E: anneanddave.chapman@outlook.com;
W: www.rspb.org.uk/groups/sevenoaks
Meetings: 7.45pm, 1st Thursday of the month (Sep-May). Otford Memorial Hall, High Street, Otford, Sevenoaks, TN14 5PQ.

THANET. (1975; 120).
Brian Short. T: 07721 452 294;
E: theRSPBthanetlocalgroup@talktalk.net;
W: www.rspb.org.uk/groups/thanet
Meetings: 7.30pm, last Tuesday of the month (Jan-Nov, Dec/see website). St Peter's Church Hall, Portland Centre, Hopeville Avenue, Broadstairs, CT10 2TR.

TONBRIDGE. (1975; no formal membership).
Martin Ellis. T: 01892 521 413;
E: rspb@ellismp.plus.com;
W: www.rspb.org.uk/groups/tonbridge
Meetings: 7.30pm, one Wednesday each month (Sep-Apr). St Philip's Church, Salisbury Road, Tonbridge, TN10 4PA.

ENGLAND

Wetland Bird Survey (WeBS) Organiser
DUNGENESS AREA. Mr D Walker.
T: 01797 321 309; E: dungenessobs@vfast.co.uk

EAST KENT. Vacant - contact WeBS Office.

NORTH KENT ESTUARIES. Mr GR Orton.
T: 07788 102 238; E: geoffortón@hotmail.com

PEGWELL BAY. Mr I Hodgson. T: 01304 617 341;
E: sbbotmail@gmail.com

THAMES ESTUARY (FOULNESS). See Essex.

WEST KENT. Vacant - contact WeBS Office.

Wildlife Trust
KENT WILDLIFE TRUST. (1958; 31,000).
Tyland Barn, Sandling, Maidstone, ME14 3BD.
T: 01622 662 012, (fax) 01622 671 390;
E: info@kentwildlife.org.uk;
W: www.kentwildlifetrust.org.uk

LANCASHIRE & NORTH MERSEYSIDE

Bird Atlas/Avifauna
The Birds of Lancashire and North Merseyside.
Steve White, Barry McCarthy & Maurice Jones
(Hobby Publications, 2008).

Atlas of Breeding Birds of Lancashire and North Merseyside 1997-2000. Robert Pyefinch & Peter Golborn (Hobby Publications, 2001).

Bird Recorder
(Incl. North Merseyside). Steve White, 102 Minster Court, Crown Street, Liverpool, L7 3QD.
T: 0151 707 2744; E: stevewhite102@btinternet.com

Bird Report
BIRDS OF LANCASTER & DISTRICT (1959-), from Peter Cook, 21 Threshfield Avenue, Heysham, Morecambe, LA3 2DU. T: 07880 541 798;
E: peter.cook33@btinternet.com.

BLACKBURN & DISTRICT BIRD CLUB REPORT (1992-), from Jonathan Fry, 20 Rhodes Avenue, Blackburn, BB1 8NP. E: birdrecorder24@gmail.com

CHORLEY AND DISTRICT NATURAL HISTORY SOCIETY ANNUAL REPORT (1975-), published online. W: www.chorleynats.org.uk

EAST LANCASHIRE ORNITHOLOGISTS' CLUB BIRD REPORT (1982-), from Tony Cooper, 28 Peel Park Ave, Clitheroe, BB7 1ET. E: anthony.cooper34@btinternet.com

FYLDE BIRD REPORT (1983-), from Kinta Beaver, 18 Staning Rise, Staining, Blackpool, FY3 0BY.
E: kinta.beaver@btinternet.com

LANCASHIRE BIRD REPORT (1914-), from Dave Bickerton, 64 Petre Crescent, Rishton, Blackburn, BB1 4RB. E: bickertond@aol.com

BTO Regional Representative
EAST. Tony Cooper. T: 01200 424 577;
E: bto.elancs@btinternet.com

MERSEYSIDE. Bob Harris. T: 01948 880 112;
E: harris@liv.ac.uk

NORTH-WEST. Jean Roberts. T: n/a;
E: jeanrbrts6@aol.com

SOUTH. Vacant - contact Dawn Balmer, BTO
T: 01842 750 050

Club
BLACKBURN & DISTRICT BIRD CLUB. (1991; 100).
Anne Wilkinson (Sec). Address: n/a.
T: 01254 812 425;
E: webmaster@blackburnbirdclub.co.uk;
W: www.blackburnbirdclub.co.uk
Meetings: 7.30pm, normally 1st Monday of the month (Oct-Apr). St Silas's Church Hall, Preston New Road, Blackburn, BB2 6PS.

CHORLEY & DISTRICT NATURAL HISTORY SOCIETY.
(1979; 130). Phil Kirk (Sec). Address: n/a.
T: 01257 266 783; E: secretary@chorleynats.org.uk;
W: www.chorleynats.org.uk
Meetings: 7.30pm, 3rd Thursday of the month (Sep-Apr). St Mary's Parish Centre, Devonshire Road, Chorley, PR7 2SR.

EAST LANCASHIRE
ORNITHOLOGISTS' CLUB.
(1955; 45).
David Chew (Sec),
Lower Wheathead Barn,
Wheathead Lane, Blacko,
Nelson, BB9 6PD.
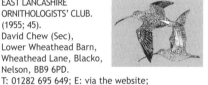
T: 01282 695 649; E: via the website;
W: www.eastlancsornithologists.org.uk
Meetings: 7.30pm, 1st Tuesday of the month (Sep-Jun). St Anne's Church Hall, Wheatley Lane Road, Fence, BB12 9ED.

FYLDE BIRD CLUB. (1982; 180).
Paul Ellis (Sec), 22 Beach Road, Preesall, Poulton le Fylde, FY6 0HQ. T: 01253 811 726 (eves);
E: paul.ellis24@btopenworld.com;
W: www.fyldebirdclub.org
Meetings: 7.45pm, 4th Tuesday of the month (all year). River Wyre Hotel, Breck Road, Poulton le Fylde, FY6 7JZ.

FYLDE NATURALISTS' SOCIETY. (1946; 90).
Julie McGough (Sec). Address: n/a. T: n/a;
E: secretary@fyldenaturalists.co.uk;
W: www.fyldenaturalists.co.uk
Meetings: 7.30pm, 2nd Wednesday of the month (Sep-Mar). Forest Gate Baptist Church Hall, off Whitegate Drive, Blackpool, FY3 9AW (unless otherwise stated in the programme).

ENGLAND

LANCASHIRE & CHESHIRE FAUNA SOCIETY. (1914; 150).
Dave Bickerton (Sec), 64 Petre Crescent, Rishton,
BB1 4RB. T: 01254 886 257;
E: bickertond@aol.com; W: www.lacfs.org.uk
Meetings: No indoor meetings held.

LANCASTER & DISTRICT BIRDWATCHING SOCIETY.
(1959; 200). Peter Cook (Sec), 21 Threshfield Ave,
Heysham, Morecambe, LA3 2DU. T: 01524 851 454
& 07880 541 798; E: peter.cook33@btinternet.com;
W: www.lancasterbirdwatching.org.uk
Meetings: 7.30pm, last Monday of the month (Sep-
Nov/Jan-Mar) - contact/see website for details.

MERSEYSIDE NATURALISTS'
ASSOCIATION. (1938; 140).
Sabena Blackbird (Chairman),
18 Ludlow Grove, Bromborough,
Wirral CH62 7JH. T: n/a.
E: chairman@mnapage.info;
W: www.mnapage.info
Meetings: Contact/see website
for details.

PRESTON BIRD WATCHING & NATURAL HISTORY
SOCIETY. (1876/Preston Scientific Society; 140).
Kayleigh Roebuck (Sec). Address: n/a.
T: 07713 975 321; E: prestonwildlife@gmail.com;
W: www.prestonsociety.co.uk
Meetings: 7.30pm, Monday evenings (Oct-Mar). St.
Mary's Church, Church Avenue, Penwortham, PR1 0AH.

ROSSENDALE ORNITHOLOGISTS' CLUB.
(1976; 135 online). Ian Brady. T: 01706 222 120;
E: n/a; W: http://rocforum.activeboard.com
Meetings: 7.15pm, 3rd Monday of the month
(check the forum for details). Weavers Cottage,
Bacup Road, Rawtenstall, BB4 7NW.

Ringing Group/Bird Observatory
FYLDE RG. Mr S Eaves. T: 07973 835 078;
E: seumus64@gmail.com

MERSEYSIDE RG. Dr R Harris. T: 01948 880 112;
E: drbobharris@gmail.com;
W: www.merseysiderg.org.uk

NORTH LANCASHIRE RG (inc. North Heysham Bird
Observatory). Mr J Wilson. T: 01524 735 899;
E: johnwilson711@btinternet.com

SOUTH WEST LANCS RG. Mr I Wolfenden.
T: 01519 311 232; E: ian.wolfenden@btinternet.com

RSPB Local Group
BOLTON. (1978; 155).
Terry Delaney. T: 0161 794 4684.
E: terry.delaney@sky.com;
W: www.rspb.org.uk/groups/bolton
Meetings: 7.30pm, 2nd Thursday of the month
(Sep-Apr). St Catherine's Academy Sports Centre,
entry by Newby Road, Bolton, BL2 5JH

LANCASTER. (1972; 130).
Val Hall. T: 01524 241 606;
E: RSPBlancaster@gmail.com;
W: www.rspb.org.uk/groups/lancaster
Meetings: 7.30pm, 3rd Wednesday of the month
(Aug-Nov, Feb-May). The Centre @ Halton, Low
Road, Halton, Lancaster, LA2 6NB. Sep meeting/
AGM held at Leighton Moss.

LIVERPOOL. (1972; 180).
Chris Tynan. T: 07831 352 870; E: christtynan@aol.com;
W: www.rspb.org.uk/groups/liverpool
Meetings: 7.30pm, 3rd Monday of the month
(Sep-Apr), 1st Monday in Dec). Mossley Hill Parish
Church Hall, Rose Lane, Liverpool, L18 8DB.

SOUTHPORT. (1974; 200).
Kathryn Hall. T: 07802 426 376;
E: SouthportRSPB@btinternet.com;
W: www.rspb.org.uk/groups/southport
Meetings: 7.45pm, 3rd Friday of the month
(Sep-May). Lord Street West Church Hall,
Duke Street, Southport, PR8 2FP.

WIGAN. (1973; 80).
Neil Martin. T: 01695 624 860;
E: neimaz07@yahoo.co.uk;
W: www.rspb.org.uk/groups/wigan
Meetings: 7.45pm, 2nd Tuesday of the month
(Sep-Apr). St Anne's Parish Hall, Church Lane,
Shevington, Wigan, WN6 8BD.

Wetland Bird Survey (WeBS) Organiser
ALT ESTUARY. Mr SJ White. T: via WeBS Office.
E: stevewhite102@btinternet.com

DEE ESTUARY (CLWYD/MERSEYSIDE). Mr CE Wells.
T: via WeBS Office; E: colin.wells@rspb.org.uk

EAST LANCASHIRE AND FYLDE. Mr S Dunstan.
T: 07985 417 755;
E: stephendunstan76@googlemail.com

MERSEY ESTUARY. Mr DJ Smith.
T: 01925 542 745 (day) & 01925 602 397 (eve);
E: dermot.smith71@gmail.com

MERSEYSIDE (INLAND). Mr K Feeney.
T: via WeBS Office; E: kvin@hotmail.co.uk

MORECAMBE BAY (NORTH). See Cumbria.

MORECAMBE BAY (SOUTH) & RIVER LUNE.
Mrs J Roberts. T: 01524 770 295 & 07815 979 856;
E: Jeanrbrts6@aol.com

NORTH LANCASHIRE (INLAND). Mr PJ Marsh.
T: 07532 433 043; E: pmrsh123@aol.com

RIBBLE ESTUARY. Mr K Abram. T: via WeBS Office;
E: bonkser.ka@gmail.com

WEST LANCASHIRE (INLAND). Mr T Clare.
T: via WeBS Office; E: Tomclare922@gmail.com

ENGLAND

Wildlife Trust
THE WILDLIFE TRUST FOR LANCASHIRE, MANCHESTER & NORTH MERSEYSIDE. (1962; 27,000). The Barn, Berkeley Drive, Bamber Bridge, Preston, Lancs PR5 6BY.
T: 01772 324 129, (fax) 01772 628 849;
E: info@lancswt.org.uk; W: www.lancswt.org.uk

LEICESTERSHIRE & RUTLAND

Bird Atlas/Avifauna
The Birds of Leicestershire and Rutland. Rob Fray, Roger Davies, Dave Gamble, Andrew Harrop & Steve Lister. (Christopher Helm, 2009).

Rutland Breeding Bird Atlas 2008-2011. Terry Mitcham (Spiegl Press, 2013)

Bird Recorder
Carl Baggott, 72 New Street, Earl Shilton, LE9 7FR
T: n/a; E: cdbaggott@gmail.com

Bird Report
LEICESTERSHIRE & RUTLAND BIRD REPORT (1946-), from Mrs S Graham, 5 Lychgate Close, Cropston, LE7 7HU. T: 0116 236 6474; E: JSGraham83@aol.com

BTO Regional Representative
David Wright. T: 01530 231 102;
E: davewrightbto@gmail.com

Club
BIRSTALL BIRDWATCHING CLUB. (1976; 50). Ken Goodrich (Sec), 6 Riversdale Close, Birstall, Leicester, LE4 4EH. T: 0116 267 4813;
E: kjgood532@aol.com; W: n/a
Meetings: 7.30pm, 2nd Tuesday of the month (Oct-Apr). Longslade Community College, Wanlip Lane, Luther King Centre, Birstall, LE4 4GH.

LEICESTERSHIRE & RUTLAND ORNITHOLOGICAL SOCIETY. (1941; 600). Brian Moore (Sec), Flat 5, 1 Henray Ave, Leicester, LE2 9QL. T: 0116 291 0411;
E: b_moore@ntlworld.com; W: www.lros.org.uk
Meetings: 7.30pm, usually 1st Friday of the month (Oct-May). Oadby Trinity Methodist Church, Harborough Road, off the central car park, Oadby, LE2 4LA alternating with The Rothley Centre, Mountsorrel Lane, Rothley, LE7 7PR. Additional meeting may be held at the Rutland Water Birdwatching Centre.

RUTLAND NATURAL HISTORY SOCIETY. (1965; 300+). Margaret Conner (Membership Sec), 24 Burrough Road, Somerby, Melton Mowbray, LE14 2PP.
T: 01664 454 532; E: mjconner100@gmail.com;
W: www.rnhs.org.uk
Meetings: 7.30pm, 1st Tuesday of the month (Oct-Apr). Voluntary Action Rutland, Lands End Way, Oakham, LE15 6RB.

SOUTH LEICESTER BIRDWATCHERS. (2006; 60). Graham & Marion Turner. Address: n/a.
T: 07852 782 002;
E: graham.turner@btinternet.com;
W: http://southleicesterbirdwatchers.uk/
Meetings: 7.15 pm, 2nd Wednesday of the month (Sep-Jun). All Saints Parish Centre, Wigston Road, Blaby, Leicester, LE8 4FA.

Ringing Group/Bird Observatory
RUTLAND WATER RG. Mr L Park. T: n/a;
E: pink_flloyd@hotmail.com

STANFORD RG. Mr A Homer. T: 07917 075 091;
E: adam@stanfordrg.org.uk; W: www.stanfordrg.org.uk

RSPB Local Group
LEICESTER. (1973; 1600/area). Graham Heninghem. T: 01455 616 098;
E: graham.heninghem@hotmail.co.uk;
W: www.rspb.org.uk/groups/leicester
Meetings: 7.30pm, usually 3rd Friday of the month (Sep-May). Trinity Methodist Hall, Harborough Road, Oadby, Leicester, LE2 4LA.

LOUGHBOROUGH. (1970; 300). Charlotte Blunt. T: 07946 660 982;
E: Lboro.RSPBgroup@talktalk.net;
W: www.rspb.org.uk/groups/loughborough
Meetings: 7.45pm, 2nd Friday of the month (Oct-May). Lecture Theatre U020, Brockington Building, Loughborough University, Epinal Way, Loughborough, LE11 3TZ.

Wetland Bird Survey (WeBS) Organiser
LEICESTERSHIRE & RUTLAND (excl. RUTLAND WATER). Mr B Moore. T: via WeBS Office;
E: b_moore@ntlworld.com

RUTLAND WATER. Mr TP Appleton.
T: 01572 770 651; E: tappleton@birdfair.org.uk

Wildlife Trust
LEICESTERSHIRE & RUTLAND WILDLIFE TRUST. (1956; 16,000).
The Old Mill, 9 Soar Lane, Leicester, LE3 5DE.
T: 0116 262 9968, (fax) 0116 251 5426;
E: info@lrwt.org.uk; W: www.lrwt.org.uk

LINCOLNSHIRE

Bird Recorder
NORTH LINCS: John Clarkson, 33 Ramsgate, Louth, LN11 0NB. T: 07734 214 603;
E: recorder_north@lincsbirdclub.co.uk

SOUTH LINCS: Phil Hyde, The Cottage, Fen Lane, East Keal, Spilsby, PE23 4AY; T: 01790 752 590;
E: philhyde55@gmail.com

ENGLAND

Bird Report
LINCOLNSHIRE BIRD REPORT (1979-), from Bill
Sterling, 'Newlyn', 5 Carlton Avenue, Healing,
NE Lincs DN41 7PW. E: wbsterling@hotmail.com

BTO Regional Representative
EAST. Philip Espin. T: 01507 605 448;
E: pmjespin@gmail.com

NORTH. Chris Gunn. T: 01777 707 888;
E: donandchris@hotmail.co.uk

SOUTH. Hugh Dorrington. T: 01778 440 716;
E: hdorrington@btconnect.com

WEST. Mike Daly. T: 01522 820 105;
E: Mike.btorrwl@gmail.com;

LINCOLNSHIRE: Nicholas Watts
(Regional Development Officer). T: n/a;
E: nicholas@vinehousefarm.co.uk

Club
LINCOLNSHIRE BIRD CLUB.
(1979; 300).
Mike Harrison (Membership
Sec), Baumber Park, Baumber,
Horncastle, LN9 5NE. T: n/a;
E: mikebparkln9@gmail.com;
W: www.lincsbirdclub.co.uk
Meetings: Local groups hold winter evening
meetings. AGM in Mar with a guest speaker.
Contact/see website for details.

LINCOLNSHIRE NATURALISTS' UNION. (1893; n/a)
c/o Lincolnshire Wildlife Trust, Banovallum
House, Manor House Street, Horncastle, LN9 5HF.
T: 01507 526 667; E: info@lnu.org; W: www.lnu.org
Meetings: 2pm, Saturdays - contact/see website
for details. Whisby Education Centre, Whisby Nature
Park, Moor Lane, Thorpe on the Hill, Lincoln, LN6 9BW.

Ringing Group/Bird Observatory
GIBRALTAR POINT BIRD OBSERVATORY.
Kevin Wilson (Warden) Gibraltar Point Field Centre,
Skegness, PE24 4SU. T: 01754 898 079;
E: lincstrust@gibpoint.freeserve.co.uk;
W: http://gibraltarpointbirdobservatory.blogspot.co.uk

MID LINCS RG. Mr E Tyler. T: n/a;
E: edward.tyler@gmail.com

WASH WADER RG. Mr P Ireland. T: n/a;
E: pli@blueyonder.co.uk; W: www.wwrg.org.uk

RSPB Local Group
GRIMSBY. (1986; n/a).
Martin Francis. T: 01472 883 436;
E: martin.francis2@ntlworld.com;
W: www.rspb.org.uk/groups/grimsby
Meetings: 7.30pm, 3rd Monday of the month
(Sep-Jun). Corpus Christi Church Hall, Grimsby
Road, Cleethorpes, DN35 7LJ.

LINCOLN. (1974; 250).
Peter Skelson. T: 01522 695 747;
E: peter.skelson@lincolnRSPB.org.uk;
W: www.lincolnrspb.org.uk
Meetings: 7.30pm, 2nd Thursday of the month
(Sep-May). Bishop Grosseteste University,
Longdales Road, Lincoln, LN1 3DY.

SOUTH LINCS SOCIAL GROUP. (1987; n/a).
Vincent Chambers. T: 01205 820 046;
E: RSPBsouthlincs@gmail.com;
W: www.rspb.org.uk/groups/southlincolnshire
Meetings: Various - contact/see website for
details.

Wetland Bird Survey (WeBS) Organiser
HUMBER ESTUARY (INNER SOUTH). Mr K Parker.
T: via WeBS Office; E: keith@ksparker.freeserve.co.uk

HUMBER ESTUARY (MID-SOUTH). Mr R Barnard.
T: 01484 868 425; E: richard.barnard@rspb.org.uk

HUMBER ESTUARY (NORTH). See Yorkshire.

HUMBER ESTUARY (OUTER SOUTH). Mr JR Walker.
T: 01507 338 038; E: dunewalker@btinternet.com

NORTH LINCOLNSHIRE (INLAND). Ms C Gunn.
T: via WeBS Office; E: donandchris@hotmail.co.uk

SOUTH LINCOLNSHIRE (INLAND). Mr RCE Titman.
T: 01778 380 695; E: bob.titman@gmail.com

THE WASH (LINCOLNSHIRE). Mr J Scott.
T: 01485 545 261; E: jim.scott@rspb.org.uk

Wildlife Trust
LINCOLNSHIRE WILDLIFE TRUST. (1948; 27,000).
Banovallum House, Manor House Street,
Horncastle, LN9 5HF.
T: 01507 526 667, (fax) 01507 525 732;
E: info@lincstrust.co.uk; W: www.lincstrust.org.uk

LONDON (GREATER)

Bird Atlas/Avifauna
The London Bird Atlas. Ian Woodward, Richard
Arnold, Neil Smith (London Natural History
Society & John Beaufoy Books, due Nov 2017).

The Birds of London. Andrew Self
(Christopher Helm, 2014).

Bird Recorder
Andrew Self, 16 Harp Island Close, Neasden, London
NW10 0DF. T: 07443 221 382; E: a-self@sky.com

Bird Report
LONDON BIRD REPORT: 20-mile radius of St Paul's
Cath. (1936-), from Catherine Schmitt, London
Natural History Society, 4 Falkland Ave, London
N3 1QR. E: catherineschmitt20@gmail.com

ENGLAND

BTO Regional Representative
LONDON, NORTH. Ian Woodward. T: n/a;
E: ianw_bto_nlon@hotmail.co.uk

LONDON, SOUTH. Richard Arnold.
T: 0208 224 1135; E: bto@thomsonecology.com

Club
MARYLEBONE BIRDWATCHING SOCIETY. (1981; 145).
Steve Ripley (Chair),
29 Berriman Road, Holloway,
London N7 7PN.
T: 0207 609 1837;
E: birdsmbs@yahoo.com;
W: www.birdsmbs.org.uk
Meetings: 7.15pm, usually 3rd
Friday of the month (Sep-Apr,
not Dec). Gospel Oak Methodist
Church, Lisburne Road, London
NW3 2NT.

THE LONDON BIRD CLUB (1858; 1000).
(Ornithology Section of London NHS).
Douglas Bilton (Sec), 75 Walcot Square, London
SE11 4UB. T: 07725 740585;
E: douglasbilton@gmail.com;
W: http://www.lnhs.org.uk/index.php/about-us/
lnhs-sections/london-bird-club
Meetings: 7.00pm, contact/see website
for details. Burgh House, New End Square,
Hampstead, London, NW3 1LT.

Ringing Group/Bird Observatory
LONDON GULL STUDY GROUP - (SE incl.
Hampshire, Surrey, Sussex, Berkshire and
Oxfordshire). Group is no longer active but still
receiving sightings/recoveries of ringed birds and
able to give information on gulls.
Dr AB Watson. T: n/a;
E: barriewatson1@yahoo.com

RUNNYMEDE RG. See Berkshire.

RSPB Local Group
BEXLEY. (1979; n/a).
Stuart Banks. T: 0208 854 7251;
E: stuartbans@hotmail.co.uk;
W: www.rspb.org.uk/groups/bexley
Meetings: 7.15pm, 2nd Friday of the month
(Sep-May). John Fisher Church Hall, 48 Thanet
Road, Bexley, DA5 1AP.

BROMLEY. (1972; 170).
David Hampson. T: 07392 790 719;
E: bromleyRSPB@gmail.com;
W: www.rspb.org.uk/groups/bromley
Meetings: 7.15pm, 2nd Wednesday of the month
(Sep-Jun). United Reformed Church (Verrall Hall),
Widmore Road, Bromley, BR1 1RY.

CENTRAL LONDON. (1974; 250).
Cher Edworthy. T: 07716 779 526;
E: RSPB.centrallondongroup@gmail.com;
W: www.rspb.org.uk/groups/centrallondon
Meetings: 6.45pm, 2nd Thursday of the month
(Sep-May). St Columba's Church Hall, Pont St,
London SW1X 0BD.

CROYDON. (1973; 500).
John Davis. T: 0208 640 4578;
E: johndavis.wine@care4free.net;
W: www.rspb.org.uk/groups/croydon
Meetings: 2.00pm & 8.00pm, 2nd Monday of the
month (not Jun). Whitgift Sports Club, The Clubhouse,
Croham Manor Road, South Croydon, CR2 7BG.

ENFIELD. (1971; 2700).
Norman Hudson. T: 0208 363 1431;
E: dorandnor@tiscali.co.uk;
W: www.rspb.org.uk/groups/enfield
Meetings: 7.45pm, 1st Thursday of the month
(Sep-Jun). St Andrews Church Hall, Silver St,
Enfield, EN1 3EG.

HAVERING. (1972; 270).
Mike Hughes. T: 01708 250 585;
E: mikeboyo15@gmail.com;
W: www.rspb.org.uk/groups/havering
Meetings: 7.45pm, 2nd Friday of the month (Sep-May).
Hornchurch Library, North Street, Hornchurch, RM11 1TB.

NORTH EAST LONDON. (2009; 200).
David Littlejohns. T: 0208 989 4746;
E: NelondonRSPB@yahoo.co.uk;
W: www.rspb.org.uk/groups/northeastlondon
Meetings: 8.00pm, 2nd Tuesday of the month.
St Mary's Church - Gwinnell Room, 207 High Road,
South Woodford, London E18 2PA.

NORTH WEST LONDON. (1983; n/a).
Bob Husband. T: 0208 441 8742;
E: bobhusband@hotmail.co.uk;
W: www.rspb.org.uk/groups/nwlondon
Meetings: 8pm, usually the last Tuesday of the
month (Sep-Mar). Wilberforce Centre, St Paul's
Church, The Ridgeway, London NW7 1QU.

PINNER & DISTRICT. (1972; 300).
Ian Jackson. T: 0208 907 3513;
E: imjpinRSPB@gmail.com;
W: www.rspb.org.uk/groups/pinner
Meetings: 8pm, 2nd Thursday of the month
(Sep-May). St John The Baptist Church Hall,
Church Lane, Pinner, Middx HA5 3AA.

RICHMOND & TWICKENHAM. (1979; 180).
Clare Million. T: 07794 835 571;
E: richmondRSPB@yahoo.co.uk;
W: www.rspb.org.uk/groups/richmond
Meetings: 7.30pm, 1st Wednesday of the month
& 2.00pm, 2nd Tuesday of the month (Sep-May).
York House, Richmond Road, Twickenham, TW1 3AA.

ENGLAND

Wetland Bird Survey (WeBS) Organiser
GREATER LONDON (excl. THAMES ESTUARY/
see Essex). Mr AV Moon. T: 01923 774 344 &
07811 847 732; E: andrew.moon@talk21.com

LEE VALLEY. See Hertfordshire.

SOUTH WEST LONDON. See Surrey.

Wildlife Trust
LONDON WILDLIFE TRUST. (1981; 14,000).
Dean Bradley House, 52 Horseferry Road, London
SW1P 2AF. T: 0207 261 0447, (fax) 0207 633 0811;
E: enquiries@wildlondon.org.uk;
W: www.wildlondon.org.uk

MANCHESTER (GREATER)

Bird Recorder
Ian McKerchar, 42 Green Ave, Astley, Manchester
M29 7EH. T: 01942 701 758 & 07958 687 481;
E: ianmckerchar1@gmail.com

Bird Report
BIRDS IN GREATER MANCHESTER (1959-), from the
Bird Recorder - see above.

*LEIGH ORNITHOLOGICAL SOCIETY BIRD REPORT
(1971-)*, download from website W: www.leighos.org.uk

BTO Regional Representative
Nick Hilton. T: 07920 494 240; E: nmhilton71@aol.com

Steve Atkins (Assistant Representative).
T: 01706 645 097; E: steveatkins@tiscali.co.uk

Club
ALTRINGHAM AND DISTRICT
NATURAL HISTORY SOCIETY. (1908; 30)
Mike Pettipher (Chairman). Address: n/a. T: n/a;
E: info@altnats.org.uk; W: www.altnats.org.uk
Meetings: 7:30pm, 2nd Tuesday of the month
(Sep-Apr). The Jubilee Centre, The Firs, Bowdon,
Altrincham, WA14 2TQ.

LEIGH ORNITHOLOGICAL SOCIETY. (1971; 115).
David Shallcross (Chairman), 28 Surrey Avenue, Leigh,
WN7 2NN. T: n/a; E: leighos.chairman@gmail.com;
W: www.leighos.org.uk
LOS Young Birders. W: www.losybc.blogspot.co.uk
Meetings: 7.30pm, uaually 1st Friday of the
month (ca. 10 talks Sep-May) - contact/see
website for details. Derby Room, Leigh Library,
Turnpike Centre, Civic Square, Leigh, WN7 1EB.

ROCHDALE FIELD NATURALISTS' SOCIETY. (1898; 90).
Joan Carter (Gen Sec), 57 Plover Close, Bamford,
Rochdale, OL11 5PU. T: 01706 524 255;
E: rfnsenquiries@talktalk.net;
W: www.rochdalefieldnaturalists.org.uk
Meetings: 7.30pm, usually 2nd Thursday of
the month (Sep-Apr). Cutgate Baptist Church,
Edenfield Rd, Rochdale, OL12 7SS.

STOCKPORT BIRDWATCHING SOCIETY. (1972; 70).
Dave Evans, 36 Tatton Road South, Stockport,
SK4 4LU. T: 0161 432 9513;
E: windhover1972@yahoo.co.uk; W: n/a
Meetings: 7.30pm, last Wednesday of the month
(Sep-Apr). The Heatons Sports Club, Heaton Moor
Stockport, SK4 2NF.

Ringing Group/Bird Observatory
LEIGH RG. Mr AJ Gramauskas. T: n/a;
E: leigh.ringing.group@gmail.com

SOUTH MANCHESTER RG. See Cheshire.

RSPB Local Group
HIGH PEAK. (1974; 130).
Richard Stephenson. T: 0161 427 4187;
E: stephenson3rj@gmail.com;
W: www.rspb.org.uk/groups/highpeak
Meetings: 7.30pm, 3rd Monday of the month
(Sep-May). Marple Senior Citizens Hall, Memorial
Park, Marple, Stockport, SK6 6BA.

STOCKPORT. (1979; 150).
Jayne Skelhorn. T: 0161 879 4680;
E: jayne.skelhorn@talktalk.net;
W: www.rspb.org.uk/groups/stockport
Meetings: 7.30pm, 2nd Monday of the month
(Sep-Apr). Stockport Masonic Guildhall,
169 Wellington Road South, Stockport, SK1 3UA.

Wetland Bird Survey (WeBS) Organiser
GREATER MANCHESTER. Mr T Wilcox.
T: via WeBS Office; via WeBS Office

Wildlife Trust. See Lancashire.

NORFOLK

Bird Atlas/Avifauna
*The Norfolk Bird Atlas: Summer and Winter
Distributions 1999-2007.* Moss Taylor & John H
Marchant (BTO 2011).

The Birds of Norfolk. Moss Taylor,
Michael Seago, Peter Allard &
Don Dorling (Christopher Helm,
1999/rep 2007).

The Birds of Blakeney Point.
Andy Stoddart, Steve Joyner
& James McCallum (Wren
Publishing, 2005).

Bird Recorder
Neil Lawton. Address: n/a; T: n/a;
E: dnjnorfolkrec@btinternet.com

Bird Report
*NAR VALLEY ORNITHOLOGICAL SOCIETY ANNUAL
REPORT (1977-)*, from Ian Black, Three Chimneys,
Tumbler Hill, Swaffham, PE37 7JG.
E: enquiries@narvos.org.uk

ENGLAND

NORFOLK BIRD & MAMMAL REPORT (1953-), from
Tony Leech, NNNS Publications, 3 Eccles Road,
Holt, NR25 6HJ. E: birdreport@nnns.org.uk

NORFOLK ORNITHOLOGISTS' ASSOCIATION ANNUAL
REPORT (1962-), from NOA, Broadwater Rd,
Holme Next the Sea, Hunstanton, PE36 6LQ.
E: info@noa.org.uk

BTO Regional Representative
NORTH-EAST. Chris Hudson. T: 01603 868 805;
E: Chris697@btinternet.com

NORTH-WEST. Bob Osborne. T: 01553 670 430;
E: rtoclass40@yahoo.co.uk

Fred Cooke (Assistant Representative)
T: 01553 631 076; E: f.cooke1@btinternet.com

SOUTH-EAST. Rachel Warren. T: 01603 593 912;
E: campephilus@btinternet.com

SOUTH-WEST. Vince Matthews. T: 01953 884 125;
E: norfolksouthwest@gmail.co.uk

Club
CLEY BIRD CLUB. (1986; 620+).
John Dicks (Chairman), Cherry Tree House, Cherry
Tree Road, Plumstead, NR11 7LQ.
T: 01263 577 354; E: j48a@hotmail.com;
W: www.cleybirdclub.org.uk/
Meetings: 7.30pm, one Wednesday monthly
(Nov-Feb). Cley Village Hall, The Fairstead, Cley,
NR25 7RJ.

NAR VALLEY ORNITHOLOGICAL SOCIETY. (1976; 125).
Ian Black (Chairman), Three Chimneys, Tumbler
Hill, Swaffham, PE37 7JG. T: 01760 724 092;
E: enquiries@narvos.org.uk; W: www.narvos.org.uk
Meetings: 7.30pm, last Tuesday of the month
(Jul-Nov & Jan-May). Barn Theatre, Convent of
The Sacred Heart, Mangate Street, Swaffham,
PE37 7QW.

NORFOLK & NORWICH NATURALISTS' SOCIETY.
(1869; 630). Dr Nick Owens
(Sec), 22 Springfield Close,
Weybourne, Holt, NR25 7TB.
T: 01263 588 410;
E: info@nnns.org.uk;
W: www.NNNS.org.uk
Meetings: 7.30pm, 2nd
Tuesday of the month
(Oct-Mar), St Andrew's Hall,
Church Lane, Eaton, NR4 6NW.

NORFOLK ORNITHOLOGISTS' ASSOCIATION. (1970; 1500).
Sophie Barker (Warden/Secretary), Broadwater Rd,
Holme-next-Sea, Hunstanton, PE36 6LQ.
T: 01485 525 406; E: info@noa.org.uk;
W: www.noa.org.uk
Meetings: AGM held in Sep.

NORTH-EAST NORFOLK BIRD CLUB. (2015; 280).
Colin Blaxill, (Membership Sec), Caitlins, Bernard
Close, High Kelling, Holt, NR25 6QY.
T: 01263 711 718; E: membership@nenbc.co.uk;
W: www.nenbc.co.uk
Meetings: 7.30pm, last Thursday of the month
(Sep-Nov, Jan-Apr, plus a social event in Dec &
May). Aylmerton Village Hall, Aylmerton, NR11 8PX.

WENSUM VALLEY BIRDWATCHING SOCIETY. (2003; 100+).
Lin Pateman (Sec). Address: n/a. T: 01263 587 262:
E: wvbs.secretary@gmail.com; W: www.wvbs.co.uk
Meetings: 7.30pm, 3rd Thursday of the month
(all year). Great Witchingham (Lenwade) Village
Hall, Hubbards Loke, Lenwade, NR9 5AZ.

Ringing Group/Bird Observatory
BTO NUNNERY RG. Mr J Walker. T: 01842 750 050;
E: justin.walker@bto.org

EAST ANGLIA GULL GROUP - contact BTO.

EAST NORFOLK RG. Mr K Brett. T: 01493 384 062;
E: kevbrett@btinternet.com;
W: http://eastnorfolkringinggroup.blogspot.co.uk/

HOLME BIRD OBSERVATORY (NOA RG). See Club - NOA.

NORTH NORFOLK RG. Mr K Herber. T: 07785 920 044;
E: keith.herber@btinternet.com;
W: http://northwestnorfolkstonechats.wordpress.com

NORTH WEST NORFOLK RG. Mr J Middleton.
T: n/a; E: johnmiddleton@bmarket.freeserve.co.uk

SHERINGHAM RG. Mr A Bull. T: n/a;
E: alanbull2010@gmail.com

SOUTH WEST NORFOLK RG. Mr T Bagworth.
T: n/a; E: tim.bagworth@btinternet.com

THETFORD FOREST RG. Dr G Conway. T: n/a;
E: greg.conway@bto.org

UEA RG. Dr I Barr. T: n/a; E: I.barr@yahoo.co.uk;
W: http://uearg.blogspot.co.uk/

WASH WADER RG. See Lincolnshire.

RSPB Local Group
NORWICH. (1971; 230).
David Porter. T: 01603 745 310 (day);
E: RSPBnorwichgroup@virginmedia.com;
W: www.rspb.org.uk/groups/norwich
Meetings: 7.30pm, 2nd Monday of the month
(Sep-Jun). Hellesdon Community Centre, (off Wood
View Road), Middletons Lane, Norwich, NR6 5QB.

Wetland Bird Survey (WeBS) Organiser
BREYDON WATER. Mr P Rowe. T: via WeBS Office;
E: via WeBS Office

NORFOLK (excl. ESTUARIES). Mr T Strudwick.
T: via WeBS Office; E: tim.strudwick@rspb.org.uk

ENGLAND

NORTH NORFOLK COAST. Mr N Lawton.
T: via WeBS Office; E: via WeBS Office

THE WASH (NORFOLK). See Lincolnshire.

Wildlife Trust
NORFOLK WILDLIFE TRUST. (1926; 35,000).
Bewick House, 22 Thorpe Road, Norwich, NR1 1RY.
T: 01603 625 540, (fax) 01603 598 300;
E: info@norfolkwildlifetrust.org.uk;
W: www.norfolkwildlifetrust.org.uk

NORTHAMPTONSHIRE

Bird Recorder
VACANT.

Bird Report
NORTHANTS BIRDS (1969-),
from RW Bullock,
81 Cavendish Drive,
Northampton, NN3 3HL.

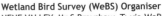

Northants Birds

County bird records for 2013

BTO Regional Representative
Barrie Galpin.
T: 01780 444 351;
E: barrie.galpin@zen.co.uk

Ben Reeve (Assistant Representative).
T: 01788 824 413; E: benreeve@outlook.com

Club
NORTHAMPTONSHIRE BIRD CLUB. (1973; 50).
Eleanor McMahon (Sec), Oriole House, 5 The Croft,
Hanging Houghton, NN6 9HW. T: 01604 880 009;
E: eleanor1960@btinternet.com;
W: https://northantsbirdclub.blogspot.com/
Meetings: 7.30pm, 1st Wednesday of the month.
(all year). The Lodge, Pitsford Water, 7 Blixworth
Road, Holcot, NN6 9SJ.

Ringing Group/Bird Observatory
NORTHANTS RG. Mr N Wood. T: 07974 980 220;
E: nicholas841@btinternet.com

ROCKINGHAM FOREST RG. Mr D Holman.
T: 07903 105 299;
E: derek.holman280@btinternet.com

STANFORD RG. See Leicestershire & Rutland.

RSPB Local Group
MID NENE. (1975; 280).
Ian Wrisdale. T: 01933 410 566;
E: wrisdale1@tiscali.co.uk;
W: www.rspb.org.uk/groups/midnene
Meetings: 7.30pm, 3rd Thursday of the month
(Sep-Mar). The Saxon Hall, Thorpe Street, Raunds,
Wellingborough, NN9 6LT.

Wetland Bird Survey (WeBS) Organiser
NENE VALLEY. Mr S Brayshaw. T: via WeBS Office;
E: via WeBS Office

NORTHAMPTONSHIRE (excl. NENE VALLEY).
Mr B Galpin. T: 01780 444 351;
E: barrie.galpin@zen.co.uk

Wildlife Trust. See Cambridgeshire.

NORTHUMBERLAND

Bird Atlas/Avifauna
Northumbria Bird Atlas. Tim Dean, Dick Myatt,
Muriel Cadwallender, Tom Cadwallender
(Northumberland & Tyneside Bird Club, 2015).

Bird Recorder
Tim Dean, 2 Knocklaw Park, Rothbury, NE65 7PW.
T: 01669 621 460; E: t.r.dean@btinternet.com

Bird Report
BIRDS IN NORTHUMBRIA (1970-), from Trevor Blake,
6 Glenside, Ellington, Morpeth, NE61 5LS.
E: trevor.1958@live.co.uk

BIRDS ON THE FARNE ISLANDS: in Northumbrian
Naturalist (1971-), from the Natural History
Society of Northumbria, Great North Museum,
Hancock, Barras Bridge, Newcastle upon Tyne,
NE2 4PT. T: 0191 208 2790; E: nhsn@ncl.ac.uk

BTO Regional Representative
Tom Cadwallender. T: 01665 830 884;
E: tomandmurielcadwallender@hotmail.com

Muriel Cadwallender
(Regional Development Officer). T: & E: as above.

Club
NATURAL HISTORY SOCIETY OF NORTHUMBRIA.
(1829; 1000+).
Natural History Society of Northumbria, Great North
Museum: Hancock, Barras Bridge, Newcastle upon
Tyne, NE2 4PT. T: 0191 208 2790;
E: nhsn@ncl.ac.uk; W: www.nhsn.ncl.ac.uk
Meetings: 7pm, Fridays (Oct-Mar) in the learning
suite of the Museum.

NORTH NORTHUMBERLAND BIRD CLUB. (1984; 250+).
Glynis Gower (Sec). Address: n/a. T: 01289 330 969;
E: ringouzel@northnorthumberlandbirdclub.co.uk;
W: www.northnorthumberlandbirdclub.co.uk

Meetings: 7.30pm, 3rd Friday
of the month (Sep) and 2nd
Friday of the month (Oct-Jun).
Bamburgh Pavilion (corner of
the green below Bamburgh
Castle).

ENGLAND

NORTHUMBERLAND & TYNESIDE BIRD CLUB. (1958; 270).
Andrew Brunt (Sec), South Cottage, West Road,
Longhorsley, Morpeth, NE65 8UY. T: 01670 788 352;
E: ntbcorg@gmail.com; W: www.ntbc.org.uk
Meetings: 7.00pm, 2nd Thursday of the month
(Sep-Apr). Northern Rugby Club, McCracken Park,
Great North Road, Newcastle upon Tyne, NE3 2DT.

Ringing Group/
Bird Observatory
NHS OF NORTHUMBRIA.
Dr C Redfern. T: n/a;
E: chris.redfern@ncl.ac.uk

Natural
History
Society of
Northumbria

NORTHUMBRIA RG. Mr B Galloway.
T: 0191 286 4850; E: bryangalloway@btinternet.com;
W: http//:northumbriaringinggroup.com

RSPB Local Group
NEWCASTLE UPON TYNE. (1969; 250).
Jeff Mason. T: 0191 289 5058;
E: newcastlerspbgroup@gmail.com;
W: www.rspb.org.uk/groups/newcastle
Meetings: 7.00pm, Tuesdays - quarterly (contact/
check wesite for details). Jurys Inn, St James
Gate, Scotswood Road, Newcastle upon Tyne,
NE1 4AD.

Wetland Bird Survey (WeBS) Organiser
LINDISFARNE. Mr A Craggs. T: 01289 381 470;
E: andrew.craggs@naturalengland.org.uk

NORTHUMBERLAND (COASTAL). Ms K Evans.
T: via WeBS Office; E: via WeBS Office

NORTHUMBERLAND (INLAND). Mr S Holliday.
T: via WeBS Office; E: steveholliday@hotmail.co.uk

Wildlife Trust
NORTHUMBERLAND WILDLIFE TRUST. (1971; 13,000).
Garden House, St Nicholas Park, Jubilee Road,
Gosforth, Newcastle upon Tyne, NE3 3XT.
T: 0191 284 6884, (fax) 0191 284 6794;
E: mail@northwt.org.uk; W: www.nwt.org.uk

NOTTINGHAMSHIRE

Bird Recorder
Andy Hall, 10 Staverton Road, Bilborough,
Nottingham, NG8 4ET. T: 0115 875 9043;
E: andy.h11@ntlworld.com

Bird Report
BIRDS OF NOTTINGHAMSHIRE (1943-), from Jenny
Swindells, 21 Chaworth Road, West Bridgford,
Nottingham, NG2 7AE.
E: j.swindells@btinternet.com

BTO Regional Representative
Lynda Milner. T: 01623 862 025;
E: milner.lynda@googlemail.com

Club
LOUND BIRD CLUB. (1990; 90).
Paul Hobson (Chairman). Address: n/a.
T: 07415 671 346; E: hoblong@hotmail.co.uk;
W: www.loundbirdclub.com
Meetings: Various talks through the year -
contact/see website for details.

NETHERFIELD WILDLIFE GROUP. (1999; 130).
Philip Burnham (Sec), 57 Tilford Road, Newstead
Village, Nottingham, NG15 0BU.
T: 01623 401 980 & 07964 037 657;
E: philip.burnham@netherfieldwildlife.org.uk;
W: www.gedlingconservationtrust.org/
netherfield-lagoons/netherfield-wildlife-group/
Meetings: No indoor meetings held.

NOTTINGHAMSHIRE BIRDWATCHERS.
(1935; 325).
Jenny Swindells (Sec),
21 Chaworth Rd, West Bridgford,
Nottingham, NG2 7AE.
T: 0115 9812 432;
E: j.swindells@btinternet.com;
W: www.nottsbirders.net
Meetings: Contact/see website for details.

WOLLATON NATURAL HISTORY SOCIETY.
(1976; 70).
E: via website;
W: www.spanglefish.com/wollatonnaturalhistory/
Meetings: 7.30pm, 3rd Wednesday of the month
(not Aug). St Leonards Community Centre,
Bramcote Lane, Wollaton, HG8 2ND.

Ringing Group/Bird Observatory
BIRKLANDS RG. Mr A Ashley. T: 07532 259 513;
E: andyashley39@gmail.com

NORTH NOTTS RG. Mr A Blackburn.
T: 01777 706 516 or 07718 766 873;
E: adrian.blackburn@sky.com

SOUTH NOTTS RG. Mr KJ Hemsley.
T: 07986 433 615; E: kjh260987@gmail.com;
W: http://southnottsringinggroup.blogspot.co.uk/

TRESWELL WOOD INTEGRATED POPULATION
MONITORING GROUP. Mr C du Feu.
T: 01427 848 400; E: chris.r.dufeu@gmail.com;
W: www.treswellwoodipmg.org

RSPB Local Group
MANSFIELD. (1986; 70).
Diane Bartlam. T: 07847 935 583;
E: dianeashplorers@hotmail.co.uk;
W: www.rspb.org.uk/groups/mansfield
Meetings: 7.30pm, 1st Wednesday of the month
(Sep-Jun). Bridge St Methodist Church, Rock
Valley, Mansfield, NG18 2HA.

NOTTINGHAM. (1974; 300).
Doreen Markam. T: 0115 912 0796;
E: RSPBnottmlgmem@gmail.com;
W: www.rspb.org.uk/groups/nottingham
Meetings: 7.30pm, 1st Wednesday of the month
(Sep-May). Nottingham Mechanics, 3 North
Sherwood Street, Nottingham, NG1 4EZ.

Wetland Bird Survey (WeBS) Organiser
NOTTINGHAMSHIRE. Prof DT Parkin.
T: 0115 932 0090 (eve); E: bluethroat@btinternet.com

Wildlife Trust
NOTTINGHAMSHIRE WILDLIFE TRUST. (1963; 10,000).
The Old Ragged School, Brook Street,
Nottingham, NG1 1EA. T: 0115 958 8242,
(fax) 0115 924 3175; E: info@nottswt.co.uk;
W: www.nottinghamshirewildlife.org

OXFORDSHIRE

Bird Atlas/Avifauna
Birds of the Heart of England (Banbury area).
TG Easterbrook (Liverpool University Press, 2013).

Birds of Oxfordshire. JW Brucker, AG Gosler &
AR Heryet (Pisces Publications, 1992).

Bird Recorder
Ian Lewington, 119 Brasenose Road, Didcot, OX11 7BP.
T: 01235 819 792; E: lewbirder@btinternet.com

Bird Report
BIRDS OF OXFORDSHIRE (1915-), from Roy Overall,
30 Hunsdon Road, Iffley, Oxford, OX4 4JE.
E: roy.overall@oos.org.uk

*BANBURY ORNITHOLOGICAL SOCIETY ANNUAL
REPORT (1966-),* from Mike Lewis, Old Mlll
Cottage, Avon Dassett, nr Southam, Warwickshire
CV47 2AE. E: mikelewisad@gmail.com

BTO Regional Representative
NORTH. Frances Buckel. T: 01608 644 425;
E: fran.buckel@btinternet.com

SOUTH. John Melling. T: 01865 820 867;
E: bto-rep@oos.org.uk

Club
BANBURY ORNITHOLOGICAL
SOCIETY (incl. parts of
Northants/Oxon/Warwick).
(1952; 100).
Frances Buckel (Sec), Witts End,
Radbones Hill, Over Norton,
Chipping Norton, OX7 5RA.
T: 01608 644 425; E: fran.buckel@btinternet.com;
W: www.banburyornithologicalsociety.org.uk
Meetings: 7.30pm, 2nd Monday of the month
(Sep-May).The Banbury Cricket Club, White Post
Road, Bodicote, OX15 4BN.

OXFORD ORNITHOLOGICAL SOCIETY. (1921; 330).
Barry Hudson (Sec), Pinfold, 4 Bushey Row,
Bampton, Witney, OX18 2JU. T: 01993 200 790 &
07788 496 847; E: secretary@oos.org.uk;
W: www.oos.org.uk
Meetings: 7.45pm, 2nd Wednesday of the month
(Sep-May). Exeter Hall, Oxford Road, Kidlington,
OX5 1AB.

Ringing Group/Bird Observatory
EDWARD GREY INSTITUTE. Dr A Gosler.
T: n/a; E: andrew.gosler@zoo.ox.ac.uk

RSPB Local Group
OXFORD. (1977; 100).
Roy Grant. T: 01865 774 659;
E: roy.otters@hotmail.co.uk;
W: www.rspb.org.uk/groups/oxford
Meetings: 7.45pm, (usually) 1st Thursday of
the month (Sep-May). Sandhills Primary School,
Terrett Avenue, Sandhills, Oxford, OX3 8FN.

VALE OF WHITE HORSE. (1977; 160).
Steve Bastow. T: 07900 213 698;
E: stevebastow@outlook.com;
W: www.rspb-vwh.org.uk
Meetings: 7.45pm, 3rd Monday of the month
(Sep-May). Didcot Civic Hall, Britwell Road,
Didcot, OX11 7HN.

Wetland Bird Survey (WeBS) Organiser
OXFORDSHIRE (NORTH). Mrs S Bletchly.
T: 01295 721 048;
E: sandra.banornsoc@btinternet.com

OXFORDSHIRE (SOUTH). Mr BR Carpenter.
T: 07920 760 986; E: beniow@yahoo.co.uk

Wildlife Trust
BERKSHIRE, BUCKS. & OXON WILDLIFE TRUST.
(1959; 54,000).
The Lodge, 1 Armstrong Road, Littlemore, Oxford,
OX4 4XT. T: 01865 775 476, (fax) 01865 711 301;
E: info@bbowt.org.uk; W: www.bbowt.org.uk

SHROPSHIRE

Bird Atlas/Avifauna
The Birds of Shropshire. Leo Smith (Liverpool
University Press, due Oct 2018).

Bird Recorder
Martyn Owen, 34 Peacock Hill, Alveley, WV15 6JX.
T: 07736 286 675; E: soscountyrecorder@gmail.com

Bird Report
SHROPSHIRE BIRD REPORT (1956-), from
E: WebManager@shropshirebirds.com

BTO Regional Representative
Jonathan Groom. T: n/a;
E: bto.shropshire@gmail.com

ENGLAND

Club
SHROPSHIRE ORNITHOLOGICAL
SOCIETY. (1955; 800).
Helen J Griffiths (Sec).
Address: n/a. T: 01743 761 507;
E: secretary@shropshirebirds.co.uk;
W: www.shropshirebirds.com
Meetings: 7.15pm, 1st
Wednesday of the month
(Oct-Apr). Bayston Hill Memorial Hall, Lyth Hill
Road, Bayston Hill, Shrewsbury, SY3 0DR.

Ringing Group/Bird Observatory
CHELMARSH RG. Mr D Fulton. T: n/a;
E: davebirder@aol.com;
W: http://chelmarshrg.blogspot.co.uk/

SHROPSHIRE RG. Dr R Harris. T: 01948 880 112;
E: drbobharris@gmail.com;
W: http://shropshirerg.wordpress.com

RSPB Local Group
SHROPSHIRE. (1991; 110).
Connie Sansom. T: 01295 676 444;
E: ShrewsburyRSPBgroup@gmail.com;
W: www.rspb.org.uk/groups/shropshire
Meetings: 7.30pm, 4th Tuesday of the month
(Sep-Apr/2nd Tuesday in Dec). Bayston Hill
Memorial Hall, Lyth Hill Rd, Shrewsbury,
SY3 0DR.

SOUTH SHROPSHIRE. (2004; 70).
Carol Wood. T: 07807 068 304;
E: carolwood772@outlook.com;
W: www.rspbsouthshropshire.co.uk
Meetings: 7.30pm, 2nd Tuesday of the month
(Sep-Apr). Culmington Village Hall, on the B4365,
Culmington, SY8 2DA.

Wetland Bird Survey (WeBS) Organiser
SHROPSHIRE. Mr MF Wallace. T: 01743 369 035;
E: michaelwallace47@gmail.com

Wildlife Trust
SHROPSHIRE WILDLIFE TRUST. (1962; 10,000).
193 Abbey Foregate, Shrewsbury, SY2 6AH.
T: 01743 284 280, (fax) 01743 284 281;
E: enquiries@shropshirewildlifetrust.org.uk;
W: www.shropshirewildlifetrust.org.uk

SOMERSET & BRISTOL/AVON

Bird Atlas/Avifauna
*The Birds of Exmoor and the Quantocks.*David
Ballance, Brian Gibbs & Roger Butcher (privately
published, 2nd ed 2016).

*Somerset Atlas of Breeding and Wintering Birds
2007-2012.* David Ballance, Rob Grimmond,
Julian Thomas & Eve Tigwell (Somerset OS, 2014).

Avon Atlas 2007-11. Richard L Bland & M Dadds
(Bristol Naturalists' Society, 2012).

A History of the Birds of Somerset. DK Ballance
(Isabelline Books, 2006).

Bird Recorder
AVON. John Martin, 34 Cranmoor Green, Pilning,
Bristol, BS35 4QF. T: 01454 633 040 &
07443 544 962; E: avonbirdrecorder@gmail.com

SOMERSET. Brian Gibbs, 23 Lyngford Road,
Taunton, TA2 7EE. T: 01823 274 887;
E: briandgibbs23@gmail.com

Bird Report
AVON BIRD REPORT (1977-), from Harvey Rose,
Arncliffe, Coast Road, Walton Bay, Clevedon,
BS21 7AS. E: h.e.rose@bris.ac.uk

SOMERSET BIRDS (1912-), from the Somerset Bird
Recorder - see above.

BTO Regional Representative
AVON. Gordon Youdale. T: 01454 881 690;
E: gordon.youdale@blueyonder.co.uk

Dave Stoddard (Assistant Representative).
T: 0117 924 698; E: dave.stoddard@tiscali.co.uk

SOMERSET. Eve Tigwell. T: 01373 451 630;
E: eve.tigwell@zen.co.uk

Penny Allwright (Assistant Representative).
T: 01458 210 345; E: penny.allwright@btinternet.com

Club
BRISTOL NATURALISTS' SOCIETY. (1862; 550).
Lesley Cox (Sec, Ornithology Section). Address: n/a.
T: 07786 437 528; E: info@bristolnats.org.uk;
W: http://bristolnats.org.uk/ornithology/
Meetings: 7.30pm, 2nd Wednesday of the month
(Oct-Mar). Usually at Westbury-on-Trym, Methodist
Church, 46 Westbury Hill, Bristol, BS9 3AA.

BRISTOL ORNITHOLOGICAL CLUB. (1967; 550).
Judy Copeland (Membership Sec),
19 St George's Hill, Easton-in-Gordano,
North Somerset BS20 0PS. T: 01275 373 554;
E: bocsecretary@hotmail.com;
W: www.bristolornithologicalclub.co.uk
Meetings: 7.30pm, 3rd Thursday of the month
(Sep-Mar). Newman Hall, Grange Court Road,
Westbury-on-Trym, BS9 4DR.

EXMOOR NATURAL HISTORY SOCIETY. (1974; 480).
Caroline Giddens (Sec), 12 King George Road,
Minehead, TA24 5JD. T: 01643 707 624;
E: carol.enhs@talktalk.net; W: www.enhs.org.uk
Meetings: 7.30pm, 1st Wednesday of the month
(Oct-Mar). Methodist Church Hall, The Avenue,
Minehead, TA24 5AY.

ENGLAND

SOMERSET ORNITHOLOGICAL SOCIETY. (1974; 475).
Jeff Hazell (Membership Sec), 9 Hooper Rd,
Street, BA16 0NP. T: 01458 443 780;
E: jeff.hazell@somersetbirding.org.uk;

W: www.somersetbirding.org.uk
Meetings: 7.30pm, 3rd Thursday
of the month (Oct-Apr, except
Dec). Village Hall, Ruishton,
Taunton, TA3 5JD.

**Ringing Group/Bird
Observatory**
CHEW VALLEY RS. Mr A Ashman.
T: 07842 242 935;
E: alan.ashman@talktalk.net;
W: www.chewvalleyringingstation.co.uk

GORDANO VALLEY RG. Mr W White.
T: n/a; E: warwickwhite@btinternet.com

RSPCA. Mr K Leighton. T: n/a;
E: kev.leighton@yahoo.com

RSPB Local Group
BATH AND DISTRICT. (1969; 260).
Jean Melksham. T: 01225 404 985;
E: jeanmelksham@blueyonder.co.uk;
W: www.rspb.org.uk/groups/bath
Meetings: 7.30pm, 3rd Wednesday of the month
(Sep-Apr). St Andrew's Community Church,
Hawthorn Grove, Combe Down, Bath, BA2 5QA.

SOUTH SOMERSET. (1979; 240).
Denise Chamings. T: 01460 240 740;
E: denise.chamings@talktalk.net;
W: www.rspb.org.uk/groups/southsomerset
Meetings: 7.30pm, 3rd Thursday of the month
(Sep-May). The Millennium Hall, Seavington St.
Mary, Ilminster, TA19 0QH.

Wetland Bird Survey (WeBS) Organiser
AVON (OTHER SITES). Mr R Higgins.
T: 0117 944 1034;
E: rupert@wessexeco.fsnet.co.uk

SEVERN ESTUARY (SOMERSET & BRISTOL).
Dr HE Rose. T: via WeBS Office;
E: H.E.Rose@bristol.ac.uk

SOMERSET LEVELS. Miss T Harper.
T: via WeBS Office; E: via WeBS Office

SOMERSET (OTHER SITES). Ms EM Tigwell.
T: 01373 451 630; E: eve.tigwell@zen.co.uk

Wildlife Trust
AVON WILDLIFE TRUST. (1980; 17,000).
32 Jacobs Wells Road, Bristol, BS8 1DR.
T: 0117 917 7270, (fax) 0117 929 7273;
E: mail@avonwildlifetrust.org.uk;
W: www.avonwildlifetrust.org.uk

SOMERSET WILDLIFE TRUST. (1964; 18,000).
34 Wellington Road, Taunton, Somerset TA1 5AW.
T: 01823 652 400, (fax) 01823 652 411;
E: enquiries@somersetwildlife.org;
W: www.somersetwildlife.org

STAFFORDSHIRE

Bird Atlas/Avifauna. See West Midlands.

Bird Recorder
Nick Pomiankowski, 22 The Villas, West End,
Stoke-on-Trent, ST4 5AQ. T: 01782 849 682;
E: staffs-recorder@westmidlandbirdclub.org.uk

Bird Report.
See West Midlands.

BTO Regional Representative
NORTH: Scott Petrek. T: n/a;
E: scott.petrek@gmail.com

Gerald Gittens (Assistant Representative).
T: 01785 815 141; E: gerald.gittens1@btopenworld.com

SOUTH: Scott Petrek/Gerald Gittens - see above.

WEST: Scott Petrek/Gerald Gittens - see above.

Club
WEST MIDLAND BIRD CLUB (STAFFORD BRANCH).
David Dodd (Chairman). Address: n/a. T: n/a;
E: stafford@westmidlandbirdclub.org.uk;
W: www.westmidlandbirdclub.org.uk/stafford
Meetings: 7.45pm, 1st Tuesday of the month
(Nov-Mar). Perkins Engines Sport & Social Club,
Tixall Road, Stafford, ST16 3UB.

RSPB Local Group
BURTON & SOUTH DERBYSHIRE. (1973; 50).
Dave Lummis. T: 01283 219 902;
E: david.lummis@btinternet.com;
W: www.basd-rspb.co.uk
Meetings: 7.30pm, 1st Wednesday of some
months between Sep-May - contact/see website
for details. All Saint's Church Hall, Branston Road,
Burton-on-Trent, DE14 3BY.

LICHFIELD & DISTRICT. (1977; 1150).
Dennis Muxworthy. T: 0121 353 6886;
E: dennis.muxworthy@btinternet.com;
W: www.rspb.org.uk/groups/lichfield
Meetings: 7.30pm, 2nd Tuesday of the month
(Sep-May). Guildhall, Bore Street, Lichfield, WS13 6LU.

NORTH STAFFS. (1982; 200).
Geoff Sales. T: 01782 618 152;
E: sgeoff31@gmail.com;
W: www.rspb.org.uk/groups/northstaffordshire
Meetings: 7.30pm, 3rd Wednesday of the month
(Sep-May). North Staffs Conference Centre (Medical
Institute), Hartshill Road, Stoke-on-Trent, ST4 7NY.

SOUTH WEST STAFFORDSHIRE. (1972; 145).
Theresa Dorrance. T: 01902 847 041;
E: tmidorrance@gmail.com;
ww.rspb.org.uk/groups/southweststaffs
Meetings: 8.00pm, 2nd Tuesday of the month
(Sep-May). Codsall Village Hall, Wolverhampton
Road, Codsall, WV8 1PW.

Wetland Bird Survey (WeBS) Organiser
STAFFORDSHIRE. Mr S Petrek. T: via WeBS Office;
E: scott.petrek@gmail.com

Wildlife Trust
STAFFORDSHIRE WILDLIFE TRUST. (1969; 15,000).
The Wolseley Centre, Wolseley Bridge, Stafford,
ST17 0WT. T: 01889 880 100, (fax) 01889 880 101;
E: info@staffs-wildlife.org.uk;
W: www.staffs-wildlife.org.uk

SUFFOLK

Bird Atlas/Avifauna
The Birds of Suffolk.
Steve Piotrowski
(Christopher Helm, 2003).

Bird Recorder
NORTH EAST. Andrew Green,
17 Cherrywood, Harleston,
Norfolk IP20 9LP.
T: 07766 900 063;
E: waveney@yahoo.com

SOUTH EAST. Scott Mayson, 8 St Edmunds Close,
Woodbridge, IP12 4UY. T: n/a;
E: smsuffolkbirder@gmail.com

WEST. Colin Jakes, 7 Maltward Avenue, Bury St
Edmunds, IP33 3XN. T: 01284 702 215;
E: colin@jakes.myzen.co.uk

SUFFOLK. National Rarities Co-ordinator.
David Walsh, 20 Netley Close, Ipswich, IP2 9YB.
T: 07947 051 223; E: davidfwalsh@hotmail.co.uk

Bird Report
SUFFOLK BIRDS (1950-), from Suffolk Naturalist's
Society, c/o The Museum, High St, Ipswich,
IP1 3QH. E: enquiries@sns.org.uk

BTO Regional Representative
Mick Wright. T: 01473 721 486; E: kupe1515@sky.com

Club
SUFFOLK ORNITHOLOGISTS' GROUP. (1973; 400).
Gi Grieco. Address: n/a. T: 07951 482 547;
E: info@sogonline.org.uk; W: www.sogonline.org.uk
Meetings: 7.30pm, last Thursday of the month
(Sep-Nov, Jan-Apr). The Wolsey Room, London
Road Holiday Inn, London Road, Ipswich, IP2 0UA
or The Cedars Hotel, Needham Road, Stowmarket,
IP14 2AJ.

WAVENEY BIRD CLUB. (n/a; n/a).
Helen Gooderham (Sec), Christmas Land Cottage,
Linstead Parva, Halesworth, IP19 0LF.
T: 01986 785 318;
E: secretary@waveneybirdclub.com;
W: www.waveneybirdclub.com
Meetings: 7.30pm, usually 2nd Monday of the
month (Oct-Mar). The Maltings Pavilion, Pirnhow
Street, Ditchingham, NR35 2RU.

Ringing Group/Bird Observatory
DINGLE BIRD CLUB. Dr D Pearson.
T: n/a; E: dpearson251@gmail.com

EAST ANGLIA GULL GROUP - contact BTO.

KESSINGLAND RG. Mrs P Walker. T: n/a;
E: patwalker663@gmail.com

LACKFORD RG. Dr P Lack. T: n/a;
E: bee.eaters@btinternet.com

LANDGUARD BIRD OBSERVATORY.
Landguard Bird Observatory, View Point Road,
Felixstowe, IP11 3TW. T: 01394 673 782;
E: langardbo@yahoo.co.uk; W: www.lbo.co.uk

LANDGUARD RG. Mr M Marsh. T: 01394 673 782;
E: mikecmarsh@tiscali.co.uk

LITTLE OUSE RG. Jacquie Clark. T: n/a;
E: nandjclark@btinternet.com

WAVENEY RG. Mr C McIntyre. T: 01379 678 345 &
07704 437 662; E: mcintyrechris@btinternet.com

RSPB Local Group
IPSWICH. (1975; 150).
Timothy Kenny. T: 01394 809 236;
E: IpswichRSPBlocalgroup@yahoo.com;
W: www.rspb.org.uk/groups/ipswich
Meetings: 7.30pm, 2nd Thursday of the month
(Sep-Apr). St Andrews Church Hall, The Street,
Rushmere,Ipswich, IP5 1DH.

LOWESTOFT. (1976; n/a).
Howard Bayliss. T: n/a;
E: LowestoftRSPBlocalgroup@gmail.com;
W: www.rspb.org.uk/groups/lowestoft
Meetings: 7.30pm, 1st Friday of the month
(all year). St Marks Church Centre, Bridge Road,
Oulton Broad, Lowestoft, NR33 9JX.

WOODBRIDGE. (1987; 320).
Paul Hetherington. T: 01728 724 504;
E: RSPBwoodbridge@paulandgill.com;
W: www.rspb.org.uk/groups/woodbridge
Meetings: 7.30pm, 1st Thursday of the month
(Oct-May). Woodbridge Community Hall, Station
Road,Woodbridge, IP12 4AU.

ENGLAND

Wetland Bird Survey (WeBS) Organiser
ALDE COMPLEX. Mr I Castle. T: 01394 450 188;
E: ian@castle-hamlett.co.uk

ALTON WATER. Mr J Glazebrook.
T: via WeBS Office;
E: johnglazebrook@btopenworld.com

BLYTH ESTUARY (SUFFOLK). Mr W Russell.
T: via WeBS Office; E: via WeBS Office

DEBEN ESTUARY. Mr N Mason. T: 07876 086 039 &
01394 411 150; E: nick.mason4@btinternet.com

ORWELL ESTUARY. Mr MT Wright.
T: 01473 721 486 & 07801 506 942;
E: kupe1515@sky.com

SUFFOLK (OTHER SITES). Mr A Miller.
T: 01502 478 788;
E: alanm@suffolkwildlifetrust.org

Wildlife Trust
SUFFOLK WILDLIFE TRUST. (1961; 28,000).
Brooke House, The Green, Ashbocking, Ipswich,
IP6 9JY. T: 01473 890 089, (fax) 01473 890 165;
E: info@suffolkwildlifetrust.org;
W: www.suffolkwildlifetrust.org

SURREY

Bird Atlas/Avifauna
Birds of Surrey. Jeffery J Wheatley (Surrey Bird
Club, 2007).

Bird Recorder
Eric Soden, Ceres, Moushill Lane, Milford, GU8 5BQ.
T: 01483 429 799; E: ericsoden@aol.co.uk

Bird Report
*SURBITON AND DISTRICT BIRD WATCHING SOCIETY
ANNUAL BIRD REPORT (1970-)*, from Thelma Caine,
21 More Lane, Esher, KT10 8AJ.
E: thelmacaine512@btinternet.com

SURREY BIRD REPORT (1953-), from Jeremy Gates,
5 Hillside Road, Weybourne, Farnham, GU9 9DW.
T: 01252 315 047; E: jeremygates@live.com

BTO Regional Representative
Penny Williams. T: 01276 857 736;
E: penny@waxwing.plus.com

Club
SURBITON & DISTRICT BIRDWATCHING SOCIETY.
(1954; 130). Gary Caine (Membership Sec),
21 More Lane, Esher, KT10 8AJ. T: 01372 468 432;
E: gary.caine@royalmail.com;
W: http://surbitonbirds.org/
Meetings: 8pm, 3rd Tuesday of each month
(not Aug). The Main Hall, Surbiton Library, Ewell
Rd, Surbiton, KT6 6AG.

SURREY BIRD CLUB. (1957; 360).
Penny Williams (Membership Sec), Bournbrook
House, Sandpit Hall Lane, Chobham, GU24 8HA.
T: 01276 857 736; E: sbc@waxwing.plus.com;
W: www.surreybirdclub.org.uk
Meetings: Contact/see website for details.

Ringing Group/Bird Observatory
HERSHAM RG. Mr A Beasley. T: n/a;
E: ajbeasley00@yahoo.co.uk

RUNNYMEDE RG. See Berkshire.

RSPB Local Group
DORKING & DISTRICT. (1982; 230).
Roy Theobald. T: 01306 889 976;
E: roytheobald@yahoo.co.uk;
W: www.rspb.org.uk/groups/dorkinganddistrict
Meetings: 8.00pm, 3rd Friday of the month
(Sep-Apr). Christian Centre, Church Street,
Dorking, RH4 1DW.

EAST SURREY. (1984; 7000+/area).
John Lawrence. T: 01737 553 316;
E: jfjlawrence@gmail.com;
W: www.eastsurreyrspb.co.uk
Meetings: 8.00pm, 2nd Wednesday of the month
(not Aug). White Hart Barn, Godstone, RH9 8DT.

EPSOM & EWELL. (1974; 50).
Timothy Tomkins. T: 0208 391 0116;
E: timothy.tomkins@yahoo.co.uk;
W: www.rspb.org.uk/groups/epsom
Meetings: 7.45pm, 2nd Friday of the month
(Sep-Jun). All Saints Church Hall, 7 Church Road,
West Ewell, KT19 9QY.

GUILDFORD & DISTRICT. (1974; 450).
Paul Graber. T: 01483 450 732;
E: Info@RSPBguildford.org.uk;
W: www.rspbguildford.org.uk
Meetings: Generally - 2.00pm, 1st Thursday
of the month (Sep-Apr). Shalford Village Hall,
Kings Road, Shalford, GU4 8JU & 7.30pm, 4th
Wednesday of the month (Sep-Apr). Onslow
Village Hall, The Square, Wilderness Road,
Guildford, GU2 7QR.

NORTH WEST SURREY. (1974; 150).
Alan Sharps. T: 01784 244 665;
E: nwsleader@yahoo.co.uk;
W: www.rspb.org.uk/groups/nwsurrey
Meetings: 7.45pm, 4th Wednesday of the month
(Sep-Jun). St Charles Borromeo School, Portmore
Way, Weybridge, KT13 8JD.

Wetland Bird Survey (WeBS) Organiser
SURREY & SW LONDON. Mrs P Williams.
T: via WeBS Office; E: penny@waxwing.plus.com

Wildlife Trust
SURREY WILDLIFE TRUST. (1959; 26,000).
School Lane, Pirbright, Woking, GU24 0JN.
T: 01483 795 440, (fax) 01483 486 505;
E: info@surreywt.org.uk;
W: www.surreywildlifetrust.org

SUSSEX

Bird Atlas/Avifauna
The Birds of Sussex. Sussex
Ornithological Society/
Adrian LR Thomas
(BTO, 2014).

Bird Recorder
Mark Mallalieu, 29 Cobbetts
Mead, Haywards Heath,
West Sussex RH16 3TQ.
T: 01444 441 425 &
07736 788 077;
E: recorder@sos.org.uk

Bird Report
SUSSEX BIRD REPORT (1948-), from John Trowell,
'Lorrimer', Main Road, Icklesham, Winchelsea,
E. Sussex TN36 4BS. E: membership@sos.org.uk

BTO Regional Representative
Helen Crabtree. T: 01444 441 687;
E: hcrabtree@gmail.com

Dave Boddington (Assistant Representative).
T: n/a; E: davebodds@yahoo.co.uk

Club
FRIENDS OF RYE HARBOUR NATURE RESERVE.
(1973; 2000+). Friends of Rye Harbour, Lime Kiln
Cottage, Rye Harbour Road, Rye, East Sussex
TN31 7TU. T: 07884 494 982;
E: rhnroffice@sussexwt.org.uk;
W: rhnrfriends.co.uk
& www.sussexwildlifetrust.org.uk/ryeharbour
Meetings: Special events, including winter talks,
held for Friends (info in newsletter).

HENFIELD BIRDWATCH. (1998; 150+).
Mike Russell, Tor-Est-In, Lower Station Road,
Henfield, West Sussex BN5 9UG. T: 01273 649 246;
E: mikerussell1@yahoo.co.uk;
W: http://henfieldbirdwatch.co.uk/

SHOREHAM DISTRICT ORNITHOLOGICAL SOCIETY.
(1953; 200). SDOS Hon. Sec, 24 Chancellors Park,
Hassocks, West Sussex BN6 8EZ. T: n/a;
E: membership@sdos.org; W: www.sdos.org
Meetings: 7.30pm, 2nd Tuesday of the month
(Oct-Apr). St Peter's Church Hall, West Street,
Shoreham-by-Sea, East Sussex BN43 5GZ.

SUSSEX ORNITHOLOGICAL SOCIETY. (1962; 2000+).
Chris Davis (Sec), 27 Salisbury Road, Seaford,
East Sussex BN25 2BD. T: 01323 891 267;
E: secretary@sos.org.uk; W: www.sos.org.uk
Meetings: Annual conference (Jan) Haywards
Heath. AGM (Apr) - contact/see website for details.

Ringing Group/Bird Observatory
BEACHY HEAD RS. Mr R Edgar. T: n/a;
E: redgar793047@gmail.com

CUCKMERE RG. Mr JAG Dunlop. T: 01323 844 642;
E: graeme2.dunlop@gmail.com

RYE BAY RG. Mr P Jones. T: n/a;
E: philjonespalace@gmail.com

STEYNING RG. Mr B Clay. T: n/a;
E: brian.clay@ntlworld.com

RSPB Local Group
BRIGHTON & DISTRICT. (1974; 190).
Mark Weston. T: 01903 606 581;
E: mark.weston@rspb.org.uk;
W: www.rspb.org.uk/groups/brighton
Meetings: 7.30pm, 4th Thursday of the month
(Sep-May, for Dec/see website). Brighton Hove
Sixth Form College, BHASVIC Sports Hall Café,
205 Dyke Road, Hove, East Sussex BN3 6EG.

CHICHESTER. (1979; 245).
Chris Furlepa. T: 01243 261 591;
E: chichesterbirds@gmail.com;
W: www.rspb.org.uk/groups/chichester
Meetings: 7.30pm, 4th Thursday of the month
(Sep-May). The Masonic Hall, 7 South Pallant,
Chichester, West Sussex PO19 1SY.

CRAWLEY & HORSHAM. (1978; 65).
Andrea Saxton. T: 01403 242 218;
E: andrea.saxton@sky.com;
W: www.rspb.org.uk/groups/crawley
Meetings: 8.00pm, 3rd Wednesday of the month
(Sep-Apr). The Friary Hall, Haslett Avenue West,
Crawley, West Sussex RH10 1HR.

EAST GRINSTEAD. (1998; 185).
Shaun Taylor. T: 01342 719 456;
E: eastgrinsteadRSPB@gmail.com;
W: www.rspb.org.uk/groups/egrinstead
Meetings: 7.45pm, last Wednesday of the month
(Sep-Jun, not Dec). Main Hall, East Court, College
Lane, East Grinstead, West Sussex RH19 3LT.

EASTBOURNE & DISTRICT. (1994; 200).
Tony Vass. T: 01424 844 304;
E: eastbourneRSPB@gmail.com;
W: www.rspb.org.uk/groups/eastbourne
Meetings: 2.15pm & 7.30pm, 1st Wednesday of
the month (Sep-Jun). St. Wilfrid's Church Hall,
Eastbourne Rd, Pevensey Bay, East Sussex BN24 6HL.

HASTINGS & ST LEONARDS. (1983; 65).
Micheal Hughes. T: 07709 892 772;
E: michealhughes2010@hotmail.co.uk;
W: www.rspb.org.uk/groups/hastings
Meetings: 7.30pm, 3rd Friday of the month. The
Taplin Centre, Upper Maze Hill, St Leonards-on-
Sea, East Sussex TN38 0LQ.

Wetland Bird Survey (WeBS) Organiser
CHICHESTER HARBOUR. Mr P Hughes.
T: via WeBS Office;
E: peter.hughes@conservancy.co.uk

SUSSEX (OTHER SITES - COASTAL).
Mr D Boddington. T: 01273 672 228 &
07771 758 105; E: davebodds@yahoo.co.uk

SUSSEX (OTHER SITES - INLAND). Dr HM Crabtree.
T: 01444 441 687 & 07989 384 281;
E: hcrabtree@gmail.com

Wildlife Trust
SUSSEX WILDLIFE TRUST. (1961; 30,000).
Woods Mill, Shoreham Road, Henfield, West Sussex
BN5 9SD. T: 01273 492 630, (fax) 01273 494 500;
E: enquiries@sussexwt.org.uk;
W: www.sussexwildlifetrust.org.uk

WARWICKSHIRE

Bird Atlas/Avifauna.
See West Midlands.

Bird Recorder
Steven Haynes. Address: n/a.
T: 01676 542 612
& 07815 675 090;
E: warks-recorder@
westmidlandbirdclub.org.uk

Bird Report.
See West Midlands.

BTO Regional Representative
Mark Smith. T: 01926 735 398;
E: mark.smith36@ntlworld.com

Club
NUNEATON & DISTRICT BIRDWATCHERS' CLUB.
(1950; 30). Address: n/a. T: n/a;
E: nuneatonbirdclub@outlook.com;
W: http://nuneatonbirdclub.wordpress.com/
Meetings: 7.30pm, 3rd Thursday of the month
(Sep-Apr). Hatters Space Community Centre,
Upper Abbey Street, Nuneaton, CV11 5DN.

Ringing Group/Bird Observatory
ARDEN RG. Mr R Juckes.T: 01789 778 748;
E: rogerjuckes24@btinternet.com

BRANDON RG. Mr D Stone. T: 01789 731488;
E: dave@rockuk.myzen.co.uk

RSPB Local Group
COVENTRY & WARWICKSHIRE. (1969; 120).
Peter Worthy. T: 01926 497 967;
E: pete@cpworthy.plus.com;
W: www.rspb.org.uk/groups/coventryandwarwickshire
Meetings: 7:30pm, 4th Friday of the month
(Sep-May). Baginton Village Hall, Frances Rd, Baginton,
Coventry, CV8 3AB.

Wetland Bird Survey (WeBS) Organiser
Mr M Griffiths. T: 01564 826 685 &
07837 138 815; E: matt_avesmaster@hotmail.com

Wildlife Trust
WARWICKSHIRE WILDLIFE TRUST. (1970; 23,000).
Brandon Marsh Nature Centre, Brandon Lane,
Coventry, CV3 3GW. T: 02476 302 912,
(fax) 02476 639 556; E: enquiries@wkwt.org.uk;
W: www.warwickshire-wildlife-trust.org.uk

WEST MIDLANDS

Bird Atlas/Avifauna
The New Birds of the West Midlands. Graham
& Janet Harrison - covers Staffordshire,
Warwickshire, Worcestershire & the former West
Midlands County (West Midland Bird Club, 2005).

Bird Recorder
Kevin Clements, 26 Hambrook Close, Dunstall
Park, Wolverhampton, West Midlands WV6 0XA.
T: 01902 568 997;
E: west-mids-recorder@westmidlandbirdclub.org.uk

Bird Report
WEST MIDLAND BIRD REPORT (inc Staffs, Warks,
Worcs & W Mids) (1934-), from Mark Rickus, 27
Ringmere Avenue, Castle Bromwich, B36 9AT.
E: secretary@westmidlandbirdclub.org.uk

BTO Regional Representative
BIRMINGHAM & WEST MIDLANDS. Steve Davies.
T: 07782 891 726;
E: stevedaviesbtorep@hotmail.co.uk

Club
WEST MIDLAND BIRD CLUB (1929; 1400).
(Staffs, Warks, Worcs & the West Midlands.
Mark Rickus (Sec), 27 Ringmere Avenue, Castle
Bromwich, Birmingham, B36 9AT. T: 0121 749 5348;
E: secretary@westmidlandbirdclub.org.uk;
W: www.westmidlandbirdclub.org.uk
Meetings: Contact/see website for branch details.

Field Trips only:
Ray Davies. T: 0121 682 4375 & 07762 061 603;
E: wmbcfieldtrips.ray@westmidlandbirdclub.org.uk
Judith Gerrard. T: 0121 427 3779 & 07975 631 430;
E: wmbcfieldtrips.judith@westmidlandbirdclub.org.uk

WEST MIDLAND BIRD CLUB (SOLIHULL BRANCH).
Humphrey Miller (Chairman), 29 Dorchester Court,
Dorchester Road, Solihull, B91 1LL. T: 0121 705 8507;
E: solihull@westmidlandbirdclub.org.uk;
W: www.westmidlandbirdclub.org.uk/solihull
Meetings: 7.30 pm, 1st Friday of the month (Oct-Mar).
Guild House, 1715 High Street, Knowle, Solihull, B93 0LN.
*# Branch future uncertain after Mar 2018 AGM
- check the website after this date.*

Ringing Group/Bird Observatory
BIRMINGHAM UNIVERSITY RG. Mrs L Kelly.
T: 07780 600 399; E: smileypinkfrog@yahoo.co.uk
W: http://www.birmingham.ac.uk/research/activity/
ornithology/people/ringing-group/index.aspx

MERCIAN RG. Mr D Clifton. T: n/a;
E: djc.dab@talk21.com

RSPB Local Group
SOLIHULL. (1983; 2600).
John Roberts. T: 0121 707 3101;
E: johnbirder@care4free.net;
W: www.rspb.org.uk/groups/solihull
Meetings: 7.30pm, (usually) 1st Thursday of the
month (Sep-Apr). Bentley Heath Community Hall,
Widney Road, Bentley Heath, Solihull, B93 9BQ.

STOURBRIDGE. (1978; 150).
David Bradford. T: 01384 390 035;
E: djbstourbridge@yahoo.co.uk;
W: www.rspb.org.uk/groups/stourbridge
Meetings: 7.30pm, 2nd Wednesday of the month
(Sep-May). Wollaston Suite, Stourbridge Town
Hall, Crown Centre, Stourbridge, DY8 1YE.

SUTTON COLDFIELD. (1986; 250).
Anna Keen. T: 01295 253 330;
E: anna.keen@RSPB.org.uk;
W: www.rspb.org.uk/groups/suttoncoldfield
Meetings: 7.30pm, normally 1st Monday of the
month (Sep-Jun). Bishop Vesey's Grammer School,
Lichfield Road, Sutton Coldfield, B74 2NH.

WALSALL. (1971; n/a).
Michael Pittaway. T: 01922 710 568;
E: michaelpittaway34@gmail.com;
W: www.rspb-walsall.org.uk
Meetings: 7.30pm, 3rd Wednesday of the month
(Sep-May). St Marys RC Primary School, Jesson Rd,
Walsall, WS1 3AY.

Wetland Bird Survey (WeBS) Organiser
WEST MIDLANDS. Mr NR Lewis. T: 0121 783 0874;
E: nick.r.lewis@virginmedia.com

Wildlife Trust
WILDLIFE TRUST FOR BIRMINGHAM
AND THE BLACK COUNTRY. (1980; 7,500).
16 Greenfield Crescent, Edgbaston, Birmingham,
B15 3AU. T: 0121 454 1199, (fax) 0121 454 6556;
E: info@bbcwildlife.org.uk; W: www.bbcwildlife.org.uk

WILTSHIRE

Bird Atlas/Avifauna
Birds of Wiltshire. J Ferguson-Lees, P Castle &
P Cranswick (Wiltshire Ornithological Society,
2007).

Bird Recorder
Nick Adams. Address: n/a; T: n/a;
E: recorder@wiltshirebirds.co.uk

Bird Report
WILTSHIRE BIRD REPORT (HOBBY) (1975-), from
John Osborne, 4 Fairdown Avenue, Westbury,
BA13 3HS. E: josb@talktalk.net

BTO Regional Representative
NORTH: Bill Quantrill. T: 01225 866 245;
E: william.quantrill@btinternet.com

SOUTH: Bill Quantrill - see above.

Club
SALISBURY & DISTRICT
NATURAL HISTORY SOCIETY.
(1952; 140).
John Pitman (Ornithology
Section). Address: n/a.
T: 01722 327 395;
E: jacpitman@btinternet.com;
W: www.salisburynaturalhistory.com
Meetings: 7.30pm, 3rd Thursday of the month
(Sep-Apr). The Meeting Room, Salisbury Baptist
Church, Brown Street, Salisbury, SP1 2AS.

WILTSHIRE ORNITHOLOGICAL SOCIETY. (1974; 500+).
Matt Prior (Chair). Address: n/a. T: n/a;
E: chair@wiltshirebirds.co.uk;
W: www.wiltshirebirds.co.uk
Meetings: 7.30pm, 2nd Tuesday of the month
(Oct-Mar). Crown Room, Crown Centre,
39 St. Johns Street, Devizes, SN10 1BL.

Ringing Group/Bird Observatory
COTSWOLD WATERPARK RG. See Gloucestershire.

NORTH WILTS RG. Mr G Deacon. T: n/a;
E: grahamd12@virginmedia.com

WEST WILTS RG. Mr S Tucker. T: 07789 438 451;
E: simonrtucker7@gmail.com

RSPB Local Group
SOUTH WILTSHIRE. (1986; 630).
Tony Goddard. T: 01722 712 713;
E: goddard543@hotmail.com;
W: www.rspb.org.uk/groups/southwiltshire
Meetings: 7.30pm, 2nd Tuesday of the month
(Sep-May). Salisbury Arts Centre, Bedwin Street,
Salisbury, SP1 3UT.

ENGLAND

Wetland Birds Survey Organiser
AVON VALLEY. See Hampshire.

COTSWOLD WATER PARK. See Gloucestershire.

WILTSHIRE. Mr W Quantrill. T: 01225 866 245;
E: william.quantrill@btinternet.com

Wildlife Trust
WILTSHIRE WILDLIFE TRUST. (1962; 17,000).
Elm Tree Court, Long Street, Devizes, SN10 1NJ.
T: 01380 725 670, (fax) 01380 729 017;
E: info@wiltshirewildlife.org;
W: www.wiltshirewildlife.org

WORCESTERSHIRE

Bird Atlas/Avifauna. See West Midlands.

Bird Recorder
Steven Payne, 6 Norbury Close, Redditch,
B98 8RP. T: 01527 60169;
E: worcs-recorder@westmidlandbirdclub.org.uk

Bird Report. See West Midlands.

BTO Regional Representative
Steve Davies. T: 01562 885 789;
E: stevedaviesbtorep@hotmail.co.uk

Harry Green (Assistant Representative).
T: 01386 710 377; E: zen130501@zen.co.uk

Club
WEST MIDLAND BIRD CLUB (KIDDERMINSTER
BRANCH). Brian Rickett (Chairman), 1 Russell
Road, Kidderminster, DY10 3HT. T: 01562 913 898;
E: kidderminster@westmidlandbirdclub.org.uk;
W: www.westmidlandbirdclub.org.uk/
kidderminster
Meetings: 7.30pm, 4th Wednesday of the month
(Sep-Apr). St Oswalds Church Centre,
off Broadwaters Drive, Kidderminster, DY10 2RY.

Ringing Group/Bird Observatory
WYCHAVON RG. Mr J Hodson. T: 01905 371 333;
E: hodson77@btinternet.com

RSPB Local Group
WORCESTER & MALVERN. (1980; 150).
Peter Butler. T: 01905 821 468;
E: peterbutler49@gmail.com;
W: www.rspb.org.uk/groups/worcester
Meetings: 7.30pm, 2nd Wednesday of the month
(Sep-May). Powick Village Hall, on A449, Powick,
WR2 4RT.

Wetland Bird Survey (WeBS) Organiser
WORCESTERSHIRE. Mr A Warr. T: 01905 28281;
E: andrew.warr3@btopenworld.com

Wildlife Trust
WORCESTERSHIRE WILDLIFE TRUST. (1967;
20,000). Lower Smite Farm, Smite Hill,
Hindlip, Worcester, WR3 8SZ. T: 01905 754
919, (fax) 01905 755 868; E: enquiries@
worcestershirewildlifetrust.org;
W: www.worcswildlifetrust.co.uk

YORKSHIRE

Bird Atlas/Avifauna
*Breeding Birds of the Sheffield Area including the
North-east Peak District.* David Wood & Richard
Hill (Sheffield Bird Study Group, 2013).

Birds of the Huddersfield Area. Paul & Betty Bray
(Huddersfield Birdwatchers Club, 2008).

The Birds of Yorkshire. J Mather (Croom Helm, 1986).

Bird Recorder
YORKSHIRE. Recorder, rarities.
Chris Robinson. Address: n/a; T: n/a;
E: sabsgull@hotmail.co.uk

EAST YORKSHIRE. Vacant.

NORTH YORKSHIRE. Ian Court, 2 Burley Mews,
Steeton, Keighley, BT20 6TX. T: 01535 658 582;
E: ian.court@mypostoffice.co.uk

SOUTH YORKSHIRE. Martin Wells, 715 Manchester
Road, Stocksbridge, Sheffield, S36 1DQ.
T: 0114 288 4211;
E: martinwells@barnsleybsg.plus.com

WEST YORKSHIRE. Andy Jowett. Address: n/a.
T: n/a; E: jowett.a@sky.com

Bird Report
*BIRDS IN HUDDERSFIELD
(1966-),* from
Michael Wainman,
2 Bankfield Avenue, Taylor Hill,
Huddersfield, HD4 7QY.
T: 01484 469 232;
E: m.wainman@ntlworld.com

*BIRDS IN THE SHEFFIELD AREA
(1973-),* from Martin Hodgson,
142 Hangingwater Road,
Sheffield, S11 7ET.
W: martin.hodgson54@
orangehome.com

*BRADFORD ORNITHOLOGICAL
GROUP REPORT (1987-), from
Mr CJ King, 7 Elder Bank,
Queensbury, Bradford,
BD13 2BT.
E: bogmembership@live.co.uk

ENGLAND

FILEY BIRD REPORT (1976-), from Janet Robinson, 31 Wharfedale, Filey, YO14 0DG.
E: ianrobinson@yorkshire.net

FLAMBOROUGH HEAD BIRD OBSERVATORY, from Tony Hood. 9 Hartendale Close, Flamborough, East Yorkshire YO15 1PL.
E: tonyhood74@gmail.com

HARROGATE & DISTRICT NATURALISTS' SOCIETY BIRD REPORT (1958-), from Jill Warwick, Sharow Grange, Sharow, Ripon, HG4 5BN. T: 01765 602 832; E: jill@swland.co.uk

SPURN WILDLIFE (1991-), from Spurn Bird Obs, Kew Villa, Kilnsea, via Patrington, Hull, HU12 0UB. T: 01964 650 479; E: friendsofspurn@hotmail.com

YORK ORNITHOLOGICAL CLUB REPORT (1966-), from Jane Chapman, 12 Moorland Road, York, YO10 4HF. T: 01904 633 558; E: secretary@yorkbirding.org.uk

YORKSHIRE BIRD REPORT (1940-), from Jill Warwick, Sharow Grange, Sharow, Ripon, HG4 5BN. T: 01765 602 832; E: jill@swland.co.uk

BTO Regional Representative
BRADFORD. Mike Denton. T: 01484 646 990; E: michael@atheta.plus.com

CENTRAL. Mike Brown. T: 01423 567 382; E: mikebtorep@gmail.com

EAST. Michael Hessey. T: n/a; E: mikeh-btora1@outlook.com

HULL. Michael Hessey - see above.

LEEDS & WAKEFIELD. Vacant - contact Dawn Balmer, BTO T: 01842 750 050

NORTH-EAST. Graham Oliver. T: 01947 811 290; E: g.h.oliver@btinternet.com

John McEachen (Assistant Representative). T: 01947 810 251; E: mceachen@btinternet.com

NORTH-WEST. Gerald Light. T: 01756 753 720; E: gerald@uwlig.plus.com

RICHMOND. Mike Gibson. T: 01677 450 542; E: mkgibson@btinternet.com

SOUTH-EAST: Aidan Gill. T: 07961 079 995; E: aidanpgill@gmail.com

SOUTH-WEST: Grant Bigg. T: n/a; E: gr_bigg@tiscali.co.uk

YORK. Rob Chapman. T: 01904 633 558; E: robert.chapman@tinyworld.co.uk

Club
BRADFORD ORNITHOLOGICAL GROUP. (1987; 100). Shaun Radcliffe (Chairman), 8 Longwood Avenue, Bingley, Bradford, BD16 2RX. T: 01274 770 960; E: shaun.radcliffe@btinternet.com; W: www.bradfordbirding.org
Meetings: 7.30pm, 1st Tuesday of the month (all year). The Link, 35 Cliffe Avenue, Baildon, Shipley, BD17 6NX.

FILEY BIRD OBSERVATORY & GROUP. (1977; 100). Contact: VACANT.
E: secretary@fbog.co.uk; W: www.fbog.co.uk

HARROGATE & DISTRICT NATURALISTS' SOCIETY. (1947; 210). Sue Coldwell (Gen Sec), 4 Abbots Way, Knaresborough, HG5 8EU. T: 01423 868 043; E: gensec@hdns.org.uk; W: www.hdns.org.uk
Meetings: 7.30pm, fortnightly, on a Wednesday (Oct-Mar). St. Roberts Centre, 2/3 Robert Street, Harrogate, HG1 1HP.

HUDDERSFIELD BIRDWATCHERS' CLUB. (1966; 80). Chris Abell (Sec), 57 Butterley Lane, New Mill, Holmfirth, HD9 7EZ. T: 01484 681 499; E: cdabell@googlemail.com; W: www.huddersfieldbirdwatchersclub.co.uk
Meetings: 7.30pm, Tuesday's fortnightly (Sep-May). The Old Court Room, Town Hall, Ramsden St, Huddersfield, HD1 2TA.

HULL VALLEY WILDLIFE GROUP. (1997; 175). Barry Warrington (Membership Sec), 51 Buttfield Road, Hessle, HU13 0AX. T: n/a; E: wildlife_barrywarrington@yahoo.co.uk; W: http://hullvalleywildlifegroup.blogspot.co.uk/

ROTHERHAM & DISTRICT ORNITHOLOGICAL SOCIETY. (1974; 80). RDOS, c/o Galaxy Four, 493 Glossop Road, Sheffield, S10 2QE; T: n/a; E: via website; W: www.rotherhambirds.co.uk
Meetings: 7.30pm, 2nd Friday of the month (Sep-Apr). Herringthorpe United Reform Church Hall, Wickersley Road, Rotherham, S60 4JN.

SCARBOROUGH BIRDERS. (1993; 50). Ian Glaves (Sec). Address: n/a.
T: 01723 859 766; E: n/a; W: www.scarboroughbirding.co.uk
Meetings: contact/see website for details. (Oct-Mar). Ye Olde Forge Valley, 5 Pickering Road, West Ayton, Scarborough, YO13 9JE.

SHEFFIELD BIRD STUDY GROUP. (1972; 260). Richard Hill (Sec), 22 Ansell Road, Sheffield, S11 7PE. T: n/a; E: Secretary@sbsg.org; W: www.sbsg.org
Meetings: 7.15pm, 2nd Wednesday of the month (Sep-May). Hicks Building Lecture Theatre 5, Sheffield University, Hounsfield Road, Sheffield, S3 7RH.

ENGLAND

SK58 BIRDERS. (1992; 50).
Paul Tennyson (Chairman),
16/18 Sheffield Road, South
Anston, Sheffield, S25 5DT.
T: 01909 569 409;
E: p.tennyson@sky.com;
W: www.sk58birders.com
Meetings: 7.30pm, last
Wednesday of the month
(Sep-Nov & Jan-May). The
Loyal Trooper Inn, Sheffield
Road, South Anston, Sheffield,
S25 5DT.

SK58 BIRDERS

SORBY NATURAL HISTORY SOCIETY. (1918; 400).
(Ornithology Section) - Sec position vacant.
E: ornithology@sorby.org.uk; W: www.sorby.org.uk
Meetings: Regularly held - contact/see website
for details.

SWILLINGTON INGS BIRD GROUP. (1989; 230).
Martin Robinson (Sec). Address: n/a; T: n/a;
E: swillingtoningsbirdgroup@gmail.com;
W: http://sibg1.wordpress.com
Meetings: 7.30pm, usually 1st Thursday of the
month (Feb, Apr, Jun, Aug, Oct, Dec).
Two Pointers, 69 Church Street, Woodlesford,
LS26 8RE.

WAKEFIELD NATURALISTS' SOCIETY. (1851; 30).
Address: n/a; T: n/a; E: via website;
W: http://wakefieldnaturalists.org
Meetings: 7.30pm, 2nd Tuesday of the month
(Sep-Apr). Quaker Meeting House, Thornhill
Street, Wakefield, WF1 1NQ.

YORK ORNITHOLOGICAL CLUB. (1965; 80).
Jane Chapman (Sec), 12 Moorland Road, York
YO10 4HF. T: 01904 633 558;
E: secretary@yorkbirding.org.uk;
W: www.yorkbirding.org.uk
Meetings: 7.30pm, 1st Tuesday of the month
(Sep-Jun). St Olaves Church Hall, Marygate Lane,
Marygate, York, YO30 7BJ.

YORKSHIRE NATURALISTS' UNION (1861; 500).
Jill Warwick (Bird Section - Sec), Sharow Grange,
Sharow, Ripon, HG4 5BN. T: 01765 602 832;
E: jill@swland.co.uk; W: www.ynu.org.uk
Meetings: No indoor meetings held.

Ringing Group/Bird Observatory
BARNSLEY RG. Mr M Wells. T: n/a;
E: martinwells@barnsleybsg.plus.com

DONCASTER RG. Mr D Hazard. T: 01302 391 120;
E: davesaringer@gmail.com

EAST DALES RG. Mrs J Warwick. T: n/a;
E: jill@swland.co.uk;
W: https://eastdalesringinggroup.wordpress.com

EAST YORKSHIRE RG (inc. Filey & Flamborough
Bird Observatories). Mr M Thomas.
T: 07803 241 452; E: mark.thomas@rspb.org.uk

Mr P Dunn (Ringing Officer) T: 07720 769 473;
E: pjd@fbog.co.uk

FILEY BIRD OBSERVATORY. See Club.

FLAMBOROUGH BIRD OBSERVATORY.
Tony Hood, (Sec) 9 Hartendale Close,
Flamborough, East Yorkshire YO15 1PL.
T: n/a; E: tonyhood74@gmail.com;
W: http://fbo.org.uk/

HUMBER WADER RG. Mrs C Barker.
T: 07949 231777; E: cbarker2@btinternet.com

PICKERING FORESTS RG. Mr I Nicholson. T: n/a;
E: ian.n1000@btinternet.com

SAND HUTTON RG. Mrs R Jones. T: n/a;
E: rebecca.j.farthing@gmail.com

SORBY BRECK RG. Dr G Mawson.
T: 01246 415 097; E: moonpenny@talktalk.net;
W: www.britishringers.co.uk

SPURN BIRD OBSERVATORY.
Mr P Collins (Warden), Spurn Bird Obs, Kilnsea,
via Patrington, Hull, HU12 0UG. T: 01964 650 479;
E: pcnfa@hotmail.com;
W: www.spurnbirdobservatory.co.uk

SWALEDALE RG. Tony Crease. T: n/a;
E: tonycrease@btinternet.com

RSPB Local Group
AIREDALE & BRADFORD. (1972; 3500/area).
Paul Barrett. T: 01274 582 078;
E: abRSPB@blueyonder.co.uk;
W: www.rspb.org.uk/groups/airedaleandbradford
Meetings: 7.30pm, 1st Friday of the month
(Sep-Apr). The Kirkgate Centre, 39A Kirkgate,
Shipley, BD18 3EH.

DONCASTER. (1984; 70).
Steve Pynegar. T: 01302 834 443;
E: steve.pynegar@gmail.com;
W: www.rspbdoncaster.com
Meetings: 7.00pm, 2nd Wednesday of the month
(Sep-May). Castle Park Rugby Club, Armthorpe
Road, Doncaster, DN2 5QB.

EAST YORKSHIRE. (1986; 120).
Paul Leyland. T: 01723 891 507;
E: EastyorksRSPB@yahoo.co.uk;
W: www.rspb.org.uk/groups/eastyorkshire
Meetings: 7.30pm, 4th Tuesday of the month
(Sep-Apr, not Dec). North Bridlington Library,
Martongate, Bridlington, YO16 6YD.

ENGLAND

HARROGATE DISTRICT. (2005; 90).
Bill Sturman. T: 01423 870 883;
E: billsturman@outlook.com;
W: www.rspb.org.uk/groups/harrogate
Meetings: 7.30pm, 2nd Monday of the month
(Sep-Apr). Christ Church Parish Centre, The Stray,
Harrogate, HG1 4SW.

HUDDERSFIELD & HALIFAX. (1981; 100).
David Hemingway. T: 01484 301 920;
E: d.hemingway@ntlworld.com;
W: www.rspb.org.uk/groups/huddersfieldandhalifax
Meetings: 7.30pm, 3rd Wednesday of the month
(Sep-Jun). New North Road Baptist Church, New
North Parade, Huddersfield, HD1 5JU.

HULL & DISTRICT. (1983; 335).
John Hallam. T: 01482 354 595;
E: jobar.hull@hotmail.com;
W: www.rspb.org.uk/groups/hull
Meetings: 7.30pm, 2nd Tuesday of the month
(Sep-Apr). Christchurch United Reformed Church,
South Ella Way, Kirk Ella, Hull, HU10 7HB.

LEEDS. (1974; 420).
Ian Willoughby. T: 0113 258 6555;
E: RSPBleeds@googlemail.com;
W: www.rspb.org.uk/groups/leeds
Meetings: 7.30pm, various Wednesdays (Sep-Apr).
Friends Meeting House, 188 Woodhouse Lane,
Leeds, LS2 9DX.

RICHMONDSHIRE & HAMBLETON. (2005; n/a).
Ted Cooper. T: 07767 886 358;
E: croftbirder@hotmail.com;
W: www.rspb.org.uk/groups/
richmondshireandhambleton
Meetings: Various - contact/see website for
details.

SHEFFIELD. (1981; 300).
Helen Ensor. T: 07749 932 806;
E: ensorhelen@gmail.com;
W: www.rspb.org.uk/groups/sheffield
Meetings: 7.30pm, 1st Thursday of the month
(Sep-May). Central United Reformed Church,
Norfolk Street, Sheffield, S1 2JB.

SKIPTON. (1986; 300).
Ewart Dawson. T: 01729 840 601;
E: ewartdawson1@gmail.com;
W: www.rspb.org.uk/groups/skipton
Meetings: 7.30pm, 2nd Wednesday of the month
(Sep-Apr). The Church Hall, Skipton Baptist
Church, Rectory Lane, Skipton, BD23 1ER.

WAKEFIELD. (1987; 100).
Duncan Stokoe. T: 01924 280 458;
E: duncanstokoe@gmail.com;
W: www.rspb.org.uk/groups/wakefield
Meetings: 7.30pm, 4th Thursday of the month
(Sep-Apr). Ossett Community Centre, Prospect
Road, Ossett, WF5 8AN.

YORK. (1972; 600).
Barry Bishop. T: 01904 639 853;
E: barryjbishop@hotmail.com;
W: www.rspb.org.uk/groups/york
Meetings: 7.30pm, usually 2nd week of the month
on a Tues, Wed or Thurs (Sep-May). Also afternoon
meetings, 2.30pm - contact/check website for
details. Clements Hall, Nunthorpe Road, York,
YO23 1BW.

Wetland Bird Survey (WeBS) Organiser
EAST YORKSHIRE AND SCARBOROUGH (excl.
THE HUMBER). Mr S Morgan. T: 01965 544 947 &
07951 075 045; E: jimmygpz@hotmail.com

HARROGATE AND YORKSHIRE DALES.
Mr WG Haines. T: 07870 828 978;
E: bill.haines@westlondonbirding.co.uk

HUDDERSFIELD & HALIFAX AREA.
Vacant - contact WeBS Office.

HUMBER ESTUARY (NORTH). Mr N Cutts.
T: via WeBS Office; E: via WeBS Office

LEEDS AREA. Mr PR Morris. T: via WeBS Office.
E: paulr.morris8@outlook.com

SOUTH YORKSHIRE. Mr J Dunning.
T: 07981 737 748; E: jamiedunning8@gmail.com

WAKEFIELD AREA. Mr P Smith. T: via WeBS Office;
E: via WeBS Office

Wildlife Trust
SHEFFIELD AND ROTHERHAM WILDLIFE TRUST.
(1985; 5,200).
37 Stafford Road, Sheffield, S2 2SF.
T: 0114 263 4335, (fax) 0114 263 4345;
E: mail@wildsheffield.com;
W: www.wildsheffield.com

YORKSHIRE WILDLIFE TRUST. (1946; 40,000).
1 St George's Place, Tadcaster Road, York,
YO24 1GN. T: 01904 659 570;
E: info@ywt.org.uk; W: www.ywt.org.uk

SCOTLAND

Bird Atlas/Avifauna
The Birds of Scotland. Ron Forrester &
Ian Andrews (Scottish Ornithologist's Club, 2007).

Bird Report
SCOTTISH BIRD REPORT (1968-, data online since
2002), from W: www.the-soc.org.uk/publications/
scottish-bird-report-online/

Club
SCOTTISH ORNITHOLOGISTS' CLUB.
See National Directory.

Wildlife Trust
SCOTTISH WILDLIFE TRUST. (1964; 41,000)
See National Directory.

ANGUS & DUNDEE

Bird Recorder
Jon Cook. 76 Torridon Road,
Broughty Ferry, Dundee, DD5
3JH. T: 01382 738 495;
E: 1301midget@tiscali.co.uk

Bird Report
ANGUS & DUNDEE BIRD
REPORT (1985-), from the
Bird Recorder - see above.

BTO Regional Representative
ANGUS. Peter Ellis. T: n/a;
E: peterellis46@gmail.com

Ken Slater (Regional Development Officer).
T: n/a; E: alisonslater19@aol.com

Club
ANGUS & DUNDEE BIRD CLUB. (1997; 200+).
Gus Guthrie. Address: n/a. T: 01575 574 548;
E: gusguthrie@btinternet.com;
W: www.angusbirding.com/html/adbc.html
Meetings: 7.30pm, 3rd Tuesday of the month
(Sep-Apr). Panbride Church Hall, 8 Arbroath Road,
Carnoustie, Angus DD7 6BL.

SOC TAYSIDE BRANCH. (1960's; 150).
Brian Brocklehurst, 146 Broughty Ferry, DD5 3EB.
T: 01382 778 348;
E: brian.brocklehurst1@btinternet.com;
W: www.the-soc.org.uk
Meetings: 7.30pm, 1st Thursday of the month
(Sep-Apr, 2nd Thursday in Jan). Methodist Church
Halls, 20 Marketgait, Dundee, DD1 1QR

Ringing Group/Bird Observatory
TAY RG. E: contact via website -
http://tayringinggroup.org/contact.htm
W: www.tayringinggroup.org/

RSPB Local Group
DUNDEE. (1972; 100).
Graham Smith. T: 01382 532 461;
E: grahamnjen@hotmail.com;
W: www.rspb.org.uk/groups/dundee
Meetings: 7.30 pm, 2nd or 3rd Wednesday of
the month (Sep-Nov/Jan-Mar plus AGM Apr &
xmas social Dec). Methodist Church,
20 West Marketgait, Dundee, DD1 1QR.

Wetland Bird Survey (WeBS) Organiser
ANGUS (excl. MONTROSE BASIN).
Vacant - contact WeBS Office.

MONTROSE BASIN. Miss A Cheshier.
T: via WeBS Office; E: acheshier@swt.org.uk

ARGYLL

Bird Atlas/Avifauna
Birds of Argyll. Tristan ap Rheinallt, Clive Craik,
P Daw, B Furness, S Petty &
D Wood (Argyll Bird Club, 2007).

Bird Recorder
Jim Dickson, 11 Pipers Road, Cairnbaan,
Lochgilphead, Argyll PA31 8UF. T: 01546 603 967;
E: meg@jdickson5.plus.com

Assistant Recorder. Malcolm Chattwood, 1 The
Stances, Kilmichael Glassary, Lochgilphead, Argyll
PA31 8QA. T: 01546 603 389;
E: abcrecorder@outlook.com
For submission of all non-rare bird records.

Bird Report
ARGYLL BIRD REPORT (1980/83-), from
Bob Furness, The Cnoc, Tarbet, Arrochar,
Dunbartonshire G83 7DG.
E: bob.furness@glasgow.ac.uk

ARRAN BIRD REPORT (1980-), from ANHS c/o
Lindsey & Robert Marr, Tiree, Brodick Road,
Lamlash, Isle of Arran, KA27 8JU.
E: marr.tiree98@btinternet.com

ISLE OF MULL BIRD REPORT (2003-), from Mr Alan
Spellman, 'Maridon', Lochdon, Isle of Mull, Argyll
PA64 6AP. T: 01680 812 448;
E: mullbirds@btinternet.com; W: www.mullbirds.com

BTO Regional Representative
ARGYLL MAINLAND, BUTE & GIGHA. Nigel Scriven.
T: 07901 636 353; E: njscriven@gmail.com.

ARGYLL (MULL, COLL, TIREE & MORVERN).
Geoff Small. T: 01680 300 002;
E: geoff.small@btopenworld.com

Sue Dewar (Regional Development Officer).
T: n/a; E: suedewar123@btinternet.com

ARRAN ONLY. James Cassels (Assistant Representative).
T: 01770 860 316; E: jim@arranbirdingh.co.uk

ISLAY, JURA & COLONSAY. David Wood.
T: 01496 300 118; E: david.wood@rspb.org.uk

Club
ARGYLL BIRD CLUB. (1985; 270).
Anne Archer (Sec), 2 The Meadows, Toward, By
Dunoon, Argyll, PA23 7UP. T: 01369 870 273;
E: archerspringbank@btinternet.com;
W: www.argyllbirdclub.org
Meetings: All-day indoor meetings are held on
a Saturday in early Mar & early Nov each year -
contact/see website for details.

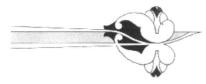

ISLE OF MULL BIRD CLUB. (2001; 150+).
Felicity Pollard (Sec), Fear nen Eun, Aros, Isle of
Mull PA72 6JP. T: 01680 300 013;
E: secretary@mullbirdclub.org.uk;
W: www.mullbirdclub.org.uk
Meetings: 7.30pm, 3rd Friday of the month
(Sep-Apr). Craignure Village Hall, PA65 6BE

Ringing Group/Bird Observatory
TRESHNISH ISLES AUK RG. Mr A Carter.
T: 01722 710 382; E: standlynch@btinternet.com

RSPB Local Group
HELENSBURGH. (1975; 35).
John Clark. T: 01436 821 178;
E: laighfield@gmail.com;
W: www.rspb.org.uk/groups/helensburgh
Meetings: 7.30 pm, 3rd Wednesday of the month
(Sep-Apr). The Guide Halls, Lower John Street,
Helensburgh.

Wetland Bird Survey (WeBS) Organiser
ARGYLL MAINLAND. Mr N Scriven.
T: 07901 636 353; E: njscriven@gmail.com

ARRAN. Mr J Cassels. T: 01770 860 316;
E: jim@arranbirding.co.uk

BUTE. Mr IL Hopkins. T: 01700 504 042 &
07702 123 170; E: hopkins0079@btinternet.com

ISLAY, JURA & COLONSAY. Mr D Wood.
T: 01496 300 118; E: david.wood@rspb.org.uk

MULL. Mr N Scriven - see above.

TIREE & COLL. Dr J Bowler. T: 01879 220 748.
E: john.bowler@rspb.org.uk

AYRSHIRE

Bird Recorder
Fraser Simpson, 4 Inchmurrin Drive, Kilmarnock,
KA3 2JD; T: n/a;
E: recorder@ayrshire-birding.org.uk

Bird Report
AYRSHIRE BIRD REPORT (1976-), from Anne Dick,
Rowanmyle House, Tarbolton, Mauchline,
KA5 5LU. E: a_m_dick@hotmail.com

BTO Regional Representative
AYRESHIRE & CUMBRAE.
Brian Broadley. T: 01290 424 241;
E: brianbroadley@picavert.com

Club
SOC AYRSHIRE BRANCH. (1962; 120).
Anne Dick, Rowanmyle House, Tarbolton,
Mauchline, KA5 5LU. T: 01292 541 981;
E: a_m_dick@btinternet.com;
W: www.the-soc.org.uk
Meetings: 7.30pm, 2nd Tuesday of the month
(Sep-Apr). Monkton Community Church,
Main Street, Monkton by Prestwick, KA9 2RN.

RSPB Local Group
CENTRAL AYRSHIRE. (1978; 85).
Anne Dick. T: 01292 541 981;
E: a_m_dick@btinternet.com;
W: www.ayrshire-birding.org.uk
Meetings: 7.30pm. 3rd Monday of the month
(Sep-Apr). Newton Wallacetown Church Hall,
60 Main Street, Ayr, KA8 8EF.

NORTH AYRSHIRE. (1976; 180).
John Tedd. T: 01294 823 434;
E: john.tedd@virgin.net; W: www.narspb.org.uk
Meetings: 7.30pm, 2nd Friday of the month
(Sep-Apr). Argyll Centre, Donaldson Avenue,
Saltcoats, Ayrshire KA21 5AG.

Wetland Bird Survey (WeBS) Organiser
AYRSHIRE (excl. ISLE OF CUMBRAE). Mr DA Grant.
T: via WeBS Office; E: daveg466@gmail.com

ISLE OF CUMBRAE. Vacant - contact WeBS Office.

BORDERS

Bird Atlas/Avifauna
*The Breeding Birds of South-east Scotland:
A tetrad atlas 1988-1994.* Ray Murray, Mark
Holling, Harry Dott & Peter Vandome. (Scottish
Ornithologists' Club, 1998).

Bird Recorder
Martin Moncrieff. Address: n/a; T: (
E: bordersrecorder@gmail.com

SCOTLAND

David Parkinson. Address: n/a; T: 01896 822 028;
E: bordersrecorder@gmail.com

Bird Report
BORDERS BIRD REPORT (1979-), from Malcolm
Ross, Westfield Cottage, Smailholm, Kelso,
TD5 7PN. T: 01573 460 699;
E: eliseandmalcolm@btinternet.com

BTO Regional Representative
Dave McGarvie. T: n/a; E: 7askja@gmail.com

Club
SOC BORDERS BRANCH. (1980; 150).
Neil Stratton, Heiton Mains, Heiton, Kelson,
TD5 8JR. T: 01573 450 695;
E: neildstratton@btinternet.com;
W: www.the-soc.org.uk
Meetings: 7.30pm, 2nd Monday of the month
(Sep-Apr, except Jan). Kingsknowes Hotel, Selkirk
Road, Galashiels, TD1 3HY.

Ringing Group/Bird Observatory
BORDERS RG. Dr T Dougall.
T: n/a; E: gilltomer@hotmail.com

Wetland Bird Survey (WeBS) Organiser
BORDERS. Mr AT Bramhall. T: 01896 755 326;
E: andrewtbramhall@gmail.com

CLYDE

Bird Atlas/Avifauna
*Arran Bird Atlas 2007-2012:
Mapping the breeding and
wintering birds of Arran.* Jim
Cassels (Arran NHS, 2014).

*The Birds of Bute: A Bird
Atlas and Local Avifauna.*
Ronald Forrester, Ian Hopkins
& Doug Menzies (Buteshire
NHS, 2012).

Bird Recorder
Recorder. Iain Gibson, 8 Kenmure View, Howwood,
Johnstone, Renfrewshire PA9 1DR.
T: 01505 705 874; E: iaingibson.soc@btinternet.com

Assistant Recorder, Rarities. Val Wilson, Flat 2/1,
12 Rawcliffe Gardens, Langside, Glasgow, G41
3DA. T: 0141 649 4512;
E: val.wilson38@btinternet.com

CLYDE ISLANDS (ARRAN, BUTE & CUMBRAE).
Bernard Zonfrillo, 28 Brodie Road, Glasgow,
G21 3SB. T: n/a; E: b.zonfrillo@bio.gla.ac.uk

Bird Report
CLYDE BIRDS (Clyde & Clyde Islands) (1973-), Val
Wilson, Flat 2/1 12 Rawcliffe Gardens, Glasgow,
G41 3DA. E: val.wilson38@btinternet.com

BTO Regional Representative
LANARK, RENFREW & DUNBARTON.
Andy Winnington. T: 01475 528 841;
E: andy.winnington@yahoo.com

Club
SOC CLYDE BRANCH. (n/a; 300).
Ian Fulton. Address: n/a. T: 0141 773 4329;
E: SOC.Clyde@btinternet.com; W: www.the-soc.org.uk
Meetings: 7.30pm, 1st Monday of the month
(Sep-Apr, except Sep & Jan/2nd Mon). Zoology
Dept, Graham Kerr Building, University of
Glasgow, G12 8QQ.

Ringing Group/Bird Observatory
CLYDE RG. Mr I Livingstone. T: 01698 871 688;
E: iainlivcrg@googlemail.com

RSPB Local Group
GLASGOW. (1972; 140).
Neil Rankine. T: 07986 580 116;
E: rspbglasgowgroupleader@gmail.com
W: www.rspb.org.uk/groups/glasgow
Meetings: 7.30pm, 2nd Wednesday of the month
(Sep-Apr). Renfield St Stephens Church Centre,
260 Bath Street, Glasgow, G2 4JP.

HAMILTON. (1976; 90).
Jim Lynch. T: 0141 583 1044;
E: birder45a@yahoo.co.uk;
W: www.rspb.org.uk/groups/hamilton
Meetings: 7.30pm, 3rd Thursday of the month
(Sep-May). Motherwell South Parish Church, 11
Gavin Street, Motherwell, ML1 2RL.

RENFREWSHIRE. (1986; 200).
Margaret Brown. T: n/a;
E: RenfrewRSPB@hotmail.com;
W: www.rspb.org.uk/groups/renfrewshire
Meetings: 7.30pm, 1st Friday of the month
(Sep-May, 2nd Friday in Jan). The McMaster
Centre, 2a Donaldson Drive, Renfrew, PA4 8LX.

Wetland Bird Survey (WeBS) Organiser
CLYDE ESTUARY. Mr J Clark. T: 01436 821 178 &
07703 211 696; E: laighfield@gmail.com

GLASGOW, RENFREWSHIRE, LANARKSHIRE.
Mr J Clark - see above.

DUMFRIES & GALLOWAY

Bird Recorder
Paul Collin, 'Gairland', Old Edinburgh Road,
Minnigaff, Newton Stewart, DG8 6PL.
T: 01671 402 861; E: pncollin@live.co.uk

Bird Report
BIRDS IN DUMFRIES & GALLOWAY (1987-), from Peter
Swan, 3 Castle View, Castle Douglas, DG7 1BG.
T: 01556 502 144; E: pandmswan@btinternet.com

SCOTLAND

BTO Regional Representative
DUMFRIES. Andy Riches. T: n/a;
E: slioch69@aol.com

KIRKCUDBRIGHT. Andrew Bielinski. T: 01644 430 418;
E: andrewb@bielinski.fsnet.co.uk

WIGTOWN. Geoff Sheppard. T: 01776 870 685;
E: geoff.roddens@btinternet.com

Club
SOC DUMFRIES BRANCH. (1964; 85).
Lesley Creamer, Braeside, Virginhall, Thornhill,
DG3 4AD. T: 01848 330 821;
E: braesideles@gmail.com; W: www.the-soc.org.uk
Meetings: 7.30pm, 2nd Wednesday of the month
(Sep-Apr). Cumberland St Day Centre, Dumfries
(off Brooms Rd car park), DG1 2JX.

SOC STEWARTRY BRANCH. (1976; 80).
Joan Howie, The Wilderness, High Street, New
Galloway, Castle Douglas, DG7 3RL.
T: 01644 420 280; E: joanospreys1@btinternet.com;
W: www.the-soc.org.uk
Meetings: 7.30pm, various Thursdays during the
month (Sep-Mar). Kells School, New Galloway,
DG7 3RU

SOC WEST GALLOWAY BRANCH. (1975; 35).
Geoff Sheppard, The Roddens, Leswalt, Stranraer,
DG9 0QR. T: 01776 870 685;
E: geoff.roddens@btinternet.com;
W: www.the-soc.org.uk
Meetings: 7.30pm, usually 1st or 2nd Tuesday of
the month (Oct-Mar). Stranraer Library, North
Strand Street, Stranraer, DG9 7LD.

Ringing Group/Bird Observatory
NORTH SOLWAY RG. Mr G Sheppard.
T: 01776 870 685; E: geoff.roddens@btinternet.com

RSPB Local Group
GALLOWAY. (1985; 120).
David Henshilwood. T: 01566 650 129;
E: david.henshilwood@btinternet.com;
W: www.rspb.org.uk/groups/galloway
Meetings: 7.30pm, irregular Mondays (Sep-Apr).
The Gordon Memorial Hall, adjoining St Ninian's
Scottish Episcopal Church, Whitepark Road, Castle
Douglas, DG7 1EX.

Wetland Bird Survey (WeBS) Organiser
AUCHENCAIRN AND ORCHARDTON BAYS.
Mr EAM MacAlpine. T: 01556 640 244;
E: js.eamm@gmail.com

DUMFRIES AND GALLOWAY (OTHER SITES).
Mr AC Riches. T: 07792 142 446 & 07376 636 341;
E: slioch69@aol.com

FLEET BAY. Mr DM Hawker. T: 01557 814 249 &
07748 590 838; E: davidhawker3@gmail.com

LOCH RYAN. Mr PN Collin. T: 01671 402 861;
E: pncollin@live.co.uk

ROUGH FIRTH. Ms J Baxter. T: via WeBS Office;
E: jbaxter@nts.org.uk

SOLWAY ESTUARY (NORTH). Mr AC Riches - see above.

WIGTOWN BAY. Mr PN Collin - see above.

FIFE

Bird Atlas/Avifauna
The Fife Bird Atlas. Norman Elkins, Jim Reid,
Allan Brown, Derek Robertson & Anne-Marie
Smout. (Privately Pub, 2003).

Bird Recorder
FIFE inc.OFFSHORE ISLANDS (NORTH FORTH) -
(excl. Isle of May). Graham Spa, 19 Inverewe
Place, Dunfermline, KY11 8FH; T: 07770 225 440;
E: grahamspa@aol.com

ISLE OF MAY. Iain English, 19 Nethan Gate,
Chantinghall Road, Hamilton, South Lanarkshire
ML3 8NH; T: 01698 891 788;
E: i.english@talk21.com

Bird Report
FIFE BIRD REPORT (1988-), from the Bird Recorder
- see above.

ISLE OF MAY BIRD OBSERVATORY REPORT (1985-),
from Stuart Rivers, Flat 8 (2F2), 10 Waverley
Park, Edinburgh, EH8 8EU.
E: slr.bee-eater@blueyonder.co.uk

BTO Regional Representative
FIFE & KINROSS. Norman Elkins. T: 01334 654 348;
E: jandnelkins@btinternet.com

Club
FIFE BIRD CLUB. (1985; 200).
The Secretary.
Address: n/a. T: n/a;
E: secretary@fifebirdclub.org;
W: www.fifebirdclub.org.uk
Meetings: 7.30pm, usually
a Thursday (Sep, Oct, Dec,
Jan, Mar, Jun) plus an AGM
- contact/see website for
details. Dean Park Hotel, Kirkcaldy, KY2 6HF.

LOTHIANS AND FIFE SWAN &
GOOSE STUDY GROUP. (1978; 12)
Allan & Lyndesay Brown, 61 Watts Gardens, Cupar,
Fife KY15 4UG. T: 01334 656 804;
E: swans@allanwbrown.co.uk

SCOTLAND

SOC FIFE BRANCH. (1950; 170).
Caroline Gordon. Address: n/a. T: 01592 750 230;
E: sweetbank101@gmail.com;
W: www.the-soc.org.uk
Meetings: 7.30pm, 2nd Wednesday of the month
(Sep-Apr). Supper Room of St Andrews Town Hall
(at corner of South Street & Queen's Gardens),
St Andrews, KY16 9TA.

Ringing Group/Bird Observatory
ISLE OF MAY BIRD
OBSERVATORY.
Margaret Thorne
(Secretary), Craigurd
House, Blyth Bridge,
West Linton, EH 46 7AH.
T: 01721 752 612;
E: craigurd@hotmail.com;
W: www.isleofmaybirdobs.org

TAY RG. See Angus & Dundee

Wetland Bird Survey (WeBS) Organiser
FIFE (excl. ESTUARIES). Mr AW Brown.
T: 01334 656 804 & 07871 575 131;
E: swansallan@gmail.com

FORTH ESTUARY (NORTH). Mr A Inglis.
T: 01383 822 115; E: aandjinglis@hotmail.com

TAY & EDEN ESTUARY. Mr N Elkins.
T: 01334 654 348; E: jandnelkins@btinternet.com

FORTH

Bird Atlas/Avifauna
The Birds of Clackmannanshire.
Neil Bielby,
Keith Broomfield &
John Grainger (Scottish
Ornithologist's Club, 2014).

Bird Recorder
UPPER FORTH. Chris
Pendlebury, 3 Sinclair Street,
Dunblane, FK5 0AH.
T: 07798 711 134;
E: chris@upperforthbirds.co.uk

Bird Report
FORTH AREA BIRD REPORT (1975-), published in
The Forth Naturalist & Historian, from
Roy Sexton, 22 Alexander Drive, Bridge of Allan,
Stirling, FK9 4QB. T: 01786 833 409;
E: RoyGravedigger@aol.com

BTO Regional Representative
CENTRAL. Neil Bielby. T: 01786 823 830;
E: neil.bielby@gmail.com

Club
SOC CENTRAL SCOTLAND BRANCH. (1968; 100).
Neil Bielby, 56 Ochiltree, Dunblane, FK15 0DF.
T: 01786 823 830; E: n64b68@gmail.com;
W: www.the-soc.org.uk
Meetings: 7.30pm, 1st Thursday of the month
(Oct-Mar). The Allan Centre, Fountain Road,
Bridge of Allan, FK9 4AT.

RSPB Local Group
FORTH VALLEY. (1995; 50).
Richard Knight. T: 07941 298 688;
E: richard.knight@blueyonder.co.uk;
W: www.rspb.org.uk/groups/forthvalley
Meetings: 7.30pm, 3rd Thursday of the month
(Sep-Apr). Hillpark Community Centre, Morrison
Drive, Bannockburn, Stirling, FK7 0HZ.

Wetland Bird Survey (WeBS) Organiser
CENTRAL (excl FORTH ESTUARY). Mr N Bielby.
T: 01786 823 830; E: neil.bielby@gmail.com

FORTH ESTUARY (INNER). Dr MV Bell.
T: via WeBS Office; E: mvbell34@gmail.com

HIGHLAND & CAITHNESS

Bird Atlas/Avifauna
The Birds of Eigg. John Chester (Isle of Eigg
Heritage Trust, 2013).

Skye Birds. RL McMillan. (Skye-Birds.com, 2nd ed 2009)

A History of Caithness Birds 1979 to 2001. Manson
Sinclair (Privately published, 2002).

The Birds of Sutherland. Alan Vittery (Colin
Baxter Photography Ltd, 1997).

The Birds of Badenoch and Strathspey. Roy Dennis
(Colin Baxter Photography Ltd, 1995).

Bird Recorder
CAITHNESS. Sinclair Manson, 7 Duncan Street,
Thurso, KW14 7HZ. T: 01847 892 379;
E: sinclairmanson@btinternet.com

HIGHLAND [ROSS-SHIRE, INVERNESS-SHIRE,
SUTHERLAND, BADENOCH & STRATHSPEY,
LOCHABER, LOCHALSH & SKYE]. Peter Stronach,
Clachan, Boat of Garten, INverness-shire PH24
3BX; T: 01479 851 272;
E: highlandrecorder@gmail.com

Bird Report
CAITHNESS BIRD REPORT (1983-97), no
longer published but the latest report can be
downloaded from website W: www.the-soc.org.uk
(local branches link)

HIGHLAND BIRD REPORT (1995-), from Lynda
Graham, 9 Burn Brae Terrace, Westhill, Inverness,
IV2 5HD. E: ljgraham50@btinternet.com

SCOTLAND

BTO Regional Representative
CAITHNESS. Donald Omand. T: 01847 811 403;
E: achreamie@yahoo.co.uk

INVERNESS (EAST & SPEYSIDE). Hugh Insley.
T: 01463 230 652; E: hugh.insley@btinternet.com

INVERNESS (WEST). Hugh Insley - see above.

ROSS-SHIRE. Simon Cohen. T: n/a;
E: saraandsimon@hotmail.com

RUM, EIGG, CANNA & MUCK. Bob Swann.
T: 01862 894 329; E: robert.swann@homecall.co.uk

SKYE. Carol Hawley. T: n/a; E: bto.skye@gmail.com

Stephen Bentall (Regional Ambassador).
E: s.bentall@talk21.com

SUTHERLAND. Lesley Mitchell. T: 07817 281 352;
E: colourflow@btinternet.com

Club
EAST SUTHERLAND BIRD GROUP. (1976; 120).
Fraser Symonds, Old Schoolhouse, Balvraid,
Dornoch, Sutherland IV25 3JB. T: 01408 633 922;
E: esbirdgroup@gmail.com; W: n/a
Meetings: 7.30pm, last Monday of the month
(Oct/Nov, Jan-Mar). Golspie Community Centre,
Back Rd, Golspie, Highland KW10 6TL.

SOC CAITHNESS BRANCH. (n/a; 50).
Angus McBay, Schoolhouse, Weydale, Thurso,
KY14 8YJ. T: 01847 894 663;
E: angmcb@btinternet.com; W: www.the-soc.org.uk
Meetings: 7.30pm, 1st Wednesday of the month
(Sep-Mar, not Jan). Castlehill Heritage Centre,
Harbour Road, Castletown, Caithness KW14 8TG.

SOC HIGHLAND BRANCH. (1955; 230).
Kathy Bonniface. Address: n/a. T: 01808 511 740;
E: kathybonniface@aol.com;
W: www.the-soc.org.uk; W: www.highlandbirds.scot
Meetings: 7.30pm, 1st or 2nd Tuesday of the
month (Sep-Apr). Culloden Library, Keppoch Road,
Culloden, IV2 7LL.

Ringing Group/Bird Observatory
CANNA RG. Mr R Swann. T: 01862 894329;
E: robert.swann@homecall.co.uk

HIGHLAND RG. Mr R Swann - see above.

RSPB Local Group
HIGHLAND. (1987; 160).
Doreen Manson. T: 01997 433 283;
E: doreen.a.manson@gmail.com;
W: www.rspb.org.uk/groups/highland
Meetings: 7.30pm, last Thursday of the month
(Sep-Apr). Greyfriars Free Church, Balloan Road,
Inverness, IV2 4PP.

Wetland Bird Survey (WeBS) Organiser
BADENOCH AND STRATHSPEY. Mr K Duncan.
T: via WEBS Office; E: via WeBS Office

CAITHNESS. Mr SAM Manson.
T: 01847 892 379;
E: sinclairmanson@btinternet.com

LOCHABER. Mr J Dye. T: via WeBS Office;
E: john.dye@virgin.net

SKYE & LOCHALSH. Mr RL McMillan.
T: via WeBS Office; E: bob@skye-birds.com

SUTHERLAND (excl. MORAY BASIN).
Vacant - contact WeBS Office.

WEST INVERNESS AND WESTER ROSS.
Dr AFG Douse. T: via WeBS Office;
E: via WeBS Office

LOTHIAN

Bird Atlas/Avifauna. See Borders.

Bird Recorder
Stephen Welch, 25 Douglas Road, Longniddry,
EH32 0LQ. T: 01875 852 802 or 07931 524 963;
E: lothianrecorder@the-soc.org.uk

Bird Report
LOTHIAN BIRD REPORT (1979-),
from Gillian Herbert, 19 Cammo Grove,
Edinburgh, EH4 8EX.
E: gillianiherbert@btinternet.com

BTO Regional Representative
Alan Heavisides. T: 0131 449 3816;
E: alanheavisides@yahoo.com

Club
LOTHIANS AND FIFE SWAN AND GOOSE STUDY
GROUP. See Fife.

SOC LOTHIAN BRANCH. (1936; 500).
Morag King, 7 Durham Terrace, Edinburgh,
EH15 1QJ. T: 0131 258 4638 & 07810 415 941;
E: abercorncottage@gmail.com;
W: www.the-soc.org.uk
Meetings: 7.30pm, 2nd Tuesday of the month
(Sep-Apr). The Guide Hall, 33 Melville Street,
Edinburgh, EH3 7JF. [Two meetings a year are
held at Waterston House, Aberlady.]

Ringing Group/Bird Observatory
LOTHIAN RG. Mr M McDowall. T: n/a;
E: m1kemcd@yahoo.co.uk

SCOTLAND

RSPB Local Group
EDINBURGH. (1974; 480).
Brian Robertson. T: 01875 340 580;
E: brianedinburghRSPB@btinternet.com;
W: www.rspb.org.uk/groups/edinburgh/
Meetings: 7.30pm, alternating between a Tuesday
& Wednesday each month (Sep-Apr). Napier
University, Lindsay Steward Lecture Theatre,
10 Napier University, Colinton Road, Craiglockhart
Campus, Edinburgh, EH14 1DJ.

Wetland Bird Survey (WeBS) Organiser
FORTH ESTUARY (OUTER SOUTH). Mr DJ Priddle.
T: 01620 827 459; E: dpriddle@eastlothian.gov.uk

LOTHIAN (excl ESTUARIES). Mr AW Brown.
T: 01334 656 804 & 07871 575 131;
E: swansallan@gmail.com

TYNINGHAME ESTUARY. Ms T Sykes.
T: via WeBS Office; E: via WeBS Office

MORAY & NAIRN

Bird Atlas/Avifauna
The Birds of Moray and Nairn. Martin Cook
(Mercat Press, 1992).

Bird Recorder
Martin Cook, Rowanbrae, Clochan, Buckie,
Banffshire AB56 5EQ. T: 01542 850 296;
E: martin.cook99@btinternet.com

Bird Report
BIRDS IN MORAY AND NAIRN (1999-), online since
2010), download from website
W: www.birdsinmorayandnairn.org

BTO Regional Representative
MORAY & NAIRN. Melvin Morrison. T: 01542 882 940;
E: wmmorrison@btinternet.com

Club
SOC MORAY BRANCH (Moray Bird Club). (2013; 60).
Martin Cook, Rowanbrae, Clochan, Buckie,
Banffshire AB56 5EQ. T: 01542 850 296;
E: martin.cook99@btinternet.com;
W: www.the-soc.org.uk;
W: www.birdsinmorayandnairn.org
Meetings: 8.00pm, 2nd Thursday of the month
(Oct-Mar). Elgin Museum Hall, 1 High Street,
Elgin, IV30 1EQ.

Wetland Bird Survey (WeBS) Organiser
LOSSIE ESTUARY. Mr R Proctor. T: 07976 456 657;
E: bobandlouise@proctor8246.fsnet.co.uk

MORAY & NAIRN (INLAND). Mr D Law.
T: via WeBS Office; E: jdavidlaw@btinternet.com

MORAY BASIN COAST. Mr RL Swann.
T: via WEBS Office; E: robert.swann@homecall.co.uk

NORTH EAST SCOTLAND

Bird Atlas/Avifauna
The Birds of North-East Scotland Then and Now.
Adam Watson & Ian Francis (Paragon Publishing,
2012).

The Breeding Birds of
North-East Scotland.
Ian Francis & Martin Cook
(Scottish Ornithologist's Club,
2011).

The Birds of North-East
Scotland. ST Buckland, MV
Bell & N Picozzi (North-East
Scotland Bird Club, 1990).

Bird Recorder
Nick Littlewood, The James Hutton Institute,
Craigiebuckler, Aberdeen, AB15 8QH.
T: 07748 965 920; E: nesrecorder@yahoo.co.uk

Bird Report
NORTH-EAST SCOTLAND BIRD REPORT (1974-),
from Dave Gill, Quarmby, Neathermuir Road,
Maud, Peterhead, Aberdeenshire AB42 4ND.
E: david@gilldavid1.orangehome.co.uk

NORTH SEA BIRD CLUB ANNUAL REPORT (1979-),
from Andrew Thorpe, OceanLab & Centre
for Ecology, Aberdeen University, Newburgh,
Aberdeenshire AB41 6AA. E: nsbc@abdn.ac.uk

BTO Regional Representative
ABERDEEN. Moray Souter. T: 01358 788 828;
E: bto_aber_rr@btintrnet.com

KINCARDINE & DEESIDE. Graham Cooper.
T: 01339 882 706; E: grm.cooper@btinternet.com

Club
SOC NORTH-EAST SCOTLAND BRANCH. (1956; 150).
John Wills, Bilbo, Monymusk, Inverurie,
Aberdeenshire AB51 7HA. T: 01467 651 296;
E: grampian.secretary@the-soc.org.uk;
W: www.the-soc.org.uk
Meetings: 7.30pm, 1st Monday of the month
(Oct-Apr, except Jan, 2nd Mon). Sportsman's
Club, 11 Queens Road, Aberdeen, AB15 4YL.

Ringing Group/Bird Observatory
GRAMPIAN RG. Mr R Duncan. T: 01224 823 184;
E: raymond@waxwing.fsnet.co.uk;
W: http://grampianringing.blogspot.co.uk

SCOTLAND

RSPB Local Group
ABERDEEN & DISTRICT. (1975; 260).
Mark Sullivan. T: 01224 861 446;
E: geolbird_abz@btinternet.com;
W: www.rspb.org.uk/groups/aberdeen
Meetings: 7.30pm, 2nd Tuesday of the month
(Oct-Apr). Aberdeen University, Main Lecture
Theatre, Zoology Building, Tillydrone Ave,
Aberdeen, AB24 2TZ.

Wetland Bird Survey (WeBS) Organiser
ABERDEENSHIRE. Mr M Souter. T: 01358 788 828;
E: bto_aber_rr@btinternet.com

ORKNEY

Bird Atlas/Avifauna
The Birds of Orkney. C Booth, M Cuthbert &
P Reynolds. (The Orkney Press, 1984).

Bird Recorder
Jim Williams, Fairholm, Finstown, Orkney
KW17 2EQ. T: 01856 761 317 & 07879 000 399;
E: jim.geniefea@btinternet.com

Bird Report
*NORTH RONALDSAY BIRD OBSERVATORY BIRD
REPORT (2011-), from* Alison Duncan, NRBO,
Twingness, North Ronaldsay, Orkney KW17 2BE.
T: 01857 633 200; E: alison@nrbo.prestel.co.uk

ORKNEY BIRD REPORT (1974-), from the Bird
Recorder - see above.

BTO Regional Representative
Colin Corse. T: 01856 874 484;
E: ccorse@btinternet.com

Club
SOC ORKNEY BRANCH. (1993; n/a).
Helen Aiton. Address: n/a. T: 01856 751 482;
E: helendavidaiton@hotmail.co.uk;
W: www.the-soc.org.uk
Meetings: 7.30pm, 1st Thursday of the month
(Oct & Nov) and 2nd Thursday of the month
(Feb & Mar). St Magnus Centre, Kirkwall.

Ringing Group/Bird Observatory
NORTH RONALDSAY BIRD OBSERVATORY.
Alison Duncan (Warden), Twingness, North
Ronaldsay, KW17 2BE. T: 01857 633 200;
E: alison@nrbo.prestel.co.uk; W: www.nrbo.co.uk

ORKNEY RG. Mr C Corse. T: 01856 874 484;
E: ccorse@btinternet.com; W: www.orkneyrg.co.uk

SULE SKERRY RG. Mr D Budworth.
T: 01283 215 188; E: dbud01@aol.com

RSPB Local Group
ORKNEY. (1985; 300/area).
Dick Matson. T: 01856 751 426;
E: P.wilson410@btinternet.com; W: n/a
Meetings: Meetings advertised in newsletter and
local press, or phone/email for details.

Wetland Bird Survey (WeBS) Organiser
ORKNEY. Mrs M Wilson. T: via WeBS Office;
E: via WeBS Office

OUTER HEBRIDES

Bird Recorder
Yvonne Benting, Suthainn, Askernish, South Uist,
HS8 5SY. T: 07501 332 803
E: recorder@outerhebridesbirds.org.uk
W: www.outerhebridesbirds.org.uk

Bird Report
*OUTER HEBRIDES BIRD REPORT
(1997-), from*
Brian Rabbitts, 6 Carinish, Isle
of North Uist, Outer Hebrides
HS6 5HL. T: 01876 580 328;
E: rabbitts@hebrides.net

BTO Regional Representative
BENBECULA & THE UISTS.
Yvonne Benting.
T: 07501 332 803;
E: uistbto@gmail.com

LEWIS & HARRIS. Chris Reynolds.
T: 01851 672 376 (summer) / 01202 854 629
(rest of yr); E: cmreynolds@btinternet.com

Ringing Group/Bird Observatory
SHIANTS AUK RG. Mr J Lennon. T: 01636 525 963;
E: jjlennon17@gmail.com

Wetland Bird Survey (WeBS) Organiser
HARRIS AND LEWIS. Ms Y Benting.
T: via WeBS Office; E: uistbto@gmail.com

UISTS AND BENBECULA. Ms Y Benting - see above.

PERTH & KINROSS

Bird Recorder
Scott Paterson, 12 Ochil View, Kinross, KY13 8TN.
T: 01577 864 248 & 07501 640 518;
E: pkrecorder@the-soc.org.uk

Bird Report
PERTH & KINROSS BIRD REPORT (1974-), digital
reports from the Bird Recorder - see above.

BTO Regional Representative
PERTHSHIRE. Michael Bell. T: 01786 822 153;
E: mvbell34@gmail.com

COUNTY DIRECTORY

SCOTLAND

Club
PERTHSHIRE SOCIETY OF NATURAL SCIENCE
(1867; Ornithological Section: 25).
Jeanne Freeman, 14 St Mary's Drive, Perth, PH2
7BY.
T: 01738 620 914; E: birdsatpsns@btinternet.com;
W: www.psns.org.uk
Meetings: 7.30pm, Wednesday - dates vary (Oct-Mar),
Sandeman Room, AK Bell Library, 17 York Place, Perth,
PH2 8EP - contact/see website for details.

Wetland Bird Survey (WeBS) Organiser
LOCH LEVEN. Mr J Squire. T: via WeBS Office;
E: jeremy.squire@snh.gov.uk

PERTH AND KINROSS (INLAND). Dr MV Bell.
T: via WeBS Office; E: mvbell34@gmail.com

TAY & EDEN ESTUARY. See Fife.

SHETLAND

Bird Atlas/Avifauna
The Birds of Shetland. P Harvey, M Pennington,
K Osborn, R Riddington, P Ellis, M Huebeck & D
Okill (Christopher Helm, 2004).

Bird Recorder
FAIR ISLE. David Parnaby, Fair Isle Bird
Observatory, Fair Isle, Shetland, ZE2 9JU.
T: 01595 760 258; E: fibo@btconnect.com

SHETLAND. Rob Fray, Sunnydell, Virkie, Shetland
ZE3 9JS. T: 01950 461 929;
E: recorder@shetlandbirdclub.co.uk

Bird Report
FAIR ISLE BIRD OBSERVATORY REPORT (1949-),
from Susannah Parnaby, Fair Isle Bird Observatory,
Fair Isle, Shetland, ZE2 9JU. T: 01595 760 258;
E: fibo@btconnect.com

SHETLAND BIRD REPORT (1969-), from the Bird
Recorder - see above.
E: reports@shetlandbirdclub.co.uk

BTO Regional Representative
Dave Okill. T: 01595 880 450;
E: david@auroradesign.plus.com

Club
SHETLAND BIRD CLUB. (1973; 200+).
Helen Moncrieff (Sec), Scholland, Virkie, ZE3 9JL.
T: 01950 460 249;
E: secretary@shetlandbirdclub.co.uk;
W: www.shetlandbirdclub.co.uk
Meetings: Occasional - contact/see website for
details.

Ringing Group/Bird Observatory
FAIR ISLE BIRD OBSERVATORY.
David Parnaby (Warden), Fair Isle Bird Observatory,
Fair Isle, Shetland ZE2 9JU. T: 01595 760 258;
E: fairisle.birdobs@zetnet.co.uk;
W: www.fairislebirdobs.co.uk

SHETLAND RG. Mr G Petrie. T: 01950 477 589;
E: gwpatocra@gmail.com

Wetland Bird Survey (WeBS) Organiser
SHETLAND. Mr PV Harvey. T: 01950 460 160 &
07879 444 612; E: paul@shetlandamenity.org

NOTES

276

WALES

Bird Report
The WELSH BIRD REPORT is published in 'BIRDS IN WALES', from the Welsh Ornithological Society. W: www.birdsinwales.org.uk

BTO Wales Officer
John Lloyd. T: 01550 750 202;
E: johnvlloyd2000@gmail.com

Club
WELSH ORNITHOLOGICAL SOCIETY.
See National Directory.

EASTERN AREA OF WALES

Bird Atlas/Avifauna
The Birds of Radnorshire. Peter Jennings (Fidedula Books, 2014).

The Birds of Gwent. WA Venables, AD Baker, RM Clarke, C Jones, JMS Lewis & SJ Tyler (Christopher Helm, 2008).

The Birds of Montgomeryshire. B Holt & G Williams (privately published, 2008).

Bird Recorder
BRECONSHIRE. Andrew King, Heddfan, Pennorth, Brecon, Powys LD3 7EX. T: 01874 658 351; E: andrew.king53@virgin.net

GWENT. Tom Chinnick, School House, Llandenny, Usk, NP15 1DL. T: 07982 719 881; E: countyrecorder@gwentbirds.org.uk

MONTGOMERYSHIRE. Mike Haigh, Tynewydd Ketch, Llanfyllin, Powys, SY22 5EU. T: 01691 648 746; E: montbird@gmail.com

RADNORSHIRE (VC43). Pete Jennings, The Old Farmhouse, Choulton, Lydbury North, Shropshire SY7 8AH. T: 01588 680 631; E: radnorshirebirds@hotmail.com

Bird Report
BRECONSHIRE BIRDS (1962-), from Clare Morgan, Brecknock Wildlife Trust, Lion House, Bethel Square, Brecon, Powys LD3 7AY. T: 01874 625 708

GWENT BIRD REPORT (1973-), from Andrew Cormack, 29 Chestnut Drive, Abergavenny, Monmouthshire NP7 5JZ. E: treasurer@gwentbirds.org.uk

MONTGOMERYSHIRE BIRD REPORT (1981/82-), from 2013 report, now available as a download from montgomerybirdblog.blogspot.co.uk/p/county-reports.html

BTO Regional Representative
BRECKNOCK. Andrew King. T: 01874 658 351; E: andrew.king53@virgin.net

GWENT. Jerry Lewis. T: 01873 855 091; E: jmsl2587@yahoo.co.uk

MONTGOMERY. Jane Kelsall. T: 01970 872 019; E: janekelsall@phonecoop.coop

RADNOR. Carlton Parry. T: 01597 824 050; E: cj.parry@tiscali.co.uk

Club
GWENT ORNITHOLOGICAL SOCIETY. (1964; 420). Trevor Russell (Sec). Address: n/a. T: n/a; E: secretary@gwentbirds.org.uk; W: www.gwentbirds.org.uk
Meetings: 7.30pm, 1st & 3rd Saturdays of the month (Sep-Apr). Goytre Village Hall, Newtown Road, Penperlleni, Pontypool, NP4 0AW.

MONTGOMERYSHIRE WILDLIFE TRUST BIRD GROUP. (1997; 110). Brayton Holt (Sec). Address: n/a. T: 01938 500 266; E: montbird@gmail.com; W: www.montgomerybirdblog.blogspot.co.uk
Meetings: 7.30pm, 3rd Wednesday of the month (Sep-Apr). Welshpool Methodist Hall, 13 High Street, Welshpool, Powys SY21 7JP.

RADNORSHIRE BIRD GROUP. (1988; 75). Pete Jennings, The Old Farmhouse, Choulton, Lydbury North, Shropshire SY7 8AH. T: 01588 680 631; E: radnorshirebirds@hotmail.com Co-ordinates bird recording and surveys in the county through the Bird Recorder.

Ringing Group/Bird Observatory
GOLDCLIFF RG. Mr R Clarke. T: 01633 615 581; E: chykembro2@aol.com

LLANGORSE RG. Mr J Lewis. T: 01873 855 091; E: jmsl2587@yahoo.co.uk

MID-WALES RG. Mr A Cross. T: 07837 521 673; E: avcross@btinternet.com

Wetland Bird Survey (WeBS) Organiser
BRECONSHIRE. Mr VA King. T: 01874 658 351; E: andrew.king53@virgin.net

GWENT (excl. SEVERN ESTUARY). Dr WA Venables. T: via WeBS Office; E: via WeBS Office

MONTGOMERYSHIRE. Ms J Kelsall. T: 01970 872 019; E: janekelsall@phonecoop.coop

RADNORSHIRE. Mr PP Jennings. T: 01588 680 831; E: ppjennings@hotmail.co.uk

SEVERN ESTUARY (WALES). Dr WA Venables.
- see above

WALES

Wildlife Trust

BRECKNOCK WILDLIFE TRUST. (1964; 1,000).
Lion House, Bethel Square, Brecon, Powys LD3 7AY.
T: 01874 625 708, (fax) 01874 610 552;
E: enquiries@brecknockwildlifetrust.org.uk;
W: www.brecknockwildlifetrust.org.uk

GWENT WILDLIFE TRUST. (1963; 9,000).
Seddon House, Dingestow, Monmouth, NP25 4DY.
T: 01600 740 600, (fax) 01600 740 299;
E: info@gwentwildlife.org;
W: www.gwentwildlife.org

MONTGOMERYSHIRE WILDLIFE TRUST. (1982; 1,400).
42 Broad St, Welshpool, Powys, SY21 7RR.
T: 01938 555 654, (fax) 01938 556 161;
E: info@montwt.co.uk; W: www.montwt.co.uk

RADNORSHIRE WILDLIFE TRUST. (1987; 1000).
Warwick House, High St, Llandrindod Wells, Powys
LD1 6AG. T: 01597 823 298, (fax) 01597 823 274;
E: info@rwtwales.org; W: www.rwtwales.org

NORTHERN AREA OF WALES

Bird Atlas/Avifauna

*The Breeding Birds of North
Wales*. Anne Brenchley, Geoff
Gibbs, Rhion Pritchard & Ian M
Spence (Liverpool University
Press, 2013).

The Birds of Meirionnydd.
Rhion Pritchard (Welsh
Ornithological Society, 2012).

The Birds of Anglesey. Peter Hope-Jones
& P Whalley (Menter Mon, 2004).

Bird Recorder

ANGLESEY. David Wright. Graig Eithin, Mynydd
Bodafon, Llanerchymedd, Anglesey LL71 8BG.
T: 07973 568 096; E: bodafondavid@yahoo.co.uk

CAERNARFONSHIRE. Rhion Pritchard, Pant Afonig,
Hafod Lane, Bangor, Gwynedd LL57 4BU.
T: 01248 671 301; E: rhion678pritchard@gmail.com

DENBIGHSHIRE. Ian M Spence, 43 Blackbrook,
Sychdyn, Mold, Flintshire CH7 6LT.
T: 01352 750118; E: ian.spence@zen.co.uk

FLINTSHIRE. Ian M Specnce - see above.

MEIRIONNYDD. Jim Dustow, Afallon, 7 Glan y Don,
Rhiwbryfdir, Blaenau Ffestiniog, Gwynedd LL41 3LW;
T: 01766 830 976; E: jim.dustow@rspb.org.uk

Bird Report

*BARDSEY BIRD AND FIELD OBSERVATORY REPORT
(1953-)*, from Jo Jones, 70 Newmarket Road,
Burwell, Cambridgeshire CB25 0AE. T: 01638 743 131;
E: jojones4@btinternet.com

CAMBRIAN BIRD REPORT (NW Wales) (1953-), from
Geoff Gibbs, Fronwen, Llanfairfechan, LL33 0ET.
T: 01248 681 936; E: geoffkate.gibbs@care4free.net

NORTH-EAST WALES BIRD REPORT (2004-), from
Ian M Spence, 43 Blackbrook, Sychdyn, Mold,
Flintshire CH7 6LT. E: ian.spence@zen.co.uk

*WREXHAM BIRDWATCHERS' SOCIETY ANNUAL
REPORT (1981-)*, from Marian Williams, 10 Lake
View, Gresford, Wrexham, LL12 8PU.
T: 01978 854 633

BTO Regional Representative

ANGLESEY. Ian Hawkins. T: 01248 430 590;
E: ian.hawkins590@btinternet.com

CAERNARFON. Geoff Gibbs. T: 01248 681 936;
E: geoffkate.gibbs@care4free.net

Rhion Pritchard (Assistant Representative).
T: 01248 671 301;
E: rhion678pritchard@btinternet.com

CLWYD EAST. Anne Brenchley. T: 01352 750 118;
E: annebrenchley@imsab.myzen.co.uk

CLWYD WEST. Mel ab Owain. T: 01745 826 528;
E: melabowain@gmail.com

Glen Heaton (Assistant Representative).

MEIRIONNYDD. Rob Morton. T: 01341 422 426;
E: r.morton1@btinternet.com

Club

BANGOR BIRD GROUP. (1947; 100).
Gareth Howells. Address: n/a.
T: 01248 714 678; E: n/a; W: n/a
Meetings: 7.30pm, every Wednesday, Autumn
and Spring terms. Brambell Building, University
of Bangor, Deiniol Road, Bangor, LL57 2UW.

CAMBRIAN ORNITHOLOGICAL
SOCIETY. (1952; 190). Julian
Thompson (Sec), Pensychnant,
Sychnant Pass, Conwy, LL32 8BJ.
T: 01492 592 595;
E: julian.pensychnant@
btinternet.com;
W: https://birdsin.wales/
counties/bird-clubs/
Meetings: 7.30pm, 1st Friday of the month
(Sep-May). Pensychnant Centre, Sychnant Pass,
Conwy, LL32 8BJ.

CLWYD BIRD RECORDING GROUP (a committee of
local birders who produce the North-East Wales
Bird Report). Giles Pepler (Sec), Rosedan, Bagillt,
Flint, Flintshire CH6 6DH. T: 01352 732 876;
E: gilesp64@gmail.com; W: www.cbrg.org.uk
Meetings: No indoor meetings held.

WALES

CLWYD ORNITHOLOGICAL SOCIETY. (1956; 45).
Angela Ross, 25 Leonard Avenue, Rhyl, LL18 4LN.
T: 01745 338 493;
E: angela.ross@talktalk.net; W: n/a.
Meetings: 7.30pm, last Tuesday of the month
(Sep-Nov & Jan-Apr). Rhuddlan Community
Centre, Parliament Street, Rhuddlan, LL18 5AW.

DEESIDE NATURALISTS' SOCIETY. (1973; 500+).
The Secretary. Address: n/a. T: n/a;
E: secretary@deenats.org.uk;
W: www.deenats.org.uk
Meetings: 7.30pm, 3rd Friday of the month
(Sep-Mar).
Connah's Quay
Community
Centre, Tuscan
Way, off Chapel
Street, Connah's
Quay, CH5 4DZ.

WREXHAM BIRDWATCHERS' SOCIETY. (1974; 90).
Marian Williams, 10 Lake View, Gresford,
Wrexham, Clwyd LL12 8PU. T: 01978 854 633;
E: n/a;
W: https://birdsin.wales/counties/bird-clubs/
Meetings: 7.30pm, 1st Friday of the month
(Sep-Apr). Gresford Memorial Hall, High Street,
Gresford, Wrexham, LL12 8PS.

Ringing Group/Bird Observatory
BARDSEY BIRD OBSERVATORY.
Steve Stansfield (Warden), Cristin, Bardsey Island,
Pwllheli, Gwynedd LL53 8DE. T: 07855 264 151;
E: warden@bbfo.org.uk; W: www.bbfo.org.uk

CHESHIRE SWAN GROUP. See Cheshire.

MERSEYSIDE RG. See Lancashire & North Merseyside.

SCAN RG. Dr D Moss. T: n/a;
E: dorianmoss16@gmail.com

RSPB Local Group
NORTH WALES. (1986; 80).
John Beagan. T: 01492 531 409;
E: colwynbooks@waitrose.com;
W: www.rspb.org.uk/groups/northwales
Meetings: 7.30pm, 3rd Friday of the month
(Sep-Apr). St Davids Church Hall, Penrhyn Bay,
Llandudno, Conwy, LL30 3NT.

Wetland Bird Survey (WeBS) Organiser
ANGLESEY. Mr I Sims. T: via WeBS Office.
E: ian.sims@rspb.org.uk

CAERNARFONSHIRE.
Mr R Pritchard. T: via WeBS Office;
E: rhion678pritchard@gmail.com

CLWYD (COASTAL).
Vacant - contact WeBS Office.

CLWYD (INLAND). Mr D Halpin. T: 07595 847 930;
E: duncan.halpin@gmail.com

DEE ESTUARY. Mr CE Wells - see Lancashire.
FORYD BAY. Mr S Hugheston-Roberts.
T: via WeBS Office; E: simon.hr@btinternet.com

MEIRIONNYDD (ESTUARIES). Mr J Dustow.
T: via WeBS Office; E: Jim.Dustow@rspb.org.uk

MEIRIONNYDD (OTHER SITES). Mr TG Owen.
T: 01766 590 302; E: via WeBS Office

Wildlife Trust
NORTH WALES WILDLIFE TRUST. (1963; 4,000).
376 High Street, Bangor, Gwynedd LL57 1YE.
T: 01248 351 541, (fax) 01248 353 192;
E: nwwt@wildlifetrustswales.org;
W: www.northwaleswildlifetrust.org.uk

SOUTHERN AREA OF WALES

Bird Atlas/Avifauna
Birds of Glamorgan. Clive Hurford &
Peter Lansdown (Privately Published, 1995).

An Atlas of Breeding Birds in West Glamorgan.
DK Thomas (Gower Ornithological Society, 1992).

Bird Recorder
GLAMORGAN (EAST). Phil Bristow, 2 Forest Oak
Close, Cyncoed, Cardiff CF23 6QN.
T: 07769 973 890; E: phlbrstw@gmail.com

GOWER. Mark Hipkin, 6 Holly Road, Neath,
SA11 3PE. T: 01639 638 475 & 07875 431 917;
E: markhipkin1@gmail.com

Bird Report
EAST GLAMORGAN BIRD REPORT (1985-), from
John Wilson, 122 Westbourne Road, Penarth, Vale of
Glamorgan, CF64 3HH. E: johndw1948@gmail.com

GOWER BIRDS (1968-), from Jeremy Douglas-Jones,
14 Alder Way, West Cross, Swansea, SA3 5PD.
T: 01792 551 331; E: jeremy@douglas-jones.biz

BTO Regional Representative
EAST GLAMORGAN (MID). Wayne Morris.
T: 01443 430 284; E: eastglambto@gmail.com

Daniel Jenkins-Jones (Assistant Representative).
T: 01292 062 1394; jenkinsjones@btinternet.com

GLAMORGAN (SOUTH). Wayne Morris / Daniel
Jenkins-Jones - see above.

GLAMORGAN (WEST). Lyndon Jeffery.
T: 01792 874 337; E: norma.jeffery@virginmedia.com

WALES

Club
CARDIFF NATURALISTS' SOCIETY. (1867; 150).
Mike Dean (Sec), 36 Rowan Way, Lisvane, Cardiff,
CF14 0TD. T: 029 2075 6869;
E: secretary@cardiffnaturalists.org.uk;
W: www.cardiffnaturalists.org.uk
Meetings: 7.30pm, various evenings (Sep-Jun).
Lecture Theatre, Room D.106 on 1st floor of the
UWIC, Llandaff Campus, Western Ave, Cardiff,
CF5 2YB.

GLAMORGAN BIRD CLUB. (1990; 250).
Ceri Jones (Sec), 26 Smithies Ave, Sully, VoG,
CF64 5SS. T: 029 2053 1769;
E: secretary@glamorganbirds.org.uk;
W: www.glamorganbirds.org.uk
Meetings: 7.45pm, generally 1st Tuesday of the
month (Oct-Apr). Kenfig NNR Visitor Centre, Ton
Kenfig, Bridgend, Mid Glamorgan CF33 4PT.

GOWER ORNITHOLOGICAL SOCIETY. (1956; 100).
Jeremy Douglas-Jones (Sec),
14 Alder Way, West Cross,
Swansea, SA3 5PD.
T: 01792 551 331;
E: jeremy@douglas-jones.biz;
W: www.glamorganbirds.org.uk
Meetings: 7.15pm, usually 4th
Friday of the month (Sep-Mar,
not Dec). The Environment Centre, Pier Street,
Swansea, SA1 1RY.

Ringing Group/Bird Observatory
FLAT HOLM RG. Mr R Facey. T: 07890 123 108;
E: faceyrj@yahoo.co.uk

GOWER RG. Mr DC Davies. T: 01639 821 353 &
07973 180 069; E: cedwyn.d@btinternet.com;
W: http://gowerbirdringinggroup.blogspot.co.uk

KENFIG RG. Mr D Carrington. T: n/a;
E: dgcarrington@sky.com;
W: http://kenfigrg.blogspot.co.uk

RSPB Local Group
CARDIFF & DISTRICT. (1973; n/a).
Huw Moody-Jones. T: 01446 760 757;
E: huwmoodyjones@hotmail.com;
W: www.RSPB.org.uk/groups/cardiff
Meetings: 7.30pm, various Fridays (Sep-May).
Llandaff Parish Hall, (next car park off) High St,
Llandaff, Cardiff, CF5 2DX.

WEST GLAMORGAN. (1985; 345).
Maggie Cornelius. T: 01792 229 244;
E: RSPBwglamgrp@googlemail.com;
W: www.rspb.org.uk/groups/westglamorgan
Meetings: Contact/see website for details.
Environment Centre, Pier Street, Swansea,
SA1 1RY.

Wetland Bird Survey (WeBS) Organiser
BURRY INLET (NORTH). Mr L Jeffery.
T: 01792 874 337; E: norma.jeffery@virginmedia.com

EAST GLAMORGAN. Mr D Jenkins-Jones.
T: 07703 607 601; E: eastglamwebs@gmail.com

SEVERN ESTUARY (WALES). See Eastern Area.

WEST GLAMORGAN. Mr L Jeffery - see above.

Wildlife Trust
WILDLIFE TRUST OF SOUTH AND WEST WALES.
(2002; 8,000).
The Nature Centre, Fountain Road, Tondu,
Bridgend, Mid-Glamorgan CF32 0EH.
T: 01656 724 100, fax 01656 726 980;
E: info@welshwildlife.org;
W: www.welshwildlife.org

WESTERN AREA OF WALES

Bird Atlas/Avifauna
Birds of Ceredigion. Hywel Roderick & Peter Davis
(Wildlife Trust, S & SW Wales, 2010).

Atlas of Breeding Birds in Pembrokeshire 2003-07.
Annie Haycock et al (Pembrokeshire Bird Group, 2009).

irds of Pembrokeshire. Jack Donovan &
Graham Rees (Dyfed Wildlife Trust, 1994).

Bird Recorder
CARMARTHENSHIRE. Gary Harper, Maesteg, Capel
Seion, Drefach, Llanelli, SA14 7BS.
T: 01269 831 496 & 07748 970 124;
E: gary.harper3@gmail.com

CEREDIGION. Russell Jones, Bron y Gan, Talybont,
Ceredigion SY24 5ER. T: 07753 774 891;
E: russell.jones@rspb.org.uk

PEMBROKESHIRE. Joint Recorder, Rarities.
Jon Green, Crud Yr Awel, Bowls Road, Blaenporth,
Ceredigion SA43 2AR. T: 01239 811 561;
E: jonrg@tiscali.co.uk

PEMBROKESHIRE. Joint Recorder. Stephen Berry,
The Old Mill, Llanychaer, Pembrokeshire SA65 9TB.
T: 01348 875 604; E: stephen.berry16@btinternet.com

Bird Report
CARMARTHENSHIRE BIRDS (1982-), from
Wendell Thomas, 48 Glebe Road, Loughhor,
Swansea, SA4 6QD. E: wendellthomas57@gmail.com

CEREDIGION BIRD REPORT (1982/85), from Wildlife
Trust of South and West Wales - see Wildlife Trust.

PEMBROKESHIRE BIRD REPORT (1981-), download
from website
W: www.pembrokeshirebirdgroup.blogspot.co.uk

WALES

SKOKHOLM BIRD REPORT (1981-), download from website: https://www.welshwildlife.org/wp-content/uploads/2015/11/Annual-Report-2016.pdf

BTO Regional Representative
CARDIGAN. Moira Convery. T: 01970 612 998;
E: moira.convery@gmail.com

CARMARTHEN. Terry Wells. T: 01267 238 836;
E: bto@twells.me.uk

PEMBROKESHIRE. Bob Haycock. T: 01834 891 667;
E: bob.rushmoor1@tiscali.co.uk

Annie Haycock (Assistant Representative). T: n/a;
E: rushmoor1@tiscali.co.uk

Club
CARMARTHENSHIRE BIRD CLUB. (2003; 140+).
Sian Rees-Harper (Sec), Maesteg, Capel Seion,
Drefach, Llanelli, SA14 7BS. T: 01269 831 496;
E: gary.harper3@gmail.com;
W: www.carmarthenshirebird.club
Meetings: 7.30pm, 2nd Wednesday of the month
(Oct-Mar). Llanelli Cricket Club, Stradey Park,
Llanelli, SA15 4BT.

PEMBROKESHIRE BIRD GROUP. (1983; 60).
Peter Royle (Sec), Orlandon Kilns, St. Brides,
Haverfordwest, SA62 3AP. T: 01646 636 970;
E: pdroyle@orlandon.co.uk;
W: http://pembrokeshirebirdgroup.blogspot.co.uk/
Meetings: No indoor meetings held.

Ringing Group/Bird Observatory
PEMBROKESHIRE RG. Mr J Hayes.
T: 01646 687 713; E: hayes313@btinternet.com;
W: http://pembsringinggroup.blogspot.co.uk/

SKOKHOLM BIRD OBSERVATORY.
Richard Brown/Giselle Eagle (Wardens), Skokholm
Island, Martins Haven, Pembrokeshire, SA62 3BJ.
T: 07971 114 303; E: skokholmwarden@gmail.com;
W: http://skokholm.blogspot.co.uk

SKOKHOLM RG. Mr R Brown - see above.

TEIFI RG. Dr W James. T: 07775 833 477;
E: wendyjames682@gmail.com;
W: www.teifimarshbirds.blogspot.co.uk

Wetland Bird Survey (WeBS) Organiser
CARMARTHENSHIRE. Mr T Wells. T: 01267 238 836;
E: terry@twells.me.uk

CEREDIGION (incl DYFI ESTUARY). Mr RJ Jones.
T: via WeBS Office; E: russell.jones@rspb.org.uk

PEMBROKESHIRE. Mrs AN Haycock.
T: via WeBS Office. E: annie@rushmoorphotos.co.uk

Wildlife Trust
WILDLIFE TRUST OF SOUTH AND WEST WALES.
See Southern Area of Wales.

NOTES

CHANNEL ISLANDS

Wetland Bird Survey (WeBS) Organiser
CHANNEL ISLANDS (INLAND). Mr HG Young.
T: 01534 860 040; E: glyn.young@durrell.org

ALDERNEY

Atlas/Avifauna
The Birds of Alderney. Jeremy G Sanders.
(Privately Published, 2007).

Bird Recorder
Alderney Wildlife Trust/Alderney Records Centre
E: ecologist@alderneywildlife.org

BTO Regional Representative
Chris Mourant. T: n/a;
E: chris.mourant@yahoo.co.uk

Ringing Group/Bird Observatory
ALDERNEY BIRD OBSERVATORY.
Paul Veron (Chairman), Alderney Bird Observatory,
Links Cottage, Route des Carriers, Alderney,
GY9 3YE. T: 01481 822 914; E: n/a;
W: https://alderneybirdobservatory.org

Wetland Bird Survey (WeBS) Organiser
Alderney Wildlife Trust Ecologist.
T: 01481 822 935; E: ramsar@alderneywildlife.org

Wildlife Trust
ALDERNEY WILDLIFE TRUST. (2002)
Shades, 48 Victoria Street, St Anne, Alderney GY9
3TA. T/fax: 01481 822 935;
E: info@alderneywildlife.org;
W: www.alderneywildlife.org

GUERNSEY

Bird Atlas/Avifauna
*Birds of the Bailiwick:
Guernsey, Alderney, Sark
and Herm.* Duncan Spencer
& Paul Hillion (Jill Vaudin
Publishing 2011).

Bird Recorder
Mark Lawlor, St Etienne,
Les Effards, St Sampsons,
Guernsey GY2 4TU.
T: 01481 258 168;
E: mplawlor@cwgsy.net

Bird Report
GUERNSEY BIRD REPORT (1992-), download from
website: W: www.guernseybirds.org.gg

BTO Regional Representative
Chris Mourant. T: n/a;
E: chris.mourant@yahoo.co.uk

Club
LA SOCIÉTÉ GUERNESIAISE. (1882).
Secretary, La Société Guernesiaise, Candie
Gardens, St Peter Port, Port Guernsey GY1 1UG.
T: 01481 725 093; E: societe@cwgsy.net;
W: www.societe.org.gg

Chris Mourant (Sec, Ornithology Section).
Address: n/a. T: 07911 130 415;
E: ornithology@societe.org.gg;
W: www.guernseybirds.org.gg
Meetings: (Ornithology Section). 7.30pm,
1st Thursday of the month. Frossard Theatre,
Candie - address, as above.

RSPB Local Group
GUERNSEY BAILIWICK. (1975; 200+).
Donna Francis. T: 01481 232 632;
E: donna@cwgsy.net; W: www.rspbguernsey.co.uk
Meetings: 7.30pm, dates vary (Sep-Apr) -
contact/see website for details. La Villette Hotel,
St Martins, Guernsey GY4 6QG.

Wetland Bird Survey (WeBS) Organiser
GUERNSEY COAST. Ms M Simmons.
T: 01481 256016; E: msim@cwgsy.net

JERSEY

Bird Recorder
Tony Paintin, 1 Ficquet House, La Verte Rue,
St Brelade, Jersey JE3 8EL. T: 01534 741 928;
E: cavokjersey@hotmail.com

Bird Report
JERSEY BIRD REPORT (1991-), from Ornithology
Section, La Société Jersiaise - see below.

BTO Regional Representative
Tony Paintin. T: 01534 741 928;
E: cavokjersey@hotmail.com

Club
SOCIÉTIÉ JERSIAISE. (1873).
La Société Jersiaise, 7 Pier Road, St Helier, Jersey
JE2 4XW. T: 01534 758 314;
E: info@societe-jersiaise.org;
W: www.societe-jersiaise.org

Roger Noel (Sec, Ornithology Section).
Address: n/a. T: n/a;
E: rogernoel1@googlemail.com
Meetings: (Ornithology Section). 8pm, 1st & 3rd
Thursdays of the month. Arthur Mourant Room -
address as above.

Wetland Bird Survey (WeBS) Organiser
JERSEY COAST. Mr R Noel. T: 01534 481 409;
E: rogernoel1@googlemail.com

NORTHERN IRELAND

Bird Recorder
George Gordon, 2 Brooklyn Avenue, Bangor,
Co Down BT20 5RB. T: 028 9145 5763;
E: nimbus10111947@gmail.com

Bird Report
IRISH BIRD REPORT (1953-), included in Irish Birds,
see BirdWatch Ireland in Republic of Ireland.

*COPELAND BIRD
OBSERVATORY REPORT*,
from David Galbraith,
Bookings Secretary.
T: 028 9338 2539 &
07934 416 668;
E: davidgalbraith903@
btinternet.com

BTO Regional Representative
BTO IRELAND OFFICER. Shane Wolsey.
T: 028 9146 7947; E:shane.wolsey@bto.org

ANTRIM & BELFAST. Adam McClure.
T: 028 9346 2562 & 07793 038 211;
E: adamdmcclure@yahoo.com

ARMAGH. Stephen Hewitt. T: n/a;
E: sjameshewitt@hotmail.com

DOWN. Kerry Leonard. T: 028 9145 2602 &
07773 982 436; E: kerrysleonard@hotmail.com

FERMANAGH. Michael Stinson. T: 07890 358 239;
E: mick.stinston@hotmail.com

LONDONDERRY. John Clarke. T: 028 7032 7675;
E: jclarke48@gmail.com

TYRONE. Michael Stinson - see above.

Club

NORTHERN IRELAND
BIRDWATCHERS' ASSOCIATION.
See National Directory.
W: http://nibirds.blogspot.co.uk/

NORTHERN IRELAND
ORNITHOLOGISTS' CLUB.
See National Directory.
W: nioc.co.uk

Ringing Group/Bird Observatory
BELFAST AND DOWN RG. Mr D Clarke.
T: 07774 780 750; E: declan@coneyisland.plus.com;
W: https://www.facebook.com/BogMeadowsCes

COPELAND BIRD OBSERVATORY.
David Galbraith (Booking Secretary).
T: 028 9338 2539 or 07934 416 668;
E: davidgalbraith903@btinternet.com;
W: www.thecbo.org.uk

RSPB Local Group
ANTRIM. (1977; 25).
Brenda Campbell. T: 028 9332 3657;
E: brendacampbell@supanet.com;
W: www.rspb.org.uk/groups/antrim
Meetings: 8pm, usually 2nd Monday of the month
(Sep-Jun). College of Agriculture Food & Rural
Enterprise, 22 Greenmount Road, Antrim, BT41 4PU.

BELFAST. (1970; 130).
Derek McLain. T: 028 9334 1488;
E: d.mclain@btinternet.com; W: n/a
Meetings: Cooke Centenary Church Hall, Park
Road, Belfast, BT7 2FW - contact for details.

COLERAINE. (1978; 45).
Peter Robinson. T: 028 7034 4361;
E: robinsonpg@btinternet.com; W: n/a
Meetings: 7.30pm, 3rd Monday of the month.
St Patricks Church, Minor Church Hall, Corner of
Brook St and Circular Road, Coleraine, BT52 1PY.

FERMANAGH. (1977; 30).
Sandra Trimble. T: 028 8952 1885;
E: rwgtrimble@googlemail.com; W: n/a
Meetings: 8pm. Cathedral Hall, Halls Lane,
Enniskillen, BT74 7DR - contact for details.

LARNE. (1974; 35).
Jimmy Christie. T: 028 2858 3223;
E: candcandjchristie@btinternet.com; W: n/a
Meetings: 7.30pm, 1st Wednesday of the month
(Sep-Mar). Larne Grammar School, 4-6 Lower
Cairncastle Rd, Larne, BT40 1PQ.

LISBURN. (1978; 30).
Richard Crothers. T: 028 9262 1866;
E: Richardcrothers@btinternet.com;
W: www.rspb.org.uk/groups/lisburn
Meetings: 7.30pm, 4th Monday of the month
(Sep-May). Friends Meeting House, 4 Magheralave
Road, Lisburn, BT28 3BD.

Wetland Bird Survey (WeBS) Organiser
ANTRIM (OTHER SITES). Mr A McClure.
T: 028 9346 2562 & 07793 038 211;
E: adamdmcclure@yahoo.co.uk

ARMAGH (excl. LOUGHS NEAGH & BEG).
Mr SJ Hewitt. T: via WeBS Office;
E: sjameshewitt@hotmail.com

BANN ESTUARY. Mr H Dick. T: 028 7032 9720;
E: via WeBS Office

BELFAST LOUGH. Mr S Wolsey.
T: 028 9146 7947; E: shane.wolsey@bto.org

DUNDRUM BAY. Patrick Lynch. T: 028 4375 1467;
E: patrick.lynch@nationaltrust.org.uk

NORTHERN IRELAND

FERMANAGH. Mr M Stinson.
T: via WeBS Office; E: via WeBS Office

LARNE LOUGH. Mrs D Hilditch. T: via WeBS Office;
E: mail18brae@btinternet.com

LOUGH FOYLE. Mr M Tickner. T: 028 9049 1547;
E: matthew.tickner@rspb.org.uk

STRANGFORD LOUGH. Mr KL Mackie.
T: 07719 537 275; E: kerrymackie9@gmail.com

Vacant sites - contact WeBS Office:

CARLINGFORD LOUGH.
DOWN (OTHER SITES).
LONDONDERRY (OTHER SITES).
LOUGHS NEAGH AND BEG.
OUTER ARDS.
SOUTH DOWN COAST.
TYRONE (excl. LOUGHS NEAGH AND BEG).

Wildlife Trust
ULSTER WILDLIFE. (1978; 12,000).
McClelland House, 10 Heron Road, Belfast, BT3 9LE.
T: 028 9045 4094; E: info@ulsterwildlife.org;
W: www.ulsterwildlife.org

REPUBLIC OF IRELAND

BirdWatch Ireland
Unit 20, Block D
Bullford Business Campus
Kilcoole, Greystones
Co. Wicklow, A63 RW83,
Eire.
T: 353 (0)1 281 9878;
E: info@birdwatchireland.ie;
W: www.birdwatchireland.ie

Bird Recorder
IRELAND (all non-rarities): BirdWatch Ireland,
P.O.Box 12, Greystones, Co. Wicklow.
E: info@birdwatchireland.ie

CLARE. John Murphy. E: murphyjohn@gmail.com

CORK. Mark Shorten. E: mshorten@gmail.com

DONEGAL. Ralph Sheppard. E: rsheppard@eircom.net

DUBLIN, LOUTH, MEATH & WICKLOW.
Declan Murphy & Dick Coombes.
E: dmurphy@birdwatchireland.ie
E: rcoombes@birdwatchireland.ie

GALWAY. Chris Peppiatt. E: chris.peppiatt@iol.ie

KERRY. Michael O'Clery & Jill Crosher.
E: moclery@tinet.ie

LIMERICK. Tony Mee, Ballyorgan, Kilfinane,
Co. Limerick.

MAYO. National Parks and Wildlife, Lagduff More,
Ballycroy, Westport.

MID-SHANNON. Stephen Heery. E: sheery@eircom.net

MONAGHAN. Joe Shannon. E: joeshan@eircom.net

WATERFORD. Paul Walsh, 16 Castlepoint,
Crosshaven, Co. Cork.
E: pmwalsh@waterfordbirds.com

WEXFORD. Tony Murray, Wexford Wildfowl
Reserve, North Slob. E: murraytony@hotmail.com

Bird Report
IRISH BIRD REPORT (1977),
contact BirdWatch Ireland.

BirdWatch Ireland Branches
There is a network of 30 branches who organise
birdwatching events and talks around the country
- they can be contacted via BirdWatch Ireland.

Ringing Group/Bird Observatory
CAPE CLEAR BIRD OBSERVATORY.
Birdwatch Ireland - see above.
E: info@birdwatchireland.ie;
W: www.birdwatchireland.ie/Birdwatching/
CapeClearBirdObservatory/tabid/567/Default.aspx

GREAT SALTEE RS. Mr AJ Walsh.
E: alynwalsh@eircom.net

IRISH MIDLANDS RG. Mr S Kingston.
E: irishmidlandsringinggroup@gmail.com

MUNSTER RG. Mr KPC Collins.
E: kevincollins062@gmail.com

BirdWatchIreland

WILDLIFE WELFARE

A number of organisations work towards the care and rehabilitation of injured, sick and abandoned birds/wildlife across the UK, and individual wildlife hospitals carry out the same role on a local basis - some of these are listed below. The RSPCA (England & Wales), SSPCA (Scotland) and USPCA (Northern Ireland) are the national charities that help and advise on injured wildlife (NOT the RSPB). You can also find an independent local rescue centre on www.helpwildlife.co.uk

ORGANISATIONS

BRITISH WILDLIFE REHABILITATION COUNCIL (1987)
Promoting the care and rehabilitation of wildlife casualties through the exchange of information between people such as rehabilitators, zoologists and veterinary surgeons who are active in this field. Organises symposiums and regional workshops. Publishes a regular newsletter, The Rehabilitator.
Contact: BWRC, PO Box 8686, Grantham, Lincolnshire NG31 0AG; E: admin@bwrc.org.uk; W: www.bwrc.org.uk

HELPWILDLIFE.CO.UK (2005)
HelpWildlife.co.uk is maintained by a very small team of people involved in British wildlife rehabilitation to fully utilise the internet to help with wildlife issues. The site aims to provide informed, unbiased advice about caring for sick or injured birds and animals. Volunteers trawl the internet for details of those who might be able to help so that assistance can be offered quickly in an emergency. Visitors to the site are invited to provide feedback on listings published to ensure they are kept as up to date as possible.
Contact: for general enquiries NOT for a specific wildlife rescue - E: enquiries@helpwildlife.co.uk; W: www.helpwildlife.co.uk

INTERNATIONAL CENTRE FOR BIRDS OF PREY (1967)
The ICBP works for the conservation of birds of prey and their habitats through public education, captive breeding, treatment and rehabilitation of wild injured birds of prey. Education is on-going to visitors and specific groups and parties, from first schools to universities. The Centre continues its captive breeding aims; to research species; maintain the collection and provide birds for demonstrations. The Centre also works with many other groups and facilities to continue to support worldwide field research projects and international conservation programmes. It accepts, treats and rehabilitates injured wild birds of prey.
The Centre is open from Feb-Nov, 10.30am-5.30pm (4.30pm Feb & Nov) and closed in Dec/Jan.
Contact: ICBP, Boulsdon House, Newent, Gloucs GL18 1JJ.
T: 01531 820 286;
E: info@icbp.org; W: www.icbp.org

PEOPLE'S DISPENSARY FOR SICK ANIMALS (1917)
Provides free veterinary treatment for sick/injured animals whose owners qualify for this charitable service and promotes responsible pet ownership.
Contact: PDSA, Whitechapel Way, Priorslee, Telford, Shropshire TF2 9PQ. T: 0800 917 2509; W: www.pdsa.org.uk

RAPTOR FOUNDATION (1989)
Involved in the care of wild, disabled birds of prey, as well as raptors rescued from breeders. The foundation researches raptor ailments and assists veterinary schools. A full 24-hour rescue service is available for injured raptors and owls and the centre assists in breed-and-release schemes to rebuild populations across Europe. Centre is open daily, 10am-5pm (4pm in winter), closed Jan 1 & Dec 25/26.
Contact: The Raptor Foundation, The Heath, St Ives Road, Woodhurst, Cambs PE28 3BT.
T: 01487 741 140; E: info@raptorfoundation.org.uk; W: www.raptorfoundation.org.uk

RAPTOR RESCUE (1978)
Raptor Rescue has evolved into one of the UK's foremost organisations dedicated to ensuring all sick and injured birds of prey are cared for by suitably qualified people, and wherever possible, released back into the wild.
Contact: Raptor Rescue. T: 0870 241 0609; E: secretary@raptorrescue.org.uk; W: www.raptorrescue.org.uk

ROYAL SOCIETY FOR THE PREVENTION OF CRUELTY TO ANIMALS (1824): RSPCA
The oldest welfare charity looking out for the needs of animals on farms, in research labs, in the wild in paddocks and in our homes. The RSPCA also operate four wildlife centres providing specialist care for the rehabilitation of wildlife throughout England and Wales (see wildlife hospitals below). In cases of animal cruelty, inspectors are contacted through their National Communication Centre, which can be reached via the Society's 24-hour national cruelty and advice line: T: 0300 1234 999
Contact: RSPCA Headquarters, Willberforce Way, Southwater, Horsham, West Sussex RH13 9RS. W: www.rspca.org.uk

WILDLIFE WELFARE

SCOTTISH SOCIETY FOR THE PREVENTION OF CRUELTY TO ANIMALS (1839): SCOTTISH SPCA

Represents animal welfare interests to Government, local authorities and others. Educates young people to realise their responsibilities. Maintains an inspectorate to patrol and investigate and to advise owners about the welfare of animals and birds in their care. Maintains a National Wildlife Rescue Centre. Bird species, including birds of prey, are rehabilitated and where possible released back into the wild.
Contact: Scottish SPCA, Kingseat Road, Halbeath, Dunfermline, Fife KY11 8RY.
T: 03000 999 999 (animal helpline 7am-11pm);
E: via website; W: www.scottishspca.org

SWAN SANCTUARY (1980s)

Founded by Dorothy Beeson, this registered charity is the largest and only completely self-contained swan hospital in the UK. It has several nursing ponds and rehabilitation lakes. 24-hr rescue service, with volunteers on hand to recover swans (and other animals).
Contact: The Swan Sanctuary, Felix Lane, Shepperton, Middlesex TW17 8NN.
T: 01932 240 790 (emergency); E: via website;
W: www.the swansanctuary.org.uk

ULSTER SOCIETY FOR THE PREVENTION OF CRUELTY TO ANIMALS (1836): USPCA

Represents animal welfare in Northern Ireland with the purpose of preventing cruelty and revlieve suffering to all animals, both pets and wildlife.
Contact: UPSCA, Unit 6, Carnbane Industrial Estate (East), Newry, Co Down BT35 6HQ.
T: 028 3025 1000; E: enquiries@uspca.co.uk;
W: www.uspca.co.uk

WILDLIFE HOSPITALS

England

SWAN LIFELINE.
Swan Rescue HQ & Treatment Centre, Cuckoo Weir Island, South Meadow Lane, Eton, BERKSHIRE SL4 6SS.
T: 01753 859 397; E: via website;
W: www.swanlifeline.org
Thames Valley 24-hour swan rescue & treatment service. Veterinary support & hospital unit. Membership available.

TIGGYWINKLES, THE WILDLIFE HOSPITAL TRUST.
Tiggywinkles, Aston Road, Haddenham, Aylesbury, BUCKINGHAMSHIRE HP17 8AF. T: 01844 292 292 (24hr helpline); E: mail@tiggywinkles.org;
W: www.sttiggywinkles.org.uk
All British species. Veterinary referrals & helpline for vets & others on wild bird treatments. Full veterinary unit & staff. Membership available.

RSPCA WILDLIFE CENTRES.
EAST WINCH, Gayton Rd, East Winch, NORFOLK PE32 1LG. T: 0300 123 0709

MALLYDAMS WOOD, Peter James Lane, Hastings, EAST SUSSEX TN35 4AH. T: 0300 123 0723

STAPELEY GRANGE, London Road, Stapeley, Nantwich, CHESHIRE CW5 7JW. T: 0300 123 0722

WEST HATCH, Cold Road,Taunton SOMERSET TA3 5RT. 0300 123 0747

RSPCA ctd.
T: 0300 1234 999 (24-hr national cruelty line);
W: https://www.rspca.org.uk/whatwedo/care/wildlifecentres

SWAN RESCUE SANCTUARY.
The Widgeons, Crooked Withies, Holt, Wimborne, DORSET BH21 7LB. T: 01202 828 166;
W: www.swan-rescue.co.uk
Rescue service for swans. Large sanctuary of ponds/lakes. Hospital and intensive care. Veterinary support. Free advice and help line. Rescue water craft for emergencies. Viewing by appointment only.

VALE WILDLIFE HOSPITAL & REHABILITATION CENTRE. Station Road, Beckford, Tewkesbury, GLOUCESTERSHIRE GL20 7AN.
T: 01386 882 288; E: info@valewildlife.org.uk;
W: www.valewildlife.org.uk
All wildlife. Intensive care. Veterinary support.

HAWK CONSERVANCY TRUST.
Visitor Centre, Sarson Lane, Weyhill, Andover, HAMPSHIRE SP11 8DY. T: 01264 773 850;
E: info@hawkconservancy.org;
W: www.hawk-conservancy.org
The HCT is an important centre for receiving injured birds of prey and has one of the only specialist birds of prey hospitals in the UK.

WILDLIFE WELFARE

RAPTOR CENTRE.
Ivy Cottage, Groombridge Place Gardens,
Groombridge, Tunbridge Wells, KENT TN3 9QG.
T: 01892 861 175; E: via website;
W: www.raptorcentre.co.uk
Birds of prey. Veterinary support. 24hr rescue
service for sick and injured birds of prey that
covers the South-East.

BERWICK SWAN & WILDLIFE TRUST.
Windmill Way East, Ramparts
Business Park, Berwick-upon-
Tweed, NORTHUMBERLAND
TD15 1TU. T: 01289 302 882;
E: swan-trust@hotmail.co.uk;
W: www.swan-trust.org
All categories of wildlife. Pools
for swans, other waterfowl.
Veterinary support.

BRITISH WILDLIFE RESCUE CENTRE.
Amerton Farm & Craft Centre, Amerton, Stafford,
STAFFORDSHIRE ST18 0LA. T: 01889 271 308;
E: admin@thebwrc.com; W: www.thebwrc.com
All species, including imprints and permanently
injured. Hospital, large aviaries and caging. Open
daily to the public. Veterinary support.

GENTLESHAW BIRD OF PREY & WILDLIFE CENTRE.
Fletcher's Country Garden Centre, Stone Road,
Eccleshall, STAFFORDSHIRE ST21 6JY.
T: 01785 850 379; E: gentleshaw1@btconnect.com;
W: www.gentleshawwildlife.co.uk
All birds of prey (incl. owls). Hospital cages and
aviaries; release sites. Veterinary support.

THE WILDLIFE AID FOUNDATION.
Randalls Farm House, Randalls Road,
Leatherhead, SURREY KT22 0AL. 24-hr Wildlife
Help & Enquiries line: 09061 800 132 (50p/min);
E: via website; W: www.wildlifeaid.org.uk
Wildlife hospital and rehabilitation centre helping
all native British species. Special housing for birds
of prey. Membership scheme and fund raising
activities. Veterinary support.

BRENT LODGE BIRD & WILDLIFE TRUST.
Cow Lane, Sidlesham, Chichester, WEST SUSSEX
PO20 7LN. T: 01243 641 672 (emergency number);
E: via website; W: www.brentlodge.org
All species of wild birds and small mammals.

ANIMAL HOUSE WILDLIFE WELFARE.
58 Dale Edge, Eastfield, Scarborough,
NORTH YORKSHIRE YO11 3EP. T: 07807 038 553;
E: birdsofprey06@gmail.com;
W: www.animalhousewildlifewelfare.com
Specialises in the rescue and rehabilitation of
birds of prey.

Scotland

HESSILHEAD WILDLIFE RESCUE CENTRE.
Gateside, Beith, AYRSHIRE KA15 1HT.
T: 01505 502 415; E: info@hessilhead.org.uk;
W: www.hessilhead.org.uk
All species. Releasing aviaries. Veterinary
support. Visits on open days.

NATIONAL WILDLIFE RESCUE CENTRE.
Scottish SPCA, National Wildlife Rescue Centre,
Fishcross, CLACKMANNANSHIRE FK10 3AN.
T: 03000 999 999; E: via website;
W: www.scottishspca.org/rehome/our-centres/
national-wildlife-rescue-centre/
No visiting, but casualties accepted at any time.

Wales

GOWER BIRD HOSPITAL.
Sandy Lane, Pennard, SWANSEA,
SA3 2EW. T: 01792 371 630;
E: admin@gowerbirdhospital.org.uk;
W: www.gowerbirdhospital.org.uk
All species of wild birds, also small
mammals. Cares for sick, injured
and orphaned wild birds and animals with the sole
intention of returning them to the wild.

Channel Islands

GUERNSEY.
GSPCA ANIMAL SHELTER,
Les Fiers Moutons,
St Andrews, GUERNSEY
GY6 8UD.
T: 01481 257 261;
(T: 07781 104 082 emergency);
E: admin@gspca.org.gg; W: www.gspca.org.gg
All species. 24-hour emergency service. Veterinary
support.

JERSEY.
JSPCA ANIMALS' SHELTER,
89 St Saviour's Road, St Helier,
JERSEY JE2 4GJ.
T: 01534 724 331;
(T: 07797 720 331 emergency);
E: info@jspca.org.je;
W: www.jspca.org.je
All species. 24-hour emergency
service. Veterinary support.
Educational Centre.

**All of the organisations and wildife hospitals
that look after the health and welfare of our
wildlife rely on funding from memberships
and/or donations.**

BIRD INFORMATION SERVICES & BIRDLINE NUMBERS

Bird Forum
Free to join, online forum. W: www.birdforum.net

BirdGuides
Offers subscription bird news services online and via email, text message and apps for Apple and Android devices. T: 020 8826 0934;
E: contact@birdguides.com; W: www.birdguides.com

Flightline
Northern Ireland's daily bird news service.
T: 07973 403 146 or 07870 863 782;
E: nibirds@live.co.uk;
http://nibirds.blogspot.co.uk

Rare Bird Alert
Offers subscription instant bird news service - available online, by pager or phone app.
T: 01603 457 016; E: admin@rarebirdalert.co.uk;
W: www.rarebirdalert.co.uk

Rare Bird Network
A free bird sightings service, which covers any bird sighting.
E: info@rarebirdnetwork.co.uk;
W: www.rarebirdnetwork.co.uk

Birdline   09068 700 222 (National number)

Scotland   09068 700 234
W: www.the-soc.org.uk/birdline-scotland

South East   09068 700 240
W: www.southeastbirdnews.co.uk

South West   09068 700 241

East Anglia   09068 700 245
W: www.birdlineeastanglia.co.uk

North East   09068 700 246

Midlands   09068 700 247

Wales   09068 700 248

North West   closed

Note:
The 09068 Birdline numbers are charged at premium line rates (65p per minute from landline or mobile + any connection charges your mobile provider may charge).

NOTES

NATIONAL DIRECTORY

Joe Mitchell

The Corn Bunting *Emberiza calandra* is one of a suite of birds that are the focus of many national conservation bodies as they work with the farming community to turn around declines in farmland bird populations.

NATIONAL ORGANISATIONS

THERE ARE MANY organisations operating across the UK. Some cater for specialist groups of people/interests, others are open to a wider audience. The majority are membership-based, please contact them directly for more information about their work and subscription rates. In addition, a number of govermental departments are listed in this section. Have a browse!

ARMY ORNITHOLOGICAL SOCIETY (1960)

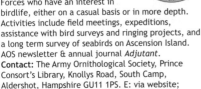

Open to any serving and ex-Army personnel, other Services and their families, MOD civil servants and members of the Commonwealth Forces who have an interest in birdlife, either on a casual basis or in more depth. Activities include field meetings, expeditions, assistance with bird surveys and ringing projects, and a long term survey of seabirds on Ascension Island. AOS newsletter & annual journal *Adjutant*.
Contact: The Army Ornithological Society, Prince Consort's Library, Knollys Road, South Camp, Aldershot, Hampshire GU11 1PS. E: via website;
W: www.armybirding.org.uk

ASSOCIATION FOR THE PROTECTION OF RURAL SCOTLAND (1926)

Works to protect Scotland's world renown landscape and the amenity of the countryside from unnecessary or inappropriate development. APRS recognise the needs of those who live and work in rural Scotland and the necessity of reconciling these needs with the sometimes competing requirements of industry and recreation. *Rural Scotland* newsletter.
Contact: Association for the Protection Rural Scotland, Dolphin House, 4 Hunter Square, Edinburgh EH1 1QW. T: 0131 225 7012; E: info@ruralscotland.org;
W: http://aprs.scot/

ASSOCIATION OF COUNTY RECORDERS AND EDITORS (1993)

The basic aim of ACRE is to promote best practice in the work of the County Recorders, proving a forum for discussions on the business of producing county bird reports and in problems arising in assessing records and managing county databases systems and archives. ACRE also provides a discussion medium for interactions of the County Recorders and Editors with British Birds Rarities Committee (BBRC), Rare Breeding Bird Panel (RBBP) and the British Trust for Ornithology (BTO).
Contact: Hugh Pulsford, Secretary. T: 01565 880 171;
E: countyrec@cawos.org

BARN OWL TRUST (1988)

A registered charity dedicated to conserving the Barn Owl and its environment. It is the main source of Barn Owl information in the UK. It carries out surveys of old buildings, due for development, and advises on Barn Owl mitigation measures. In 2012 the Trust published a definative guide to Barn Owl conservation, 'The Barn Owl Conservation Handbook'. Other publications are available. Trust members have erected more than 2,000 nestboxes and is closely involved in habitat creation both on its own land and through farm visits. Events held.
Contact: Barn Owl Trust, Waterleat, Ashburton, Devon TQ13 7HU. T: 01364 653 026;
E: info@barnowltrust.org.uk;
W: www.barnowltrust.org.uk

BIRD OBSERVATORIES COUNCIL (1946)

The BOC co-ordinates and promotes the work of bird observatories at a national level. All accredited bird observatories (20 at present) affiliated to the Council undertake a ringing programme and provide a ringing experience to those interested. Most are also able to provide accommodation for visiting birdwatchers.
Contact: Alison Duncan, The Secretary BOC, North Ronaldsay Bird Observatory, Twingness, North Ronaldsay, Orkney KW17 2BE. T: 01857 633200;
E: info@birdobscouncil.org.uk; www.birdobscouncil.org.uk

BIRD STAMP SOCIETY (1986)

Quarterly magazine *Flight* contains philatelic and ornithological articles. Lists all new issues and identifies species. Runs a quarterly Postal Auction - number of lots of between 500 to 700 per auction, depending on stock levels.
Contact: Graham Horsman (Membership Sec), 23a East Main Street, Blackburn, West Lothian EH47 7QR. T: 01506 651 029; E: graham_horsman7@msm.com;
W: www.birdstampsociety.org

BIRDING FOR ALL (2000)

Formally known as The Disabled Birder's Association, Birding For All (2010) is a registered charity and international movement, which aims to promote access to reserves and other birding places and to a range of services, so that people with different needs can follow the birding obsession as freely as able-bodied people. Membership is currently free (donations welcomed) and is open to everyone - new members are needed to help send a stronger message to those who own and manage nature reserves to improve access when they are planning and improving facilities. BFA also seeks to influence those who provide birdwatching services and equipment. In the past, BFA have also runs overseas trips.
Contact: Bo Beolens (Chairman), Birding For All, 18 St Mildreds Road, Cliftonville, Margate, Kent CT9 2LT.
E: bo@birdingforall.com; W: www.birdingforall.com

BIRDWATCH IRELAND (1968, network of over 30 branches)

The largest independent conservation organisation in Ireland with over 15,000 members. Its primary objective is the protection of wild birds and their habitats in Ireland through the efforts of its staff, members and volunteers alike. It carries out extensive research and survey work, operates applied conservation projects and manages a network of reserves nationwide. It publishes e*Wings* (electronic) magazine and *Irish Birds* (annual journal).
Contact: BirdWatch Ireland, Unit 20, Block D, Bullford Business Campus, Kilcoole, Greystones, Co. Wicklow, A63 RW83 Ireland. T: +353 (0)1 2819 878;
Fax: +353 (0)1 281 0997; E: info@birdwatchireland.ie;
W: www.birdwatchireland.ie

BRITISH BIRDS RARITIES COMMITTEE (1959)
The Committee adjudicates records of species of rare occurrence in Britain (marked 'R' in the Checklists, P.55) and publishes its annual report in B*ritish Birds*. The BBRC also assesses records from the Channel Islands. In the case of rarities trapped for ringing, records should be sent to the Ringing Office of the British Trust for Ornithology, who will in turn forward them to the BBRC.
Contact: Chas Holt (Secretary), British Birds Rarities Committee, 307 St John's Way, Thetford, Norfolk IP24 3PA. E: secretary@bbrc.org.uk; W: www.bbrc.org.uk

BRITISH DECOY & WILDFOWL CARVERS ASSOCIATION (1990)
The Association is a non-profitmaking organisation, run by carvers to promote all aspects of their art. It produces three *Wingspan* magazines p.a.; keeps members in touch with the art; promotes regional groups; generates local interest; holds competitions and exhibitions; and cares for the interests of bird carvers. Each Sept the BDWCA stages the 'Festival of Bird Art' in Bakewell, in the Peak District, and includes the National Bird Carving Championships.
Contact: E: bdwcaenquiries@bdwca.org.uk; W: www.bdwca.org.uk

BRITISH DRAGONFLY SOCIETY (1983)
The BDS aims to promote the recording and the conservation of dragonflies. Members receive two issues of *Dragonfly News* and *BDS Journal* each year and *Darter*, the annual magazine for dragonfly recorders. There are countrywide field trips, an annual members' day, and training is available on aspects of dragonfly identification and ecology.
Contact: Henry Curry (Sec), British Dragonfly Society, 23 Bowker Way, Whittlesey, Cambs PE7 1PY.
T: 01733 204 286; E: secretary@british-dragonflies.org.uk; W: www.british-dragonflies.org.uk

BRITISH FALCONERS' CLUB (1927)
The BFC is the oldest and largest falconry club in Europe and has a number of regional branches in the UK. Its aim is to encourage responsible falconers and conserve birds of prey by breeding, holding educational meetings and providing facilities, guidance and advice to those wishing to take up the sport. Publishes *The Falconer* and a newsletter.
Contact: British Falconers' Club, Westfield, Meeting Hill, Worstead, North Walsham, Norfolk NR28 9LS.
T: 01692 404 057;
E: admin@britishfalconersclub.co.uk;
W: www.britishfalconersclub.co.uk

BRITISH LIBRARY SOUND ARCHIVE - WILDLIFE SOUNDS (1969)
The most comprehensive collection of bird sound recordings in existence. Consists of 240,000+ wildlife recordings including more than 10,000 species (birds, mammals, amphibians, reptiles, fish & insects) from around the world, many accessible for free listening. Copies or sonograms of most recordings can be supplied for private study or research and, subject to copyright clearance, for commercial uses. Contribution of new material and enquiries on all aspects of wildlife sounds and recording techniques are welcome. Publishes a number of magazines and periodicals, CD guides to bird songs and other wildlife, including ambience titles. Catalogue available on-line at http://cadensa.bl.uk/uhtbin/cgisirsi/x/x/0/49/
Contact: Cheryl Tipp, Curator, Wildlife Sounds, The British Library, 96 Euston Road, London NW1 2DB.
T: 020 7412 7403; E: wildlifesound@bl.uk;
W: www.bl.uk/reshelp/findhelprestype/sound/wildsounds/wildlife.html

BRITISH NATURALISTS' ASSOCIATION (1905)
The association was founded to promote the interests of nature lovers and bring them together. It encourages and supports schemes and legislation for the protection of the country's natural resources. It organises meetings, field weeks, lectures and exhibitions to help popularise the study of nature. BNA publishes two magazines, *Country-Side* and *British Naturalist* and has a number of local branches.
Contact: British Naturalists' Association BM 8129, General Secretary, London WC1N 3XX.
T: 0844 892 1817; E: info@bna-naturalists.org;
W: www.bna-naturalists.org

BRITISH ORNITHOLOGISTS' CLUB (1892)
The Club's objects are 'the promotion of scientific discussion between members of the BOU, and others interested in ornithology, and to facilitate the publication of scientific information in connection with ornithology'. The Club maintains a special interest in avian systematics, taxonomy and distribution and publishes the B*ulletin of the British Ornithologists' Club* quarterly, as well as a continuing series of publications. It also holds a number of evening meetings each year (see website for details).
Contact: BOC, c/o Natural History Museum at Tring, Akeman Street, Tring, Herts HP23 6AP.
T: 02208876 4728 & 07919 174 898;
E: info@boc-online.org; W: www.boc-online.org

BRITISH ORNITHOLOGISTS' UNION (1858)
The BOU is one of the world's oldest and most respected ornithological societies. It aims to promote ornithology within the scientific and birdwatching communities, in Britain and around the world - this is largely achieved by the publication of its quarterly international journal, *Ibis*, featuring work at the cutting edge of our understanding of the world's birdlife. It also runs an active programme of meetings, seminars and conferences covering major ornithological topics and issues of the day - the proceedings are published free on the BOU website. Via social media (see website for links) the BOU acts as a global ornithological hub providing details of newly published research articles, conferences, jobs, PhD opportunities and more. Work being undertaken around the world can include research projects that have received financial assistance from the BOU's on-going programme of Small Research Grants and Career Development Bursaries (for ornithological students).

NATIONAL ORGANISATIONS

The BOU's Records Committee (see below) maintains the official British List. It has also published a series of country/island group 'checklists'.
Contact: British Ornithologists' Union, P.O. Box 417, Peterborough, PE7 3FX. E: via website;
W: www.bou.org.uk

BRITISH ORNITHOLOGISTS' UNION RECORDS COMMITTEE

A standing committee of the BOU, the BOURC's function is to maintain the British List, the official list of birds recorded in Great Britain - the up-to-date list can be viewed on the BOU website. Where vagrants are involved it is concerned only with those which relate to potential additions to the British List (i.e. first records). In this it differs from the British Birds Rarities Committee. It also examines, where necessary, important pre-1950 records, monitors introduced species for possible admission to, or deletion from, the List, and reviews taxonomy and nomenclature relating to the List. BOURC reports are published in Ibis and are also available via the BOU website. **Contact:** as above (BOU)

BRITISH TRUST FOR ORNITHOLOGY (1933)

The BTO is an independent charitable research institute that combines professional and citizen science aimed at using evidence of change in wildlife populations, particularly birds, to inform the public, opinion-formers and environmental policy/decision makers.

Through the fieldwork of 40,000+ volunteer birdwatchers, in partnership with professional research scientists, the BTO collects high quality monitoring data on birds and other wildlife. Surveys include the National Ringing Scheme, the Nest Record Scheme, the Breeding Bird Survey (in collaboration with JNCC/RSPB), the Wetland Bird Survey, in particular Low Tide Counts (in collaboration with WWT/RSPB/JNCC) which all contribute to an integrated programme of population monitoring. The BirdTrack recording system is an important resource for recording bird data and all birdwatchers are encouraged to use it to log their bird sightings. The Trust has a network of voluntary regional representatives (see County Directory) who organise fieldworkers for the BTO's programme of national surveys in which members participate. The results of these co-operative efforts are communicated to government departments, local authorities, industry and conservation bodies for effective action. For details of current activities see National Projects. Members receive *BTO News* regularly throughout the year and have the option of subscribing to *Bird Study* (four times yearly) and *Ringing & Migration* (twice yearly). Local meetings are held in conjunction with bird clubs and societies, there are regional and national birdwatchers' conferences, and specialist courses in bird identification and modern censusing techniques. Grants are made for research, and members have the use of a lending and reference library at Thetford and the Alexander Library at the Edward Grey Institute of Field Ornithology.

Contact: British Trust for Ornithology, The Nunnery, Thetford, Norfolk IP24 2PU. T: 01842 750 050; Fax: 01842 750 030; E: info@bto.org; W: www.bto.org

BTO SCOTLAND (2000)

BTO Scotland's main functions are to promote the work of the Trust and develop wider coverage for surveys in Scotland, by encouraging greater participation in survey work. With a landscape and wildlife so different from the rest of the UK, BTO Scotland ensure that the Trust's work is not just related to the priorities of the UK as a whole but is also focused on the priorities of Scotland.
Contact: BTO Scotland, Biological and Environmental Sciences, University of Stirling, FK9 4LA.
T: 01786 466 560; Fax: 01786 466 561;
E: scot.info@bto.org; W: www.bto.org

BRITISH WATERFOWL ASSOCIATION

The BWA is an association of enthusiasts interested in keeping, breeding and conserving all types of waterfowl, including wildfowl and domestic ducks and geese. It is a registered charity, without trade affiliations, dedicated to educating the public about waterfowl and the need for conservation as well as to raising the standards of keeping and breeding ducks, geese and swans in captivity. Publishes *Waterfowl* magazine for members three times a year.
Contact: Kate Elkington, BWA Secretary, The Old Bakehouse, Ashperton, Ledbury, HR8 2SA.
T: 01531 671 250; E: info@waterfowl.org.uk;
W: www.waterfowl.org.uk

BUGLIFE (2000)

The only organisation in Europe devoted to the conservation of all invertebrates, actively engaged in halting the extinction of Britain's rarest slugs, snails, bees, wasps, ants, spiders, beetles and many more. It works to achieve this through practical conservation projects; promoting the environmental importance of invertebrates and raising awareness about the challenges to their survival; assisting in the development of helpful legislation and policy; developing and disseminating knowledge about how to conserve invertebrates; and encouraging and supporting invertebrate conservation initiatives by other organisations in the UK, Europe and worldwide.
Contact: Buglife, Bug House, Ham Lane, Orton Waterville, Peterborough, PE2 5UU.
T: 01733 201 210; E: info@buglife.org.uk;
W: www.buglife.org.uk

CAMPAIGN FOR THE PROTECTION OF RURAL WALES (1928)

Its aims are to help the conservation and enhancement of the landscape, environment and amenities of the countryside, towns and villages of rural Wales and to form and educate opinion to ensure the promotion of its objectives. It gives advice and information upon matters affecting protection, conservation and improvement of the visual environment.

Contact: Tŷ Gwyn, 31 High Street, Welshpool, Powys SY21 7YD.
T: 01938 552 525 or 01938 556 212;
E: info@cprwmail.org;
W: www.cprw.org.uk

NATIONAL ORGANISATIONS

CENTRE FOR ECOLOGY & HYDROLOGY (CEH)
The work of the CEH, a component body of the Natural Environment Research Council, includes a range of ornithological research, covering population studies, habitat management and work on the effects of pollution. The CEH has a long-term programme to monitor pesticide and pollutant residues in the corpses of predatory birds sent in by birdwatchers, and carries out detailed studies on affected species. The Biological Records Centre (BRC), which is part of the CEH, is responsible for the national biological data bank on plant and animal distributions (except birds). Also see BRC website: www.brc.ac.uk
Contact: Centre for Ecology & Hydrology, Maclean Building, Benson Lane, Crowmarsh Gifford, Wallingford, Oxfordshire OX10 8BB. T: 01491 838 800; E: via website; W: www.ceh.ac.uk

CLA (Country Land and Business Association) (1907)
The CLA is at the heart of rural life and is the voice of the countryside for England and Wales, campaigning on issues which directly affect those who live and work in rural communities. Anyone who ownes rural land or runs a rural business will benefit from joining the CLA and its members range from some of the largest landowners, with interests in forest, moorland, water and farming, to some with little more than a paddock or garden.
Contact: Country Land and Business Association Ltd, 16 Belgrave Square, London SW1X 8PQ. T: 020 7235 0511; Fax: 020 7235 4696; E: mail@cla.org.uk; W: www.cla.org.uk

CONSERVATION FOUNDATION (1982)
Created by David Bellamy and David Shreeve, it provides a means for people in public, private and not-for-profit sectors to collaborate on environmental causes. Over the years its programme has included award schemes, conferences, promotions, special events, field studies, school programmes, media work, seminars and workshops etc. The Conservation Foundation has created and managed environmental award schemes of all kinds. For information about how to apply for current award schemes visit the website.
Contact: Conservation Foundation, 1 Kensington Gore, London SW7 2AR. T: 020 7591 3111; E: info@conservationfoundation.co.uk; W: www.conservationfoundation.co.uk

CPRE (Campaign to Protect Rural England) (1926)
CPRE now has a branch in every county and over 200 district groups. It highlights threats to the countryside and promotes positive solutions. In-depth research supports active campaigning, and through reasoned argument and lobbying, CPRE seeks to influence public opinion and decision-makers at every level. Membership is open to all.
Contact: Campaign to Protect Rural England, 5-11 Lavington Street, London SE1 0NZ. T: 020 7981 2800; Fax: 020 7981 2899; E: info@cpre.org.uk; W: www.cpre.org.uk

EARTHWATCH INSTITUTE (1971)
Earthwatch developed the innovative idea of engaging the general public into the scientific process by bringing together individual volunteers and scientists on field research projects, thereby providing an alternative means of funding, as well as a dedicated labour force for field scientists. Since 1971 Earthwatch have invested in nearly 1400 conservation research projects in more than 120 countries.
Contact: Earthwatch Institute (Europe), Mayfield House, 256 Banbury Road, Oxford, OX2 7DE. T: 01865 318 838; E: info@earthwatch.org.uk; W: http://eu.earthwatch.org

EDWARD GREY INSTITUTE OF FIELD ORNITHOLOGY (1937)
The EGI takes its name from Edward Grey, first Viscount Grey of Fallodon, a life-long lover of birds and former Chancellor of the University of Oxford. The Institute now has a permanent (research) staff of research students, senior visitors and post-doctoral research workers. Field research is carried out mainly in Wytham Woods near Oxford and on the island of Skomer in West Wales. In addition there are laboratory facilities and aviary space for experimental work.
The Institute houses the Alexander Library of Ornithology, one of the largest collections of 20th Century material on birds in the world, which is supported by the British Ornithologists' Union who provide much of the material. It also houses the British Falconers Club library. The Library is open for reference use only to all holders of a university card or valid Bodleian Library card. External visitors are welcome on a one-off day pass by arrangement - contact: sophie.wilcocx@bodleian.ox.ac.uk
Contact: Lynne Bradley, PA to Prof. Ben Sheldon, The EGI, Department of Zoology, University of Oxford, The John Krebs Field Starion, Wytham, Oxford, OX2 8QJ; T: 01865 271 234; E: ben.sheldon.pa@zoo.ox.ac.uk; W: www.zoo.ox.ac.uk/egi/

ENVIRONMENT AGENCY (1996)
A non-departmental body, sponsored by the Department for Environment, Food and Rural Affairs, which aims to protect and improve the environment and to contribute towards the delivery of sustainable development through the integrated management of air, land and water. Functions include pollution prevention and control, waste minimisation, management of water resources, flood defence, improvement of salmon and freshwater fisheries, conservation of aquatic species, navigation and use of inland and coastal waters for recreation.
Contact: Environment Agency, National Customer Contact Centre, PO Box 544, Rotherham, S60 1BY. General enquiries - T: 03708 506 506 (Mon-Fri, 8am - 6pm). Environment incident hotline T: 0800 80 70 60; floodline (24 hrs) T: 0345 988 1188;
E: enquiries@environment-agency.gov.uk;
W: www.gov.uk/government/organisations/environment-agency

NATIONAL ORGANISATIONS

EURING (1963)

EURING co-ordinates bird-ringing schemes throughout Europe. It aims to promote and encourage: Scientific and administrative co-operation between national ringing schemes; development and maintenance of high standards in bird ringing; scientific studies of birds, in particular those based on marked individuals; and the use of data from bird ringing for the management and conservation of birds. These objectives are achieved mainly through co-operative projects, the organisation of meetings and the collection of data in the EURING Data Bank.
Contact: E: enquiries@euring.org; W: www.euring.org

FIELD STUDIES COUNCIL (1943)

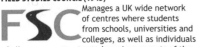 Manages a UK wide network of centres where students from schools, universities and colleges, as well as individuals of all ages, can stay to study various aspects of the environment under expert guidance. Courses include many bird related themes. Research workers and naturalists wishing to use the records and resources are welcome. There are centres in England, Scotland, Wales and Northern Ireland - see website for contacts and courses available. FSC also publish many id charts, guides and handbooks.
Contact: Field Studies Council, Preston Montford, Montford Bridge, Shrewsbury, SY4 1HW.
T: 01743 852 100; T (FSC publications): 01952 208 910;
E: enquiries@field-studies-council.org;
W: www.field-studies-council.org

FIELDFARE TRUST

Fieldfare works with people with disabilities and countryside managers to improve access to the countryside for everyone. It provides advice and training services to countryside management teams, supported by its research into national standards for accessibility under the BT Countryside for All Project. For members of the public, it runs projects which can enable them to take action locally, provide information on accessible places to visit and run events like the Fieldfare Challenge,encouraging young people to get active in the countryside.
Contact: Fieldfare Trust, 69 Crossgate, Cupar, Fife KY15 5AS. T: 01334 657 708; E: info@fieldfare.org.uk;
W: www.fieldfare.org.uk

FORESTRY COMMISSION (1919)

The government department responsible for the protection and expansion of Britain's forests and woodlands, it runs from national offices in England and Scotland. Its objectives are to protect Britain's forests and resources, conserve and improve the biodiversity, landscape and cultural heritage of forests and woodlands, develop opportunities for woodland recreation and increase public understanding and community participation in forestry.

Contact: *FC England.* National Office, 620 Bristol Business Park, Coldharbour Lane, Bristol, BS16 1EJ.
T: 0300 067 4000; E: fe.england@forestry.gsi.gov.uk;
W: www.forestry.gov.uk

FC Scotland. Silvan House, 231 Corstorphine Road, Edinburgh EH12 7AT. T: 0300 067 6156;
E: fcscotland@forestry.gsi.gov.uk;
W: www.scotland.forestry.gov.uk

Wales. See under listing for Natural Resources Wales.

FRESHWATER HABITATS TRUST (1988)

Formally Pond Conservation, Freshwater Habitats Trust aim is to protect freshwater life in ponds, streams, rivers and lakes through research, surveys and practical conservation work. Practical projects are targeted on the places that will bring the greatest benefits for freshwater life at regional and UK scale. The Million Ponds Project has already created over 1,000 new ponds and aims to construct another 30,000 by 2020
Contact: Freshwater Habitats Trust, Bury Knowle House, North Place, Headington, Oxford, OX3 9HY.
T: 01865 595 505; E: info@freshwaterhabitats.org.uk;
W: www.freshwaterhabitats.org.uk

FRIENDS OF THE EARTH (1971)

The largest international network of environmental groups in the world, represented in over 75 countries. In the UK it has a unique network of campaigning local groups, working in communities in England, Wales, Northern Ireland and Scotland, with over 200 local groups. It is largely funded by supporters with more than 90% of income coming from individual donations, the rest from special fundraising events, grants and trading.

Contact: Friends of the Earth, The Printworks, 139 Clapham Road, London SW9 0HP.
T: 020 7490 1555; W: www.foe.co.uk

Friends of the Earth Cymru
33 Castle Arcade Balcony, Cardiff, CF10 1BY.
T: 029 2022 9577; E: cymru@foe.co.uk;
W: www.foe.cymru

Friends of the Earth Northern Ireland
7 Donegall Street Place, Belfast BT1 2FN.
T: 028 9023 3488; E: foe-ni@foe.co.uk;
W: www.foe.co.uk/northern-ireland

Friends of the Earth Scotland
Thorn House, 5 Rose Street, Edinburgh EH2 2PR.
T: 0131 243 2700; W: www.foe-scotland.org.uk

FWAG ASSOCIATION (2011)

The FWAG Association succeeded FWAG in 2011. It represents a coming together of the local Farming & Wildlife Advisory Groups which continue to serve the farming community up and down the country today, according to the original FWAG standards and values.
Contact: FWAG Association. E: hello@fwag.org.uk;
W: www.fwag.org.uk

Local FWAG Groups:
East Midlands FWAG
E: info@eastmidlandsfwag.co.uk;
W: www.eastmidlandsfwag.co.uk

FWAG East (Cambs, Herts, Essex & Beds)
T: 01223 841 507; E: hello@fwageast.org.uk;
W: www.fwageast.org.uk

FWAG South East
T: 01483 810 887 & 07713 333 182;
E: shaun.page@fwagadvice.co.uk;
W: www.fwagadvice.co.uk

FWAG South West (including Herefordshire)
T: 01823 660 684; E: admin@fwagsw.org.uk;
W: www.fwagsw.org.uk

Norfolk FWAG
T: 01603 814 869; E: advice@norfolkfwag.co.uk;
W: www.norfolkfwag.org

Suffolk FWAG
T: 01728 748 030; E: tim.schofield@suffolkfwag.co.uk;
W: www.suffolkfwag.co.uk

GAME AND WILDLIFE CONSERVATION TRUST (1931)

A registered charity which uses science to promote game and wildlife management as an essential part of nature conservation and support best practice for field sports that contribute to improving the biodiversity of the countryside. More than 100 staff, including many scientists, run over 60 research projects. The results are used to advise government, landowners, farmers and conservationists on practical management techniques which will benefit game species, their habitats and other wildlife. In June the *Annual Review* lists papers published in the peer-reviewed scientific press.
Contact: Game & Wildlife Conservation Trust, Burgate Manor, Fordingbridge, Hampshire SP6 1EF.
T: 01425 652 381; Fax: 01425 655 848;
E: info@gwct.org.uk; W: www.gwct.org.uk

GAY BIRDERS CLUB (1994)

A voluntary society for gay, lesbian, bisexual or transgender birdwatchers, their friends and supporters, over the age of consent, in the UK and worldwide. The club has a network of regional contacts and organises day trips, weekends and longer events at notable birding locations in the UK and abroad (ca.100 p.a.). Members receive a quarterly newsletter *Out Birding* with details of all events. There is a 'Grand Get Together' every two years.
Contact: E: contact@gbc-online.org.uk;
W: www.gbc-online.org.uk

HAWK AND OWL TRUST (1969)

A registered charity dedicated to the conservation and appreciation of wild birds of prey and their habitats. Publishes a newsletter members' magazine, *Peregrine* and educational materials for all ages. The Trust achieves its major aim of creating and enhancing nesting, roosting and feeding habitats for birds of prey through projects which involve practical research, creative conservation and education, both on its own reserves and in partnership with landowners, farmers and others. Members are invited to take part in fieldwork, population studies, surveys, etc. The Trust manages three main reserves: Sculthorpe Moor in Norfolk; Shapwick Moor on the Somerset Levels; and Fylingdales Moor conservation area in North Yorkshire. Its Sculthorpe reserve near Fakenham, Norfolk offers schools and other groups cross-curricular environmental activities.

Contact: Hawk and Owl Trust, Turf Moor Road, Sculthorpe, Fakenham, Norfolk NR21 9GN.
T: 01328 850 590; E: enquiries@hawkandowl.org;
W: www.hawkandowl.org

INTERNATIONAL WADER STUDY GROUP (1970)

An association of wader enthusiasts, both amateur and professional, from all parts of the world, the Group aims to maintain contact between them, help organise co-operative studies, and provide a vehicle for the exchange of information. Publishes *Wader Study* three times a year and holds annual meetings throughout Europe.
Contact: International Wader Study Group, c/o British Trust for Ornithology, The Nunnery, Thetford, Norfolk IP24 2PU. E: membership@waderstudygroup.org;
W: www.waderstudygroup.org

IRISH RARE BREEDING BIRDS PANEL

In Ireland, the (UK) RBBP is responsible for collating data on rare breeding species rare within the whole of the UK which breed or attempt to breed in Northern Ireland, but not in the Republic of Ireland. The IRBBP operates across the whole of Ireland.
Contact: E: irbbp.secretary@gmail.com

IRISH RARE BIRDS COMMITTEE (1985)

Assesses records of species of rare occurrence in the Republic of Ireland. Details of records accepted and rejected are incorporated in the *Irish Bird Report*, published annually in *Irish Birds*. The Committee operates under the auspices of BirdWatch Ireland and also works closely with the Northern Ireland Birdwatchers' Association Rarities Committee to maintain a comprehensive records of birds found on the island of Ireland.
Contact: E: secretary@irbc.ie; W: www.irbc.ie

JOINT NATURE CONSERVATION COMMITTEE (1990)

A committee with members from Natural Resourses Wales, Northern Ireland's Council for Nature Conservation and the Countryside, Natural England and Scottish Natural Heritage as well as the Northern Ireland Environment Agency. Their role is to provide evidence, information and advice so that decisions are made to protect natural resources and systems, specifically to work on nature conservation issues the UK as a whole and internationally. The committee is the UK Government's nature conservation advisor in European and global fora, taking issues forward from the four home countries to inform policy development and then provide support to ensure that European and international requirements are met.
Contact: Joint Nature Conservation Committee, Monkstone House, City Road, Peterborough, PE1 1JY.
T: 01733 562 626;
Fax: 01733 555 948;
E: comment@jncc.gov.uk;
W: www.jncc.defra.gov.uk

NATIONAL ORGANISATIONS

LINNEAN SOCIETY OF LONDON (1788)
Named after Carl Linnaeus, the 18th Century Swedish biologist, who created the modern system of scientific biological nomenclature, the Society promotes all aspects of pure and applied biology. It houses Linnaeus' collection of plants, insects and fishes, library and correspondence. The Society has a major reference library consisting of books, journals and archives. Publishes the *Biological, Botanical* and *Zoological* Journals, and the *Synopsis of the British Fauna* series. Contact: Linnean Society of London, Burlington House, Piccadilly, London W1J 0BF. T: 020 7434 4479 (ext. 210); E: info@linnean.org; W: www.linnean.org

MAMMAL SOCIETY (1954)
The Mammal Society is the only organisation solely dedicated to the study and conservation of all British mammals. It seeks to raise awareness of mammal ecology and conservation needs, to survey British mammals and their habitats to identify the threats they face, and to promote mammal studies in the UK. Contact: The Mammal Society, 18 St John's Church Road, London, E9 6EJ.T: 0238 001 0981; E: info@themammalsociety.org; W: www.mammal.org.uk

MARINE CONSERVATION SOCIETY (1983)
MCS is the UK charity that campaigns for clean seas and beaches around the British coastline, sustainable fisheries, and protection for all marine life. MCS is consulted on a wide range of marine issues and provides advice primarily to government, but also to industry, on topics ranging from offshore wind, oil and gas, to marine strategies and fisheries reform. It provides advice to ensure that further action is taken to conserve our seas and reduce the effect of marine activities on marine habitats and species. It has an extensive programme for volunteers, ranging from fund-raising and an annual clean-up of UK beaches, to surveys of species such as basking shark. Contact: Marine Conservation Society, Overross House, Ross Park, Ross-on-Wye, HR9 7US. T: 01989 566 017; E: via website; W: www.mcsuk.org

NATIONAL TRUST (1895)
The charity works for the preservation of places of historic interest or natural beauty in England, Wales and Northern Ireland. It has a membership of over 4.5 million and over 61,000 volunteers (contributing five million hours of work). Over 22 million visits are made to the pay-for-entry sites and it is estimated that 100 million visits are made to the open air properties. The Trust protects 240,000 ha of land and 775 miles of coastline and over 500 historic houses, castles, ancient monuments, gardens and parks and nature reserves (many of the latter SSSIs/ASSIs, NNRs, Ramsar sites and SPAs). Contact: The National Trust (Membership), PO Box 574, Manvers, Rotherham, S63 3FH . T: 0344 800 1895; E: enquiries@nationaltrust.org.uk; W: www.nationaltrust.org.uk

NATIONAL TRUST FOR SCOTLAND (1931)
The charity protects and promotes Scotland's natural and cultural heritage for present and future generations to enjoy. Amongst its responsibilities it looks after 129 buildings, nearly 70 gardens, 190,000 acres of countryside - including seven National Nature Reserves and 46 Munro mountains. Contact: The National Trust for Scotland, Hermiston Quay, 5 Cultins Rd, Edinburgh EH11 4DF. T: 0131 458 0200; E: information@nts.org.uk; W: www.nts.org.uk

NATURAL ENGLAND
Natural England is the government's adviser for the natural environment in England, helping to protect England's nature and landscape for people to enjoy and for the services they provide. Responsibilities include helping land managers and farmers to protect wildlife and landscapes; improving public access to the coastline; managing 140 National Nature Reserves; managing programmes that help restore and create wildlife habitats; and providing evidence to help make decisions affecting the natural environment. Contact: Natural England, Head Office, 4th Floor, Foss House, Kings Pool, 1-2 Peasholme Green, York, YO1 7PX. T: 0300 060 3900 (enquiries); E: enquiries@naturalengland.org.uk; W: www.gov.uk/government/organisations/natural-england

NATURAL HISTORY MUSEUM AT TRING (1937)
Founded by Lord Rothschild, the museum has 4,000 specimens on public display including many rarities and extinct species. The galleries are open daily 10am-5pm (2pm-5pm on Sun) except Dec 24-26. Bird Group: the Museum at Tring looks after one of the largest ornithological collections in the world - with over a million skins, skeletons, nests, sets of eggs and specimens preserved in spirit, and there is an extensive ornithological library with 75,000 works. The Bird Group collection and library are not open to the public but can be visited by researchers (enquire by E: via website). Contact: The Walter Rothschild building, Akeman Street, Tring, Herts HP23 6AP. T: 020 7942 6171; W: www.nhm.ac.uk/visit/tring.html

NATURAL RESOURCES WALES (2013)
Natural Resources Wales brings together the work of the Countryside Council for Wales, Environment Agency Wales and Forestry Commission Wales, as well as some functions of Welsh Government. Its purpose is to ensure that the natural resources of Wales are sustainably maintained, enhanced and used, now and in the future. Contact: Natural Resources Wales, Customer Care, Tŷ Cambria, 29 Newport Road, Cardiff CF24 0TP. customer care T: 0300 065 3000 (Mon-Fri, 9am-5pm); incident hotline T: 0300 065 3000, then 1 (24 hrs); floodline T: 0345 988 1188 (24 hrs); E: enquiries@naturalresourceswales.gov.uk; W: https://naturalresources.wales/

NATIONAL ORGANISATIONS

NEXT GENERATION BIRDERS (2011)
A different perspective on birding through the eyes of a new generation. An active and growing group of 13-25 year olds who have taken upon themselves to encourage other young people to enjoy their obsession and passion.
Contact: E: ngbirders@gmail.com;
W: http://nextgenerationbirders.blogspot.co.uk/

NORTH SEA BIRD CLUB (1979)
The Club aims to: provide a recreational pursuit for people employed offshore; obtain, collate and analyse observations of all birds seen offshore; produce reports of observations, including an annual report; promote the collection of data on other wildlife offshore. Currently it holds over 120,000 records of birds, cetaceans and insects reported since 1979.
Contact: The North Sea Bird Club, Ocean Laboratory and Culterty Field Station, Newburgh, Aberdeenshire AB41 6AA. T: 01224 274 428; E: nsbc@abdn.ac.uk; W: www.abdn.ac.uk/nsbc/

NORTHERN IRELAND BIRDWATCHERS' ASSOCIATION (1991)
NIBA publishes the Northern Ireland Bird Report and is responsible for Flightline, a local rate telephone hotline for rare bird sightings. The NIBA Records Committee assesses the records in N Ireland.
Contact: NIBA. T: 028 9146 7408 (Flightline);
E: nibirds@live.co.uk; W: http://nibirds.blogspot.com

NORTHERN IRELAND ORNITHOLOGISTS' CLUB (1965)
Formed to focus the interests of active birdwatchers in Northern Ireland. There is a regular programme of lectures (Oct-Apr) and field trips for members and the Club organises an annual photographic competition.
Contact: Carol Gillespie (Hon Sec), NIOC, 4 Demesne Gate, Saintfield, Co. Down BT24 7BE.
T: 028 9751 9371; E: carolgillespie@btinternet.com;
W: www.nioc.co.uk

NORTHERN IRELAND RARE BIRDS COMMITTEE (1997)
NIRBC manages the records of birds in Northern Ireland.
Contact: NIRBC. E: NIRBComm@gmail.com;
W: https://nirbc.blogspot.co.uk

RARE BREEDING BIRDS PANEL (1972)

Rare Breeding Birds Panel

With a representative from BTO, JNCC, RSPB, three independent members and a Secretary, the RBBP collects all information on rare breeding birds in the UK, so that changes in status can be monitored as an aid to conservation and is stored for posterity. Bespoke recording forms are used (obtainable from the website). Records should be submitted via county and regional recorders. RBBP also monitor breeding by scarcer non-native species and seek records of these in the same way. An Annual report is published in *British Birds*. For details of species covered by RBBP see 'Checklists' section.
Contact: The Secretary, Rare Breeding Birds Panel, The Old Orchard, Grange Road, North Berwick, East Lothian EH39 4QT. T: 01620 894 037;
E: secretary@rbbp.org.uk; W: www.rbbp.org.uk

ROYAL AIR FORCE ORNITHOLOGICAL SOCIETY (1965)
Open to any serving and ex-RAF personnel, other Services, MOD civil servants and their families. Organises field meetings and expeditions at home and abroad and undertakes surveys and ringing operations. Publishes a newsletter and a journal.
Contact: E: rafos_secretary@hotmail.com;
W: www.rafornithology.org.uk

ROYAL NAVAL BIRDWATCHING SOCIETY (1946)

RNBWS is open to anyone with a common interest in birds at sea. Maintains an extensive seabird database with records received from most sea areas of the world. Publishes a newsletter four times a year and an annual report - *The Sea Swallow*.
The RNBWS administers a fund left by the late Cpt David Simpson with small grants available for scientific seabird studies.
Contact: Warrant Officer Steve Copsey RN (Gen Sec).
E: secretary@rnbws.org.uk; W: www.rnbws.org.uk

ROYAL PIGEON RACING ASSOCIATION (1897)
Promotes the sport of pigeon racing and controls pigeon racing within the Association. Organises liberation sites, issues rings, calculates distances between liberation sites and home lofts, and assists in the return of strays. May be able to assist in identifying owners of ringed birds found.
Contact: Royal Pigeon Racing Association, The Reddings, Cheltenham, GL51 6RN. T: 01452 713 529;
E: via website; W: www.rpra.org

ROYAL SOCIETY FOR THE PROTECTION OF BIRDS (1899)
UK Partner of BirdLife International and, with over one million members (incl. over 200,000 youth members - see RSPB Phoenix/RSPB Wildlife Explorers), is Europe's largest voluntary wildlife conservation body. The RSPB, a registered charity, is governed by an elected body. Its work in the conservation of wild birds and habitats covers a range of areas including: the acquisition and management of nature reserves; research and surveys; monitoring; responding to development proposals, land use practices and pollution which threaten wild birds and biodiversity; and the provision of an advisory service on wildlife law enforcement.
The RSPB currently manages 200 nature reserves in the UK, covering almost 130,000 ha and home to 80% of Britain's rarest or most threatened bird species. The aim is to conserve a countryside network of reserves with all examples of the main bird communities and with due regard to the conservation of plants and other animals.
There is an active network of 145 local groups (see County Directory) which hold regular indoor and outdoor meetings. 13,000 people volunteer in a wide range of capacities, including working on the RSPB's nature reserves.
The RSPB's International Dept works closely with Birdlife International and its partners in other countries and is involved with numerous projects overseas, especially in Europe and Asia.

NATIONAL ORGANISATIONS

Contact: RSPB, The Lodge, Potton Road, Sandy, Bedfordshire SG19 2DL.
T: 01767 680 551;
Membership enquiries:
T: 01767 693 680 (9am-5.15pm);
Wildlife enquiries:
T: 01767 693 690 (9am-5.15pm);
E: (firstname.name)@rspb.org.uk;
W: www.rspb.org.uk

Regional Offices:
ENGLAND
Eastern England: Stalham House, 65 Thorpe Road, Norwich, NR1 1UD. T: 01603 661 662. **Covers:** Bedfordshire, Cambridgeshire, Essex, Hertfordshire, Lincolnshire, Norfolk, Suffolk.

London Office: 5th Floor, 50 Southwark Street, London SE1 1UN. T: 0207 940 3050.

Midlands: 46 The Green, South Bar, Banbury, Oxfordshire OX16 9AB. T: 01295 253 330. **Covers:** Buckinghamshire, Derbyshire, Herefordshire, Leicestershire, Northamptonshire, Nottinghamshire, Oxfordshire, Rutland, Shropshire, Staffordshire, Warwickshire, West Midlands, Worcestershire.

Northern England:
Denby Dale Office, Westleigh Mews, Wakefield Road, Denby Dale, Huddersfield, HD8 8QD. T: 0300 7772 676.

Newcastle Office, 1 Sirius House, Amethyst Road, Newcastle Business Park, Newcastle-upon-Tyne, NE4 7YL. T: 0300 7772 676.

Lancaster Office, 7.3.1 Cameron House, White Cross Estate, Lancaster, LA1 4XF. T: 0300 7772 676.

Covers: Cheshire, Cleveland, County Durham, Cumbria, East Riding of Yorkshire, Greater Manchester, Lancashire, Merseyside, Middlesbrough, North Yorkshire, North East Lincolnshire, North Lincolnshire, Northumberland, South Yorkshire, Tyne & Wear, West Yorkshire.

South East: 1st Floor, Pavilion View, 19 New Road, Brighton, BN1 1UF. T: 01273 775 333. **Covers:** East Sussex, Hampshire, Isle of Wight, Kent, Surrey, Berkshire, West Sussex.

South West: 4th Floor (North Block), Broadwalk House, Southernhay West, Exeter, EX1 1TS. T: 01392 432 691. **Covers:** Bristol, Cornwall, Devon, Dorset, Somerset, Gloucestershire, Wiltshire.

NORTHERN IRELAND
Northern Ireland Headquarters: Belvoir Park Forest, Belfast, BT8 7QT. 028 9049 1547. **Covers:** Co. Antrim, Co. Armagh, Co. Down, Co. Fermanagh, Co. Londonderry, Co. Tyrone.

SCOTLAND
Scotland Headquarters: 2 Lochside View, Edinburgh Park, Edinburgh EH12 9DH. T: 0131 317 4100.

East Scotland: 10 Albyn Terrace, Aberdeen, Aberdeenshire AB10 1YP. E: esro@rspb.org.uk; T: 01224 624 824. **Covers:** Aberdeen, Aberdeenshire, Angus, Dundee, Fife, Moray, Orkney, Perth and Kinross, Shetland.

North Scotland: Etive House, Beechwood Park, Inverness, IV2 3BW. T: 01463 715 000; E: nsro@rspb.org.uk **Covers:** Eilean Siar, Highland.

South and West Scotland: 10 Park Quadrant, Glasgow, G3 6BS. T: 0141 331 0993; E: glasgow@rspb.org.uk **Covers:** Argyll and Bute, Clackmannanshire, Dumfries and Galloway, East Ayrshire, East Lothian, East Dunbartonshire, East Renfrewshire, Midlothian, North Ayrshire, North Lanarkshire, Renfrewshire, Scottish borders, South Ayrshire, South Lanarkshire, Stirling, West Dunbartonshire, West Lothian.

WALES
Wales Headquarters: Castlebridge 3, 5-19 Cowbridge Road East, Cardiff CF11 9AB. T: 029 2035. 3000; E: cymru@rspb.org.uk **Covers:** Blaenau Gwent, Bridgend, Caerphilly, Cardiff, Carmarthenshire, Ceredigion, Merthyr Tydfil, Monmouthshire, Neath Port Talbot, Newport, Pembrokeshire, Powys, Rhondda Cynon Taff, Swansea, Torfaen, Vale of Glamorgan.

North Wales Office: Uned 14, Llys Castan, Ffordd Y Parc, Parc Menai, Bangor, Gwynedd LL57 4FD. T: 01248 672 850. **Covers:** Conwy, Denbighshire, Flintshire, Gwynedd, Isle of Anglesey, Wrexham.

RSPB WILDLIFE EXPLORERS (4-19) / RSPB PHOENIX (13+)
Junior section of the RSPB (formally the YOC), with a local network of around 80 youth groups. Activities include projects, holidays, roadshows, competitions, and local events for children, families and teenagers. All members receive *Wild Explorer* (6 pa.), Pheonix members also receive *Wingbeat*, the only environmental magazine written by teenagers for teenagers (4 pa.).
Contact: RSPB - as above.
W: www.rspb.org.uk/discoverandenjoynature/families/children/

SCOTTISH BIRDS RECORDS COMMITTEE (1984)
Set up by the Scottish Ornithologists' Club to ensure that records of species not deemed rare enough to be considered by the British Birds Rarities Committee, but which are rare in Scotland, are fully assessed; also maintains the official list of Scottish birds.
Contact: Chris McInerny (Sec), SBRC, 10 Athole Gardens, Glasgow, G12 9AZ E: chris.mcinerny@glasgow.ac.uk; W: www.the-soc.org.uk/bird-recording/records-committee/

SCOTTISH NATURAL HERITAGE (1991)
SNH is funded by the Scottish Government. Its purpose is to promote and care for Scotland's natural heritage; to help people enjoy nature responsibily; to enable greater understanding and awareness of nature; and to promote the sustainable use of Scotland's natural heritage.
Contact: SNH HQ, Great Glen House, Leachkin Road, Inverness, IV3 8NW. T: 01463 725 000; E: enquiries@snh.gov.uk; W: www.snh.gov.uk

NATIONAL ORGANISATIONS

SCOTTISH ORNITHOLOGISTS' CLUB (1936)
The SOC promotes the study, enjoyment and conservation of wild birds and their habitats across Scotland. The Club has 15 branches (see County Directory), each with a programme of indoor meetings and field trips. The SOC organises an annual weekend conference in the autumn and a joint SOC/BTO one-day birdwatchers' conference in spring. *Scottish Birds* is published quarterly. The SOC is based in a large resource centre which offers panoramic views of Aberlady Bay and houses the George Waterston Library.
Contact: The SOC, Waterston House, Aberlady, East Lothian EH32 0PY. T: 01875 871 330;
E: mail@the-soc.org.uk; W: www.the-soc.org.uk

SCOTTISH WILDLIFE TRUST (1964)
A member of The Wildlife Trusts partnership. The Trust's vision is for 'a connected network of healthy, resilient ecosystems supporting Scotland's wildlife and people.' Its main activities focus on managing 120 wildlife reserves and undertaking practical conservation tasks; influencing and campaigning for better wildlife-related policy and action; inspiring people to enjoy and find out more about wildlife.
Contact: Scottish Wildlife Trust, Harbourside House, 110 Commercial Street, Edinburgh, EH6 6NF.
T: 0131 312 7765; Fax: 0131 312 8705;
E: enquiries@scottishwildlifetrust.org.uk;
W: www.scottishwildlifetrust.org.uk

SEABIRD GROUP (1966)
The group promotes and helps to coordinate the study and conservation of seabirds. It maintains close links with other national and international ornithological bodies and organises regular conferences on seabird biology and conservation topics. Small grants available to assist with research/survey work on seabirds. Publishes regular newsletters and the journal '*Seabird*'.
Contact: Holly KIrk (Secretary).
E: secretary@seabirdgroup.org.uk;
W: www.seabirdgroup.org.uk

SOCIETY FOR CONSERVATION IN AVICULTURE (1993)
The Society aims to promote and develop all species and varieties of birds kept by aviculturists, with special regard to threatened and endangered species both in the wild and in captivity. Officers play an active role in promoting responsible care and ownership of all birds. Members do not have to be bird keepers.
Contact: M Williamson, c/o MECNW, Monks Ferry, Wirral, CH41 5LH. E: via website; W: www.thesca.org.uk

SOCIETY OF WILDLIFE ARTISTS (1964)
Registered charity that seeks to generate an appreciation of the natural world through all forms of fine art. The Natural Eye exhibition held annually in Oct/Nov at the Mall Galleries, London. Through bursary schemes, the Society has been able to help young artists with awards of up to £750 towards travel, education or the cost of materials.
Contact: The Federation of British Artists, 17 Carlton House Terrace, London SW1Y 5BD.
T: 020 7930 6844; E: info@mallgalleries.com;
W: www.swla.co.uk

SWIFT CONSERVATION (2009)
An advice service aiming to reverse the decline in the UK's Swifts. Swift Conservation runs a website providing extensive information on Swifts, and on how to both preserve existing and set up new Swift nest sites. Swift Conservation also runs a lecture and training service, providing guidance for the general public, planners, developers and architects. It supplies local advice and help via a network of volunteers, and has links to similar assistance across Europe, Central Asia and North America. It campaigns for better protection of Swifts and other birds that rely on nest places in or on buildings.
Contact: E: mail@swift-conservation.org;
W: www.swift-conservation.org

THE CONSERVATION VOLUNTEERS (formerly BTCV) (1959)
The Conservation Volunteers helps thousands of people each year to reclaim local green spaces. Through their own environmental projects and through a network of community groups people are enabled to take responsibility for their local environments. TCV has published a series of practical handbooks (digital format/subscribe online).
Contact: TCV, Sedum House, Mallard Way, Potteric Carr, Doncaster, DN4 8DB. T: 01302 388 883;
E: information@tcv.org.uk; W: www.tcv.org.uk

WADER QUEST (2012)
A voluntary charity dedicated to supporting wader conservation through fundraising and increasing awareness about the acute problems facing wader populations around the world. Specialises in supporting community wader conservation projects by purchasing equipment and materials from the charity's Grants Fund. Members (Friends of Wader Quest & Sponsors) receive a quarterly e-newsletter. Talks and events are undertaken throughout the year in partnership with other organisations.
Contact: Rick and Elis Simpson, Wader Quest, 20 Windsor Avenue, Newport Pagnell, Bucks, MK16 8HA.
T: 07484 186 443; E: waderquest@gmail.com;
W: www.waderquest.org

WELSH ORNITHOLOGICAL SOCIETY (1988)
Promotes the study, conservation and enjoyment of birds throughout Wales. Runs the Welsh Records Panel which maintains then Welsh bird list and produces an annual report of accepted rare birds in Wales. Publishes the journal *Birds In Wales* twice a year and organises an annual conference.
Contact: E: membership@birdsin.wales;
W: www.birdsinwales.org.uk

NATIONAL ORGANISATIONS

WILDFOWL & WETLANDS TRUST (1946)
Founded by Sir Peter Scott to conserve wetlands and their biodiversity, WWT has 10 wetland centres (see below). The centres are nationally, or internationally, important for wintering wildfowl. Walks, talks and events are available for visitors, and resources and programmes are provided for school groups. All the centres, except Caerlaverock and Welney, have collections of wildfowl from around the world, including many endangered species. The Trust's conservation programmes focus on a variety of aspects including science and processes that underpin conservation action, threats to wetlands and their wildlife and threatened species. WWT Consulting undertakes commercial contracts and Wetland Link International promotes the role of wetland centres for education and public awareness. Publishes the journal *Wildfowl* annually.
Contact: Wildfowl and Wetlands Trust, Slimbridge, Gloucestershire GL2 7BT. T: 01453 891 900; E: enquiries@wwt.org.uk; W: www.wwt.org.uk

WWT WETLAND CENTRES:
WWT Arundel, Mill Road, Arundel, Sussex BN18 9PB. T: 01903 883 355; E: info.arundel@wwt.org.uk

WWT Caerlaverock, Eastpark Farm, Caerlaverock, Dumfriesshire DG1 4RS. T: 01387 770 200; E: info.caerlaverock@wwt.org.uk

WWT Castle Espie, 78 Ballydrain Road, Comber, Co Down, N Ireland BT23 6EA. T: 028 9187 4146; E: info.castleespie@wwt.org.uk

WWT Llanelli,Llwynhendy, Llanelli, Carmarthenshire SA14 9SH. T: 01554 741 087; E: info.llanelli@wwt.org.uk

WWT London, Queen Elizabeth's Walk, Barnes, London SW13 9WT. T: 020 8409 4400; E: info.london@wwt.org.uk

WWT Martin Mere, Fish Lane, Burscough, Lancashire L40 0TA. T: 01704 895 181; E: info.martinmere@wwt.org.uk

WWT Slimbridge, Bowditch, Slimbridge, Gloucs GL2 7BT. T: 01453 891 900; E: info.slimbridge@wwt.org.uk

WWT Steart Marshes, Steart, Somerset, TA5 2PU. T: 01278 651 090; E: info.steart@wwt.org.uk

WWT Washington, Pattinson, Washington, Tyne & Wear NE38 8LE. T: 0191 416 5454; E: info.washington@wwt.org.uk

WWT Welney, Hundred Foot Bank, Welney, Nr. Wisbech, PE14 9TN. T: 01353 860 711; E: info.welney@wwt.org.uk

WILDLIFE SOUND RECORDING SOCIETY (1968)
Works closely with the Wildlife Section, British Library Sound Archive. Members carry out recording work for scientific purposes as well as for pleasure. A field weekend is held each spring, and members organise meetings locally. Four CD sound magazines of members' recordings are produced for members each year, and a journal, *Wildlife Sound*, is published twice a year.

Contact: David Mellor (Hon Membership Secretary), WSRS, Fuchsia Cottage, Helperthorpe, Nr Malton, North Yorks YO17 8TQ; E: membership@wildlife-sound.org; W: www.wildlife-sound.org

WILDLIFE TRUSTS (1995)
Founded in 1912 and now the largest UK charity dedicated to conserving all habitats and species, with a membership of more than 800,000 in 47 individual county trusts (see County Directory). Collectively, they manage about 2,300 nature reserves covering more than 95,000 ha. The Trusts also lobby for better protection of the UK's natural heritage and are dedicated to protecting wildlife for the future. Members receive their local Trust magazine which includes a UK News section.
Contact: The Wildlife Trusts, The Kiln, Waterside, Mather Road, Newark, NG24 1WT. T: 01636 677 711; Fax: 01636 670 001; E: enquiry@wildlifetrusts.org; W: www.wildlifetrusts.org

WILDLIFE WATCH (1977)
The junior branch of The Wildlife Trusts with 150,000 members. There are around 260 Wildlife Watch groups across the UK where children can join in a wide range of activities. Membership is through a local Trust as a junior member.
Contact: Wildlife Watch - address as above. T: 01636 670 000; E: watch@wildlifetrusts.org; W: www.wildlifewatch.org.uk

WWF-UK (1961)
WWF is the world's largest independent conservation organisation, working in more than 100 countries. It works to conserve habitats and species, protect endangered spaces, and address global threats to nature by seeking long-term solutions with people in government and industry, education and civil society. Members receive *Action* magazine three times a year.
Contact: WWF-UK, The Living Planet Centre, Rufford House, Brewery Road, Woking, Surrey GU21 4LL. T: 01483 426 444; E: via website; W: www.wwf.org.uk

ZOOLOGICAL PHOTOGRAPHIC CLUB (1899)
Circulates black and white and colour prints of zoological interest via a series of postal portfolios. Membership limited to 28.
Contact: John Tinning (Hon. Secretary). E: john.tinning@btinternet.com; W: www.zpc-naturefolio.org.uk

ZOOLOGICAL SOCIETY OF LONDON (1826)
Carries out research, organises symposia and holds scientific meetings. Manages the Zoological Gardens in Regent's Park (first opened in 1828) and Whipsnade Wild Animal Park near Dunstable, Beds, each with extensive collections of birds. The Society's library has a large collection of ornithological books and journals. Publications include *Journal of Zoology, Animal Conservation* and *The International Zoo Yearbook*.
Contact: Zoological Society of London, Regent's Park, London NW1 4RY. T: 0344 225 1826; E: info@zsl,org; W: www.zsl.org

Predatory Bird Monitoring Scheme

LEE WALKER explains the work of the PBMS (see CEH listing, page 293)

THE CENTRE FOR ECOLOGY & HYDROLOGY (CEH) runs the Predatory Bird Monitoring Scheme (PBMS), working with regulators and industry to try to minimise unintentional risk to wildlife from pollutants. Operating for over 50 years, the PBMS is now the longest-running scheme of its kind anywhere in the world.

We detect and quantify current and emerging chemical threats. We do this by measuring the levels of priority contaminants accumulated in the carcasses and eggs of predatory birds. Our data provide information on the extent of risk from chemicals, and how and why this risk varies over time and geographically. Priority chemicals we currently monitor include rodenticides (used to control rodent damage, estimated to cost hundreds of millions of pounds per year), lead from ammunition and shot, mercury and various organic industrial pollutants such as flame retardants.

The PBMS relies on citizen science. Each year, members of the public typically send in 300 to 400 carcasses of birds of prey that they have found dead (often road traffic victims). Specially licensed bird ringers also send us around 150 failed eggs. We analyse these samples for chemical residues and retain them in a unique tissue and egg archive, which contains more than 40,000 samples collected since the late 1960s, representing a collection asset of some £4-5 million.

The PBMS is a partner in the Wildlife Disease & Contaminant Monitoring & Surveillance Network (WILDCOMS, www.wildcoms.org.uk), a collaboration between UK surveillance schemes that monitor disease and contaminants in vertebrate wildlife. We work closely with WILDCOMS and associated partner schemes to share samples and data, thereby widening the value of the PBMS. We contribute samples to projects that monitor the prevalence of wildlife diseases such as Trichomoniasis and West Nile Virus. We also share resources, samples and data with three WILDCOMS partners to provide a national overview of the exposure of red kites to rodenticides.

****

What to do if you find a dead BoP

If you find a dead bird of prey and are able to pick it up please contact us by calling 01524 595 830 or emailing pbms@ceh.ac.uk We will then send you out a submission pack that will allow you to post the bird back to the PBMS free of charge. We carry out a post mortem examination of every bird we receive, the results of which we send back to you, and tissues are retained in our archive for our monitoring programme and future studies.

When picking up a carcass ensure that it is safe for you to do so – especially if it is beside a road. It is a good idea to minimise skin contact with the carcass, for example, use an inverted plastic bag to pick up the bird. ALWAYS wash your hands thoroughly with soap and water after handling the carcass.

For more information about the work of the scheme please go to our website: http://pbms.ceh.ac.uk

Help us protect
predatory birds

Our research monitors pollutants in birds of prey

WE NEED YOUR HELP

If you find a dead bird of prey, collect it and call the Predatory Bird Monitoring Scheme (PBMS) on
01524 595830

✉PBMS@ceh.ac.uk; 🐦@PBMSatCEH
📘www.facebook.com/COLLECTRAPTORS
http://pbms.ceh.ac.uk

Photo – ©fotogenix.www.fotosearch.co.uk

NATIONAL PROJECTS

NATIONAL ORNITHOLOGICAL PROJECTS depend for their success on the active participation of amateur birdwatchers. In return they provide birdwatchers with an excellent opportunity to contribute in a positive and worthwhile way to the scientific study of birds and their habitats, which is the vital basis of all conservation programmes. The following entries provide a description of each particular project and a note of whom to contact for further information.

BIG GARDEN BIRDWATCH
An RSPB Survey
The Big Garden Birdwatch, first launched in 1979, has grown into fun for all the family. All you need to do is count the birds in your garden, or a local park, for one hour during (usually) the last weekend of January. In 2017 over 500,000 people recorded a total of 8,074, 966 birds, with the House Sparrow remaining in top spot. The long-term trends of birds coming into gardens can be monitored.
Contact: RSPB.

BIRD CONSERVATION TARGETING PROJECT
Joint project organised in partnership between BTO, RSPB, Natural England & Scottish National Heritage
The project has been developed to target management and resources towards important sites for scarce and declining farmland and woodland birds. Records are brought together from a wide range of sources, including BirdTrack, individual birdwatchers, county bird clubs and national surveys. The project produces distribution maps which are used to guide the spending of millions of pounds to benefit birds through agri-environment and woodland grant schemes, and to influence woodland management to benefit birds on publicly owned woodland. The targeting maps help to ensure that government grant schemes are allocated to put the right conservation measures in the right places.
Contact: RSPB.

BIRDTRACK
Organised by BTO on behalf of BTO, RSPB, BirdWatch Ireland, SOC & WOS

BirdTrack is a free, online bird recording system for birdwatchers to store and manage bird records from anywhere in Britain and Ireland. The idea is simple: make a note of the birds that you see/hear at any time and then enter your observations on an easy-to-use web page (W: www. birdtrack.net) - registration required - (complete lists are preferred but casual records and incomplete lists can also be entered). There's also a free App for Android and iPhone smartphones through which you can log your sightings whilst you're in the field and upload them at the click of a button.

Exciting real-time outputs are generated by BirdTrack, including species reporting-rate graphs and animated maps of sightings, all freely-available online. The data collected are used by researchers to investigate migration movements and the distribution of scarce birds, and to support species conservation at local, national and international scales.
Contact: BTO. E: birdtrack@bto.org

BREEDING BIRD SURVEY (BBS)
Supported by BTO, JNCC & RSPB
First started in 1994, the BBS is the main scheme for monitoring population changes of the UK's common breeding birds and provides an indicator of the health of the countryside. It is dependent on volunteer birdwatchers throughout the country, about 2800 of them anually. Two visits (early-Apr/mid-May and mid-May/late-Jun) of about five hours in total, are made to survey the breeding birds in a 1x1km square. Survey squares are picked at random by computer to ensure that all habitats and regions are covered. BBS trends are produced annually for over 100 species. Since its inception, BBS has been a tremendous success - now more than 3,500 squares are covered by the survey and 200+ species are recorded annually.
Contact: BTO, Sarah Harris (National Organiser) or your local BTO Regional Representative (see County Directory). E: bbs@bto.org

CONSTANT EFFORT SITES (CES) SCHEME
Funded by a partnership between BTO, JNCC, The National Parks & Wildlife Service (Ireland) & ringers
The CES scheme, run since 1983, coordinates standardised summer ringing at over 130 sites across Britain and Ireland. The scheme allows the BTO to monitor trends on abundance of adults and juveniles, productivity and adult survival rates for 24 species of common songbirds.
Information from CES complements demographic information collected by other BTO surveys and feeds into the BTO's Integrated Population Monitoring programme which highlights the causes of changes in bird populations. Results are updated annually and published on-line as part of the BirdTrends Report (W: www.bto.org/about-birds/birdtrends).
Contact: BTO. E: ces@bto.org

GARDEN BIRD FEEDING SURVEY (GBFS)
A BTO project
Starting in 1970/71, the Garden Bird Feeding Survey is the longest-running study of garden birds in Britain. Each year, a network of householders record the numbers and variety of birds using the different food supplements, feeders and water that they have provided in their garden - the results examine the effects on birds using these resources. Participation is limited to about 250 gardens each year. Observations are made on a weekly basis from October to March inclusive, with two recording periods (Oct/Dec & Jan/Mar). Gardens are selected by region and by type - from city flats to suburban semis, rural houses to outlying farms - to give a good spread of sites.
Contact: BTO. E: gwb@bto.org

NATIONAL PROJECTS

BTO GARDEN BIRDWATCH (GBW)

A BTO project

Started in January 1995, this project is a year-round survey that monitors the use that birds and other species groups of wildlife make of gardens. Participants from all over the UK and Ireland keep a weekly log of species using their gardens. The data collected are used to monitor regional, seasonal and year-to-year changes in the garden populations of our commoner birds, mammals, butterflies, reptiles and amphibians. To cover running costs there is an annual subscription of £17. Participants receive a quarterly magazine and all new joiners receive a garden bird book. Results/more information are available online: www.bto.org/volunteer-surveys/gbw
Contact: BTO. E: gbw@bto.org

GARDEN WILDLIFE HEALTH

A joint scheme of Zoological Society of London, BTO, Froglife & RSPB

This project aims to monitor the health of, and identify disease threats to, British garden wildlife. The particular focus is on garden birds, amphibians, reptiles and hedgehogs. Members of the public are asked to submit reports of sick or dead wildlife and to submit samples for analysis.
Contact: Garden Wildlife Health vets
T: 0207 449 6685; E: gwh@zsl.org;
W: www.gardenwildlifehealth.org

GOOSE AND SWAN MONITORING PROGRAMME (GSMP)

Organised by WWT and funded in partnership with JNCC & Scottish National Heritage

Geese and swans are a cornerstone of the Wildfowl and Wetland Trust's conservation work. The UK supports 14 native goose and migratory swan populations, 13 are monitored through the GSMP network. During winter, geese and swans from Canada to central Russia undertake arduous migrations to reach their wintering grounds in the UK. In order to safeguard them WWT tracks how many individuals are in each population, where they are found, and the overall trend of the population (increasing, decreasing or remaining stable). Other demographic measures - most importantly productivity (how many young are born each year) and survival (or mortality) rates - help to understand the reasons behind any increases or decreases. To gather the information the WWT use a number of techniques and tools, including counts and capture/marking. A large amount of this work is carried out by volunteer birdwatchers who give their time to assist with the data collection.
Contact: WWT. E: enquiries@wwt.org.uk;
W: http://monitoring.wwt.org.uk/our-work/

HERONRIES CENSUS

A BTO project

This survey, started in 1928, has been carried out under the auspices of the BTO since 1934 and represents the longest continuous series of population data for any European breeding bird (Grey Heron). Counts of apparently occupied nests are made at as many UK heronries as possible each year, to provide an index of current population levels.

Data from Scotland and Wales is relatively scant, and more contributions from these countries would be especially welcomed, as would notification of new colonies elsewhere. Herons may be hit hard during periods of severe weather and are vulnerable to pesticides and pollution. Little Egret and other incoming species of colonial waterbird such as Cattle Egret are now fully included, whether nesting with Grey Herons, or on their own. Counts of Cormorant nests at heronries are also encouraged. Periodically Heronries Surveys are undertake and the data added to the Heroneries Census database.
Contact: BTO. E: herons@bto.org

IRISH WETLAND BIRD SURVEY (I-WeBS)

A joint project of BirdWatch Ireland, the National Parks & Wildlife Service of the Dept of Arts, Culture & the Gaeltacht

The Irish Wetland Bird Survey (I-WeBS) is the scheme that monitors wintering waterbirds in Ireland. The survey runs from September to March each winter. Wetlands of all types and sizes are monitored, including

I-WeBS

estuaries, coastlines, bays, rivers, turloughs, lakes, streams and flooded fields. Each winter, more than 350 people take part counting waterbirds at over 250 wetlands throughout the country. The counts are undertaken once a month on predefined count days by skilled volunteers, as well as by professional staff of the National Parks and Wildlife Service and BirdWatch Ireland. New counters welcomed!
Contact: I-WeBS Office, BirdWatch Ireland.
T: 353 (0)1 281 9878; E: iwebs@birdwatchireland.ie

NATIONAL BEACHED BIRD SURVEY

An RSPB project

In its current format the NBBS has been running since 1971. The results of the annual survey are used in conjunction with those from other European countries and aim to contribute to international monitoring efforts to document trends in chronic marine oil pollution and to promote adequate methods of controlling illegal oil discharge to help reduce seabird mortality.
Contact: RSPB. Sabine Schmitt, Senior Research Asst.
E: sabine.schmitt@rspb.org.uk

NEST BOX CHALLENGE

A BTO project

NBC is an on-line survey which aims to monitor the breeding success of birds in Britain's green spaces. Participants are asked to register one or more nests, or nest boxes, in their garden or local green space, monitoring their progress via regular nest inspections and recording the number of eggs and/or chicks present at each visit. Records of unused boxes are also valuable as they can be used to determine next box occupancy rates. Anyone who has a nest box or nest in their garden or local park can take part. Over 4000 boxes were monitored in 1500 gardens in 2016.
Contact: BTO. E: nbc@bto.org

NEST RECORD SCHEME

A BTO Project carried out with funding from JNCC
The scheme monitors changes in the nesting success and the timing of breeding of Britain's bird species by gathering information on nests found anywhere in the country, from a Blackbird in a garden to an Oystercatcher on a Scottish loch. Participants locate nests and monitor their progress over several visits, making counts of the number of eggs and/or chicks on each occasion and recording whether they are successful.

Information from NRS complements demographic information collected by other BTO surveys and feeds into the BTO's Integrated Population Monitoring, highlighting the causes of changes in bird populations. Since the scheme started in 1939, 1.25 million nest record histories have been collected and now more than 30,000 nest records (of 160-170 species) are submitted to the BTO each year by over 600 volunteer surveyors. The results are updated annually and published online as part of the BirdTrends Report. Guidance on how to become a BTO nest recorder, including best practice guidelines on minimising disturbance while visiting nests, is available online. A free starter pack is available on request.
Contact: BTO. E: nrs@bto.org

RETRAPPING ADULTS FOR SURVIVAL (RAS) SCHEME

Funded by a partnership between BTO, JNCC, The National Parks & Wildlife Service (Ireland) & ringers
Under the RAS scheme, started in 1999, ringers aim to catch or re-sight at least 50 adult birds of a single species in a study area in the breeding season. This data allows the BTO to monitor survival rates in adult birds and is particularly useful for those species not widely covered by CES scheme. and forms part of the BTO's Integrated Population Monitoring framework. Results are updated annually and published as part of the BirdTrends Report.
Contact: BTO. E: ras@bto.org

RINGING SCHEME

Funded by a partnership between BTO, JNCC (on behalf of the Country Agencies), The National Parks & Wildlife Service (Ireland) & ringers
Marking birds with individually numbered metal rings allows us to study survival, productivity and movements of British and Irish birds. Over 2,600 trained and licensed ringers operate in Britain and Ireland, marking nearly one million birds each year. Training to be a ringer takes at least a year, but more often two or more years, depending on the aptitude of the trainee and the amount of ringing they do. A restricted permit can usually be obtained more quickly. Anyone can contribute to the scheme by reporting ringed or colour-marked birds seen or found W: http://blx1.bto.org/euring/main/index.jsp or contact BTO HQ. Anyone finding a ringed bird should note the ring number, species, when and where found and, if possible, what happened to it. If the bird is dead, it may also be possible to remove the ring, which should be kept in case there is a query. Anyone reporting a ringed bird will be sent details of where and when the bird was originally ringed.
Check out the 'Demog Blog' for up to date news and stories: http://btoringing.blogspot.co.uk
Contact: BTO. E: ringing@bto.org

WATERWAYS BREEDING BIRD SURVEY

A BTO project, supported by the Environment Agency
WBBS uses transect methods of surveying, like those of the Breeding Bird Survey, to record bird populations along randomly chosen stretches of rivers and canals throughout the UK (covering from just 500m to a maximum of 5km). Just two survey visits are needed during April-June, all birds seen or heard are recorded. WBBS began in 2008 taking over from the Waterways Bird Survey (which started in 1974) as the main monitoring scheme for birds in this habitat.
Contact: BTO Regional Representative to enquire if any local stretches require coverage (see County Directory), otherwise BTO HQ. E: wbbs@bto.org

WETLAND BIRD SURVEY (WeBS)

Run by BTO in a partnership funder by BTO, RSPB, JNCC and in association with WWT
The Wetland Bird Survey (WeBS) is the monitoring scheme for non-breeding waterbirds in the UK. The principal aims of the scheme are:

1. To identify population sizes of waterbirds.
2. To determine trends in numbers and distribution.
3. To identify important sites for waterbirds.

WeBS Core Counts are made annually at around 2000 wetland sites of all habitats, although estuaries and large still waters predominate. Monthly coordinated counts are made mostly by volunteers, principally between September and March, with fewer summer observations.

Estuaries in the UK provide an important habitat for non-breeding waterbirds. Low Tide Counts are made on about 20 of them each winter to identify important feeding areas (Core Counts tend to quantify birds present at high tide roosts).

Counts are relatively straightforward and can take from a few minutes up to a few hours, depending on the size of the site -numbers of all target species in the count area are recorded.

The WeBS data is used to designate important waterbird sites and protect them against adverse development, for research into the causes of declines, for establishing conservation priorities and strategies, and to formulate management plans for wetland sites and waterbirds.

WeBS participants receive an annual newsletter and a comprehensive annual report. New counters are always welcome - contact the local WeBS Organiser (see County Directory).

Contact: Heidi Mellan (General Webs Enquiries), WeBS Office, BTO. E: heidi.mellan@bto.org or E: webs@bto.org

INTERNATIONAL DIRECTORY

Neil Gartshore

Going abroad?
Before you go it is worth checking out the local BirdLife partner's website to see what's going on there - for Lesvos (Greece) it will be the Hellanic Ornithological Society (HOS). Birders visiting a hide overlooking the excellent Kalloni Saltpans.

BirdLife
INTERNATIONAL

The BirdLife Partnership: www.birdlife.org
BirdLife is a Partnership of non-governmental
organisations (NGOs) with a special focus on nature
and people. Each NGO Partner represents a unique
geographic territory/country.

The BirdLife Network explained:

Secretariat: The co-ordinating and servicing body of
BirdLife International.

Partners: Membership-based NGOs who represent
BirdLife in their own territory. Vote holders and key
implementing bodies for BirdLife's Strategy and
Regional Programmes in their own territories.

Partners Designate: Membership-based NGOs
who represent BirdLife in their own territory, in a
transition stage to becoming full Partners. Non-vote
holders.

Affiliates: Usually NGOs, but also individuals,
foundations or governmental institutions when
appropriate. Act as a BirdLife contact with the aim of
developing into, or recruiting, a BirdLife Partner in
their territory.

SECRETARIAT ADDRESSES

BirdLife Global Office
The David Attenborough Building
1st Floor, Pembroke Street
Cambridge CB2 3QZ, UK
T: 01223 277 318
Fax: 01223 281 441
E: birdlife@birdlife.org

Birdlife Africa Regional Office
Volker's Garden on Terrace Close
off Rhapta Road
Westlands
Nairobi, Kenya

Postal Address
PO Box 3502 - 00100 GPO
Nairobi, Kenya
T: +254 020 247 3259
T: +254 020 806 8314
Fax: +254 020 806 8315
E: birdlife-africa@birdlife.org

Birdlife West Africa Sub-Regional Office
35A Sam Nujoma Rd
North Ridge
Accra, Ghana

Postal Address
PO Box GP 22521
Accra, Ghana
T: +233 (0) 302 255 015
T: +233 (0) 261 737 101

BirdLife Americas Regional Office
Juan de Dios Martinez N35-76 y
Av. Portugal
Quito, Ecuador

Postal address
BirdLife International
Casilla 17-17-717
Quito, Equador
T: +593 2 2277 059
Fax +593 2 2469 838
E: americas@birdlife.org

BirdLife Asia Regional Office
[Japan]
TM Suidobashi Building
4F, Misaki-cho 2-14-6
Chiyoda-ku
Tokyo 101-0061, Japan
T: +81 (3) 5213 0461
Fax.+81 (3) 5213 0422
E: info@birdlife-asia.org

[Singapore]
354 Tanglin Road
#01-16/17
Tanglin International Centre
Singapore 247672
T: +65 6479 3089
Fax: +65 6479 3090
E: singapore.office@birdlife.org

BirdLife Europe
Avenue de la Toison d'Or 67
(2nd floor), B-1060 Brussels
Belgium
T: +32 2280 08 30
Fax +32 2230 38 02
E: europe@birdlife.org

BirdLife Middle East Regional Office
Khalda
Salameh El-Ma'aaytah Street
Building No 6.
Amman, Jordan

Postal address
PO Box 2295
Amman 11953, Jordan
T: +962 6 564 8173
Fax: +962 6 564 8172
E: me@birdlife.org

BirdLife Pacific Regional Office
10 MacGregor Road
Suva, Fuji

Postal address
GPO Box 18332
Suva, Fuji
T: +679 331 3492
Fax: +679 331 9658
E: suva.office@birdlife.org

AFRICA

PARTNERS

Burkina Faso
NATURAMA 01 B.P. 6133, 01, Ouagadougou.
E: info@naturama.bf; W: www.naturama.bf;
Pub: *Naturama (newsletter)*

Ethiopia
Ethiopian Wildlife and Natural History Society
(EWNHS), PO Box 13303, Addis Ababa.
E: ewnhs.ble@gmail.com; W: www.ewnhs.org.et;
Pub: *Agazen (school magazine); Ethiopian Wildlife &
Nat. Hist. Soc. (quarterly newsletter); Walia (semi-
scientific journal)*

Ghana
Ghana Wildlife Society (GWS), PO Box 13252,
Accra. E: info@ghanawildlifesociety.org;
W: www.ghanawildlifesociety.org; Pub: *NKO
(magazine)*

Kenya
NatureKenya, PO Box 44486, 00100 GPO, Nairobi.
E: office@naturekenya.org;
W: www.naturekenya.org;
Pub: *Nature Net (newsletter); Kenya Birding
(magazine); Journal of East African Natural History
(scientific); Scopus (scientific)*

INTERNATIONAL ORGANISATIONS

Mauritania
Nature Mauritania, 2647, Nouakchott.
E: djibril.diallo@natmau.mr; W: www.natmau.mr

Nigeria
Nigerian Conservation Foundation (NCF), PO Box 74638, Victoria Island, Lagos. E: info@ncf-nigeria.org

Seychelles
Nature Seychelles, Roche Caiman, Box 1310, Victoria, Mahe.
E: nature@seychelles.net; W: www.natureseychelles.org;
W: www.cousinisland.net; Pub: *Zwazo (magazine)*

Sierra Leone
Conservation Society of Sierra Leone (CSSL), 4C Main Motor Road, Tengbeh Town, Freetown.
E: cssl_03@yahoo.com

South Africa
BirdLife South Africa (BLSA), Private Bag X5000, Gauteng, ZA, 2121. E: info@birdlife.org.za;
W: www.birdlife.org.za; Pub: *e-newsletter; African BirdLife (magazine); Ostrich (scientific)*

Tunisia
Association Les Amis des Oiseaux (AAO), Bureau No 4 au 2eme etage, 14 Rue Ibn El Heni, 2080 Ariana.
E: aao.org@gmail.com; W: www.aao.org.tn; Pub: *(newsletter)*

Uganda
NatureUganda (NU), The EANHS, PO Box 27034, Kampala. E: nature@natureuganda.org;
W: www.natureuganda.org; Pub: *The Naturalist (newsletter)*

Zimbabwe
BirdLife Zimbabwe (BLZ), PO Box RVL 100, Runiville, Harare. E: birds@zol.co.zw; W: www.birdlifezimbabwe.org;
Pub: *The Babbler (newsletter); Honeyguide (scientific)*

PARTNERS DESIGNATE

Botswana
BirdLife Botswana (BLB), Kgale Siding, Plot K1069, Unit B1, Gaborone. E: blb@birdlifebotswana.org.bw;
W: www.birdlifebotswana.org.bw; Pub: *The Babbler (scientific); Familiar Chat (newsletter); Birds and People (conservation newsletter)*

Burundi
Association Burundaise pour la Protection de la Nature (ABN), PO Box 7069, Bujumbura.
E: info@aboconservation.org; W: http://www.abn.bi

Madagascar
Asity Madagascar, Lot IIN 83DM Analamahitsy, Antananarivio. E: contact@asity-madagascar.org;
W: www.asity-madagascar.org

Zambia
BirdWatch Zambia, Box 33944, Lusaka 10101.
E: birdwatch.zambia@gmail.com;
W: www.birdwatchzambia.org;
Pub: *BirdWatch Zambia (newsletter)*

AFFILIATES

Cameroon
Cameroon Biodiversity Conservation Society (CBCS), PO Box 3055, Messa, Yaoundé. E: cbcs_cam@yahoo.fr

Djibouti Nature
Djibouti Nature, Nasser A. Othman Building, Marabou-Djibouti, PO Box 3088, Djibouti.
E: naturedjibouti@gmail.com; W: www.djiboutinature.org;
Pub: *The Eye (newsletter/quasi-scientific journal)*

Egypt
Nature Conservation Egypt, 56A Mahrousa St, Aguouza, 1st Floor, Apt 20, Giza. E: info@natureegypt.org;
W: www.natureegypt.org

Ivory Coast
SOS-FORETS (SF), 22 BP 918, Abidjan 22.
E: sosforets@hotmail.com; W: www.sosforets.ci

Liberia
Society for Conservation of Nature in Liberia (SCNL), Monrovia, PO Box 2628, Monrovia, LR, 1000.
E: scnlliberia@yahoo.com; W: www.scnliberia.org

Malawi
Wildlife & Environmental Society of Malawi (WESM), Private Bag 578, Limbe. E: wesm-hq@wesm.mw;
W: www.wildlifemalawi.org; Pub: *WESM News (newsletter)*

Mauritius
Mauritian Wildlife Foundation, Grannum Road, Vacoas.
E: executive@mauritian-wildlife.org;
W: www.mauritian-wildlife.org; Pub: *(newsletter)*

Morocco
GREPOM, Scientific Institutre Av Ibn Battota, BP 703, Agdal, 10090, Rabat. E: grepom@grepom.org;
W: www.grepom.org

Rwanda
Association pour la Conservation de la Nature au Rwanda (ACNR), PO Box 4290, Kigali.
E: conserverwanda@yahoo.com; W: www.acnrwanda.org

AMERICAS

PARTNERS

Argentina
Aves Argentina (AOP), Matheu 1246/8 (C1249AAB), Buenos Aires.
E: info@avesargentinas.org.ar
W: www.avesargentinas.org.ar;
Pub: *The Hornero (scientific); Aves Argentinas (magazine); Nuestras Aves (magazine)*

Bahamas
Bahamas National Trust (BNT), PO Box 4105, Nassau.
E: bnt@bnt.bs; W: www.bnt.bs; Pub: *Trust Notes (newsletter)*

Belize
Belize Audubon Society (BAS), PO Box 1001, 12 Fort St, Belize City. E: base@btl.net; W: www.belizeaudubon.org;
Pub: *Belize Audubon Society (newsletter)*

Bolivia
Asociacion Armonia, Avenidad Lomas de Arena 400, Casilla 3566, Santa Cruz. E: armonia@armonia-bo.org;
W: www.armoniabolivia.org

INTERNATIONAL ORGANISATIONS

Canada
Bird Studies Canada (Bsc), PO Box 160, 115 Front Street, Port Rowan, Ontario N0E 1M0.
E: generalinfo@bsc-eoc.org; W: www.birdscanada.org; Pub: *Bird Studies Canada (annual report); Birdwatch Canada (newsletter)*

Canada
Nature Canada, 85 Albert Street, Suite 900, Ottawa, K1P 6A4. E: info@naturecanada.ca; W: www.naturecanada.ca

Ecuador
Aves y Conservación, Pasaje Joaquin Tinajero E3-05 y Jorge Drom, Casilla 17-17-906, Quito.
E: aves_direccion@avesconservacion.org; W: www.avesconservaccion.org

Falkland Islands
Falklands Conservation, 41 Rodd Road, Jubilee Villas, Stanley, FIQQ 1ZZ. E: info@falklandsconservation.com; W: www.falklandsconservation.com; Pub: *Falklands Conservation (newsletter); Wildlife Conservation (magazine)*

Panama
Panama Audubon Society (PAS), Apartado 0843-03076, Panama City. E: info@panamaaudubon.org; W: www.panamaaudubon.org; Pub: *Toucan (newsletter)*

Paraguay
Guyra, Av. Cnel. Carlos Bóveda, Parque Ecológico Capital Verde, Viñas Cué, Asunción, CC 1132.
E: guyra.paraguay@guyra.org.py; W: www.guyra.org.py; Pub: *Memoria Anual (annual report)*

United States
Audubon, 225 Varick Street, 7th Floor New York, NY, 10004. E: international@audubon.org; W: www.audubon.org; Pub: *Audubon (magazine)*

AFFILIATES

Brazil
SAVE Brasil, Rua Fernão Dias, 219 conj 2 Pinheiros, São Paulo SP, 05427-010. E: aves@savebrasil.org.br; W: www.savebrasil.org.br; Pub: *annual activity report*

Chile
Comité Nacional Pro Defensa de la Flora y Fauna (CODEFF), Ernesto Reyes 035, Providencia, Santiago. E: administra@codeff.cl; W: www.codeff.cl; Pub: *Ecos Codeff (newsletter)*

Cuba
Centro Nacional de Áreas Protegidas (CNAP), Calle 18a, No 1441, 41 y 47, Playa, Havana. E: cnap@snap.cu; W: www.snap.cu

Dominican Republic
Grupo Jaragua (GJI), Calle El Vergel No 33, Ensanche, El Vergel, Santo Domingo. E: jaragua@tricom.net; W: www.grupojaragua.org.do

El Salvador
SalvaNATURA (SN), Finca Vista Alegre Km 3½, Planes de Randeros, San Salvador. E: info@salvanatura.org; W: www.salvanatura.org

Mexico
Pronatura, 1 Calle Pedro Moreno esq. Benito Juárez, Barrio Santa Lucia, San Cristobal de las Casas, Chiapas, 29200.
E: pronatura@pronatura.org.mx; W: www.pronatura.org.mx; Pub: *Pronatura (newsletter)*

Puerto Rico (to USA)
Sociedad Ornitológica Puertorriqueña, Inc. (SOPI), PO Box 195166, San Juan, 00919-5166.
E: directivasopi@yahoo.com; W: www.avesdepuertorico.org; Pub: *El Bien-Te-Veo (magazine)*

Uruguay
Aves Uruguay (GUPECA), Canelones 1164, Montevideo. E: info@avesuruguay.org.uy; W: www.avesuruguay.org.uy; Pub: *Achara (magazine)*

ASIA

PARTNERS

Bhutan
Royal Society for the Protection of Nature, PO Box 325, Building #25, Lhado Lam Kawajangsa, Thimphu-11001. E: rspn@rspnbhutan.org; W: www.rspnbhutan.org

Hong Kong
Hong Kong Birdwatching Society, (HKBWS) 7C, V Ga Building, 532 Castle Peak Road, Lai Chi Kok, Kowloon. E: hkbws@hkbws.org.uk; W: www.hkbws.org.hk; Pub: *Hong Kong Bird Report; HKBWS quarterly bulletin*

India
Bombay Natural History Society (BNHS), Hornbill House, Shaheed Bhagat Singh Road, Mumbai, 400 001.
E: rahmani.asad@gmail.com; W: www.bnhs.org; Pub: *Hornbill (magazine); Journal of BNHS (scientific)*

Japan
Wild Bird Society of Japan (WBSJ), Maruw Bldg, 3-9-23, Nishi-Gotanda, Shinagawa-ku, Tokyo 141-0031.
E: hogo@wbsj.org; W: www.wbsj.org; Pub: *Wild Bird (magazine); Toriino (magazine); Strix (scientific)*

Malaysia
Malaysian Nature Society (MNS), PO Box 10750, Kuala Lumpur 50724.
E: mns@mns.org.my; W: www.mns.my; Pub: *Pencinta Alam (newsletter); Tapier (school newsletter); Suara Enggang (bulletin); Malaysian Naturalist (magazine); Malayan Nature Journal (scientific)*

Philippines
Haribon Foundation, 2/F, Santos and Sons Building, 973 Aurora Blvd, Cubao, Quezon CIty 1109.
E: act@haribon.org.ph; W: www.haribon.org.ph

Singapore
Nature Society (Singapore) (NSS), 510 Geylang Road, #02-05, The Sunflower, 398466. E: contact@nss.org.sg; W: www.nss.org.sg; Pub: *Nature News (newsletter); Nature Watch (magazine)*

Taiwan
Chinese Wild Bird Federation (CWBF), 1F, No. 3, Lane 36 Jing-Long St., 116 Taipei. E: mail@bird.org.tw; W: www.bird.org.tw; Pub: *Feathers (newsletter)*

INTERNATIONAL ORGANISATIONS

Thailand
Bird Conservation Society of Thailand (BCST), 221 Moo 2, Soi Ngamwongwan 2, Tambol Bangkhen, Ampur Meung, Nontaburi 11000. E: bcst@bcst.or.th; W: www.bcst.or.th; Pub: *BCST (bulletin)*

PARTNERS DESIGNATE

Nepal
Bird Conservation Nepal (BCN), PO Box 12465, Lazimpat, Kathmandu. E: bcn@birdlifenepal.org; W: www.birdlifenepal.org

AFFILIATES

Indonesia
Burung Indonesia, Jl. Dadali 32, Bogor 16161. E: birdlife@burung.org; W: www.burung.org

Myanmar (Burma)
Biodiversity and Nature Conservation Association (BANCA), No.943, Second Floor (right), Kyeik Wine Pagoda Road, Ward (3), Mayangone Township, Yangon. E: bancamayanmar@gmail.com; W: www.banca-env.org

Sri Lanka
Field Ornithology Group of Sri Lanka (FOGSL), Dept of Zoology, Univ of Colombo, Colombo 03. E: fogsl@cmb.ac.lk; W: http://fogsl.cmb.ac.lk; Pub: *Malkoha (bulletin)*

BIRDLIFE DIRECT ACTION PROGRAMMES

Cambodia
BirdLife International Cambodia Programme, Street 476, 2, Toul Tom Poung I Chamkar Morn, PO Box 2686, Phnom Penh. E: admin@birdlifecambodia.org

China
China Programme, 7C, V Ga Building, 532 Castle Peak Rd, Lai Chi Kok, Hong Kong. E: info@chinabirdnet.org

Vietnam
BirdLife International in Vietnam, Viet Nature Conservation Centre, PO Box 89, 6 Dinh Le, Hanoi. E: birdlife@birdlife.org.vn

EUROPE & CENTRAL ASIA

PARTNERS

Austria
BirdLife Austria, Museumplatz 1/10/8, AT-1070 Wien. E: office@birdlife.at; W: www.birdlife.at; Pub: *Vogelschutz in Osterreich (magazine); Egretta (scientific)*

Belarus
BirdLife Belarus (APB), PO Box 306, Minsk, 220050. E: info@ptushki.org; W: www.ptushki.org; Pub: *Homeland Security birds (newsletter); Birds and Us (magazine); Subbuteo (Belarusian Ornithological newsletter)*

Belgium
(Flanders) Natuurpunt, Coxiestraat 11, Mechelen, BE-2800. E: info@natuurpunt.be; W: www.natuurpunt.be; Pub: *various newsletters*

(Wallonia) Natagora, Rue Nanon 98, Namur, BE-5000. E: philippe.funcken@natagora.be; W: www.natagora.be; Pub: *The Aves (newsletter); Natagora (magazine)*

Bulgaria
Bulgarian Society for the Protection of Birds (BSPB), PO Box 50, Sofia, BG-Sofia 1111. E: bspb_hq@bspb.org; W: www.bspb.org; Pub: *Living Nature (magazine/english)*

Cyprus
BirdLife Cyprus, PO Box 12026, Nicosia, CY-2340. E: birdlifecyprus@birdlifecyprus.org.cy; W: www.birdlifecyprus.org; Pub: *Annual Bird Report; e-news (newsletter)*

Czech Republic
Czech Society for Ornithology (CSO), Na Belidle 252/34, Prague, CZ-150 00 Praha 5. E: cso@birdlife.cz; W: www.birdlife.cz; Pub: *Zpravy Ceske Spolecnosti Ornitologicke (newsletter); Ptaci Svet (magazine); Sylvia (scientific)*

Denmark
Dansk Ornitologisk Forening (DOF), Vesterbrogade 140, Copenhagen , DK-1620 Copenhagen V. E: dof@dof.dk; W: www.dof.dk; Pub: *Fuglearet (bird report); Fugle & Natur (magazine); Dansk Ornitologisk Forenings Tidsskrift (scientific)*

Estonia
Estonian Ornithological Society (EOS), Veski 4, Tartu, EE-51005. E: eoy@eoy.ee; W: www.eoy.ee; Pub: *Tiiutajat (newsletter); Hirundo (magazine)*

Finland
BirdLife Suomi, Annankatu 29 A 16, Helsinki, FI-00101. E: toimisto@birdlife.fi; W: www.birdlife.fi; Pub: *Tiira (newsletter); Linnut (magazine & yearbook); Ornis Fennica (scientific)*

France
Ligue pour la Protection des Oiseaux (LPO), Fonderies Royale, 8 rue de Docteur Pujos, BP 90263, FR-17305. E: lpo@lpo.fr; W: www.lpo.fr; Pub: *Ornithos (newsletter); L'Oiseau (magazine); L'Oiseau (magazine for juniors); Rapaces de France (magazine)*

Germany
Nature and Biodiversity Conservation Union (NABU), Charitestr. 3, Berlin, D-10117. E: nabu@nabu.de; W: www.nabu.de; Pub: *Naturschutz Heute (magazine)*

Gibraltar
Gibraltar Ornithological & Natural History Society (GONHS), The Gibraltar Natural History Field Centre, Jew's Gate, Upper Rock Nature Reserve, PO Box 843, Gibraltar. E: info@gonhs.org; W: www.gonhs.org; Pub: *Gibraltar Bird Report; Gibraltar Nature News (magazine); Iberis (scientific)*

Greece
Hellenic Ornithological Society (HOS), Themistokleous 80, Athens, GR-10861. E: info@ornithologiki.gr; W: www.ornithologiki.gr; Pub: *newsletter*

Hungary
Magyar Madártani és Természetvédelmi Egyesület (MME), Kolto u. 21, Budapest, H-1121. E: mme@mme.hu; W: www.mme.hu; Pub: *newsletter; Madártavlat (magazine); Ornis Hungarica (scientific)*

INTERNATIONAL ORGANISATIONS

Ireland
BirdWatch Ireland, Unit 20, Block D, Bullford Business Campus, Kilcoole, Co Wicklow. E: info@birdwatchireland.org; W: www.birdwatchireland.ie; Pub: *eWings (newsletter); Wings (magazine); Irish Birds (scientific)*

Israel
Society for the Protection of Nature in Israel (SPNI), Hanagev 2, Tel-Aviv 66186. E: ioc@inter.net.il; W: www.natureisrael.org; Pub: *SPNI News (bulletin)*

Italy
Lega Italiana Protezione Uccelli (LIPU), Via Udine 3/a, Parma, IT-43100. E: info@lipu.it; W: www.lipu.it; Pub: *Ali & Ali Junior (magazines), newsletter*

Kazakhstan
Association for the Conservation of Biodiversity of Kazakhstan (ACBK), Beibitshilik 18, Astana, 020000. E: acbk@acbk.kz; W: www.acbk.kz; Pub: *ACBK News (annual bulletin)*

Latvia
Latvian Ornithological Society (LOB), A.k. 105, Riga, LV-1046. E: putni@lob.lv; W: www.lob.lv; Pub: *Putni Daba (magazine)*

Luxembourg
Natur&ëmwelt, Kraizhaff, 5 Route de Luxembourg, Kockelscheuer, L-1899. E: secretariat@naturewelt.lu; W: www.naturemwelt.lu; Pub: *newsletter*

Malta
BirdLife Malta, 57 /28, Triq Abate Rigord, Ta' Xbiex, XBX 1120. E: info@birdlifemalta.org; W: www.birdlifemalta.org; Pub: *Il-Huttafa (children's magazine); Bird's Eye View (magazine)*

Netherlands
Society for the Protection of Birds (VBN), PO Box 925, NL-3700 AX. E: info@vogelbescherming.nl; W: www.vogelbescherming.nl; Pub: *newsletter; Vogels (magazine)*

Norway
Norwegian Ornithological Society (NOF), Sandgata, Trondheim, N-7012. E: nof@birdlife.no; W: www.birdlife.no; Pub: *Var Fuglefauna (magazine); Fuglevennen (magazine); Ornis Norvegica (scientific)*

Poland
Polish Society for the Protection of Birds (OTOP), ul. Odrowaza 24, Marki 05-270. E: office@otop.org.pl; W: www.otop.org.pl; Pub: *Ptaki (magazine)*

Portugal
Portuguese Society for the Study of Birds (SPEA), Avenida Columbano Bordalo Pinheiro, 87, 3.° Andar, 11070-062, Lisboa. E: spea@spea.pt; W: www.spea.pt; Pub: *newsletters; Pardela (magazine)*

Romania
Romanian Ornithological Society (SOR)/BirdLife Romania, Bd. Hristo Botev, nr. 3, ap 6, Bucuresti, 030231. E: office@sor.ro; W: www.sor.ro; Pub: *newsletter*

Slovakia
SOS/BirdLife, Zelinarska 4, Bratislava, SK-821 08. E: vtaky@vtaky.sk; W: www.birdlife.sk; Pub: *Vtáky (magazine); Tichodroma (scientific)*

Slovenia
BirdLife Slovenia (DOPPS), Tržaška 2, p.p. 2990, Ljubljana, SI-1001. E: dopps@dopps.si; W: www.ptice.si; Pub: *Svet Ptic (magazine); Acrocephalus (scientific)*

Spain
SEO/BirdLife, Melquiades Biencinto 34, Madrid, ES-28053. E: seo@seo.org; W: www.seo.org; Pub: *Aves y Naturaleza (magazine); Ardeola (scientific)*

Sweden
Swedish Ornithological Society (SOF), Stenhusa Gard, Morbylanga, SE-380 62. E: info@birdlife.se; W: www.birdlife.se; Pub: *Vår Flågelvärld (magazine); Ornis Svecica (scientific)*

Switzerland
SVS/BirdLife Switzerland, PO Box Wiedingstrasse 78, Zurich, CH-8036. E: svs@birdlife.ch; W: www.birdlife.ch; Pub: *newsletters; Ornis/Ornis Junior (magazines); Info BirdLife Suisse/Schweiz (magazines)*

Ukraine
Ukrainian Society for the Protection of Birds (USBP), PO Box 33, Kyivv, 01003. E: uspb@birdlife.org.ua; W: www.birdlife.org.ua; Pub: *'Bird' (magazine)*

United Kingdom (see National listing)
Royal Society for the Protection of Birds (RSPB), The Lodge, Sandy, Bedfordshire, SG19 2DL. E: www.rspb.org.uk/contactus/; W: www.rspb.org.uk

PARTNERS DESIGNATE

Azerbaijan
Azerbaijan Ornithological Society (AOS), M. Mushbig Street 4B, Ap. 60, Baku, AZ1021. E: info@aos.az; W: www.aos.az

Iceland
Fuglavernd - BirdLife Iceland (ISPB), Skulatun 6, Reykjavik, IS-105. E: fuglavernd@fuglavernd.is; W: www.fuglavernd.is

Turkey
Doğa Derneği (DD), Kizilay Mah,Menekse 2 Sokak 33/5, Ankara. E: doga@dogadernegi.org; W: www.dogadernegi.org; Pub: *newsletter; Kuş Sesi (magazine)*

AFFILIATES

Andorra
Associació per a la Defensa de la Natura (ADN), Baixa del Moli, num 5, 1r-1a, Andorra La Vella, AD500. E: adn@adn-andorra.org; W: www.adn-andorra.org; Pub: *El Mussol (newsletter); Aiguerola (magazine)*

Armenia
Armenian Society for the Protection of Birds (ASPB), Paruyr Sevak 7, Yerevan, 0014. E: armbirds@yahoo.com; W: www.aspbirds.org

Croatia
Association BIOM, Preradoviceva 34, Zagreb, 10000. E: info@biom.hr; W: www.biom.hr; Pub: *Pogled U Divljindu (magazine)*

INTERNATIONAL ORGANISATIONS

Faroe Islands
Faroese Orginithological Society (FOS), Postboks 1230,
FO-110 Torshavn. E: ffff@kallnet.fo; W: www.faroenature.net

Kyrgyzstan
Nature Kyrgyzstan, Ul, Tabatshnaja 24, Bishkek, 720011.
E: nabu-kirgistan@infotel.kg; W: www.wildlife.kg

Liechtenstein
Botanish-Zoologische Gesellschaft (BZG), Im Bretscha
22, Schaan, Furstentum, FL-9494. E: bzg@bzg.li or
renat@renat.li; W: www.bzg.li

Lithuania
Lithuanian Ornithological Society (LOD), Naugarduko
St. 47-3, Vilnius, LT-03208. E: lod@birdlife.lt;
W: www.birdlife.lt; Pub: *Paukščiai (magazine)*

Macedonia
Macedonian Ecological Society (MES), Ul. Vladimir
Nazor 10, Skopji, 1000. E: contact@mes.org.mk;
W: www.mes.org.mk

Montenegro
Center for Protection & Research of Birds of
Montenegro (CZIP), Veliše Mugoše bb, Podgorica,
81 000. E: czip@czip.me; W: www.czip.me

Serbia
Bird Protection and Study Society of Serbia, Radnička
20a, Novi Sad, 21000. E: sekretar@pticesrbije.rs;
W: www.pticesrbije.rs; Pub: *Detlić (magazine); Ciconia
(scientific)*

Uzbekistan
Uzbekistan Society for the Protection of Birds (UzSPB),
Off. 501, Institute of Gene Pool of Plants & Animals of
Academy of Science, 32-Durmon-yuki Street, Tashkent
100125. E: roman.kashkarov@iba.uz; W: www.uzspb.uz;
Pub: *newsletter*

BIRDLIFE DIRECT ACTION PROGRAMMES

Russia

MIDDLE EAST

PARTNERS

Jordan
Royal Society of the Conservation
of Nature (RSCN), PO Box 6354,
Jubeiha-Abu-Nusseir Circle 11183,
Amman. E: adminrscn@rscn.org.jo;
W: www.rscn.org.jo

Lebanon
Society for the Protection of Nature in Lebanon (SPNL),
Awad Bldg, 6th Floor Abdel Aziz Street, PO Box: 11-5665,
Beirut. E: spnlorg@cyberia.net.lb; W: www.spnl.org;
Pub: *Wings & Waves (newsletter)*

Palestine
Palestine Wildlife Society (PWLS), PO Box 89, Beit
Sahour, Palestine. E: pwls@wildlife-pal.org;
W: www.wildlife-pal.org

AFFILIATES

Bahrain
Bahrain Natural History Society (BNHS), Box 1858,
Manama. E: saeed@alreem.com

Iraq
Nature Iraq, House 25, Street 27, Qtr 104 Ashti,
Sulaymaniyah. E: info@natureiraq.org;
W: www.natureiraq.org; Pub: *newsletter*

Kuwait
Kuwait Environment Protection Society (KEPS),
PO Box 1896, Safat 13019. E: info@keps.org.kw;
W: www.keps.org.kw

Qatar
Friends of the Environment Centre, Villa No 92, zone
52, Mekka St, Dohar. E: fec.org.qa@live.com;
W: www.fec.qa

Saudi Arabia
Saudi Wildlife Authority (SWA), Riyadh.
E: ncwcd@zajil.net; W: www.swa.gov.sa

Syria
Syrian Society for Conservation of Wildlife (SSCW),
Al-Mazza- Al-Sheikh Saad, Shabaan Building No. 20 - 1st
Floor, Damascus. E: sscw.syria@gmail.com

PACIFIC

PARTNERS

Australia
BirdLife Australia, Suite 2-05, 60 Leicester Street,
Carlton, VIC 3053. E: info@birdlife.org.au;
W: www.birdlife.org.au; Pub: *Australian BirdLife
(magazine); Australian Field Ornitghology (scientific);
Emu - Austral Ornithology (scientific); BirdLife (e-news)*

Cook Islands
Te Ipukarea Society (TIS), PO Box 649, Rarotonga.
E: 2tis@oyster.net.ck or info@tiscookislands.org;
W: www.tiscookislands.org; Pub: *newsletter*

French Polynesia
Société d'Ornithologie de Polynésie (MANU), Residence
du plateau Mitirapa, Lot 48, Impasse Des Acacias B.P.
7023, Taravao, 98719, Tahiti. E: sop@manu.pf;
W: www.manu.pf; Pub: *Te Manu (newsletter)*

New Zealand
Forest & Bird, 90 Ghunzee Street, Wellington 6140.
E: office@forestandbird.org.nz; W: www.forestandbird.org.nz;
Pub: *newsletters, Forest & Bird (magazine); Kiwi
Conservation Club (magazine for children); Forest &
Bird (annual report)*

Palau
Palau Conservation Society (PSC), PO Box 1811, Koror,
96940. E: pcs@palaunet.com; W: www.palauconservation.org;
Pub: *Ngerel a Biib (newsletter); annual report*

PARTNERS DESIGNATE

New Caledonia (to France)
Société Calédonienne d'Ornithologie (SCO);
41 rue du 18 Juin, Nouméa. E: president@sco.asso.nc;
W: http://sco.over-blog.org/

AFFILIATES

Fiji
Nature Fiji, 14 Hamilton-Beattie Street, Suva.
E: support@naturefiji.org; W: www.naturefiji.org;
Pub: *newsletter*

SPECIAL INTEREST ORGANISATIONS

AFRICAN BIRD CLUB

c/o Birdlife International - see below.
E: info@africanbirdclub.org
E (membership & sales):
membership@africanbirdclub.org
W: www.africanbirdclub.org
Pub: *Bulletin of the African BC*

BIRDLIFE INTERNATIONAL

The David Attenborough Building, Pembroke
Street, Cambridge CB2 3QZ. T: 01223 277 318;
Fax: 01223 281 441
E: birdlife@birdlife.org
W: www.birdlife.org
Pub: *World Birdwatch*

EAST AFRICA NATURAL HISTORY SOCIETY

(see Kenya/Nature Kenya under BirdLife Africa)

EURING (European Union for Bird Ringing)

Euring Data Bank
c/o BTO, The Nunnery, Theford, Norfolk IP24 2PU.
T: 01842 750 050
E: enquiries@euring.org; W: www.euring.org

FAUNA AND FLORA INTERNATIONAL

The David Attenborough Building, Pembroke
Street, Cambridge CB2 3QZ.
T: 01223 571 000
Fax: 01223 461 481
E: info@fauna-flora.org
W: www.fauna-flora.org
Pub: *Fauna & Flora Update; Flora & Fauna
(magazine); Oryx (journal)*

LIPU-UK
(Italian League for the Protection of Birds)

David Lingard, Fernwood, Doddington Road,

Whisby, Lincs LN6 9BX.
T: 01522 689 030
E: mail@lipu-uk.org
W: www.lipu-uk.org
Pub: *Ali (Wings)*

NEOTROPICAL BIRD CLUB

(Middle & South America and the Caribbean)
c/o The Lodge, Sandy, Bedfordshire, SG19 2DL.

E: secretary@neotropicalbirdclub.org
W: www.neotropicalbirdclub.org
Pub: *Neotropical Birding; Cotinga*

ORIENTAL BIRD CLUB

P.O.Box 324, Bedford, MK42 0WG.
E: mail@orientalbirdclub.org
W: www.orientalbirdclub.org
Pub: *Forktail; BirdingASIA*

ORNITHOLOGICAL SOCIETY OF THE MIDDLE EAST,
THE CAUCASUS AND CENTRAL ASIA (OSME)

c/o The Lodge, Sandy, Bedfordshire
SG19 2DL.
E: secretary@osme.org
W: www.osme.org
OSME Pub: *Sandgrouse*

TRAFFIC International
(the wildlife trade monitoring network)

The David Attenborough Building, Pembroke
Street, Cambridge CB2 3QZ.
T: 01223 277 427
E: traffic@traffic.org
W: www.traffic.org
Pub: *TRAFFIC Bulletin, Newsletters*

WEST AFRICAN ORNITHOLOGICAL SOCIETY

Tim Dodman (Membership Secretary), Hundland,
Papa Westray, Orkney KW17 2BU.
E: tim@timdodman.co.uk
W. www.malimbus.free.fr
Pub: *Malimbus*

WETLANDS INTERNATIONAL

PO Box 471, 6700 AL Wageningen, Netherlands.
T: +31 (0) 318 660 910
Fax: +31 (0) 318 660 950
E: post@wetlands.org
W: www.wetlands.org
Pub: *Wetlands*

WORLD OWL TRUST

Millstones, Bootle, Cumbria
LA19 5TJ. T: 01229 718 080
E: jen@owls.org
W: www.owls.org

WORLD PHEASANT ASSOCIATION

Barbara Ingman (administrator),
WPA, Middle, Nimebanks, Hexham,
Northumberland NE47 8DL.
T: 01434 345 526
E: office@pheasant.org.uk
W: www.pheasant.org.uk
Pub: *WPA News*

WORLD WIDE FUND FOR NATURE/WWF

The Living Planet Centre,
Rufford House, Brewery Road,
Woking, Surrey GU21 4LL.
T: 01483 426 444
E: info@wwf.org.uk
W: www.panda.org
W: www.wwf.org.uk

QUICK REFERENCE SECTION

Neil Gartshore

The Whimbrel *Numenius phaeopus* is protected under Schedule 1 of the Countryside and Wildlfe Act 1981 and is a red listed bird of conservation concern (BOCC).

SUNRISE & SUNSET TIMES FOR 2018

Predictions are given for the times of sunrise and sunset on every SUNDAY throughout the year. For places on the same latitude as the following, add FOUR minutes for each degree of longitude west (subtract if east).

These times are in GMT, except between 01:00 on Mar 25th and 01:00 on Oct 28th, when the times are in BST (one hour in advance of GMT).

		London		Manchester		Edinburgh	
		Rise	Set	Rise	Set	Rise	Set
January	7	08:05	16:09	08:23	16:08	08:41	15:58
	14	08:00	16:19	08:18	16:18	08:35	16:09
	21	07:54	16:31	08:10	16:31	08:26	16:23
	28	07:45	16:43	08:01	16:44	08:15	16:37
February	4	07:34	16:55	07:49	16:57	08:02	16:52
	11	07:22	17:08	07:36	17:11	07:47	17:08
	18	07:09	17:21	07:21	17:25	07:31	17:23
	25	06:55	17:34	07:06	17:39	07:14	17:38
March	4	06:40	17:46	06:50	17:52	06.57	17:53
	11	06:24	17:58	06:34	18:05	06:39	18:08
	18	06:08	18:10	06:17	18:18	06:21	18:22
	25	06:52	19:22	07:00	19:34	07:02	19:37
April	1	06:36	19:34	06:43	19:44	06:44	19:51
	8	06:21	19:45	06:26	19:57	06:26	20:05
	15	06:05	19:57	06:10	20:10	06:08	20:19
	22	05:51	20:09	05:54	20:22	05:51	20:34
	29	05:37	20:20	05:39	20:35	05:34	20:48
May	6	05:24	20:32	05:25	20:48	05:18	21:02
	13	05:12	20:43	05:12	21:00	05:04	21:15
	20	05:02	20:53	05:01	21:11	04:52	21:28
	27	04:54	21:02	04:52	21:21	04:41	21:40
June	3	04:48	21:10	04:45	21:30	04:33	21:49
	10	04:44	21:16	04:41	21:36	04:28	21:57
	17	04:43	21:20	04:39	21:41	04:26	22:02
	24	04:44	21:22	04:40	21:42	04:27	22:03

SUNRISE & SUNSET TIMES FOR 2018

		London		Manchester		Edinburgh	
		Rise	Set	Rise	Set	Rise	Set
July	1	04:48	21:21	04:44	21:41	04:32	22:01
	8	04:53	21:17	04:51	21:37	04:39	21:57
	15	05:01	21:12	04:59	21:30	04:48	21:49
	22	05:10	21:04	05:09	21:21	04:59	21:39
	29	05:20	20:54	05:19	21:10	05:11	21:26
August	5	05:30	20:42	05:31	20:58	05:24	21:12
	12	05:41	20:29	05:43	20:44	05:38	20:57
	19	05:52	20:15	05:55	20:29	05:52	20:40
	26	06:03	20:00	06:07	20:13	06:05	20:23
September	2	06:15	19:45	06:20	19:57	06:19	20:05
	9	06:26	19:29	06:32	19:40	06:33	19:47
	16	06:37	19:13	06:44	19:23	06:46	19:28
	23	06:48	18:57	06:56	19:05	07:00	19:10
	30	06:59	18:41	07:09	18:48	07:14	18:51
October	7	07:11	18:25	07:21	18:32	07:27	18:33
	14	07:23	18:10	07:34	18:15	07:42	18:15
	21	07:35	17:55	07:47	17:59	07:56	17:58
	28	06:47	16:41	07:00	16:45	07:11	16:42
November	4	06:59	16:29	07:14	16:31	07:26	16:26
	11	07:12	16:17	07:27	16:18	07:41	16:12
	18	07:24	16:08	07:40	16:08	07:55	16:00
	25	07:35	16:00	07:52	15:59	08:09	15:51
December	2	07:45	15:55	08:03	15:53	08:21	15:43
	9	07:54	15:52	08:13	15:50	08:31	15:39
	16	08:01	15:52	08:20	15:50	08:39	15:38
	23	08:05	15:55	08:24	15:52	08:43	15:41
	30	08:06	16:00	08:25	15:58	08:44	15:47

QUICK REFERENCE

Reproduced with permission from HMNAO, UKHO and the Controller of Her Majesty's Stationery Office.

TIDE TABLES: USEFUL INFORMATION

BRITISH SUMMER TIME

In 2018 BST applies from 01:00 on March 25th to 01:00 on October 28th.
Note that all the times in the following tide tables are GMT.

Shetland 42, 43
Orkney 44, 45

During British Summer Time one hour should be added.
Predictions are given for the times of high water at Dover throughout the year.

The times of tides at the locations shown here may be obtained by adding or subtracting their 'tidal difference' as shown opposite (subtractions are indicated by a minus sign).

Tidal predictions for Dover have been computed by the National Oceanographic Centre. Copyright reserved.

Map showing locations for which tidal differences are given on facing page.

TIDE TABLES 2018

Example 1
To calculate the time of the afternoon high water at Herne Bay on January 5th, 2018:
1. Look up the time at Dover (13:15)*
   = 13:15 pm
2. Add the tidal difference for Herne Bay
   = plus 1 hour, 28 minutes
3. Therefore the time of the afternoon high water at Herne Bay = 14:43 pm

Example 2
To calculate the time of the morning high water at Blakeney on 28th July, 2018:
1. Look up the time at Dover (11:27)*
   = 11:27 am
2. Add 1 hour for British Summer Time
   = 12:27 pm
3. Subtract the tidal difference for Blakeney = minus 4 hours, 7 minutes
4. Therefore the time of the afternoon high water at Blakeney = 08:20 am

NB: *All Dover times are shown on the 24-hour clock.
Following the time of each high water, the height of the tide is given in metres. This height only applies to the high water level at Dover and may be different in other areas around the country.

TIDAL DIFFERENCES

1 Dover	See pp 318-321	23 Morecambe	0 20
2 Dungeness	-0 12	24 Silloth	0 51
3 Selsey Bill	0 09	25 Girvan	0 54
4 Swanage (lst H.W.Springs)	-2 36	26 Lossiemouth	0 48
5 Portland	-4 23	27 Fraserburgh	1 20
6 Exmouth (Approaches)	-4 48	28 Aberdeen	2 30
7 Salcombe	-5 23	29 Montrose	3 30
8 Newlyn (Penzance)	5 59	30 Dunbar	3 42
9 Padstow	-5 47	31 Holy Island	3 58
10 Bideford	-5 17	32 Sunderland	4 38
11 Bridgwater	-4 23	33 Whitby	5 12
12 Sharpness Dock	-3 19	34 Bridlington	5 53
13 Cardiff (Penarth)	-4 16	35 Grimsby	-5 20
14 Swansea	-4 52	36 Skegness	-5 00
15 Skomer Island	-5 00	37 Blakeney	-4 07
16 Fishguard	-3 48	38 Gorleston	-2 08
17 Barmouth	-2 45	39 Aldeburgh	-0 13
18 Bardsey Island	-3 07	40 Bradwell Waterside	1 11
19 Caernarvon	-1 07	41 Herne Bay	1 28
20 Amlwch	-0 22	42 Sullom Voe	-1 34
21 Connahs Quay	0 20	43 Lerwick	0 01
22 Hilbre Island		44 Kirkwall	-0 26
(Hoylake/West Kirby)	-0 05	45 Widewall Bay	-1 30

QUICK REFERENCE

NB. Care should be taken when making calculations at the beginning and end of British Summer Time. See worked examples above.

TIDE TABLES JANUARY–APRIL 2018

Tidal Predictions : HIGH WATERS 2018

Datum of Predictions = Chart Datum : 3.67 metres below Ordnance Datum (Newlyn)

British Summer Time Dates for 2018 : 25th March to 28th October (data not adjusted)

DOVER — January

Day	Morning time	m	Afternoon time	m
1 M	09:48	6.75	22:21	6.75
2 Tu	10:40	6.90	23:14	6.91
3 W	11:33	6.96		
4 Th	00:05	6.98	12:24	6.92
5 F	00:54	6.96	13:15	6.78
6 Sa	01:40	6.85	14:03	6.57
7 Su	02:26	6.67	14:51	6.31
8 M	03:13	6.43	15:43	6.01
9 Tu	04:06	6.14	16:43	5.72
10 W	05:09	5.86	17:53	5.51
11 Th	06:20	5.68	19:06	5.47
12 F	07:30	5.67	20:11	5.59
13 Sa	08:31	5.79	21:05	5.80
14 Su	09:23	5.96	21:50	6.03
15 M	10:07	6.12	22:30	6.22
16 Tu	10:45	6.24	23:05	6.37
17 W	11:21	6.32	23:39	6.48
18 Th	11:53	6.36		
19 F	00:12	6.53	12:24	6.36
20 Sa	00:44	6.53	12:55	6.32
21 Su	01:15	6.49	13:27	6.25
22 M	01:46	6.41	14:00	6.15
23 Tu	02:21	6.31	14:41	6.03
24 W	03:04	6.20	15:32	5.89
25 Th	04:00	6.05	16:36	5.76
26 F	05:06	5.93	17:48	5.69
27 Sa	06:20	5.89	19:03	5.75
28 Su	07:33	6.01	20:17	5.99
29 M	08:41	6.26	21:21	6.30
30 Tu	09:41	6.52	22:16	6.52
31 W	10:35	6.74	23:06	6.85

DOVER — February

Day	Morning time	m	Afternoon time	m
1 Th	11:26	6.86	23:54	6.99
2 F			12:14	6.88
3 Sa	00:39	7.02	12:59	6.80
4 Su	01:21	6.95	13:41	6.64
5 M	02:00	6.80	14:22	6.41
6 Tu	02:42	6.57	15:06	6.13
7 W	03:28	6.25	15:57	5.80
8 Th	04:22	5.87	16:58	5.46
9 F	05:30	5.51	18:15	5.25
10 Sa	06:50	5.35	19:33	5.28
11 Su	08:03	5.43	20:38	5.51
12 M	09:03	5.65	21:28	5.80
13 Tu	09:49	5.89	22:09	6.06
14 W	10:27	6.09	22:44	6.28
15 Th	10:59	6.24	23:15	6.45
16 F	11:30	6.36	23:48	6.57
17 Sa			12:00	6.45
18 Su	00:30	6.64	12:32	6.48
19 M	00:51	6.65	13:04	6.46
20 Tu	01:22	6.61	13:37	6.39
21 W	01:55	6.53	14:15	6.28
22 Th	02:36	6.40	15:03	6.10
23 F	03:28	6.19	16:03	5.86
24 Sa	04:35	5.93	17:18	5.63
25 Su	05:54	5.74	18:45	5.58
26 M	07:21	5.78	20:10	5.81
27 Tu	08:38	6.05	21:16	6.18
28 W	09:38	6.36	22:09	6.54

DOVER — March

Day	Morning time	m	Afternoon time	m
1 Th	10:30	6.62	22:54	6.80
2 F	11:15	6.77	23:38	6.97
3 Sa	11:58	6.83		
4 Su	00:18	7.02	12:38	6.78
5 M	00:57	6.96	13:15	6.66
6 Tu	01:33	6.82	13:52	6.47
7 W	02:11	6.58	14:31	6.21
8 Th	02:51	6.26	15:15	5.88
9 F	03:38	5.84	16:09	5.50
10 Sa	04:41	5.40	17:21	5.16
11 Su	06:06	5.11	18:50	5.08
12 M	07:31	5.16	20:05	5.29
13 Tu	08:37	5.42	21:00	5.62
14 W	09:25	5.72	21:42	5.94
15 Th	10:01	5.98	22:15	6.21
16 F	10:31	6.21	22:47	6.43
17 Sa	11:00	6.39	23:18	6.60
18 Su	11:32	6.54	23:51	6.72
19 M	00:24	6.77	12:06	6.62
20 Tu	00:57	6.75	12:40	6.63
21 W	01:33	6.65	13:16	6.56
22 Th	02:15	6.48	13:56	6.41
23 F	03:09	6.19	14:45	6.19
24 Sa	04:19	5.85	15:47	5.88
25 Su	05:45	5.61	17:04	5.60
26 M	07:20	5.67	18:37	5.53
27 Tu	08:36	5.97	20:03	5.79
28 W	09:32	6.29	21:05	5.97
29 Th	10:18	6.52	21:54	6.50
30 F	10:59	6.66	22:36	6.74
31 Sa			23:15	6.89

DOVER — April

Day	Morning time	m	Afternoon time	m
1 Su	11:37	6.73	23:54	6.93
2 M			12:14	6.71
3 Tu	00:31	6.87	12:49	6.62
4 W	01:06	6.72	13:24	6.46
5 Th	01:40	6.49	13:59	6.24
6 F	02:16	6.18	14:38	5.96
7 Sa	02:58	5.80	15:25	5.60
8 Su	03:54	5.37	16:30	5.24
9 M	05:15	5.04	17:55	5.04
10 Tu	06:47	5.01	19:18	5.17
11 W	07:57	5.26	20:18	5.49
12 Th	08:48	5.59	21:03	5.84
13 F	09:24	5.91	21:39	6.16
14 Sa	09:55	6.19	22:12	6.42
15 Su	10:27	6.43	22:45	6.63
16 M	11:01	6.62	23:20	6.78
17 Tu	11:39	6.73	23:57	6.85
18 W			12:18	6.74
19 Th	00:36	6.82	13:00	6.66
20 F	01:18	6.69	13:46	6.48
21 Sa	02:06	6.46	14:40	6.24
22 Su	03:06	6.15	15:44	5.95
23 M	04:17	5.82	16:57	5.70
24 Tu	05:43	5.63	18:26	5.65
25 W	07:14	5.71	19:45	5.87
26 Th	08:23	5.96	20:44	6.17
27 F	09:16	6.21	21:31	6.43
28 Sa	09:59	6.39	22:12	6.62
29 Su	10:36	6.51	22:51	6.73
30 M	11:13	6.58	23:30	6.75

National Oceanography Centre (www.noc.ac.uk)

TIDE TABLES MAY-AUGUST 2018

Time Zone: **UT(GMT)** Units: **METRES**

Tidal Predictions : HIGH WATERS 2018

Datum of Predictions = Chart Datum : 3.67 metres below Ordnance Datum (Newlyn)

British Summer Time Dates for 2018 : 25th March to 28th October (data not adjusted)

DOVER — May

Day	Morning time	m	Afternoon time	m
1 Tu	11:50	6.60	12:26	6.55
2 W	00:06	6.70	13:00	6.43
3 Th	00:42	6.56	13:34	6.26
4 F	01:15	6.36	14:10	6.03
5 Sa	01:49	6.10	14:53	5.75
6 Su	02:27	5.79	15:48	5.45
7 M	03:18	5.45	16:58	5.23
8 Tu	04:27	5.16	18:16	5.23
9 W	05:48	5.06	19:23	5.46
10 Th	07:01	5.22	20:13	5.79
11 F	07:55	5.52	20:55	6.12
12 Sa	08:38	5.86	21:33	6.41
13 Su	09:16	6.18	22:12	6.65
14 M	09:54	6.45	22:51	6.81
15 Tu	10:33	6.65	23:34	6.88
16 W	11:15	6.78	—	—
17 Th	—	—	12:02	6.80
18 F	00:11	6.84	12:51	6.72
19 Sa	01:11	6.69	13:45	6.58
20 Su	02:07	6.47	14:40	6.37
21 M	03:07	6.20	15:38	6.14
22 Tu	04:13	5.94	16:44	5.93
23 W	05:30	5.76	18:00	5.84
24 Th	06:51	5.76	19:14	5.93
25 F	07:57	5.90	20:14	6.11
26 Sa	08:49	6.06	21:03	6.28
27 Su	09:33	6.20	21:47	6.42
28 M	10:12	6.33	22:27	6.50
29 Tu	10:51	6.42	23:07	6.53
30 W	11:29	6.48	23:46	6.50
31 Th	—	—	12:06	6.47

DOVER — June

Day	Morning time	m	Afternoon time	m
1 F	00:23	6.40	12:42	6.41
2 Sa	00:57	6.25	13:16	6.29
3 Su	01:31	6.07	13:51	6.14
4 M	02:06	5.85	14:29	5.94
5 Tu	02:49	5.62	15:14	5.73
6 W	03:43	5.41	16:09	5.55
7 Th	04:48	5.29	17:14	5.47
8 F	05:55	5.33	18:20	5.56
9 Sa	06:57	5.53	19:19	5.79
10 Su	07:51	5.83	20:11	6.09
11 M	08:39	6.14	20:57	6.38
12 Tu	09:24	6.41	21:43	6.62
13 W	10:11	6.63	22:30	6.79
14 Th	11:00	6.77	23:19	6.86
15 F	11:51	6.83	—	—
16 Sa	00:12	6.84	12:46	6.82
17 Su	01:07	6.74	13:39	6.73
18 M	02:04	6.56	14:30	6.56
19 Tu	02:59	6.34	15:22	6.39
20 W	03:56	6.10	16:19	6.18
21 Th	05:00	5.88	17:24	6.00
22 F	06:10	5.75	18:33	5.92
23 Sa	07:18	5.75	19:37	5.95
24 Su	08:16	5.84	20:33	6.05
25 M	09:06	5.98	21:22	6.16
26 Tu	09:51	6.14	22:07	6.26
27 W	10:32	6.28	22:48	6.33
28 Th	11:10	6.38	23:27	6.35
29 F	11:48	6.44	—	—
30 Sa	00:05	6.32	12:24	6.44

DOVER — July

Day	Morning time	m	Afternoon time	m
1 Su	00:39	6.25	12:58	6.39
2 M	01:12	6.14	13:31	6.30
3 Tu	01:45	6.01	14:05	6.18
4 W	02:21	5.86	14:41	6.03
5 Th	03:02	5.72	15:25	5.90
6 F	03:54	5.60	16:19	5.79
7 Sa	04:55	5.55	17:22	5.75
8 Su	06:00	5.61	18:27	5.84
9 M	07:06	5.78	19:31	6.03
10 Tu	08:06	6.03	20:29	6.28
11 W	09:03	6.31	21:24	6.53
12 Th	09:57	6.57	22:16	6.72
13 F	10:51	6.77	23:09	6.84
14 Sa	11:43	6.90	—	—
15 Su	00:03	6.87	12:35	6.95
16 M	00:57	6.81	13:24	6.91
17 Tu	01:50	6.68	14:11	6.79
18 W	02:38	6.47	14:57	6.60
19 Th	03:27	6.22	15:46	6.36
20 F	04:20	5.95	16:42	6.08
21 Sa	05:22	5.70	17:48	5.84
22 Su	06:33	5.57	19:00	5.72
23 M	07:42	5.60	20:06	5.77
24 Tu	08:42	5.76	21:03	5.90
25 W	09:31	5.97	21:50	6.06
26 Th	10:13	6.18	22:32	6.19
27 F	10:51	6.34	23:09	6.27
28 Sa	11:27	6.46	23:44	6.32
29 Su	00:17	6.33	12:01	6.52
30 M	00:48	6.29	12:35	6.53
31 Tu	—	—	13:06	6.49

DOVER — August

Day	Morning time	m	Afternoon time	m
1 W	01:19	6.22	13:36	6.41
2 Th	01:49	6.12	14:07	6.31
3 F	02:24	6.02	14:44	6.20
4 Sa	03:08	5.90	15:32	6.06
5 Su	04:06	5.77	16:34	5.91
6 M	05:14	5.67	17:45	5.83
7 Tu	06:30	5.69	19:01	5.90
8 W	07:46	5.88	20:12	6.12
9 Th	08:54	6.20	21:15	6.41
10 F	09:51	6.53	22:09	6.67
11 Sa	10:42	6.81	23:01	6.85
12 Su	11:30	6.99	23:51	6.92
13 M	00:40	6.89	12:18	7.08
14 Tu	01:25	6.76	13:02	7.05
15 W	02:08	6.56	13:44	6.92
16 Th	02:51	6.30	14:26	6.72
17 F	03:38	5.99	15:10	6.43
18 Sa	04:36	5.66	16:01	6.07
19 Su	05:47	5.40	17:04	5.70
20 M	07:08	5.37	18:22	5.46
21 Tu	08:17	5.56	19:41	5.48
22 W	09:11	5.85	20:45	5.68
23 Th	09:54	6.12	21:35	5.92
24 F	10:30	6.34	22:15	6.12
25 Sa	11:03	6.50	22:48	6.27
26 Su	11:35	6.61	23:19	6.38
27 M	—	—	23:49	6.45
28 Tu	00:19	6.47	12:06	6.66
29 W	00:48	6.45	12:36	6.66
30 Th	01:18	6.38	13:05	6.61
31 F	—	—	13:34	6.53

QUICK REFERENCE

National Oceanography Centre (www.noc.ac.uk)

TIDE TABLES SEPTEMBER-DECEMBER 2018

Time Zone: UT(GMT)

Units: **METRES**

Tidal Predictions : HIGH WATERS 2018

Datum of Predictions = Chart Datum : 3.67 metres below Ordnance Datum (Newlyn)

British Summer Time Dates for 2018 : 25th March to 28th October (data not adjusted)

DOVER — September

Day	Morning time	m	Afternoon time	m
1 Sa	01:52	6.28	14:09	6.41
2 Su	02:33	6.13	14:55	6.22
3 M	03:28	5.91	15:57	5.96
4 Tu	04:41	5.73	17:17	5.73
5 W	06:08	5.58	18:46	5.72
6 Th	07:39	5.77	20:09	5.99
7 F	08:48	6.17	21:12	6.35
8 Sa	09:43	6.56	22:03	6.66
9 Su	10:30	6.87	22:50	6.86
10 M	11:13	7.06	23:34	6.94
11 Tu	11:55	7.14		
12 W	00:16	6.91	12:36	7.10
13 Th	00:56	6.80	13:14	6.96
14 F	01:34	6.60	13:52	6.72
15 Sa	02:13	6.36	14:33	6.41
16 Su	02:57	6.04	15:20	6.04
17 M	03:50	5.68	16:21	5.56
18 Tu	05:00	5.33	17:43	5.23
19 W	06:28	5.20	19:13	5.24
20 Th	07:48	5.39	20:24	5.50
21 F	08:45	5.73	21:15	5.81
22 Sa	09:29	6.06	21:52	6.08
23 Su	10:03	6.33	22:22	6.29
24 M	10:34	6.53	22:50	6.45
25 Tu	11:04	6.67	23:18	6.57
26 W	11:34	6.76	23:48	6.64
27 Th	12:04	6.79		
28 F	00:19	6.65	12:35	6.76
29 Sa	00:52	6.59	13:07	6.68
30 Su	01:28	6.47	13:45	6.52

DOVER — October

Day	Morning time	m	Afternoon time	m
1 M	02:11	6.27	14:32	6.25
2 Tu	03:08	5.97	15:38	5.90
3 W	04:24	5.67	17:05	5.63
4 Th	05:58	5.55	18:45	5.64
5 F	07:31	5.79	20:07	5.97
6 Sa	08:38	6.20	21:06	6.34
7 Su	09:29	6.58	21:54	6.63
8 M	10:12	6.87	22:34	6.81
9 Tu	10:51	7.04	23:13	6.88
10 W	11:30	7.10	23:51	7.04
11 Th	12:09	7.04		
12 F	00:28	6.79	12:45	6.89
13 Sa	01:04	6.63	13:21	6.65
14 Su	01:41	6.40	13:58	6.33
15 M	02:21	6.12	14:42	5.94
16 Tu	03:09	5.76	15:37	5.50
17 W	04:11	5.39	16:57	5.14
18 Th	05:35	5.17	18:33	5.08
19 F	07:03	5.26	19:49	5.33
20 Sa	08:07	5.58	20:42	5.67
21 Su	08:53	5.93	21:19	5.98
22 M	09:29	6.24	21:48	6.25
23 Tu	10:00	6.48	22:16	6.46
24 W	10:30	6.67	22:45	6.64
25 Th	11:01	6.80	23:18	6.76
26 F	11:35	6.87	23:54	6.79
27 Sa	12:10	6.86		
28 Su	00:33	6.73	12:48	6.75
29 M	01:15	6.58	13:31	6.53
30 Tu	02:03	6.34	14:25	6.23
31 W	03:04	6.05	15:36	5.89

DOVER — November

Day	Morning time	m	Afternoon time	m
1 Th	04:18	5.78	17:02	5.65
2 F	05:46	5.68	18:39	5.69
3 Sa	07:12	5.87	19:55	5.96
4 Su	08:17	6.20	20:51	6.26
5 M	09:07	6.51	21:36	6.49
6 Tu	09:49	6.74	22:15	6.65
7 W	10:28	6.88	22:51	6.74
8 Th	11:07	6.92	23:28	6.77
9 F	11:45	6.88		
10 Sa	00:05	6.72	12:21	6.74
11 Su	00:42	6.61	12:57	6.52
12 M	01:18	6.43	13:33	6.25
13 Tu	01:55	6.20	14:12	5.93
14 W	02:37	5.92	15:01	5.57
15 Th	03:30	5.60	16:06	5.24
16 F	04:36	5.33	17:29	5.07
17 Sa	05:56	5.26	18:50	5.18
18 Su	07:09	5.44	19:49	5.47
19 M	08:02	5.74	20:32	5.80
20 Tu	08:44	6.07	21:07	6.11
21 W	09:20	6.36	21:40	6.39
22 Th	09:55	6.60	22:16	6.62
23 F	10:32	6.78	22:54	6.78
24 Sa	11:11	6.89	23:36	6.84
25 Su	11:54	6.89		
26 M	00:22	6.81	12:39	6.77
27 Tu	01:12	6.68	13:30	6.57
28 W	02:06	6.49	14:29	6.30
29 Th	03:03	6.26	15:35	6.03
30 F	04:07	6.04	16:48	5.81

DOVER — December

Day	Morning time	m	Afternoon time	m
1 Sa	05:20	5.90	18:11	5.75
2 Su	06:38	5.93	19:25	5.87
3 M	07:44	6.10	20:24	6.05
4 Tu	08:39	6.31	21:12	6.23
5 W	09:25	6.48	21:54	6.39
6 Th	10:07	6.59	22:33	6.51
7 F	10:48	6.65	23:11	6.59
8 Sa	11:27	6.64	23:48	6.61
9 Su	12:05	6.56		
10 M	00:25	6.57	12:41	6.41
11 Tu	01:01	6.46	13:16	6.22
12 W	01:36	6.31	13:52	6.00
13 Th	02:13	6.11	14:32	5.75
14 F	02:55	5.88	15:20	5.49
15 Sa	03:45	5.64	16:20	5.28
16 Su	04:45	5.47	17:29	5.22
17 M	05:53	5.45	18:36	5.34
18 Tu	06:57	5.61	19:33	5.60
19 W	07:52	5.88	20:22	5.91
20 Th	08:39	6.18	21:08	6.23
21 F	09:24	6.46	21:52	6.50
22 Sa	10:09	6.69	22:38	6.71
23 Su	10:55	6.83	23:27	6.84
24 M	11:44	6.88		
25 Tu	00:17	6.88	12:36	6.83
26 W	01:09	6.84	13:30	6.69
27 Th	02:00	6.72	14:24	6.49
28 F	02:51	6.55	15:21	6.24
29 Sa	03:45	6.33	16:20	5.99
30 Su	04:45	6.11	17:27	5.78
31 M	05:53	5.95	18:39	5.70

National Oceanography Centre (www.noc.ac.uk)

Time Zone: UT(GMT) Units: METRES

Tidal Predictions : HIGH WATERS 2019

Datum of Predictions = Chart Datum : 3.67 metres below Ordnance Datum (Newlyn)

British Summer Time Dates for 2019 : 31st March to 27th October (data not adjusted)

DOVER — January

Day	Morning time	m	Afternoon time	m
1 Tu	07:03	5.92	19:47	5.75
2 W	08:06	5.99	20:45	5.90
3 Th	09:02	6.12	21:34	6.08
4 F	09:50	6.25	22:17	6.26
5 Sa	10:33	6.35	22:56	6.41
6 Su	11:13	6.41	23:33	6.50
7 M	11:51	6.41		
8 Tu	00:09	6.54	12:26	6.36
9 W	00:44	6.52	13:00	6.27
10 Th	01:18	6.44	13:32	6.13
11 F	01:50	6.31	14:03	5.97
12 Sa	02:23	6.15	14:39	5.80
13 Su	03:00	5.98	15:23	5.62
14 M	03:47	5.80	16:18	5.47
15 Tu	04:45	5.66	17:24	5.41
16 W	05:52	5.62	18:33	5.49
17 Th	07:01	5.74	19:41	5.71
18 F	08:04	5.98	20:42	6.02
19 Sa	09:01	6.28	21:36	6.34
20 Su	09:54	6.55	22:28	6.63
21 M	10:45	6.77	23:18	6.85
22 Tu	11:36	6.89		
23 W	00:09	6.98	12:28	6.91
24 Th	00:57	7.01	13:19	6.83
25 F	01:45	6.95	14:09	6.66
26 Sa	02:30	6.79	14:56	6.42
27 Su	03:16	6.56	15:45	6.12
28 M	04:08	6.26	16:42	5.81
29 Tu	05:09	5.93	17:50	5.55
30 W	06:21	5.69	19:07	5.46
31 Th	07:36	5.64	20:18	5.58

DOVER — February

Day	Morning time	m	Afternoon time	m
1 F	08:42	5.76	21:15	5.81
2 Sa	09:36	5.94	22:01	6.05
3 Su	10:21	6.12	22:40	6.26
4 M	10:59	6.25	23:16	6.42
5 Tu	11:34	6.33	23:51	6.52
6 W	12:07	6.36		
7 Th	00:24	6.56	12:39	6.34
8 F	00:54	6.54	13:07	6.28
9 Sa	01:23	6.47	13:34	6.19
10 Su	01:50	6.36	14:03	6.08
11 M	02:21	6.25	14:39	5.95
12 Tu	03:00	6.09	15:27	5.77
13 W	03:53	5.89	16:30	5.57
14 Th	05:02	5.69	17:45	5.45
15 F	06:21	5.62	19:09	5.53
16 Sa	07:40	5.78	20:25	5.84
17 Su	08:48	6.10	21:27	6.23
18 M	09:45	6.45	22:18	6.60
19 Tu	10:36	6.73	23:07	6.89
20 W	11:26	6.90	23:54	7.07
21 Th	12:15	6.96		
22 F	00:39	7.13	13:01	6.91
23 Sa	01:23	7.07	13:45	6.75
24 Su	02:03	6.90	14:26	6.51
25 M	02:45	6.64	15:10	6.20
26 Tu	03:33	6.28	16:02	5.83
27 W	04:30	5.85	17:06	5.46
28 Th	05:43	5.46	18:28	5.25

DOVER — March

Day	Morning time	m	Afternoon time	m
1 F	07:09	5.33	19:50	5.33
2 Sa	08:24	5.48	20:54	5.61
3 Su	09:21	5.73	21:41	5.91
4 M	10:06	5.97	22:20	6.17
5 Tu	10:42	6.15	22:54	6.37
6 W	11:13	6.28	23:27	6.50
7 Th	11:43	6.37	23:58	6.58
8 F	12:12	6.41		
9 Sa	00:27	6.59	12:39	6.40
10 Su	00:53	6.55	13:04	6.35
11 M	01:18	6.49	13:33	6.28
12 Tu	01:48	6.41	14:07	6.17
13 W	02:25	6.26	14:52	5.97
14 Th	03:17	6.00	15:54	5.69
15 F	04:28	5.68	17:16	5.44
16 Sa	05:57	5.51	18:51	5.45
17 Su	07:29	5.66	20:14	5.79
18 M	08:40	6.03	21:15	6.23
19 Tu	09:36	6.41	22:05	6.62
20 W	10:24	6.70	22:50	6.91
21 Th	11:11	6.88	23:34	7.09
22 F	11:55	6.94		
23 Sa	00:17	7.13	12:38	6.89
24 Su	00:57	7.06	13:18	6.74
25 M	01:36	6.87	13:57	6.52
26 Tu	02:15	6.58	14:38	6.22
27 W	03:00	6.20	15:27	5.86
28 Th	03:55	5.73	16:27	5.45
29 F	05:07	5.30	17:48	5.17
30 Sa	06:39	5.13	19:15	5.20
31 Su	07:59	5.30	20:24	5.48

DOVER — April

Day	Morning time	m	Afternoon time	m
1 M	08:58	5.58	21:14	5.80
2 Tu	09:42	5.86	21:53	6.08
3 W	10:16	6.08	22:27	6.30
4 Th	10:45	6.24	22:57	6.45
5 F	11:12	6.36	23:27	6.54
6 Sa	11:40	6.44	23:54	6.59
7 Su	12:08	6.48		
8 M	00:22	6.59	12:38	6.46
9 Tu	00:51	6.55	13:09	6.40
10 W	01:24	6.46	13:47	6.26
11 Th	02:05	6.27	14:35	6.03
12 F	03:00	5.97	15:40	5.73
13 Sa	04:16	5.65	17:06	5.50
14 Su	05:51	5.50	18:41	5.54
15 M	07:21	5.69	19:59	5.87
16 Tu	08:30	6.04	20:57	6.28
17 W	09:23	6.38	21:45	6.62
18 Th	10:08	6.62	22:28	6.86
19 F	10:51	6.82	23:11	6.99
20 Sa	11:33	6.82	23:52	7.01
21 Su	12:14	6.79		
22 M	00:32	6.91	12:53	6.66
23 Tu	01:10	6.71	13:31	6.48
24 W	01:50	6.43	14:12	6.22
25 Th	02:33	6.07	14:57	5.91
26 F	03:25	5.66	15:53	5.55
27 Sa	04:33	5.27	17:04	5.25
28 Su	05:58	5.08	18:29	5.19
29 M	07:20	5.19	19:41	5.39
30 Tu	08:20	5.46	20:33	5.69

QUICK REFERENCE

National Oceanography Centre (www.noc.ac.uk)

MAP OF SEA AREAS

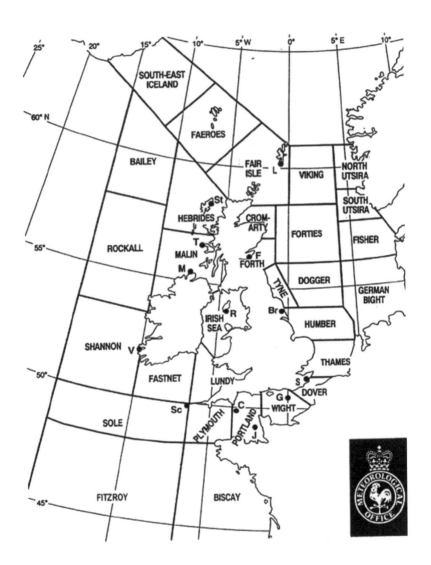

STATIONS WHOSE LATEST REPORTS ARE BROADCAST IN THE 5-MINUTE FORECASTS

Br Bridlington; C Channel Light-Vessel Automatic; F Fife Ness; G Greenwich Light-Vessel Automatic; J Jersey; L Lerwick; M Malin Head; R Ronaldsway; S Sandettie Light-Vessel Automatic; Sc Scilly Automatic; St Stornoway; T Tiree; V Valentia.

BEAUFORT WIND SCALE (SEA)

Scale	Description	MPH	Knots	State of the sea
0	Calm	<1	<1	Sea surface smooth and mirror-like.
1	Light Air	1-3	1-3	Scaly ripples/no crests.
2	Light Breeze	4-7	4-6	Small wavelets, crests glassy - no breaking.
3	Gentle Breeze	8-12	7-10	Large wavelets, crests begin to break, scattered whitecaps
4	Moderate Breeze	13-18	11-16	Small waves - becoming longer, fairly frequent whitecaps.
5	Fresh Breeze	19-24	17-21	Moderate waves taking longer form, many whitecaps, some spray.
6	Strong Breeze	25-31	22-27	Large waves, whitecap common, more spray.
7	Near Gale	32-38	28-33	Sea heaps up & white foam streaks off breaking waves.
8	Gale	39-46	34-40	Moderately high waves of greater length, edges of crests begin to break into spindrift, foam blown in streaks.
9	Strong Gale	47-54	41-47	High waves, dense streaks of foam, sea begins to roll, spray may reduce visibility.
10	Storm	55-63	48-55	Very high waves with overhanging crest, sea white with densely blown foam, heavy rolling, lowered visibility.
11	Violent Storm	64-72	56-63	Exceptionally high waves, foam patches cover sea, visibility more reduced.
12+	Hurricane	≥73	≥64	Air filled with foam, waves over 45ft, sea completely white with driving spray, visibility greatly reduced.

THE COUNTRYSIDE CODE

Launched on 12 July 2004, this Code for England has been produced through a partnership between the Countryside Agency and Countryside Council for Wales.

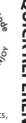

The Countryside Code has been revised and re-launched to reflect the introduction of new open access rights (Countryside & Rights of Way Act 2000) and changes in society over the last 20 years.

• **Be safe - plan ahead**
Follow any signs, even when going out locally, it's best to get the latest information about where and when you can go; for example, your rights to go onto some areas of open land may be restricted while work is carried out, for safety reasons or during breeding seasons. Follow advice and local signs, and be prepared for the unexpected.

• **Leave gates and property as you find them**
Please respect the working life of the countryside, as our actions can affect people's livelihoods, our heritage, and the safety and welfare of animals and ourselves.

• **Protect plants and animals and take your litter home**
We have a responsibility to protect our countryside now and for future generations, so make sure you don't harm animals, birds, plants, or trees.

• **Keep dogs under close control**
The countryside is a great place to exercise dogs, but it's every owner's duty to make sure their dog is not a danger or nuisance to farm animals, wildlife or other people.

• **Consider other people**
Showing consideration and respect for other people makes the countryside a pleasant Environment for everyone - at home, at work and at leisure.

BIRDS OF CONSERVATION CONCERN (BOCC) 4

The 4th list of the BOCC was published in December 2015 - the species under the 'Red', 'Yellow' and 'Green' categories are listed below. The full details of the assessment was published in *British Birds* 108, 708-746:

Eaton MA, Aebischer NJ, Brown AF, Hearn RD, Lock L, Musgrove AJ, Noble DG, Stroud DA and Gregory RD (2015). Birds of Conservation Concern 4: the population status of birds in the United Kingdom, Channel Islands and Isle of Man.

RED LIST
White-fronted Goose
Pochard
Scaup
Long-tailed Duck
Common Scoter
Velvet Scoter
Black Grouse
Capercaillie
Grey Partridge
Balearic Shearwater
Shag
Red-necked Grebe
Slavonian Grebe
White-tailed Eagle
Hen Harrier
Corncrake
Lapwing
Ringed Plover
Dotterel
Whimbrel
Curlew
Black-tailed Godwit
Ruff
Red-necked Phalarope
Woodcock
Arctic Skua
Puffin
Roseate Tern
Kittiwake
Herring Gull
Turtle Dove
Cuckoo
Lesser Spotted Woodpecker
Merlin
Golden Oriole
Red-backed Shrike
Willow Tit
Marsh Tit
Skylark
Wood Warbler
Grasshopper Warbler
Savi's Warbler
Aquatic Warbler
Marsh Warbler
Starling
Ring Ouzel
Fieldfare
Song Thrush
Redwing
Mistle Thrush
Spotted Flycatcher
Nightingale
Pied Flycatcher
Black Redstart
Whinchat

House Sparrow
Tree Sparrow
Yellow Wagtail
Grey Wagtail
Tree Pipit
Hawfinch
Linnet
Twite
Lesser Redpoll
Yellowhammer
Cirl Bunting
Corn Bunting

YELLOW LIST
Mute Swan
Bewick's Swan
Whooper Swan
Bean Goose
Pink-footed Goose
Greylag Goose
Barnacle Goose
Brent Goose
Shelduck
Wigeon
Gadwall
Teal
Mallard
Pintail
Garganey
Shoveler
Eider
Goldeneye
Smew
Quail
Red Grouse
Black-throated Diver
Great northern Diver
Fulmar
Manx Shearwater
Storm Petrel
Leach's Petrel
Gannet
Bittern
Spoonbill
Black-necked Grebe
Honey Buzzard
Marsh Harrier
Montagu's Harrier
Osprey
Spotted Crake
Crane
Stone Curlew
Avocet
Oystercatcher
Grey Plover
Bar-tailed Godwit

Turnstone
Knot
Curlew Sandpiper
Sanderling
Dunlin
Purple Sandpiper
Common Sandpiper
Green Sandpiper
Spotted Redshank
Greenshank
Wood Sandpiper
Redshank
Snipe
Great Skua
Black Guillemot
Razorbill
Guillemot
Little Tern
Sandwich Tern
Common Tern
Arctic Tern
Black-headed Gull
Mediterranean Gull
Common Gull
Lesser black-backed Gull
Yellow-legged Gull
Caspian Gull
Iceland Gull
Glaucous Gull
Great black-backed Gull
Stock Dove
Tawny Owl
Short-eared Owl
Nightjar
Swift
Kingfisher
Kestrel
Shorelark
House Martin
Willow Warbler
Dartford Warbler
Short-toed Treecreeper
Dipper
Redstart
Dunnock
Meadow Pipit
Water Pipit
Bullfinch
Mealy Redpoll
Scottish Crossbill
Parrot Crossbill
Snow Bunting
Lapland Bunting
Reed Bunting

BIRDS OF CONSERVATION CONCERN (BOCC) 4

GREEN LIST
Tufted Duck
Red-breasted Merganser
Goosander
Ptarmigan
Red-throated Diver
Great Shearwater
Sooty Shearwater
Great Cormorant
Little Egret
Grey Heron
Little Grebe
Great Crested Grebe
Red Kite
Goshawk
Sparrowhawk
Buzzard
Golden Eagle
Water Rail
Moorhen
Coot
Golden Plover
Little Ringed Plover
Little Stint
Jack Snipe
Pomarine Skua
Long-tailed Skua
Little Auk

Black Tern
Little Gull
Rock Dove
Wood Pigeon
Collared Dove
Barn Owl
Long-eared Owl
Green Woodpecker
Great Spotted Woodpecker
Hobby
Peregrine
Chough
Magpie
Jay
Jackdaw
Rook
Carrion Crow
Hooded Crow
Raven
Goldcrest
Firecrest
Blue Tit
Great Tit
Crested Tit
Coal Tit
Bearded Tit
Woodlark
Sand Martin

Swallow
Cetti's Warbler
Long-tailed Tit
Chiffchaff
Blackcap
Garden Warbler
Lesser Whitethroat
Whitethroat
Sedge Warbler
Reed Warbler
Waxwing
Nuthatch
Treecreeper
Wren
Blackbird
Robin
Stonechat
Wheatear
Pied Wagtail
Rock Pipit
Brambling
Chaffinch
Greenfinch
Crossbill
Goldfinch
Siskin

SCHEDULE 1 SPECIES

Under the provisions of the Wildlife and Countryside Act 1981 the following bird species (listed in Schedule 1 - Part I of the Act) are protected by special penalties at all times.

Avocet
Bee-eater
Bittem
Bittern, Little
Bluethroat
Brambling
Bunting, Cirl
Bunting, Lapland
Bunting, Snow
Buzzard, Honey
Chough
Corncrake
Crake, Spotted
Crossbills (all species)
Divers (all species)
Dotterel
Duck, Long-tailed
Eagle, Golden
Eagle, White-tailed

Falcon, Gyr
Fieldfare
Firecrest
Garganey
Godwit, Black-tailed
Goshawk
Grebe, Black-necked
Grebe, Slavonian
Greenshank
Gull, Little
Gull, Mediterranean
Harriers (all species)
Heron, Purple
Hobby
Hoopoe
Kingfisher
Kite, Red
Merlin
Oriole, Golden

Osprey
Owl, Barn
Owl, Snowy
Peregrine
Petrel, Leach's
Phalarope, Red-necked
Plover, Kentish
Plover, Little Ringed
Quail, Common
Redstart, Black
Redwing
Rosefinch, Scarlet
Ruff
Sandpiper, Green
Sandpiper, Purple
Sandpiper, Wood
Scaup
Scoter, Common
Scoter, Velvet
Serin

Shorelark
Shrike, Red-backed
Spoonbill
Stilt, Black-winged
Stint, Temminck's
Stone-curlew
Swan, Bewick's
Swan, Whooper
Tern, Black
Tern, Little
Tern, Roseate
Tit, Bearded
Tit, Crested
Treecreeper, Short-toed
Warbler, Cetti's
Warbler, Dartford
Warbler, Marsh
Warbler, Savi's
Whimbrel
Woodlark
Wryneck

The following birds and their eggs (listed in Schedule 1 - Part II of the Act) are protected by special penalties during the close season, which is Feb 1 to Aug 31 (Feb 21 to Aug 31 below high water mark), but may be killed outside this period - Goldeneye, Greylag Goose (in Outer Hebrides, Caithness, Sutherland, and Wester Ross only), Pintail.

QUICK REFERENCE

INDEX TO RESERVES

INDEX TO RESERVES

QUICK REFERENCE

INDEX TO RESERVES